THE ECONOMIC STATE OF NEW ENGLAND

The Economic State of

NEW ENGLAND

Report of the Committee of New England of the

National Planning Association

DIRECTORS OF RESEARCH AND EDITORS

Arthur A. Bright, Jr., APRIL 1951–MAY 1953

George H. Ellis, APPOINTED JULY 1953

STAFF ECONOMISTS

William H. Miernyk, Ray S. Kelley, Jr., Edward K. Smith

CONTRIBUTING ECONOMISTS

John H. Bragg, Robert A. Nelson

PUBLISHED BY ARRANGEMENT WITH THE NEW ENGLAND COUNCIL

NEW HAVEN: YALE UNIVERSITY PRESS, 1954

London: Geoffrey Cumberlege, Oxford University Press

This study of the New England economy is a memorial to the vision, the wisdom and the labors of Arthur A. Bright, Jr., director of research for the Committee of New England who died suddenly on May 14, 1953.

Arthur Bright was a thoroughly able, impartial, scientific economist with a sincere devotion to the public interest and the ability to bring divergent groups together constructively. It was inevitable that the results of research guided by such a man should become a landmark in the development of regional economics. The project was a challenge which he approached with dedicated zeal and from which he derived the pleasure born of work honestly and conscientiously done.

But apart from his professional life, he was an exceptionally fine person. Dates and places do little to convey the reality of a man. Suffice it to say that Arthur Bright was born May 17, 1918. He was very young as leaders go, yet everything he did was touched with distinction. He was graduated from Dartmouth College *summa cum laude* in 1939 and the following year was awarded a master's degree with highest honors by the Amos Tuck School of Business Administration. He was a member of Phi Beta Kappa. From the University of Chicago he received an A.M. in economics in 1942 and the Ph.D. in 1949. He was the author of a book, *The Electric-Lamp Industry* (Macmillan, 1948), which remains the definitive work in its field. At thirty-four, he was director of research for the Federal Reserve Bank of Boston. By such milestones are earthly accomplishments measured.

The magnitude of the loss of the man whose achievements these were is less easily calculated. Words—the abstract words which men employ to name the qualities they admire in each other—are poor things for painting a portrait which can make a man live for those who did not know him. Kindness, humility, warmth, fairness, intelligence, humor—those who knew Arthur Bright can testify that he embodied all these and more, and to them, though their bereavement is great, he can never be completely lost.

To those who did not know Arthur Bright, this volume is his identification. Though others have helped to complete it, essentially it is his. It is his gift to New England which he loved and in which he believed.

Leonard Carmichael

Foreword

THE NATIONAL PLANNING ASSOCIATION is an independent, nonpolitical, non-profit organization established in 1934. It is an organization in which leaders of agriculture, business, labor, and the professions join in developing programs to maintain and strengthen private initiative and enterprise. Members of its standing committees on national and international policy and its special and regional committees are chosen because of their leadership in their respective fields. They serve without compensation and as individuals rather than as representatives of firms or organizations.

The National Planning Association for many years has stressed the interdependence of economic groups and of geographic areas in the achievement of our national goals. We have emphasized, too, that the nation cannot achieve its objectives unless the economic, social, and cultural possibilities of all of our great regions are fully developed. Experience has demonstrated that both the nation and the region can profit from objective studies which pool the knowledge of a cross-section of responsible leaders from the major economic groups, who are thoroughly familiar with their own area's problems and therefore well equipped to state regional goals and point out feasible action.

This was the NPA approach when, at the request of the Joint Committee on the Economic Report of the United States Congress, we formed the Committee of New England. The Joint Committee was interested in receiving from New Englanders a report on the impact of federal policies on their region's economy, prepared along lines similar to a report issued earlier under the auspices of the NPA Committee of the South, to which there had been a highly favorable reaction.

The NPA Board of Trustees was pleased when members of the Committee of New England decided to broaden their objective to provide a basis for a unified program of constructive action for New England. Although the NPA as such has not participated in the preparation or criticism of this series of reports, we are pleased to authorize their publication in the belief that they will contribute materially to public understanding of the economic functions of this important region of the United States.

The New England Council has played a particularly vital role by underwriting publication expenses. The Council's willingness to assume the financial risk of issuing the reports in pamphlet form insured the successful publication of the completed study. The Committee of New England is especially grateful for the vision and confidence the New England Council displayed by its contributions.

NPA is grateful to many individuals and institutions, too numerous to name here, for the unfailing cooperation which has been very helpful in this undertaking. Our thanks go especially to members of the New England Committee and its chairman Leonard Carmichael; members of the Research Advisory Committee and its chairman Sumner H. Slichter; and the research staff and its directors, Arthur A. Bright, Jr. and George H. Ellis.

H. CHRISTIAN SONNE
Chairman, NPA Board of Trustees

Washington, D.C.
May 1, 1954

Preface

THE COMMITTEE OF NEW ENGLAND was organized by the National Planning Association at the request of the Joint Committee on the Economic Report of the United States Congress. It was composed of 95 leaders active in the region's agriculture, business, manufacturing, labor organizations, educational and financial institutions, government agencies, and press and radio. At the organizing meeting on November 13, 1950, it chose as its initial objective the conduct of "an honest self-appraisal of New England's economic problems on which strong, effective action could be based."

Seven study panels composed of Committee members were given the responsibility for work on a wide range of subjects important to New England's economic and social development. At the same time, a Research Advisory Committee, composed of 35 well-known experts in economic and social problems—including faculty members from 14 New England universities—was established to work closely with the Committee and the research staff.

Each of the reports on *The Economic State of New England* has been approved for publication by the appropriate Committee study panel as indicated by the table of contents. The panels took an active role in aiding the planning of the reports and they provided valuable comments and suggestions for revision of the initial drafts.

Publication does not imply agreement by all members of the Committee with all the findings and conclusions of the report. Prior to publication drafts of each report were sent to all Committee members. The Committee's operating plan has provided for an expression of views that differ from those contained in the reports. Dissenting opinions, where expressed, have been included with the appropriate reports.

Responsibility for the editorial content of this volume rests on the Committee's Directors of Research. The Committee was exceptionally fortunate to secure Arthur A. Bright, Jr., as its first director of research. Dr. Bright laid the detailed plans for the research, obtained and directed the professional staff, and worked closely with the study panels and the Research Advisory Committee in developing and revising the initial drafts prepared by the staff economists. At the time of his death on May 14, 1953, Dr. Bright had brought the study near to completion. To finish the research and see the study through to publication the Committee appointed George H. Ellis as its second director of research.

The Research Advisory Committee under the chairmanship of Sumner H. Slichter has counseled the staff and provided information and suggestions throughout the research program. Reading committees composed of a few specially qualified members of the Research Advisory Committee have certified the technical competence of the reports as indicated by the Research Advisory Committee membership list in the appendix.

It would be impossible to list all the persons whose support and cooperation have made it possible to carry out the Committee of New England project. I should like to make special acknowledgment of the aid of Harold B. Shepard, Donald G. White, Thomas D. Rice, Patrick McHugh, New England representatives of the United States Fish and Wildlife Service, Louis A. Zehner, staff members of the state agricultural colleges, the Boston Regional Office of the Bureau of Mines, R. Leigh Fitzgerald, Joseph C. Knox, Theo G. Morss, Joseph A. Reddy, Edward T. O'Donnell, Arthur C. Gernes, Edward Medley, Wendell D. Macdonald, Bernard Fahres, Marguerite I. Coughlin, Harry B. Ernst, Parker B. Willis, R. C. Gill, and Everett Smith.

This has been a truly New England-wide group undertaking. In behalf of the Committee, I wish here to express appreciation to all those who have assisted in so many ways. I am especially grateful for the editorial assistance of Mrs. Arthur A. Bright, Jr., whose contributions in proofreading the manuscript and preparing the index were invaluable. May I also express gratitude to the many New England individuals and organizations whose contributions have made it possible to finance this project locally.

LEONARD CARMICHAEL
*Chairman, Committee of New England
of the National Planning Association*

Contents

I

Transition in New England

Drafted by George H. Ellis.

INTRODUCTION

The economic activities of any region such as New England are closely integrated with similar activities in the United States and the world. Regions like nations have their individual capabilities, problems, and opportunities. By virtue of its age, geographic location, and historical development, New England has both unique problems and unique opportunities. These distinctive features are described and analyzed in the reports that follow. But first it is important to recognize that New England's present economic structure is merely one stage in a process of transition that has been in progress since the founding of Plymouth Colony.

From New England's beginning as a few cleared fields in a forest wilderness, through the colonial period, and into the early years of the young republic, the region's economic characteristics have undergone continuous change. At the time of the earliest federal census, New England contained 26% of the national population. This entitled the area to 27% of the representatives and 63% of the senators in the newly formed national Congress. Since that date New England has made great strides. New lands were cleared, developed into farms, and some have since been returned to forest land. Manufacturing plants sparked the growth of great manufacturing cities and continue as the main source of income to the region. Population expanded ninefold, and the income at the disposal of each member of that larger population increased many times.

Much of this activity of the growing region was providing for the vigorous development of new geographic areas of the nation. New England products, skills, finance, and New England people all played important roles. By this very process the region diminished its own relative importance in comparison with other regions of the United States. For example, by 1950 the region contained only 6% of the nation's population and counted only 6% of the representatives and 13% of the senators in our national Congress.

The building of a great nation inevitably means that the original nucleus constitutes an ever-decreasing share of many national economic statistical totals. From this viewpoint, the declines in New England's shares of national economic totals become milestones of achievement. It means, for example, that our machine-tool industry has been successful in building the looms and the sewing machines, the lathes and the presses which provided new regions with the wherewithal to make their living. As the nation continues to develop, more such milestones will be inevitable. This report is not concerned with quoting those decreasing shares to support contentions of New England's economic decline. We have sought instead to describe and analyze the basic changes in economic activities over the years and to describe the current economic situation in terms of resources, problems, and opportunities. The younger regions of the nation long ago developed their own industrial capacities and rose to challenge their forerunners in the older regions. These new challenges provide the framework for analysis of New England's current position.

TRANSITION IN NEW ENGLAND'S ECONOMIC ACTIVITIES

New England's economic activities have been in continual transition since colonial days. Farming, as a way of life, was very soon supplemented by fishing and international trade. The growth of local markets for manufactured products, together with the time and cost of importing manufactured products from European countries, provided early incentives for resourceful men to undertake manufacturing activities in the colonies. Capital accumulated in whaling or trading became available for investment in domestic industrial enterprises, and provided the savings necessary to launch New England as a manufacturing center.

New England is the birthplace of many of the earliest firms in the nation's great industries. In 1638 Stephen Daye set up the first printing press in the colonies in Cambridge, Massachusetts. The first foundry was established in Saugus, Massachusetts, in 1643. Samuel Slater established a textile mill in Pawtucket, Rhode Island, in 1790. Many other examples also attest the fact that New England achieved an early start in the field of manufacturing. As early as 1850 two-thirds of New England's labor force was devoted to nonagricultural activities. Not until 1910 did the nation achieve this degree of industrialization.

New Englanders quickly learned the advantages of manufacturing local or imported raw materials and shipping them to the rest of the nation or to the world. That activity provided the original basis for the region's prosperity and continues to be the all-important method by which New Englanders make their living. On the average, one out of every three workers in New England works in a factory. Growing manufacturing employment, therefore, has constantly been regarded as the basic indicator of a prosperous and soundly expanding economy. In the years following 1920 when manufacturing employment declined in New England, there was general pessimism and alarm that the area had passed its prime. It was feared it must deteriorate because of inability to compete with the younger, more vigorous competitors it had helped to build. Yet New England has recovered lost ground, has expanded its manufacturing employment to new peaks, and has raised its income to new record levels. The explanation lies in historical changes in the region's economic activities.

Relationship of Economic Activities and Income Levels

In 1691 Sir William Petty wrote: "There is much more to be gained by *Manufacture* than *Husbandry;* and by *Merchandise* than *Manufacture* . . ."[1] He went on to point out that the high level of income per person in Holland in 1691 depended upon the employment of a large proportion of the Dutch population in manufacturing and commercial enterprises. That generalization might well be taken as the major theme running through the story of New England's economic development.

Writing in 1940, Colin Clark, a noted Australian economist, picked up this theme and went on to demonstrate two relationships of great significance to New England. After an intensive investigation of the available statistics of many countries covering a period of years, Clark generalized that the process of economic development is accompanied by a predictable shifting in the labor force. At first the proportion of the working population engaged in agriculture declines as the proportion engaged in manufacturing and construction activities increases. As economic development continues, the proportion engaged in agriculture declines still further and the proportion of workers engaged in service occupations, such as transportation, finance, communication, and personal services, increases, even at the expense of the proportion engaged in manufacturing enterprises. Clark maintained that the proportion devoted to manufacturing tends to reach a maximum and decline thereafter. His statistics indicate that this process of development is accompanied by a rising level of "per person income."

Clark postulated that varying rates of increasing productivity explain this process of economic development. Rapid strides in bettering farm output by using fertilizers, machines, and improved techniques permitted us to devote decreasing proportions of our labor force to raising food to supply our expanding population. Our manufacturing and construction industries multiplied their effectiveness many times by using machines, power sources, and techniques that are products of our advancing technology. The great contributions made by these two sectors of our economy were possible only because we also increased the relative size and effectiveness of our service industries. Transportation, power, communication, financing, and distribution facilities expanded greatly to meet the needs of our more complex economy. The higher levels of income provided by these improvements permitted individuals to hire more dentists, lawyers, musicians, and others

1. Quoted in Colin Clark, *Conditions of Economic Progress* (1st ed. London, Macmillan, 1940), p. 176.

in the personal service occupations. In this category there is less evidence of advances in productivity.

The thesis proposed by Sir William Petty and developed by Colin Clark is demonstrated by two sorts of statistical evidence. Chart I-1 presents visually the relationship discovered by Clark between average real income per person and the proportion of the working population engaged in service occupations in 33 countries during the ten-year period 1925–34. It is very clear that in those nations with the highest income per person the largest share of the working population was in the service occupations.

CHART I-1

Real Income per Person and Working Population in Service Occupations, 31 Countries, 1925–34

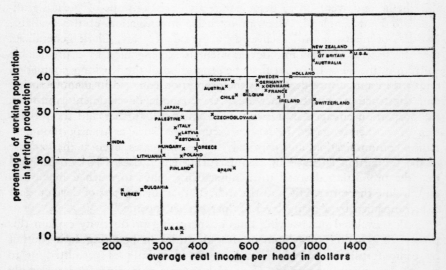

Source: Colin Clark, *Conditions of Economic Progress* (1st ed. Macmillan, 1940), p. 180

The historical statistics describing the economic development of the United States provide further support for Colin Clark's description of the process of economic development. Chart I–2 emphasizes the changing roles played by the three major categories of the working population in the 130-year span before 1950. With uninterrupted steadiness the proportion of our working population engaged in primary occupations (farming, forestry, and fishing) has decreased. The proportion engaged in manufacturing occupations (including mining and construction) rose until 1920 when it seemed to reach a leveling point. The proportion engaged in service occupations (transportation, clerical work, distribution, communication, finance, and education) has risen steadily ever since 1820.

Careful observation clearly reveals the pattern of changing occupations as economic development proceeds, but even more care is required in the analysis of causal relationships behind that development. A high proportion of working population devoted to service occupations is the *combined* result of the requirements of a highly industrialized economy and demand for personal services resulting from a high level of income. It would be inaccurate to claim that countries have a high level of per capita income just

CHART I-2

Changing Occupations in the United States and New England
1820–1950

(1) *Farming occupations* include agriculture, forestry, and fishing.
(2) *Manufacturing occupations* include manufacturing, mining, and construction.
(3) *Service occupations* include transportation, clerical, distribution, communication, finance, and education.

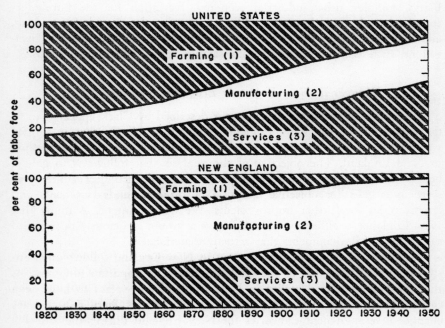

Source: United States figures calculated from Colin Clark, *Conditions of Economic Progress,* 2d ed., p. 404. New England figures were calculated from U.S. Census of Population. Regional figures for 1860, 1880, and 1890 are not available. Regional data for 1910, 1920, and 1930 were adjusted for comparability with 1940. No adjustments were made for the changes in Census definition for other years.

because they have a large proportion of their working population engaged in service occupations. It would be equally inaccurate to claim that a nation has a large share of its working population engaged in service occupations just because it has a high level of per capita income.

The demand for workers in service activities stems from two sources, industrial and personal. In the first instance all economic systems, whether pastoral or urban-industrial, require many services. The demand for these services increases as the system becomes more industrialized. There must be continuous association and contact among operating units, and this requires increased communication and transportation. Raw materials must be procured and assembled, and this stimulates the need for extensive transportation facilities. The goods must be produced, and production requires many services furnished by public utilities. The goods must be sold, and their sale requires an elaborate network of retail outlets, financing and credit facilities.

A second major factor in determining the demand for service activities is the pattern of consumer demand for personal services. Studies of consumption patterns have shown that personal services, recreation, education, and travel become of greater relative importance as incomes rise. In a highly complex urban-industrial economy, recreation for the family becomes relatively more important. The family must also provide for security, and that need fosters the establishment of many specialized financial institutions, such as insurance companies, savings banks, and mutual funds.

Changes in New England's Economic Structure

The process of economic development described by Clark appeared to fit the experience of the New England economy so closely that it seemed worth while to check the statistical evidence and apply the analytical method to New England. The objective of the analysis that follows is to gain a better understanding of past changes in economic activities which may serve as a basis for objective appraisal of prospective developments and opportunities for further improvements. We do not intend to imply that New Englanders, either individually or as a group, consciously determined the pattern of developments that actually materialized.

The history of economic development in New England follows a pattern strikingly similar to that of the United States. The important difference is that the process started earlier in New England and seems to have been carried beyond the national stage of development. Chart I–2 portrays changes in employment categories for New England during the past 100 years. Frequent changes in census tabulation procedures seriously weaken the reliability of the available statistics. Nevertheless, grouping occupations by broad categories clearly reveals the transition in New England occupations.

By 1850 New England was well ahead of the nation in the process of economic development. The manufacturing sector of the region's labor force was just twice as large, relatively, as that in the nation's labor force. During the next 100 years that sector in New England expanded its relative share by only 16%, while the national manufacturing sector expanded by 83%. The service sectors in both the region and nation grew with remarkable similarity and by 1950 were virtually identical in both areas. The great bulk of growth in service occupations was accounted for by increased demand for trade, financial, and professional services.

By 1910 New England had reached a stage of advanced economic development. Only 10% of her civilian labor force was engaged in farming, forestry, or fishing activities. The possibility of drawing from this reservoir of labor to build up manufacturing employment was greatly restricted. Nevertheless, during the next 30 years the number of workers engaged in those primary occupations declined by approximately 92,000 workers or about 29%. Even though the primary category was squeezed tightly, it could provide an increase of only 6% to the manufacturing labor force in the region. That was almost exactly the record obtained during the 1910–40 period. Newcomers, the other source of labor force expansion in the region, provided about 800,000 workers; this was just about the total increase in number of persons occupied in service occupations during the 30-year period. Even by devoting all of the net increase in its labor force to the service occupations, New England barely held its own in the grand sweep of economic progress. By 1950 income had expanded further and New England was still slightly below the historical average relationship in proportion of workers engaged in service occupations.

The national experience during this 1910–40 period was vastly different. At the start about 32% of the national labor force was employed in primary occupations. The number of workers so employed declined 14% during the next 30 years. That decline released more than 1,750,000 workers which helped to swell the manufacturing labor force by 17%. In addition, the nation's manufacturing labor force increased another 24% by drawing upon the new entrants to the labor force. Other newcomers to the labor force joined service occupations, allowing that category to double itself and preserve the historical average relationship between income and the proportion of workers engaged in service occupations.

A thoughtful reading of this historical record provides two critical insights—one looking backward and one forward. Looking backward we see how improbable it was that New England's manufacturing labor force would grow at a rate matching that of the nation. Such a growth would have required a 41% expansion in manufacturing employment during the period 1910–40. Just to preserve the 1910 relationships between the farming, manufacturing, and service categories of the labor force, the total labor force would have needed to expand by 373,000 workers more than it actually did during that period in New England. This would have required the net in-migration of at least 675,000 persons. Those who complain that New England did not expand its manufacturing employment as fast as the nation are, in effect, complaining that in-migration has not been high enough. During the 1940–50 decade net migration into New England reached an estimated 158,000 persons.[2] During the previous two decades the migration flow caused a net loss to the region's labor force. Continued improvements in employment opportunities in New England in comparison with other areas may induce a continued net inflow of workers. But it would be unrealistic to expect a net inflow of sufficient magnitude to cause the region's labor force to grow as rapidly as the nation's.

The historical record, examined with an eye to the future, shows that New England must look very carefully at the opportunities for raising its income level. We can no longer expect the large gains in income that come from shifting from primary to manufacturing occupations. That shift has already been made. In the future we must look within the category of manufacturing employment for the changes necessary to provide higher income.[3]

After 1919 New England was able to expand her proportion of workers engaged in service occupations only by contracting the proportion engaged in manufacturing categories. By virtue of hindsight, it is possible to see that New England's expansion in service occupations was possible only because the total number of persons engaged in manufacturing activities was not expanded sharply. This analysis of the region's economic history ought not, however, to be interpreted as evidence that New England should abandon its dependence upon manufacturing as its prime source of income. New England's high and growing level of income and its high and growing level of employment in service occupations are equally dependent upon growth and improvement in manufacturing employment.

Potentials for Future Changes in Occupations

If changing occupations and rising per capita incomes are so closely connected, what will result from New England's efforts to continue expansion in per capita incomes? In what way may the labor force expect to change in the future? What goals may be established and what measurements may be used to judge achievements?

In considering those questions it is useful to remember that economic development has not been uniform throughout New England. Let us examine the stage of economic development of each of the New England states. Chart I–3 compares the position of each of the New England states

2. See our report No. 7, "The People of New England and Their Employment."
3. Higher incomes may also be provided by improving the output of New England farms. See our report, "Agriculture in New England" (No. 3).

with the other states of the United States for the year 1950. The mark for
each state indicates its per capita income in relation to the proportion of
its labor force engaged in tertiary occupations. Although the pattern for
this single year 1950 does not show as high a degree of relationship as that
portrayed in the averages for the ten-year period shown by Clark, the
chart does show a strong relationship between the level of per capita income
and the proportion of workers engaged in tertiary occupations.

CHART I-3

Per Capita Income and Labor Force in Service Occupations
United States, 1950

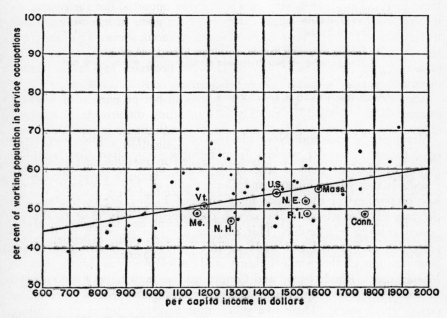

Source: U.S. Census of Population, 1950

Chart I-3 and the table immediately below the chart show that the six
New England states have widely varying proportions of their labor force
in agriculture. In one respect, however, all six are uniform. Each of the
six is below the expected average relationship for the 48 states in the nation.
The average proportion of labor force in service occupations in relation to
different levels of per capita income is indicated on the diagram by a straight
line. All the marks indicating the relationship for the New England states
fall below that line. In the case of Rhode Island and Connecticut, they are
considerably below the expected average relationship. This evidence does

not support contentions that workers in New England have been forced into the service occupations to such an extent that the ratios in New England states are out-of-line in relation to the state income levels. New England is not burdened by having an excessive proportion of its labor force engaged in nonagricultural or nonmanufacturing activities.

Table I–1. Labor Force Occupations in New England, 1950

STATE	PROPORTION OF LABOR FORCE IN		
	FARMING[1]	MANUFACTURING[2]	SERVICES[3]
Maine	11.11	39.80	49.08
New Hampshire	6.72	46.54	46.74
Vermont	18.58	31.11	50.31
Massachusetts	2.13	42.98	54.89
Rhode Island	1.72	49.57	48.70
Connecticut	3.01	48.52	48.47
NEW ENGLAND	3.96	44.28	51.76
UNITED STATES	12.46	33.69	53.86

1. *Farming occupations* include agriculture, forestry and fishing.
2. *Manufacturing occupations* include manufacturing, mining, and construction.
3. *Service occupations* include transportation, clerical, distribution, finance, communication, and education.
Source: U.S. Census of Population, 1950

Vermont, Maine, and New Hampshire each have considerably more opportunity to transfer workers from farming occupations into manufacturing occupations than is true of the other three states in the region. Rhode Island, Massachusetts, and Connecticut already have exceptionally low proportions of their labor force engaged in farming occupations. In the case of Massachusetts, the service component is very close to the expected average relationship. This may be a combined result of the concentration of financial and trade services provided by Boston and of the concentration of the textile industry and its employment adjustments in Massachusetts. Rhode Island and Connecticut are both heavily concentrated in manufacturing employment and are considerably below average in service employment. These two states must look to a future of adjusting their manufacturing growth to the rate of growth in their labor force. They may seek to increase the incomes of existing workers by continued improvements within the manufacturing category.

We cannot regard an increase in the proportion of the labor force devoted to service occupations as conclusive evidence of economic growth. Indeed, in the short run a sudden spurt in service occupations may prove to be a sign that an escape valve is needed for the pressure of unemployment in other occupations. In some cases, a shift to the tertiary services may serve to moderate a fall in income rather than accompany an increase. During a time of depression the impact of industrial unemployment is lessened as laid-off workers seek employment in other occupations. This sort of shift is usually only a stopgap measure: to many workers a shift to tertiary industries is preferable to idleness or government relief. At a later date some of the working population in the tertiary industries are attracted back into secondary industries or move to other geographic areas where their former type of employment is more readily available.

A short-run shift to service occupations, resulting from the pressure of unemployment, does not contradict the generalization that rising levels of per capita income over a long period of time are associated with rising employment in service occupations. We do not seek to write off the seriousness of unemployment and "sick" secondary industries by pointing out growth in service industries; we do emphasize that service employment cushioned the impact of unemployment as the cotton textile industry contracted. Parallel growth rates in the secondary and service categories have maintained the ratios within New England that would be expected, judging from the income level.

New England has the goal of providing a rising level of individual income for a growing population. If historical development processes continue true to form the rising level of per capita income in New England will probably be associated with a slowly increasing proportion of the labor force being devoted to service occupations. Obviously the small proportion of the labor force engaged in farming occupations cannot be squeezed much further. It is apparent that the proportion devoted to manufacturing occupations may have to contract or at least not expand. To a region traditionally dependent upon manufacturing, this conclusion is loaded with serious implications.

In recent decades the region's labor force has grown at a rate of about 1%, or 34,700 workers, a year. *Rapid in-migration would provide faster growth. However, in the absence of a sharp increase in net in-migration, we may expect an expansion in the manufacturing labor force of only about 15,000 workers a year during the next few years. This expectation sets a minimum goal for New England. We must employ our million and a half manufacturing and construction workers continuously, and we must provide at least 15,000 new manufacturing jobs a year and an ever-increasing flow of individual income.* Manufacturing is the heart of New England's economic well-being. Can that heart continue to pump out increasing levels of income while receiving such a small annual increment of workers? The solution lies in changes in manufacturing activity that have been going on in recent decades and must continue in the future.

TRANSITION IN NEW ENGLAND MANUFACTURING

Relying heavily on statistical tools, we have described the New England economy in terms of changing occupations of the labor force. This treatment is not intended as a substitute for an analytical explanation of the causes for the changes observed. Each of our reports analyzes in considerable detail the events leading up to the present position of the various segments of the New England economy. Before proceeding to individual cases, however, it is worth while considering some fundamental changes that have affected all the different segments of the economy.

Changes in New England's Competitive Position

Over the years since the first establishment of industrial activity in New England, probably the most fundamental change in the competitive position of New England's manufacturers has been the westward geographic shift of industrial and consumer markets. This movement was inextricably linked with developments in the methods of transportation. New England's seaboard location and established shipping facilities were great advantages to the early manufacturers in the region. As long as water remained the main highway of commerce, the region's manufacturers were at the door to the markets of the nation and the world.

As the interior markets of the American continent were opened, the development of railroads permitted New England manufacturers to serve those markets. With the passing of time those newer areas developed their own industrial facilities and began to make use of their own resources. Today most New England manufacturers measure their market areas in terms not of the total national market but of reaching into the concentrated markets of the industrial Northeast. Our report on "Freight Rates and New England's Competitive Position" shows that the average manufacturer relies heavily on markets in New England and the Middle Atlantic States. It is estimated that 50% of the manufactured products shipped by rail from New England go to the Middle Atlantic States.[4]

A second change in New England's competitive position arose out of the shift in sources of power used in our industrial economy. While water power was the prime energy source used in manufacturing, the area had a distinct advantage. Its many streams and waterfalls provided power sites which were adequate in the early stages of industrialization. However, rapidly expanding energy requirements led to the development of fuel-based energy, the invention of electric lights and motors, and the transporting of power over electrical circuits. The absence of commercially usable sources of coal, oil, or natural gas forced New England into the position of importing these now predominant sources of energy at a cost inclusive of transportation from distant sites. The development of power transmission by electricity and the use of individual machine power units outmoded the belt-shaft transmission system so universal throughout the region. This development was a first step tending to make New England's huge textile

4. See our Staff Memorandum No. 1, *Origins and Destinations of New England's Rail Traffic, 1949.*

factories obsolete. Viewed in this perspective, the potential development of economical electric power based upon atomic energy is seen to be an immensely important development that may well have a profound effect on manufacturers in the New England region.

A third fundamental change in the competitive position of New England's manufacturers has been the general transition to a metals-based economy. World War II stimulated the transition so that by 1950 more than half the nation's manufacturing labor force was employed in durable-goods industries.

Continued progress in our knowledge of how to work on both hot and cold metals, together with the invention of new methods of transportation, communication, cooking, washing, heating, and other household activities, has provided the basis of the nation's great metal-producing and metal-consuming industries. Prior to this development, New England's prominence in the fields of textiles and shoes guaranteed national importance in the manufacturing field. The new developments related to metals emphasized the lack of basic commercial ores or fuels in the region. The versatility of New England manufacturers has in many cases enabled them to import the basic metals, to manufacture them, and to export them competitively to other areas of the United States. Nevertheless, the lack of the basic resources has precluded the growth of the basic heavy industries in New England. This development need not be a self-perpetuating disability. As our knowledge expands further, the tendency to shift toward lighter metals may redound to New England's advantage if facilities for producing those metals can be located within the region. Tied in with this development is the possibility that the nation will become increasingly dependent upon overseas sources for basic raw materials. As this transpires New England's advantage resulting from her seaboard location may again become of paramount importance.

Historical Industrial Shifts

The fundamental changes in New England's competitive position did not occur abruptly or simultaneously. Their impact registered on different industries at different times. Some firms adjusted their production and marketing processes to meet changing conditions and continued to thrive. Other firms, notably in the cotton textile industry, were forced to liquidate their New England facilities and close or move to other locations. Throughout this transition period new firms were established as the result of the vision and ambition of young enterprisers who saw opportunities to develop new fields in New England. New England's manufacturing activity has always been changing and growing, but the intensity of this readjustment increased in the years following World War I. In the 20-year period ending in 1939, New England lost about 158,000 textile jobs and another 38,000 jobs in its shoe and leather industries. These were jolts that could not be taken lightly, but they were not death blows. In retrospect, it appears that the increased diversity resulting from the transition has been an improvement to the employment structure of the region.

Expressed simply, the transition in New England manufacturing may be described as an increase in the relative importance of metal-working and metal-using industries. In general, industries producing durable goods such

CHART I–4

Manufacturing Shifts in New England, 1919–52
Distribution of Employment by Major Categories

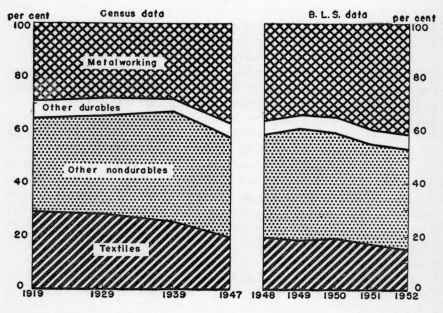

Source: Calculated from U.S. Census of Manufactures and Bureau of Labor Statistics by Department of Research and Statistics, Federal Reserve Bank of Boston

as airplanes and machinery have expanded while industries producing nondurable goods, particularly textiles, have contracted their employment. Chart I–4 shows the changes in relative importance of the four largest categories of manufacturing employment. It is evident that the region's great dependence on soft-goods industries was materially reduced as the proportion of the working force engaged in durable-goods industries rose from 36% in 1919 to 47% in 1952. The chart does not present, however, the absolute changes that have occurred. In the 28 years ending in 1947, durable-

goods industries expanded by a total of 97,000 workers; during the same
period about 30,000 workers were released to nonmanufacturing occupations, as the nondurable goods industries contracted employment by about
127,000 persons.

Since 1947 the rate of this transition has accelerated. In the six years
ending in 1953, the durable-goods industries expanded their working forces
by approximately 85,000 workers while the nondurable-goods industries
contracted their working forces by approximately 44,000 persons. The expansion in metal-working activity in the region since World War II has
been more than sufficient to offset continued contraction in the still important textile industry. Over the span of years since 1919, expansion of
employment in the durable-goods industries has almost exactly offset the
contraction of employment in the nondurable-goods industries, with a net
increase of about 10,000 workers.

Problems of the Manufacturing Shifts

It is not surprising to find that a transition of such magnitude left problems in its wake. The problem of concentrated areas of unemployment
became immediately apparent; a second potential problem of increased
vulnerability to cyclical fluctuations remains uncertainly in the future.

Although New England has always been widely known for the diversity
of her manufacturing, many of her cities have made their name by concentrating on the production of a single type of commodity. The names
of Fall River, New Bedford, Lowell, Lawrence were virtually synonymous
with textiles. The cities of Brockton, Haverhill, Lynn, and Marlboro tied
their fortunes to the shoe industry. Many smaller towns and cities throughout the region became one-industry towns or even one-firm towns, and
trusted their luck to either the textile or shoe industries. Readjustments in
those two industries were inevitably reflected in unemployment difficulties
in specialized cities. The situation was aggravated by a geographic transition within the region's shoe industry, in which growth in the northern tier
of New England states partially offset declining employment in that industry in the three southern New England states. Redistribution and
relocation of the industry resulted in leaving unemployed work forces
behind.[5]

The core of New England's unemployment problem is the small group
of cities that have relied excessively on a single industry for their livelihood.
At the bottom of the 1949 recession in New England, four cities, with 4.3%
of the region's population, accounted for 14.4% of the unemployed. In June
1953, three years after the start of the Korean War, New England unem-

5. See our Staff Memorandum No. 2, *Chronic Unemployment in New England from 1947
to 1951.*

ployment had shrunk to 64,784 workers, but those same four cities accounted for 15.0% of the region's unemployed.

New England's unemployment with its pattern of concentration in specific cities is not unique, but it is more acute than in other areas of the United States. In some communities in the Pennsylvania coal fields, for example, the problem is similar because of reliance upon a single occupation—coal mining. On an over-all basis, New England has had more than its share of surplus labor markets. At the bottom of the 1949 recession, New England had 50% of the nation's areas of substantial labor surplus. Although stimulation of manufacturing as a result of the defense build-up transferred some New England communities from the surplus into the shortage market categories, nevertheless, in July of 1953 the region still had 18.8% of the nation's substantial labor surplus areas.

Some communities have seized the initiative and speeded up the transition necessary for conversion from one-industry towns into diversified communities. One example is the industrial expansion in Nashua, New Hampshire, after Textron curtailed its operations. Partial closing of Textron's operations there in 1948 left approximately 3,000 unemployed. The community went to work to lease its vacant floor space to small diversified industries. By October of 1950 Nashua's unemployment had been reduced to 700. The town was converted from a textile-dependent status to one in which no one industry or plant employed over 14% of the labor force. By this action, the community reduced not only its pool of unemployed persons but also its vulnerability to future unemployment as a result of excessive dependence on a single industry.

The transition of New England manufacturing from the nondurable-goods to durable-goods industries carries with it the threat of greater vulnerability to the impact of business fluctuations. It has been repeatedly demonstrated that the first industries to feel the impact of reduced business in times of business stress are the machine-tool and metal-working industries. As New England continues its shift into those industries, the likelihood grows that as an area it will increase its sensitivity to the business cycle. In the past, employment in New England has demonstrated more than average stability as a reflection of its greater dependence on the more stable nondurable-goods industries. To say that this stability will be lessened is not to assert that the region's cyclical sensitivity will be greater than that of the nation.

The advantages of achieving greater industrial diversity are as pertinent to those cities dependent upon metal-working industries as to those dependent on nondurable-goods industries. For example, analysis of the experience of Connecticut cities during the 1949 recession vividly illustrates the fact that employment dropped more sharply in the metal-working centers than it did in the diversified industrial areas. While New England is adjusting itself to the loss of its nondurable-goods industries, it should not repeat the error of overconcentration in any line of industrial activity. Metal-working centers such as Bridgeport, Hartford, Waterbury, and New Haven should be as ardent supporters of diversification as the cities of Lawrence, Lowell, Brockton, and Haverhill.

THE ECONOMIC STATUS OF NEW ENGLAND

New England's transition in manufacturing activities has been a forced response to changing competitive conditions. It has also been a fortunate alternative that permitted the region to maintain and even expand the income level of its residents. Dependence upon manufacturing is forced upon the region by virtue of its resources and location. *Success in transforming its manufacturing activities is a testimonial to the region's basic adaptability. No other region in the country has faced these problems in similar magnitude and demonstrated to the same degree an ability to meet changing conditions with changing economic activities.*

Changes in Workers' Earnings

Statistics cannot supply a definitive answer to the question of whether or not New England workers have gained by this general change in their working activity. Statistics of average earnings do not supply the entire answer. Unmeasurable psychological and social values are involved when workers change jobs. Transition within manufacturing activities also brings to communities a greater diversity of their industrial base together with a lessening of social costs of unemployment. These side advantages are immeasurable in monetary terms.

New England's employment transition has left in its wake problems of concentrated unemployment and idle facilities but at the same time has created new industries, provided new forms of employment, and stimulated the construction of new industrial facilities. The losses of employment and income are recorded in many newspapers and in the minds of many people. Nevertheless, in the aggregate it is perfectly clear that New England's income has not suffered because of the employment transition. It is difficult to assess the degree of improvement in monetary income that has resulted, but it is unquestionable that the direction of movement has been toward betterment. Differences in working conditions, length of working hours, and stability of employment all serve to confuse a picture which might be drawn based entirely on average hourly earnings by workers in the various industries.

Wherever statistics are available, they indicate the advantage of durable-goods employment in contrast with the nondurable-goods variety. For example, in 1951 the average annual payment of salary and wages per employee in the nondurable-goods industries in New England was 15%

lower than the comparable payment in durable-goods industries. The average annual payment in the textile industry was lower than that in any of the metal-working industries. Geographic differences and differences in length of work week affect this kind of comparison, so it is useful to compare average hourly earnings. In Connecticut during the mid-week of May 1953 the average *hourly* earnings in the textile industry were lower than, those in all but three of the state's 18 industry groups—above only apparel, furniture and wood, and miscellaneous metal industries. The average *weekly* earnings in the textile industry for that week were lower than those of all but two of the 18 industry groups. A sample of 1,772 representative manufacturing establishments in Massachusetts during May 1953 revealed that average weekly payments per production worker in the nondurable-goods industries were 19% lower than similar payments in the durable-goods industries. Payments in the textile mill industry were 12% lower than the lowest of the several metal-working industries.

Our study of straight-time hourly earnings by labor market areas provided additional data to support the view that both within and outside New England workers in durable-goods industries tend to receive higher payments than their fellow workers in the nondurable-goods industries.[6] In individual communities the incoming firms do not always match the wage levels of the outgoing textile or shoe firms. For example, many of the jobs in electronics firms have substantially lower hourly rates than the hourly rates in the textile or shoe industries. Even allowance for longer work weeks in electronics firms does not insure higher weekly earnings. On balance, however, the evidence is strong that New England's transition from nondurable to durable-goods industries has worked to the advantage of the region by providing more higher paying jobs.

The realignment of manufacturing activity was not only a critical requirement to maintain New England's level of income, it was also a fundamental cause of the employment shift toward the service industries. Manufacturing activities made possible the high level of income which supported consumers' desires to increase their consumption of personal services. At the same time, the manufacturing segment increased its requirements for such services as transportation, communication, finance, and distribution.

It cannot be claimed that the transition to service occupations acted to raise or maintain New England's income level. While the evidence is not conclusive, it does suggest that monetary remuneration in the service occupations does not match that in the manufacturing occupations. In 1950 average wages and salary (including supplementary) payments in manufacturing occupations in the nation were about $3,510. Similar payments in service occupations ranged from $3,930 in the transportation category down to $2,260 in the personal service category. The average for all service

6. See Table 9–5 in our report No. 9, "Wages in New England."

occupations was about $3,100. Difficulties in correctly estimating the value of intangible supplements to income make these figures useful only as general guides to the relative magnitudes.

The available statistics describing New England's income go back only to 1929. Total income is obviously affected by the size of the region's labor force and by the growth of population. For this reason, it is convenient to judge changes in income on the basis of the income received in relation to the population in the region. Chart I–5 indicates the changes in New England's per capita income contrasted with those of the nation.

CHART I–5

Per Capita Income in New England and United States
1929–52

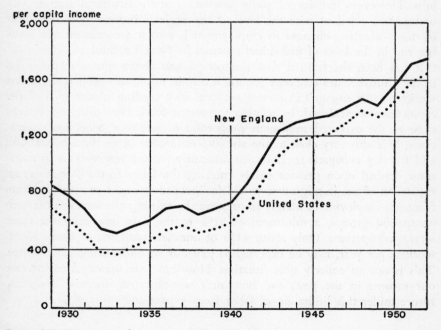

Source: U.S. Department of Commerce, "State Income Payments in 1952," *Survey of Current Business,* August 1953

New England's per capita income has been consistently higher than that of the nation and has fluctuated less rapidly. Between 1929 and the depth of the depression in 1933, per capita income in the region dropped 39% in comparison with the 46% drop in the nation. Our report on "Wages in New England" explains the greater stability of New England's income. It is sufficient here to emphasize that throughout the period for which income information is available the region's income has remained above the national average in spite of the thoroughgoing change-over of basic economic activity which was taking place. At the time of the last survey, in 1952, New England's per capita income stood 6.7% above the national average.

New England's Income Position

In retrospect, it appears that the transition to durable-goods manufacturing has served to raise the level of New England's income. The number of higher paying jobs in durable-goods industries expanded as the number of lower paying jobs in nondurable-goods industries contracted. Simultaneously the shift in manufacturing occupations supported the growth of employment in service occupations. Transfer of workers from manufacturing into service occupations generally meant a move to lower paying jobs. However, transfer of some workers from agricultural into service occupations acted to raise the level of the region's income. The net effect of these offsetting changes in employment has been a continued but slowing rise in the level of individual incomes in New England.

It has been determined that production and consumption relationships in the United States economy require a certain minimum proportion of our workers to be engaged in service occupations according to the level of per capita income achieved. In relation to income level, New England is very close to the expected minimum proportion of workers in service occupations. It is also very close to the absolute minimum of workers in farming and forestry occupations. If its manufacturing employment is to grow, it must depend upon persons newly entering the labor force. Obviously, an expansion of net in-migration would facilitate more rapid growth of manufacturing employment. Merely to preserve the existing relationships between occupation groups, a minimum of 52% of the new workers must enter service occupations. Only about 44% of our new workers, or about 15,000 workers per year, may be expected to join our manufacturing labor forces. This is not an entirely new situation. How have we managed to increase our income in the past, and how may we expect to increase it in the future under this limitation of labor force expansion?

"Upgrading" as a Method to Expand Income

New England must take a hard look at its own opportunities for raising its income level. We cannot expect in the future to make large gains in income by shifting our workers from farming to manufacturing occupations. The opportunity must lie in upgrading present employment. By upgrading we mean increasing the value of the output from the working hour of each laborer. There are at least four closely related methods by which this upgrading may be achieved.

1. It is well understood that the value of output per worker in manufacturing varies from industry to industry. The value of each worker's hourly output in the automobile industry, for example, is greater than the market value of the output of each worker in the garment industry. By shifting workers from one industry to another, the value of workers' output can be increased. In substance this is the process we have witnessed as cotton textile workers have been displaced by higher paid metal workers. By this test the loss of New England's textile industries, *insofar as it results in shifts to higher paying employment,* is a necessary concomitant of the process of upgrading.

2. The production of some products within an industry classification sometimes results in a higher value of output per worker than does the production of other products within the same industry. By shifting the product emphasis within an industry, the value of worker output can be increased. For example, within the textile industry the shift from production of cotton gray goods to the production of cotton specialty products has resulted in an increase in the value of output per worker in the industry.

3. The value of workers' output can be increased by improved management, more machinery, and other methods to secure a larger physical output within a given industry making a given product. The introduction of new types of tools and new methods of production is an example of this method of increasing the value of workers' output.

4. Upgrading may occur as a result of a change in the price structure which enhances the value of the workers' output within a given industry making a given product.

In general, it is very difficult to isolate the specific contribution to increased worker output resulting from the various methods of upgrading. Fortunately such definitive description or analysis is unnecessary. What is vitally necessary is to realize that upgrading of manufacturing activity is the key to higher incomes in New England.

NEW ENGLAND'S AWARENESS
OF ITS ECONOMIC STATUS

New England's economic life has been a theme for writers for hundreds of years. Early visitors from Europe used to write home in glowing terms of the industry and resourcefulness of the colonists. Alarm about the economic future has also been perennial. As early as 1736 Peter Faneuil, the builder of Faneuil Hall in Boston, protested the English restriction on colonial trade, complaining, "Wee have forty-three sales of vessells now a Building in this Town, and there is nothing but Disapointment to be expected from them."[7]

7. Quoted in William B. Weeden, *Economic and Social History of New England* (Boston, Houghton Mifflin, 1894), p. 612.

During the 19th century our economic life became more complex. Economic problems seemed more pressing and more information became available. In Massachusetts a census of industrial statistics was prepared in 1837, 1845, and every ten years thereafter. In 1793 the governor of Massachusetts was endorsing grants to aid "cotton manufacturing" at Beverly and "glass manufacturing" at Boston. In 1810 the governor of Vermont devoted part of his legislative message to discussing the expediency of encouraging domestic manufactures. By 1822 a new governor was dwelling on the importance of transportation facilities to local industries. Forty-one years later another governor was tracing improved business to improved transportation facilities. In the last half of the century reports on capital investment by industry, population growth, and comparison of business conditions were frequent.[8]

During the 1920's the exodus of the cotton industry from New England brought increasing public awareness of the region's economic problems. A flood of publications devoted their attention to New England economic issues. The Massachusetts legislature showed its concern in 1929 by passing a "resolve providing for an investigation by the Massachusetts Industrial Commission of the conditions affecting the textile industry . . ."[9]

The depression years of the 1930's stimulated an outpouring of studies of *regional* economy, as distinct from descriptions of individual states or industries. The United States Department of Commerce issued extensive descriptions of the commercial and industrial structure of New England.[10] A group of distinguished students of the New England scene were induced to write a series of reports on New England's prospect in 1933.[11] Three years later the National Resources Committee released an extensive report on regional planning in New England.[12] Expanded statistical services by both state and federal governments provided more information for increased analysis of the region's economy.

Economic research on New England slowed down during the war years as efforts were devoted to furthering the war effort. In the postwar years, however, it increased in variety and intensity. The Federal Reserve Bank of Boston instituted a continuing study of all aspects of economic activity in the region. The area's universities and colleges increased their research on regional topics. State legislatures and development agencies sponsored

8. Hasse, Adelaide R., *Index of Economic Materials in Documents of the State of Massachusetts,* and *Index of Economic Materials in Documents of the State of Vermont,* Carnegie Institution of Washington, 1908.

9. General Court Resolves of 1929, Chapter 54, House Document 70.

10. U.S. Department of Commerce, *Commercial Structure of New England,* Domestic Commerce Series No. 26, Washington, 1929 and *Industrial Structure of New England,* Series No. 28, Washington, 1930.

11. Wright, John K., ed., *New England's Prospect: 1933,* American Geographical Society, 1933.

12. National Resources Committee, *Regional Planning,* Part III, "New England," Washington, 1936.

or conducted studies of economic significance to their states. Newspapers and periodicals gave increasing attention to the problems of the region.

New Englanders have been gaining in awareness and understanding of their economic situation. Their activities tell the story. The formation, support, and expansion of the activities of the New England Council testify to the region-wide consciousness of the governors of the six New England states and those who participate in the activities of the Council. The rapid spread, during postwar years, of community activities, such as industrial foundations, industrial districts, industrial development committees, and state development credit corporations, provides irrefutable evidence that New England communities are increasingly aware of their problems and opportunities in the area of economic development.

New Englanders have consistently displayed resourcefulness in adapting to changing conditions in changing times. Never in the region's history have the citizens been more alert to the need for economic understanding and the value of intelligent appraisal of the opportunities to forge ahead in economic development. To this audience, and with full confidence in the future, the Committee of New England offers its contribution to the economic understanding of New England.

SELECTED REFERENCES

1. Bean, L. H., "International Industrialization and Per Capita Income," National Bureau of Economic Research, *Studies in Income and Wealth,* Vol. *8,* Pt. 5, New York, 1946.

2. Bidwell, Percy Wells, "Rural Economy in New England at the Beginning of the Nineteenth Century," *Transactions of the Connecticut Academy of Arts and Sciences* (New Haven, 1916), *20,* 241–399.

3. *Boston Herald, Commercial and Financial New England,* 1906.

4. Clark, Colin, *Conditions of Economic Progress,* London, Macmillan, 1940.

5. Federal Reserve Bank of Boston, "Shifts in New England's Labor Force," *Monthly Review,* March 1947.

6. Hasse, Adelaide R., *Index of Economic Materials in Documents of the State of Massachusetts* and *Index of Economic Materials in Documents of the State of Vermont,* Carnegie Institution of Washington, 1908.

7. Massachusetts General Court Resolves of 1929, Chapter 54, House Document No. 70.

8. National Resources Committee, *Regional Planning,* Pt. III, "New England," Washington, 1936.

9. U.S. Department of Commerce, *Commercial Structure of New England,* Domestic Commerce Series No. 26, Washington, 1929, and *Industrial Structure of New England,* Series No. 28, Washington, 1930.

10. Weeden, William B., *Economic and Social History of New England,* Boston, Houghton Mifflin, 1894.

11. Wright, John K., ed., *New England's Prospect: 1933,* New York, American Geographical Society, 1933.

1

The Forests of New England

Drafted by Ray S. Kelley, Jr., under the direction of Arthur A. Bright, Jr.

INTRODUCTION

More than three-fourths of the land area of New England is forested. Although the region contains only 2.1% of the nation's land area, it has 6.7% of the commercial forest area in the United States. Maine and New Hampshire, with 84.5 and 83.9% of their land in forests, rank well above any other state in the country. All the New England states are more than 60% forested. Only three other states in the country have such a high percentage.

This forest land is extremely important to the New England economy. It is a capital asset for 244,000 forest-property owners, and it provides an important source of raw materials for the timber and wood-consuming industries in the region.

The value of New England forests to their owners is considerable. The standing timber alone is worth more than half a billion dollars, at current prices. The annual value of the New England timber harvest is estimated to be between $30,000,000 and $35,000,000 on the stump, before any other values are added.

Two groups of New England industries are in various degrees supported by forests—those that depend on withdrawn timber for raw materials and those that use the forests without withdrawing any timber. Some industries depend on both types of forest support, of course, but usually one type of use predominates.

The first group includes all logging and manufacturing of lumber and lumber products, wooden containers, pulp, paper, paperboard, wooden furniture, veneer and plywood, and numerous other wood-processing industries. These industries give direct employment to between 135,000 and 145,000 New England workers in an average year, almost 10% of the region's industrial labor force. Indirectly, they provide employment for many more. In 1950 the wood-consuming industries of New England paid almost $300,-000,000 in wages, and their total value added by manufacture in that year exceeded $640,000,000. Their annual shipments of finished products have a value in excess of a billion dollars.

The second group of forest-based industries includes all the activities that depend in whole or in part on standing forests. The region's vacation business, for example, relies heavily on the New England forests to attract tourists, because forests improve the outdoor environment in a number of ways. New England agriculture needs the forests to help prevent erosion and floods by slowing and stabilizing stream flows. The forests are similarly important to many other industries dependent on a steady supply of water power or process water.

The nonconsuming users of forests are of considerable importance to the New England economy, of course, but they are not discussed in this report.[1] They are concerned not so much with the productive ability of the forests as with their mere presence. The consuming users, however, are dependent largely on the productive capacity of the forests. Most wood-consuming industries favor sites near dependable supplies of raw materials. Without productive forests New England would be severely handicapped in attracting new wood-consuming manufactures and might lose many that it now has.

At present the region has to import large quantities of timber from both domestic and foreign sources to meet its requirements. Annual lumber consumption in New England is well over two billion board feet, yet only about half that amount is produced in the region. To meet its remaining lumber needs New England resorts to imports primarily from the West Coast, the South, and Canada. The imported lumber supplements the local supply and also fills requirements to which native lumber is not adapted.

New England paper and paperboard manufacturers require wood pulp equivalent to 2,700,000 cords of pulpwood in an average year. In addition, some of the woodpulp made in New England goes to manufacturers of synthetic fibers and plastics. To add to the demand, the New England pulp industry is planning an expansion program which will increase capacity nearly 175,000 tons annually. While most of the present pulpwood supply comes from New England forests, eastern Canada has been shipping in about one-third of the pulpwood or its pulp equivalent which New England mills consume. On the other hand, New England exports some pulpwood to New York State and wood pulp to other points.

The supply from Canada is not a certainty. The expanding Canadian paper industry is requiring steadily larger quantities of pulpwood, and it could eventually absorb the output of the eastern Canadian forests. Furthermore, the pulpwood forests of eastern Canada have suffered seriously from a spruce budworm epidemic. Millions of cords of Canadian spruce and fir timber have been killed since 1938.

Information is not readily available for determining to what extent other New England wood-consuming industries depend on imports, but there are indications that local supplies are not fully adequate.

Under these circumstances, it is important to the New England economy that the productivity of the region's forests be increased to make their maxi-

1. See the Committee's reports on "The Agriculture of New England" (No. 3), "Water, Fuel, and Energy in New England" (No. 5), and "The Vacation Business of New England" (No. 6).

mum contribution to income and employment. The first part of this report is devoted to a discussion of the condition of the New England forests and to the factors that affect their yields. The rest of the report considers ways in which forest output can be increased and suggests a program for the progressive rehabilitation of New England forest land.

THE STATUS OF NEW ENGLAND FORESTS

While New England surpasses all other regions of the country in the percentage of forested land area, land area is not a good measure of forest condition. Of the 30,811,000 acres of commercial forest land in the region, 45% is in saw timber. There are about 52 billion board feet of saw timber standing on saw-timber areas in New England. While this may sound impressive, it amounts to only about 3,660 board feet per acre. It is believed that when the first settlers came to America the New England forests had about 15,000 board feet of timber to the acre. In the United States as a whole, including the virgin stands of the West, there are currently about 7,550 board feet per acre in saw-timber stands.

The saw-timber stands are New England's best forests. The other 55% of the region's commercial forests are predominantly in smaller trees. Twenty-seven per cent of the forested area is pole-timber land, which contains trees of 5″ d.b.h. and up to saw timber size.[2] That timber can be used for pulpwood, poles, posts, and a few other purposes, if it is of the right type and quality.

New England's forest land is obviously far less productive than it could be under proper harvesting and forestry practices. In this respect it is similar to the forest land in much of the rest of the nation. The forests of the West Coast are in better condition, but at the present rate of drain and under present methods of cutting and management many of the western forests are also deteriorating. Management practices in European forests, on the other hand, are generally far superior to those in this country.

Comparisons of the state of New England's forests with those in other regions mean little by themselves. If New England does not have enough wood to supply its industries with raw materials, it does not help to say, "Well, neither can the South, or New York State, or the West Coast." It is of the utmost importance for New England to use its valuable forestry resources as efficiently as possible. To keep their employees profitably at work the region's wood-using industries must have the necessary raw materials, independent of other parts of the country.

2. Diameter at breast height, 4.5 feet above the ground.

Forest Growth

In 1944 the total commercial timber growth in New England was estimated by the United States Forest Service at 897,000,000 cubic feet a year,
or 29 cubic feet per acre. Over half that growth was in hardwoods. Saw-
timber growth was 1,799,000,000 board feet a year, of which 910,000,000 was

CHART 1-1

Estimated Timber Growth on Commercial Forest Land in
New England, by States and Wood Type, 1944
(in millions of cubic feet)

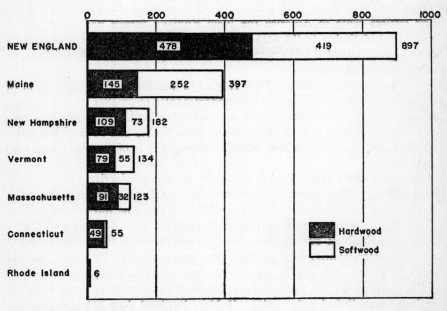

Source: U.S. Forest Service

softwood growth and 889,000,000 was hardwood. Average saw-timber growth
per acre was 58 board feet. The United States average of growth per acre
was also about 29 cubic feet for all timber, but for saw timber it was 77 board
feet an acre. Chart 1-1 shows the timber growth on commercial forest land in
New England, by states.

New England's forest area is theoretically capable of producing more than
11 billion board feet annually—more than 350 board feet per acre per year.
Such an ideal is extremely unlikely of achievement. A degree of forest
management resulting in a doubling or trebling of the present total output

is a more realistic goal. There are numerous examples in the region of rates of growth in excess of 400 feet per acre per year; *there is ample opportunity for improving New England's forests and increasing their total production.*

Forest-management Practices in New England. The principal reason for the low growth rate of New England forests is their past lack of proper management. Even present management practices are generally inadequate to bring the forest stock up to a level sufficient to prevent depletion of the better grades and types of timber. In fact, according to a recent sample study conducted for the Northeast Pulpwood Research Center, it was estimated that during the five-year period 1945–49 about one-fourth of the timber cut in New England was cut under practices which actually deteriorated the forests. Less than 1% of the volume was cut under practices that could be considered "high order," and only 14% following practices which could be rated as good. (See Table 1–1.) According to the sample estimates, Maine had the best record of any New England state, while New Hampshire and Rhode Island had the worst.[3]

Table 1–1. Grades of Forest Cutting Practices in New England, 1945–49 Average vs. 1945

Area	BETTER				POORER		
1945–49 AVERAGE	HIGH ORDER	GOOD	FAIR	TOTAL	POOR	DESTRUCTIVE	TOTAL
Maine	0.1	16.0	67	83.1	15	1.9	16.9
New Hampshire	0.5	7.5	26	34.0	54	12.0	66.0
Vermont	0.2	7.2	72	79.4	20	0.6	20.6
Massachusetts	5.1	17.8	40	62.9	20	17.1	37.1
Rhode Island*	1.0	1.0	8	10.0	58	32.0	90.0
Connecticut	9.0	36.0	25	70.0	24	6.0	30.0
NEW ENGLAND	.7	14.0	59.0	73.7	22.1	4.2	26.3
1945—NEW ENGLAND†	0	7	58	65	29	6	35

* Estimate.
† U.S. Forest Service appraisal as of January 1, 1945.
Source: Northeast Pulpwood Research Center, *Forest Practice Survey Report,* Gorham, N. H., 1952

The Research Center survey helped to bring up to date a study conducted by the United States Forest Service in 1945. That study reported no high-order cutting practices in New England, 7% good, 58% fair, and 35% poor or destructive. The later survey, therefore, indicates increased use of both "high-order" and "good" cutting practices. *Although there has been an improvement, opportunities for further improvement are great. The New England forests need far better management than they have had in the past.*

What are the causes for the low level of forest management in New England? There are a number of reasons, but a principal one seems to be the lack of knowledge by most woodland owners and their lack of interest in putting to work what knowledge they do have. Many woodland owners, especially the small ones, do not understand forest management. They often feel that

3. The Rhode Island figures should be interpreted with caution, since the sample for that state was not considered statistically sound.

there is no point in bothering about their holdings, since their lots are so small that even under the most economical management they would realize only a relatively small income from them. Forestry is usually neither their sole income nor a major source of it. The ownership pattern of New England's forests, therefore, is an important reason for the poor level of forest management in the region.

The United States Forest Service found that in 1944 New England's forests were 95% privately owned. It is doubtful if the percentage has changed much since then. The 5% that was publicly owned was divided as follows: about half by the Federal Government, one-third by the states, and most of the remainder by the towns and cities of the region. A very small percentage was owned by the counties. Of the 29,000,000 acres privately owned in 1950, about 6,100,000 (20%) were owned by the farmers of the region (1950 Census of Agriculture).

In all, there were 243,958 private owners of forest land in New England in 1944. The average holding was 120 acres. Among the owners 99.9% owned less than 5,000 acres. Those small woodland owners, however, held title to only 60% of the region's forest land, and their average holding was but 72 acres. The remaining 40% of the private commercial forest land was held by just 239 owners, 0.1% of the total. Forty-five of them held 32% of the region's private commercial forests.

According to the United States Forest Service, in 1945 more than half the New England forest land in small holdings (under 5,000 acres) was without any forest management. None of it was intensively managed. The 1945 survey indicated not only that the management of small tracts is much inferior to that on the large holdings but also that the large owners could greatly increase the productiveness of New England's forest by increasing the intensity of their management.

Small woodland owners in the aggregate hold title to more land than the large owners, but there are so few large owners that they can be much more easily approached by those interested in good forestry practices. Moreover, the large holders typically work their forests for income and are more concerned with increasing the growth of timber on their land. It is undoubtedly not lack of education, lack of knowledge, or lack of desire for profits that prevents more intensive management on the large holdings, but the problem of profitability of high-level management. Among the small owners, however, the poor practices seem to be largely due to lack of education or just plain lack of interest, which is probably a symptom of lack of education.

The Small Woodland Owner of New England. A survey made in 1949 by the Northeastern Forest Experiment Station studied the small woodland owners of New England to determine their occupations and why they held forest land. The sample covered 23 New England towns. Among other things the survey found that 96% of the owners, holding three-fourths of the small woodland acreage, had occupational interests that did not require the use of their forest land for timber. (See Table 1–2.) Furthermore, over half the properties and two-fifths of the acreage were held for reasons other than their timber values. (Table 1–3.) About two-thirds of the owners lived in the town where the property was located or in an adjacent town, 17% lived elsewhere in the same state, and 18% lived outside the state.

Table 1–2. Occupational Interests of Small Woodland Owners in
New England, 1949*

OCCUPATION	PER CENT OF AREA	PER CENT OF OWNERS
Wood-using plant operations	23.6	3.8
Business and professional	18.6	18.2
Full-time farmers	11.6	18.8
Retired	9.5	10.2
Laborers and clerical workers	8.4	17.8
Housewives	6.0	9.9
Recreation resort operators†	5.5	2.3
Public utilities	3.2	0.4
Dealers in forest land	3.1	2.8
Other	10.5	15.8
TOTAL	100.0	100.0

* In 23 surveyed towns in New England.
† Includes sporting clubs.
Source: Solon Barraclough and James Rettie, The Ownership of
Small Private Forest-Land Holdings in 23 New England
Towns, Northeastern Forest Experiment Station, Up-
per Darby, Pa., 1950

These facts point up the major problems in getting sound management on the small woodlands. They show that many of the owners are hard to reach; they do not receive forestry education as part of their work; they do not live near their lots; and they do not hold the land for its timber value.

A second major reason for the low level of forest management is the uncertainty many timber owners feel about its profitability. The condition of each tract is different from that of every other tract, and so are the objectives of the owners. High-order cutting is generally looked upon as a more expensive way of obtaining a given quantity of timber than are the less desirable methods of cutting. The immediate yields under intensive management may be lower, even though the long-run yields are generally greater. Thus the conflict is between present and future income, and the decision requires some balancing of the costs of building up the woodland against the anticipated revenues. Since a period of years may be required to reap the rewards of high-order management, and since future timber prices are unknown, there has been some skepticism about whether good forestry management does "pay."

Good forest management, like many other operations, results in by-products. If a market can be found for them, or if an existing market can be broadened, forest management can be profitably intensified. *The major by-*

products of forest management are so-called logging waste, "weed" species, and poorly formed trees. At present, markets for these by-products are limited. That limitation has been a third major deterrent to intensive management of forest land in New England, as well as in other sections of

Table 1–3. Reasons Small Woodland Owners Held Timber Land in
New England, 1949*

FOREST PROPERTIES BEING HELD FOR	PER CENT OF OWNERS†	PER CENT OF AREA†
Timber values	43	62
Recreational purposes	20	23
Satisfaction of owning land	15	12
Residential use	15	9
Sale later at a higher price	15	10
Use as pasture	8	6
Other uses	9	10

* In 23 surveyed towns in New England.
† Total greater than 100% because some owners gave more
than one reason for holding land.
Source: Ibid.

the country, even though many progressive woodland owners realize that thinning and weeding operations often more than pay for themselves in enhanced capital values and increased future yields.

Types of Forest Drain

There are numerous types of forest drain, but in New England the largest is from man's harvesting of timber. This includes the material removed from the woods as timber products, and all forms of logging residues. The combined forest drain from destructive agents such as fire, disease, insects, and wind is also significant. On the basis of information pieced together from a number of sources, published and unpublished, New England's annual postwar drain from all causes has been estimated to be about 800,000,000 cubic feet for all types of commercial timber and about 2.5 billion board feet for saw timber. Chart 1–2 summarizes the various drains.

Cutting Drains. Annual postwar cutting drains have been about 671,000,000 cubic feet, of which 394,000,000 has been softwoods and 277,000,000 hardwoods. The region's sawmills are the largest consumers of timber. In 1947 there were 2,359 active sawmills in New England, 4.4% of the national total. Their production of 1.14 billion board feet, however, was only 3.2% of the nation's lumber output. The average annual lumber production per sawmill in New England was about 484,000 board feet. Eighty-five per cent of the mills cut less than a million feet of lumber each and produced 44% of the regional output. Only seven New England mills sawed more than 5,000,000 board feet of lumber in that year.

To reach this output, the sawmills of New England used an estimated 228,000,000 cubic feet of timber, assuming that five board feet of lumber were produced from each cubic foot of timber. While a board foot is 12″ x 12″ x 1″, a cubic foot of New England saw timber yields only about five board feet of lumber because of the shrinkage from slabs, sawdust, and other residual materials.

About 2,000,000 cords of timber are cut annually for pulpwood in New England. Chart 1–3 shows the cut by states for selected postwar years. In an average cord of pulpwood there is about 90 cubic feet of timber, so annual cut

CHART 1–2

Estimated Annual Postwar Timber Drains from the Commercial Forests
of New England, by Sources
(in millions of cubic feet)

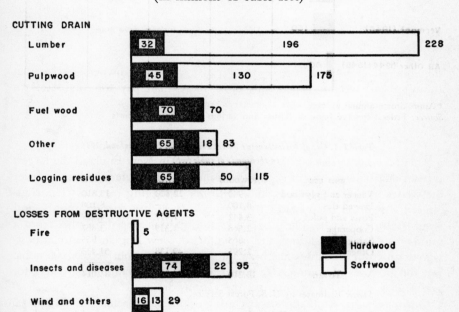

Source: Data or estimates of the Federal Reserve Bank of Boston and the U.S. Forest Service

for pulpwood is about 175,000,000 cubic feet. The most desired species are the softwoods, especially spruce and fir. About two-thirds of the New England pulpwood cut in 1944 was spruce or fir.

The other primary wood-using industries of New England consumed about 83,000,000 cubic feet of the region's timber in 1944. Table 1–4 shows the breakdown of consumption among some of the "miscellaneous" wood-using industries. Veneer and plywood mills have been among the largest of these users, followed by producers of hewed ties.

CHART 1-3

Wood Cut for Pulpwood in the New England States in Recent Years
(in thousands of cords)

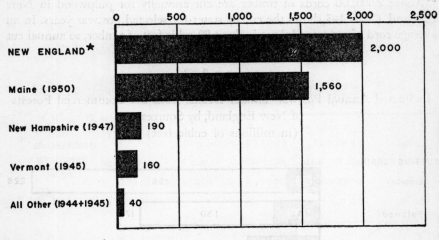

* Approximate annual average.
Source: Federal Reserve Bank of Boston and various state forestry reports

Table 1-4. Cut of Miscellaneous Forest Products in New England, 1944
(in thousands of cubic feet)

END USE	SOFTWOODS	HARDWOODS	TOTAL
Veneer and plywood	940	12,870	13,810
Hewed ties	8,100	—	8,100
Posts and poles	3,442	1,477	4,919
Cooperage	2,568	1,319	3,887
Shingles	865	—	865
Other	2,295	49,138	51,433
TOTAL	18,210	64,804	83,014

Source: Estimates by U. S. Forest Service

In timber operations of all kinds, there are large amounts of by-products that are not used commercially. These by-products are referred to as "waste" or "residual materials," whether or not their utilization is economically feasible. There are two types of timber residues, logging residue and primary manufacturing residue. Logging residues include all unutilized stems, or parts of stems, tops, and limbs of cut trees left in the forests, plus all damage done to other trees as a result of timber operations. Primary manufacturing residues include both coarse materials, such as slabs, edgings, and trimmings, and fine materials such as sawdust and shavings. In addition to the timber residues, some manufacturing operations produce large quantities of unutilized chemical residues, bark, and other materials.

The harvesting of timber is often inefficient, especially on small woodlands where loggers are likely to be unskilled and supervision poor. Much good timber is undoubtedly lost because too much wood is left in the stumps. As much as 5% of the best wood can be lost by cutting stumps too high. Also, loggers are often careless about where trees fall, causing needless destruction or damage to growing trees. And when logs are skidded or dragged out of

CHART 1–4

Wood Waste in New England, 1944 *

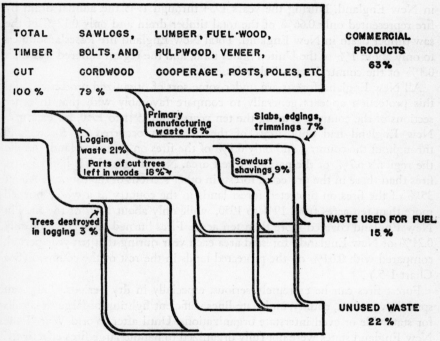

TOTAL	SAWLOGS,	LUMBER, FUEL-WOOD,	COMMERCIAL
TIMBER	BOLTS, AND	PULPWOOD, VENEER,	PRODUCTS
CUT	CORDWOOD	COOPERAGE, POSTS, POLES, ETC	63%
100%	79%		

Primary manufacturing waste 16%

Slabs, edgings, trimmings 7%

Logging waste 21%

Parts of cut trees left in woods 18%

Sawdust shavings 9%

Trees destroyed in logging 3%

WASTE USED FOR FUEL 15%

UNUSED WASTE 22%

* Primary manufacture only, excluding wood pulp.
Source: Federal Reserve Bank of Boston, based on 1944 study by U.S. Forest Service

the forest carelessly, the same sort of damage results. Finally, logs are too seldom cut to grade specifications which foresee their highest economic utilization.

In 1944 only 63% of the commodity timber drain from the New England forests ended up as commercial products. (See Chart 1–4.) The remainder was residual material of one type or another. Over 42% of the residual material was used for fuel, though often not efficiently. The logging residues exceeded manufacturing residues by nearly 30%. In Chart 1–2 only the logging residues were shown separately; manufacturing residues were included in the figures for each of the other cutting drains.

The amount of wood residues in New England is truly impressive, but it still is not as large relatively as in other parts of the country. In the United States as a whole, wood residues represented 57% of the total commodity drain in 1944. Only about one-third of that residual material was used for fuel. *While New England's position in the generation and use of residues compares favorably with that of the United States as a whole, the region should not be satisfied as long as there are opportunities to improve the efficiency with which its timber is used.*

Fire Losses. Losses from fire have not been a major source of timber drain in New England. During the years 1934 through 1943 the annual drain by fire represented only 0.66% of the total timber drain and only 0.12% of the saw-timber drain in New England. Total New England fire losses amounted to only about 1% of the United States total, and the region suffered less than 0.4% of the country's saw-timber losses.

All New England forests are under some sort of organized protection, and this protection appears generally to compare favorably with that in other sections of the country. During the ten years from 1941 to 1950, for example, New England had only 2.7% of the fires that occurred on forest land throughout the country, and only 6.1% of the fires on protected land, despite the region's 6.7% of the nation's forest area. New England has had smaller fires than those in the protected forests in other sections of the country. About 35% of the fires on protected forest lands in the country as a whole burned more than ten acres from 1941 to 1950, while only about 10% of the fires in New England covered more than ten acres. Fires burned an average of only 0.24% of New England's forested area each year during that ten-year period, compared with 0.64% on the protected lands in the rest of the country. (See Chart 1–5.)

Forest fires can be extremely serious, especially in dry periods. They can spread over town, county, and state lines. Efficient fighting of large fires calls for statewide or even interstate organizations. Until after World War II the New England states were not fully organized to handle large fires effectively. There was too much reliance on inadequately trained local forces, and there was little central control for coordinating fire-fighting efforts. Since the war the central authority of the states has been strengthened, especially in Maine.

Since the great New England forest fires of October 1947 there has also been conspicuous interstate cooperation in working out a system for fire control. Most notable was the establishment of the Interstate Forest Fire Protection Compact, which covers all the New England states and New York. These seven states, with the approval of the United States Congress, have ratified and implemented the agreement. Although they have not yet joined, New Jersey, Pennsylvania, Quebec, and New Brunswick are eligible for inclusion. The member states are bound by the compact to render all possible aid to other member states in combatting, controlling, or preventing forest fires, with due regard to the maintenance of protection at home.

New England can be proud of its forest-fire record and the forward-looking legislation its states have enacted to aid in forest-fire protection. Nevertheless, opportunities for improvement still remain in some areas. Further improvements are being made continuously, and some further reduction in the overall forest drain from this source can be anticipated.

CHART 1–5

Area Burned by Forest Fires in New England and the United States
on Protected Lands, 1941–50
(per cent of total area)

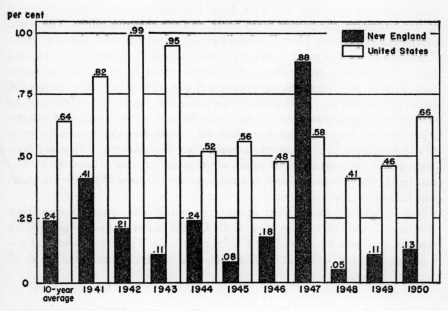

Source: U.S. Forest Service

Losses from Insects, Disease, and Wind. Almost 16% of New England's total timber drain each year and about 10% of the region's saw-timber drain are due to natural destructive agents such as wind, insects, and disease. There is little that can be done to prevent windstorm losses except to remove the more susceptible, older trees before they blow over and to salvage wind-thrown timber. Younger trees ordinarily bend more readily with the wind and are often sheltered by larger trees. There is a larger percentage of loss from wind in saw timber than in timber of other types.

Losses from insects and disease are far larger than losses from wind, as

Chart 1–2 shows. The figures there are conservative estimates by the United States Forest Service for an average year during the period 1934–43. Some individual states have made estimates that are substantially higher. It is difficult to determine precisely the loss from disease and insects, because many of the trees attacked are not killed outright. Attack by these pests frequently results in deformation and decay, or in retardation of the rate of growth.

There are two types of insect and disease destruction, endemic losses and epidemic losses. The former result from the normal activities of established insects and disease pests, the latter from outbreaks that spread rapidly and markedly affect the forests. Examples of endemic losses are heart rots, blister rusts, and most of the insects and diseases that attack tree leaves and stems without killing the tree. Endemic *disease* losses are far more serious in New England than endemic *insect* losses.

Examples of epidemic losses in New England are those caused by the spruce budworm, the bronze birch borer, and the chestnut blight. The latter completely wiped out New England's stands of commercial chestnut trees. Epidemic losses are more difficult to control than fire, once they obtain a foothold. *The best preventions for epidemic forest losses are sound forest management and vigorous early action if the disease or insect strikes. A healthy, fast-growing, well-managed forest is less likely to be damaged by insects or diseases than a poorly managed forest. Unfortunately, not enough is yet known about many of the insects and diseases that devastate large areas of our forests for us to be able to prevent their depredations. There has been considerable research on those problems, especially by the United States Department of Agriculture, but much more research is needed by private, state, and federal groups.*

New England's total timber losses from wind, insects, and disease from 1934 to 1943 were more than 12% of the United States total, and the region's saw-timber losses were nearly 9% of the nation's. Those losses are far too high for a region with but 5.2% of the total timber volume and 3.6% of the saw timber.

Net Growth or Drain in the New England Forests

Chart 1–6 shows in summary the estimated annual postwar forest growth and forest drain in New England. Although the over-all annual forest growth currently exceeds the total drain by about 97,000,000 cubic feet on a volume basis, the drain on the timber of saw-log size exceeds the growth by about 697,000,000 board feet a year. The average size of the trees in the woods is gradually becoming smaller. Continuation of the present ratio of drain to growth of saw timber will affect the future supply adversely. On the other hand, because most of the growth is in the poorer trees, many of them of sprout origin, the oversupply of small and inferior material is gradually increasing. Our forests are being taken over by timber which is not well suited to the established uses. Many local forest-dependent industries are meeting increasing difficulties in finding opportunities to buy suitable timber and logs.

This progressive depletion and gradual deterioration of the softwoods, particularly those mainly utilized for saw timber, and the pressure on certain of the higher grades of hardwoods must be replaced by progressive rehabilitation and increased productivity if the region's forests are to contribute to the economic growth of New England.

CHART 1–6

Estimated Annual Postwar Forest Growth and Total Forest Drain in New England, by Type of Timber

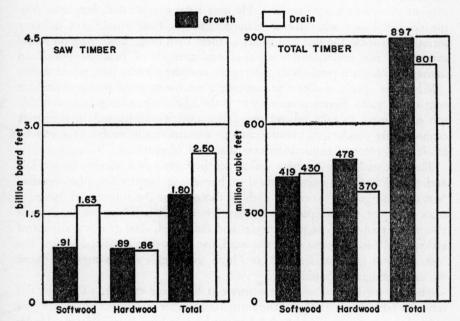

Source: Based on data and estimates of the U.S. Forest Service

The initial objective of a New England forest policy, therefore, should be achievement of at least a balance between annual growth in the forests and the yearly requirements of the established wood-using industries. The policy should also aim toward additional future growth sufficient to permit expansion of these and new wood-consuming industries. Such an objective should have two principal components: better use of the present timber resources and an increase in the over-all productivity of the forests.

The first objective can be accomplished by reducing wastes in the harvesting and processing of timber, by finding economic uses for underutilized timber types, and by reducing losses from insects, disease, and fire. The second objective can be accomplished by improving forest-management practices. Under our free enterprise system, incentives are important considerations in the improvement of present practices. In the following section we shall suggest some ways of increasing these incentives.

A PROGRAM FOR THE PROGRESSIVE REHABILITATION OF NEW ENGLAND FOREST LAND

Improving Forest Management

An old forester once claimed that a lot of people think forest management consists of shooting woodpeckers. He may have exaggerated, but most people do not know what forest management is. That would not be very serious, except for the fact that many of them own forest land. A great many owners do not understand even the fundamentals of practical woodland management. As a result both the region and the owners themselves suffer.

When we speak of forest management we mean good management for continuous yield. Forest management is the efficient handling and profitable use of a forest to take advantage of the capacity of its soil in the most economically productive manner and to maximize the profits that can be made on a piece of timberland over a period of years.

The first settlers in America looked on the forests as a mine to be worked and then left. The typical method of harvesting lumber was the so-called "cut out and get out" method, without thought for the future. All the good trees were cut, all the poor trees were left standing. There was a gradual rise in the proportion of poor species and deformed, slow-growing timber of all types. When one area was exhausted, the work continued elsewhere. The "cut out and get out" method, or "high grading," is even now far more widespread than it should be.

Another method of working a forest is by "clear cutting." This practice removes both the mature and the immature timber and leaves an empty plot of land that may not yield another harvest for two human generations. Under certain conditions the clear cutting of limited areas does not violate the principle of good management, particularly in inaccessible parts of northern New England, but normally the method is wasteful and destructive.

Still another method of working a forest is by "cutting to a diameter limit," which means that the trees above a certain diameter are all cut and those below the limit are left standing. While this is a definite improvement over widespread clear cutting or high grading, it still leaves much to be desired.

Foresters realize the shortcomings of the "cut out and get out" method and of the other inferior practices. They have learned that if most forests are given even a minimum of good treatment they can yield a continuous income for their owners. Forest management is analogous to the management of a herd of cattle. Both should be handled so that the stock reproduces and grows all the time and younger stock is always coming along to replace the older slow-growing stock that is taken out and sold.

A forest is in many ways like a garden. It will do better if it is weeded and cultivated. There are weed trees—undesirable species—and poorly formed trees. Weeds interfere with the growth of the desirable trees and make the forests less profitable. Since the owner gets his income from the growth of trees, the annual growth rate per acre is an indicator of how profitable a forest is. Increasing the growth of the forests depends on the practices adopted by the woodland owners. By working to increase his forest growth and his own profits, the individual owner can also help the wood-using industries of New England and the region as a whole.

How can an owner increase the rate of growth of timber on his land? To get the fastest growth, he should see that his land is well stocked with the most thrifty trees. He should make full use of the land, but it should not be crowded. The best number of trees per acre depends on the age of the trees, the species, and the growing conditions. A rough rule of thumb followed by many foresters for determining the proper spacing between two adjacent trees is to divide the sum of their diameters in inches by two and add six, which gives the distance in feet. If trees grow too far apart they are likely to be excessively branchy and have badly shaped trunks. These trees yield knotty, poorly shaped logs. When trees are crowded, they lose vigor and grow slowly. Proper spacing is an important part of sound forestry, aimed at producing vigorous, healthy, and well-formed trees of desirable species.

Thus the slow-growing trees, the deformed trees, and those of inferior species should be removed as early as possible in the management program. Improvement of the forest may involve any of a number of treatments: weeding, thinning, or the harvesting of salable lumber by partial cuttings.

Partial cuttings remove mature trees, singly or in small blocks, to make room for the young, faster growing timber. The speed with which a tree grows depends on the climate, soil, type of tree, influence of surrounding trees, and the care it is given. A vigorous New England white pine increases its volume at the peak of productivity by as much as 14 board feet a year. (See Chart 1-7.) If the purpose is to obtain maximum volume production, these trees should ordinarily be cut when their diameters reach 18 to 20 inches. Obtaining maximum volume production may not always be the governing principle, however, particularly with respect to individual trees. Trees that are of inferior species or are deformed, defective, or dying take room from faster growing or otherwise more desirable trees. If it is not profitable to remove these "weeds," they should at least be killed by girdling or some other method. Ideally, a forest property should consist of trees of all ages, for then part of the forest is continually reaching maturity. A forest property that is managed well will tend toward this ideal, though it is not an absolute necessity for profitability.

Along with partial or selective cutting, the woodland owner should see that his land is protected against fire as much as is economically possible. Furthermore, when the timber is harvested, he should see that waste and damage to standing timber are minimized.

A well-managed forest can contain upward of 15,000 board feet of timber

CHART 1–7

How White Pine Trees Increase in Volume

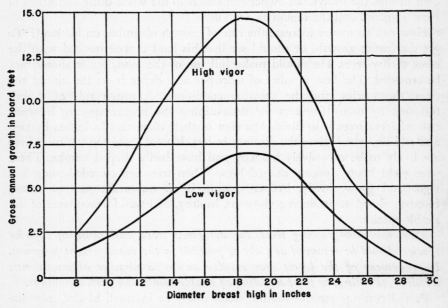

Source: Federal Reserve Bank of Boston, from New England Forestry Foundation

per acre, and it can grow at an annual rate of over 300 feet per acre.[4] Varying periods of years are required for individual forests to reach that level, but forests can be profitable before such an ideal state is reached.

We have showed that in recent years only a very small percentage of New England woodland owners engaged in even moderately sound forest management. The small owner, especially, followed poor management practices. From that discussion it seemed clear that a large number of small owners

4. This is an expression of a practical objective for whole forest properties. Pure white pine may grow at an annual rate of 1,200 board feet per acre or more and attain a total volume of more than 40,000 feet per acre under highly favorable conditions.

would improve the level of management, if they could be reached and if good forestry could be explained to them. *For the small woodland owners the problem of better forest management is largely one of education. Many agencies, both public and private, have been carrying on extensive educational programs.* The state and federal forest services and departments of agriculture, the state development commissions, the lumber producers and dealers, contractors, box manufacturers, paper manufacturers, and other trade developmental groups all have a deep interest in building up the condition of the forests. *They should develop and carry out an improved, concerted educational program among small woodland owners and the public. For maximum effectiveness, it should be cooperative and fully coordinated.*

There are other small owners who just do not want to be bothered with their woodlands. They feel that the absolute return would be so small it would not be worth their effort. They would probably not respond well to education. What can be done about them? *One method is for them to turn over the management of their woodland to someone else, a consulting forester, a company, or an association organized to provide forest-management services.*

Of course, some of these owners would have to be convinced that the harvesting of timber on their land would not affect the other values of their forests. They may still think of timber harvesting as clear cutting. Where they can be shown that their forest land would be improved they might be more interested, especially since it would relieve them of the burden of personal supervision. Such an arrangement has many advantages, particularly for absentee owners or others not in a position to give direct attention to management of the property or removal and sale of the forest products.

The New England Forestry Foundation. Several new private organizations have been formed in New England to assist the small woodland owner in improving his forest management while also increasing his long-term profits and capital values. A leading organization of this type is the New England Forestry Foundation. The foundation is a private, nonprofit corporation which provides complete forestry service at cost. Trained foresters operate from the foundation's forest-management centers scattered throughout New England. In 1952 there were ten such centers and two subcenters. More are planned.

The foundation offers a number of services. Its foresters will examine a tract, work out a forest-management plan, mark the timber on the area for cutting, and market the timber. All the details of managing, cutting, and selling the timber are taken care of if the owner so desires. Cuttings are made at five- or ten-year intervals, and the value of the standing timber is steadily improved.

By the end of 1952 the foundation had served more than 1,000 clients owning a total of 231,069 acres. While that is only a little more than 1% of the forest land in New England held by small owners, the foundation's work has been increasing at a rapid pace. It has cut selectively, according to long-range plans, more than 52,000,000 board feet of timber. As its activities spread, it will become better known and its clientele should continue to expand. *The work of the New England Forestry Foundation can be a major force in reaching New England's forest goals, and it deserves region-wide support and use.*

Connwood, Incorporated. A small woodland owner can also be relieved of the problem of marketing his timber by joining or using a marketing cooperative. There are several local forest-products cooperatives in New England. One of them is Connwood, Incorporated, which was formed in Connecticut in 1945 and operates there and in adjacent areas. Its chief function is to market the timber of its members and of others that call on it in order to maximize the price received. It insists on good forestry practices, however, before it will handle the timber. Connwood provides special services, such as mapping, estimating, and planting for woodland owners, but those are not its major functions.

Connwood's approach to the problem of small woodland management is sound. It does not offer all the services of the Forestry Foundation, but it does offer small owners a definite inducement to improve their forestry practices while they also benefit from maximum returns on the cuttings.

Timber Owners of New England, Inc., and the Small Woodland Owner. Another example of how private interests can help to improve the level of forest management in New England, while securing a good financial return, is the recently formed Timber Owners of New England, Inc. This company's objective is to acquire woodland properties and manage them over time for maximum long-term profits. Advance estimates for the first two lots acquired by the company indicate a substantial annual return. The prospect of income taxation at the capital-gains rate is an important consideration in this undertaking.

The company's present properties are all in New Hampshire, where it has the advantage of a yield tax instead of the usual property tax. Stockholders purchase stock in exchange for either cash or forest property. All timber is cut selectively to build up the stand for increased and sustained yield. The separate lots can be cut in rotation to produce an annual income. *This pooling of interests by investors in managing a group of separate woodlots for financial return is a promising departure from conventional forest ownership. If it grows as a device, it can become a significant element in increasing the yield of New England's forests.*

Other Aids to Woodland Owners. There are numerous other sources of private, public, and quasi-public aids to woodland owners in New England. All the New England states maintain forestry departments which, with the cooperation of the Federal Government, maintain staffs of county foresters whose advice is available to small woodland owners. The forestry departments administer the state-owned woodlands as well as maintain forest-fire and disease protection in cooperation with federal agencies. The Federal Government helps to maintain state extension foresters who also bring forestry advice and education to woodland owners.

Private associations other than those previously mentioned, such as the Society for the Protection of New Hampshire Forests and the forest and park associations of Massachusetts and Connecticut, promote sound forestry by education and demonstration programs. Private consulting foresters and firms of timber cruisers and surveyors also offer management and cutting services.

Indirectly, many other groups are aiding the woodland owner, by carrying on basic and applied research in many areas of silviculture, marketing, and protection from disease and insects. Most of the state universities and some private universities are carrying on research in their forestry departments. The Northeastern Forest Experiment Station of the United States Forest Service, the Northeast Pulpwood Research Center, the New England Council, and the Federal Reserve Bank of Boston are examples of public, private, and quasi-public groups that are sponsoring or carrying on research to help forestry in New England.

In sum, the available aids to woodland owners are substantial. Many owners fail to avail themselves of the opportunities to learn about or to apply improved practices, however, because they do not know about them or are not sufficiently interested. This situation underscores the need for co-ordination and improvement in the educational activities of the organizations concerned.

Conclusions on the Small Woodland Owner's Role in Improving the Forests. The aggregate opportunity for improvement in the quality of forest management in New England is far greater on the small woodlands than on the large holdings. What is the likelihood of such improvements? It will probably be slow. The lack of knowledge and interest will be difficult to overcome. Much can probably be accomplished eventually, however, through the sustained joint efforts of the interested public and private groups.

Whatever the eventual improvements on the small woodlands, a more rapid way to achieve higher growth rates would seem to be to induce the large owners to step up the intensity of their forest management. The 239 owners of tracts 5,000 acres or more in extent control 11,600,000 acres of the region's forests. If they were to raise the level of their forest management so that the average acre had an annual growth of 200 board feet, imports of forest products could be reduced considerably. We could reasonably expect higher yields to result, moreover, from widespread application of more intensive forest management. Would more intensive management be profitable for the large forest owner?

A great deal has been written about the profitability of intensive forest management, but there is still no generally accepted view on the subject. Indeed, there does not seem to be a single simple answer. In many cases truly intensive management probably would pay well, while in others it might not be profitable under present economic conditions. Each situation has to be analyzed separately.

Even if intensive management is not profitable in every instance, those who have the most to gain by increasing the profitability of their forests have not yet experimented extensively to test the value of the method. *Few large forest owners in New England apply intensive management. At least some of those who do follow such management practices are convinced that the extra costs, if any, are more than compensated by the increased yield and improved certainty of future supply. It would seem that many more large forest owners would benefit from high-level forest management.*

In appraising the profitability of improved management, one should remember that timber growing is a long-run venture. Present costs should be balanced against expected future timber prices in determining the most profitable level of management. Timber requirements in this country are still increasing, and the supply of timber has been decreasing. It appears quite likely that future timber prices will rise above the general level of wholesale prices, just as they have in the past. Changing technology and the rise of new materials have reduced the demand for timber for some uses, but the demand for other uses has increased. It does not appear likely that the upward trend in stumpage values will be reversed in the foreseeable future by overproduction resulting from improved forest management. An increase in the supply of readily usable material, beyond amounts needed by existing industries, could be expected to attract new uses and lead to even greater demand.

The rate at which good forest management advances in New England will depend in part on the availability of labor adapted to work in the woods. Logging and pulpwood operations are in continuous competition with other industries able to offer employment terms and conditions that are more attractive to many workers. In spite of the many improvements in working conditions brought by mechanization, greatly improved living quarters and diets in the camps, higher wages, and other inducements, the pulpwood producers of northern New England have had to depend heavily on permit labor brought in from Canada. In southern New England there is a shortage of men willing to go into the woods who possess even moderate skills for the job.

Present signs point toward continuation of the shortage of woods labor as at least a moderate deterrent to the application of improved forest-management practices in New England. One of the industry's problems is how to build up a more favorable attitude toward woods work without excessively increasing costs.

Since the relationship between stumpage prices and costs is so important to owners working their forests for profit, we shall consider some of the ways in which this relationship can be changed in favor of the woodland owner. Concentration of effort should be on reducing the costs of more intensive forest management, to minimize the possible competitive disadvantages from generally higher stumpage prices. Where the growing timber can be used more economically, however, even an increase in stumpage prices need not result in increased costs to the wood-consuming industries, as we shall see in discussing the marketing of wood residues and surplus wood.

The rest of this section contains brief discussions of four major problems in changing the relationship between timber prices and costs: forest taxation, forest-fire insurance, forest credit, and the increased utilization of surplus and waste wood. They are the ones that have been most widely discussed and seem most likely of success. In each case, our concern is primarily for the woodland whose owner's chief concern is making a profit on his timber.

Forest Taxation

So far as possible taxes on the forests should be levied to increase rather than diminish the incentives of owners to adopt good forestry practices. Unfortunately, most present forest taxation dulls the owner's incentive to practice good forestry. New Hampshire's recent universal forest-yield tax is the most important exception to that general condition.

In most of New England except New Hampshire the preponderance of forest land is taxed under the general property tax laws, as if standing timber were short-term commercial inventory rather than a long-term investment. Owners of timber are continually threatened with increased assessments as the timber stands are improved, and they always face the possibility of an increased rate of taxation. Such a tax policy discourages good forest management.

In Massachusetts and Connecticut forest land owners can request that their timber and land be assessed separately, and they can pay a modified yield or severance tax on the timber removed from classified forest land. Few owners take advantage of this procedure, partly because of the special effort and complicated procedure of the optional plan, and partly because of lack of knowledge about the plan.

Neither Vermont nor Rhode Island has a special forest-land tax law. In the organized towns of Maine, forest taxation is administered by each town, usually under the general property tax laws. The taxation in the unorganized towns and in the so-called "wild lands" is handled by the state. The state has adopted a policy of low valuations and moderate tax rates which has contributed to stable ownership and conservative management.

Much of the forest land in New England, especially in the three southern states, will require years of good management before the growing stock can be built up sufficiently to yield a substantial return to the owner. If the standing timber is subjected to taxes each year, the owner is faced with the necessity of investing more money to pay the taxes, with no financial returns for many years. The owner may be unable to tie up the extra money and may liquidate part or all of his timber assets before they have reached the proper age for cutting. If the timber were not subject to tax until it was cut, however, the owner would not face that added pressure and would have the opportunity to build up his forest for a maximum yield. Moreover, over time the larger yields would produce increased tax revenues for the communities. These are the advantages of a severance or yield tax. The yield tax should apply automatically to all commercial timberland and make it unnecessary for the owner to apply for special treatment. The land itself, of course, should be taxed according to the general property tax laws. If the land is equitably assessed so high that forestry is unprofitable, this should be an indication that the land is better adapted to other uses.

The forest-yield tax adopted by New Hampshire in 1949 has the advantages mentioned above, plus additional incentives for good forestry management. No other state in the union has a forest taxation law that is so progressive. It abolished the annual property tax on all standing timber and substituted a yield tax of 10% of the stumpage value when the timber is cut. The tax is reduced to 7% if the state forester verifies that the cutting conforms to good forestry practices as outlined in the law itself. Since many towns necessarily experienced a temporary reduction in tax revenue as a result of the law, a state reimbursement fund was established to compensate towns temporarily for any resulting loss of revenue.

The New Hampshire tax law lowers the cost of improved management and increases the economic incentive for good forestry, but it is not a cure-all for poor forest management. According to a recent study by the Northeastern Forest Experiment Station: "The greatest long-run value of the new law is in its educational effect. Widespread public discussion has been aroused by the passage and application of the new law. Some knowledge of desirable forest practices has been acquired by selectmen, landowners, and operators throughout the state. Forestry has a more realistic meaning to these people now than it had two years ago." [5]

While improved forest taxation does not guarantee the best forest practices, the individual state governments could hardly adopt any more effective legislation for promoting sound forestry. *We strongly recommend the adoption by the other New England states of forest taxation laws similar to that of New Hampshire.* *

5. Solon Barraclough and Ernest M. Gould, Jr., *A Preliminary Appraisal of New Hampshire's Forest-yield Tax,* Northeastern Forest Experiment Station, U. S. Forest Service, November 1951.

* *Dissenting opinion by Committee member.* I do not join in this recommendation for all states, as I am not sure that the New Hampshire yield tax is applicable to the situation in Maine at the present time, and I believe that there is much to be said in favor of trying to improve the assessment method.—Edward E. Chase.

Forest-Fire Insurance

One obstacle to good forest management is the risk of forest fires. It takes years to convert a poor or mediocre forest into a well-stocked, fast-growing stand. This rehabilitation process often requires the investment of capital as well as time. Many timberland owners hesitate to make the necessary outlays because they fear that a fire could wipe out all or a large share of the investment.

Forest-fire insurance is one means of reducing the risk. If a woodland owner could insure his timber at a reasonable rate, he would be more inclined to improve his stand and delay cutting his timber. The safety of the owner's investment would be more assured at all stages of the trees' growth. An insured owner should also find it easier to obtain a loan for forest improvements, if necessary. The fire insurance would make him a better risk.

Forest-fire insurance is not a new idea. Some European countries have had it for many years. A forest-fire insurance company existed in New Hampshire for several years during and after World War I with fair success, but its lack of sufficient reserves induced it to sell out to a larger insurance company. In 1927 the United States Chamber of Commerce made a study of forest-fire insurance possibilities in the United States and found such insurance unlikely to be successful. At that time, however, organized fire protection in the country was far less widespread than it is today, and lumber prices were so low that there was less incentive to protect the forests or improve forestry practices.

The interest in fire insurance has recently been renewed in New England by the United States Chamber of Commerce and other public and private groups, especially the New Hampshire Forestry and Recreation Commission and the New England Council. Insurance companies are also taking an active interest in its development.

Most of northern New England is an especially good risk for forest-fire insurance. Besides being well protected by organized fire control, most of the area has a wet humus soil, high humidity, abundant and fairly even precipitation, numerous roads, farms, and other natural fire barriers.

To be successful, forest-fire insurance must be inexpensive and readily available to small and medium woodland owners. Some large owners may be less interested in full-coverage insurance because their holdings are self-insuring to some extent against ordinary fires. If it were available, however, they might find some form of conflagration or catastrophe insurance attractive. The pulp and paper companies with large timber holdings realize the importance of their forests as dependable sources of pulpwood and the importance of maintaining high fire-protection standards. They cooperate with and supplement the state forest-fire organizations directly and through private protection associations. Many large users of timber favor the idea of insurance, and some of those with large holdings might be expected to buy insurance for their own protection as well as to encourage small woodland owners to follow suit.

Some insurance companies sell forest-fire insurance today, but it apparently has not had many takers, in part because of a lack of concerted promotion and in part because of resistance to the premium rates charged. One of the large New England stock fire-insurance companies, for example, has offered such insurance during the last 10 or 12 years for as low as $8 per $1,000 of value in some particularly favorable cases, but it has had less than one inquiry a week about it.

If forest-fire insurance and its benefits are to become widespread in New England, there must be much more activity in publicizing its advantages, both to woodland owners and to the insurance companies. The insurance companies have been reluctant to undertake a full-scale promotion campaign until they have explored the situation more thoroughly. The New England Council's Forestry and Wood Industries Committee has planned a full investigation of the possibilities and profitability of forest-fire insurance in New England.

The extensive use of forest-fire insurance would probably help improve forestry practices in some cases, especially if the insurance companies keyed their rates realistically to the aggregate of forest-fire losses. Its effect would probably be greatest on the small and medium woodland owners, to whom the loss from an ordinary fire can be a real catastrophe. Probably fire insurance is less important than improved forest taxation or the greater utilization of surplus wood and waste, but it would be one additional stimulant to good forestry.

Forest Credit

The rehabilitation of much of New England's forest area will be expedited if it can be given the benefit of improvement work on timber stands such as thinning, weeding, and in some cases replanting. Such work often requires a net cash outlay because the cost exceeds the value of the salable or usable material produced. Some young timber stands in need of such treatment contain nothing of immediate economic value to offset the cost of improvement. Shortage of capital funds to finance this needed work is one of the recognized handicaps to the forest rehabilitation program. Various methods of overcoming it have been suggested. One suggestion that has received widespread attention is that timber owners might tap new sources of capital through the use of credit.

Forest properties are generally less acceptable as collateral security for loans, however, than most other types of property, particularly for terms as long as would be needed for this type of financing. In part this is because the publicity given to forest fires has created excessively unfavorable impressions of the risk of loss. National banks are prohibited by law from making loans on unimproved property, and the Comptroller of the Currency has specifically ruled that forests are not improved properties within the meaning of the law. Some state bankers' associations have suggested modifications of this ruling. Production loans, with standing timber forming a part of the collateral security, are quite common where immediate cutting operations are planned, but long-term credits are less frequent. Recently four large life insurance companies have announced long-term lending programs for forest owners, but so far they have apparently confined their operations largely to the South.

This venture by the insurance companies into a new type of credit appears to be based on the assumption that many owners are unable to undertake the work essential to rehabilitation of their forest properties because of their limited financial resources. The venture also apparently rests on a belief that the rehabilitation will be accompanied by increases in values and yields more than sufficient to liquidate the loan within the term specified in the agreement. The maximum amount loaned is presumably a percentage of the value of the whole property which is pledged as security when the loan is made.

Thrifty stands of timber are frequently cut just as they are entering their period of greatest productivity, because the owners need or want their current value in cash. Some of these stands would more than double in volume and triple in value in another 15 years or so if they could be left to grow. With some forest management, they would do still better. If the destruction of these stands could be prevented through the use of credit or some other device, the benefits would be significant. More timber would become available for the wood-using industries, and the owners would have more profitable investments.

Forest credit and other possible methods of meeting forestry's need for increased capital funds should continue to engage the attention of foresters and others concerned with the problem. Lending institutions should take an active part in the search for improved methods of extending credit that are mutually satisfactory to the borrower and the lender. Fortunately, there are signs that some headway is being made in the solution of this problem.

Utilization of Residues and Surplus Wood

Directly and indirectly, one of the greatest contributions to better forest management would be reduction of the amount of wood residues and greater use of timber by-products. As we have said, there are three principal types of by-products, logging residues, manufacturing residues, and surplus wood. What are the chances of reducing wood residues in New England? Can better use be made of surplus wood and of that residue which is unavoidable?

Logging residues could and should be reduced by adopting better harvesting methods and by making it more profitable to remove much of the cut and damaged timber that is now left in the forests. The best method of eliminating incomplete harvesting of timber is close supervision by experienced foresters, though that is not always possible. Another important method is continuing education of small woodland owners in proper harvesting methods to show them how to increase their forestry returns. Such education can probably be conducted best by the various public and semipublic forestry agencies, but private groups should cooperate actively in the effort.

Wood left in the forest is frequently usable for pulpwood, fuel, fence posts, or other products. Handling and transportation costs sometimes make removal of this material impractical, but in many cases failure to put it to use is due to the prevalent practice of "one-product" logging. Operations are commonly undertaken to produce nothing but saw logs, often softwood saw logs only, and the operators may show little interest in the market prospects of other products. Fortunately the benefits and economies of "integrated" logging are coming to be increasingly understood in New England and elsewhere.

It is to be hoped that the time will not arrive in New England, as it did years ago in most of Europe, when every branch and twig will be removed from the forest. Some wood should be left to decay and restore humus to the soil. Leaving excessive amounts, however, not only augments the waste volume but also raises the hazard of damage from fire, insects, and disease.

Improved transportation facilities are needed in some forested areas, as are improved marketing channels. Insufficient roads of access frequently make it difficult to apply adequate management practices in certain parts of the region. The improvement of marketing channels has been aided by organizations like Connwood and the New England Forestry Foundation, which provide woodland owners with marketing services that incorporate the principle of integrated operation. In contrast to "one-product" operation, they give attention to the market prospects of *all* the material ripe for removal.

Logging residue is a serious nationwide as well as regional problem. It deserves a great deal of study and constructive effort by public and private groups. In the past, when wood was plentiful, many inefficient logging practices were condoned. These practices have been passed down from generation to generation, and they are difficult to change. They must be changed, however, if New England is to realize the potential of its forest resources.

The second important source of residues is the manufacture of primary wood products. More than half of this type of residue is the result of sawmill operations. Another 14% arises from the manufacture of pulp and paper, largely in the form of chemical residues. What are the chances of reducing these residues?

There is probably little hope of substantially reducing the amount of manufacturing residue, especially in sawmill operations, as long as lumber is the prime sawmill product. Logs are round, and lumber is rectangular. There will necessarily be a more or less constant proportion of slabs and other coarse material. Furthermore, unless new mechanical methods are developed, most woodworking operations will produce sawdust and shavings. There is some avoidable residue, however, due to decay of wood awaiting processing. This is even true in the pulp industry, which has to maintain substantial inventories of pulpwood, sometimes for considerable periods. Nevertheless, it is unlikely that any great strides in reducing manufacturers' residue will be made in the near future, so the major task is to find more uses for the residue.

The limited market for logging residues, surplus wood, and manufacturing residues has been a major factor in their inefficient use. This limitation has been a marked deterrent to good forest management. So far as the wood-using industries are concerned, they obviously receive less revenue per unit of raw timber than they would if their by-products could be sold or used profitably. If satisfactory markets existed for all the industrial by-products, raw timber values would tend to rise. This would increase the incentive for more intensive forest management. Both the woodland owner and the manufacturer stand to gain, therefore, from any technological or institutional changes which make possible better use of the by-products.

It has been estimated that the total by-product volume available for use in New England amounts to about 7,000,000 tons a year (approximately 315,000,000 cubic feet), including logging residue, surplus wood, and manufacturing residue. What are the reasons for the present limited by-product utilization? The most important are limitations of concentration points, limitations of technical knowledge, and lack of market development for new products made largely from waste.

One of the major problems in finding economical uses for waste in New England is the small number of major waste-concentration points. As we have pointed out, only seven of New England's 2,359 active sawmills in 1947 produced over 5,000,000 board feet of lumber. Furthermore, there are few concentration yards in New England for drying, surfacing, and grading lumber. As a result, sawmill operations and their by-products are scattered widely throughout the region. It has been difficult to utilize much of the waste except as fuel.

There are a few major points of waste concentration, however, that may afford enough raw material in waste form for economical operation of certain kinds of waste-using industries. In 1949 the Federal Reserve Bank of Boston made a research grant to the Northeastern Wood Utilization Council to conduct a survey of manufacturing wood waste in New England. Among other things, the study revealed some important wood-waste concentrations. (See Map 1–1.) The largest accumulation within a roughly 15-mile radius was found at Bryant Pond, Maine (the Bethel-Norway-Paris area), with 105,000 tons annually. Waste at other areas was much smaller,

MAP 1-1

Where Manufacturing Wood Waste Is Concentrated in New England

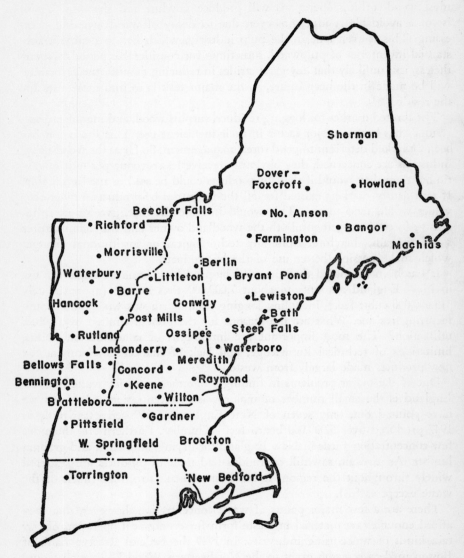

Source: Federal Reserve Bank of Boston, based on 1949 Survey by Northeastern Wood Utilization Council

ranging between 5,000 and 45,000 tons annually. The average at all concentration points except Bryant Pond was 14,650 tons. The waste was quite evenly balanced between the coarse materials and the fine shavings and sawdust.

The values producible by present methods of waste conversion do not permit long-distance transportation. If a manufacturer is to use it, the waste must ordinarily be available in sufficient quantities near his plant. Is there enough waste at any one of these points to provide raw material for any particular waste-using manufacturer? Does it meet specifications with respect to species, moisture content, bark content, reliability of supply, and in other possible respects? So far, not enough is known to give an unqualified answer to this question for most industries. Much depends on technical knowledge and on the costs and prices of alternative materials and competing products.

Intensive and continuing research is needed to overcome the deficiencies in technical knowledge about both new uses for wood waste and more economical wood-using processes. There has been a great deal of research progress in recent years, especially since World War II, but much more is needed. Government research has played a large and important part in the development of knowledge about wood utilization. The United States Forest Products Laboratory at Madison, Wisconsin, and the state agricultural experiment stations have been especially active in this work.

There are indications that private research on wood utilization in New England has not been as widespread as it should be. There are also signs, however, that more New England firms are becoming research-minded. Most pulp and paper companies already spend substantial sums on the development of new and improved paper and paper products. Privately endowed colleges and universities and other private organizations have also contributed to research on these problems. One private agency that has been especially active is the Northeastern Wood Utilization Council. This was organized in 1942 as a nonprofit organization to attack the problem of utilizing low-grade wood and wood residues. It is supported by companies and individuals interested in the problem. The council's objective is to assemble information and ideas on wood use from various sources at home and abroad and to encourage applied research in this field.

There have already been some important technological changes in wood utilization that are significant for more effective use of the region's wood resources. The most promising has been the development of processes for using hardwoods for the manufacture of wood pulp, both paper pulp and dissolving pulp for rayon and other products. These processes provide opportunities for using species and grades of wood formerly unutilized. Numerous limitations on the use of hardwoods for pulp have been removed, and progress is still being made.

One large paper company is working toward shifting one of its pulp mills over entirely to hardwoods for its raw material, and other companies are using larger percentages of hardwoods than formerly. Defibrating plants, which manufacture roofing and floor coverings, are also absorbing considerable amounts of hardwoods. There is now a potentially even more important new use for large quantities of hardwood. The Great Northern Paper Company has announced plans to construct a $30,000,000 mill at East Millinocket, Maine, for making pulp for newsprint paper from hardwoods by the new chemi-groundwood process. The mill is expected to produce about 120,000 tons of newsprint paper a year from formerly unutilized timber.

The large-scale use of fine manufacturing residue has also been growing. Wood flour is being produced in larger and larger quantities. There are now five plants in Maine alone which have a combined capacity of about 100,000 tons of wood flour annually. Wood flour is produced entirely from bark-free, dry pine shavings and sawdust and is used as an extender or filler in the manufacturing of linoleum, bakelite-type resins, and other plasticizers. The possibilities for future expansion of wood-flour production in New England depend largely on the course of linoleum demand, on the development of other uses, and on the availability of a continuous, high-quality supply of suitable woodworking waste.

Approximately 15,000 tons of wood are used annually in New England for the production of a semihardboard at Wilton, New Hampshire. Logs, sawmill residue, and edgings are used as raw materials. The residue used is softwood, and it need not be bark-free. In this instance, however, the mill uses the residues as an alternative source of supply, not as an attack on the residue problem. There have been investigations of the feasibility of setting up hardboard plants and plants to manufacture other types of wallboard in New England which would use wood residues and other currently unused materials.

Other technical advances in utilization of wood residue have been of particular importance to small woodland owners. The development of portable charcoal kilns by the Connecticut Agricultural Experiment Station has opened the way for one more use of residues and surplus wood. The woodland owner, under present economic conditions, may not make much profit from charcoal, but under favorable circumstances the revenue should help defray the expenses of weeding and thinning operations. Better wood laminations have also been made possible through the development of improved glues. Thin strips can be glued together to form structural timbers that are often cheaper and stronger than solid wood. Wood chips, shavings, and sawdust are being used for soil improvement and as bedding for livestock and poultry. Sawdust is used in the manufacture of insulating material. Numerous other possibilities are being explored, though a large number of known uses are still not economical because of high costs, local lack of sufficient quantities of raw materials, or other limiting factors.

CONCLUSIONS

The forests of New England are one of the region's richest resources. Under present management practices their timber yield is less than the region's consumption. Moreover, the yield is only a fraction of what the 31,000,000 acres of commercial timberland in New England could produce. To increase the productivity of the forests and their contribution to the New England economy, there are many positive actions which should be taken by private and public organizations. The following are some of the more important ones:

1. More intensive management of forest properties by large owners.

2. An improved, coordinated educational program about the meaning of and need for better forest management among small woodland owners and the public.

3. Greater use by small woodland owners of forest-management or marketing specialists, such as the New England Forestry Foundation and Connwood, Inc.

4. Adoption in the other five New England states of progressive forest taxation laws similar to that of New Hampshire.*

5. Reduction of logging wastes by the use of better harvesting methods and by utilization of much timber now left in the forests.

6. Continued intensive research by private and public agencies to develop new uses for wood waste and improved wood-using processes.

7. Vigorous market development of New England's products made from wood residues.

8. Increased use of forest-fire insurance in New England, especially by small and medium woodland owners.

9. Further pooling of interests by investors in multiple forest holdings, such as the Timber Owners of New England, Inc.

10. Continued search by lending institutions and others for improved methods of extending long-term forest credits.

11. Further improvements, where opportunities exist, in forest-fire protection by cities and states.

12. Increased research by public and private agencies on the prevention and control of destructive insects and diseases.

SELECTED REFERENCES

1. Baldwin, Henry I., in collaboration with Edgar L. Heermance, *Wooden Dollars,* Federal Reserve Bank of Boston, 1949.
2. Barraclough, Solon, and Gould, Ernest M., Jr., *A Preliminary Appraisal of New Hampshire's Forest-Yield Tax,* Station Paper No. 45, Northeastern Forest Experi-

* Edward E. Chase did not join in this recommendation. See note on page 48 for a statement of his views.

ment Station, Forest Service, U. S. Department of Agriculture, Upper Darby, Pa., November 1951.

3. Federal Reserve Bank of Boston, *Monthly Review* (Boston): "New England Forests," July 1948; "Nature's Self-storing Warehouse," August 1948; "The Right Key to Forest Profits," September 1948; "Budgeting a Forest," January 1949; "Forest Taxation," June 1949; "Who Owns Forest Land," August 1949; "Wood Waste," November 1949; "Forest Fire Menace," April 1950; "Eastern White Pine," September 1950; "New England Pulp and Paper Industry," August 1951; "Forestry in an Urban State," February 1952; "Good Forest Management Will Make New England's Woodlands More Productive," July 1952.

4. Northeast Pulpwood Research Center, *Forest Practice Survey Report,* Gorham, N. H., 1952.

5. Northeastern Wood Utilization Council, Inc., *Wood Yeast for Animal Feed,* Bulletin No. 12, New Haven, Conn., 1946.

6. ———— *Problems in the Utilization of Wood Waste,* Bulletin No. 16, New Haven, Conn., 1947.

7. ———— *The Pulping of Southern New England Hardwoods,* Bulletin No. 20, New Haven, Conn., 1948.

8. ———— *Wood Waste Utilization,* Bulletin No. 30, New Haven, Conn., 1949.

9. ———— *Connwood Incorporated,* Bulletin No. 34, New Haven, Conn., 1951.

10. Shepard, H. B., *Forest Fire Insurance in the Northeastern States,* Technical Bulletin No. 651, Forest Service, U. S. Department of Agriculture, Washington, D. C., 1939.

11. U. S. Department of Agriculture, *Trees,* Yearbook of Agriculture, Washington, 1949.

12. U. S. Department of Agriculture, Forest Service, *Forests and National Prosperity,* Misc. Publication No. 668, Washington.

13. ———— Reappraisal Reports, Washington:
No. 1. *Gaging the Timber Resources of the United States,* 1945.
No. 2. *Potential Requirements for Timber Products in the United States,* 1945.
No. 3. *The Management Status of Forest Lands in the United States,* 1945.
No. 4. *Wood Waste in the United States,* 1946.
No. 5. *Protection against Forest Insects and Diseases in the United States,* 1947.
No. 6. *Forest Cooperatives in the United States,* 1947.

14. Williams, Ellis T., *Forest Insurance,* Station Paper No. 26, Northeastern Forest Experiment Station, Forest Service, U. S. Department of Agriculture, Upper Darby, Pa., June 1949.

2

The Fisheries of New England

Drafted by Ray S. Kelley, Jr., under the direction of Arthur A. Bright, Jr.

The accessibility of one of the world's most prolific ocean fishing banks and bountiful supplies of shellfish in many harbors and estuaries along the coast made the fishing industry "the cornerstone of New England's prosperity" for 150 years. Fishing has continued to be of great importance to many New England coastal communities, though more rapid expansion in other industries has substantially reduced its relative importance to the region as a whole.

The New England fishing industry appeared to be hard pressed for a few years after World War II. While the outlook has improved since 1947, the industry still faces serious problems. If those who depend on it for their livelihood are to prosper, the market for New England fish products must be extended; adequate supplies of high-quality, low-priced fish must be assured; and all segments of the industry—dealers, boat owners, fishermen, and shore workers—must cooperate more closely in a sustained program of industry improvement. Fishing is the oldest industry in New England, but there remains a multitude of opportunities for expansion and improvement.

What changes are needed to increase the demand for New England fishery products? How can the supply of fish and shellfish be increased? What changes in labor-management relations would aid the industry? After sketching the history and organization of the industry, we shall suggest some answers to these questions.

HISTORY AND ORGANIZATION OF THE NEW ENGLAND FISHING INDUSTRY

Fishing was once the most important industry in New England. As the region developed and other employment opportunities expanded, it became relatively less and less important to the economy. By 1880 the New England fishing industry employed only 37,000 men out of a total labor force of a million and a half. In 1950 there were about 24,000 fishermen and 14,000 shore workers engaged in processing and transporting fish, but the region's labor force had grown to about 4,250,000.

To the early colonist fishing was a necessity for survival. During the last half of the 17th century the fishing interests became by far the most important source of wealth in the region. It was the availability of fish above all else that provided cargoes for trading vessels and made New England's great sea trade possible.

Paradoxically, the wealth of the New England fisheries was partially responsible for the relative decline of the fishing industry. The first manufacturers in New England produced supplies for the fishermen and traders. The New England brass industry sprang from the market for ship chandlery. The sugar, hides, gold, and silver brought to Boston in payment for fish stimulated sugar refining, shoemaking, and jewelry production. Capital accumulated in fishing and trade was invested in new industries, especially textiles. New England came to employ a larger and larger percentage of its population in manufacturing.

To become less important does not mean to become unimportant, however. In certain coastal districts of the region fishing is still by far the most important industry. About 30% of the labor force in Gloucester is employed in catching, processing, or distributing fish. Another 40% depend indirectly upon fishing for their livelihood. In Provincetown the percentage engaged directly in fishing during the winter months is nearly 35%. Similar conditions exist in other towns up and down the coast.

New England's fishing industry, both past and present, has owed its existence to the prolific fishing grounds of the Northwest Atlantic. Off the coast lie 260,000 square miles of one of the world's finest fishing grounds. The Northwest Atlantic region is characterized by a wide continental shelf, which in some places extends out from the coast for hundreds of miles. Large areas of the shelf rise to form submerged plateaus. On those banks there is a vast population of bottom-living fishes, called groundfish.

Taken together, the groundfish are the most important marine resource of New England and the third most valuable in the United States. Eight kinds of groundfish—haddock, ocean perch, cod, flounder, pollock, whiting, cusk, and hake—constituted nearly 60% of the weight and value of fish landed at New England ports in 1950. In addition to the groundfish, there are such valuable pelagic species as herring and mackerel. Fisheries for lobsters, clams, oysters, and scallops are also important along the New England shore.

In 1950 over 80 species of fish and shellfish were sold at New England ports. The largest item in the catch was ocean perch, with landings amounting to 208,000,000 pounds worth over $9,000,000 to the fishermen. Sea herring ranked second in weight but fifth in value. Third in poundage and first in value was haddock, with a yield of 158,000,000 pounds worth nearly $12,000,-000 at the pier. Cod, flounder, whiting, and pollock were the only other species taken in quantities exceeding 25,000,000 pounds. The catches of 17 others exceeded a million pounds each, and landings of about 60 minor species amounted to less than a million pounds apiece.

The total catch in 1950 was slightly over one billion pounds, worth $60,-600,000 to the fishermen. That was a record volume, which topped the landings in 1949 by about 7,000,000 pounds. For each of the three years 1948–50 the catch far exceeded that recorded for any previous year. (See Chart 2–1.)

CHART 2-1

New England's Total Catch of Fish and Shellfish
1887–1950 *

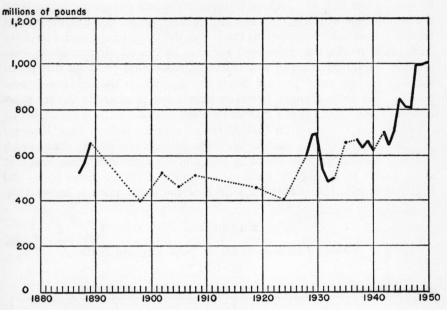

millions of pounds

* Dotted lines indicate data unavailable for intervening years.
Source: U.S. Fish and Wildlife Service

The pattern of landings has shown an irregularly rising trend since the
twenties, with the most rapid increase during and after World War II.

New England specializes in fresh and frozen fish products. It has been
estimated that 85% of the New England catch is sold in those forms. Large
amounts are packaged. In 1951 New England plants produced 165,000,000
pounds of packaged fresh and frozen fish and shellfish, while all other
plants in the United States and Alaska produced only 41,000,000 pounds.
With its 80% share of domestic production of packaged seafood, New England has an excellent opportunity to expand its sales over the nation.

Before World War I New England produced large quantities of salt fish,
especially salt cod. After the war there was a rapid shift to fresh and frozen
fish. Since the late 19th century the New England fishing industry had been
losing salt-fish business to other nations which had cost advantages over the
domestic producers. The rapid rise in "large-package" sales to institutions
and restaurants after World War I was made possible by the introduction
of the filleting and quick-freezing processes. The adoption of brand names

and the entrance of chain stores into the business stimulated the packaging of fresh fish for home consumption.

During the twenties and early thirties the domestic market for New England fish was still limited largely to the New York–New England region because of the lack of adequate transportation and storage facilities. With the introduction of refrigerator cars and cold-storage warehouses, the market for fish was extended somewhat; but it was the fairly recent introduction of frozen-food trucks, the widespread adoption by grocers of frozen-food lockers, and the introduction of easy-to-handle, one-pound packages that paved the way for the rapid postwar boom through which the industry is now passing. The same changes, however, have made possible the deeper penetration of the United States market by foreign producers.

During the 35 years prior to 1942 Boston was the leading New England port in quantity of fish landed. With the development of the ocean perch industry, Gloucester went ahead in 1942 and has remained in the lead ever since, except in 1947. New Bedford has ranked third in recent years, and Portland fourth. (See Chart 2–2.) Each of the major ports is highly indi-

CHART 2–2

Fishery Landings at Major New England Ports
1893–1951 *

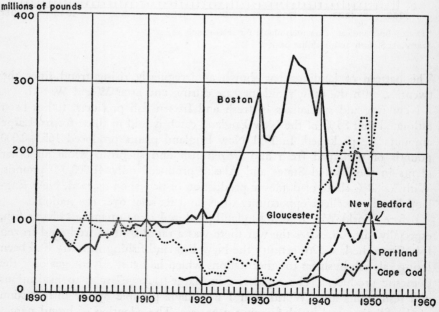

* For Portland, New Bedford, and Cape Cod, figures are not available prior to years shown.
Source: U.S. Fish and Wildlife Service

vidualized. Their catch, gear, and methods of operation are all quite distinct.

Boston is the principal haddock port of the world. In 1950, 107,000,000 pounds of this species, worth $13,500,000 to the fishermen, were landed there. Haddock represented 62% of the port's total catch by weight and 68% by value. Next in rank was cod, which amounted to only 8% of the quantity but 13% of the value. (See Table 2–1.)

Table 2–1. The Catch of Leading Species at Various Massachusetts Ports and in the State of Maine, 1950

SPECIES	WEIGHT OF LANDINGS (IN POUNDS)	PER CENT OF TOTAL WEIGHT	VALUE OF LANDINGS	PER CENT OF TOTAL VALUE
Boston				
Haddock	107,379,298	62.4	$ 9,179,523	67.7
Cod	14,360,086	8.3	1,786,633	13.2
Flounder	10,028,340	5.8	924,076	6.8
Pollock	9,885,717	5.7	451,386	3.3
All other	30,379,915	17.8	1,214,907	9.0
TOTAL	172,033,356	100.0	$13,556,525	100.0
Gloucester				
Ocean perch	120,291,028	61.4	$ 5,692,334	62.8
Whiting	16,981,201	8.7	556,544	6.1
Haddock	9,983,522	5.1	791,914	8.7
Flounder	7,443,946	3.8	538,710	5.9
All other	41,231,641	21.0	1,481,303	16.5
TOTAL	195,931,338	100.0	$ 9,060,805	100.0
New Bedford				
Trash fish*	56,040,749	47.9	$ 458,062	4.0
Flounder	29,411,614	25.2	3,723,581	32.8
Scallop (meat)	11,982,185	10.2	5,589,956	49.3
Haddock	11,513,628	9.8	990,997	8.7
All other	7,963,248	6.9	580,258	5.2
TOTAL	116,911,424	100.0	$11,342,854	100.0
Cape Cod Ports				
Whiting	11,617,529	30.8	$ 288,321	11.3
Flounder	5,912,330	15.7	676,987	26.4
Trash fish*	5,542,251	14.7	50,038	2.0
Cod	3,034,535	8.0	230,957	9.0
All other	11,653,335	30.8	1,313,259	51.3
TOTAL	37,759,980	100.0	$ 2,559,562	100.0
Maine				
Herring, round	185,481,490	57.5	$ 1,269,467	8.6
Ocean perch	79,281,327	24.6	3,102,352	21.1
Lobsters	18,352,570	5.7	6,412,311	43.7
Whiting	15,538,493	4.8	190,120	1.3
All other	24,034,948	7.4	3,714,492	25.3
TOTAL	322,688,828	100.0	$14,688,742	100.0

* Fish for reduction and animal food.
Source: U.S. Fish and Wildlife Service

Three important innovations led to a rapid rise in Boston's haddock catch during the 1920's: the introduction of the beam or otter trawler in 1905, the invention of the filleting process in 1922, and the improvements in freezing and storing fish in the late twenties. Furthermore, Boston's predominantly Newfoundland fishermen were accustomed to taking long fishing trips and to working day and night. Boston was also the nearest major port to the prolific Georges Bank haddock ground.

The pursuit of haddock by the Boston fleet has had a considerable effect on the structure of its fishing industry. Haddock is taken primarily by otter trawler, especially the large otter trawler. Of the 66 large trawlers in the 1950 New England fishing fleet, 48 operated out of Boston. (See Table 2-2.)

Table 2-2. The Home Ports of New England's Fishing Vessels, 1950 (number of vessels)

	BOSTON	GLOUCESTER	NEW BEDFORD	PORTLAND	ALL OTHER	TOTAL
Small vessels (under 50 tons)	51	60	113	52	289	565
Medium vessels (50–150 tons)	30	114	33	9	25	211
Large vessels (over 150 tons)	48	13	3	1	1	66
TOTAL	129	187	149	62	315	842

Source: Official Yearbook of the Fishing Masters Association, Boston, Mass., 1950

Since a large trawler costs more than $300,000 at present prices, few are owned individually. In 1950 the five largest fish dealers in Boston owned 60% of the port's large trawler fleet. The companies which owned most of the boats also bought most of the fish. For example, dealer-boat owners purchased more than 85% of the fish landed at Boston during 1947.[1]

Corporate ownership of a large part of the fleet has created a situation in which the owner, skipper, and crew are no longer neighbors who meet and work together on a personal basis. More important, the dealer-boat owner has somewhat divergent objectives regarding the price of fish from those of the individual boat owners and the fishermen. The individual boat owners and the fishermen benefit from high prices at the pier. The boat owner who is also a dealer has mixed objectives. As an owner he wants a high price for the fish caught by his own vessels, but as a dealer he wants low prices on the fish he buys. For example, since the filleting of haddock yields only about 40% clear meat, a dealer can save 2.5 cents a pound in fillet production for every cent the cost of raw fish is reduced.

Gloucester is the major port for ocean perch. In 1950 over 61% of the weight and 63% of the value of the total Gloucester catch were ocean perch. Haddock ranked a poor second by value, with less than a tenth of the Boston catch. The structure of the industry in Gloucester is different from Boston's.

1. Since 1950 the two largest dealer-boat owners have reduced their vessel holdings, however, and the six newest trawlers are owned by companies that are not dealers.

Ocean perch are landed at Gloucester principally by medium otter trawlers. Since less capital is needed to purchase the smaller vessels, more are owned individually or on a partnership basis. The canning and processing companies do own some boats, nevertheless.

Gloucester's fish business is less concentrated today than it was 35 years ago. Before World War I the Gorton-Pew Company was by far the largest dealer in the salt-fish business and owned 60% of the 200 boats operating. Expansion of the ocean perch fisheries after 1935 resulted in the formation of many new firms. Gorton-Pew is still the largest purchaser of fish landed, however, and the largest producer of fresh and frozen fillets. At present that firm handles about 20% of all fish landed at Gloucester.

New Bedford is the scallop and flounder port. Over half the nation's sea scallop supply comes from that port. Before 1937 New Bedford was a relatively unimportant seafood-producing center. Although it had a fairly large fishing fleet of small and medium-sized trawlers, or draggers, most of the catches were landed at New York City. After 1937, with the development of freezing and filleting and the stimulation of war demands, new concerns entered the market. The fleet also expanded rapidly during the same period.

The principal landings in the Cape Cod area during 1950 were whiting, flounder, cod, and trash fish. Total landings in that year amounted to about 38,000,000 pounds valued at over $2,500,000. The major landings on Cape Cod are made at Provincetown and Woods Hole, which have small fleets that fish primarily the inshore grounds.

By far the most valuable species of seafood taken along the Maine coast is lobster. Lobsters are caught in baited pots by thousands of individual lobstermen. The most important fish landings at Maine ports are ocean perch and sea herring. The major Maine port for ocean perch is Portland, but Rockland has also been expanding in recent years. In 1949 a large Portland concern opened a modern icing plant in Rockland. Two large Boston concerns operate the two largest ocean perch and whiting plants in Portland. The bulk of the herring catch, mostly canned as sardines, is taken in the northern coastal districts, especially in the Eastport area.

Since World War II landings have increased at a number of smaller ports. Point Judith, Rhode Island, and Stonington, Connecticut, are examples of that expansion. Large amounts of shellfish are also taken along the Rhode Island coast, especially along the shores of Narragansett Bay.

INCREASING THE DEMAND FOR NEW ENGLAND FISH PRODUCTS

If the New England fishing industry is to prosper and continue to provide employment for even its present small proportion of the region's labor force, it must sell more fish. To sell more it must catch more, and must create a demand for the increased catch. Creating the demand may well be the more difficult of the two major problems.

The fishing industry in New England, like any competitive industry in any location, has two principal sources of competition—from other products which satisfy the same basic demand and from the same industry in other areas. The first is often of greater importance, both as a source of competitive pressure and as an opportunity for further development. The extent of competition from other products, such as meat, poultry, and dairy products, often is not given sufficient weight in considering the problems of the New England fishing industry.

Most of the domestic producers of fishery products in other areas specialize in fresh fish for their local markets or in canned fish products. The Pacific Coast is the largest producer outside New England, for example, but sells primarily canned salmon, tuna, pilchards (California sardines), and mackerel. Thus the competition of other American regions is largely from somewhat different products.

Canada and Newfoundland, now part of Canada, have always been the largest foreign suppliers of fresh and frozen groundfish to the United States. Since 1939 American imports of Canadian fish have increased considerably. (See Table 2–3.) Trade with Iceland, a large supplier of cured fish, dimin-

Table 2–3. *United States Imports of Groundfish Fillets, by Country of Origin, 1940–52*
(in pounds)

YEAR	CANADA*	ICELAND	NORWAY	ALL OTHER	TOTAL
1940	9,676,367	46,507	—	16,979	9,739,853
1941	9,930,806	224	—	—	9,931,030
1942	16,634,082	40,000	—	—	16,674,082
1943	15,651,192	672,224	—	—	16,323,416
1944	23,865,073	680,496	—	—	24,545,569
1945	41,766,873	1,402,283	—	—	43,169,156
1946	44,930,834	4,234,437	1,818	4,000	49,171,089
1947	30,927,723	4,165,712	—	—	35,093,435
1948	49,594,425	3,964,554	395,767	8,800	53,963,546
1949	41,685,312	5,130,528	506,425	—	47,322,265
1950	49,211,661	12,767,478	1,715,590	1,104,982	64,799,711
1951†	57,669,763	24,162,173	3,883,077	1,327,068	87,042,081
1952	55,000,000‡	36,000,000‡	11,000,000‡	5,802,447‡	107,802,447†

* Includes Newfoundland and Labrador.
† Preliminary.
‡ Estimated.
Source: U.S. Fish and Wildlife Service

ished during World War II. Since 1945, however, that country has greatly expanded its shipments of frozen groundfish to the United States, and imports of frozen fish from Norway and other European countries have been rising. The imports of other types of fishery products have also grown. Since New England's sales of seafood to other parts of the United States consist largely of fresh and frozen fillets, the New England fishing industry has been most conscious of these imports and this source of direct competition.

Competition from Other Products

Total per capita consumption of meat, fish, cheese, and poultry in the United States was 242 pounds in 1951. Fish consumption was 11.4 pounds, of which about 6.5 pounds was fresh and frozen fish. American consumption of fish is low in comparison with many other countries. (See Table 2–4.)

Table 2–4. *Annual Per Capita Consumption of Fish and Shellfish in Various Foreign Countries before World War II*

	POUNDS		POUNDS		POUNDS
Japan	55	Netherlands	29	Uruguay	12
Sweden	52	Germany	18	Argentina	10
Norway	44	Belgium	17	Italy	9
Denmark	39	Spain	16	Chile	8
Portugal	37	New South Wales	15	Egypt	7
England and Wales	35	France	14		
Canada	29	Australia	13		

Source: U.S. Fish and Wildlife Service

The lower American figure is partly the result of this nation's higher per capita income and its greater ability to produce meat, partly of the country's relatively large inland concentration of population. A smaller proportion of Americans is "fish conscious," and until comparatively recently the costs and risks of transporting fresh fish for long distances made it difficult to build up the inland markets. Where the bulk of the population lives near the coast, as in Japan and Western Europe, the closer associations with the sea have supported fish consumption.

The consumption of fish is not uniform throughout the United States. Usually it is largest in the areas where production is largest. New York City has an annual per capita consumption of 32 pounds, and Jacksonville 18 pounds, while the figures for such inland cities as St. Louis and Louisville are nine and six pounds respectively.

Competition from meats and other protein-rich foods has produced the greatest downward pressure upon the demand for fish products. *A major problem of the New England fishing industries is how to make the large interior population of the country more fish conscious. Just a small shift of preference to fish can produce a greatly expanded demand. To change buying habits and tastes takes money, work, and time, especially in the face of large promotional expenditures by the nation's meat producers. It seems almost certain, however, that a proper mobilization of the industry's energies can attain important success in that objective.*

The industry has actually made considerable gains in recent years. Between 1933 and 1950 United States per capita consumption of fresh and frozen fish increased from 4.2 to 6.5 pounds, largely because of increased Western consumption of New England fish. Since 1946 the entire American fishing industry has been engaged in a nationwide campaign to increase fish consumption through its trade organization, the National Fisheries Institute.

For a short period the trade organizations in New England ports tried to publicize New England fish products actively. The Boston dealers' trade association raised $30,000 for that purpose in 1947, and a Gloucester trade association raised about $100,000 annually for advertising purposes for a few years after the war. Both programs have been discontinued, however, because they were not considered successful by members of the industry. The larger firms, of course, have been advertising their products for years, *but large-scale industry advertising of New England fish should be reconsidered, not to replace but to supplement individual advertising.*

The United States Fish and Wildlife Service has also been active in educating the public about the merits of fish. At present the Service is carrying on educational work with the National School-Lunch Program by fish cookery demonstrations to increase the use of fish in planning school meals.

The broader problems of merchandizing are fully as important in building a greater demand for New England's fish products as in other industries. Packaging and the improvement of marketing channels are especially critical areas. The relatively recent introduction of the one-pound package has been an outstanding success. Aggressive firms in the New England fishing industry see great possibilities for further market development in that direction. It costs money to increase demand, but the prospects for returns on that investment are high. Often midwestern and southern grocers have to be canvassed by salesmen, by mail, and by other advertising to induce them to adopt new products. One local firm has a man visiting every grocery in the southeastern states explaining the merits of fish products, displaying the products, and educating the grocers in methods of selling fish. It is important to convince grocers about the merits of frozen-fish products, because frozen-food cabinet space is still so small relative to total store space and many grocers have hesitated to use it for new or untried products. As cabinet space increases, however, or as frozen fish becomes more popular, the space given to fish products should increase. Also, there are still many underexploited species of fish off the New England coast, some of which can conceivably become profitable new products. New forms of processing, such as the new packaged precooked fish and the packaged "complete fish dinner," can benefit from consumer satisfaction with older products.

Even the best packaging, promotion, and missionary sales effort will fail if a product does not live up to its advance billing. If the inland market for New England fish is to grow, quality must be kept uniformly high. This is a problem for the industry itself to control. *Market competition and the promotion of national brands help develop quality-consciousness. In addition, self-policing through the dealers' associations would be highly desirable, as, for example, through the use of a port-wide or New England-*

wide seal of quality approval on packaged fish which meets minimum specifications.[2] High quality not only holds customers for existing products but also increases their receptiveness to new products.

In New England the typical handling of fish on vessels and at the pier has been seriously deficient and has been an especially important cause of deterioration in quality. The larger fish are generally pitchforked at least three times before they reach the carts in which they are hauled to the dealers' shops: from the deck into the hold, from the hold into the pens, and from the pens into unloading baskets at the pier where the fish are dumped into a box on a scale. After weighing, the fish may be forked again into the carts which haul them away. Besides the direct damage to the fish, fork punctures allow bacteria to enter and hasten deterioration. Some fish still are left uncovered in the carts without ice for many hours. While the poor practices have been reduced considerably in recent years, there is room for further improvement. *Inefficient and destructive handling should be eliminated by industry-wide consultation and cooperative action.* Modern equipment to remedy conditions may be costly but far less so than inaction.

Improved methods of processing are also important ways of increasing quality and reducing cost. Unfortunately the New England fishing industry as a whole has not done as much as it should about either. Only a few firms have research facilities of any kind, and most others have been slow to adopt new ideas. The continued leadership and success of the few should stimulate the rest of the industry. Research is admittedly expensive and beyond the reach of most individual firms, but it is not beyond their collective reach. The prospects of improving quality, reducing cost, and creating new products seem to be excellent.

The New England fishing industry should invest more in its own future, as have the meat packers and other groups whose products compete with fish, as well as the fishing industry of the West Coast. The research carried on by the United States Fish and Wildlife Service on fish technology, fish biology, methods of catching fish, and other problems is valuable to the industry, but it is not a substitute for the industry's own efforts. A New England fish-products research institute might well be established, supported by the entire industry for its collective benefit.[3] The best way to meet competition is to keep ahead of it.

In working to expand its long-term market throughout the country, the fishing industry in New England has had to guard against the temptation of taking unduly high profits in the short run. The sales of fresh fish formerly were typically priced on a policy of "charging what the traffic will bear." Markups by wholesalers and retailers were high because of the risk of loss in handling a highly perishable product. Prices fluctuated from day

2. For an extensive discussion of the quality problem, see Donald J. White, *The New England Fishing Industry,* Harvard University Press, August 1954.

3. See White's book for further development of this topic.

to day as market conditions changed. High meat prices have made it tempting, especially for distributors and retailers, to push up the price of fish and draw larger profits per pound from the established market. High prices for meat have also provided an excellent opportunity for permanently increasing fish sales. With relatively low prices for fish, the chances for market expansion have been better, and greater interest in using fish in the interior of the country has helped to retain the gains even after meat prices began to decline.

Available evidence indicates that the New England dealers have been pursuing a cautious pricing policy. This is partly because they are aware of the importance of extending the market, partly because of the inflow of directly competing products from abroad, and partly because products and methods of distribution have changed.

Now the fishing industry is becoming more and more a segment of the frozen-food industry. The risk of loss in frozen-fish handling has been greatly reduced, removing the major excuse for high distributive markups. Dealers in branded products aim at price stability largely because of the pressure from retailers and consumers. The more constant price lessens the risk of inventory loss for the retailer and assures the consumer of a stable price regardless of the day or time of year when the fish is purchased.

Foreign Competition

The growth in American imports of fresh and frozen groundfish fillets from 9,740,000 pounds in 1940 to 107,802,000 pounds in 1952 has alarmed some parts of the New England fishing industry about the future. Though the New England catch and sales of groundfish have increased sharply over the same period, the rise in imports has been more rapid. Some groups maintain that foreign imports are flooding the market and that ruin lies ahead of the industry. They have called for higher tariffs, import quotas, and even for governmental price supports.

In view of the success of the New England fishing industry as a whole during recent years, the situation does not seem unduly alarming. Those concerns that have not shared in the growth cannot blame foreign imports when their nearby competitors have expanded and prospered. Their lack of success testifies rather to their own past and present shortcomings than to the havoc wrought by foreign competition.

It is true, of course, that a continued rapid increase in imported fish products would be a real test of the capacity of the industry. If the total domestic market for fish should remain constant, parts of the New England industry would undoubtedly suffer. But the total market actually has expanded considerably, and there is opportunity for much more expansion. It seems quite possible for the New England fishing industry to prosper alongside still larger imports from abroad, provided necessary adjustments are made within the industry.

In the past, imports of fresh and frozen fish have come largely from the Maritime Provinces of Canada. (See Table 2–3.) They have risen sharply since 1940, and there is no indication that they will not remain high. But the aggregate statistics do not reveal adequately the true nature of that competition. Much of the fresh and frozen fish from Canada is cod, a species which New England banks cannot supply in sufficient quantity to meet market demands. Many Canadian fish-processing plants are operated by or for American firms, including several New England firms. A large proportion of Canadian imports, therefore, supplement rather than compete with the local operations of New England firms. There has been a definite swing to diversification in the product lines of the leading fish dealers, with specialized plants for particular species located close to principal producing banks.

The Maritime Provinces have certain competitive advantages over the New England states in the matter of fish products. Their labor costs are lower, in spite of the higher productivity of New England fishermen and shore workers. The prices of fish at the pier are often three to four times as high in New England as in Canada, and the supply of certain species is nearer the Maritime fishing ports. Labor costs are not the only determinants of competitive position, however, and the Maritime Provinces have certain offsetting disadvantages. For example, the costs of most manufactured materials—packages, machinery, parts—are higher in the Maritimes, for they must usually be brought in from distant sources. Skilled technicians are scarcer; and the distance from the market means higher transportation costs. Moreover, the appreciation of the Canadian dollar during the last two years has seriously affected the competitive position of Maritime fish producers in the American market.

The Maritimes are disadvantageously located in respect to the American market. New England firms are better able to adapt their operations to the changing demands of the market. Wherever the market is a sensitive one, as it is for fish products, this element of flexibility can help compensate for the lower costs of distant competitors. To compete effectively a company must have warehouses and freezers near the market, as well as sales offices. In Newfoundland and Nova Scotia phone service and delivery to American customers are slower. A firm close to the market can often capture a big order by a quick phone call and promise of rapid truck delivery, while the relatively isolated firm cannot. The observed differences in prices of fish at the pier are themselves an indication of the marketing advantages of New England dealers, since the prices in New England ports are established by auctions. If the dealers were unable to compete on the basis of those differentials, their top bids would decline and the gap would tend to narrow.

The growth of Canadian imports, therefore, has resulted largely from the integration of American marketing advantages with Canadian production advantages. The disadvantages for an independent firm in the Maritimes are still serious if it tries to market its products independently. The largest independent producer in Newfoundland, for example, currently sells only about one-fifth of its output independently; the remainder is packaged for New England dealers. It appears probable that most future expansion in Canadian production for sale in the United States will continue to be by branch plants of American firms or by independents packing for American dealers.

Competition from other major producers of groundfish fillets, especially Iceland, has increased rapidly since the war. Iceland has competitive advantages over New England in labor costs and fish costs even greater than those of the Maritime Provinces. The Icelandic industry is controlled by the government. Wages are about 65 cents an hour for shore workers, and the price of fish is fixed by the government at 2 cents a pound for cod and 1.25 cents for all other species. Iceland's fishing equipment, due in part to Marshall Plan aid, is extremely good. Its large trawlers can hold 1,000,000 pounds of fish, compared to about 400,000 pounds for New England's large trawlers. There are many fishing banks near Iceland which have not been tapped intensively.

The fishing industry in Iceland also has all the marketing disadvantages faced by the independent Canadian producer in the American market. Distances are great and communications slow. The Icelandic industry lacks smooth, efficient marketing channels in this country. Some of its costs are also higher, for it must import all its raw materials, even wood.

The rapid increase in American fish imports from Iceland after the war was primarily the result of the economic chaos in Europe. Europe, especially England and Italy, were Iceland's leading markets before the war. Since the war, however, England has limited the importation of fish, and Italian currency is not sufficiently strong to be acceptable to the Icelanders. As a result, Iceland has turned to the United States market for badly needed dollars, and the State Department has encouraged Icelandic exports to increase the economic strength of that strategically located island. Fish represent about 98% of Iceland's exports, so curtailment of fish exports would be a serious blow to the economy.

Norway has also increased its exports of groundfish fillets to the United States recently, and larger imports from Germany, Denmark, Great Britain, and Holland can be expected. Those countries have both the advantages and disadvantages of location shared by Iceland and Canada. Furthermore, the quality of fish from Denmark, Holland, and Germany is apt to be below that of New England-caught fish, for the vessels of those countries must travel far from port to make catches. They do not threaten serious competition to the New England industry.

What effects will these expanded imports of fish have on the New England industry? One important effect may be to produce a gradual relative shift of emphasis in New England from production to distribution of fish products. This does not mean a decline in production employment but rather a more rapid expansion in distribution employment. Growth in the domestic market offers an opportunity for at least relative stability and probably some further increase in New England's total employment at sea and in shore processing plants.

There will probably also have to be a gradual adjustment in the relative emphasis upon the various species by the New England industry. It does not appear that Boston or New Bedford will be greatly affected, even by a substantial further increase in imports. The threat to Gloucester and other ocean perch ports is greater, for Iceland is potentially a large supplier of that species. Even there, marketing advances and sufficient development of the inland market would seem to offer substantial protection. Moreover, adaptation of those ports' equipment and fishing effort to other species is not an impossibility. At Gloucester there has been a gradual shift to whiting fishing, and one company is experimenting with freezing tuna at sea. *Gloucester's best protection against future uncertainty would undoubtedly be to reduce its extreme dependence upon the fishing industry while it is adapting its fisheries to new products. It needs a more diversified economic base.* Increased manufacturing activity is more desirable than increased tourist business, since the latter has the same seasonal peak as the fisheries.

At present there is a tariff on fish products, but it has had relatively little effects on imports. The present duty is 1⅞ cents a pound on imports of whole or filleted groundfish up to 15% of average domestic consumption of fillets during the previous three years, and 2.5 cents a pound on all imports in excess of the 15%. The duty on all other fillets is a straight 2.5 cents. The increase in fish prices during recent years and the shift from roundfish to fillet marketing have decreased the relative importance of the tariff in total costs.

Although most members of the New England fishing industry have not suffered seriously from foreign competition and may not suffer greatly in the future, some of them have advocated an increase in the import duty on fish or an import quota. Many of the smaller dealers and vessel owners have joined the fishermen and shore workers in the request.

We do not believe that either an increase in tariffs or a quota is the most desirable solution to the New England fishing industry's future problems. For one thing, the amount of tariff relief that is available without a change in the basic law is not enough to make a great deal of difference in the competitive situation. The recent shift in rates of exchange between the American and Canadian dollars has had more effect than an increased tariff would have. Furthermore, the broader international issues involved, especially in connection with Canadian and Icelandic imports, seem clearly to dominate the sectional interests of the New England industry. Most important of all, alertness and aggressiveness by the industry itself seem to offer its own best protection, as well as the greatest service to the American consumer. A quota would not only protect inefficient domestic producers but also tend to create an artificial scarcity and raise fish prices. This might create even more serious future problems if it led to excessively intensive fishing.

Expansion of the market is a most promising avenue of development, but research in products and improvements in processing offer further opportunities to the New England industry that will help greatly in offsetting the region's higher labor costs. *In brief, we have sufficient faith in the stimulating effects of healthy competition to believe that the New England industry will continue to survive and even grow, and that the gradual adjustments necessary will be within the ability of the industry to accomplish. If that faith is misplaced, the special interests of the regional industry do not in our opinion overbalance the national interest to the extent of meriting greater tariff or quota protection.*

INCREASING THE SUPPLY OF FISH

As long as American demand for New England's fish specialties increases more rapidly than the importation from other areas, the New England industry can grow, provided there is a local supply of fish available to meet that demand. If a shortage develops on the local banks, New England fishermen have to travel greater distances, with consequent effects on the quality and cost of their fish. There are two principal ways to increase supplies: by improved technology and by more efficient utilization of existing fishing grounds. Improved technology does not increase the quantity of fish on the banks, of course, but it can lead to reductions in unit costs. Improved methods can permit the capture of fish that otherwise would never be caught, for example on distant banks that are not at present economical to fish.

Technological Changes

Since the introduction of the large otter trawler and the small trawler or dragger, few significant technological changes have been made in catching groundfish. Otter trawlers generally limit their efforts to fishing grounds with smooth bottoms, for on rough grounds the nets snag and tear. Over rough bottoms fishermen use the less productive line trawl or gill netting.

The development of major new techniques of catching fish is a slow and irregular process. The New England fishing industry has not pioneered in working out important new procedures or equipment. Most of the fundamentally new ideas, such as the otter trawl back in 1906, have come from abroad. Now a new idea called electronarcosis has come from a German scientist.

This method of catching groundfish, still in the experimental stages, makes use of a net similar to the otter trawl, but the effective net opening is enlarged by placing electrodes on the tow lines ahead of and away from the net. The fish are stunned by electrical impulses and tumble into the net. The inventors claim that by varying frequencies and voltages, they can select various sizes and even species of fish. Moreover, the net can be drawn through the water at a height where rough sea bottoms do not interfere.

Whether or not the electrical method proves practicable, *it is important that studies of fish catching be continued. New Englanders have much to gain by taking part in these and by experimenting with new proposals. In such ventures industry-wide cooperation and research programs would hasten development.*

Another technological change which could increase the supply of New England fish indirectly is freezing whole fish at sea, as the tuna fleet has done in the Pacific. The Fish and Wildlife Service has carried out limited experiments to determine the feasibility of the process. Preliminary tests indicate that it might improve the quality of edible fish and make the whole waste of the fish (usually gutted at sea) available for the expanding by-products industry. Furthermore, since a trawler could remain at sea for a longer period without affecting the quality of the fish, the ratio of fishing time to days in port or sailing to banks could be increased. The annual catch of the trawler therefore could be increased. *The New England industry as a whole would be well advised to participate actively in the Fish and Wildlife experiments on freezing at sea and not leave major responsibility for the work to that agency.*

The Scarcity Problem

New Englanders have been worried for centuries about depletion of their fishery resources. As early as 1668 the General Court of Massachusetts passed a law that "no man shall kill any cod, haddock, hake or pollock in December or January because of spawning, nor mackerel to barrel up in May or June."

Many groups have studied the problem of depletion. There have been hearings, discussions, articles, and speeches on the subject, but as yet no completely satisfactory answer has been found, which is not surprising in view of the great number of variables that can affect the catch of fish. Fish populations are characterized by extreme local fluctuations due to natural causes alone. The fish may fail to spawn successfully in some years, they may migrate to other areas, or they may be hit by an epidemic. On the other hand, fewer fish may be caught because demand is poor, because fewer vessels or men are available, or because the weather is bad. Also, more may be caught after the introduction of some new invention. Pollution or the absence of fish ladders may prevent the spawning of certain species. Finally, the catch may fall because there has been previous overfishing.

With so many factors affecting catch, the diagnosis of the supply situation requires a great deal of accurate information covering many years. Collecting the necessary data is expensive and complicated by the fact that fishing banks are international. The Grand Banks of Newfoundland, for example, are fished, among others, by Americans, Canadians, Norwegians, French, Portuguese, and Spaniards.

The most important local bank, Georges Bank off Cape Cod, is fished primarily by Americans; hence the best data are available for that bank, but even these are incomplete. While biologists and statisticians of the Fish and Wildlife Service have studied many phases of the problem, they have not had sufficient funds for a complete investigation even of local supply conditions. Any discussion of depletion, therefore, is handicapped by lack of sufficient reliable data. As we have said, there is a genuine need for more information in the fields of fishing technology, biology, market development, and related topics. *The shifting of some federal funds from agriculture, which in 1945 received over $7.00 for each ton of food produced, to the fisheries, which received only 82 cents per ton of food produced, might provide increased benefits for the nation without increased federal disbursements.*

Through centuries of fishing the original abundance of the New England banks has undoubtedly been reduced, yet they remain highly productive and a large fleet of vessels lands many millions of pounds at New England and foreign ports every year. Unquestionably, the American market will absorb more of certain species than our own banks will be able to supply economically. To help meet that demand, New England fishermen already make many trips to the more distant banks off Nova Scotia and Newfoundland. When stocks on adjacent banks are temporarily or permanently reduced to such an extent that it is less profitable to fish on them, the boats move to more distant sources.

In 1950 about 29% of the fish landed at the leading New England ports came from the banks off Nova Scotia, and about 70% came from the New England banks. Those percentages vary from year to year as the relative abundance changes on the local banks. In 1928, for example, about 82% of the catch came from the New England banks, but in 1934 a larger volume of fish was taken off Nova Scotia by New England fishermen than on the adjacent banks. The data for the period 1904–50 for all species of fish are shown in Chart 2-3. The catch on the Nova Scotian banks tends to increase in poor years of fishing off New England and to fall off when New England banks are more prolific. But there is no indication that Nova Scotian banks are replacing New England banks as a source of total supply.

CHART 2–3

Catches of United States Fishing Vessels in Selected Areas of the
North Atlantic Landed at Principal Ports
1904–50

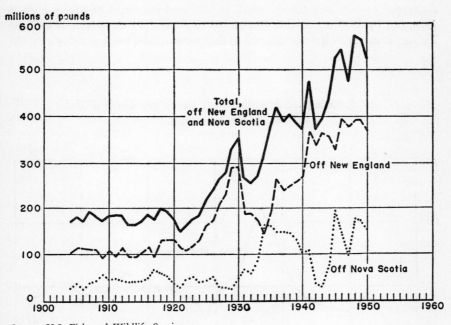

Source: U.S. Fish and Wildlife Service

*While the trend in catch on Nova Scotian banks has been increasing since
the twenties, the trend for the New England banks has increased still faster.
So far as the aggregate catch is concerned, these figures do not show that
the fish supplies on our local banks are becoming scarce.*

A full discussion of the depletion problem, however, requires consideration
of individual species of fish. There are claims that certain species are becoming scarce. Let us see if a critical situation exists for any of the major
species of fish.

Haddock: The chief source of the world's haddock supply is Georges
Bank off Cape Cod. As has been pointed out, Boston early became the leading haddock port. With the introduction of otter trawling, filleting, and
quick-freezing, the catch and demand for haddock increased rapidly, reaching a peak of 258,000,000 pounds for the total American catch in 1929. The
catch from Georges Bank reached a peak of 223,000,000 pounds the same
year and remained high in 1930. During the next few years it fell off sharply,
and reached a low of 50,000,000 pounds in 1934. Since that year landings of

haddock from Georges Bank have averaged 97,000,000 pounds and have not exceeded 122,000,000 pounds. (See Chart 2–4.)

Under the relatively static methods of fishing that had existed in New England since the twenties, the weight of catch per day's fishing is an index of the relative population density on the banks. Since 1917 that measure has fluctuated widely. It reached a peak in 1927 and remained relatively high in 1928, but by 1930 it had slid downward to about half the previous average. Those lower yields have continued to the present. The catch per day's fishing

CHART 2–4

Total Landings of Haddock and Catch per Day's Fishing
from Georges Bank
1917–51

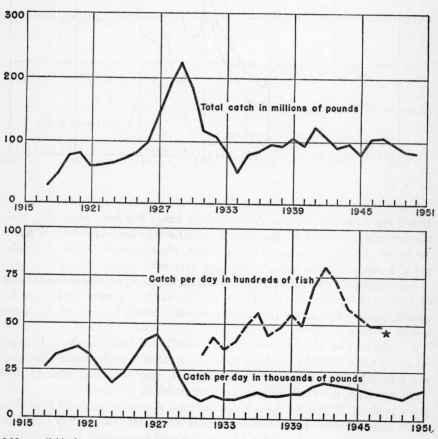

* Not available for more recent years.
Source: U.S. Fish and Wildlife Service

in number of fish has also fluctuated since 1931, but the trend has been very slightly upward.

These figures on catch per day were supplied by the North Atlantic Fisheries Investigation of the U.S. Fish and Wildlife Service at Woods Hole. Their most recent analysis indicates that the haddock fisheries on Georges Bank have essentially stabilized. Future landings will probably fluctuate about the average of the past few years, if fishing intensity remains the same. Of course, fluctuations in spawning success and other natural conditions will cause year-to-year fluctuations in the haddock population, but there is no present indication of a continuing decline in production with the present intensity of fishing.

While haddock remains fairly abundant on Georges Bank, it is fairly certain that production could be increased considerably by a simple conservation measure. Over 90% of the haddock landed at New England ports are caught by otter trawlers, which drag a large net along the bottom of a bank. Those nets are not selective; they take everything in their paths not too small to escape through the mesh. That the net picks up unmarketable fish which must be thrown back not only makes the fisherman's task more difficult but also destroys many small cod or haddock which later would reach marketable size. Throwing the small fish overboard does no good, as most of the fish are dead or dying when discarded. In 1947 an estimated 17,000,000 baby haddock too small to market were discarded on Georges Bank alone.

Haddock grow rapidly in their early years of life. The average one-year-old fish weighs 0.16 pounds. At three years the average weight is 1.56 pounds, about ten times as much. The lack of foresight in destroying those young fish is obvious. Furthermore, since haddock on Georges Bank spawn for the first time when two to three years old, a great number will be able to spawn at least once if they are given some protection until they reach that age.

Several methods have been considered for protecting baby haddock: (1) closed nursery grounds; (2) closed seasons; (3) minimum market size; and (4) larger mesh in the cod end of otter trawls. Since baby haddock are found in many places on Georges Bank, closed nursery grounds would mean an almost complete cessation of fishing. Furthermore, a closed season appears unworkable because baby scrod are found on the Bank all year. A minimum market size alone would not help greatly, because the small fish are destroyed on or before surfacing.

The Fish and Wildlife Service made a study to see if the larger mesh size would release baby haddock. A large number of experimental tows showed that only one-fifth as many baby scrod were taken in the larger mesh as in the standard nets. Furthermore, the tests showed no reduction in catch of 1.5 to 2.5 pound scrod, and the catch of large haddock was increased. They also found that the larger mesh nets were (1) less costly, (2) easier to handle because of the relative absence of trash, (3) easier to mend because of fewer knots, and (4) lighter, thus increasing towing speeds.

American fishery officials estimate that haddock production on Georges Bank could be increased 50% in ten years by the general adoption of a larger mesh size. The Fish and Wildlife Service proposed that the International Commission for the Northwest Atlantic Fisheries (to be discussed later) recommend such a regulation. The commission recommended legislation to Canada and the United States; and the larger mesh size went into effect for American fishermen on June 1, 1953.

Ocean Perch: The rosefish,[4] or "ocean perch" as it has been renamed, is a relative newcomer to the commercial fisheries. Prior to 1933, when it was discovered that it could be filleted and frozen successfully, ocean perch had been discarded as trash. Shortly after its introduction a heavy demand sprang up in the Middle West for the low-priced, small, white fillets with the mild taste and texture of fresh-water perch. From 118,000 pounds in 1930, landings at New England ports reached 237,000,000 pounds worth over $10,000,000 in 1949. Seventy-five per cent of the ocean perch fillet production is consumed in the midwestern market.

CHART 2–5

Sources of Ocean Perch Landed at New England Ports
1935–50

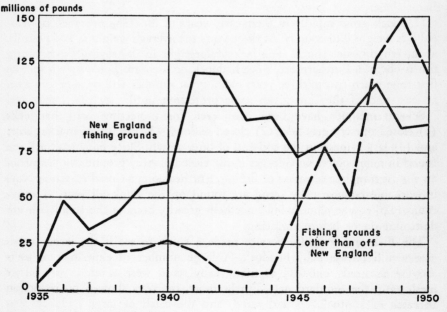

Source: U.S. Fish and Wildlife Service

4. Known by fishermen in most countries as redfish.

Gloucester took principal advantage of the development of ocean perch fillets, for a number of reasons. It is closer than Boston to the ocean perch grounds in the Gulf of Maine, and, more important, it had unused buildings, vessels, and manpower which could be converted quickly to their exploitation. The gear and fishermen of Gloucester were traditionally employed for short trips and daytime operations. Ocean perch are caught only during daylight hours, because the fish scatter or rise off the bottom at night.

Less is known about ocean perch than about haddock, but present indications are that the population adjacent to New England will not supply the growing United States demand. At first most ocean perch were taken in the Gulf of Maine, but as demand increased boats went increasingly to Nova Scotia for their catch. They now go to the Grand Banks of Newfoundland as well. By 1948 less than half the ocean perch landings at New England ports were taken from the adjacent grounds. (See Chart 2-5.)

The ocean perch catch from the New England banks increased until 1941. Since that year, the total catch has been somewhat less. The Fish and Wildlife Service believes the catch per day's fishing (Table 2-5) and the total landings indicate a fairly stabilized condition. The apparent stability, they admit, has been due in part to the discovery of new ocean perch grounds within the New England banks. Grounds show a rapid decrease after three or four years of fishing; then the vessels move to other areas.

Table 2-5. *Catch of Ocean Perch Per Day's Fishing From New England Banks, 1935–49*
(in thousands of pounds)

1935	14.6	1940	9.9	1945	9.9
1936	9.3	1941	13.0	1946	10.5
1937	9.6	1942	11.2	1947	9.9
1938	8.9	1943	11.8	1948	10.1
1939	10.0	1944	6.4	1949	7.2

Source: U.S. Fish and Wildlife Service

The history of other species, such as haddock, has indicated that when a new fishery is established catch increases rapidly for several years, holds steady for a few years, then falls off considerably and stabilizes at a lower level, usually with a smaller average size. That has apparently happened in the Gulf of Maine ocean perch grounds, and it may happen on the Nova Scotian grounds in a few years if the intensity of fishing remains constant. The ocean perch requires at least nine years to mature, and when the initial lush abundance is skimmed off, the catch falls to a lower but steady yield.

Whether or not the *total* catch falls off depends on a number of factors. Recently large fisheries of ocean perch were found along the outer edge of the Grand Banks and in deeper waters off New England. If a method for exploiting those grounds can be found, the total New England landings may increase substantially.

The ocean perch has been studied intensively only since 1942, a short time when the subject of study is so complex. The present research program of the Fish and Wildlife Service includes investigations of variations in abundance, the extent of the breeding season, the fecundity of female fish of different sizes, age and growth of mature fish, and the number of the breeding stock in the various areas.

Because so little is yet known about the species, no official recommendations for conservation of ocean perch have been made. Fishermen have often suggested that certain nursery grounds be closed or that legislation be enacted to make it unlawful to take ocean perch during spawning season. The Fish and Wildlife Service states that fishermen report an abundance of small fish, so it is difficult to argue that the breeding stock has been overfished.

Flounder: Nearly 67,000,000 pounds of flounders were landed at New England ports in 1950, the latest year for which complete data are available. The principal flounder port was New Bedford. Its 1950 total of 29,000,000 pounds worth $3,700,000 represented a considerable decline from the peak of 36,700,000 pounds in 1942.

Until the introduction of otter trawling, the flounder fisheries were hardly touched. The small mouths of many of the species saved them from the hooks of line trawls, and no market existed for some of the more abundant species. In 1900 only 4,500,000 pounds were landed. The otter trawl and filleting process stimulated production. Today about 97% of the catch is taken by otter trawl, and most of it is filleted.

In New England at least six types of flounder are brought to market from nearby coastal waters and from offshore banks. In relative importance they are the yellowtail, blackback, gray sole, lemon sole, dab, and fluke. The halibut is often included in the flounder group.

The history of the yellowtail flounder is closely analogous to that of the ocean perch. Prior to 1935 it was considered trash. Then it won acceptance as a table fish, and production rapidly expanded. Peak production was reached in 1942 when 65,000,000 pounds were landed in New England. Since then landings have fallen off to a 1950 total of only 23,000,000 pounds.

At first the catch of yellowtail was made in the southern coastal waters of New England, but high production was maintained only by going farther to sea. Landings from the more distant Georges Bank increased from 10% of New Bedford's catch in 1942 to 62% during the first eight months of 1949. Catch per day's fishing fell from 9,600 pounds in 1942 to 4,800 pounds in 1948.

Studies by the Fish and Wildlife Service indicate that the decline in yellowtail abundance is due primarily to overfishing and changing migratory habits. Not enough is known about the species to predict safely a reasonable stabilization level. The studies do indicate, however, that *supplies of yellowtail could be increased somewhat by setting a minimum size limit of 11 inches.*

Blackback or winter flounder is the second most important species of North Atlantic flounder. Annual catch in the early thirties was 50,000,000 pounds. Since then it has fallen to about 22,000,000 pounds. The decline was apparently due in part to a decline in fish population and in part to a shifting of fishing resources to other species, especially yellowtail.

While blackbacks are found from New Jersey northward to Canada, the principal stocks occur off New York, Connecticut, Rhode Island, and southern Massachusetts. The desired market size is over ten inches, but many are caught between eight and ten inches. Since the growth rate is very rapid, the blackback can survive intense fishing. *For better utilization of the blackback resource, the Fish and Wildlife Service has recommended a minimum size limit of ten inches. Adherence to that minimum should increase the fishermen's catch by increasing the number of spawning adults.*

About 7,000,000 pounds of gray sole, 3,800,000 pounds of lemon sole, and 4,900,000 pounds of dab were landed at New England ports in 1950. The biology of these flounders and the potentialities of the local supplies are still unknown.

Other Groundfish: In the 19th century, when New England salted much of its fish, *cod* supported the largest fishery in the United States. Since the introduction of filleting and quick-freezing, the market for other species has developed, and the demand for cod has declined.

Some cod is taken along with haddock on Georges Bank, but fishermen primarily in search of cod generally go to the Nova Scotian banks or beyond. About half the United States landings since 1931 have come from Georges Bank and the Gulf of Maine; but the species becomes more abundant off Nova Scotia and Newfoundland. The abundance of cod varies from year to year, and the reasons for the variation are not known. While the United States catch as a whole has fallen since 1896, the productivity of the western Atlantic fishery as a whole has neither increased nor decreased markedly. Without further study it is uncertain what, if any, conservation recommendations need be made, and no study of cod is underway at present.

In 1950 *whiting,* or silver hake, ranked fifth in poundage of fish landed. Landings in that year were nearly 65,500,000 pounds worth more than $1,300,000, a sharp rise from the 1939 catch of only 8,000,000 pounds. Whiting are taken commercially from Sable Island to Virginia, but Gloucester's landings of 17,000,000 pounds in 1950 gave it first rank as the whiting supplier. The Cape Cod catch of 11,600,000 pounds of whiting exceeded the weight of all other individual species landed at the Cape Cod ports in 1950. New Englanders eat very little whiting. St. Louis and Kansas City are the principal markets, where it is popular in fried-fish sandwiches.

Knowledge about the whiting population, rate of growth, and size at maturity is extremely limited. Only fragmentary data are available regarding nursery grounds. Reports have come to the Fish and Wildlife Service from local fishermen that the species is becoming scarcer. The Service has not been able to conduct a study of the whiting fishery to determine the facts.

Sizable landings of *pollock* have been made at New England ports in recent years. The 1950 catch was close to 26,000,000 pounds. Boston landings of 10,000,000 pounds surpassed those of any other port. Production could probably be increased if a larger demand could be created for the slightly off-color meat of the species. The off-color meat lies directly under the skin. Use of newly developed fish-skinning machines set to remove the skin and off-color meat from fillets would, it is believed, create a greater demand. Also, recent success in frozen and precooked fillets may enlarge the market. Little is known about the biology of pollock or the extent of its supply in American waters.

Two types of *hake* are sold commercially by New England fishermen. Landings of white hake were 14,000,000 pounds in 1950, all of which were sold as food fish. The catch of red hake, most of which is used in the trash market, amounted to over 40,000,000 pounds during the same period. White hake fishermen have been receiving a good price, but red hake sells for less than a cent a pound. Red hake, while a good-flavored species, is so soft-bodied that it does not keep well fresh or frozen. During World War II the Army bought large quantities of red hake for use in chowders, but since then its demand as food fish has fallen off. At present some is frozen at New Bedford for use on animal farms. The biology and population of the hakes are also relatively unknown, but the Fish and Wildlife Service believes the fishery could be expanded if the market warranted.

Herring and Mackerel: Two pelagic or migratory species are important to New England fishermen. In 1950 herring landings totaled 195,000,000 pounds valued at $1,350,000, and the landings of mackerel were over 14,000,000 pounds. Over the years the catch of each species has fluctuated widely, but most experts agree that the fluctuations have resulted primarily from natural causes rather than overfishing.

In 1951 the Maine herring catch fell off considerably. The Fish and Wildlife Service, the Maine Sardine Packers Association, and the Maine Department of Sea and Shore Fisheries are cooperating on a study of the herring to determine the causes of the recurring shortages, but they have not yet reached conclusions about its control. Fortunately it appears that the 1952 Maine herring catch was larger than average. Herring were taken in places where they had seldom been found in the past.

Summary for Leading Species: We have considered briefly New England's nine most important species of fish. They account for 85% of the weight and 95% of the value of total New England fish landings. None of them appears in danger of extinction, nor is the over-all productivity of the banks where they are caught declining seriously. It is striking, however, that this important national food resource has received so little study over the years that its potential yields are not well known. The most efficient use of the resource requires much better knowledge of its characteristics and extent.

On the basis of existing information, it appears that haddock, ocean perch and certain species of flounder on the banks adjacent to New England are being fished near capacity in terms of present fishing methods. Other species, such as whiting, pollock, and hake, are probably not being fully exploited.

With no change in technology, demand, or conservation measures, it would seem that the New England production of most principal species can be maintained. The nearby catch of ocean perch and yellowtail flounder may decline, but ocean perch production could be maintained by extension of the fishery to more distant banks if costs and other competitive conditions permit. The production of some species, especially haddock and certain flounders, could be increased by instituting the conservation measures recommended by the Fish and Wildlife Service or by an international conservation program.

The first step in an international conservation program was taken when 11 nations (Canada, Denmark, France, Iceland, Italy, Newfoundland, Norway, Portugal, Spain, the United Kingdom, and the United States) signed the International Convention for the Northwest Atlantic Fisheries in Washington, D.C., in February 1949. The convention was designed to promote international cooperation in coordinating, correlating, and disseminating information concerning the fisheries of the northwest Atlantic Ocean. Canada, Denmark, Iceland, Norway, Portugal, the United Kingdom, and the United States had ratified it by July 1952.

The convention established the Northwest Atlantic Fisheries Commission and selected a Massachusetts man as chairman. That commission may propose joint government action prescribing fishing seasons, spawning grounds, size and catch limits, and regulations governing gear and appliances. It has recommended the use of a larger mesh size in otter-trawl nets in area V (Gulf of Maine and Georges Bank), which might increase the haddock catch, in particular, by a substantial percentage.

There is no reason to suppose that New England's fish production, either over-all or from the New England banks, cannot continue to grow. In the last twenty years species once considered trash have come into widespread demand as food fishes, for example ocean perch, yellowtail flounder, and whiting. Similar changes may occur in the future. Cusk, pollock, pout, red hake, or even skates might well become much more valuable and important with improved processing and marketing methods. Improvements in fishing gear could also open sources of supply not yet tapped.

These changes can be hastened by the introduction of more research programs by the industry itself and by state and federal agencies. A fishery school at Gloucester, which has been under consideration by the Massachusetts legislature, would be a step in that direction. The industry itself should take the lead. A fish-products research institute, which we have already suggested, would aid the industry in adapting its actions to the changing problems and opportunities.

Salmon, Alewife, and Shad: The relatively poor current showing of three major andromous species of fish is the result of a long decline in their abundance, caused by overfishing, pollution, and exclusion from their spawning grounds. In early New England history nearly every stream was well stocked with salmon and shad; and alewife was so plentiful it was used as fertilizer. As industrialization took place, dams blocked the fish from their spawning grounds. Sawdust, pulp waste, bleaches, dyes, other factory wastes, and city sewage discouraged fish from entering the mouths of rivers. In recent years salmon have been taken regularly in New England only on the Penobscot, Dennys, and Narraguagus rivers in Maine. The 1949 catch for all New England was but 800 pounds, compared to about 400,000 in 1873.

If the salmon population is to be increased, extensive study and action will be necessary. Much salmon has been lost permanently as a consequence of industrialization, and it would be futile to attempt to correct the situation in every instance. *But in many localities salmon could be restored quite inexpensively by the addition of fish ladders.*

The first steps in a limited salmon-restoration program have been undertaken by the Fish and Wildlife Service in cooperation with the Maine Atlantic Sea-run Salmon Commission, the Maine Department of Fish and Game, the Maine Sea and Shore Fisheries, and the University of Maine. In June 1948 those agencies agreed to pool their resources. The State of Maine contributes $20,000 a year and the Federal Government about $75,000. The money has been used so far for fish ladders, restocking, and studies of river suitability. Other states might adopt similar programs to restore the salmon fisheries. The return on investment could be high.

Shad, though it has fared a little better than salmon, is another example of mismanagement of a resource. Once shad was one of the most abundant fish along the Atlantic coast. New England's catch in 1896 was 1,800,000 pounds. In 1950 it was less than 300,000 pounds, restricted largely to the Connecticut River. Like salmon, the decline resulted primarily from overfishing, pollution, and the erection of dams.

Shad runs can be increased by erection of suitable fish ladders around dams in some coastal rivers. Regulating fishing to moderate levels also helps, as has been demonstrated in the Hudson River since 1935. Restricted fishing spares the spawning adults and rebuilds the runs by natural reproduction. Exploratory work on the possibility of reestablishing shad runs in Maine has been undertaken by the Atlantic States Marine Fisheries Commission in cooperation with the Fish and Wildlife Service, but more study and effort are needed if shad runs are to approach their former levels in New England.

Alewife production has also declined, from about 12,000,000 pounds in 1896 to 5,700,000 pounds in 1950. The drop has not been a matter of as much concern as the loss of the salmon and shad fisheries, for alewife are small fish with many fine bones and are disdained by most American consumers. They sell for only slightly more than a cent a pound. Despite their declining abundance, they are so easily fished that they continue to be taken from the tightly packed schools which run in the small Maine and Massachusetts streams. Most of the produce is pickled and shipped to the West Indies or is used by offshore fishermen for bait.

THE SHELLFISH INDUSTRIES OF NEW ENGLAND

The problems of the shellfish industries in New England are in many respects the same as those of the fish industry. There are similar objectives of increasing both supplies and consumer demand, especially demand for the lesser known varieties. There are some important differences between the two industries, however, in organization, methods of operation, and problems. Moreover, the deep-sea fishing grounds are primarily international, while the shellfisheries are largely properties of the individual states and are subject to state regulation.

The shellfisheries accounted for only 6% of the weight of the total New England seafood catch in 1950 but for 35% of the value. Furthermore, while their gear and appliances require less capital investment, more persons were employed directly in the shellfisheries than in all the other New England fisheries. The principal types of shellfish taken during 1950, in order of their importance, were lobsters, scallops, and clams. In addition, mussels and oysters are produced in certain parts of the region.

Lobsters

The lobster fishery is the third most important in the region. The 1950 New England lobster catch was 22,558,700 pounds, worth $8,108,404. Of those landings 80% were taken in Maine, most of the rest in Massachusetts. Demand for the northern lobster is high, though most of the catch is consumed within the region. New England's production has increased rapidly in recent years, and prices have more than doubled since 1939, both despite an increase in imports from 15,000,000 pounds in 1939 to 35,000,000 pounds in 1950.

The major problem facing the industry is possible depletion of the lobster resources. While total production has increased considerably in recent years, annual catch per lobster trap fell from a peak of 177.5 pounds in 1887 to 34 pounds in 1940, in spite of improved technology. The reproduction rate of lobsters is low. Mature females spawn every two years, but the 30,000 eggs they produce may yield only two grown lobsters.

To conserve this valuable resource the separate New England states have attempted to enforce minimum size limits. In addition, Maine has a maximum size limit to protect the larger spawners. The eventual success of the size limitations in maintaining and increasing the lobster population cannot yet be judged. The Fish and Wildlife Service and the states have conducted considerable research on the lobster in the past and have gathered much valuable information, but a final decision about conservation measures will require further biological studies. In the meantime *the present size regulations should be strictly enforced*.

Scallops

For about two decades the scallop fishery of the United States has been centered at the port of New Bedford. In 1949, 19,804,000 pounds of scallop meats worth $7,792,000 were landed in the United States, and 11,707,000 pounds worth about $4,500,000 were landed in New Bedford.

In Europe the entire scallop is eaten, but in this country the only part consumed is the "eye," the large adductor muscle that controls shell movements. The remainder is discarded or used as trash. Sea scallops are found on sandy and rocky bottoms at depths of two to 150 fathoms. The sea scallop cannot close its shell tightly. It dies soon after it is caught and spoils unless it is shucked immediately. Little is known about the biology of the sea scallop or about the possibility of maintaining or increasing production.

Bay scallops, as the name implies, live in bays and estuaries, most frequently on sandy or muddy flats covered with eel grass. The bay scallop is smaller than the deep-sea scallop. It brings a good price and is highly prized. Bay scallops spawn but once in a lifetime during their first summer. New England state and town regulations permit the capture only of adult scallops, so the size of the commercial catch does not influence the propagation of the species. Pollution of coastal waters, however, has an important effect upon their numbers.

Clams and Oysters

Two major types of clam are produced in New England—the soft-shell and the hard-shell, or quahog. New Englanders prefer the former in home-made chowders, at clam bakes, and fried. The quahog is usually the raw material for canned clam chowder and minced clams.

In 1950 New England's commercial clam production was slightly less than 14,000,000 pounds valued at $3,424,000. Rhode Island's production of hard-shelled clams exceeded that of any other New England state, while Maine was the leading producer of the soft-shelled variety.

Soft-shelled clams supplement many a New Englander's income. Since this variety lives along the shoreline, requirements for entering the clam business are a clam fork, time, and energy. A good worker with average luck and skill can dig about four bushels of clams during the few hours when the tide is out. Hard-shelled clams are found in deeper water and require a somewhat larger investment for commercial production.

Recently there has been a noticeable decrease in the abundance of clams, especially the soft-shelled variety. Biologists do not know the exact causes for the decline, but pollution, excessive digging, and natural hazards are apparently among the leading factors. Steps are being taken in parts of New England to decrease the losses from pollution, and biologists are looking for means of reducing the natural hazards, especially losses from starfish attacks. A long-range project is now being conducted at the Narragansett Marine Laboratory in Rhode Island to find out more about the quahog. Such projects should be of great service to the New England shellfish industry.

Some measures have been undertaken to reduce excessive digging. Since control of clam digging is divided between state and township no uniform regulations exist, but many New England towns require a two-inch minimum size for both soft-shelled clams and quahogs. Most towns bar nonresident diggers and issue either family or commercial licenses to residents only.

One potential method for increasing the production of clams is scientific cultivation by public or private groups. There has been some cultivation, but not nearly enough to increase production substantially. One reason for the lack of cultivation has been the refusal of state and local governments to lease grounds to private interests for this purpose. It appears that refusal is not always in the public interest and that adequate safeguards for the public could be written into leases to private groups.

The situation for oysters, which is not discussed in detail, is somewhat similar to that for clams. In 1950 the New England fisheries produced $1,681,000 worth of oysters. New England's oyster fisheries lie along the southern coast of the region, and, while small in total, they are of some local importance. Pollution, natural enemies, and heavy exploitation have decreased the productivity of the oyster beds.

Mussels

Despite the abundance of mussels along the New England coast and their reputation as a delicacy in Europe, the region's mussel production has been small. Mussels are similar in many respects to clams, but their shells are thinner. The mussel's richness in protein and vitamins would make it a valuable addition to the American diet.

New England canners used only 15,000 pounds of Maine mussels in 1942. They experienced no difficulty in preparing or marketing mussels when they increased their pack to 1,500,000 pounds in 1943. By 1950, however, total New England catch had dropped to about 57,000 pounds as the wartime demand receded.

In Cape Cod Bay and other waters of southern New England, mussels inhabit fairly deep water where dredges are necessary. In Maine, however, where the black mussels are exposed during low tide, one man in a day can gather from 15 to 30 bushels with a clam hoe, rake, or pitchfork. *Maine canners might well give greater attention to exploiting this resource.*

Conclusion

The question of supply seems to be more critical than demand for most of the New England shellfisheries. To penetrate the interior markets on a larger scale, quantities must be increased. The quick-freezing of precooked scallops and clams, the live canning and quick-freezing of lobsters, and the rapid air and truck delivery of live lobsters are but a few examples of the recent developments in packaging and marketing techniques. Supply and market expansion must go together. As with the finny fish, it is important that the shellfish industry and the state and federal agencies concerned cooperate intensively in increasing knowledge about shellfish biology and control, in order to increase the potential yields of lobsters, scallops, clams, and oysters.

INTRA-INDUSTRY RELATIONS

Faced as it is by problems of competition and supply, the New England fishing industry can ill afford internal dissension. Constant disagreement and strife between employers and unions can hinder efforts at improvement and adjustment to changing conditions.

Labor relations within the deep-sea fisheries portion of the industry have been stormy at times. Distrust and past disagreements still prevent smooth cooperation between employers and employees. Each group typically attempts to further its own immediate interests in its own way. It is important that the opposing groups recognize more clearly their community of interest if the industry is to improve its position.

Two unions represent most workers in the principal groundfish ports of New England. The Seafood Workers' Union, affiliated with the International Longshoremen's Association, A. F. of L., represents employees of the shore processing plants. The Atlantic Fishermen's Union, which represents the fishermen themselves, is affiliated with the Seafarers International Union, A. F. of L. The histories of the two groups have been quite different.

The Seafood Workers' Union

The Seafood Workers' Union has locals in each of the major New England fishing ports. Each local has exclusive jurisdiction within its port and is responsible directly to the International Longshoremen's Association. The

Boston and Gloucester locals were formed about 1938; New Bedford and Portland were organized somewhat later.

The Boston union negotiates with the Massachusetts Fisheries Association, which represents most of the dealers, but the dealers sign contracts individually. Union membership in 1952 was about 1,500 in Boston, although it has dropped below 1,000 at times. Between 1940 and 1950 wage rates at Boston increased 60 per cent to $1.50 an hour for cutters. In 1950 two new increases totaled 11.5 cents an hour. The union negotiated and secured a guaranteed 40-hour week in 1946, plus paid vacations and holidays and a union shop.

While wage rates in Gloucester and Portland are below those in Boston, there have also been substantial increases in those ports since the union was organized. Union membership in Gloucester is about 1,800. Though the employers sign individual contracts, they bargain through an informal but effective group arrangement. A 14-week strike of seafood workers occurred at Gloucester during the summer of 1950.

In New Bedford and Portland the local unions have bargained with the employers individually. New Bedford was the scene of the only jurisdictional struggle in which the seafood workers have been involved. In 1944 a dispute broke out between the Amalgamated Meatcutters, A. F. of L., and and the International Longshoremen's Association, resulting in victory for the latter.

Except at Gloucester, there have been relatively peaceful relations between the Seafood Workers' Union and the employers. Prior to World War II the union seems to have lacked bargaining power, since more men were looking for work than there were jobs. During and after the war the prosperity of the industry has allowed employers to make sufficiently attractive wage offers to minimize conflict.

The Atlantic Fishermen's Union

The history of the fishermen's union has been much more stormy and complex. A union was organized in 1915, but it lost strength after 1921, when a court decision outlawed the closed shop and the union lost a six-month strike. In 1937 the present Atlantic Fishermen's Union was formed at Boston to replace the former union. The ports of Gloucester and New Bedford were organized late in 1939. Since that time total membership has fluctuated between 3,000 and 4,000 in those three ports and at Portland and New York.

Collective bargaining between the fishermen and the boat owners is usually conducted through an employers' association. The Federated Fishing Boats of New England and New York represents the Boston trawler owners. At Gloucester and New Bedford the boat owners' representatives are the Gloucester Fishing Vessels Association and the Seafood Producers Association, respectively. There is no association at Portland, where the union has few contracts. The draggers and small-vessel owners of Boston also have no association, but the union's agreements with the more prominent dragger owners are usually followed by the others.

Like most unions, the Atlantic Fishermen's Union has had the primary objectives of (1) improving working conditions and (2) increasing the take-home pay of its members. The first objective has been approached largely through collective bargaining. Under the unique compensation arrangements in the fishing industry, however, the second objective can be attacked only partially in that manner.

Fishermen are paid for each trip in shares of the net proceeds from the catch of that trip. The boat owner and crew bear all or a stipulated part of specific expenses and share the balance of the proceeds under the terms of a "lay" agreement. The fishermen can increase their earnings, therefore, either by bettering the terms of the lay or by enhancing the value of their catch. They have approached changes in the lay primarily through collective bargaining. To enhance the value of their catch they have used various indirect methods more than collective bargaining. Their policies have centered on increasing prices, especially through the establishment of selling rooms to insure competitive markets, through direct limitations on production or the establishment of minimum prices, and through indirect limitations on production.

To increase their share of the proceeds of a catch by bettering the terms of the lay, the fishermen may attempt either to change the lay split or to reduce the expenses allocated to them. In the past the union has had some bitter disputes with the boat owners in trying to better the terms of the lay. With a few exceptions, the issue has now been resolved. The lay split is currently 60–40 in favor of the fishermen on most vessels except the scallop boats, where it is 65–35. In general, the present lay split is probably about as good as the fishermen can expect. A split more favorable to the fishermen could affect the owner's ability to continue the vessels in operation.

The allocation and control of lay expenses are still bones of contention. The union has attempted to shift below-the-line expenses, which are deducted from the fishermen's gross share, to the above-the-line category. (See item (c) in the Boston Lay agreement shown in Table 2–6.)

The union has not had marked success in reallocating expenses. In 1940 the union won its demand that payment for ice during the summer months be an above-the-line expense on Boston trawlers. The owners of the smaller draggers, at both Boston and the other ports, have also accepted that change. The only other change has been a shift in the mate's bonus to the status of a joint expense for those vessels sailing from New Bedford.

Where the union has been unable to secure reallocation of expenses, it has been interested in controlling the expenses which remain below the line to make sure they are at a minimum. The boat owners generally pay for all supplies and deduct their cost from the fishermen's gross share. *In none of the ports has the union formed its own cooperative for the purchase of provisions, oil, or ice, a logical method of ensuring fair prices for these below-the-line expenses, although union officials have tried to interest their members in such a scheme.* Currently, the fishermen are paying close to retail prices for many supplies and provisions. In Boston alone these items amount to around $750,000 each year, and the fishermen could profit substantially if materials and supplies were obtained at wholesale prices.

Table 2–6. The Boston Lay

The owner agrees that the lay shall be the 60–40 lay as follows:

There shall first be deducted from the gross stock the following items:

Ice for three months actual fishing starting

June 1	Actual cost
Wharfage	Actual cost
Scales	Actual cost
Exchange fee	Actual cost
Chief engineer	$25 per trip
2d engineer	$15 per trip
Mate	$20 per trip
Sounding	$1.50 per day
Watching	Actual cost

(b) The balance of the remaining stock shall then be divided as follows: sixty (60) per cent thereof for the crew and forty (40) per cent for the owner.

(c) From the crew's said sixty (60) per cent of the remaining stock there shall be deducted the following items:

Fuel	Actual cost
Lubricating oil	Actual cost
Ice	Actual cost
Icing up	Actual cost
Groceries and provisions	Actual cost
Cook's per	$15 per trip
Water	Actual cost
5 Lumpers and a checker if used on a 17-man crew, or 7 lumpers if a 15-man crew is used	Actual cost

Note: In case of a "broker" or unsatisfactory trip due to breakdown, the owners agreed under this contract to pay all expenses and to pay the fishermen a per diem up to ten days as follows: fishermen, $5.00; mate, $6.00; chief engineer, $6.00; 2d engineer, $6.00; cook, $6.00.

Source: Federal Reserve Bank of Boston, *Monthly Review*, February 1950 (from the Uniform Trawler Agreement between the Atlantic Fishermen's Union and the Federated Fishing Boats of New England and New York, May, 1946)

To obtain a fully competitive market for fish the union has pressed for selling rooms which will bring sales and prices into the open. The aim is to bring the full weight of dealers' demand for fish to bear in the determination of prices. The union has been successful in establishing selling rooms in both Gloucester and New Bedford. The rules require that all union-manned vessels sell their catch through the selling room, that all sales be made at specific times each day, and that sales slips be exchanged between buyer and seller.

At Boston labor relations are complicated by the fact that many of the trawlers are dealer owned. As has been pointed out, dealers who are also boat owners have mixed incentives about the price of fish. Most fish landed in Boston are sold through the New England Fish Exchange, which has only dealer members. Since 1919 the Exchange has operated under rules of a consent decree specified by the federal courts. The union has pressed unsuccessfully since 1937 for the right to be represented on the board of directors of the Exchange and for changes in the selling rules, especially elimination of the so-called sell-over provision.

The sell-over has been one of the greatest sources of bad feeling and strife in the Boston fishing industry. The rules of the Exchange provide for the sale of all catches to the highest bidder, with the further provision that any purchaser may stop taking fish at the first sale price if any part of the catch falls below standard quality. When unloading is stopped, the balance of the catch must be resold, or sold-over, to the highest bidder. Any dealer may bid in the sell-over, including the original purchaser. The sell-over nearly always results in lower prices for the rest of the fish on the boat.

If the fishermen challenge the dealer's protest about quality, an arbitration board is called to settle the dispute. The board consists of the dealer, the fishermen's representative, and any mutually acceptable third person willing to serve. If a third party is not agreed upon, the Exchange manager determines the quality.

While the sell-over is designed to recognize differences in the quality of fish, the union argues that it is used most often when the market for fish is poor. The union claims that the same quality of fish may be sold as top quality on one day, when supply is short, and as second quality the next day, when supplies are plentiful. During the war period, 1942–46, when the demand for fish was exceptionally high, there were practically no sell-overs.

The Boston dealers claim that the sell-over provision actually results in a higher average price for the fishermen's catch. Without it, they argue, it would be impossible for them to bid extra amounts for the higher quality fish. Neither party to the controversy has apparently made a serious attempt to solve the problem by attacking its real cause, the question of evaluating fish quality. *Since appraisal of quality is now largely a matter of judgment, the opposing interests of the two groups will perpetuate the conflict until objective and measurable standards of quality are developed and incorporated into the selling rules. The two groups might support jointly the technical studies necessary to develop such standards and methods of applying them.*

Since the Boston union has been unable to change the selling rules of the Exchange or to seat a representative on the board of directors, it has turned to other methods for securing "fair prices." Until the summer of 1947, when it was enjoined by the Superior Court of Suffolk County, the union attempted to safeguard the incomes of its members by directly limiting production during periods of depressed prices.

On February 17, 1947, trawlers arrived at Boston with about 1,500,000 pounds of fish. Prices fell drastically. When the union found the prices unacceptable, the crews refused to unload their vessels. Total unloaded fish reached 2,000,000 pounds by the end of the week, as more trawlers arrived. The following week, the fish were unloaded when the Superior Court of Suffolk County issued a temporary injunction against the union on the petition of the attorney general of Massachusetts. On August 28, 1947, the injunction was made permanent. It ordered the union, its officers, and its members to cease and desist from (1) preventing the sale of fresh fish at its fair market price, (2) discriminating between buyers, (3) fixing prices above the fair market level, and (4) limiting production. The court held that the union's actions had constituted a monopoly in violation of the common law and were contrary to public policy. On appeal the Supreme Judicial Court of Massachusetts affirmed in substance the decree of the Superior Court. The Supreme Court of the United States refused to review the decision.

Since the union can no longer affect prices by direct production limitations, it has used indirect methods of restricting the catch such as limits on trip length, increased periods ashore between trips, and actual limits on numbers of trips. The fishermen have argued strongly for their position, in view of the irregularity of supplies and prices and the effects on their incomes. Extensive general restrictions of that sort tend to raise unit costs, however, and to injure the competitive position of the New England industry on which the fishermen depend for their livelihood, though perhaps some limit on trip length might be beneficial in reducing the amount of poor quality fish and the need for sell-overs. *Policies of general limitation of production run counter to the long-run interests of all groups in the industry. Urging on dealers increased product research and market development would appear to be a far more satisfactory way for the union to raise the earnings of its members.*

Low prices at particular periods are primarily the result of insufficient demand at such times in relation to new landings. The best solution is the maintenance of demand at high levels, a problem in marketing and inventory control. While temporary gluts still exist at times, the increased proportion of the catch that is quick-frozen tends to lessen the depressing effects of unusually large landings. Freezing fish at sea might assist even more in stabilizing prices, as well as in improving quality. *For their part, the dealers could demonstrate their good faith by admitting a union representative to the Exchange and by working out with the union improvements in the sell-over procedure.*

Future relations between the union and individual boat owners are still unsettled. *The bargaining groups have been without a contract in Boston for five years. Though each side professes to want a contract, talks have moved slowly. Unless the major disagreements can be resolved and a reasonable contract drawn up, each group may suffer seriously, harming others in the process.* The solution lies with them.

CONCLUSIONS

This study of the New England fishing industry indicates that the position of the industry has improved considerably since the end of World War II and that even greater improvement can be made in the future. To assure and hasten that improvement, we have recommended a number of specific changes, including the following:

1. Increased emphasis on the promotion of New England fish products by individual firms, by trade associations, by labor unions, and by government groups.

2. Continuing analysis and improvement of packaging and merchandizing techniques to be made by individual firms and trade associations.

3. Keeping quality at a high level, either by educational programs among members of the industry, by self-policing of the industry through dealers' associations, or through the use of a port-wide or New England-wide seal of quality.

4. Placing increased emphasis on industrial research. The establishment of an industry-sponsored research laboratory to study fish processing and technology.

5. Further research by the Fish and Wildlife Service on fish technology, fish biology, methods of catching fish, and other basic industry problems.

6. Searching out better ways of using foreign supplies to supplement New England's own production, rather than looking to increased tariffs or to import quotas for protection against increased foreign imports.

7. Adopting various recommended conservation measures in order to avoid critical scarcity of any major species of New England fish and to make greater catches possible. Continued support of the International Commission for the Northwest Atlantic Fisheries and its conservation program.

8. Initiation by state and local governments of a more liberal policy for leasing shellfishing grounds to private persons for the commercial cultivation of clams and other shellfish.

9. Speeding up negotiations between Boston vessel owners and the Atlantic Fishermen's Union for a collective bargaining contract.

10. The establishment of a cooperative for buying provisions which the fishermen pay for and consume while fishing.

SELECTED REFERENCES

1. Ackerman, Edward A., *New England's Fishing Industry,* Chicago, 1941.
2. *Atlantic Fisherman* (monthly), Goffstown, N.H.
3. Burtt, Everett J., "An Economic Appraisal of the New England Fishing Industry" (unpublished doctoral dissertation), Duke University, 1950.
4. McFarland, Raymond, *A History of the New England Fisheries,* New York, 1911.

5. U.S. Department of the Interior, Fish and Wildlife Service: *Fisheries of the United States and Alaska* (annual); *New England Fisheries* (annual); *Frozen Fish* (monthly and annual); *Canned Fish and By-products* (annual); *Packaged Fish* (annual); *Manufactured Fishery Products* (annual); *Maine Landings* (monthly and annual); *Massachusetts Landings* (monthly and annual); *Imports and Exports of Fishery Products* (annual); *Fishery Statistics of the United States* (annual); *Fishery Products Report*—Boston (daily, monthly, and annual).

6. U.S. Senate, *Fishery Resources of the United States*. Letter of the Secretary of the Interior transmitting, pursuant to law, a report on a survey of the fishery resources of the United States and its possessions, 79th Congress, 1st Session, 1945.

7. White, Donald J., "Union Policies in the New England Fishing Industry" (unpublished doctoral dissertation), Harvard University, 1949.

8. ———— "The New England Fishing Industry: America's Oldest Industry Faces Crisis," *Monthly Review*, Federal Reserve Bank of Boston, March 1950.

3

Agriculture in New England

*Drafted by John H. Bragg under the direction
of Arthur A. Bright, Jr.*

INTRODUCTION

Even in a highly industrialized area such as New England, agriculture plays a significant role in the regional economy. The gross income of New England farmers in 1951 was $775,000,000 and their net income was about $273,000,000; the region's farm labor force during the same year averaged 223,000. Agriculture ranks as one of New England's larger industries, though it provides less than 2% of the region's total net income.

The contribution of New England agriculture is far broader, however, than measurements of its size alone would suggest. Most of the area's farm products are raised for consumption within the region, and the agricultural community is closely tied to the other economic life of the six states. The principal products are highly specialized and often highly perishable. Some crops are important "export" items which help New England to earn its living.

Table 3–1. Net Agricultural Income in New England
and the United States, 1951*

AREA	AGRICULTURAL INCOME AS PER CENT OF TOTAL INCOME	PER CENT OF N.E. AGRICULTURAL INCOME
Maine	3.7	16
New Hampshire	3.0	8
Vermont	9.2	17
Massachusetts	1.0	31
Rhode Island	0.6	3
Connecticut	1.6	25
NEW ENGLAND	1.7	100
UNITED STATES	7.6	—

* Includes net income of farm proprietors, farm wages, and
net rents to landlords living on farms.
Source: Estimated from U.S. Department of Commerce data

While Vermont is the only New England state which draws a larger than national proportion of its total income from agriculture, the share of agriculture is also above the regional average in Maine and New Hampshire. (See Table 3–1.) Even in the three southern states of the region, the dairy, poultry, truck, tobacco, cranberry, and other specialized farms make important contributions to the prosperity of scores of communities. In fact, virtually

half of New England's agricultural income is produced in its two largest
industrial states, Massachusetts and Connecticut.

This report presents a brief summary of the nature and characteristics of
agriculture in New England, including discussions of the leading individual
products and a consideration of the major problems and opportunities for
further progress.

THE NATURE OF NEW ENGLAND'S AGRICULTURE

It is well known that New England consumes more agricultural produce
than it raises. The region contains only 2.1% of the nation's land area, yet it
houses 6.1% of the population. A larger proportion of New England's surface

CHART 3-1

Cash Receipts per Acre of Cropland and Pasture, Ten Leading States, 1950
(in dollars)

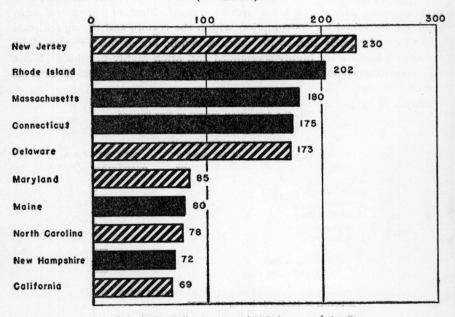

Source: U.S. Bureau of Agricultural Economics and U.S. Bureau of the Census

is covered by forest than that of any other region in the United States. Only
31% of New England's land area is devoted to agriculture, in comparison
with 61% of the nation's. Despite these limitations, New England farmers
produced about 2.5% of the total value of the country's farm output in 1950.

Cropland in New England in 1950 totaled only 4,216,000 acres, 1.03% of
the national total, and a fifth of it was limited to use as pasture. Illinois and

Iowa each contain five times as much agricultural land as the six New England states combined. When the total of cropland and pasture in all New England is compared with that in each of the other 42 states, New England ranks 37th.

One of the most striking characteristics of New England agriculture is the ability of the region's farmers to produce so much on so little land. Through intensive farming of specialized products well suited to the soils, climate, and markets, the region's cash receipts per acre from farm marketings rate high. Five of the New England states rank in the top ten of the nation. Vermont's large amount of pasture land pulls its ranking down to 21st. (See Chart 3–1.)

Even on an aggregative basis, however, certain parts of New England rate highly as producers of farm products. Surprisingly, some of the region's leading industrial areas are among the largest agricultural producers of the United States. In 1949 two New England counties were among the top 100 of the approximately 2,500 counties of the nation in value of all farm products sold. Aroostook County, Maine, ranked 16th, and Hartford County, Connecticut, ranked 26th.

Composition of New England Farming

As we have noted, much of New England's agriculture is highly specialized. Of the 51% of the region's farms specifically classified in the 1950 census of agriculture, dairy farms outnumbered each other type in all New

Table 3–2. New England's Cash Receipts from Farm Marketings,
by Commodity, 1951 (in thousands of dollars)

COMMODITY	VALUE	PER CENT OF TOTAL
Poultry	$270,976	35.0
Dairy products*	224,129	28.9
Miscellaneous crops	76,924	9.9
Meat animals†	62,524	8.1
Potatoes	59,071	7.6
Tobacco	32,591	4.2
Fruit	30,875	4.0
Truck crops	18,093	2.3
ALL FARM PRODUCTS	$775,183	100.0

* Does not include income from sale of cull cows and veal calves.

† Approximately 95% of this amount was income to dairymen from the sale of cull cows and veal calves. See page 108.

Source: U.S. Department of Agriculture, Bureau of Agricultural Economics.

England states. Commercial poultry farms were the second most common type, except in Maine. In 1951 cash receipts from marketings of dairy and poultry products constituted 63.9% of the total cash receipts from New

England agriculture. (Table 3–2.) Five other commodities accounted for all but 9.9% of the remainder.

A large proportion of the raw materials and equipment that New England farmers use is imported into the region. Through the economies of cooperative purchasing, farmers have been able to obtain these items more cheaply than they could by individual purchasing. In addition, through their cooperatives farmers have developed seed, feeds, and fertilizers particularly well suited to New England conditions.

The present structure of agriculture in New England is far different from what it was in the past. There have been constant changes since the Pilgrims first planted their crops in the fields around Plymouth. New developments and shifts in competition have required flexibility and adaptability of the region's farmers. For example, improved transportation and the opening of the West ended the early role of the Connecticut and Champlain valleys as the granaries of New England. The rise of refrigerated freight cars stimulated the growth of meat packing in the Middle West. New England's sheep industry moved to the Far West. The coming of the automobile meant the loss of southern Maine's market for its principal cash crop, hay for Boston's horses.

Although some established enterprises waned and agriculture in the region shrank in relative importance over the years, new specializations rose to fill much of the gap. Back in 1838 a report stated that in Aroostook County, Maine, "the staple crop is, and must ever be, wheat." Since that report, Aroostook County has become the largest potato-producing area of the country. Now, because of tremendous increases in yields and smaller per capita consumption of potatoes, many acres that formerly grew potatoes have been released to the production of vegetables for freezing, beef, and milk.

The farmers of southern Maine had a difficult time finding an alternative source of income when they lost their market for hay. About 1935, however, they started to raise chickens for meat on a commercial basis. The industry expanded rapidly. By 1951, there were 21,145,000 broilers raised in Maine, 63 times as many as the 1935–39 average.

The refrigerated transportation that caused the region to lose most of its fresh-meat industry at the same time permitted an expansion of Boston's milkshed. Milk is now produced in the northern sections of Vermont and in Maine for the region's metropolitan areas. Not only do consumers obtain more milk at reasonable prices but farmers in more distant areas also ship fresh fluid milk for a higher return than they could realize on cream, butter, and cheese. The improved transportation also makes western grain available for the region's dairy herds and poultry flocks.

As patterns of agricultural production and consumption continue to change, New England farmers must be alert to the necessity and opportunity for making further adjustments.

Size of New England's Farms

A basic shift in New England farm operations occurred during the last generation, a change from subsistence to commercial farming. This shift has accompanied the gradually increasing specialization of the region's agriculture.

The transition to more commercial farming has also produced an increase in the size of New England farms. According to the 1950 census of agriculture, the average farm in the region contains 121.5 acres. (See Table 3–3.) The averages vary from 185.2 acres in Vermont and 137.7 acres in Maine down to 73.5 acres in Rhode Island. While the New England figures are considerably smaller than the national average of 215.3 acres, they represent substantial increases over the averages of 25 years ago. Some farms that are now operated as one unit were two or more independent farms a generation ago, yet most of the larger units are still considered family farms. Changes in census definitions make it impossible, however, to draw precise contrasts between present and previous averages.

Table 3–3. Size of New England Farms, 1950

SIZE IN ACRES	NUMBER OF FARMS	PER CENT OF TOTAL
Under 3	3,447	3.3
3–9	9,552	9.3
10–29	15,097	14.6
30–49	9,947	9.6
50–69	9,698	9.4
70–99	11,165	10.8
100–139	12,995	12.6
140–179	9,208	8.9
180–219	6,293	6.1
220–259	4,005	3.9
260–499	9,058	8.8
500–999	2,352	2.3
1,000 and over	408	0.4
TOTAL	103,225	100.0

Source: U.S. Bureau of the Census, 1950 Census of Agriculture

The acreage of a farm is only one indication of its size. A better measure is the value of products sold. In 1949, 3.5% of New England's farms sold products valued at $25,000 or more and 28% had sales of $5,000 or more. The national proportions were 2.5 and 23%, respectively. The New England percentages are affected by the 14% of the region's farms classified as part-time and the 29% classed as residential. These percentages are larger than the comparable national figures of 12 and 19%. Elimination of the part-time and residential farms further improves the regional picture. In 1949, 6.2% of the commercial farms in New England sold products valued in excess of $25,000, and 50% had sales of $5,000 or more.

As one would expect, there are important variations from the New England averages among the six states. For instance, 35% of New Hampshire's farms are residential, a higher percentage than in any other New England state, although Maine's 33% is almost as large. In Vermont, on the other hand, where commercial farming is of greater relative importance, the proportion of residential farms is the lowest in New England, only 21%. In the three southern states the proportion of residential farms is about the same as the regional average. Variations in the percentages of part-time farms follow a similar geographical pattern. New Hampshire's 17% is the highest in New England, and Vermont's 10% is the lowest.

These rural residences and part-time farmers help furnish stability and an important reserve strength to the New England economy. While they do not yield sufficient income to support families, they do supplement the families' other income with small amounts of cash and especially with home-grown produce. If the owner is temporarily unemployed, he and his family can raise and preserve most of their food and perhaps realize some income from the sale of excess eggs, milk, vegetables, and woodlot products. Since manufacturing in New England is widely spread among many small towns, the farm-factory family is common throughout the region.

The residential and part-time farms are generally high-cost units from an over-all economic point of view. Their small tillable acreage and their small volume of output do not justify mechanization. From the producers' point of view, however, these units may involve low cash costs of production. The labor used, for example, has little alternative value. Only the additional costs, if any, are chargeable to the farming operation.

The smaller average size of New England farms is reflected in a higher percentage of owner-operators than in other regions. For example, in 1950 more than 95% of the New England farm operators were either full or part owners of their farms, compared to 73% for the nation. Only 3.7% of the region's farm operators were tenants, as opposed to 27% for the nation. Almost half of the few farm tenants in New England were cash tenants.

It appears that a larger than national proportion of the region's farm tenants have agreements to purchase the farms they are working. These agreements are typically used as steps to ownership, frequently between father and son. Most New England farms cannot support more than one family, which hinders father-son partnerships. A purchase agreement, however, can give the son a responsibility in management and the security of knowing the farm will ultimately be his. At the same time, it helps to keep the farm in full production and to give the parents security and independence in their old age.

New England's Portion of National Production

While New England farmers produced only 2.4% of the value of the nation's farm output in 1951, the relative importance of the region was far greater for several products. On the other hand, there are many agricultural products which New England raised not at all or in negligible amounts. The nation depends on other regions, for example, for its cotton, citrus fruits, wheat, sugar beets, and rice. The products in which New England makes its largest national contribution are typically those which lend themselves best to the climate and soils of the region, such as potatoes and cranberries, or which grew from the initiative and ability of the region's farmers, such as poultry.

In their competition with producers in other areas, New England farmers face certain cost disadvantages. Feed, fertilizer, and labor costs, among others, are higher in New England. But large nearby markets pay premium prices for quality produce. By improving the quality of their products and by adopting better production and marketing techniques, New England farmers have maintained the competitive position of their specialized products in these markets.

Dairying is New England's largest single source of cash farm income. Most of the region's dairy products are produced for consumption within the six states. At the beginning of 1952 the region had 3.0% of the nation's cows and heifers two years old or more that were kept for milk. Cash receipts from the sale of dairy products by New England dairymen in 1951 were 5.2% of the national total. These percentages substantially exceeded the region's 2.5% share of all farm output combined.

The poultry business is New England's second largest source of agricultural income. On January 1, 1951, 4% of the nation's hens were on New England farms. Income to New England's poultrymen from the sale of eggs in 1951 was 7.1% of that for the nation. Three major factors led to the higher percentage of income from eggs than the percentage of hens on the farms: (1) higher than national egg production per bird, (2) lower mortality, and (3) more direct marketing and premium prices paid for eggs.

Another favorable factor in New England's high income from eggs is the baby chick business. In 1949 New England hatcheries incubated and hatched 4.8% of the nation's baby chicks. In addition, there were large "export" shipments of hatching eggs, which commanded premium prices. Approximately 40% of the eggs set in hatcheries in or near the large broiler area of the Delaware-Maryland-Virginia peninsula were New England eggs.

In 1951 New England raised 16% of the potatoes grown in the United States. Maine is the leading potato-producing state in the nation; in 1951 it produced 87% of the potatoes raised in the region and 14% of those raised in the United States. Potatoes are the principal agricultural export of the region. Only 19% of the domestic rail shipments of Maine potatoes went to New England destinations in 1951; the remainder went to 38 other states. Maine not only excels in the production of the tablestock potatoes but also produces almost half the certified seed potatoes raised in the nation.

The South Shore and Cape Cod areas of Massachusetts produce more cranberries than the rest of the country combined. In both 1950 and 1951 Massachusetts' share of the quantity and value of the national cranberry crop exceeded 60%. Nevertheless, the over-all importance of this specialized crop is small, for it yielded only 3.9% of the total cash receipts from farm marketings in Massachusetts during 1951.

Apples, blueberries, raspberries, and strawberries are also raised in significant amounts in New England, though they do not have the national importance of the region's cranberries. In 1950 New England produced 7.3% of the nation's commercial apple crop. The production of blueberries is especially important in the eastern counties of Maine. The region's commercial production of strawberries and raspberries is usually as a supplement to other products. Despite the limited range of products, cash receipts to New England farmers from the sale of fruit were virtually the same proportion of total cash receipts as for the nation as a whole.

The Connecticut Valley has long been famous for its high quality cigar binder and wrapper tobacco. On 1.3% of the country's tobacco acreage, Connecticut Valley farmers produced 1.5% of the 1951 crop. The cash receipts from its sale were 2.8% of the national total. This higher proportion of gross income than acreage resulted from the type and high quality of tobacco grown. Limiting the comparison only to cigar-binder and cigar-wrapper types provides an even better measure of the importance of New England as a tobacco area. New England grew 49% of the nation's cigar-binder tobacco in 1950 and 58% of the cigar-wrapper tobacco. In 1951 the percentages were 70 and 55, respectively.

New England's maple products, while a relatively small portion of the region's total agricultural income, are of considerable national significance. In 1951, 51% of the nation's maple sugar and 49% of its maple syrup were produced on New England farms.

Nature and New England Agriculture

The agriculture of New England is conditioned heavily, of course, by the region's climate and other physical characteristics. The patterns of precipitation, temperature, and soils provide both advantages and disadvantages to farming. In general, they are favorable to dairying and the raising of poultry, potatoes, tobacco, and certain other crops in various parts of the region. Even the specialized products to which New England is best suited, however, are always subject to the uncertainties of nature, as is true of almost all agriculture.

The average annual precipitation varies from approximately 35 inches in the northern parts of Maine, Vermont, and New Hampshire to almost 50 inches in southern New England. The average for New England as a whole from 1886 to 1952 was 41.29 inches, with about 10 inches of precipitation in each of the four seasons. Although many agricultural regions in the nation have as much or more rainfall, none has such a favorable distribution.

Both droughts and floods are fairly common in New England, but they are less frequent than in many other parts of the nation. There has never been a crop failure that extended throughout all of Aroostook County, Maine. Portions of the tobacco crop in the Connecticut Valley are occasionally damaged by local hail storms. Sometimes prolonged rainy spells during the haying season cause losses to dairymen when they are unable to cure the hay or are delayed in harvesting it. On the other hand, the hay-curing problem can be partially overcome by the increased use of mow driers or by utilizing the crop for grass silage.

Soil erosion is not as much of a problem in New England as in many parts of the nation because so much of our farm land is in grass. Sheet erosion does occur on many of the cultivated hillsides, and occasionally there is some gully erosion.

A large part of New England is mountainous. The northern part of the Appalachian chain extends through western Massachusetts and a good deal of Vermont, New Hampshire, and Maine. The coastal plain is narrow. Much of the region gives evidence of its glacial past in the familiar ledges projecting through the earth's surface and the rocks and boulders strewn over fields and pastures. The many stone walls that line country roads and rim farmers' fields are silent reminders of the ice sheet that once buried the entire region. While the mountainous terrain reduces the potential farm acreage, it also gives rise to numerous streams and rivers which flow through fertile valleys to the sea.

The severe New England winters have always been a hindrance to many types of agriculture. Snowfall varies from over 100 inches in the northern section and in the mountains to about 30 inches along the southern coastline. The mean temperature of January ranges from 10° F. in northern Maine to 26° F. in southern New England. Along the southern shore and on Cape Cod the mean is 32° F. The average number of frost-free days is 120 in northern Maine and about 180 days in the lower part of the region. The cool nights and short growing season are not suitable for the production of field corn and various other crops, and alfalfa does not survive the winters in many portions of northern New England or in the hill country of southern New England. In addition, the pasture season is relatively short; most livestock has to be barn-fed for six months each year. The short season also limits many truck farmers in the number of crops that can be raised each year. Aroostook County has ideal climate and soil for the production of potatoes, but farmers must plan to ripen and harvest their crop before the ground freezes in October.

In the spring and fall, cranberry growers have to guard their bogs against frost. New England apple and blueberry producers also face the danger of frost during the bloom. These growing problems give some indication of why poultry raising has become so important in the region.

NEW ENGLAND'S PRINCIPAL AGRICULTURAL PRODUCTS

Each type of farming has its own problems and opportunities. This section of the report contains brief discussions of New England's leading agricultural commodities—dairy products, poultry, potatoes, and tobacco. While the sale of meat animals yields more cash income than the region's tobacco crop, we do not discuss New England's meat animals separately since most sales result from culls from dairy herds. Woodlot products are considered briefly as a supplement to other farm products.[1] The production of cranberries, maple products, and other farm items is of national significance, but these represent only a small portion of the region's agricultural output and are not treated separately.

Dairying

As we have noted, dairying provides the largest source of income to New England farmers. The dairymen's income is derived mainly from the sale of dairy products and the sale of cull cows and veal calves. In 1951 cash receipts from the sale of dairy products alone were $224,129,000, 29% of the region's

Table 3–4. Cash Receipts from Marketings of Dairy Products*
in All New England States, 1951
(in thousands of dollars)

STATE	VALUE	PER CENT OF STATE TOTAL	POSITION AMONG ALL SOURCES OF FARM INCOME
Maine	$31,751	17.6	3rd
New Hampshire	18,365	26.8	2d
Vermont	73,030	61.5	1st
Massachusetts	49,352	23.4	2d
Rhode Island	9,248	35.2	1st
Connecticut	42,383	24.8	2d
NEW ENGLAND	$224,129	28.9	2d

* Excludes income from sale of cull cows and veal calves.
Source: U.S. Department of Agriculture, Bureau of Agricultural Economics

gross agricultural income and second only to the cash receipts from marketings of poultry and poultry products as a source of agricultural income. (See Table 3–4.) In the same year, New England farmers received $52,282,000 from the sale of all cattle and calves, approximately 95% of which came from the sale of dairy animals. The combined cash receipts from dairy products and cull animals was $273,916,000.

The 27% of New England farms classified as dairy farms undoubtedly

1. There is a more extensive treatment of woodlot problems in report No. 1 on "The Forests of New England."

takes in all the larger herds, but there are many other smaller dairies in New England included in more general classifications.

Between 1944 and 1949 the number of cows and heifers two years old and over on New England farms declined 12.6% from 819,892 to 653,197. There was virtually no change, however, in the volume of milk sold over the same period. It was 3,471,000,000 pounds in 1944 and 3,419,000,000 pounds in 1949. The production of milk per cow increased sufficiently to maintain total production despite the smaller number of cows. Since 1949, however, both the number of cows and quantity of milk produced have increased.

Increased efficiency in milk production has been the product of improved breeding, better feeding, and other advances in animal care. Perhaps the outstanding improvement has been the development of higher yielding stock through the greatly expanded use of artificial insemination. The percentage of cows artificially bred in New England rose from 1.9% in 1945 to 24.5% in 1951. (See Table 3–5.)

Table 3–5. *The Artificial Insemination of Cows in All New England States, 1951*

STATE	NUMBER OF COWS ON FARMS JANUARY 1*	NUMBER OF FIRST SERVICES	PERCENTAGES OF COWS ARTIFICIALLY BRED
Maine	114,000	42,102	36.9
New Hampshire	66,000	22,330	33.8
Vermont	276,000	40,589	14.7
Massachusetts	126,000	39,821	31.6
Rhode Island	20,000	1,754	8.8
Connecticut	118,000	30,016	25.4
NEW ENGLAND	720,000	176,612	24.5

* The number of cows on New England farms remained relatively stable throughout 1951.
Source: The six New England artificial breeding cooperatives and New York Artificial Breeders Cooperative

Each New England state has an artificial breeding cooperative. In five states, the cooperatives operate on a statewide basis. In Vermont, the New Hampshire and New York associations also cover portions of the state. There is close cooperation among the various associations in New England and in other states. As techniques improve, it may prove desirable for one or more of the state associations to merge their bull studs. *From the standpoint of efficiency, lower costs, broader sire selection, and better service to New England dairymen, a federated New England bull stud owned by the state associations is a desirable goal.*

While artificial insemination is playing a vital role in improving milk production per cow, the New England Green Pastures Program is helping farmers to reduce feed costs through the use of more and improved home-grown feed. This important program originated in New Hampshire in 1947 and has operated since 1948 on a New England-wide basis. The objectives are primarily educational, but they also involve a contest among dairy farmers as to the quality of their pastures and recognition of outstanding performance. This program is designed to show dairymen how they can better utilize their land to grow a higher proportion of their herd's feed and to make the highest quality feed possible. The ultimate aim is a higher degree of efficiency of New England dairymen through better use of the region's natural resources.

From the start the program has received the financial support of industries serving New England dairymen. It would be expected that fertilizer companies, and farm machinery and equipment dealers would support it, since they stand to profit by its success. Feed manufacturers have also been among the most generous supporters in the interests of the sound growth of dairying in New England.

Dairying has expanded rapidly in various parts of New England during recent years, and especially in Aroostook County, Maine. With fewer acres needed to produce the nation's potato crop, dairying offers Aroostook farmers an opportunity to diversify their products and supplement their incomes. Between 1946 and 1951 the county's three principal milk receiving plants showed an increase in receipts from 7,500,000 to 35,288,000 pounds. Income from dairying rose from $330,000 to $1,800,000 in the same period.

> Northern Maine has many advantages for dairying including the best summer pasture conditions in the East. The principal disadvantages, as contrasted with other dairy areas, are the short pasture and long winter feeding season. Ample supplies of higher quality silage, economically handled by mechanical means, can go a long way toward offsetting that disadvantage.
>
> As a matter of fact, with abundant homegrown oats and quality forage the year around, northern Maine appears to have conditions about as favorable for economical milk production as exist anywhere in this country.[2]

Dairy marketing techniques have also changed to keep pace with changing conditions. At the insistence of producers, Congress passed the Agricultural Marketing Agreement Act of 1937. One section of this act provides for federal milk orders. Under these orders, the Boston market adopted, in June 1946, a butter-powder formula to set the price of milk. This formula replaced the cumbersome procedure of holding hearings each time a price adjustment was necessary. The butter-powder formula would have produced such erratic prices, however, that the formula was set aside most of the time. In practice, the market price was named in emergency "suspension" orders issued by the secretary of agriculture. In April 1948 the butter-powder

2. Allen W. Manchester, Harry I. Bell, and Clement S. Dunning, *Dairying on Aroostook Potato Farms*, Maine Extension Bulletin 415, October 1951.

formula was abandoned in favor of the "Boston Milk Price Formula." The fundamental objective of the new formula was to maintain price levels that would foster a good balance between the milk supply and the fluid milk demand, avoiding both milk shortages and troublesome surpluses. Class I, or fluid milk prices, are kept in line with changes in general wholesale prices, consumer buying power, grain and labor costs, and the supply of milk relative to fluid milk sales.

The supply-demand adjustment in price is a unique feature of the Boston formula. This procedure has been adopted by about 12 other markets with federal milk orders, and others are considering its adoption. Basically, this provision tends to correct any persistent condition which upsets the normal balance between supply and demand. Under the original supply-demand adjustment, if the proportion of milk used for manufactured dairy products in the most recent 12-month period went below 33%, the price of fluid milk was adjusted upward 44 cents a hundred pounds until the situation was corrected. Conversely, if the 12-month volume of milk used for manufacture were more than 41% of the total, the price was adjusted downward 44 cents.

Since the adoption of the formula in 1948, this method of pricing milk has gained general favor. With so many variables and no previous experience to use as a guide, however, the initial formula needed some refinements. On April 1, 1952, the formula was revised to provide for the substitution of the Index of New England Consumer Income (after taxes) for the New England Index of Department Store Sales. On September 1, 1952, the mechanics of the formula were revised substantially. Provision was made for eight seasonal adjustments in price instead of four; for the substitution of the year 1951 as the base period in place of the 1925–29 benchmark; and for the reduction of time from one year to two months in the computation of supply-demand adjustments.

The dairy marketing development that milk distributors in Massachusetts and Alabama adopted simultaneously in 1942 without each other's knowledge was every-other-day delivery. Shortly afterward, in order to save gas, tires, and manpower, the Office of Defense Transportation ordered the nation's milk distributors to eliminate special deliveries and call backs for collection purposes and to reduce mileage an additional 25%. This had the effect of making every-other-day delivery, a marketing technique that New England had helped to develop, compulsory throughout the nation.

On the other hand, New Englanders have been slow in accepting the elimination of Sunday deliveries. The milk truck drivers have opposed its adoption in New England because of the possibility that fewer delivery men would be needed. *Sunday deliveries are being eliminated in some New England cities, however, and the increased efficiency of delivery should help distributors to hold down prices as higher wages and equipment costs are pushing their expenses upward.*

Poultry

Poultry raising has increased rapidly in New England, and it offers potentials of considerable further development. By 1951 cash receipts for the region's poultry products were slightly more than those for dairy products (Table 3–6) though the dairy industry as a whole was a larger source of income due to the sale of cull cows and veal calves.

Table 3–6. Cash Receipts from Marketings of Poultry and Poultry Products
in All New England States, 1951
(in thousands of dollars)

STATE	VALUE	PER CENT OF STATE TOTAL	POSITION AMONG ALL SOURCES OF FARM INCOME
Maine	$63,448	35.2	1st
New Hampshire	34,858	50.9	1st
Vermont	11,046	9.3	3rd
Massachusetts	88,189	41.8	1st
Rhode Island	8,406	32.0	2d
Connecticut	65,029	38.9	1st
NEW ENGLAND	$270,976	35.0	1st

Source: U.S. Department of Agriculture, Bureau of Agricultural Economics

In 1950 commercial poultry farms represented 13% of New England farms. A large number of farms whose sale of poultry products accounted for a sizable portion of their income were undoubtedly included in the general and miscellaneous classifications. Thirteen New England counties ranked among the 100 leading counties of the nation in egg production in 1949, and four were among the 25 top counties—Middlesex and Worcester counties in Massachusetts, Hillsboro County, New Hampshire, and Windham County, Connecticut.

The New England market for poultry products is highly favorable to the present and future growth of this type of farming in the region. New Englanders consume more eggs and poultry meat (excluding broilers) than are produced in the area. They prefer fresh eggs and chickens of high quality from nearby farms, and they are willing to pay premiums over the prices of western poultry and eggs to obtain fresh, quality products.

New England's production of poultry products in 1951 was 2,715,000,000 eggs, 132,000,000 pounds of chicken other than broilers, 209,000,000 pounds of broilers, and 19,000,000 pounds of turkey. On the basis of national consumption averages for poultry products, the region's production was insufficient to meet its needs for all except broilers. Egg production fell short of requirements by about 28%. Chicken production was 15% less than consumption, and the region's farmers raised only 38% of the turkeys which New Englanders ate.

The one poultry product which the region produces in surplus is broilers.

In 1951 production outran consumption by more than 70%. Most of the New England broilers were shipped to the New York market, where they commanded a premium of .5 to 1.5 cents a pound over those from other areas, primarily because of their superior quality. The trend is now toward marketing broilers in the eviscerated or "oven-ready" style. *If New England hopes to maintain its markets, the region's broiler processing plants must be equipped for evisceration.*

From the point of view of both New England consumers and New England producers, the flow of western eggs into the regional market is desirable. Western eggs act as a supplement to New England eggs and help to stabilize the market. When local eggs are in short supply, the high price attracts western eggs to help fill the demand. Conversely, when local eggs are plentiful, their lower price effectively reduces the number of western eggs which enter the local markets.

From the consumer's standpoint, the availability of western eggs in New England tempers the price rise during the season of lower local production and assures a plentiful supply throughout the year. From the producer's standpoint, western eggs lower his prices somewhat, but he profits because the year-round supply of eggs at reasonable prices encourages their increased consumption.

Many poultry leaders in the northeastern part of the United States have long been concerned over competition from poultry raised in the grain belt. It would seem that farmers in that area could produce eggs and poultry meat more cheaply than farmers in New England, since the price of scratch grains is lower in the Midwest. Laying mash is about the same price in both areas, however, and New England has important offsetting advantages that have produced a major increase in the region's poultry population during the past 25 years. The principal reasons for the New England increase have been the growing markets for high quality products, the region's better bred stock, its good poultry climate, and more know-how. *While competition from other areas is likely to remain keen, it would appear that New England poultrymen can continue to maintain and possibly even improve their position.*

Perhaps the single most important advantage of the region in egg production is the high yield of its flocks. New England's production per hen was 200 eggs in 1951, about 25 eggs more than the average for the nation. When the 48 states of the nation are ranked according to egg production per bird, the New England states hold six of the first seven places. (See Chart 3–2.) In addition, the mortality of chicks raised for replacements was only 9% in New England during 1948, compared with 13% in the nation, while the mortality of hens the first year in the laying house was 13% in New England and 17% in the nation.

Production of hatching eggs and baby chicks is another outstanding part of the region's poultry business. New England produces enough hatching eggs to supply its own needs and leave approximately 50% for shipment to poultrymen in other parts of the country. In 1951 the hatching eggs shipped out of New England were valued at an estimated $11,500,000.[3]

New England's hatching-egg flocks in 1951 totaled approximately 4,600,000 birds. Assuming an average annual production of 10 dozen eggs per bird [4]

CHART 3–2

Annual Egg Production per Lay, Ten Leading States, 1951

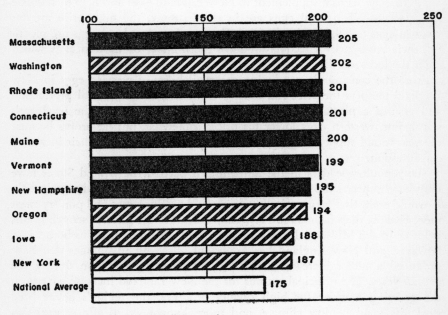

Source: U.S. Bureau of Agricultural Economics

and the use of from 40 to 60% of the eggs produced by these flocks for hatching purposes, about 25,000,000 dozen New England eggs were used as hatching eggs in that year. (Table 3–7.) About 3,700,000 dozen eggs are required annually for replacements for laying flocks and 8,300,000 dozen for broiler chicks. The remainder are sent to other areas, where poultrymen have long sought hatching eggs and baby chicks from New England's vigorous strains.

The New England poultry industry was not active in broiler production

3. Estimates on hatching eggs were supplied largely by Frank D. Reed, poultry specialist, Maine Agricultural Extension Service.

4. The estimate of 10 dozen eggs is less than the average for all layers, since many hatching-egg birds are kept for only six months. In addition, production is typically lower in hatching-egg flocks than in table-egg flocks.

prior to 1940. The growth of the market for broilers was stimulated by the red-meat shortage of the 1940's, by growing population, by higher income levels, and by the increased efficiency of broiler growers. As a result of research in the development of new breeds, feeds, etc., poultrymen now can raise a 3.5-pound broiler in two weeks less time than ten years ago on 1.75 pounds less feed and with half the labor.

Table 3-7. *Production and Use of Hatching Eggs in New England, 1951*

STATE	BIRDS IN HATCHING-EGG FLOCKS* (THOUSANDS)	EGGS PRODUCED BY HATCHING-EGG FLOCKS (THOUSANDS OF DOZENS)	EGGS USED AS HATCHING EGGS	
			PER CENT	THOUSANDS OF DOZENS
Maine	1,197	11,970	60%	7,180
New Hampshire	1,559	15,590	60	9,350
Vermont	191	1,916	60	1,150
Massachusetts	1,029	10,290	40	4,120
Rhode Island	57	570	40	230
Connecticut	560	5,600	50	2,800
TOTAL	4,593	45,936	54%	24,830

* Based on number of birds tested for pullorum.
Source: Estimates by Frank D. Reed, Maine Agricultural Extension Service

New England, with its established hatching-egg business, was a natural location for expansion of broiler production. In the past 15 years the broiler industry has grown phenomenally in New England. By 1951 the number of broilers raised in New England reached 60,142,000 and was ten times as large as the average annual production from 1935 to 1939. While there are commercial broiler enterprises in every New England state, eastern Connecticut and Waldo County, Maine, are the two areas of largest concentration. Maine's production zoomed from almost nothing before the war to more than 21,000,000 by 1951.

This extraordinary growth of the broiler industry in New England, and especially in Maine, could not have taken place without the large amounts of credit obtained from processors and feed dealers. The cost of this credit is high, though the lenders have also provided supervision and counsel as part of their service. Resurgent competition from red meats and a narrower cost-price margin are now eliminating some of the high-cost broiler producers and adding to the pressure on the more efficient enterprises. *Credit in the future may not be so readily available, and producers who have high mortality records and low feed-conversion ratios may have difficulty in finding processors who will contract with them. For continued prosperity, the broiler producers of New England will have to strive for even more efficient production, improvement in preparation and marketing techniques, and the development of new markets.*

In view of New England's large deficit in home-grown turkeys, this would seem to be one type of poultry enterprise that could profitably be expanded in the region. Aroostook County appears to be a section in New England where turkeys could be produced on a large commercial scale at costs competitive with those in the Midwest. Home-grown grains could be produced for turkey feed on acreages that have been retired from potato production or that are in a potato rotation. The high quality clover and grass that is grown in the potato rotation makes excellent range for poults and young turkeys. The cool climate and the early advent of cool weather in the fall also appear as favorable factors for obtaining early and prime "finish" of the birds.

Potatoes

Potatoes accounted for 7.6% of New England's gross agricultural income in 1951 and ranked third in dollar volume among the major types of agricultural products. The high rating of potatoes as a source of income in the region is due largely to the cash receipts of Maine farmers, rather than to the general importance of potatoes throughout New England. (Table 3–8.) In Maine the 1951 cash income from potatoes was $49,077,000, 27% of the gross income of Maine farmers and 83% of the total cash receipts of New England farmers from the sale of potatoes.

Table 3–8. *Cash Receipts from Marketings of Potatoes in All New England States, 1951 (in thousands of dollars)*

STATE	VALUE	PER CENT OF STATE TOTAL	POSITION AMONG ALL SOURCES OF FARM INCOME
Maine	$49,077	27.3	2d
New Hampshire	1,365	2.0	5th
Vermont	923	0.8	7th
Massachusetts	2,688	1.3	8th
Rhode Island	1,579	6.0	4th
Connecticut	3,439	2.0	6th
NEW ENGLAND	$59,071	7.6	3rd

Source: U.S. Department of Agriculture, Bureau of Agricultural Economics

Potatoes are the principal surplus agricultural product grown in New England. In 1951 New Englanders consumed about 16,145,000 bushels of potatoes and produced 52,746,000 bushels. Virtually 70% of the crop was exported for consumption in other areas.

New England produced 16.2% of the nation's 1951 potato crop on 9.7% of the national potato acreage. Since most of New England's potatoes are grown in Maine, the productivity of that state dominates the regional yields. Maine had 79% of New England's potato acreage and produced 87% of New England's potato crop. *Maine producers have made tremendous strides in increasing potato yields during recent years.* The average yield per acre was 266 bushels in 1940. By 1950 it had risen to 480 bushels, and in 1951 it was 445 bushels. These yields were almost double the United States average of 132 bushels in 1940, 253 bushels in 1950, and 241 in 1951. In New Hampshire, Connecticut, and Rhode Island, yields were also above the national average.

The high level and great increase in Maine's potato yields per acre have been the result of improved seed, the development of higher yielding varieties, the heavier use of fertilizer, and improved techniques and materials to control insects and disease. The acreage allotments in effect during the postwar period in connection with the price support program provided a strong impetus to obtain increased yields per acre. Facing a curtailment of acreage, producers withdrew their lowest yielding land from production and used more intensive practices on those acres still in production. The effect of these intensified practices is indicated to some extent by the decline in yield per acre from 1950 to 1951, the first postwar year without price supports or acreage allotments for potatoes.

The majority of the farms in Aroostook County are specialized potato farms, while in the other New England states potatoes generally are raised as a supplementary crop to a dairy, poultry, or tobacco enterprise. Because of major reductions in acreage through acreage allotments and the need to continue smaller acreages due to increased yields and lower per capita consumption of potatoes, more progress has been made in the diversification of Aroostook County farms recently than was true prior to 1946.

The developments of the last few years have also produced a rapid shift from research on potato production alone to combined research on production and marketing techniques. So far, there has been comparatively little research on new methods of merchandising and selling potatoes. Packaging has undergone a radical change, however, as the trend toward smaller homes and kitchenette apartments has led to a substitution of 5- to 15-pound paper sacks for the old 50- and 100-pound burlap bags.

The physical facilities of most of the Maine potato houses which do the bulk of consumer packaging are still inadequate. Their work areas are typically too small to accommodate the grading, sizing, and packaging equipment necessary to do the job efficiently. *Correction of these plant inadequacies is part of the program necessary for future prosperity of potato growing in Maine. In addition, if Maine is to hold its present potato markets and develop new ones, the growers and distributors must improve their marketing practices. More of the recommendations of research already completed should be adopted, and an intensified long-range marketing-research program should be undertaken for the future.*

Tobacco

The New England tobacco industry is located in the lower Connecticut Valley, mostly in the towns bordering the river. For the most part, Havana Seed tobacco is raised in Massachusetts, Broadleaf tobacco on the east side of the river in Connecticut, and both varieties on the west side of the river in

Hartford County, Connecticut. A third type, Shade tobacco, is raised primarily in Connecticut. The outdoor tobacco is used largely for cigar binders, although some of it finds use as cigar wrappers. Shade tobacco is used almost entirely for wrappers. The portions of both crops not suitable for either wrappers or binders are used as filler, scrap chewing tobacco, or the manufacture of various by-products.

During recent years the cigar-tobacco growers of New England have faced problems somewhat different from those of the growers of tobacco in other parts of the country. For one thing, there has not been the market expansion for cigars that there has been for cigarettes. The average consumption of cigars by each adult male in the United States declined from 265 per year during the first decade of the 20th century to 130 by the mid-1930's. Except for a small increase since 1950, average consumption has since remained fairly stable.

Markets and foreign competition have both been greatly affected in the last decade by the consequences of World War II. Prior to 1941 Sumatra and Indonesia produced a large share of the world's cigar-wrapper tobacco. During the Japanese occupation production ceased, production facilities were destroyed, and a large amount of tobacco land was acquired by the natives to grow food. Full production of tobacco had not yet been restored in Sumatra and Indonesia by 1952.

Foreign supplies were short during the war and postwar periods, and this shortage led to higher prices for Connecticut Valley tobacco, which encouraged an expansion of acreage and production. After the war, exports of wrapper and binder tobacco increased and acted as a support to New England's increased tobacco production. Annual exports of binder tobacco have been at an estimated 5% of total production since 1945, compared to 1% from 1920 to 1945. Exports of shade-grown cigar-wrapper types of tobacco were about 25% of total production in 1951.

The foreign demand will almost certainly be short-lived, however. Exports of binder tobacco from the beginning have been limited by the demand for a leaf that can also be used for wrappers and by the low dollar balances of many importing countries. The substantial exports of wrapper tobacco under the European Payments Union can be expected to drop sharply when Sumatran production recovers. The Sumatran leaf is thinner and more desirable, and European nations will probably prefer to purchase tobacco in sterling areas to conserve their dollar balances.

Tobacco growing in the Connecticut Valley faces the probable need for a sizable cut in production. Like all agricultural production, however, tobacco acreage is slow to retract during periods of unfavorable prices. When the export market is cut off, responsible leaders in the industry believe that there will be a surplus of wrapper tobacco of approximately 25% of total production and that the shade growers will face a situation similar to that of the outdoor growers.

These developments help explain the recent attitudes of New England tobacco growers to price supports and acreage limitations. Under the Price Control Act of 1942, tobacco was classified as an essential commodity and was eligible for price support at 90% of parity through the device of nonrecourse crop loans by the Federal Government. The law was later amended to make the acceptance of marketing quotas a prerequisite to price supports. After several years of quotas, the binder growers voted them out for the 1952 crop, only to reverse their position for the 1953 crop. During 1951, the last year of the acreage controls and price supports, binder growers in the Connecticut Valley put under loan about 24% of the Havana Seed crop and 13% of the Broadleaf crop.

Overexpansion of Connecticut Valley tobacco production is being adjusted in part through the loss of many fertile acres to industrial sites and urban developments. The Connecticut Valley is one of the most highly industrialized and rapidly growing areas of New England. High wages and extensive employment opportunities are producing a large influx of population. Hartford County is the center of the tobacco industry in the valley. Twenty-two of its 29 municipalities experienced a population increase of 20% or more from 1940 to 1950; 18 had increases of more than 30%; and 11 grew more than 40%.

Further adjustments in tobacco production will probably be necessary as the foreign demand for domestic tobacco lessens. Many Connecticut Valley tobacco farms already have increased their output of other products, such as potatoes, dairy products, and truck crops. This type of transition is typical of New England's past record of agricultural flexibility. Tobacco growers should give careful thought to their planting and diversification plans in advance of a possible critical period.

Woodlot Products

There are 103,087 farms with woodlots in New England, according to the 1945 United States Forest Service Reappraisal. They total 6,477,000 acres and average 63 acres per farm. *The woodlots permit farmers to supplement their regular operations and provide them with a profitable use of their time during slack seasons.*

There are numerous markets for the products of the small woodlot owner, although the type and location of the woodlot heavily influence the nature of its use. In some areas, for instance, pulpwood is in demand, while in others nearby cities provide a ready market for fireplace wood. In areas where balsam fir or spruce abound, the cutting of Christmas trees may prove a profitable venture. Many acres formerly cleared for pasture and meadow in New England are now reverting to forest growth. With an increasing scarcity of well-shaped Christmas trees each year, it appears that Christmas-tree plantations can provide an attractive return per acre from much land that otherwise would have no earning power for many years.

Many New England farms have no local markets for their surplus forest products, or their woodlots are too small to make the sale of the products worthwhile. Still there are many uses for forest products around the farm. Fence posts and stovewood are the most frequent uses. Many farmers also have their own sawlogs custom-sawed into rough lumber for farm building, repairs, or modernization.

The farm woodlots of New England are not as efficiently used, however, as they should be. A large proportion of them would be more productive under better forest management. Either through lack of interest or ignorance, many farmers ignore the potentials of their woodlots. Thinning, weeding, and selective cutting, for example, offer opportunities for larger yields of more valuable products. More education of farmers is needed through radio, literature, demonstrations, and other means to point up the possibilities of woodlot development.

The sugarbush offers many farmers in northern New England an excellent opportunity to utilize their own labor and that of their hired help during the winter months. In 1951 the gross farm income from New England maple products was $3,473,000. Although there are other farm enterprises that pay a higher return per man-hour of work, early spring is usually a slack time on many farms. Since the investment in equipment and the upkeep of the trees are relatively inexpensive, production of maple products is often a good way to increase farm income. Studies of factors affecting land use indicate that the extra income obtained from the sugarbush adds greatly to the probability that farms in certain parts of northern New England will continue in operation. When the sugarbush is cut off, many farms in these areas are abandoned.

The 1938 hurricane seriously affected the production of New England maple products. Vermont lost a fifth of its trees and New Hampshire almost a third. Since trees usually are not tapped until they are 50 years old and 12 inches in diameter, the replacement of lost trees has been slow. Farmers in northern New England should give close attention to building up the productivity of their sugar trees. While use of the sugarbush for pasture may not appreciably affect current production, future production is hurt as the young maples are broken or browsed off. In nonpastured bush, a small amount of work in the selective thinning of young trees, in cutting out dead, diseased, and weed trees can maintain and increase future production.

SOME AGRICULTURAL PROBLEMS IN NEW ENGLAND

So far, this report has presented various highlights of New England's agriculture. In a brief treatment such as this, it is not possible to consider all aspects of the complex agricultural economy of the region. There are a number of general problems, however, which affect many or all segments of New England's agriculture. Some of these problems are discussed in this section.

Mechanization and Productivity

The more efficient use of the time of farm workers is an important method of reducing production costs in agriculture. Man-hour productivity is of special importance in New England farming, since agricultural wages in the region are high in order to meet the competition of industrial wages. Many other farm costs are also higher in New England than in other parts of the United States. Since the knowledge of agricultural techniques is well disseminated throughout the country, the ability of New England farmers to meet competition depends heavily on their operating efficiency and their technical skills.

New England farms are highly mechanized. In 1951 the region's average of 1.95 tractors for each 100 acres of cropland was second only to the Middle Atlantic states figure of 2.22 tractors per 100 acres. The national average was only 1.06, and in the Mountain states there was but .66 of a tractor for each 100 acres of cropland. (See Table 3–9.) In 1945, the latest year for which data are available, New England farms had the greatest investment in machinery and power equipment per acre of cropland for any region in the country. Stated in 1935–39 prices, the value per acre of horses and mules, tractors, trucks, automobiles, and other farm equipment was $38.75 in New England. The national average was $16.10, and the lowest figure was $11.80 for the West North Central region.

Table 3–9. *Number of Tractors per 100 Acres of Cropland,* by Regions, 1920–51*

REGION	1920	1930	1940	1945	1950	1951
NEW ENGLAND	0.05	0.36	0.76	1.34	1.63	1.95
Middle Atlantic	0.08	0.56	0.91	1.40	1.94	2.22
East North Central	0.09	0.43	0.77	1.04	1.43	1.57
West North Central	0.07	0.22	0.40	0.53	0.71	0.75
South Atlantic	0.03	0.17	0.21	0.49	1.07	1.34
East South Central	0.02	0.09	0.15	0.36	0.93	1.18
West South Central	0.04	0.12	0.24	0.52	0.78	0.96
Mountain	0.08	0.17	0.28	0.41	0.58	0.66
Pacific	0.11	0.34	0.49	0.75	1.18	1.33
UNITED STATES	0.06	0.24	0.42	0.64	0.94	1.06

* Includes acreages from which one or more crops were harvested and acreages of crop failure and summer fallow.
Source: Data for 1920–40 from U.S. Department of Agriculture's Miscellaneous Publication No. 630, *Progress in Farm Mechanization* by Martin R. Cooper, Glen T. Barton and Albert P. Brodell. Data for 1945–51 supplied by Martin R. Cooper

Rural electrification has been a primary factor in increasing the mechanization of New England agriculture. Few farms in the region could be operated profitably without the use of electricity. Besides the usual uses of electricity, electric power has replaced manual labor in such operations as silo unloading, gutter cleaning, hay hoisting, refrigeration, poultry feeding, and watering.

New England, with its relatively short distances between farms, was one of the pioneering regions in rural electrification and helped to set the pace in making electricity available to rural people. There are only three regions in the nation that exceed it in the percentage of farms electrified. Electricity had reached 92.8% of the region's farms by the end of 1951, compared with the national figure of 86.5%. (Table 3–10.)

Table 3–10. Percentage of Farm Electrification, by Regions, 1945–51
(as of December 31)

REGION	1945	1946	1950	1951
NEW ENGLAND	81.0	85.8	92.3	92.8
Middle Atlantic	80.8	86.8	93.3	94.2
East North Central	73.8	80.7	94.2	96.6
West North Central	41.3	47.7	82.2	87.7
South Atlantic	41.3	49.0	80.2	85.8
East South Central	30.0	36.2	70.7	75.4
West South Central	36.9	45.8	76.4	81.1
Mountain	54.6	60.7	78.0	83.2
Pacific	84.5	89.8	93.0	95.6
UNITED STATES	50.0	56.9	82.2	86.5

Source: Bureau of the Census, U.S. Department of Commerce, and Edison Electric Institute

While the high degree of mechanization makes it possible to reduce labor requirements, New England farmers have a relatively large investment in machinery and power equipment to be supported by their small acreage of cropland. The intensity of land use in New England partially explains why farms in this region are so heavily mechanized. The crops produced require more hours of care per acre than do those in the Midwest. Moreover, the topography of New England's many small rocky fields reduces the efficiency of tractors and tractor-drawn equipment. Midwestern farms, despite their fewer tractors per 100 acres of cropland, usually have more powerful tractors and can use them more efficiently. Tractor power is also used on many New England dairy and poultry farms, however, for such tasks as filling silos, hauling manure, sawing wood, and plowing snow. The higher New England investment in equipment per acre of cropland results both from the smaller proportion of cropland in the region's agriculture and from a larger investment per farm.

Despite the cost of farm equipment it would appear necessary for New England farmers to maintain and extend their investment in labor-saving machinery if they are to hold down total costs and preserve or improve their competitive positions. At the same time, each individual farmer must assess carefully the prospective benefits of new equipment to avoid overburdening himself with capital and maintenance costs. The pooled or cooperative use of some types of equipment is often more economical than individual ownership and use.

Agricultural productivity has increased greatly in recent decades, but the largest increases have been in products which are not produced in quantity in New England. The national average of man-hours required to produce 100 bushels of corn, for example, fell from 135 in the period 1910–14 to 67 in the years 1945–48. Over the same period, man-hours required to produce 100 bushels of wheat fell from 106 to 34. *Since these are crops in which mechanization has been most effective, New England's agricultural output per man-hour has not kept up with the progress in the nation.*

There have been important improvements in the man-hour output of the farm products of greatest importance to New England, however, and the region has a creditable record of them. Ten years ago one man per 5,000 to 6,000 broilers was standard. Today, the standard is 10,000 to 15,000. Requirements for producing 100 pounds of milk fell from 3.8 man-hours in 1910–14 to 2.7 man-hours in 1945–48, and requirements for the production of 100 eggs dropped from 2.0 to 1.3 man-hours. Available data indicate that New England farmers produce more eggs per man-hour of labor than farmers in any other region of the country and that milk output per man-hour is also above the national average. (Table 3–11.)

While the region's dairy farmers have not surpassed the efforts of dairymen in all other regions, they have adopted new techniques which have permitted them to meet most competition. *It is clear that further progress is possible, however, and the dairy industry in New England should continue and intensify its support of the programs of breeding improvements, improved pasturage, mechanization, and other opportunities for increased efficiency.*

Table 3–11. Average Man-hour Requirements and Production per Man-hour of Milk and Eggs, by Region, 1943–45 Average

REGION	MAN-HOUR REQUIREMENTS		PRODUCTION PER MAN-HOUR	
	PER COW	PER 100 HENS	POUNDS OF MILK	NUMBER OF EGGS
NEW ENGLAND	157	162	35	94
Middle Atlantic	141	167	41	77
East North Central	140	168	38	72
West North Central	135	162	33	71
South Atlantic	138	161	28	60
East South Central	127	163	26	56
West South Central	123	145	25	67
Mountain	143	166	35	70
Pacific	141	158	46	87
UNITED STATES	136	161	34	71

Source: U.S. Department of Agriculture, *Gains in Productivity of Farm Labor*, Technical Bulletin 1020

The Agricultural Labor Force

New England is still a region of family farms, despite the trend toward larger acreages and increased farm business. During the period 1945–49, 73% of New England farm workers, on the average, were members of the operators' families. The seven months from April through October require the most farm labor in New England. Even during August, September, and October, when apples, onions, potatoes, tobacco, and cranberries are harvested, farm families constitute about 60% of the New England farm labor force.

New England's agricultural labor force is not entirely self-sufficient. Each year large numbers of workers from Puerto Rico or Jamaica are brought in to work through the summer months. The Connecticut Valley tobacco growers recruit school children from the southern states to work in the tobacco fields, while Aroostook County farmers bring in Canadians to supplement the local and migratory farm labor during the potato harvest.

Other sources of labor that help fill seasonal demands in various parts of the region are school children, housewives, and city people who are able to work extra hours on farms. The latter group is becoming increasingly important. *Active mobilization of these supplementary sources of seasonal farm labor has usually been sufficient to harvest New England's crops, though workers have not always been as plentiful as farmers would like. It is possible that improved communications directed to prospective seasonal workers would produce an increased supply.*

Dependable year-round labor, however, has frequently been difficult or impossible to get because of competition from steady jobs in industry. This problem has been especially acute in southern New England since the increased defense activity which started in 1950. Even the farmers in the three northern states of the region have felt the pinch of a shortage of reliable year-round hired labor as many agricultural workers have migrated to industrial areas or have gone to work in the factories which have expanded or sprung up in the smaller towns.

Competition from industry is reflected in farm wage rates in New England which are among the highest in the nation. The composite farm wage rate for the region in 1951 was 75.9 cents an hour, compared with the national average of 62.5 cents an hour. The average rate in the region's three southern states was 80.7 cents an hour, and that in the three northern states was 73.1 cents an hour. While these rates are still far below those for most other types of work, they represent an important portion of farm costs and show signs of further increase during a period when many farm prices have been falling. *As long as industrial activity remains high, there is little indication that either the labor supply or wage levels will be eased. The squeeze on farmers is serious and points up the need for sustained improvements in productivity through better techniques and through the use of more labor-saving equipment.*

Marketing Methods

New England is a deficit food area. With the exception of potatoes, broilers, cranberries, maple products, and tobacco, virtually all New England produce is consumed within the region. The major marketing problems for most products, therefore, are associated with serving the regional market.

New England farmers send their produce to nearby markets primarily by truck. Transportation charges are small in comparison to those paid by farmers in some regions. In times of falling agricultural prices, when freight charges remain fixed, New England farmers are in a more favorable position than their counterparts in most of the rest of the country.

But the New England farmer, because of his very nearness to the market, is faced with a difficulty that confronts the near-by producer around all large consuming centers. He has a market for his entire crop —good, bad, and indifferent. Scabby, wormy apples are salable at some price. Someone will buy over-ripe tomatoes or dirty, undersized potatoes and be glad to get them at a low price. However low the price of these low-quality products may be, they are sold, because the cost of marketing is practically nothing. Often they are sold to consumers at a roadside stand right on the farm. Or they may be brought to market along with something else.

It would be disastrous for many of the poorer consumers if a supply of this low-grade produce were not available at low prices. The local producer is the only one who can afford to supply such produce. He can supply it, does supply it, and will continue to supply it because it will bring enough in the market to pay for transporting and selling it. On the other hand, mainly because of freshness, a large part of the local supply of such products as milk, eggs, sweet corn, asparagus, and apples is of better quality than that of any similar product that could possibly be brought into the local markets from distant sections. The New England farmer, then, produces and sells some of the finest and some of the poorest of the food products sold in New England and can be expected to continue to do so. But products of poor quality placed on the market are in many cases injuring the reputation of local products in general and tending to decrease their sales.[5]

The principal solution to this difficulty is through better grading and labeling of New England produce. Some products now carry brands telling of their origin, such as "State of Maine Potatoes," "Vermont Maple Syrup," and "Cape Cod Cranberries." These brands denote quality products which have met grading standards. The New England branded items, however, are largely those sold extensively outside the region. Branding has helped maintain their sales in the rest of the country in competition with produce raised in other regions, but less attention has been given to grading and branding other New England products sold in the local markets. *The use of New England brands for the region's quality agricultural products should be greatly expanded. Adequate policing of market areas and grade inspection can hold abuses of brand names by unethical dealers to a minimum.*

New England farmers and distributors dare not be complacent about their

5. Frederick V. Waugh, "The Marketing of New England's Farm Products: Demand Factors," *New England's Prospect: 1933,* ed. by John K. Wright, pp. 175–176.

present favorable market situation. Improved transportation techniques permit high quality products from other areas to enter into direct competition with local produce on New England markets. To meet this competition, a more effective marketing program must be developed. This program should include: (1) closer grading for quality and size, (2) standardization of items in a package, (3) further use of labels signifying that the product is from New England or a New England state, and (4) more effective promotional programs acquainting the consumer with the advantages of New England produce and, just as important, acquainting farmers and packers with the necessity for offering quality packages. Marketing cooperatives offer one way in which producers can do these things effectively and efficiently.

Marketing techniques for food products have been changing rapidly to meet the consumer demand for food more nearly ready for the table. Entirely new retailing methods have been developed to display frozen and prepackaged foods in self-service super markets. Fresh and frozen foods are now displayed and sold in small units, many of them ready to cook or serve with no further preparation.

This type of merchandising widens the market spread, because the middlemen perform many functions formerly done in consumers' kitchens. There are certain savings to be realized through more efficient use of specialized labor in the retail store, as well as less labor per unit of sales, but there are also some added costs. In addition to the cost of preparing and packaging the produce, expensive refrigerated display cases and sometimes entirely new stores are necessary. This entire development increases the importance of grading and branding. *Where they have not already done so, the region's farmers should adapt their operations to the more exacting demands of the market and work with distributors to improve the competitive position of New England produce.*

The wholesale markets in New England are, for the most part, antiquated and inefficient. They are not adequate to handle either the large trucks that now bring produce to market or their present large volume of business. These conditions result in inefficiency and add to the consumer's food bill, as well as reduce the returns to the farmer. As the population of the region's metropolitan areas continues to grow, the marketing problem will become increasingly acute.

New market facilities are urgently needed, especially in Boston. In general, it is desirable for new markets to be built by private capital, but the problem of acquiring land in a satisfactory location and the large costs sometimes make it difficult for private enterprise to carry out the entire project. In smaller cities or in cities where present market facilities need only enlarging, it may be feasible for the city itself to undertake the project. For large building programs, it is occasionally desirable for the state to aid in the financing. Where state or local governments do the financing in whole or in part, the costs should be assessed on those who use the facilities rather than on the taxpayers in general.

Transfers of Ownership

Young farmers who want to buy their own farms have capital problems similar to those in any new business, but the amount of capital required to buy a modern farm is greater than that needed for many other types of business. As farm size and machinery requirements have increased, capital needs have kept pace. Many capable prospective farmers have turned to other occupations for lack of sufficient capital. Frequently, critics of lending institutions imply that lack of credit is preventing young farmers from acquiring their own farms. *In New England, it is not lack of credit so much as lack of capital that excludes many capable young farmers from farm ownership.*

This obstacle to ownership exists in all industries, of course, but it has a special importance in agriculture. It hinders the transfer of many farms owned by older couples who are no longer able to carry on a full schedule of farm work. Such farms are, at best, in partial production, and much of their productivity is wasted. In some cases, they become so run down that they are eventually abandoned.

Even for those who do have the necessary capital, the present system of farm transfer by "selling out and buying in" every generation creates a heavy debt burden. Many observers feel that this method of transfer is antiquated and that new methods must be found if New England is to maintain its individually owned and operated farms.

One logical step toward farm ownership is farm tenancy. Since only 3.7% of New England's farms were rented in 1950, compared to 27% in the nation, this possible avenue to farm ownership is much more restricted in New England than in other regions. The smaller average size of New England farms is also an obstacle to transfers. In other regions, where more farms can support more than one family, father-son partnerships are common. A small farm size limits the opportunity for such arrangement.

There are many farms in the region, however, on which production could be increased. Some dairymen, with the help of agronomists and extension personnel, have done a notable job of increasing the production of home-grown feed to support larger numbers of cows. More dairymen in the region can increase their net incomes in the same way. Where the primary farm product cannot be expanded economically, total farm business can often be enlarged through the expansion of an established sideline. The small poultry flock might be enlarged or the small orchard expanded. There are possible secondary enterprises, such as raising crops for canning or freezing, beef animals, and small fruits.

Where a going farm of adequate size is owned by a farmer past his physical prime, a young man could get a start as a hired man with some management responsibility. After a probationary period, he could progress to the sharing of responsibility and profits, with a legal agreement to purchase the farm upon the death of the owner or on a yearly payment plan. *This type of arrangement seems well suited to New England agriculture, and might advantageously be used more extensively.* It offers an opportunity to young men to get started in farming, allows older men to retire completely or partially without the entire loss of income, and at the same time keeps many good farms in full production.

Agricultural Credit

Credit plays a primary role in modern agricultural operations. With the substantial investment in land, buildings, and equipment and the large seasonal operating costs, few farmers are able to finance their operations entirely from their own capital.

The ratio of cash farm operating expenses to farm capital has risen substantially during the last half century. While profits from farming can be far greater now than they were 50 years ago, the high cash costs of production can more quickly wipe out a farmer's capital in a period of low prices. Most new developments in production techniques involve further increases in cash operating costs. Forward-looking agricultural lenders are recognizing this new relationship and are reappraising their lending practices in the light of these constantly changing conditions.

During recent years, farmers have had access to extensive credit facilities of a wide variety of types. The Federal Government has created financial institutions for the benefit of farmers to supplement the broad range of private sources of funds. Despite the ready availability of credit for most agricultural purposes, this credit has not always been in the best interests of the farmer nor has it always been of the type best adapted to agriculture.

One desirable change in agricultural lending would be the greater availability of equipment loans for intermediate terms. With the shift from light horse-drawn machinery to expensive tractors and self-propelled machinery and the greater use of more elaborate equipment has come a need for machinery loans running from three to five years. *These loans would be necessarily limited by the individual bank's ability and willingness to lend demand deposits in what to commercial banks are long-term investments.*

In New England, as in the nation, the largest source of farm real estate loans is individuals and "miscellaneous" lenders. In order of the volume of loans outstanding on January 1, 1952, the principal type of lending institutions in the farm-mortgage field were (1) commercial banks and savings banks, (2) Federal Land Banks, (3) insurance companies, and (4) the Farmers' Home Administration. In most business centers in agricultural areas, one or more banks and a national farm loan association (local organization of a Federal Land Bank) are in direct competition for farm mortgages. Insurance company representatives usually cover a larger area. While most of the loans held by insurance companies are made directly to farmers, in some instances banks that are short of loanable funds act as representatives of insurance companies in extending mortgage credit to their customers.

Credit granted farmers by dealers is probably their largest single source of short-term agricultural credit. The other principal lending agencies for short-term credit are (1) commercial banks, (2) production credit associations, and (3) the Farmers' Home Administration. The production credit associations were originally organized with capital provided by the Federal Government. They have repaid the government in installments. On January 1, 1953, 10 of the 16 associations serving New England were fully farmer-owned. The remaining percentage of government ownership in the other eight is small. Although the terms are sometimes unsuitable, the availability of short-term credit for New England farmers seems to be adequate in virtually all areas.

The financing of commercial broiler enterprises is one of the knottiest problems that has confronted New England agricultural lenders in the post-war period. Commercial broiler production is risky at best. Rapid fluctuations in price can wipe out a producer's margin in a short time. New England poultrymen and lenders are fortunate, however, that the additional problem of disease has been less serious than in some other broiler areas.

New England banks and production credit associations have been reluctant to grant operating loans to broiler producers, unless the producer has had a strong net worth that would justify another loan if there were a loss on the first batch of birds. Instead, banks have financed feed dealers, hatcheries, and processors, who in turn have financed the producers. New England banks have received sharp criticism for their conservative policy on broiler loans. The bankers have a strong case for their position in view of the high risk, low returns, and highly specialized knowledge required for adequate supervision of loans. The rapid growth of the industry, despite its credit problems, indicates that adequate credit has been available. The unfortunate feature is that credit has been extended indirectly at high cost through feed dealers, hatcheries, and processors rather than directly to the broiler producers.

Real Estate Taxation

New England farmers pay higher real estate tax rates than farmers in any other region of the United States. In 1951 farmers in Maine, New Hampshire, and Massachusetts paid higher average rates per $100 of full valuation on farm property than farmers in any other state. The average rates in the other three states of the region were also above the national average.

While the burden of property taxes depends on valuation practices as well as on rates, it appears that farm property is taxed relatively higher in New England than in the United States as a whole. There are several reasons. New England farms are generally smaller than those in the farm states. More buildings per acre result in higher valuation and more people per acre means a greater demand for public services such as schools and roads. In addition, New England states emphasize property taxation, and state aid to local governments is less freely given, while a high level of services is still maintained. Not only is there a small amount of farm land available, but also much of the land classified as "farm land" is situated near populated centers and the valuation reflects alternative uses of the property. Thus, as an example, New Jersey and Connecticut, states with similar urban-rural characteristics, had about the same average farm taxation in 1951.

The problem of property taxes in New England is not restricted solely to agriculture, of course, nor is property taxation the only tax concern of farmers.[6] Farmers share the common interest, nevertheless, in the construction and administration of equitable tax systems, and they should support the periodic review and revision of state and local tax laws and practices. Equity of property assessments is of special importance.

Federal Price Policies

Agricultural price and acreage policies of the Federal Government during the last decade have had an important effect on all Americans, whether as producers or consumers of farm products. In general, New Englanders have been more affected as consumers. Even the region's farmers, for the most part, have noted the influence of the price support program on costs rather than on prices received.

Although many commodities produced by New England farmers have been subject to price supports, the direct support operations in the region under the program have been limited largely to potatoes and tobacco. As we have noted, price supports and acreage restrictions helped to hold up prices for the Connecticut Valley tobacco growers for several years. There were no purchases of New England eggs under the egg support program, however, though purchases in the Midwest strengthened egg prices in that area and narrowed the price spread between eastern and western markets. With a large portion of New England's milk used as fluid milk, the price support program did not help New England dairymen as much as those in the North Central states. Purchases of dry skim milk and butter did help bolster the price of milk used in manufactured dairy products. There were some purchases of dry milk powder in New England during the flush seasons.

The price support program did prevent a debacle in New England potato prices, especially in Maine, but it produced some deep-seated dislocations in the potato industry. The Federal Government supported the price of potatoes for the crops of 1942 through 1950 under the Steagall Amendment to the Price Control Act of 1942. The original purpose of the plan was to encourage increased production of potatoes as wartime insurance against inadequate

6. For a more extensive discussion of these problems see report No. 17 on "State and Local Taxation and Expenditures in New England."

crops of small grains. As it happened, there was no grain shortage, but it was probably a sound wartime safety measure to have encouraged greater output of potatoes. In 1943 potato farmers exceeded the goal of 3,260,000 acres set by the Department of Agriculture and produced a larger crop than was requested. In 1944 the goal was increased to 3,519,000 acres, but actual acres harvested fell short by 634,000. In all subsequent years the growers also failed to meet the acreage goals, although through high yields per acre they regularly exceeded the production goals.

Potato growers responded promptly to the wartime need for increased production. When potato requirements declined, farmers reduced their acreage. Yet huge surpluses accumulated as sustained national prosperity led to a decline in per capita consumption of potatoes. In addition, improved farming techniques and the withdrawal from production of low-yielding acres increased yields faster than plantings were reduced.

The government policy of purchasing surplus potatoes in areas of concentrated production had two major detrimental effects on the Maine potato industry. The unfavorable publicity which surrounded the disposal of surplus potatoes was centered on Maine, and it has injured the prestige of the industry. Even more important, government purchases of substantial portions of the Maine crop permitted competing areas to capture some of Maine's regular markets. While this made little difference in the income of potato growers at the time, it had serious repercussions after the withdrawal of price supports. *Maine's lost markets can be regained and held only with considerable effort, through improved marketing techniques and a high-grade promotional program.*

More recently, in 1952, there was a potato shortage rather than a surplus. Reaction against previous overproduction, in combination with a price ceiling for potatoes, created a set of conditions that disrupted normal marketing procedures and intensified the shortage. The following are excerpts from a statement on the potato situation by Representative Clifford G. McIntire before the House of Representatives:

During these years of adjustments, in which surpluses were a serious problem, and also the same years in which price support operations were in effect, returns to growers were substantially below parity. The crop of 1950 returned to growers 53% of parity. Approximately two-thirds of the 1951 crop returned growers only 73% of parity. It developed, however, as the 1951 marketing season progressed, that the supply was not in surplus as had been true in previous years, and prices began to strengthen. Beginning with early October it became apparent that the supply situation in Canada was also lower than in previous years, that the supply in the United States was not in surplus, and prices moved upward. On December 29, 1951, the Department of Agriculture officially determined that potato prices received by growers were 105% of parity on December 15, 1951. This was the first month prices had reached parity since June of 1948. The United States Department of Agriculture later reported that the supply of potatoes on hand January 1, 1952, was 97,000,000 bushels which was only 5,250,000 bushels lower than the supply of the previous year, excluding Government purchases after January 1, 1951. It seemed to many familiar with the industry that, while the supply was in balance with demand, no serious shortage existed, providing normal economic practices could prevail for the remaining portion of the season. On January 9 the Office of Price Stabilization invoked a ceiling order CPR 113, effective on the 19th of January 1952. . . .

In my opinion, this order has created a black market, and it is my considered opinion that the shortage that exists currently is directly chargeable to the operations of OPS in their complete disruption of the normal distributive pattern of the industry. In addition, it is my opinion that the crop in storage in January has moved to market 10% faster than would have been the case had there been some price incentive in holding some portion of the crop for later delivery. The order has affected the acreage planted in the early and intermediate early States. The price available to producers in the southern early States has offered no incentive for orderly marketing. Florida, with only a 6% increase in acreage, had shipped, as of April 30, 4,755 carlot equivalents as compared with 1,790 carlot equivalents on the same date in 1951. This has meant that consumers have not had as good quality and the crop was not fully matured. Early harvesting has resulted in a 15% lower yield per acre.[7]

The problems of the potato industry are summarized here as an example of the difficulties which agricultural price supports can create and because potatoes are the leading commodity in New England that has been directly affected by price supports, ceilings, and acreage allotments. New England potato growers have not been alone in their difficulties. Producers of other crops throughout the nation have faced and are facing similar situations.

Despite the distortions that sometimes have been created by federal agricultural price policies, the use of farm price supports is a valuable part of the nation's efforts to maintain economic stability. Price supports are desirable provided they are not so high that they keep high-cost producers in business. The ideal level for supports would prevent a wholesale loss of farms such as occurred in 1932 yet would not encourage excessive production, as the price supports of the late 1940's and the present supports at 90% of parity have done. A price support program should act as a cushion for farm income and as disaster insurance. It is somewhat similar in concept to unemployment insurance for industrial workers. A support price should act as a stop-loss in years of low prices, but it should be low enough so that acreage allotments are unnecessary. *A support price should not be so high that it interferes with the*

7. *Congressional Record,* May 26, 1952.

natural adjustments of production from one area to another or guarantees the
producer a profit. Finally, a support price should be set low enough so that
at most times the actual prices are set by market forces which give important
consideration to quality.

Because of the types of agriculture most prevalent in New England, price
supports, price ceilings, and acreage allotments have affected the New
England farmer more as a consumer than as a producer. This is especially
true of government policies on grain. Price supports for grain have tended to
maintain feed prices at high levels, while generally the prices of New England dairy and poultry products have been bolstered only by price support
operations in other sections of the nation. This frequently has caused un-
natural relationships between the price of feed and prices received from
marketings. The New England farmer would be equally concerned with the
relationship between the ceiling price of hogs and the ceiling price of corn.
Many New England farmers remember the corn shortage of 1944, when midwestern farmers found it more profitable to feed their corn to hogs and sell
it as meat than to ship it east as dairy and poultry feed. In view of their
geographical position at the end of the grain pipeline, the region's farmers
fear that a similar situation might arise again if price ceilings are placed on
grain.

Agricultural price policies, of course, also affect the nonfarmer consumer.
It seems clear that New England consumers in the past have paid more
through higher taxes and higher prices than the region's farmers have bene-
fited under the price support programs. This is to be expected, however, in
an area which raises but a fraction of its agricultural requirements. The indirect benefits of a prosperous agriculture are important to New England, as
well as to the nation as a whole. *The best interests of all consumers can be*
served by the development of a sound price support program with supports
at a level that neither encourages excessive production nor hinders natural
adjustments in supply to meet changing conditions. If supplies should rise
abruptly beyond "normal" levels and depress farm prices, the support operation would cushion the loss and give the farmer enough to start his next
year's crop. A program such as this would not place a heavy burden on the
taxpayer or consumer, and it would assure adequate supplies of foodstuffs
and other agricultural produce each year.

Support prices for the major crops were set at a rigid 90% of parity by the
1952 amendment to the Defense Production Act. The restoration of the 90%
guarantee replaced the 75 to 90% sliding scale of supports fixed by the Agricultural Act of 1949. The American Farm Bureau Federation and the
National Grange opposed the 1952 amendment. They believed that nonfarm
taxpayers resented the high expenditures required under a rigid 90%
guarantee and that such a high guarantee would encourage excessive increases in production and tend to perpetuate acreage allotments and other
government controls. Their opposition seems to have been justified. *The*

reinstatement of rigid 90% price supports was a step backward in farm legislation.

Other Federal Agricultural Policies

This discussion cannot consider in detail a great number of other agricultural programs of the Federal Government. Some of them should be mentioned, however, in concluding this consideration of the region's agricultural problems.

There are three agencies whose work is wholly or partly in the field of soil conservation. In New England, at least, there has been no serious overlapping of work between these agencies.

The Extension Service's program is one of education. The Soil Conservation Service makes complete land use plans for a farm and provides technical aid and in some instances equipment to carry out these plans. Agricultural conservation payments, administered by the Production and Marketing Administration, encourage farmers who have a definite conservation plan, whether it is for the entire farm or not, to carry out certain desirable conservation practices through the use of subsidized lime, fertilizer, and seed.

It is these payments to farmers from the United States Treasury that have recently been under such severe criticism. There is some question as to whether or not these direct payments are a desirable way in which to further soil-conserving practices. Most of the better farmers recognize the value of these practices and would carry them out whether paid to do so or not. While the withdrawal of payments would cause some reduction in the tonnage of lime and fertilizer used by farmers, it does not appear sound to use tax money to subsidize practices which increase farmers' incomes.

Under the Morrill Act of 1862, the states were assured of partial federal support through income from the sale of public lands for the establishment of colleges to teach agriculture, home economics, and engineering. With this federal aid, each New England state created a land grant college to teach agriculture. The agricultural colleges have played an important part in the agricultural development of New England, as well as of the rest of the nation.

Agricultural leaders soon recognized the need for agricultural research and for personnel to disseminate the findings of that research. To fill this need the Hatch Act of 1887 and the Smith-Lever Act of 1914 provided partial federal support for the state agricultural experiment stations and extension services. Although the proportions vary from state to state, the experiment stations receive approximately a fourth of their funds and the extension services receive half of their funds from the Federal Government. The balance of the cost and resident teaching are provided by the states. The importance of the experiment stations is suggested by the contribution of the Connecticut Agricultural Experiment Station to the nation through the development of hybrid corn, probably the greatest single piece of research in the history of American agriculture.

These three federal laws have provided the farmers in each state with an agricultural program with a triple purpose. The land grant colleges provide resident teaching to young prospective farmers and homeowners. The agricultural experiment stations develop and test new plant varieties, disease and insect control, production and harvesting techniques, feeds, feeding methods, grading, packaging and marketing techniques, and other improvements in farm methods. The extension services, through their county agents, home demonstration agents, and 4-H club agents, disseminate the new techniques to farmers, homemakers, and rural youth. All three functions are of huge importance to the future of New England agriculture.

CONCLUSIONS

New England is a deficit area for all but a few types of agricultural products. Most of its farm products are consumed within the region. The most important influence on the prosperity of New England agriculture is the prosperity of the region's industry and trade, which provide its customers with income. Because of the composition of agriculture in the region, sustained urban prosperity is more important to the well-being of the New England rural economy than the present high level of price supports. Nevertheless, supports at a lower level to act as disaster insurance would be desirable.

The New England farmer is favored with markets that demand and pay premium prices for high quality local produce. The production of bulky and perishable products close to markets reduces marketing costs and rewards producers with a higher proportion of the consumer's food dollar than is true in many regions. If New England farmers are to meet the keen competition from other areas, however, a better marketing program must be developed, including better grading, standardization, and packaging, improvement in transportation techniques to reduce bruising, more effective promotion of New England farm products, and better retailing techniques. Continued and more aggressive experimentation and research will be necessary to develop the kind of program that is needed.

As New England industry grows and the increased population pushes farther into rural areas, more of the region's productive farm land will be taken out of production for use as industrial and residential sites. To maintain agricultural output, the remaining land will have to be used more intensively and farming techniques will have to improve steadily.

If the region's dairymen are to continue supplying all of the fluid milk needed by this expanding population, New England's milk production will have to be increased. This can be done by further reducing the seasonality of the milk supply, by increasing milk production per cow, by keeping more cows, by raising more high-quality roughage, or by a combination of all these methods.

The prospects of population growth provide opportunities for expanded production of poultry products, with the exception of broilers. The outlook is especially promising in sections such as Aroostook County, Maine, where the shift of some land from potatoes to small grains offers a good inexpensive ration for turkeys.

The problem of transferring farm ownership so that young farmers may get started is important in New England. The small proportion of rented farms and the high capital investments necessary for modern farming make it necessary to develop new methods of transferring farms as going concerns. Agricultural credit is generally adequate, although some shift in lending from short to intermediate terms would be desirable. Present real estate taxes place a significant differential burden on farmers in most New England states, a burden that could be lightened through a more equitable distribution of local taxation.

Flexibility and adaptability have characterized New England agriculture from its earliest days. Increasing specialization of products for local markets and shifts to products for which the region is singularly well suited have kept in production many farms that would otherwise have gone out of production due to the loss of basic crops such as wheat and hay. Leadership in the use of improved farming techniques, alertness to changing consumption patterns, and improvements in marketing practices can add further to the strength of agriculture in the region.

Although New England agriculture is small in comparison to the region's industrial activity, it provides a balancing and stabilizing force in the regional economy, as well as producing an important part of the food supply. Farming is also a way of life as well as a business. Compensations from farming other than income must be considered in planning farm programs and appraising agriculture's contribution to the New England economy.

SELECTED REFERENCES

1. Black, John D., *The Rural Economy of New England,* Cambridge, Mass., 1950.
2. Federal Reserve Bank of Boston:
   New England Farm Finance News (monthly)
   Monthly Review: "An Appraisal of New England Agriculture," May 1950; "A Report on New England Agriculture," May 1951; "New England Produces Broilers!" May 1952; "Agriculture in the Connecticut River Country," March 1953.
3. U.S. Bureau of the Census, *Census of Agriculture,* 1950.
4. U.S. Department of Agriculture, *Agricultural Statistics* (annual).
5. U.S. Department of Agriculture, Bureau of Agricultural Economics:
   Agricultural Prices (monthly)
   Crop Production (monthly)
   Commodity Situation Reports (monthly and quarterly)
6. Waugh, Frederick V., "The Marketing of New England's Farm Products: Demand Factors," *New England's Prospect: 1933,* ed. John K. Wright, American Geographical Society, Special Publication No. 16, New York, 1933.

4

Minerals and New England

Drafted by Ray S. Kelley, Jr., under the direction
of Arthur A. Bright, Jr.

INTRODUCTION

All sections of the United States, and especially the industrialized areas, are extremely dependent on minerals. It is significant to the economy of the highly industrialized New England states, therefore, that they are among the nation's least richly endowed states in mineral resources. There are no important commercial deposits of mineral fuels in the region. All coal, petroleum products, and natural gas are imported from other parts of the United States or from abroad. The region's iron and steel production and consumption are based almost completely on imported materials, as are most of the production and consumption of nonferrous metals. With few exceptions, the same is true for the other major minerals and mineral products, including salt, sulphur, cement, and gypsum.

The only large-volume minerals which New England produces within its borders in quantities approximating its consumption are sand, gravel, stone, and structural clays. The region does, however, produce significant quantities of a few of the "minor" minerals.

In view of its dependence on minerals and its own meager mineral resources, it is apparent that New England relies heavily upon the effectiveness of its transportation connections with the rest of the country and the rest of the world. The New England economy can continue to function, as it has in the past, as long as the necessary mineral supplies are somewhere available and can be transported to where they are needed in the region. The critical matter, therefore, is the availability of minerals within economical transportation distances, rather than their physical existence within the region.

Naturally, distance has an important bearing on transportation cost, which in turn has an effect on the competitive position of mineral users. The matter of transportation cost is of real importance to New England for coal, iron and steel, and a few other minerals. It is much less important for the minerals whose value is higher in relation to weight, for those which are used in small quantities, and for those which are available in most localities.

This report on "Minerals and New England" has two principal objectives. The first is to delineate the role of minerals in the New England economy, with special reference to their use as industrial raw materials. The second is to describe the mineral resources that New England has, the uses to which they are put, their direct and indirect contribution to the regional economy, and their potentials for further development. We have concentrated on the nonfuel minerals, although we have also sketched out briefly the region's mineral-fuel situation. The topic of fuels is considered in a broader frame of reference in the report on "Water, Fuel, and Energy in New England."

THE ROLE OF MINERALS IN THE NEW ENGLAND ECONOMY

Just how do minerals fit into the New England economy, both those produced within the six-state area and those imported from elsewhere? The later discussion of the mineral resources of the region will be more meaningful when viewed in relation to the general minerals situation.

New England's position with respect to mineral fuels can be summarized simply. The region has no known commercial deposits of any size within its borders,[1] but it uses enormous amounts for generating electric power, heating, and motive force. All coal, petroleum products, and natural gas consumed in New England are brought in from outside. Their continued flow is vital to the operation of almost all phases of the region's life.

In 1949 New England had a net inflow by railroad and water of more than 36,650,000 tons of coal and petroleum products. That tonnage approximated the region's consumption, although there was some additional inflow by truck. About a third of the total tonnage was bituminous coal, largely for power generation and industrial use. Fuel, road, and residual oils represented an additional fifth. The tonnages of crude petroleum, gasoline, anthracite coal, and kerosene were also large.[2] Table 4-1 presents the net inflows by type of product and by general source. More than half the total tonnage came by water from other parts of the United States. The rest was divided fairly evenly between shipments by rail from the rest of the country and by water from foreign countries. New England is not unfavorably located for water shipments of petroleum products, but it is at a cost disadvantage for the overland movement of fuels.

Fuels are vital to thousands of jobs in the region's transportation services and public utilities. According to the United States Bureau of Labor Statistics, the average New England employment during 1947 by firms in these industries was 227,600. Some electric generating stations use water power, to be sure, but most of the electric-utility employment is based on coal- or oil-burning steam plants, and the proportion of steam-generated power has been rising.

Minerals are also of tremendous direct importance to New England's manufacturing industries. Their dependence on fuels is obvious. Moreover, of the

1. The low-grade anthracite deposits of Massachusetts and Rhode Island are not at present suitable for commercial use. Their possibilities are discussed briefly in a later section.
2. In terms of Btu content, oil was by far the most important fuel brought into New England in 1949.

region's 1,472,000 total manufacturing employees in 1947, the latest year for which full census data are available, more than 44% worked in industries whose principal raw materials are mineral in origin. (See Table 4–2.) The comparable figure for the United States as a whole was 47%. Most of the

Table 4–1. Sources of New England's Coal and Petroleum Products, 1949; Brought in by Rail and Water (net imports (−) and exports (+), in tons)

PRODUCT	BY RAIL	BY WATER, DOMESTIC	BY WATER, FOREIGN	TOTAL
Anthracite coal	−3,386,000	−135,000	+165	−3,521,000
Bituminous coal	−5,145,000	−6,740,000	−40,000	−11,925,000
Crude petroleum	+2,400	−908,000	−4,218,000	−5,124,000
Asphalt	+49,000	−33,000	−19,000	−4,000
Gasoline	−24,000	−4,652,000	+46,000	−4,631,000
Fuel, road, and residual oils	+12,000	−3,998,000	−3,329,000	−7,315,000
Lubricating oils and greases	−79,000	−112,000	+14	−191,000
Other refined petroleum products, including kerosene	−203,000	−3,747,000	+1,700	−3,949,000
TOTAL	−8,774,000	−20,325,000	−7,558,000	−36,658,000

Note: Details may not add to totals because of rounding.
Source: Unpublished compilation by the Federal Reserve Bank of Boston from data of the Corps of Army Engineers and the Interstate Commerce Commission

New England mineral-based employment was in the metalworking industries. Electrical and nonelectrical machinery alone accounted for 297,900 jobs in the region. Metal fabrication added 108,900 more. Despite the almost complete lack of locally produced metallic minerals, New England producers

Table 4–2. Employment in the Principal Mineral-based Manufacturing Industries, New England and the United States, 1947

INDUSTRY OR INDUSTRY GROUP	AVERAGE NUMBER OF EMPLOYEES NEW ENGLAND	UNITED STATES	N.E. AS PER CENT OF U.S.
Machinery (other than electrical)	202,100	1,546,000	13.1
Fabricated metals	108,900	971,000	11.2
Electrical apparatus	95,800	801,000	12.0
Primary metals	61,500	1,157,000	5.3
Transportation equipment	51,300	1,180,000	4.3
Jewelry, silverware, etc.	48,200	103,000	46.7
Instruments (scientific, etc.)	36,400	232,000	15.7
Stone, clay, and glass	21,500	462,000	4.7
Petroleum and coal products	3,700	212,000	1.7
TOTAL, listed above	629,400	6,664,000	9.4
TOTAL, all manufacturing	1,472,800	14,292,000	10.3
Per cent, principal mineral-based to all	44%	47%	—

Source: U.S. Bureau of the Census, Census of Manufactures, 1947

even gave employment to 61,500 persons in the primary-metal industries. Transportation equipment, jewelry and silverware, and instruments added another 135,900. There were a few thousand more in some small metalworking and chemical industries that are not included in the table.

The other major mineral-based manufacturing industries in New England are the stone, clay, and glass group, and petroleum and coal products. The latter group is entirely based on raw materials brought in from outside the region. Even in the stone, clay, and glass category several thousand of the 21,500 jobs were in the manufacture of "imported" raw materials.

New England's principal stone, clay, and glass industries were the production of abrasives (6,689 employees), asbestos products (2,800 employees), products of purchased glass (2,789 employees), cut stone and stone products (2,201 employees), concrete products (1,475 employees), gaskets and packings (926 employees), and brick and hollow tile (906 employees). The other 23 industries in the stone, clay, and glass group accounted for only 3,732 employees.

The relative importance of the mineral-based industries as a whole varies considerably from state to state, as is indicated in Table 4–3. The proportion is largest by far in Connecticut, with its great concentration in steel and nonferrous metal fabrication. The ratio is also fairly high in Rhode Island, Massachusetts, and Vermont. It is low in Maine and New Hampshire. The table also shows that the manufacture of machinery is the largest mineral-based industry group in each of the states except Rhode Island. The sequence of the other groups differs considerably among the states.

Table 4–3. Employment in New England's Principal Mineral-based Manufacturing Industries, by State, 1949
(hundreds of employees)

INDUSTRY OR GROUP	CONN.	R. I.	MASS.	VT.	N. H.	MAINE
Machinery (other than electrical)	78.2	17.3	86.8	7.1	6.2	6.4
Fabricated metals	55.8	7.8	41.0	0.8	1.6	1.9
Electrical apparatus	33.4	5.3	55.6	0.5	1.0	(a)
Primary metals	34.9	5.1	19.8	0.6	0.6	0.4
Transportation equipment	29.5	0.3	18.3	0.1	(a)	3.4
Jewelry, silverware, etc.	13.9	20.0	13.4	0.1	0.6	0.1
Instruments (scientific, etc.)	17.2	1.7	16.7	0.2	0.5	0.1
Stone, clay, and glass	5.7	1.1	10.5	2.6	1.0	0.6
Petroleum and coal products	0.3	0.7	2.5	0.2	—	(a)
TOTAL, listed above	268.9	59.3	264.6	12.2	11.5	12.9
TOTAL, all manufacturing	399.0	146.3	717.7	34.9	74.8	100.2
Per cent, principal mineral-based to all	67	41	37	35	15	13

(a) Less than 50 employees.
Source: Ibid.

There are continual changes in employment from year to year, of course, as business conditions change. *New England's 44% ratio of employment in mineral-based industries to total manufacturing employment in 1947 was much higher than the corresponding 33% figure for 1939. That increase occurred despite the fact that less than 3% of the employment in the region's mineral manufacturing rested primarily on indigenous raw materials.*

One more source of New England employment based on minerals deserves special mention. Construction activities employed an average of about 126,000 workers in the six states during 1947. The steelworkers, concrete workers, masons, plasterers, road builders, electricians, plumbers, and many others all worked primarily with mineral products. While we cannot tie a precise number of jobs to these kinds of work, the total is undoubtedly a large proportion of total construction employment. As we shall see shortly, most of New England's minerals output is consumed within the region in building, highway, and other construction.

TRANSPORTATION AND NEW ENGLAND'S MINERAL USE

We have already noted the extent and sources of New England's inbound movements of mineral fuels. A similar summary for the other principal minerals adds substance to previous statements concerning the heavy dependence of the region's manufacturing activities upon imported raw materials. It also shows the extensive outward movement of certain manufactured products made from minerals. During their stay in New England many of those materials receive a great deal of additional value through the manufacturing process. The ratios of inbound and outbound tonnages, therefore, are not at all an indication of the ratios of inbound and outbound values.

Table 4–4 presents in some detail New England's net imports and exports by rail and water of the principal nonfuel minerals and their manufactures during 1949. Accurate truck shipments cannot be included in the table because of lack of data, though interregional truck movements are of considerable importance for finished stone products, many metal products, and others. Also, many of New England's foreign imports and exports move by rail or truck from or to New York and other ports outside the region, rather than New England ports. Thus the table does not show the complete commodity flows for minerals and their products but it does provide a rough indication of the direction and relative importance of the over-all movements.

The table shows the extent of New England's net tonnage imports of non-fuel minerals and their products. Most of the net inflow is by land from the rest of the United States. Inbound water movements are of considerable importance, however, for a few minerals. New England receives large quantities of phosphate fertilizers and sulphur by water from domestic sources, and it receives sizable shipments of iron ore and gypsum by water from foreign countries.

The region is a net importer, so far as rail and water shipments are concerned, of all the basic materials except finished stone products and broken stone and rock. It is a net exporter of such high-value metal products as machinery, electrical equipment, hardware, and abrasive products. For the rest, the tonnage movements are more heavily in than out. In some instances the net imports approximate New England's total requirements, in others

Table 4–4. New England's Net Imports and Exports of the Principal Nonfuel Minerals and Their Manufactures, 1949; by Rail and Water
(net imports (−) and exports (+), in tons)

PRODUCT	BY RAIL	BY WATER, DOMESTIC	BY WATER, FOREIGN	TOTAL
Iron and steel:				
Ore and concentrates	−215,000	—	−82,000	−297,000
Pig iron	−126,000	−8,000	−5,000	−139,000
Semimanufactured iron and steel	−126,000	−28	—	−126,000
Finished iron and steel	−1,239,000	−11,000	−7,000	−1,256,000
Machinery and parts	+115,000	+1,500	+21,000	+138,000
Transportation equipment	−490,000	+78	+284	−489,000
Electrical equipment and parts	+73,000	—	—	+73,000
Hardware	+17,000	—	—	+17,000
All other iron and steel products	−106,000	+94	+507	−106,000
Scrap	+486,000	+16,000	−59	+502,000
Nonferrous metals:				
Ores and concentrates	−1,500	+33	−9,000	−11,000
Semimanufactures	−221,000	+115	+323	−221,000
Copper, brass, and bronze products*	+11,000	+947	−684	+11,000
Scrap	+28,000	—	—	+28,000
Clay products:				
Clay and bentonite	−221,000	−815	−17,000	−239,000
Brick, building tile, and refractories	−244,000	+599	+127	−243,000
Sewer pipe and drain tile	−80,000	—	—	−80,000
Chinaware, crockery, and earthenware	−5,000	−40	−5,000	−9,000
Sand products:				
Industrial sand	−99,000	—	—	−99,000
Glass, all types	−214,000	+29	−166	−214,000
Crude construction materials:				
Gravel and sand	−40,000	−4,000	+76	−45,000
Broken stone and rock	+88,000	—	—	+88,000
Furnace slag	−24,000	—	—	−24,000
Stone products:				
Rough stone	−2,200	−1,600	—	−4,000
Finished stone	+18,000	+7,000	−4,000	+21,000
Cement	−1,403,000	+180	+64	−1,403,000
Lime	−71,000	—	—	−71,000
Abrasives, not crude	+20,000	—	—	+20,000
All other	−8,000	—	—	−8,000
Other minerals:				
Salt	−332,000	—	—	−332,000
Phosphate rock	−49,000	—	—	−49,000
Fertilizers (largely phosphates)	−155,000	−124,000	+7,000	−272,000
Sulphur	−38,000	−93,000	—	−131,000
Sulphuric acid	−2,300	−18,000	+161	−21,000
All other minerals (largely gypsum)	+105,000	+565	−267,000	−161,000
Plaster	−15,000	—	—	−15,000
NET, LISTED PRODUCTS	−4,566,000	−234,000	−368,000	−5,168,000

Note: Details may not add to totals because of rounding.
* Many other copper, brass, and bronze products were incorporated in finished products of iron and steel shipped out of New England by rail or water, or were shipped out by truck.
Source: Unpublished compilation by the Federal Reserve Bank of Boston from data of the Corps of Army Engineers and the Interstate Commerce Commission

they supplement greater or lesser quantities of production within the region.

The necessity for bringing in such large quantities of mineral raw materials does not affect all New England's mineral-based industries in the same way. The stone, clay, and glass products group, for example, uses mostly indigenous materials. In general, New England firms in that group report that their competitive position, as compared with firms outside the region, is not injured by their location with respect to domestic raw materials. (See Table 4-5.) While foreign raw materials are little used by most producers of stone, clay, and glass products, those who express a strong opinion on that topic seem to feel that they are competitively favored by their New England coastal location.

Table 4-5. The Competitive Effects of New England's Location with Respect to Minerals; Opinions of Manufacturers, 1949

		PERCENTAGES OF COMPANIES WHO REPORTED THEY WERE AT			
		AN	AN		
	NO. OF	IMPORTANT	IMPORTANT		NO
INDUSTRY GROUP	COMPANIES	ADVANTAGE	DISADVANTAGE	NEITHER	ANSWER
For domestic materials:					
Instruments (scientific, etc.)	19	42	0	58	0
Stone, clay, and glass products	25	36	8	44	12
Electrical apparatus	35	29	23	48	0
Fabricated metals	78	19	28	47	5
Primary metals	27	15	30	48	7
Machinery (except electrical)	94	11	23	61	5
Transportation equipment	9	11	56	33	0
For foreign materials:					
Instruments (scientific, etc.)	19	5	0	47	47
Stone, clay, and glass products	25	8	0	40	52
Electrical apparatus	35	8	3	43	46
Fabricated metals	78	5	4	35	56
Primary metals	27	7	7	33	52
Machinery (except electrical)	94	2	4	63	31
Transportation equipment	9	22	22	22	33

Note: Percentages may not add to 100 because of rounding.
Source: Federal Reserve Bank of Boston, from unpublished compilations based on the study of "The Present Position and Prospects of New England Manufacturers," reported in the Bank's *Monthly Review*, July, August, and September 1949

Producers of scientific and other instruments in New England give a very high rating to their location with respect to raw materials. None of the 19 instrument firms covered by the Federal Reserve Bank of Boston survey reported an important competitive disadvantage in that respect for either domestic or foreign materials.

For large numbers of companies in the principal other major industry groups based on metals, however, a New England location apparently presents important competitive problems of access to domestic raw materials. This applies particularly in the transportation-equipment and primary-metal industries, but it is also of importance in the production of fabricated metals and electrical and nonelectrical machinery.

Some broad conclusions stand out from the opinions reported in Table 5. First, the patterns of opinions about the competitive aspects of location with respect to domestic raw materials differ substantially among the mineral-based industry groups of New England. There are somewhat similar patterns for related groups, however. For the largest employment producers among those groups, a sizable minority of firms feel that they are at an important competitive disadvantage in this respect.

Second, the appraisals of locations, with respect to domestic raw materials, vary considerably from firm to firm, even within industry groups. Differences in location in New England, size, and products made probably account for most of the variation.

Third, in almost all groups close to half the companies stated that their competitive position with respect to both foreign and domestic raw materials was neutral, neither an important advantage nor an important disadvantage. That was just as true in the machinery group, with its large metal requirements, as it was in the instrument group.

Fourth, a large proportion of companies in each group expressed no opinion about the competitive effect of their location with respect to foreign raw materials. Their failure to respond suggests that they believe the matter is of little importance, probably because they are not currently large users of foreign materials. To the extent that advantages or disadvantages were cited, however, the advantages typically equaled or exceeded the disadvantages.

From this brief picture of New England's interregional trade in nonfuel minerals and their products and the effects on the competitive position of manufacturers in the region, it seems clear that New England has a strong interest in improving the availability and reducing the cost of such minerals and products, particularly iron and steel. Even if one discounts the seriousness of some of the claimed disadvantages, the importance of the problem cannot be denied. After discussing New England's mineral resources and their use, we shall appraise the situation as a whole to see how the regional goals of increased availability of the nonfuel minerals can best be attained.

Before leaving the topic of the effect of minerals on the competitive position of New England manufacturers, we should add a few general comments on the effect of minerals on industrial location. Most of the value of finished products made from minerals, as well as most of the employment they generate, is added by the manufacturing process. Since labor skills and costs, capital costs, and many other elements are of great importance in total costs, it is frequently desirable to transport the raw or only slightly processed minerals long distances before they are manufactured. This is especially true for metals of high value that are used in conjunction with many other materials. Cobalt, mercury, molybdenum, and tin, for example, sold for an average of $1.00 or more a pound in 1949. The values of nickel, antimony, copper, aluminum, zinc, beryllium concentrates, and even lead were also fairly high relative to their weight. Manufacturers are not likely to locate near the sources of supply for such metals unless other locational factors are also favorable.

Iron is the principal exception to what is otherwise almost the rule among metals. The value of iron is relatively low and it is used in large quantities. Fabrication has typically been concentrated about steel-processing centers, and areas without sufficient steel facilities of their own have been at a transportation-cost disadvantage. As we have noted, that situation applies to many New England metalworking firms. But even for iron and steel the possession of rich ores alone has not been a major element in industrialization. The Mesabi Range has not made Minnesota a major steel center. Typically, the iron ore has moved toward a supply of coking coal, or both iron and coal have moved toward the market.

Most nonmetallic minerals other than fuels are covered by the generalization that applies to the nonferrous metals. If the mineral has a high value, transportation costs are relatively unimportant. If the mineral is used in relatively small quantities, it exerts almost no locational pull, regardless of value. If the mineral is available in most locales, it has little attractive power. Finally, if its use is largely in nonmanufacturing activities, it has little influence on manufacturers.

Except for steel, then, most nonfuel minerals do not have a major locational pull on manufacturing. The lack of such minerals is not necessarily a great handicap to a region, even if it raises the total transportation bill slightly, unless it also interferes with their ready availability. It is an advantage to possess them, but an area cannot expect to become industrialized because of them.

So far as transportation costs and New England's competitive position are concerned, therefore, iron and steel and mineral fuels present the greatest problems among all mineral items. The region's lack of coal is especially important, because of its relatively low value and high transportation cost. The problem of steel in New England is a special case. In a later section we shall discuss briefly the proposals that New England's steel capacity be expanded.

THE MINERALS PRODUCTION
OF NEW ENGLAND

How important is New England's own production of minerals, both to the United States as a whole and to the regional economy? New England's total mineral extraction is almost insignificant when compared to United States production. Only about 0.4% of the total value of United States output comes from New England. For every hundred dollars of United States output, New England accounts for only 40 cents.

The largest minerals-producing state in New England is Vermont, yet it contributed only 0.17% of United States dollar output of minerals in 1949, and it ranked 39th as a producing state. The other states—Massachusetts, Maine, Connecticut, New Hampshire, and Rhode Island—ranked 40th, 44th, 45th, 46th, and 47th, respectively. (See Table 4–6.) All the New England states are among the ten lowest minerals-producing states; four are in the bottom five.

Table 4–6. Value of Total Mineral Production in New England, by State, 1949

STATE	VALUE OF PRODUCTION	PER CENT OF U.S. TOTAL	STATE RANK
Vermont	$17,384,000	.17	39
Massachusetts	12,449,000	.12	40
Maine	6,742,000	.06	44
Connecticut	4,887,000	.05	45
New Hampshire	1,384,000	.01	46
Rhode Island	929,000	.01	47
New England	43,776,000	.41	—
United States	10,554,234,000	100.00	—

Note: Details may not add to totals because of rounding.
Source: U.S. Department of the Interior, Bureau of Mines, *Minerals Yearbook*, 1949

Although its minerals production is small in the aggregate, New England makes a substantial contribution to the national output of certain minerals. From data in the 1949 *Minerals Yearbook* and other publications of the United States Bureau of Mines, we estimate that New England's portion of national production in 1949, in terms of value, was 80% of the asbestos, 36% of the beryllium concentrates, 32% of the slate, 26% of the marble, 23% of the feldspar, 22% of the granite, 21% of the quartz, 21% of the graphite, 14% of the basalt, 12% of the peat, 10% of the talc, and 5% of the sheet mica.

These percentages require some qualification. Though most United States-produced asbestos came from Vermont, for example, only a small amount of the domestic consumption was from that source. Asbestos worth nearly $40,000,000 was imported, including shipments from Canada valued at $27,500,000. New England's production, therefore, represented only about 5% of United States consumption in 1949.

About 8% of the beryllium concentrates consumed in the United States was from domestic sources, so only about 3% of the nation's consumption came from New England. Also, a large percentage of the nation's requirements for quartz, and all that of high quality, was imported. About two-thirds of the graphite for domestic consumption was imported. While New England's output of graphite represented about a fifth of the country's total, it accounted for only 6% of the United States consumption.

The low production of minerals in New England without doubt rests primarily on the lack of major mineral deposits in the region, but two other important factors have lessened its portion of national output over the years. First, the area's percentage of output has naturally declined as other sections of the country have developed their mineral deposits. Second, since the region was settled much earlier than most other sections of the country, it has used up a large amount of its higher quality mineral reserves. Unlike fish or timber resources, minerals are nonrenewable; when they are removed, they are gone forever.

It has also been suggested that because of New England's coastal location water-transportation costs have been low, and so minerals have been available at relatively low prices from other parts of the world. Because of that accessibility, so the argument goes, New Englanders have not been forced to rely heavily on their own resources.

There is, of course, some truth to the theory. Were New England mineral imports cut off for any sustained period, undoubtedly some of the low-grade iron, copper, zinc, lead, and manganese ore deposits would be worked. During the early colonial period, when iron was very expensive, there was production from the region's bog-iron deposits. New England copper production in the mid-19th century was much higher than it is today, partly because of the high price of copper elsewhere at that time. Also, if imports were cut off, there would be more prospecting for minerals within the region, and some new discoveries might well be made.

Table 4–7. Employment in New England Minerals Production,
by State, 1940 and 1950
(number of employees)

STATE	1940	1950	PER CENT CHANGE
Vermont	1,455	1,853	+27
Massachusetts	1,515	1,453	−4
Connecticut	594	537	−10
Maine	562	617	+10
New Hampshire	318	188	−39
Rhode Island	189	175	−7
NEW ENGLAND	4,633	4,823	+4
UNITED STATES	913,000	971,000*	+6

* Preliminary.
Source: U.S. Bureau of the Census, Census of Population, 1950

In general, however, the theory is not a good explanation of New England's low minerals production. As it points out itself, many unworked New England deposits contain such low-grade ore that they cannot be worked economically under existing conditions. If prices were to rise sharply relative to costs, or if imported supplies were cut drastically, many submarginal deposits in the region would be reopened. But that is true throughout the country, not just in New England. Moreover, as we have seen, New England is a heavy net direct importer from abroad for only a few particular minerals. It relies most heavily on other regions of the United States, and it is with the rest of the country that its output primarily competes.

Employment in minerals extraction amounted to about 4,800 workers in New England during 1950. That total was less than 0.2% of the region's

Table 4–8. Mineral Production in New England and the United States, 1949
(value figures in thousands of dollars)

PRODUCT	NEW ENGLAND		UNITED STATES		N.E. AS PER CENT OF U.S.	
	WEIGHT	VALUE	WEIGHT	VALUE	WEIGHT	VALUE
Quantities in thousands of tons:						
Stone[a]	4,769	20,148	224,027	341,442	2.13	5.90
Sand and gravel	17,089	9,091	319,104	248,443	5.36	3.66
Slate	199	3,925	740	12,164	26.89	32.27
Cement	199	2,526	38,943	475,074	0.51	0.53
Lime (open-market)	187	2,373	6,303	68,908	2.96	3.44
Asbestos	35	2,100	43	2,614	80.67	80.32
Copper (Cu content)	3	1,250	753	296,582	0.40	0.42
Talc	65	788	462	7,523	13.97	10.48
Clays	799	629	28,000	74,619	2.81	0.84
Feldspar	76	525	406	2,278	18.71	23.06
Peat	10	120	129	1,020	7.65	11.77
Quartz from pegmatites and quartzite	17	102	108	475	15.62	21.37
Graphite	1	99	5*	475	8.44	20.78
Sand and sandstone (ground)	2	10	611	5,258	0.25	0.18
Quantities in thousands of pounds:						
Beryllium concentrates	254	41	692	111	36.71	36.60
Mica	1,018	20	66,226	928	1.54	2.19
(Scrap)	(990)	(13)	(65,712)	(796)	(1.51)	(1.64)
(Sheet)	(28)	(7)	(514)	(132)	(5.45)	(5.45)
Quantities in troy ounces:						
Gold (Au content)	120	4	1,762,367	61,683	.007	.007
Silver (Ag content)	27,446	25	34,638,896	31,350	.08	.08
All other[g]	—	—	—	8,922,751	—	—
TOTALS		$43,776		$10,554,000		0.41

Note: Details may not add to totals because of rounding. * Estimated on the basis of incomplete data. † Less than 500 tons or $500. a. For breakdown, see Appendix A. b. Does not include miscellaneous stone production. c. Output of commercial producers estimated. d. May include value of a small amount of mineral water. e. Includes value of 50 tons of rose quartz. f. Includes value of other minerals not mentioned, presumably of little total value. g. Includes such important minerals as coal, iron, petroleum, zinc, lead, etc., which are not produced in New England.
Source: U.S. Department of the Interior, Bureau of Mines, Minerals Yearbook, 1949, for all figures except estimates

3,692,000 labor force in the same year, and it was less than 0.5% of the United States employment in minerals production. The direct employment contribution of minerals production is very small, therefore, in New England as a whole.

Table 4–7 shows the number of mine and quarry workers for each New England state and the changes that took place from 1940 to 1950. The increase in New England was smaller than that in the rest of the nation, though there were great variations from state to state. Employment in minerals pro-

Table 4–8 (cont'd.) Mineral Production in New England and the United States, 1949
(value figures in thousands of dollars)

	MAINE		NEW HAMPSHIRE		VERMONT		MASSACHUSETTS		RHODE ISLAND		CONNECTICUT	
	WEIGHT	VALUE	WEIGHT	VALUE	WEIGHT	VALUE	WEIGHT	VALUE	WEIGHT	VALUE	WEIGHT	VALUE
	259	2,026	7	381	442	8,276	2,291	6,553	75[b]	451[b]	1,696	2,461
	4,605	1,394	2,351[c]	624[c]	1,582	728	5,505	4,379	398	379	2,648	1,587
	15*	301	—	—	184	3,624	—	—	—	—	—	—
	199	2,526	—	—	—	—	—	—	—	—	—	—
	20*	260[e]	—	—	29	356	108	1,360	—	—	30*	397[d]
	—	—	—	—	35*	2,100*	—	—	—	—	—	—
	—	—	—	—	3*	1,250*	—	—	—	—	—	—
	—	—	—	—	65	788	—	—	—	—	—	—
	28	25	26	20	300*	232*	156	136	—	—	289	217
	19	130	43*	300*	—	—	—	—	—	—	14	95
	3	79	†	†	—	—	1	7	—	—	6	33
	—	—	—	—	—	—	1	4	—	—	16	97
	—	—	—	—	—	—	—	—	1*	99[f]	—	—
	—	—	—	—	—	—	2	10	—	—	—	—
	4*	1*	250*	40*	—	—	—	—	—	—	—	—
	90	1	928*	19*	—	—	—	—	—	—	—	—
	(90)	(1)	(900)*	(12)*	—	—	—	—	—	—	—	—
	—	—	(28)*	(7)*	—	—	—	—	—	—	—	—
	—	—	—	—	120	4	—	—	—	—	—	—
	—	—	—	—	27,446	25	—	—	—	—	—	—
	—	—	—	—	—	—	—	—	—	—	—	—
		$6,742		$1,384		$17,384		$12,449		$929		$4,887

duction rose only in Vermont and Maine. In each other state, and especially in New Hampshire, there was a drop.

The contribution of indigenous minerals to employment in New England is greater, however, than the direct employment in the mines and quarries alone. Indirectly, mining and quarrying add many jobs in transportation and other necessary services. Also, most of the region's employment in stone, clay, and glass manufacturing exists only because of the local availability of raw materials.

As we have noted, Vermont and Massachusetts are the leading mineral-producing states in the region. Table 4–8 shows in some detail the production of the individual minerals in the New England states during 1949, in relation to that in the United States. Because of government disclosure rules, some of the figures are estimates.

The small proportion of the region's mineral production that represents raw materials for manufacturing industry stands out clearly in Chart 4–1.

Roughly four-fifths of the value of output goes into construction. Most of New England's stone production is used in the construction of buildings, memorials, roads, and walkways, and so are most of the sand and gravel output and some of the other minerals.

CHART 4–1

Value of Mineral Production in New England, by Type, 1949
(in millions of dollars)

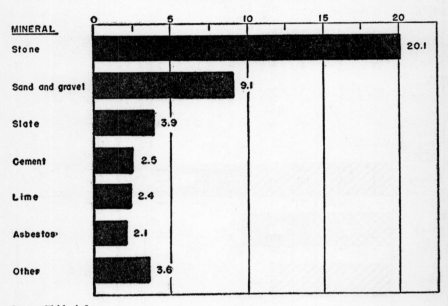

Source: Table 4–8

Stone Production

The $20,148,000 value of stone production in New England during 1949 represented almost half the region's total mineral production. As Chart 4-2 shows, granite accounted for about half the value of total stone production, and basalt, marble, and limestone made up most of the balance. Vermont and Massachusetts produced nearly three-fourths of the region's stone.[3] If slate production is added to the totals for stone, and if lime and cement, which are by-products of limestone, are also included, the total value of stone products was 66% of all mineral production in the six-state area. Sand and gravel production added another 20%, leaving only 14% of value for all other kinds of minerals.

Stone is sold primarily as dimension stone, or in crushed or broken form.

3. See Appendix 4-A for more complete details of production, by state and by type of stone.

The term "dimension stone" is applied to all blocks or slabs of natural stone which are cut to definite shapes and sizes. It is used primarily for buildings and monuments, but some is used for paving blocks, curbing, or flagging. Crushed and broken stone is used in many ways. The most important uses are as a filler for concrete and for road construction, railroad ballast, and riprap. Dimension stone is far more valuable than crushed and broken stone, though the ratios vary from mineral to mineral. The former averaged about $32 a ton in 1949, the latter about $1.50.

About 60% of the value of New England's stone production is dimension stone. It represents about 23% of the United States production. Crushed and broken stone production in New England, on the other hand, represents only about 3% of total United States production.

CHART 4-2

Value of Stone Production in New England, by Type, 1949
(in millions of dollars)

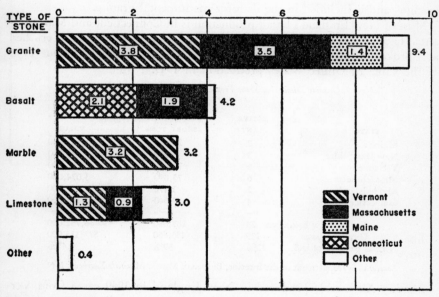

Source: Appendix 4-A

Granite. Granite is by far the most important stone produced in New England, and it is the most widely distributed. Most of it is sold as dimension stone. The production of granite dimension stone in New England and the United States during 1949 is shown in Table 4–9. Georgia is the nation's largest granite-producing state in terms of tonnage, with Massachusetts second and Vermont third. In terms of value Vermont leads, Massachusetts is second, and Georgia is third. Those three states account for nearly half of United States production.

Most of the Vermont granite comes from the Barre district. In 1949 granite produced by Barre quarrymen sold for $3,529,000, 94% of the state total. In Massachusetts most of the granite quarries are in the eastern part of the state, principally along the coast between New Bedford and Cape Ann. Maine quarries also lie primarily along the coast or on coastal islands.

New Hampshire's quarries are small. Those it has are on the slopes of the White Mountains, around Concord, and near the Vermont and Massachusetts state lines. In 1949 the "Granite State" produced less than 4% of the total New England output, less than that of every other New England state but Rhode Island. The Rhode Island and Connecticut quarries are near Long Island Sound, though there are a few in the western part of Connecticut and along the Connecticut River.

Basalt. The second most valuable stone product in New England is basalt, or traprock, a dark-colored rock used mostly in crushed or broken form. Sometimes it is used for memorials, but when so used it is classed as "black granite" and is included in the data for monumental granite.

Most of New England's basalt production is in Connecticut and Massachusetts. Those states rank fifth and sixth, respectively, as producers of crushed and broken basalt in the United States. The region produced about 14% of the value of United States production in 1949.

Table 4-9. Granite Dimension Stone Produced in the New England States, 1949

| | ACTIVE | PRODUCTION | |
STATE	PLANTS	SHORT TONS	VALUE
Maine	7	21,890	$1,342,000
New Hampshire	3	3,970	377,000
Vermont	6	72,820	3,553,000
Massachusetts	6	75,890	3,074,000
Rhode Island	2	3,470	268,000
Connecticut	4	9,640	138,000
TOTAL, NEW ENGLAND	28	187,680	$8,752,000
UNITED STATES	139	485,860	$21,315,000
N.E. as per cent of U.S.	20%	39%	41%

Source: U.S. Department of the Interior, Bureau of Mines, *Minerals Yearbook, 1949*

Marble. All marble produced in New England in 1949 came from Vermont, and it was almost entirely dimension stone. A small quantity of marble scrap from Vermont is ground as Atomite, for use in the manufacture of rubber. Vermont's production represented 26% of the United States output of all marble and about 29% of the dimension stone produced. Vermont and Tennessee are the largest producers of marble among the 48 states. Since our figure for Vermont's production was estimated in part, it is not clear which was the leader. In any event, the difference was small.

The major marble deposits of Vermont are west of the Green Mountains, but there are some less important deposits on the east side of the mountains. There are also a few small deposits in Berkshire and Hampden counties, Massachusetts, and in Connecticut, but in 1949 only the Vermont quarries were operating.

Limestone. Limestone is also an important stone product of New England. After it leaves the quarry, it is used in four major forms: (1) as limestone dimension stone; (2) as crushed or broken limestone for railroad ballast, riprap, fluxing, and many other industrial and agricultural purposes; and (3) as a raw material for making lime or (4) cement. About two-thirds of the United States production is sold crushed or broken, about one-fourth is used in cement, and about 5% is used in lime. Less than 0.3% is used as dimension stone. The value of New England's limestone production for those four uses was about $8,000,000 in 1949, divided as follows:

Type of Use	Value
Crushed or broken	3,032,000
Cement	2,526,000
Lime	2,373,000
Dimension stone	313

Limestone was produced in each of the New England states except New Hampshire during 1949, but Vermont and Massachusetts accounted for over two-thirds of the value of production in the region. The important limestone-producing sections in Massachusetts are in Berkshire County; in Maine, Knox County; in Vermont, Addison, Chittenden, Franklin, Rutland, and Windsor counties; in Connecticut, Fairfield and Litchfield counties; and in Rhode Island, Providence County.

New England is a deficit producer of both lime and cement. The only cement producer in New England is at Thomaston, Maine. Its production in 1949 was about 199,000 tons (1,057,000 barrels), while New England's consumption in 1949 was approximately 1,560,000 tons (8,280,000 barrels). *In view of the large import requirements and the substantial transportation charges from production points outside the region, it would seem that cement production in New England could profitably be expanded.*[4] The savings in transportation charges would probably more than offset New England's higher fuel costs. The capacity of the Thomaston plant has been expanded by 50%, but other new facilities would also seem to be in order. It might be feasible to produce cement near Boston or New Haven by bringing in limestone from Maine or Canada on the return of colliers.

Slate. Slate production in New England was valued at nearly $4,000,000 in 1949. Vermont's production was by far the most important in New England and was second only to Pennsylvania in the United States. Slate is used in three forms: (1) dimension slate, or blocks and slabs cut to specific

4. Arthur D. Little, Inc., *A Survey of Industrial Opportunities in New England,* report to the Federal Reserve Bank of Boston (August 1952), pp. 335–337.

sizes and shapes for roofing, structural purposes, blackboards, flagstones, and sidewalks; (2) slate granules, which are used in surfacing prepared roofing; and (3) slate flour, a by-product of granule manufacturing used in paints, roofing material, linoleum, and as a filler in asphalt road-surface mixtures. About 80% of the nation's production was used as granules or flour.

There was only one Maine producer of slate in 1929. It was located near Monson, in Piscataquis County. There were 27 operators in Vermont, more than in any other state in the country. Vermont's production is in four distinct districts. The most important district extends for 26 miles along the Vermont-New York line, southeast of the town of Sudbury, in Rutland County, to Rupert, in Bennington County. Another district runs north along the Connecticut River for more than two-thirds the length of the state. The third district runs from the Canadian line to the middle of the state, along the east flank of the Green Mountains. The fourth district is only two or three square miles in size near Lake Champlain in the township of Benson.

Sand and Gravel Production

The tonnage of sand and gravel produced in New England is nearly four times as large as that of stone, but because of their low value sand and gravel accounted for only 20% of the total value of minerals produced in New England during 1949. The tonnage of gravel was more than twice that of sand. Massachusetts was the largest producer of both sand and gravel. Almost all the region's production of those minerals in 1949 was used in building and paving. Chart 4–3 shows the value of output for each major use, by state. New England produced about 5% of the nation's sand and gravel by weight, and about 3% by value.

In a 1929 study by the United States Department of Commerce, *Industrial Structure of New England,* appears the statement: "Supplies of sand and gravel suitable for building and other purposes occur generally throughout New England in adequate quantities for all local requirements." Apparently, a similar situation existed in 1949, although this is also true for most other parts of the country. However, a small portion of the region's needs for sand and gravel were met by shipments into New England, principally from the Middle Atlantic states.

Asbestos Production

New England's asbestos production is entirely from a chrysotile mine near Belvidere Mountain in Vermont. The Vermont deposits are apparently a southern extension of the asbestos area in Quebec. The mine is owned by the Vermont Asbestos Mines Division of the Ruberoid Company, and it accounts for most of the United States production.

There has been a shortage of asbestos in the United States, especially the long-fiber type. Most asbestos consumed in the United States is imported from Canada and South Africa. Although the New England output is only a small percentage of total domestic consumption, it is important to the nation's security. Output at the Belvidere Mine was increased in 1949, and in the same year a new fiber-processing mill was put into operation at Lowell, Vermont.

CHART 4–3

Value of Sand and Gravel Production in New England, by Major Use, 1949
(in millions of dollars)

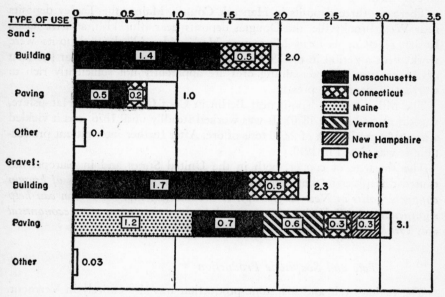

* Does not include output of commercial producers in New Hampshire.
Source: U.S. Department of the Interior, Bureau of Mines, *Minerals Yearbook, 1949*

Copper Production

The small copper output of New England is also entirely in Vermont, though there are unworked deposits in both New Hampshire and Maine. The 3,000-ton figure in Table 4–8 is only an approximation of total Vermont production in 1949. Because of the government's disclosure rule, actual production figures were not released by the Bureau of Mines.

New England's copper production in 1949 came entirely from the Elizabeth Mine at South Strafford, Vermont. It is operated by the Vermont Copper

Company, and in 1949 it ranked as the 20th largest producer in the United States. Other copper deposits are located in Strafford at the Ely Mine, also owned by the Vermont Copper Company; in Hancock County, Maine; and in Coos County, New Hampshire. None of those deposits was in production during that year.

The Ely Mine was once the largest producer of copper in the United States. The deposit, discovered in 1820, produced as much as 3,200,000 pounds of copper in 1880. During the last 30 years the mine has been idle, but estimated production over its active life was 400,000 tons of ore averaging 3.3% copper. At present, sections are filled with water, and the tunnels are caved and inaccessible. Since the ore is low in grade, it is doubtful if the mine will be reopened.

There are three deposits in Hancock County, Maine: the Tapley deposits near West Brooksville, the Douglas deposits near Blue Hill, and the Cape Rosier Zinc-Copper-Lead Mine near Harborside. All three deposits were worked for a period in the 19th century, but they were closed near the turn of the century. The remaining ores are apparently not sufficiently rich to warrant reopening at present.

The Milan copper deposit near Berlin in Coos County, New Hampshire, was discovered in the 1870's. It was worked steadily until 1876, and it yielded a monthly production of 2,600 tons of ore. After further intermittent production, it was closed in 1910.

The shortage of copper, both in the United States and in Europe, has caused difficulties in the current defense production. *On the basis of known copper deposits in New England, it seems unlikely that the region can help significantly in alleviating the copper shortage, unless some more economical way can be found to utilize the low-grade ore.*

Talc and Soapstone Production

The region's talc and soapstone production was also entirely in Vermont. In 1949 output was valued at $788,000. Vermont is the fourth largest producing state in the country.

Talc and soapstone are used in many manufacturing industries, but 85% of the nation's consumption is concentrated in the production of ceramics, paint, rubber, insecticides, roofing, and paper. A large amount of Vermont's talc production is used as a filler in the manufacture of paper products. A portion is used in making prepared roofing, rubber tires, and other rubber products, in oils and greases, and for foundry facings. It is also used in fire-clay products and in twine and cordage, as well as in the manufacture of paint and wall plaster and the finishing of textiles.

The present talc-producing centers of Vermont are at Johnson, in Lamoille County; at Reading, in Windsor County; at Waterbury, in Washington County; and at Windham, in Windham County. Soapstone is produced only at Chester, in Windsor County, where there are also two talc-processing mills.

Talc was in short supply in the United States during the first half of 1952, but the shortage was apparently not critical.

Products of Pegmatites

New England's pegmatites, or coarse granite, are a source of many important minerals, especially feldspar, mica, quartz, and beryllium. Production of these four minerals in New England is high relative to the United States totals.

Granite pegmatites occur in many sections of New England. They vary in the relative quantities of each kind of mineral. Mines classed as mica mines usually have by-products of feldspar; those classed as feldspar mines usually have by-products of mica. No New England pegmatite has been mined for beryl or quartz alone, but the Beryllium Corporation is considering opening a beryl deposit near Rumford, Maine.

About 99% of the ground feldspar produced in 1949 was consumed by the ceramic industry. Most of the rest was used in soaps and abrasives, but a small quantity of carefully selected crude feldspar was used in the manufacture of artificial teeth.

New Hampshire ranked second in value of feldspar output among the 48 states. The important New Hampshire sources of high-grade feldspar are the mica mines north of Keene, in Cheshire County. Connecticut has deposits south and west of Hartford in Middlesex and Hartford counties. Maine's most important deposits are in Oxford and Sagadahoc counties, and there are small deposits elsewhere.

The leading mica deposits of New England are in New Hampshire, though Maine and Connecticut both produce small quantities. The principal New Hampshire deposits are in Cheshire, Grafton, and Sullivan counties. There are also small quantities of mica in Merrimack, Strafford, and Coos counties. Maine mica is largely a by-product of feldspar mined in Oxford, Sagadahoc, Cumberland, and Androscoggin counties. Mica has been produced in Connecticut in Middlesex, Hartford, Fairfield, and Litchfield counties.

The mica produced in both New England and the country as a whole is largely scrap mica, which is ground up for use in the manufacture of roofing, paint, rubber and other products. Imports provide most of the country's needs for sheet mica, which has its principal uses in the production of electrical equipment.

New England's quartz production is mostly in Connecticut. Quartz is used for crushed or coated abrasives, pottery, and as a refractory. In its crude or roughly crushed state, quartz is used for metallurgical flux, for making ferro-silicon, for filling acid towers, and for grinding to silica flour.

Beryllium is a light metal of about the same density as magnesium. It is used as a hardening agent for other metals, especially for copper-beryllium alloys, and for windows in X-ray tubes and electrodes and targets in vacuum tubes. It has other specialized uses, however, such as in reaction rods for the production of atomic energy.

Many of the New England pegmatites contain other rare minerals, but they are usually found in such small quantities that it is uneconomical to extract them. Perhaps in the future, with changes in technical knowledge, the production of rare alkalies—lithium, rubidium, and cesium—will increase. A possible future use of these alkalies is in high temperature alloys, for the addition of small quantities may save large quantities of such scarce alloy metals as nickel, columbium, and cobalt. Considerable research is under way at present in this field. In the meantime, the alkalies remain largely interesting specimens that furnish collectors with more or less ornamental and uncommon minerals.

Peat Production

New England's peat production in 1949 was primarily in Connecticut and Maine, though Massachusetts and New Hampshire added small amounts. The region's output was almost 12% of the value of national production. Peat is not generally used as a fuel in the United States, because of the ready availability of higher quality fuels. More than 90% of peat consumption is for soil improvement and mixed fertilizers.

Clay Production

Common clay is widely distributed throughout the New England region, and there are producing deposits in every state except Rhode Island. Vermont, Connecticut, and Massachusetts lead in production within the region. New England's output is only a small proportion of national production, however, and it has been inadequate to meet the needs of the region. None of the highest grades of clay was produced in New England during 1949. The region's output of the coarser structural clays went primarily into the local production of brick and tile. *It seems that the region might expand its brick production, particularly by using special techniques adapted to the available raw materials.*

Graphite Production

One of the largest producers of graphite in the country is a mine in Rhode Island. The Rhode Island deposits are not large, however, and they occur with deposits of graphitic coal. The majority of the nation's consumption of natural graphite is based on imports, for use in the manufacture of foundry facings, batteries, lubricants, crucibles, pencils, and many other products.

Other Production

The preceding sketches complete the listing of the minerals produced in New England in 1949, except for small quantities of gold and silver from Vermont that are insignificant in total national production. There has also been a small production of magnesium and calcium in the region recently, however, through the reduction of dolomitic limestone and calcium carbonate in Canaan, Connecticut.

Other minerals are known to exist in New England, but their deposits are generally of such low grade or so small that commercial production has not been economical under recent conditions. It is possible that as technical knowledge increases or as richer deposits elsewhere are depleted, it may become profitable to extract additional minerals. We shall consider a few such possibilities shortly.

THE NATION'S MINERAL SITUATION AND NEW ENGLAND

In view of the small employment and value of output provided by New England's mineral industries, and in view of their nature, there seems to be little opportunity for the region as a whole to increase its over-all economic health appreciably by expanding its minerals output. Increases in output can be of considerable importance to particular communities, of course, but even a 10% increase in the *total* minerals output of New England would be equivalent only to the addition of one fair-sized manufacturing plant.

The role of minerals is broader, however, than just their direct effects on a region. Under present international conditions and the need for increasing national security, it is important to maintain adequate supplies of essential minerals. Shortages and threats of shortages have occurred for many metallic and nonmetallic minerals during the recent past.

The problem of shortages has resulted partly from the tremendous expansion in minerals production during and after World War II, which cut sharply into the nation's high-grade mineral reserves. There has been a great increase in demand for minerals by manufacturers during recent years, and the Federal Government has built up stockpiles to help preserve national security. Many important deposits have been exploited so fully that their rates of production cannot economically be increased. Moreover, the discovery and development of new domestic deposits have declined for several important minerals, so that new deposits have not been forthcoming rapidly enough to replace the old ones.

The most critical metal shortages during 1951 were in aluminum, beryllium, copper, magnesium, selenium, tin, zinc, platinum, cobalt, columbium, molybdenum, nickel, tantalum, and tungsten. During the same period there were shortages of many nonmetallic minerals, including asbestos, industrial diamonds, fluorspar, graphite, mica, talc, and certain rare earths, especially in the strategic grades.

Of the 38 principal industrial minerals listed by the Bureau of Mines for the year 1951, there were only nine which the United States produced in sufficient quantity to meet or exceed domestic consumption. There were ten

CHART 4–4

United States Import Percentages of Strategic Minerals, 1951

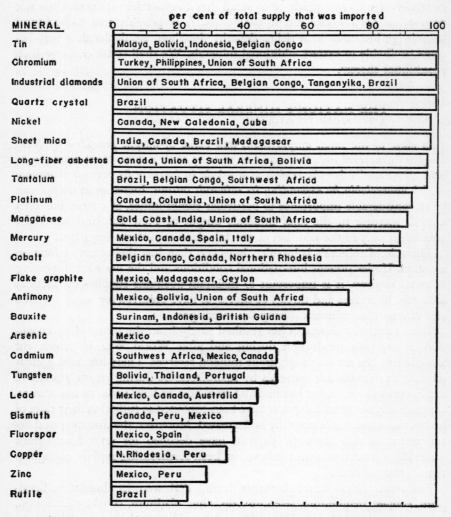

MINERAL	per cent of total supply that was imported
Tin	Malaya, Bolivia, Indonesia, Belgian Congo
Chromium	Turkey, Philippines, Union of South Africa
Industrial diamonds	Union of South Africa, Belgian Congo, Tanganyika, Brazil
Quartz crystal	Brazil
Nickel	Canada, New Caledonia, Cuba
Sheet mica	India, Canada, Brazil, Madagascar
Long-fiber asbestos	Canada, Union of South Africa, Bolivia
Tantalum	Brazil, Belgian Congo, Southwest Africa
Platinum	Canada, Columbia, Union of South Africa
Manganese	Gold Coast, India, Union of South Africa
Mercury	Mexico, Canada, Spain, Italy
Cobalt	Belgian Congo, Canada, Northern Rhodesia
Flake graphite	Mexico, Madagascar, Ceylon
Antimony	Mexico, Bolivia, Union of South Africa
Bauxite	Surinam, Indonesia, British Guiana
Arsenic	Mexico
Cadmium	Southwest Africa, Mexico, Canada
Tungsten	Bolivia, Thailand, Portugal
Lead	Mexico, Canada, Australia
Bismuth	Canada, Peru, Mexico
Fluorspar	Mexico, Spain
Copper	N. Rhodesia, Peru
Zinc	Mexico, Peru
Rutile	Brazil

Source: U.S. Department of the Interior, Bureau of Mines, *Information Circular,* 1952

strategic minerals for which the nation was more than 90% dependent on foreign nations. (See Chart 4-4.) The imports of eight others exceeded domestic production. More than half of those 18 minerals were on the shortage list in 1951.

It is impossible for the United States to be completely self-sufficient for all minerals. It is important, nevertheless, for the country to have domestic sources of vital materials to the fullest extent possible under present conditions. The expansion of production in mines and quarries that are now operating, the development of known but unworked deposits, and the discovery of new deposits all present opportunities.

Despite its small output of minerals, New England should participate actively in the expansion of mineral production in the interest of national security. There are known deposits of beryllium, copper, zinc, asbestos, graphite, mica, and talc in New England, and many of them are in production. Vermont's asbestos production has been expanded already, and increased production of slate, feldspar, lime, clay, and other minerals and their products is possible.

New England also presents opportunities for expanded sulphur production. The Brown Company of Berlin, New Hampshire, is now extracting sulphur from the tailings of a Vermont copper mine. Even larger production in the region can come from the iron-sulphide deposits in the Mt. Katahdin area of Maine. At least two large national companies already have holdings of those deposits, apparently largely as a protection against the diminishing reserves of elemental sulphur along the Gulf Coast. *New England would benefit from an aggressive development of the Maine sulphide reserves, and it is hoped that these companies will systematically open them for production as economic considerations permit.* In addition, the extraction of sulphur would yield a substantial by-product of iron.

There is also the possibility that previously unknown deposits of strategic minerals in short supply may be discovered in New England. Many parts of the region have not been prospected, and other parts have received only cursory examination. *Since the question of national security is so closely involved, it is clear that the Federal Government is, and should be, actively concerned with the expansion of New England's output of strategic minerals, just as it is in the rest of the country.* The Bureau of Mines established a special Boston office to aid the states in a detailed examination of the region's mineral potentialities, as part of the joint federal-state study of the region's natural resources by the New England and New York Interagency Committee. We hope that the final report of that committee, which is expected in 1954, will be able to present detailed new information about the mineral deposits of New England.

If the further investigations of New England's mineral resources turn up additional deposits of scarce strategic minerals of commercial grade that are needed for the national security, they should be developed by private con-

cerns. If the deposits are of less than commercial grade, decisions about development must rest on their quality in relation to the probable need for the mineral and the quality and reliability of other sources, both domestic and foreign. If the development of submarginal New England sources is in the national interest, federal subsidies would be in order, since the benefit would accrue to the nation as a whole far more than to New England. Decisions on such matters must rest primarily on military and technical considerations.

The completion of the Interagency Committee's report will not exhaust the possibilities for exploration, however. *The United States Bureau of Mines and the states, as well as private industry, should continue to press their investigations.* New Hampshire has made excellent progress in its long-range geologic mapping of the entire state. Vermont and Maine have stepped up their own geologic and prospecting activities. *The need for further work is especially great in Maine, with its large undeveloped area. Massachusetts, the only state in the region without a state geologist, should give official recognition and greater support to this aspect of the state's economy and its relation to national problems.*

Without the benefit of detailed original studies, we are not in a position to offer new information about specific opportunities for developing unexploited minerals in New England. A few recent developments have aroused so much interest, however, that we should mention them briefly.

Manganese Deposits in Maine

In recent years there has been a great deal of interest in the manganese deposits of Aroostook County, Maine. Despite their abundance, the ores so far examined are too low in grade to be developed commercially at present prices. There are four major manganese sites in the Aroostook area: the Dudley deposits, west of Mapleton; the Maple Mountain-Hovey Mountain deposits, west of Bridgewater; and the Littleton Ridge and Carpenter farms deposits, northwest of Houlton. Although manganiferous iron ore was first discovered in Aroostook County in 1837, there has never been any manganese production. Some deposits were worked for iron during the 19th century.

The deposits were first seriously prospected for manganese in 1941 by the State of Maine, in cooperation with the Federal Geological Survey. In 1942 the Manganese Ore Company, a subsidiary of the M. A. Hanna Company, also began prospecting in the area. Presumably, it did not consider the deposits a worthwhile investment for the company, as investigatory work soon ceased. The strategic importance of manganese and the great dependence of the nation on distant foreign sources prompted a resumption of investigations in 1949 by the Bureau of Mines. The studies are continuing. The bureau's metallurgical laboratories at College Park, Maryland, have run tests on thousands of pounds of ore samples taken from the four deposits. Tests are also under way at the University of Pittsburgh to develop a method for using the ore commercially.

According to a 1947 report by the Maine state geologist, reasonably assured reserves of metallic manganese in the state were 1,300,000 tons, and an additional reserve of 800,000 tons seemed probable. Subsequent prospecting has undoubtedly increased the figure, and the eventual total may be far larger. The average manganese content of the ore is about 11%, though the content of some ores may be as high as 20%. Currently acceptable ores contain 40% manganese, but 28% ore was used during World War II when costs were a secondary consideration. The Maine ore also contains considerable silica and 10 to 30% iron, which make it difficult to extract the manganese economically. *Most experts agree that an advance in technical knowledge, direct government subsidies, or both, will be necessary before there can be any substantial production of Maine's manganese. The strong support of research looking to a solution of the technical problem is of great long-term interest to New England, for it would make possible use of the ores during peace time. Moreover, if it becomes feasible to produce manganese in Maine, there should be a substantial production of iron as a by-product, or a form of ferro-manganese could be produced directly.*

Other Potentials

As has been pointed out, most domestic production of mica is "scrap" mica; and the nation's strategic sheet mica, most of which comes from abroad, is in short supply. A recently announced technical development indicates that it is possible to make synthetic mica sheets from ground mica. A new Vermont plant began production using the process in 1952. If the synthetic sheets can become a satisfactory substitute for the natural product, New England's mica deposits will take on a new national significance. Some of New Hampshire's mica mines were also reopened and a mica purchase depot was established at Franklin, New Hampshire.

There has been a recent resurgence of interest in the possible low-grade anthracite coal deposits of southern Massachusetts and northern Rhode Island. The occurrence of the deposits has been known for a long time, but their size and physical properties have not yet been fully determined. They have never been developed commercially. According to the Bureau of Mines, it is even questionable whether the deposits are anthracite coal or graphite. Further technical studies by the Bureau of Mines are currently under way. *It is to New England's interest to support continued research into the nature of the deposits and possible methods of using them. If their characteristics are satisfactory, there should presumably be a periodic reappraisal of the costs of extraction and use, until, if ever, the development becomes economically attractive.*

FOREIGN SOURCES OF MINERALS

Without doubt, the most dependable source of minerals for the United States is deposits within this country. But the availability of minerals from Canada and Mexico is almost as good. The other countries of Central and South America too are usually more secure sources for minerals than those on other continents. *It is important to the nation, therefore, to maintain friendly relations with all nations in the Western Hemisphere and to work with them in the discovery and development of their minerals for mutual benefit.*

The Development of Canadian Minerals

New England has a special interest in the development of minerals in eastern Canada. Geographically the New England seaboard is the American industrial center closest to that part of Canada. A portion of its output could flow economically to New England by all-season ocean carrier for fabrication. In the past New England has not taken adequate economic advantage of its proximity to Canada as a source of raw materials. *It would be desirable for many of the manufacturers and industrial development agencies of the region to give closer scrutiny to the growing minerals output of eastern Canada in planning their future actions.*

Canada has made great progress in its minerals development during recent years. As Chart 4 showed, Canada supplies important parts of United States consumption of nickel, sheet mica, asbestos, platinum, mercury, cobalt, cadmium, lead, and bismuth. It exports other minerals to this country as well.

The future of Canadian minerals looks even more promising. There are still enormous areas of the country that have not been prospected, and undoubtedly many important new discoveries will be made. *It is to the interest of both the United States as a whole and New England to aid Canada as much as possible in its minerals development.*

Titanium

Canadian titanium offers an important possibility for New England manufacturers. The strength, light weight, resistance to corrosion, and high melting point of titanium make it steadily more attractive for many applications as its price drops. Canadian smelting of titanium ore at Sorel, Quebec, has been growing, and a few New England firms are already actively working on its reduction or experimenting on its fabrication. More New England firms should be engaged in that preliminary examination, for the metal will almost certainly become an important industrial raw material, perhaps in time a major one. The opportunity for New England to participate actively in reduction of the ores to metallic titanium is limited at present by the region's high cost of electric power, since electrolytic processes are the leading methods for preparation of the metal. *As greater opportunities for employment develop in the fabrication of titanium, however, New England metalworking establishments should take full advantage of the new metal to improve both their products and their competitive positions.*[5]

Titanium fits uniquely into New England's gradual shift to metalworking. As we have noted, the more valuable minerals can bear the transportation charges for fairly long hauls. From that point of view, New England does not at present have a significant competitive edge in taking advantage of Canada's titanium. Its advantage lies in the closeness of its economic, political, and social ties with the eastern provinces. The transportation-cost advantage may come later, as the price of titanium falls.

Iron Ore

Many New Englanders have viewed with pleasure the development of the rich Labrador-Quebec iron ore deposits. Those deposits are of sufficient size and quality to rival the famed Mesabi Range of Minnesota. The railroad which will bring out the ore will unload its cargo at Seven Islands, a port on the lower Saint Lawrence River. All-year ocean freighters could carry the ore to a New England coastal location for manufacture into steel.

The decision to develop the Labrador ores, along with the Supreme Court decision that outlawed basing-point pricing in the steel industry, and recent technological advances in the steel industry, stimulated the New England Council and others to press for the establishment of an integrated steel mill in the region. Such a mill could reduce the delivered prices steel users in the region would have to pay and would be one of the most important mineral developments that New England could experience. It would give a strong boost to the growth of metalworking that has been taking place in the region despite the absence of a local source of steel.

New England's large consumption of steel and the region's heavy dependence on "imports" stood out in our earlier discussion of transportation in relation to New England's mineral use. Steel is one of the relatively few primary mineral products which has to be carried long distances and for which transportation cost is highly significant. Comparative transportation costs have been gradually pushing steel-production facilities away from the locations of the raw materials and toward the markets. Since New England is a deficit steel area, it seemed that the region would be a favorable location for a steel mill, especially in view of the Canadian iron ore development. The

5. New England's greatest opportunity to participate in the expanding use of other light metals—aluminum, magnesium, and zirconium, for example—is also largely in their manufacture into finished or semifinished products. The power requirements of the electrolytic reduction processes used for each of them and the distances from sources of raw ore make this region less fitted than others for the production of the metals themselves. *Ibid.*, pp. 69–76.

prospective benefit to the region was primarily the assistance to steel users, both existing companies and new ones, rather than the direct employment and income that would be created by the steel mill itself, large though that might be.

On the basis of the various factors favoring the New England location, the proposed mill for the New London area received a federal certificate of necessity early in 1951 as part of the defense-facilities program. It would have been permitted rapid write-off for federal income-tax purposes of a large part of the construction and equipment cost. Engineering studies found the project feasible if it were operated as a unit of an existing steel company, but no existing steel mill chose to take part in the project. The required investment was too great for some companies; others had already committed themselves fully to expansion of facilities elsewhere; others decided that new locations outside New England would be more advantageous to them; and others were not convinced of the profitability of the New England location.

The burst of defense-period expansion of steel capacity passed, therefore, without the construction of an integrated mill in New England. Some of the East Coast expansion will be helpful to New England manufacturers, but a new mill within the region could be even more helpful to many of them. This important goal for New England will have to await some new wave of expansion in the steel industry before it can be revived.

A new proposal has been advanced more recently for the possible construction of a new specialty steel mill in New England.[6] The proposed mill would make carbon and alloy bars, for which the New England market is strong, in an electric-furnace mill of about 140,000 tons annual capacity. The use of a scrap charge would eliminate the need for coke and blast-furnace facilities and hold down the necessary investment to a fairly small total. Steel scrap is plentiful in New England. *A specialty steel mill of this sort is an attractive possibility for New England, and the industrial development and financial agencies of the region should encourage its further examination and possible establishment.*

Latin-American Minerals

The list of strategic minerals which the United States imports from Central and South America is long and impressive—tin from Bolivia, industrial diamonds from Brazil, tantalum from Brazil, platinum from Colombia, mercury from Mexico, graphite from Mexico, and many more. Besides the nonfuel minerals, Venezuela is a major source of imported petroleum. The discovery and development of large new iron ore deposits in South America add further to the ore reserves and supplies available to the United States.

The United States has sponsored or cooperated in many of the past min-

6. *Ibid.*, pp. 32–57.

erals developments in Latin America. It should continue those relationships, both through direct private investment by American firms and through federally sponsored technical assistance. There are undoubtedly many important mineral deposits that have not yet been found in those countries. Their discovery and development can assist both the countries themselves and the United States.

Since New England industry is so highly dependent on the availability of minerals, it is in the region's interest as well as the nation's to examine carefully and support all sound programs for the development of mineral resources in the Latin American countries.

CONCLUSIONS

From this discussion of the various ramifications of New England's minerals situation, we can reach a number of major conclusions:

1. The region's indigenous minerals contribute only a small amount to the employment and income of the people of New England. The extent to which they can make a further direct contribution is small.

2. Some of the region's minerals and the discovery of new deposits may have greater significance to the country as a whole, from the point of view of national security, than they do to the New England economy.

3. The manufacturing industries of the region are tremendously dependent on minerals brought in from outside New England. The dependence is absolute for mineral fuels, iron and steel, and many other important raw materials and products.

4. The dependable availability of most minerals from sources *anywhere* is far more important to the region than their discovery or development within the six-state area, particularly where the local deposits are of low grade. Since their value is high relative to weight, they can stand the charges of even long transportation hauls. To the extent possible, however, the region should work for transportation economies and improvements in facilities that will assist in making those minerals economically available.

5. Transportation charges are significantly high for coal and iron and steel. The region's emphasis on coal should continue to be upon methods of reducing transportation costs. New England should continue to seek lower cost steel, both through the eventual construction of more steel-making facilities in the region and through encouraging the development of other nearby sources and transportation economies.

6. The increasing extent to which the United States is turning abroad for mineral supplies has improved New England's competitive position because of its seacoast location, though the region has not yet taken full advantage of its changing position. New England should support the minerals development of the entire Western Hemisphere and the rest of the Atlantic basin.

Appendix 4-A. The Value of New England's Stone Production, by Type and State, 1949

(in thousands of dollars)

ITEM	MAINE	N. H.	VT.	MASS.	R. I.	CONN.	TOTAL, N.E.	U.S.	PER CENT N.E. OF U.S.
Granite	1,360	381	3,753	3,453	280	139	9,366	42,566	22
Dimension stone	1,342	377	3,553	3,074	268	138	8,752	21,315	41
Crushed or broken	17	4	200[b]	379	12	1[a]	614	21,251	3
Basalt	41		0	1,942	100	2,074	4,158	30,486	14
Dimension stone	0		0	0	0	1[a]	1	98	1
Crushed or broken	41		0	1,942	100	2,073	4,156	30,389	14
Marble	0		3,231	0	0	0	3,231	12,293	26
Dimension stone	0		3,231[b]	0	0	0	3,231	11,153	29
Crushed or broken	0		0	0	0	0	0	1,140	0
Limestone	527		1,292	895	71	247	3,033	222,513	1
Dimension stone	0		0	0	0	*	*	12,671	*
Crushed or broken	527		1,292	895	71	247	2,032	209,842	1
Sandstone	0		0	4	0	0	4	19,906	*
Dimension stone	0		0	4	0	0	4	4,660	*
Crushed or broken	0		0	0	0	0	0	15,246	0
All other stone	97		0	259	0	0	356	13,677	3
Dimension stone	0		0	0	0	0	0	1,850	0
Crushed or broken	97		0	259	n.a.	0	356	11,827	3
TOTAL	$2,026	$ 381	$8,276	$6,553	$ 451[c]	$2,461	$20,148	$341,442	6

Note: Details may not add to totals because of rounding.

* Less than $500 or 0.5%.

n.a. = Not available.

a. Connecticut crushed or broken granite and basalt dimension stone not given separately. Total of both was $2,000; $1,000 assigned to each.

b. The value of Vermont's crushed or broken granite and marble dimension stone totaled $3,431,000. Total crushed granite production was $354,000 for Connecticut, Idaho, New York, New Jersey, New York, South Dakota, and Vermont. Of those states, the only large producer of dimension granite was South Dakota. We estimate Vermont's ground or broken granite production at $200,000 and have assigned the remaining $3,231,000 for Vermont to marble dimension stone.

c. Totals do not include "all other" stone.

Source: U.S. Department of the Interior, Bureau of Mines, Minerals Yearbook, 1949

7. New England shares the broad national interest in low tariffs and the elimination of import restrictions for all minerals.

8. The region should work toward a greater integration of its manufacturing structure with the current development of the mineral resources of eastern Canada. In addition to the eventual possibilities of Labrador iron ore, Canadian titanium offers important future prospects.

9. Some specific developments in mineral use in New England provide possible opportunities for the economic progress of the region, including expansion of mica, cement, and brick production and the extraction of sulphur from iron-sulphide deposits. The establishment of a specialty steel mill for the production of carbon and alloy bars is another important possibility.

SELECTED REFERENCES

1. Canadian Department of Mines and Resources, *Geology and Economic Minerals of Canada,* 1947.
2. Little, Arthur D., Inc., *A Survey of Industrial Opportunities in New England* (report to the Federal Reserve Bank of Boston), August 1952.
3. Maine Development Commission, *Report of the State Geologist* (biannual), 1942–50.
4. ———— *Bulletins,* Nos. 1–5, 1944–48. (Geological surveys of peat, pyrrhotite, manganese, and pegmatite deposits within the state, and a quadrangle survey.)
5. New Hampshire State Planning and Development Commission, *Mineral Resources Survey,* Pts. 1–14, 1940–50. (Surveys of deposits of various New Hampshire minerals.)
6. ———— *New Hampshire Minerals and Mines,* 1941.
7. ———— Quadrangle Studies, Pts. 1–16, 1935–50. (Geological surveys of 16 of the New Hampshire quadrangles.)
8. The President's Materials Policy Commission, *Resources for Freedom:* Vol. *1, Foundations for Growth and Security;* Vol. *2, The Outlook for Key Commodities;* Vol. *3, The Outlook for Energy Sources;* Vol. *4, The Promise of Technology;* Vol. *5, Selected Reports to the Commission,* Washington, June 1952.
9. U.S. Bureau of Mines, *Minerals Yearbook, 1949.*
10. ———— *Reports of Investigations,* 1947–50, Nos. 4395, 4409, 4410, 4412, 4423, 4425, 4443, 4701, and 4718. (Investigations of various New England mineral deposits, including copper, mica, beryl, limonite, feldspar, and manganese.)
11. U.S. Department of Commerce, *Industrial Structure of New England,* 1930.

5

Water, Fuel, and Energy in New England

Drafted by Ray S. Kelley, Jr., under the direction
of Arthur A. Bright, Jr.

INTRODUCTION

Water, fuel, and electric energy are vital to the successful operation of an industrial society. They both supplement and compete with each other, depending on the use in question and on local conditions. Because of their complex interrelationships, it is advisable to give joint consideration to the topics of availability, use, and potentials.

Except during extraordinary droughts, most parts of New England have ample rainfall, runoff, and surface and ground-water supplies to meet present and forseeable nonpower requirements for water. In certain areas, indeed, there are sometimes damaging floods. In some sections of New England, however, pollution has seriously reduced the usefulness of much of the water supply.

On the other hand, New England has almost no deposits of fuel within its borders. It produces no coal, no oil, and no natural gas. It has to meet fuel needs by imports. Because the sources of fuel are at a considerable distance, the cost of transportation causes fuel costs to be high relative to those in most other sections of the country.

The major New England rivers, except those in Maine, are highly developed for electric power, but only a fourth or fifth of the electric power produced in the region is from hydroelectric generators. New England rivers cannot provide enough power to meet more than a fraction of the local needs economically, and steam generators supply the bulk of power requirements. Steam generation requires large quantities of fuel, and with fuel in New England relatively expensive it is not surprising that electric rates are above the national average.

This report discusses the New England situation for water, fuel, and electric energy and the implications of this situation for the regional economy. The first section is devoted largely to the nonpower uses of water. The second section reviews fuel consumption, sources, and costs.

The final section summarizes the principal aspects of electric power production and consumption in the region. It draws heavily on the facts presented in the first two sections, which condition many aspects of power generation and use.

NONPOWER WATER USES AND PROBLEMS

New England is fortunate in its possession of large quantities of surface and ground water available for many uses in addition to hydroelectric power. The generation of power from falling water utilizes its quantity and *velocity*. For most other purposes, except water transportation, it is the quantity and *quality* of water that are important. New England water is of high natural quality. It is softer than supplies in most other regions of the country, and it is less contaminated by natural pollution. Municipal, farm, and industrial pollution have destroyed part of the high natural quality, however, and have reduced water supplies for some purposes.

Precipitation in New England is above the national average. It varies from an average of less than 35 inches a year in the northern inland areas to 50 inches in the southern coastal area along Long Island Sound. Runoff, the amount of water available for use after evaporation and transpiration, ranges from 15 to 30 inches a year in various sections of the area. While New England has more rain than the midwestern states, a smaller proportion of the annual rainfall comes in the summer months and so its contribution to crops is less. The additional rain does increase the ground-water level, however, and thereby stimulates forest growth. New England receives less runoff and rainfall than do states in the Southeast, but the natural quality of the water is usually higher.

In general, New England enjoys ample water supplies, and droughts are infrequent. A more frequent problem, but still not a major one, is too much water. Early New England mills located on streams near sources of water power. Towns such as Lowell, Nashua, Springfield, and Holyoke grew around the mills in the river flood plains. Considerable flood damage has occurred in limited areas during highwater years.

Water Use in New England

Water has many uses. Some is withdrawn or diverted from streams, lakes, or the ground, but the greater proportion is used without withdrawal. Even water that is withdrawn from a stream is often returned and used again for the same or other purposes.

Water withdrawn from surface or underground sources goes into five major categories of use: municipal water supplies, industrial use from private sources, irrigation, other rural uses, and the generation of electric power. Municipal water systems provide for fire protection, for drinking and sanitary purposes, for flushing streets, and for industrial uses. Rural uses for water in addition to irrigation include the watering of livestock and poultry and all other applications not served by public supply systems.

Water uses that require neither withdrawal nor diversion are extremely

Table 5-1. Estimated Withdrawal Uses of Water in New England and the United States, 1950 (millions of gallons per day)

STATE	MUNICIPAL		INDUSTRIAL[a]		RURAL[b]		IRRIGATIONAL		TOTAL, FOUR CATEGORIES		WATER POWER[c]
	GROUND WATER	SURFACE WATER	GROUND WATER	SURFACE WATER	GROUND WATER	SURFACE WATER	GROUND WATER	SURFACE WATER	GROUND WATER	SURFACE WATER	
Maine	8	70	15	970[e]	9	9	neg.	neg.	32	1,049	39,292
New Hampshire	7	20	10	75	15	1	neg.	neg.	32	96	18,732
Vermont	10	20	5	60	15	2	neg.	neg.	30	82	14,272
Massachusetts	75	320	100	250	40	1	3	3	218	574	14,272
Rhode Island	15	50	15	80	7	1	neg.	neg.	37	131	696
Connecticut	9	180	40	1,500[d]	15	7	1	neg.	65	1,687	5,262
NEW ENGLAND	124	660	185	2,935	101	21	4	3	414	3,619	92,526
UNITED STATES	3,584	10,056	5,525	71,961	2,858	706	20,204	68,486	32,171	151,209	1,100,000
NEW ENGLAND, PER CENT OF UNITED STATES	3.5	6.6	3.3	4.1	3.5	3.0	.02	.004	.013	2.4	8.4

a Other than from municipal supplies.
b Excluding irrigation.
c All from surface water.
d 1,000 mgd was brackish.
e 190 mgd was brackish.
Source: U.S. Geological Survey

important to New England. Navigation, bathing, fishing, pleasure boating, conservation of wildlife, and waste and sewage disposal all use the water where it is and do not diminish its quantity, though all in various degrees do affect its quality.

CHART 5-1

Rainfall, Runoff, and Nonpower Water Withdrawal,
New England and the United States, 1950
(millions of gallons per day)

NEW ENGLAND
130,000

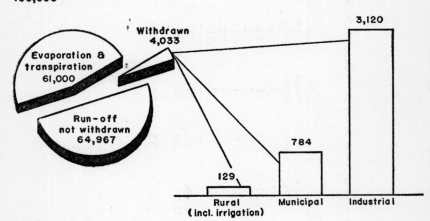

UNITED STATES
4,300,000

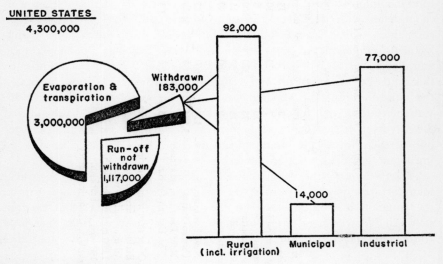

Source: U.S. Geological Survey

Table 5–1 shows the estimated withdrawal uses of water in 1950 for each of the New England states and for the United States. Since water used for hydroelectric generation is returned to the stream immediately after use, the large quantity of water withdrawn for power production has been excluded from the total of the other major withdrawal uses. Even that total involves some double counting, however, from repeated withdrawal, use, and discharge along individual streams. The repeated use of water is emphasized by the fact that in New England the use for power purposes alone exceeds total runoff.

The relationships between rainfall, runoff, and withdrawal uses other than for power generation are illustrated in Chart 5–1. New England withdraws only 5.8% of its runoff, while in the United States as a whole the withdrawal is 14.1%. New England uses only 2.2% of all the water withdrawn in the United States for nonpower purposes. The principal reason for the less intensive withdrawal in New England is the greater relative abundance of water in the region. With only 2.1% of the country's land area, New England has 3.0% of the rainfall and 5.3% of the runoff. Another major reason for New England's less intensive withdrawal is the relatively small amount of irrigation in the area as compared with the United States as a whole, where the use of water in irrigation exceeds that in industry. Industry is by far the largest consumer of water in New England, excluding power generation. Municipal utilization is only a fourth as large as total industrial use, and combined rural and irrigational use is very small in the region.

New England's water provides one of the region's outstanding advantages as an industrial location. That conclusion was substantiated by a manufacturers' opinion survey conducted by the Federal Reserve Bank of Boston in cooperation with the New England Council in 1949. Executives of 663 companies, which accounted for about 20 per cent of the region's manufacturing employment, answered questionnaires on "The Present Position and Prospects for New England Manufacturers." Their reports indicated that in 1949 "adequacy of water supply" led all other location factors in the ratio of companies which reported it as an important competitive advantage to those that reported it as an important competitive disadvantage.[1] Twenty-five per cent of the respondents considered the availability of water one of their important locational advantages; only 2% considered it an important competitive disadvantage.

Table 5–2 shows the variations in opinions about water supplies among manufacturers in the various states and industries. As one might expect, the situation is most favorable in the three northern states, but even in southern New England the companies reported overwhelmingly that local water conditions provide them with a significant advantage. The importance

1. Federal Reserve Bank of Boston, "New England Manufacturing—Its Future Prospects," *Monthly Review*, September 1949.

of New England's water availability differs among industries. It is apparently of greatest importance in the woolen and worsted branch of the textile group and in the lumber, paper, primary-metal, food, and rubber-products industries.

For manufacturing, for good living, and for the recreation business, it is obvious that New England's inland waters are one of the region's greatest natural resources. At the same time, it must be realized that while

Table 5-2. How Satisfied Are New England Manufacturers with Their Water Supplies?

	NUMBER OF COMPANIES	PERCENTAGES OF COMPANIES REPORTING WATER AS			
		IMPORTANT COMPETITIVE ADVANTAGE	OF LITTLE COMPETITIVE IMPORTANCE	IMPORTANT COMPETITIVE DISADVANTAGE	NO OPINION EXPRESSED
BY STATE					
Maine	35	43	43	0	14
New Hampshire	72	32	51	4	13
Vermont	46	41.5	54.5	2	2
Massachusetts	291	20.5	66.5	3	10
Rhode Island	38	13	79	3	5
Connecticut	171	23	68	1	8
More than one state	10	10	60	0	30
NEW ENGLAND	663	25	64	2	9
BY INDUSTRY					
Durable goods	359	21	70	2	7
Lumber products	15	40	53	0	7
Primary metals	27	37	55	0	7
Fabricated metal products	78	27	65	1	6
Furniture	56	20	66	3	11
Stone, clay, and glass	25	20	60	8	12
Machinery products	129	15	78	2	6
Other durables	29	17	83	0	0
Nondurables	304	28	57	2	12
Paper and allied products	44	39	48	0	14
Textiles	87	38	53	2	7
Cotton	21	24	71	5	0
Woolen and worsted	35	57	37	3	3
All other	31	26	58	0	16
Rubber products	14	36	43	7	14
Food products	24	33	46	0	21
Chemicals	26	31	61	4	4
Printing and publishing	20	15	60	0	25
Leather products	43	14	63	5	19
Other nondurables	46	13	74	2	11

Source: Federal Reserve Bank of Boston

quantity and natural quality are high, pollution can reduce the usefulness of New England's water resources for many purposes. New Englanders and their governmental representatives can do little to control the total quantity of the region's water resources, but they can and should exercise some control to see that their value is not reduced by abuses which can result from indifference.

Pollution

While there is ample water in New England as a whole for industrial, municipal, and rural uses, the value of water for these uses depends largely on its quality and presence in the right places at the right time. Both population and industrial activity are most heavily concentrated in the three southern states. These concentrations require enormous quantities of water for municipal and industrial uses. They also produce large amounts of waste which intensify the problem of maintaining the high natural quality of the water. Fortunately, in addition to their own runoff, the southern New England states receive large amounts of the runoff, from the northern states, especially Vermont and New Hampshire. Most of the major rivers of those states drain southward. The added supply raises both water quality and quantity in southern New England.

Since water is abundant, New England's cities and towns have generally been able to segregate and protect their water supplies. Few municipalities depend on rivers or streams for drinking water; most of them have established reservoirs in nearby hilly country and guard them carefully against pollution. In general, they have planned far ahead to meet the steadily growing public demand for water, and they look forward confidently to meeting all anticipated needs. Metropolitan Boston, for example, obtains most of its water through a long aqueduct system from Quabbin Reservoir in the middle of Massachusetts. Many other cities similarly located on rivers have reached out considerable distances to tap sources of high-quality water that do not require treatment before use. In comparison with many large population centers in other parts of the country, which must process river or lake water for drinking purposes, New England is singularly favored.

In general, ample municipal water supplies are available in New England throughout the year. In some parts of Maine, however, there are periodic shortages of drinking water during the summer months, and the infrequent more general drought conditions sometimes require restrictions on water use for short times in other states. During the drought of 1949–50, 44 of the 260 Massachusetts towns with public water supplies experienced shortages that forced some limitations in use. Such conditions are not common and affect but a small part of the region's population when they do occur. *The local shortages are problems that can and should be solved by the communities affected, either individually or in conjunction with neighboring localities.*

Municipal water supplies meet the needs of urban households, businesses, and many industrial users. Other industrial users rely on private sources of water, usually through water rights on a river or stream. The multiplicity of streams throughout the region provides adequate quantities of industrial water for practically all companies.

Manufacturers typically withdraw water from streams as it flows by their plants, use the water, and discharge their liquid wastes downstream. Industrial users normally do not compete with municipalities in New England for the same water, nor do industrial wastes usually affect public water supplies. Municipal wastes dumped in rivers often affect industrial users, however. Other conflicts of interest sometimes exist among different industrial users or between manufacturing use and various nonwithdrawal uses of water such as fishing, bathing, wildlife conservation, and boating.

The Federal Reserve Bank survey indicates that pollution has not yet become a critical region-wide problem for New England's manufacturers, but it has become a matter of serious local concern in many parts of the region. In some areas the seriousness is rapidly increasing.

New England's water was once unsurpassed in quality, and in most parts of the region was soft and clear in its natural state. Growing population and industrialization have resulted in great quantities of municipal, industrial, and farm wastes being dumped into the streams. Sections of some streams are but open sewers and cannot be used for any other purpose, except perhaps for navigation. Others are still suitable for recreation and fishing but unfit for drinking water or industrial use.

The worst pollution occurs in the three southern states. In Connecticut alone, for example, about 200 of the 5,000 miles of stream channels are excessively polluted, and 400 miles are detrimentally polluted. In Rhode Island, stretches of the Blackstone River below Woonsocket and Pawtucket are grossly polluted, as are sections of the Moshassuck River. The coastal sections of most Massachusetts rivers are contaminated, and even inland portions of the Connecticut River suffer serious pollution from industrial wastes and sewage.

Nor are the northern New England states free from pollution. In Maine most major streams show some deterioration. The Androscoggin, Penobscot, and Kennebec are in serious condition. The Presumpscot River is classed as "excessively contaminated" below Westbrook, and the Saco is heavily contaminated below Biddeford and Saco.

The damages from pollution have been great. The majority of New England manufacturers who require water for processing have had to install treatment plants to prepare the water for use. Many who have done this add their own contamination to the water that flows back into the river. The damage to recreational bathing, hunting, and fishing has been extensive. Large shore areas have been contaminated so that shellfish were killed off or rendered unfit for consumption. Small streams have been rendered unfit for watering livestock and for irrigation.

Pollution arises from four major sources: municipal sewage, industrial wastes, farms, and soil erosion. City sewers discharge hundreds of millions of gallons of waste daily, from households, hospitals, hotels, laundries, restaurants, and other businesses. Industries discharge acids, oils, dye wastes, grease, animal and vegetable materials, sawdust, metal shavings, dissolved metals, and toxic materials. Farm waste consists of drainage from all types of livestock, from milk processing, and other refuse. Sediment from soil erosion is another source of pollution, though this is not a serious New England problem except in a few areas.

Industrial wastes are usually the most damaging to water quality. Bacteria in water and in the waste itself "eat up" and decompose the organic wastes in streams. The organic materials turn into nitrites, nitrates, and finally harmless ammonium compounds. Decomposition requires oxygen, however, and removes that needed for further decomposition and for animal life. Fish, shellfish, beneficial insects, and their larvae may be destroyed. Oxygen demand is one of the technician's yardsticks in determining the degree of pollution in any water, in addition to the tests for poisonous or corrosive materials. It has been found that industrial waste of an organic nature usually requires more oxygen for purification than domestic waste. Packinghouse waste, for example, requires about ten times as much oxygen as domestic waste, while tannery waste solids require about two and a half times as much oxygen.

The United States Public Health Service made a preliminary report in 1951 on the status of water pollution in the New England drainage basins.[2] This report was based on information currently available to state pollution control agencies. Since the classification of New England's streams had not yet been completed, many important details will not be available until the Health Service's final report is issued.

The report noted 2,178 sources of pollution in the New England drainage basins, including 1,031 municipal sewer systems and 1,147 factory waste outlets. Despite the reduction of waste by 392 treatment plants (250 municipal and 142 industrial), the untreated waste was still excessive. The report recommended the construction, enlargement, or rebuilding of 692 municipal plants in New England, as well as 671 new industrial treatment plants, 69 enlarged industrial treatment plants, and eight replacements for existing treatment plants. Treatment needs for an additional 303 municipal and 96 industrial sources of pollution were still unascertained. The total cost of recommended projects was estimated at $250,000,000.

Some action has been taken since the release of the report. Of the 1,440 projects recommended, 57 were in the planning or construction stage by mid-1952, and 44 other sources of contamination were under orders from state pollution control agencies to abate pollution. Another 300 or more sources of contamination had been notified by official correspondence to prepare plans to abate pollution or show cause why a hearing should not be held.

Progress in pollution abatement has several handicaps. Municipalities and

2. U.S. Public Health Service, Federal Security Agency, *New England Drainage Basins* (summary report on water pollution), Washington, 1951.

industrial plants have little incentive to initiate expensive treatment projects which primarily benefit the downstream water users. The conflicts among users often cannot be worked out easily without intervention by state or federal agencies. Such agencies have had only limited funds to conduct needed surveys and investigations. Moreover, there have been difficult technical problems in developing suitable methods of treating certain types of industrial wastes, such as those of textile and paper mills.

Long-range planning for reducing pollution has been made possible by recent state and federal legislation. The Taft-Barkley Bill, passed in 1948 by the 80th Congress, instructed the United States Public Health Service to "collect and disseminate information relating to water pollution and the prevention and abatement thereof." Under that law, if pollution in one state affects the public health or welfare of a neighboring state, the United States Surgeon General, with the approval of the state water-pollution control agency, can make investigations, hold public hearings, and institute action in federal courts.

All the states in New England have pollution control legislation in effect. All but Maine are signatory members of the New England Interstate Water Pollution Control Commission, a compact established in 1947 for the control and coordination of antipollution work. Article 5 of the compact gives the commission authority to "establish reasonable physical, chemical and bacteriological standards of water quality satisfactory for various classifications of use." Each signatory state is to "prepare a classification of its interstate waters . . . according to present and proposed highest use" and "to submit its classification . . . to the Commission for approval." After commission approval, the states "will work to establish programs of treatment of sewage and industrial wastes which will meet standards established by the commission for classified water." *While drainage from Maine has only a minor effect on the rivers of the other New England states, it would appear desirable for Maine to join the commission as well as to revise its pollution-control laws.*

The programs to be undertaken by the federal, interstate, and state pollution agencies will take many years to complete, but they will generally employ the following procedure. The first step in a comprehensive antipollution program is to determine the sources and amounts of pollution in each stream. Once the streams are classified, the most suitable use for each stream is determined, because treatment of wastes varies according to the quality of water required by the users. Quality standards are established for each water use. Finally, a program for treatment-plant construction is formulated.

The most difficult and most controversial portion of the antipollution program is undoubtedly the determination of the most suitable use for each stream, lake, or underground reservoir. Industrialists who use streams to dispose of their wastes and who would have to pay for many new treatment plants are likely to demand low-use classifications. Property owners along the banks, especially those holding recreational sites, can be expected to press for higher-use classifications. Many of the conflicting classification demands will be difficult to justify economically, because supporting data will be hard to obtain.

There are also serious problems in determining who is to pay for the hundreds of additional projects. Persons and businesses not located near streams generally resist paying for treatment plants in other towns. Downstream groups complain against paying for treatment plants to purify the water polluted upstream. Upstream groups despair when water is drawn off their lakes to abate pollution downstream. These conflicts of interest are bound to arise.

If the region's water-pollution problems are to be solved speedily, each water user must view his own interests objectively in the light of all conflicting interests. The industrialist must recognize that real estate values decline rapidly as pollution on adjacent streams increases. The property owner must recognize that the industrialist is operating in a competitive market, and that treatment plants increase manufacturing costs and may impair competitive positions. Water conditions represent one of the few physical advantages which New England's manufacturers enjoy in competing with producers in some other regions. All must recognize that useless water is as bad as no water and that all suffer from excessive pollution.

The present extent of water pollution in New England has resulted from the lack of restraint by water users in their pursuit of self-interest over a long period of time. *If those with conflicting interests are not willing to reach amicable solutions themselves, it will be increasingly necessary for the state, interstate, and federal pollution-control agencies to take direct action to achieve the regional goal of restoring water quality, as they have done in recent years. There has been decided progress of late in pollution abatement in many parts of New England, but much more improvement is needed before its streams can achieve adequate levels of purity.*

Flood Control

The threat of floods—which can take human life, wipe out homes, destroy factories, ruin crops, erode farm lands—is not so serious in New England as in some other regions of the country. There have been serious floods in New England's history, nevertheless, especially in the towns on the flood plains of the Connecticut, Merrimack, and other major rivers. The social costs of floods are also great. In the 1936 floods more than 1,600 individuals in the New Hampshire portion of the Merrimack drainage basin alone required rehabilitation, 3,400 experienced special hardships, 10,000 registered for Red Cross aid, and 17,700 received flood emergency aid.

Reports of water conditions in New England's rivers go back many years. Authentic records for the Connecticut are available as far back as the flood of 1639. Records of the Merrimack indicate the presence of flood conditions of greater or lesser intensity fourteen times since 1852. Rhode Island's worst flood was in 1886. In recent times New England's worst floods were in 1927, 1936, and 1938. There has been little loss of life, but total damages over the years have probably approached half a billion dollars.

New Englanders, with aid from federal agencies, have done much to combat the threat from floods. Reservoirs, dams and dykes, channels, and flood warning systems have been installed in numerous river basins throughout the region.

In Connecticut there are flood control installations on the Connecticut River and its tributaries in the Hartford area. There are projects under way on the Shetucket, Natchang, and Mad rivers. Other projects are being considered by the Army Engineers and the state government at Andover Dam on the Hop River and at Thomaston Dam on the Naugatuck River. A comprehensive project is planned for the Housatonic River.

In Maine flood walls have been erected privately at Madison and Rumford on the Kennebec and Swift rivers. There has been further incidental regulation of rivers in the state by reservoirs built for power production.

Massachusetts is protected by constructions at Springfield, West Springfield, Holyoke, Chicopee, and Northampton on the Connecticut River, at Haverhill and Lowell on the Merrimack, and at Fitchburg on the Whitman River. Projects are in progress at Adams and North Adams to control the Hoosic River. Three flood control reservoirs have been built in Massachusetts on tributaries of the Connecticut and Merrimack rivers by the Army Engineers. Fifteen more such projects are planned.

New Hampshire's streams are regulated by power reservoirs and by flood control reservoirs of the Army Engineers. Local protection works are provided on the Merrimack at Nashua by channels, floodways, and dykes.

In Vermont three flood control reservoirs have been built by the Army Engineers in the Winooski basin and one in the Connecticut basin. Six more are to be built in the Connecticut basin. Vermont is also protected in part by power reservoirs.

Rhode Island's swamps, ponds, and reservoirs built for other purposes provide considerable flood protection in that state. A new project has been suggested for the lower Pawtucket basin, but so far it has not been considered economically justified.

The region has benefited considerably from past flood control projects. The Corps of Army Engineers estimates, for example, a two-to-one ratio of benefits to costs for all projects in the Connecticut drainage basin. The estimated cost of past projects in the basin is $39,700,000, of which $34,400,000 was supplied by the Federal Government. Funds raised by the Federal Government through some form of taxation have been used, therefore, to defray seven-eighths of the construction costs. Total estimated annual charges for these projects are about $1,900,000, of which $1,500,000 comes from federal funds. Authorized projects in the Connecticut basin will cost the Federal Government an estimated additional $90,000,000. Other recommended projects would cost about $25,000,000 more.

Existing flood control installations have been of considerable help in minimizing flood damage, but in certain areas much more protection is needed as population and industrial concentration increase on lands subject to overflow. No single kind of protection can meet all situations. A few large single-purpose dams and reservoirs are most economical and effective in controlling major floods. Such large installations disrupt the economic and social lives of upstream residents for the benefit of downstream groups, however, and rich agricultural lands are often flooded and damaged or destroyed. Moreover, a few large dams cannot protect the majority of communities from flash floods, which occur fairly often on the smaller streams in the more mountainous and hilly sections of New England. Protection against flash floods requires many small, local, single- or multipurpose reservoirs.

An "ideal" flood protection system for New England requires a combination of large and small dams on the region's principal rivers and their tributaries. Past developments have been in that direction, and future installations should continue the same pattern. It would be almost impossible, however, to establish a system that would provide complete protection against all flood losses in the region. Runoff conditions vary from basin to basin and from year to year. Peak floods occur at unpredictable intervals, and new peaks can always exceed those recorded in the past. Absolute protection against all conceivable flash or general flood conditions would require an enormous expansion of installations. The downstream damages they prevented would be offset in part by upstream damages they caused. Also, as the installations were expanded, the ratio of costs to benefits would rise steadily until costs exceeded benefits. Costs would include the relocation of highways, buildings, and other facilities, as well as direct construction costs. Accordingly, the level of flood control protection must necessarily be a reasonable compromise which inevitably will be less than 100% effective.

New England's cost-benefit ratios of the past suggest that the status of flood control protection in the region is still less than "ideal." The completion of projected plans throughout the region will improve the situation materially. Further planning will have to weigh carefully the total costs of new projects in relation to their anticipated benefits. The cost-benefit ratio is the best economic measure for appraising a particular project, but the social cost of floods can seldom be determined. *It is impossible to put a price on a lost life or a disrupted home, but among anticipated benefits recognition should be given to social as well as economic benefits.*

To guard against floods which even an "ideal" flood control system cannot handle, flood warning services should be improved. While the warning service of the United States Weather Bureau is fairly adequate in the Connecticut and Merrimack basins, warning systems should also be provided for the Winooski, Androscoggin, Saco, and other drainage basins subject to floods.

With few exceptions, flood control projects are undertaken by governmental bodies. Costs of projects are large, and benefits usually are spread through one or more states. While the states individually or jointly have been accustomed to carrying on flood control activities under present conditions, much of the responsibility for doing something about the flood problem rests on the Federal Government. Under its constitutional authority, Congress has directed the Corps of Army Engineers to supervise the construction and maintenance of flood control projects. The flood control act of 1944 stated that "hereafter, Federal investigations and improvements to rivers and other waterways for flood control and allied purposes shall be under the jurisdiction of the War Department under the Secretary of War and the supervision of the Chief of Engineers." The Army Engineers have made a good start on the work in New England.

In addition to the federal activities, the legislatures and governors of the four New England states in the Connecticut River basin have ratified an interstate flood control compact which Congress approved in June, 1953. Primarily, the purpose is to formulate a means of reimbursing Vermont and New Hampshire for the losses resulting from the taking of land for flood control measures which benefit other states.

Since most flood control projects are financed largely by the Federal Government, their costs are distributed by taxation over the entire country. Those persons located in areas subject to overflow pay through taxation but a small proportion of the bill for their own protection. Those who live in areas free from floods help pay for the protection of others. This is desirable, if the determination of needed projects employs accurate and reasonable criteria of costs and benefits and if the criteria are applied uniformly in all parts of the country.

New England and its people should lend their continuing support to the design and construction of an adequate and fairly conceived flood control program on a national scale. The standards of evaluating proposed projects are of particular importance. In its sharing of the costs through taxation and the benefits through new construction, the region should exercise the same restraint and objectivity that it desires in other parts of the country.

Damaged property, lost lives, and disrupted homes are not the only losses by floods. Floods also waste water. Millions of tons of flood waters race to the sea without being used. The reservoirs and dams that hold back the torrent help in power generation, in "cleaning" polluted streams during periods when water is in shorter supply and in controlling water flow for industrial use. Even a perfect flood control system, nevertheless, would not save all flood waters.

The most important flood problem in New England is the protection of life and property. If shortages of water were forseeable, extreme measures combining flood control and conservation might be justified. But at the present time a continuation of the compromise method followed in the past is clearly indicated.

THE NEW ENGLAND FUEL SITUATION

Consumption of Fuel in New England

Large quantities of fuel are used in New England's homes and businesses, and the total is greatly augmented by the use for automotive purposes. In 1949 the total amount used in homes and businesses was the equivalent of approximately 41,700,000 tons of anthracite coal or 170,000,000 barrels of fuel oil.[3]

CHART 5–2

Fuel Consumption in New England by Types, 1949
(in trillion BTU's)

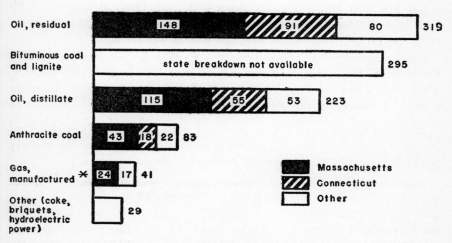

* No natural or mixed gas was used in New England in 1949.
Source: U.S. Bureau of Mines

3. For much of the data contained in this section, the Committee of New England is indebted to a special unpublished report of the U.S. Bureau of Mines, prepared originally for the use of the New England–New York Interagency Committee.

Fuel oils constituted more than half the total, and bituminous coal added another 30%. Most of the rest was anthracite coal and manufactured gas, though the region also consumed some coke, coal briquets, and hydro-electric power for fuel. (See Chart 5–2.) Since 1949 natural gas has entered New England, and in a few years natural or mixed gas should be available in most large centers of population in the region.

In spite of its climate and industrialization New England's consumption of nonautomotive fuels is low in comparison to the national figure. New England's residential, commercial, and industrial consumers used only about 4% of the total United States consumption in 1949, even though the region has over 6% of the nation's population and about 9% of its manu-facturing establishments, and despite the long, cold winters. One reason for this low level of fuel consumption is the high cost of fuel in the region. Industries which require large quantities of fuel in the production process generally do not locate in New England. But even the residential con-sumers burn less fuel than the national average.

Massachusetts accounts for approximately half the region's fuel consump-tion, and Connecticut takes another fourth. A few large categories of use absorb most of the fuel. Manufacturing industries require about a third of the total, and residential and commercial uses for heating and cooking take another third. Electric utilities, gas utilities, and railroads consume most of the rest.

By far the largest consumer of fuel among New England's manufacturing industries in 1947 was the textile industry group, which consumed 81 trillion Btu's. The next largest was the paper and paper-products industry, with 75 trillion Btu's. Other major industrial consumers of fuel in the region were the primary-metals industry (36 trillion Btu's), and the machinery industry (33 trillion Btu's). These four industry groups consumed about two-thirds of the fuel used by manufacturers in New England during 1947.

Sources of New England's Fuel Supply

With the exception of a little peat and some cordwood, New England produces no fuel. It depends primarily upon other regions of the country for its fuel supplies and, to a lesser extent, on foreign countries.

TYPE OF FUEL	DOMESTIC SOURCES	FOREIGN SOURCES	TOTAL
	(thousands of tons)		
Bituminous coal	11,885	40	11,925
Anthracite coal	3,521	*	3,521
Crude petroleum	906	4,218	5,124
Fuel, road, and residual oils	3,986	3,329	7,315
Other refined petroleum products	8,801	28	8,774
TOTAL	29,099	7,558	36,658†

* Less than 500 tons.
† Details may not add to totals because of rounding.

In 1949 a net of 36,658,000 tons of mineral fuels of all types came into the region by water and rail, all but 7,558,000 tons from domestic sources. The net tonnages were divided as indicated in the table on p. 186.[4]

Fuel moves into the region by a variety of types of transportation, depending on the type of fuel shipped and its origin. All but about 5% of the anthracite coal consumed in New England comes from northeastern Pennsylvania, primarily by all-rail transportation. Over half the region's bituminous coal requirements come from Virginia and southern West Virginia. That coal, as well as eastern Kentucky coking coal, moves to New England by water from Hampton Roads, Virginia. Another 38% of the bituminous coal comes from the central Pennsylvania fields by all-rail transportation. The remaining bituminous coal shipments enter New England by combined rail and water movement from northern West Virginia and central Pennsylvania.

The largest supplies of fuel oil move to New England from the Texas Gulf coast ports via water, and the rest comes from Louisiana, Mississippi, and Venezuela. Most of the fuel oil is refined before it reaches New England, although a small percentage is refined in the region. The Esso refinery at Everett, Massachusetts, is the largest in New England, but its capacity of 40,000 barrels a day is small in comparison with refineries in other regions. There are also three still smaller refineries in New England: one owned by Cities Service at East Braintree, Massachusetts, which is now used as a storage dump; and the Socony-Vacuum and Texas Company refineries at East Providence, both of which are operated for asphalt. The total capacity of all four refineries is only about 66,500 barrels a day, which can supply but a small fraction of the New England needs for petroleum products.

Both crude and refined fuel oils arriving in New England are unloaded from tankers at bulk plants at Portland and Searsport, Maine; Portsmouth, New Hampshire; Boston, Quincy, Everett, Braintree, Danversport, and Fall River, Massachusetts; Providence, Rhode Island; Stamford, South Norwalk, Bridgeport, New Haven, New London, Norwich, and Hartford, Connecticut. From the bulk plants, fuel oil is distributed throughout New England by underground pipelines, railroad tank cars, river-plying barges, and tank trucks.[5]

In view of the large New England consumption of petroleum products and the increasing reliance of the United States on foreign crudes, the prospects of establishing a large new refinery in New England within the next few years appear increasingly promising. In addition to a possible lowering of costs, such a facility would help alleviate the shortages of

4. See our report No. 4, "Minerals and New England," for further data on the transportation of mineral fuels into the region.

5. See our report No. 13, "New England's Transportation System and Its Use."

petroleum products which have occasionally occurred in New England and aid in the region's general economic development.[6]

The recent construction of natural gas pipelines into New England has provided another source of fuel. The plan to distribute gas to all large population centers in southern New England and to certain cities in New Hampshire will be of particular benefit to residential users for heating and cooking. It may also supplement other fuels in some commercial and industrial uses. Numerous delays have held up completion of the program, but natural gas deliveries have started in many parts of the region. *Conflicts of interest between the two corporate distributors in the region have interfered with prompt commencement of service throughout all the area to be served.*

The Cost of Fuel in New England

The almost total lack of fuel resources in New England has inevitably raised the delivered prices of most types of fuel above the national average. Transportation charges for fuels are large in relation to their prices at the mine or at the oil or gas fields. Table 5–3 shows how fuel costs varied

Table 5–3. *Fuel Costs in Manufacturing Industries, by Regions, 1947 (cents per million Btu's)*

REGION	FUEL OIL	BITUMI- NOUS COAL	ANTHRA- CITE COAL	COKE	MANUFAC- TURED GAS	NATURAL GAS
Middle Atlantic	48.2¢	24.0¢	23.4¢	40.6¢	46.2¢	34.1¢
East North Central	50.3	22.3	28.8	48.0	40.7	33.1
West North Central	46.2	21.9	22.5	52.0	41.5	16.9
South Atlantic	42.5	24.7	27.7	39.9	32.7	21.6
East South Central	54.7	21.6	27.7	41.5	33.4	17.2
West South Central	43.4	18.8	29.6	55.5	19.4	08.0
Mountain	44.5	20.8	30.1	46.4	22.0	13.7
Pacific	32.4	32.0	36.3	67.6	78.0	21.3
NEW ENGLAND	43.5	37.0	34.8	62.3	100.5	—
UNITED STATES	45.9	23.8	24.9	44.4	43.6	16.2

Source: Leland W. McCloud, *Comparative Costs of Competitive Fuels*, West Virginia University Business and Economic Studies, Vol. 1, No. 4, June 1951 (based on 1947 Census of Manufactures)

in 1947 for manufacturers in the various regions of the nation. While the actual costs have changed since 1947, the general situation is still much the same. Moreover, the pattern of costs for other users is similar to that for manufacturers. Geographical relationships among sources and users is the principal cause of the interregional variation.

The New England cost exceeded the average in every other region for bituminous coal and manufactured gas. It exceeded the average in all but the Pacific region for anthracite coal and coke. New England also did not have the benefit of natural gas, which is typically a low-cost fuel. Fuel oil is the only major fuel for which New England, with its coastal location,

6. See Arthur D. Little, Inc., *A Survey of Industrial Opportunities in New England*, report to the Federal Reserve Bank of Boston (August 1952), pp. 80–86.

has an advantage over a number of other regions. Since fuel oil is cheaper in relation to other fuels in New England than in most other regions, it is used relatively more extensively in this area as an industrial fuel.

While natural gas is cheaper than manufactured gas, even for this type of fuel increased distances from the principal producing fields raise transportation costs sharply. The average cost of natural gas in New England of necessity will remain above that in all other regions of the country, so long as the geographical pattern of supply remains as it is at present, and it will probably remain higher than that of various competing fuels. *Unless the supply of gas piped to New England expands far above that planned at present, natural gas is not likely to have much direct effect on the fuel costs of most New England manufacturers. The importance of natural gas in the region lies primarily in its benefits to residential consumers.*

Despite the higher than average cost of fuel in New England, fuel costs represent a smaller proportion of value added by manufacturing in this region than in the nation as a whole. The New England percentage was only 2.0% in 1947, contrasted with 3.2% for the United States. This low percentage resulted directly from the region's high fuel costs, for New England has not attracted many industries which consume large quantities of fuel. The six largest fuel-consuming industries, in terms of value of product, are these:

	Per Cent
Blast furnaces	36.7
Steel foundries	25.5
Lime	19.0
Cement	15.3
Brick and hollow tile	14.6
Sewer pipe	11.9

Only 0.18% of New England's value added by manufacturing came from these industries in 1947, in contrast to 1.38% for the United States. The New England value added by the six industries was less than 1% of the corresponding national total.

Even though New England industry has adapted itself to the high fuel costs in the region, they represent a disadvantage for manufacturers in the six-state area in competing with producers in most other parts of the country. As we shall see shortly, the higher than average costs of fuel are critical in causing a similar situation for power costs. Since most electric power in the region is produced by fuel-burning steam generating plants, the two conditions go together.

Both fuel and power costs are small proportions of total product value in most of New England's major manufacturing industries, but the differentials can accumulate with other unfavorable cost factors to produce a significant interregional differential in total costs for some producers.

Opportunities for Reductions in Fuel Costs

There is little prospect of immediate or significant decreases in fuel costs that will materially improve New England's competitive position, but there are a number of possibilities that can help to some extent. Electric utilities, manufacturers, railroads, and other large users of fuels are vitally concerned with the problem, and there has been a continuing effort to improve the situation.

The approaches to lower fuel costs fall into these general categories: (1) reductions in cost of extraction, (2) reductions in cost of transportation, (3) substitution of cheaper for more expensive fuels, and (4) increased efficiency in the utilization of fuels. While New England has a large stake in each approach, it is important to remember that improvements in methods which benefit New England usually benefit other parts of the country as well and may not change the region's relative position.

There is continuous research on methods of coal mining and petroleum drilling and recovery. In view of its lack of commercial petroleum and coal deposits, New England cannot easily take a major role in this effort. Nevertheless, manufacturers and research laboratories in the region may be able to make some contribution to improvements in methods of extraction for mineral fuels. Underground gasification of coal has been proposed as one possible method of lower cost extraction of coal, but it has not yet been found commercially practicable. Further research on methods of mining and using the low-grade anthracite coal deposits of southeastern Massachusetts and Rhode Island may in time lead to their commercialization.[7]

Since transportation costs for fuel are high in relation to their value at the point of extraction, the development of cheaper methods of fuel transportation is especially important to New England. New England already uses water transportation of coal and petroleum products extensively, but the region's coastal coal consumers do not receive the same benefits of low rail rates for coal shipped in by combined rail and water transport that its inland consumers obtain from rail-water-rail shipments. *It would appear that the region should press for similarity of rate treatment by the coal-carrying railroads of the Southeast, whether or not there is a second rail haul in New England.*

Other recent experiments in lower cost transportation include long conveyor-belt systems for moving large quantities of coal, and pipelines for the shipment of powdered coal. Each of these has potential applications in New England, and the region's major coal consumers should participate actively in the research and developmental efforts.

Another possible method of reducing transportation costs is to shift to closer sources of fuels. There appears to be little further opportunity for

7. These deposits are discussed in our report No. 4, "Minerals and New England."

New England to reduce its fuel costs in this fashion. The more extensive use of foreign fuels does seem to offer more opportunity for cost reduction, however, especially in conjunction with any new refinery facilities in the region. New England already obtains a sizable proportion of its petroleum products from the Caribbean area, but quota and tariff restrictions have tended to hold down the inflow from that source. *In view of the increased tendency of the United States to import petroleum from abroad, it would appear desirable to reduce import restrictions on these products. New England would be a major beneficiary of such a change, though not the only one.*

The substitution of cheaper fuels in New England offers some opportunities for economies, but most large users are already taking advantage of the substitutability of existing fuels. Coal and oil are used interchangeably by most tidewater steam electric plants and large manufacturers. Railroads in the region have shifted largely to diesel locomotives to take advantage of their economies. Natural gas offers only limited economies to manufacturers and electric utilities, since little of it will be available for nonresidential uses, and transportation costs raise its delivered price in the region close to the price of competing fuels.

The most promising opportunity for the substitution of fuels in New England is the commercialization of nuclear fuels, though their extensive use will probably require many more years of development. The possible impact of nuclear fuels is of such great importance to New England, however, that the region, and its large fuel and power users in particular, should take an active part in the development program. New England is ideally suited to be the site of one of the early experimental plants for the generation of electric power from atomic fuels.

Finally, the impact of high fuel costs can be reduced by economies in use. Improved combustion, heat exchange, conversion of power, and greater use of power all reduce fuel costs per unit of energy produced or consumed. In 1948 New England utilities required 13% more than the United States Btu average to generate a kilowatt-hour of electricity. By 1951 the differential had been reduced to only 2%. Installation of new, efficient, fuel-using equipment was an important step in reducing fuel costs per unit of output. In 1942, 35.6% of all fuel-generated power in New England (excluding Maine) was produced by equipment which required as much as 16,000 or more Btu's per kilowatt-hour of power. By 1952 that proportion had been reduced to 7.1%.

Great technological progress has been made and further progress is possible. However, with today's high construction costs it is generally not economical to replace existing steam plants built in low-cost periods. For stand-by reserve purposes or for generation during peak-load hours, the low fixed charges frequently associated with the low construction costs of existing steam plants more than offset their higher fuel consumption. *New England utilities must constantly weigh increased capital costs against lower operating costs in order to maximize the economic rate of construction of facilities and minimize the operation of obsolete fuel-using equipment.*

NEW ENGLAND'S ELECTRIC POWER SITUATION

A modern industrial society requires an ample, dependable, low-cost electric supply. Electric power has freed industry from its former dependence on direct water power and the other types of power. It provides a flexibility and economy that cannot be obtained from other power sources.

The use of electric power by industrial, commercial, residential, and other consumers has increased phenomenally in the United States during the last half century. Even during periods of recession or depression, demand has expanded steadily. As an established industrial area, New England was an early leader in the development and use of electrical power.

The Availability and Use of Electric Power

As the applications of electricity have grown and been accepted and as its availability and reliability have increased, public interest has shifted gradually from the problems of getting electric power and using it to problems of its cost. This transition has been especially marked in New England. In many parts of the world, and even in some other parts of the United States, power supply is inadequate to meet current demands, either in terms of generation or distribution facilities. Power shortages in the Pacific Northwest, for example, are still fairly frequent. Rural electrification at the end of 1951 was only 86.5% complete in the United States.

In New England, on the other hand, dependable rural electrical service is practically complete. Almost 93% of the region's farms had electric power in 1951. The infrequent power shortages have been limited to some parts of Maine and Vermont, which still depend primarily on hydroelectric power and are subject to occasional periods of low water. These local inadequacies are rapidly being eliminated.

For industrial users and other consumers in almost the entire region, power supplies are sufficient to meet peak demands and are dependable. This fact, while overlooked in some discussions of the New England power situation, is of the utmost importance. New England manufacturers, in expressing their opinions in 1949 to the Federal Reserve Bank of Boston about the competitive aspects of their locations in the region, gave a high rating to the availability and dependability of electric power.[8] Only 22 (3%) of the 663 manufacturers who participated in the study claimed that inadequacy or unreliability of power was an important competitive disadvantage for them.

Since the demand for power is growing steadily in New England, as else-

8. *Op. cit.*

where, electric utilities, government agencies, and others in the region have been concerned chiefly with how the new power is to be supplied, by whom, and by what type of generation. The need for adequacy of supply is taken for granted. The major question and point of controversy is costs. Because New England is a relatively high-rate area, the issue has taken on considerable economic and even greater political significance. Before discussing the question of rates and costs, however, it is important to consider the present electric system of the region and its operation.

At the beginning of 1951 the investment of electric utilities in generating, transmitting, and distributing facilities in the United States was well over $21 billion. It was still expanding rapidly. Investments in New England utilities approached $1.6 billion, about 7.4% of the national total.

During 1952 the electric generators of New England's utility and industrial plants produced 22.1 billion kw-h. of electricity. A little more than three-fourths was produced by thermal generators, principally by steam power. The remaining fourth was generated by the falling water of New England streams. The utility plants which provide power to the public served about 3,230,000 customers in the region and produced about 80% of New England's total electrical power consumption.

The installed capacity of all electric generators in New England at the beginning of 1953 was about 6,000,000 kw., of which over 77% was turned by steam or internal-combustion engines. About three-fourths of the total capacity was operated by privately owned utilities. Industrial concerns owned most of the rest, though municipally owned utilities operated a small amount. Industrial power capacity in New England has been declining gradually in relative importance as manufacturing concerns have shut down uneconomical power plants or put them on a stand-by basis and have switched over to utility supplies. The Federal Government neither owned nor managed any electric generators in New England.

Both capacity and generation have increased rapidly in New England and the United States in recent decades. (Table 5–4.) From 1940 to 1952 the production of electric power by privately owned utilities increased more than 115% in New England, and utility capacity increased about 67%. The rates of expansion were even greater in the nation as a whole, however, because of the more rapid population and industrial growth outside the region and the spreading use of electricity in other parts of the country. New England's share of national capacity and output has declined since 1920, as is to be expected, while the underdeveloped parts of the country have been catching up to New England.

Installed capacity and annual production alone do not give a complete picture of the reliable availability of power, however. Electric power cannot be stored in large quantities. It must be generated as it is required. The demand for electricity fluctuates widely throughout the day, the week, and the year. Capacity must be available to meet the greatest "instantaneous peak demand" during the period. Nor is installed capacity always a measure of dependable capacity. The dependable capacity of a hydroelectric plant, for example, depends on the amount of water available at the time the power is

Table 5–4. *Capacity and Production of Privately Owned Electric Utilities, New England and the United States, 1920–52*

YEAR	INSTALLED CAPACITY ON JANUARY 1 (MILLIONS OF KILOWATTS)			PRODUCTION DURING YEAR (BILLIONS OF KILOWATT-HOURS)		
	NEW ENGLAND	UNITED STATES	NEW ENGLAND AS PER CENT OF UNITED STATES	NEW ENGLAND	UNITED STATES	NEW ENGLAND AS PER CENT OF UNITED STATES
1920	1.1	12.0	9.1	2.5	37.7	6.6
1930	2.5	30.3	8.3	5.6	86.1	6.5
1940	2.7	34.4	7.8	8.4	125.4	6.7
1945	3.1	40.3	7.7	11.5	180.9	6.4
1946	3.1	40.3	7.7	12.0	181.0	6.6
1947	3.3	42.0	7.9	13.0	208.1	6.2
1948	3.4	45.4	7.5	14.0	228.2	6.1
1949	3.8	50.5	7.5	13.9	233.1	6.0
1950	3.9	55.2	7.1	15.8	266.9	5.9
1951	4.1	60.2	6.8	17.1	301.8	5.7
1952	4.5*	64.2†	7.0†	18.1†	322.3†	5.6†

* Preliminary.
† Estimated.
Source: Federal Power Commission

demanded. Because water is not always available in sufficient quantities, dependable capacity is somewhat less than total reported capacity. Areas which depend heavily on hydroelectric generation, such as Maine and the Pacific Northwest, are particularly affected by this condition. *The ratio between dependable capacity and peak demand in 1952 gave New England a reserve position of 13.8%, in contrast to the national reserve of 12.1%.*

Dependable reserve capacity is the difference between dependable capacity and peak demand. In effect, this is the capacity not often utilized but available for a few hours when demand is at its peak or when water conditions are at their worst. In New England utilities have been able to plan their construction of new plants to maintain sufficient dependable reserve capacity. This is of great importance in modern electrical usage.

Despite the adequate supply and general availability of electric power in New England and the longer record of use, average consumption is below the national average. In 1952, for example, the average residential use in New England was only 1,731 kw-h., as compared with 2,130 kw-h. for the entire United States. (Table 5–5.) Average consumption by large commercial and industrial customers of electric utilities was an even smaller proportion (only 67%) of the national average. To a considerable extent, the smaller consumption of power by industrial concerns is a result of the composition of industry and the cost of electric power in New England, as is true for the consumption of fuels. We shall return to this topic shortly.

Table 5–5. *Average Consumption of Electric Power, by Principal Types of Service, New England States and the United States, 1952* (*in kilowatt-hours*)

AREA	RESIDENTIAL	SMALL COMMERCIAL AND INDUSTRIAL	LARGE COMMERCIAL AND INDUSTRIAL
Maine	1,828	6,792	170,145
New Hampshire	1,748	6,016	731,748
Vermont	1,907	9,064	898,936
Massachusetts	1,538	5,941	483,964
Rhode Island	1,407	6,281	486,052
Connecticut	2,205	9,375	452,779
NEW ENGLAND	1,731	6,921	419,594
UNITED STATES	2,130	11,019	652,992

Source: Edison Electric Institute

The Electric Power System of New England

As the electric generating capacity of New England grows to provide for the expanding population and business, attention is turning increasingly to possibilities for maintaining adequacy of supply while reducing the costs of producing power. This is a difficult problem. It involves the complex theories of electric generation and distribution as well as costs of construction, fuels, and operation. This section discusses some of the important considerations involved in meeting New England's future power needs.

Individual Electric Systems: Most large electric utilities in New England have several generating plants. In many instances part of the capacity is hydroelectric and part is thermal electric. The problems of deciding which type of plant to construct when expanding and how to use the various plants in conjunction with each other are complex.

In the years before 1935 hydroelectric generation capacity fluctuated between 23% and 31% of all installed capacity in New England. Since 1935 the trend has been gradually toward an increasing proportion of steam generation. More than three-fourths of the region's generating capacity is now in steam plants. In some of the less developed regions of the country, water power is still the predominant type of generation. As a region becomes more industrialized and as the demand for electric power rises, however, it is normal to depend increasingly on steam generators.

There are a number of reasons for the shift from hydro to steam. One major reason is that economic sites for locating plants were first put to use before the advent of electricity. The best sites naturally were developed first and converted to electric power generation first. In New England, as a result, hydroelectric development has been more intensive than in any comparable region. While from an engineering point of view there is still considerable undeveloped power potential in New England's rivers, there are important limitations on the economic feasibility of many of the sites.

In spite of a widespread public belief to the contrary, water power is not always cheaper than steam power. While the operating costs of hydroelectric generation are much lower than those for steam generation, the capital costs of a hydroelectric project are usually much higher than for a steam plant of equivalent capacity. Furthermore, hydroelectric plants frequently must be located at great distances from load centers, involving costly transmission systems and transmission losses. Cost comparisons between hydro- and steam-generated power must take into consideration both the operating expenses and the capital and other fixed charges, as well as probable trends in future expenses and demand.

There have been conflicting forces at work on the comparative costs of steam and hydroelectric generation. *Economies in the use of fuels and the efficiency of steam-plant operation have reduced the amount of coal required to produce a kilowatt-hour of electricity from four pounds in 1902 to 0.7 pound in a modern plant. However, the generation of power from steam is still relatively inefficient compared to the 90% efficiency of hydroelectric generators, and there is a greater potential for further improvement in steam plants than in hydro plants. Each of these factors has encouraged the shift from hydro to steam, but the most important reason is that hydro plants cannot be depended upon for full capacity at times of low water.*

Since the cost of hydroelectric-plant construction includes the costs of land damages and relocation of facilities, the steady growth of the population and industrialization of New England's river valleys has caused some hydro sites, otherwise economically feasible, to become too expensive for development. This is true particularly of the lower reaches of New England rivers in all states except Maine. Yet the major load centers are located in such areas. Sites on the upper reaches of the rivers, particularly in Maine, are more feasible for construction of hydroelectric plants, but they are handicapped competitively by being far removed from the larger markets.

On the other hand, the large increases in fuel prices during recent years have tended to stimulate renewed interest in hydroelectric developments. Since most costs of hydroelectric generation are fixed, there is an incentive during inflationary periods to avoid the risk of further increases in fuel prices by building new hydroelectric facilities. Improved construction techniques have also made some hydroelectric sites feasible which once were turned down for various reasons. Moreover, growing regional markets and the rise of new load centers increase the attractiveness of sites which were once thought too far from the markets. In fact, the availability of the undeveloped power sometimes serves to attract potential users.

It is difficult to generalize about cost comparisons between new steam and hydroelectric plants in New England. Too many factors affecting the situation are applicable only to individual cases. *Each set of alternatives must be appraised in light of the particular conditions and the needs of the system which is adding the capacity.*

One factor which encourages the addition of more hydroelectric capacity, sometimes even at a higher unit production cost than steam, is the need to obtain additional peaking capacity. Steam and hydro plants complement each other to a considerable extent. It takes several hours for a modern steam turbine, starting cold, to get warmed up and put into full production. Because of this time lag, sudden unexpected increase in demand for electricity might cause trouble unless electricity could be purchased from another system, or unless steam turbines had previously been warmed up and were idling. A hydroelectric plant is not subject to a time lag of this sort. It has flexibility and an ease of starting which makes it admirably suited for short-period use at times of peak demand. In addition, hydroelectric power can be used to carry the base load during wet periods when stream flow is large and storage capacity is limited.

Another factor in the development of hydroelectric power is public pressure. Some persons believe that water is a God-given gift and that none should be wasted, almost regardless of the cost of its use. This group has pushed hard for the development of all hydroelectric potentials that are feasible from the engineering view, primarily through governmental action. *An alert public that keeps its interests before the public utilities is highly desirable, but indiscriminate public pressure for hydroelectric development without a full understanding of the complexities of generation, transmission, distribution, serves no useful purpose.*

Intersystem Connections. Sometimes a utility cannot meet all the power demand of its consumers because of unexpected breakdowns or insufficient generating capacity. Under such circumstances, if the utility is properly interconnected with others it can purchase power at any time from another system. Furthermore, it may be to the financial advantage of both buyer and seller to handle a portion of regular or peak requirements in this manner, thereby making use of generating plants of the highest available efficiency.

Physical interconnections among two or more utility systems permit such purchases and sales to meet emergencies and to pool the generating capacity of a large area for most efficient use. The major utilities throughout New England are interconnected, with the exception of the systems in the state of Maine. Maine has an emergency connection with the rest of New England, but it is not used for interchanges on a regular basis. The other five states are also partially interconnected with the systems in the eastern seaboard area extending south to Washington, D.C. *Interconnection is a major factor in holding down power rates for two primary reasons: it reduces the necessary investment in production facilities and it reduces actual production expenses.*

There are at least three important ways in which investment in production facilities can be reduced through interconnections:

First, if the instantaneous peak loads of two or more utility systems do not coincide, a smaller total dependable capacity is needed if the systems are interconnected than if they are operated in isolation. The saving in required generating capacity is equal to the difference between the sum of the individual system peaks and the peak of the combined systems. For example, if three systems have peaks of 240,000 kw., 300,000 kw., and 265,000 kw., they would require dependable capacity of 805,000 kw. in isolation, plus reserves. If the interconnected systems had a peak load of 755,000 kw., however, only this amount of dependable capacity plus reserves would be needed, resulting in a saving of at least 50,000 kw. of capacity with equally reliable service.

Second, the necessary amount of reserve capacity is lower in an interconnected system than in a number of isolated systems. Most small utilities maintain a minimum reserve capacity sufficient to replace the largest generating unit in the system. This largest unit may be a large portion of the total capacity of an isolated system.

Third, savings in investment are possible through "staggering" construction programs to meet future needs. A system in isolation can meet annual growth requirements either by adding small units approximately equal to the expected annual load growth or by installing more efficient large units less frequently and waiting for the load increase to build up to that capacity. Both methods are uneconomical. Where two or more systems are interconnected, they can stagger construction to make possible the building of large plants along with more complete utilization.

Interconnection also produces savings in operating costs, primarily because the larger units it makes possible permit economies of large-scale operation. In addition, in interconnected systems the least efficient stand-by plants are required less frequently to meet peak demands.

In general, New England's public utilities have integrated their capacity expansion programs, transmission systems, and day-to-day operations to raise the level of their efficiency to high standards. According to the Electric Coordinating Council of New England, the last large isolated system in Massachusetts, New Bedford, is now interconnected with the other Massachusetts utilities. The small-capacity connection between southern Connecticut and the New England system has also been enlarged.[9]

The one major gap in the intra-New England connection is the state of Maine. Under the Fernald Act of 1909, Maine utilities may not export hydroelectric power. The state contains the majority of New England's undeveloped hydroelectric capacity, however, and its existing developed water power provides the bulk of Maine's requirements at rates lower than the

9. Electric Coordinating Council of New England, *Power Supply and Load for New England—Past, Present and Future,* Boston, 1952.

New England average. The original intent of the Fernald law was apparently to attract industry to Maine by keeping power within the state. It does not appear that the anticipated results have been obtained, for Maine's industrial development has not been appreciably faster than that of New Hampshire. Indeed, Maine's heavy dependence on hydroelectric capacity may have been something of a handicap in industrial development. There has not been enough steam-plant capacity to complement the variable hydro generation. A few years ago a severe summer drought caused a critical shortage of electric power. The Navy had to rush a floating steam generating plant to Portland to meet the emergency. Now Maine's utilities are adding steam capacity to provide a better balance, despite the many undeveloped hydroelectric sites.

It appears that both Maine and the rest of New England would benefit from repeal of the Fernald Act and full interconnection into a New England-wide grid. While the quantity of hydroelectric power that could be exported from Maine might be small for some years, the greater efficiency in planning and operation should reward both parts of New England with the cost reductions possible through interconnection and Maine would be able to obtain a more dependable power supply. Interconnection would bring the Maine utilities under the regulation of the Federal Power Commission, however, since they would be operating across state lines. *The Maine utilities are apparently reluctant to accept such control with its attendant increased administrative expense, but it would seem to be in the interests of both the state of Maine and the rest of the region for them to do so.*

A more extreme step might even be desirable for New England. The small size of the region, its closely knit economic ties, and the need for power integration might produce even greater efficiency if all New England were served by a single power company. While the complex ramifications of such a merger preclude a definite recommendation of this sort, the idea deserves careful study to determine what additional economies, if any, it might bring.

Industrial Power Rates and Costs

Electric power rates have been the focus of considerable attention and controversy in New England during recent years. Much of the argument has rested on emotional and political premises rather than economic reasoning. It is important to view power rates and costs in their proper perspective in evaluating the New England situation.

Role of Power in Manufacturing Costs and Industrial Location. Electric power is a small but important element in the manufacturing operations of most industrial companies. For some companies, it is a major item. The availability and reliability of the necessary quantities of power are of paramount importance to successful manufacturing. The cost of that power is of secondary importance for many companies, but it is rarely unimportant.

Power costs are similar to certain other types of costs, such as fuel costs, state and local tax costs, and transportation costs, in that for most companies they represent but a small percentage of total costs and they vary considerably among different geographical areas. In 1947, the latest year for which census information is available, power costs represented only 1.86% of the value added by manufacture in New England.[10] The comparable national figure was 1.70%. These proportions were only about half as large as they had been in 1936, since power rates did not change appreciably over the period and many other costs rose substantially. Since 1947 power rates have risen somewhat, but most other prices and costs have risen more rapidly. Accordingly, power costs are at present an even smaller proportion of value added by manufacture than they were in 1947.

Wages and salaries constitute the largest single item in value added by manufacture, and purchased materials and supplies represent an even larger proportion of the total value of manufactured products. A 1% increase in labor costs would roughly equal a 16% increase in power costs in all industry as a whole, and a 1% increase in material costs is comparable to a 38% increase in power costs.

These low ratios of power costs, nevertheless, are not characteristic of all industries. The variations are rather large. While power costs represented only 0.5% of value added by manufacture in New England's apparel industry in 1947, they were 5.5% of the value added in the region's paper industry. Power costs are also of substantial importance in the primary-metals, textile, chemicals, stone, clay, and glass, and rubber industries. In some branches of the primary-metal and chemical industries which rely on electrolytic processes, power costs are a dominant item.

As we shall see shortly, power rates and costs in New England are above the national average. Industries which require large quantities of low-cost power have been slow to expand in the region or are not present at all, with the exception of the paper industry in the northern part of New England, where sufficient hydroelectric power was developed in a period of much lower construction costs. Other industries have tended to adapt their product lines and production processes to avoid those that require unusually large quantities of power.

The higher than average power rates and costs in New England as a whole have undoubtedly had some effect on the industrial development, though less than is asserted by some of the region's internal and external critics. *The principal way high power costs have been felt has been in their*

10. Value added by manufacture is a measure of the increment in value of product created by the manufacturing process. It excludes the value of purchased materials and supplies, containers, fuel, and purchased power.

influence on the location decisions of certain types of new manufacturing establishments and in the rates of expansion of some existing establishments. While power costs are usually a minor factor in a location or expansion decision, there are situations where they are not. In such situations, the above-average rate areas of New England have without question lost plants they otherwise might have obtained. Even there, however, the decisions have normally rested on an evaluation of many complex factors, not power costs alone.

CHART 5-3

Price of Purchased Industrial Power* in Large Cities in New England†
and Some Competing States, January 1, 1952

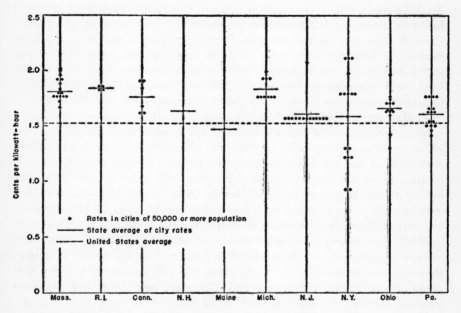

* Based on published data for 200,000 kw-h. monthly consumption with a maximum demand of 1,000 kw.
† Vermont has no large cities.
Source: Federal Power Commission

So far as the relocation of existing manufacturing plants is concerned, it appears that power costs alone are rarely an important factor. The costs of moving a plant are so great that even elimination of power costs would represent but a minor offsetting item. In New England, the out-migration of some companies and the in-migration of others have resulted from relative differences in the combination of all costs, in which power costs have been just a small fraction.

In brief, power costs are of major importance in industrial growth for only a handful of industries, and in the rest they play a small but occasionally significant role along with other cost elements. While they should not be ignored or glossed over as a factor in the economic state of New England, neither should they be given excessive blame for depressed economic conditions in a specific industry or community or held out as *the* key to future industrial development. Lower power costs in many parts of New England in relation to those elsewhere would be helpful, and the region should continue to work toward such a goal, but New Englanders should conceive this task as but one rather small phase of a many-pronged approach to the economic problems and opportunities of the region.

Industrial Power Rates in New England. Power rates can vary considerably from city to city, even within a geographical region or state. In the New England states, which are small in size and closely interconnected, the rates for most cities are fairly similar, yet there are some striking differences. Chart 5–3 presents the rate situation for one category of industrial use as of January 1, 1952, for large cities in New England and certain competing states. The chart shows average rates for monthly consumption of 200,000 kw-h. with a maximum demand of 1,000 kw. The situation is fairly characteristic of the pattern for other categories of consumption and demand.

As the chart indicates, the New England rates are in most instances somewhat above the United States average of city rates, though the difference is not as great as some persons may believe. Moreover, in most New England states at least one city has rates below the national average for this category of use. There are large cities in the region which have rates below the lowest of any large city in Pennsylvania, New Jersey, Michigan, Indiana, and Mississippi, to mention only a few. The lowest rates in Massachusetts are only slightly above the lows in North Carolina and South Carolina.

While these examples were selected to show that the New England rates are not uniformly above those elsewhere, other examples would, of course, show the reverse situation for many cities. Rates in subsidized public power areas of the Pacific Northwest and Tennessee are about half those in southern New England and are well below those in northern New England. Other southern and far western states also have very low rates. Of greater importance than the selected illustrations, nevertheless, is the fact that the average level of industrial power rates in New England is not far above that in the other states of the industrial northeast.

The relative gap between New England's industrial power rates and those in the country as a whole has narrowed somewhat in recent years. In 1950 the cost of power to the average large industrial customer in New England's large cities was 14.9% above the United States average. (See Table 5–6.) By 1953 that gap had narrowed to 13.2%. Similar relative improvements were made in the cost of power to smaller industrial users. *The weighted New England average industrial rate is at present roughly 12% higher than the weighted national industrial rate.*

Commercial and residential power rates in New England have not shown the same relative improvements. Table 5–6 shows that, with the exception of residential rates in small cities, the differentials in power cost between New England and the United States average have been widening in the three-year period, January 1, 1950 to January 1, 1953.

Table 5–6. Comparisons of "Typical Bills" for Electricity, New England vs. United States

		PER CENT BY WHICH NEW ENGLAND EXCEEDS UNITED STATES		
KILOWATT-HOURS		JAN. 1, 1950	JAN. 1, 1951	JAN. 1, 1952	JAN. 1, 1953
Residential (cities of 2,500 and more population)					
25		13.8%	14.0%	14.6%	FPC report
100		14.6	14.4	14.4	not avail-
250		18.6	18.5	18.6	able as of
					Oct. 9, 1953
Residential (cities of 50,000 and more population)					
25		12.9%	12.9%	13.7%	11.7%
100		15.9	16.3	16.5	16.8
250		21.0	21.6	21.6	21.3
500		13.5	14.5	14.5	14.8

MAXIMUM DEMAND (KILOWATTS)	MONTHLY CONSUMPTION (KILOWATT-HOURS)				
Commercial light (cities of 50,000 and more population)					
.75	50	19.1%	20.5%	20.0%	20.6%
3.0	375	29.0	28.8	28.6	31.0
6.0	750	27.2	28.6	28.5	32.4
Commercial power (cities of 50,000 and more population)					
3.0	375	24.4%	25.2%	25.1%	26.6%
12.0	1,500	13.6	16.8	16.1	21.2
30.0	6,000	6.3	8.5	9.4	10.9
Industrial (cities of 50,000 and more population)					
150	30,000	8.2%	8.8%	10.1%	7.0%
300	60,000	11.1	11.7	13.1	9.0
1,000	200,000	14.9	15.2	17.2	13.2

Source: Federal Power Commission

Power Costs and the Opinions of Manufacturers. Although rates are basic, they are not the only determining factor in the purchaser's cost of power per kilowatt-hour. The unit charge to a customer declines as his load factor consumption increases.[11] A large user of power or a high load factor customer may have a lower unit cost than another user despite a higher rate structure.

On the average, New England manufacturers are smaller users of power than manufacturers in the country as a whole. As Table 5–7 indicates, in

11. The term "load factor" refers to the relation between a customer's average power use per hour and his maximum use of power during the billing period.

1947 only in Maine did the average manufacturing establishment consume more than the national annual average of 585,000 kw-h. The Maine average was heavily influenced by its numerous large paper and textile mills. If they were available, more recent data would undoubtedly show the same general situation. It is evident that the structure of industry is an important determinant of power use, since the average consumption of New York State was well under that for New England.

Table 5–8 shows the variations in consumption of power by industry group in 1947. New England's manufacturers were smaller users of power than their counterparts in the rest of the nation in 14 of the 20 major manufacturing groups, though the variations from industry to industry were rather large.

Table 5–7. Consumption of Electric Power by Manufacturers in New England and Some Competing States, 1947 (thousands of kilowatt-hours)

STATE OR REGION	CONSUMPTION PER ESTABLISHMENT
UNITED STATES	585
NEW ENGLAND	427
Maine	1,043
New Hampshire	514
Vermont	248
Massachusetts	347
Rhode Island	312
Connecticut	469
New Jersey	440
Michigan	880
Ohio	1,012
Pennsylvania	773
New York	282
North Carolina	676
Tennessee	1,676

Source: Census of Manufactures, 1947

The lower average consumption of power by New England manufacturers has several causes. The size of plants is one element. While New England has a larger than national proportion of middle-sized plants, it lacks the number of industrial giants that pulls up the average in some other regions. Furthermore, the larger plants tend to operate at higher load factors, which further increases the differential in use. Above-average power rates in most parts of the region have also been a factor, as some manufacturers have held down their use of power for cost reasons. An additional important factor has been the greater average age of New England industry. The larger proportions of older plant and equipment tend to hold down average power consumption, in contrast to areas where industrial plant and machinery are newer. New plants and machinery are increasingly designed for greater utilization of electric and mechanical power relative to human energy. As an older industrial area which has departed more slowly from traditional methods of plant layout, work flows, and other methods of factory operation,

New England industry has been slower on the whole to step up its use of electric energy. Insofar as it has any effect, the influence of relatively high electric rates is in the direction of holding back plant modernization.

The combination of a somewhat higher average rate structure and lower load factor and average consumption per establishment produces a rather substantial excess of the average cost of electric power to New England manufacturers over the national average. According to a study by the Federal Reserve Bank of Boston, in 1947 the average of costs per kilowatt-hour was 42% higher for New England industry as a whole than for all industry in the United States, after adjustment for variations in the composition of industry between the two areas.[12] It is apparent that differences in composition are an important element in the over-all power-cost situation,

Table 5-8. Consumption of Electric Power in New England and the United States by Major Industries, 1947
(thousands of kilowatt-hours)

INDUSTRY GROUP	CONSUMPTION PER ESTABLISHMENT		N.E. AS PER CENT OF U.S.
	UNITED STATES	NEW ENGLAND	
Food	255	136	53
Tobacco	202	8	4
Textile	1,227	1,358	111
Apparel	27	32	119
Lumber	89	59	66
Furniture	107	63	59
Paper	3,750	3,890	104
Printing and publishing	44	41	93
Chemical	1,947	528	27
Petroleum and coal	4,685	1,388	30
Rubber	3,937	2,413	61
Leather and products	108	127	118
Stone, clay, and glass	678	232	34
Primary metals	7,579	1,470	19
Fabricated metals	233	208	89
Machinery	331	364	110
Electrical equipment	910	1,112	122
Transportation equipment	1,633	730	45
Instruments	210	253	120
Miscellaneous	79	152	192
ALL INDUSTRIES	585	427	73

Source: Ibid.

since the New England excess without this adjustment was 61%. It must be emphasized that these differentials are due to the manner in which the industries utilize their power. If New England industries increased their power use to the national level by increased hours of operation and further electrification, the differential in average cost per kilowatt-hour would reduce to the differential in industrial rate levels or about 12%.

The figures in Table 5-9 were derived from the census data, which are now nearly seven years old. The percentage variations might be slightly

12. "Industrial Power Costs in New England," Monthly Review, June 1950.

more favorable for New England today, but it is probably still true that
the average cost of electricity per kilowatt-hour consumed is higher in New
England than the United States average in every major industry group
except apparel. The estimated unit cost of power consumed by each major
industry in the United States and in New England is shown in Table 5-9.

Table 5-9. Power Costs in New England and the United States, by Industries, 1947
(cents per kilowatt-hour consumed)

INDUSTRY GROUP	NEW ENGLAND	UNITED STATES	N.E. AS PER CENT OF U.S.
Apparel	2.44¢	2.45¢	100
Miscellaneous	1.80	1.67	108
Leather and products	2.13	1.85	115
Paper	0.96	0.82	117
Machinery	1.62	1.33	122
Printing and publishing	2.33	1.90	123
Fabricated metals	1.85	1.47	126
Instruments	1.77	1.41	126
Transportation equipment	1.43	1.08	132
Electrical equipment	1.48	1.09	136
Food	1.74	1.28	136
Furniture	2.27	1.62	140
Textile	1.44	1.00	144
Rubber	1.30	0.90	144
Lumber	1.95	1.26	155
Stone, clay and glass	1.55	0.90	172
Chemical	1.35	0.70	193
Primary metals	1.45	0.60	242

Source: Federal Reserve Bank of Boston, "Industrial Power Costs in New England," *Monthly
Review,* June 1950 (estimated from Census of Manufactures, 1947)

The greatest differentials existed for primary metals and chemicals, but
they were also high for stone, clay, glass, and lumber products. Paradoxically, in only three cases was the differential for an industry group greater
than the unadjusted differential for all manufacturing, and in only six cases
was it greater than the adjusted differential. This apparent contradiction is
due to the structure of industry in New England compared to that in the
rest of the United States.

How do manufacturers appraise the effects of these power rates and costs
on their competitive situation? The opinions of 663 manufacturers on this
subject were expressed in a 1949 questionnaire survey on "The Present Position and Prospects for New England Manufacturers." [13] Of the executives
who expressed opinions about the effects of their power costs on their
competitive positions, 14% felt that power costs provided their concerns
with an important advantage over their competitors outside New England,
60% felt they were of little competitive importance to them, and 26% believed them an important competitive disadvantage. At most, therefore,
about a fourth of New England's manufacturing concerns feel that they are
unfavorably affected to a significant extent by the region's higher than

13. *Op. cit.*

average power rates, and even this may be a little high, for further information received by the Federal Reserve Bank of Boston suggests that some of the claims of injury may have been somewhat exaggerated. On the other hand, about a seventh of New England manufacturers evidently benefit competitively from the present situation.

As Tables 5–10 and 5–11 indicate, the situation varies from state to state and from industry to industry. In general, while more firms in each category reported a disadvantage than an advantage, the proportion which reported that power costs were a disadvantage was usually substantially below a third.

As we noted previously, the same survey also explored the effects of availability and dependability of power in New England on competitive position. Only 3% of the respondents felt that their firms were handicapped by inadequate power supplies, while 34% stated that adequacy of power supply was a definite competitive advantage to them over competitors outside New England.

The opinions on power costs substantiate what has been stated earlier in this section about the effects of power cost on industrial development and industrial location. *Power rates and costs are not a universal problem in New England, but they do affect individual industries, companies, and localities. Taken alone, they represent a small competitive obstacle for the New England economy as a whole.*

Table 5–10. Opinions of New England Manufacturers about Power Costs, by State, 1949

PERCENTAGES OF COMPANIES REPORTING POWER COSTS AS

STATE	NUMBER OF COMPANIES	IMPORTANT COMPETITIVE ADVANTAGE	IMPORTANT COMPETITIVE DISADVANTAGE	OF LITTLE COMPETITIVE IMPORTANCE	NO OPINION EXPRESSED
Maine	35	23	20	43	14
New Hampshire	72	11	29	50	10
Vermont	46	24	37	37	2
Massachusetts	291	11	25.5	54.5	9
Rhode Island	38	11	26	58	5
Connecticut	171	15	14	64	7
Plants in more than one state	10	—	30	60	10
NEW ENGLAND	663	13	24	55	8

Source: Ibid.

The Cost of Producing Power in New England

Why are power rates higher, on the average, in New England? The simplest answer is that higher costs necessitate higher charges. But such a simple answer merely serves to direct attention to the major categories of cost in an effort to determine why they are higher. Tables 5–11 and 5–12 present a selection of methods by which we may appraise the operating experiences of the larger privately owned utilities in New England and the United States.

Higher profit rates are not a cause of the higher electric rates in New England, though we also note that high costs have not materially reduced the profit rate on sales in the region. In the United States utilities, 20.66 cents of every dollar of electric operating revenue became net operating revenue in 1952, but the net revenue share in New England was only 19.16 cents of each revenue dollar. Also, New England utilities earned only 5.85% on their net plant investment in comparison with a return of 5.97% by United States utilities during 1952. Although profit rates in relation to investment are not high in New England, earnings in relation to kilowatt-hour sales are 26% above the national average. This is a reflection of much higher average investment in relation to generating capacity in New England.

As we examine the reasons for higher electric rates in New England, we should remember that rates of return on investment in New England utilities must be established by the regulating commission at levels high enough to attract the new investment funds constantly needed for expansion and improvement of service. It does not appear that earnings and rates of return on electric utility investment in New England have been excessive. It is possible, however, that more effective operations and better equipment might reduce the 26% differential between New England and United States utilities in earnings per kilowatt-hour of sales.

It is a common practice to compare the revenues and expenses of utilities on a kilowatt-hour of total sales basis. Unfortunately, that basis is unsound. In New England, about 33% of total kilowatt-hour sales are sales by one utility to another as power is generated by one company and sold to another for resale. In the United States, the comparable proportion is only 15%. The comparisons presented in columns 1 to 3 of Table 5–12 endeavor to eliminate this objection. Revenues and expenses have been expressed on a basis of total kilowatt-hour sales, excluding sales to other private utilities. Cost of power purchased from private utilities and revenues from sale of power to private utilities have both been excluded. In deriving comparable 1952 estimates for the United States, it has been necessary to use 1949 relationships in estimating both the costs and revenues to be excluded and the number of kilowatt-hours generated by private utilities but sold to cooperatives or governmentally owned systems. The value of the comparisons rests not in their detailed accuracy but in the general relationships revealed.

Another drawback in using kilowatt-hours of sales as a basis of comparison is that power costs vary as a result of differences in requirements and use of power, quite aside from differences in the technical characteristics and operations of the utility facilities. Different patterns of power use cause differences in cost of power, irrespective of the system that produces the power. A utility system that sells power to many small power users who

Table 5-11. Revenues and Expenses for Class A and B Utilities in New England and United States, 1952

	TOTAL OPERATING REVENUES AND EXPENSES			EXPENSES BY CATEGORY AS A PER CENT OF TOTAL DEDUCTIONS		
	N.E.	U.S.	PER CENT	N.E. PER CENT	U.S. PER CENT	DIFFERENCE
Electric operating revenues* (thousands of dollars)	400,061	5,333,154	7.5			
Operating expenses (thousands of dollars)						
Fuel	71,898	906,178	7.8	22.23	21.41	.82
Other production expenses* (including purchased power)	31,515	374,348	8.4	9.75	8.85	.90
Total production expense*	103,413	1,280,526	8.1	31.98	30.26	1.72
Transmission expenses	5,921	94,793	6.3	1.83	2.24	(.39)
Distribution expenses	35,902	494,086	7.3	11.10	11.68	(.58)
Customer accounting and collecting	15,102	184,901	8.2	4.67	4.37	.30
Sales promotion	6,061	92,014	6.6	1.87	2.17	(.30)
Administration and general	31,816	365,785	8.7	9.84	8.64	1.20
Total operating expenses*	198,215	2,512,105	7.9	61.29	59.36	1.93
Depreciation	35,456	508,039	7.0	10.96	12.01	(1.05)
Taxes	89,733	1,211,429	7.4	27.75	28.63	(.88)
Total deductions*	323,404	4,231,573	7.6	100.00	100.00	—
Net operating revenue†	76,657	1,101,581	7.0			
Kilowatt-hour sales (thousands)	16,004,672	291,705,023	5.5			
Kilowatts dependable capacity	4,408,849	70,280,836	6.3			
Kilowatts peak load	3,871,996	62,681,979	6.2			
Net electric plant investment (thousands of dollars)	1,310,753	18,441,970	7.1			
Number of customers	2,910,661	37,855,546	7.7			

* Operating revenues, production expenses, and kilowatt-hour sales have been adjusted to exclude the effects of intercompany purchase and sale of electric power. Adjustment of the United States data was based on 1949 relationships between power purchased and sold by private utilities in dealing with municipal and government utilities and with cooperatives.

† Net operating revenue is calculated by subtracting "total deductions" from "electric operating revenues."

Source: Calculated from Federal Power Commission

Table 5-12. Operating Ratios for Class A and B Utilities in New England and United States, 1952

REVENUES AND EXPENSES

	PER KILOWATT-HOUR OF SALES			PER DOLLAR OF NET PLANT INVESTMENT			PER DOLLAR OF TOTAL ELEC. OP. REVENUES			PER CUSTOMER		
	(1) N.E. CENTS	(2) U.S. CENTS	(3) DIFF. CENTS	(4) N.E. CENTS	(5) U.S. CENTS	(6) DIFF. CENTS	(7) N.E. CENTS	(8) U.S. CENTS	(9) DIFF. CENTS	(10) N.E. DOL.	(11) U.S. DOL.	(12) DIFF. DOL.
Electric operating revenues* (thousands of dollars)	2.50	1.83	.67	30.52	28.92	1.60	100.00	100.00	—	137.45	140.88	(3.43)
Operating expenses* (thousands of dollars)												
Fuel	.45	.31	.14	5.48	4.91	.57	17.97	16.99	.98	24.70	23.94	.76
Other production expenses* (including purchased power)	.19	.13	.06	2.41	2.03	.38	7.88	7.02	.86	10.83	9.89	.94
Total production expense*	.65	.44	.21	7.89	6.94	.95	25.85	24.01	1.84	35.53	33.83	1.70
Transmission expenses	.04	.03	.01	.45	.52	(.07)	1.48	1.78	(.30)	2.03	2.50	(.47)
Distribution expenses	.22	.17	.05	2.74	2.68	.06	8.97	9.26	(.29)	12.34	13.05	(.71)
Customer accounting and collecting	.09	.06	.03	1.15	1.00	.15	3.78	3.47	.31	5.19	4.89	.30
Sales promotion	.04	.03	.01	.46	.50	(.04)	1.52	1.72	(.20)	2.08	2.43	(.35)
Administration and general	.20	.13	.07	2.43	1.98	.45	7.95	6.86	1.09	10.93	9.66	1.27
Total operating expenses*	1.24	.86	.38	15.12	13.62	1.50	49.55	47.10	2.45	68.10	66.36	1.74
Depreciation	.22	.17	.05	2.70	2.76	(.06)	8.86	9.53	(.67)	12.18	13.42	(1.24)
Taxes	.56	.42	.14	6.85	6.57	.28	22.43	22.71	(.28)	30.83	32.00	(1.17)
Total deductions*	2.02	1.45	.57	24.67	22.95	1.72	80.84	79.34	1.50	111.11	111.78	(.67)
Net operating revenue†	.48	.38	.10	5.85	5.97	(.12)	19.16	20.66	(1.50)	26.34	29.10	(2.76)

* Operating revenues, production expenses, and kilowatt-hour sales have been adjusted to exclude the effects of intercompany purchase and sale of electric power. Adjustment of the United States data was based on 1949 relationships between power purchased and sold by private utilities in dealing with municipal and government utilities and with cooperatives.

† Net operating revenue is calculated by subtracting "total deductions" from "electric operating revenues."

Source: Calculated from Federal Power Commission

concentrate their use into a few hours of the day will inevitably have higher power costs per kilowatt-hour than if it could sell all its power to a few large users with steady hourly consumption rates. For this reason, we need to understand the differences between New England's power consumers and those in the nation.

The average sale to each customer by New England private utilities was about 5,215 kw-h. or $132 in 1952. In the United States the average sale was 7,433 kw-h. or $136 to each customer. *It is readily apparent that the 42% larger average kilowatt-hour sale by United States utilities explains a significant but undetermined portion of the difference in power cost between the region and nation.*

Total electric operating revenues per kilowatt-hour of sales in New England were .67 cents (37%) higher than the comparable United States figure in 1952.[14] An undetermined portion of that difference was due to the differing patterns of customer sales. Column 3 of Table 5–12 indicates how differing power-use patterns and other differences intermingle to make up the .67 cents per kilowatt-hour difference. Apparently, three other characteristics are dominant in explaining New England's higher power costs: the relative technical costs of providing power to consumers in New England, the relative administrative costs of operating New England utility systems, and relatively higher investment in utility facilities.

In 1952 New England utilities devoted 49.55 cents of each dollar of sales to operating expenses, 2.45 cents more than the United States average. (See Table 5–12, columns 7 to 9.) About 75% of that difference was due to the higher power generation expenses. Fuel expenses alone accounted for 40% of the difference. Considering costs in relation to kilowatt-hour of sales (see column 3), 31% of the region's difference from the national average was explained by higher production costs, and fuel expenses alone accounted for 21% of the difference.[15] In addition to the higher prices of fuel in New England, power producers were handicapped by higher operating costs of somewhat older plant equipment and less intensive utilization than that in the country as a whole. *These handicaps indicate the likelihood that higher generating expenses probably explain 50% or more of the higher power costs in New England.*

Higher "administration and general" expenses of New England utilities caused a significant portion of the differences between New England and United States operating expenses in 1952. They were more than enough to offset some advantages in expenses per customer for transmission, distribution, and sales promotion. (See Table 5–12, columns 10 to 12.) New England utilities devoted 16% more of their average sales dollar to administration and general expenses than the national average. Although the revenues per customer in New England were only 3% less than the United States

14. Excluding sales to other private utilities.
15. *Ibid.*

average, administration and general expenses per customer were 13% above the United States average. Some accounting practices by New England utilities may be sufficiently different from the United States pattern to explain a small part of the difference. Other factors are of greater importance however. Of chief importance, perhaps, is the relatively large number of small utilities in the region. New England has 21% of the nation's privately owned Class A and B utility companies, but only 7.5% of the nation's electric utility operating revenues. General administration expenses, such as the salaries of executive officers and of the legal, personnel, engineering, and general accounting staff, have to be carried by the relatively

CHART 5–4

Average Production Expenses of Major Steam Electric Plants
in New England and the United States, 1947 and 1950
(cents per kilowatt-hour generated)

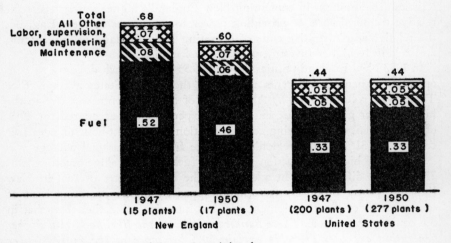

Source: Compiled from Federal Power Commission data

smaller earning capacities of the smaller utilities. Other expenses such as pension and employee welfare benefits, insurance costs, and financing and legal fees may also tend to be relatively higher in New England. Opportunities to lower administration and general costs are obviously limited by the organizational structure of New England utilities, but efforts to reduce the 13% New England–United States differential should be stressed. *Reduction of administration and general expenses by New England utilities to a level comparable with the United States average might reduce New England's power cost "disadvantage" by 5%.*

Higher electric-plant investment in relation to output and capacity contributes significantly to New England's higher average power costs. In 1952 investment by New England utilities in relation to kilowatt-hour sales was 29% and investment in relation to peak load on the system was 35% above the national average. Higher construction costs and greater dependence on hydro power play important roles in explaining the higher investment requirements. All of these factors point to the importance of continued improvements in operating efficiency.

Chart 5–4 presents a breakdown of production expenses for major steam electric plants in New England and the United States. These plants account for the bulk of steam-plant generation in each area. *The New England plants as a group achieved a substantial reduction in production expenses from 1947 to 1950, especially for fuel. While still well above production expenses in the nation, they narrowed the gap, since the group of plants in the country as a whole showed no change in production expenses.*

As we have noted, both higher fuel prices and lower plant utilization account largely for the higher production expenses in New England. Table 5–13 gives measures of these factors for both 1947 and 1950. In each instance there was a substantial gain for the region over the period in relation to progress made by plants in the rest of the country. In New England, fewer employees were needed to produce a given amount of power, plant utilization rose, and efficiency of fuel use increased. While fuel prices rose, they rose less in New England than in the country as a whole. Flexibility in the use of oil and coal permits New England steam plants to shift from one to the other as their relative prices change. Both plant expansion and modernization were factors in the improvement. Nevertheless, each of the measures in 1950 was still adverse for the New England plants as a group, and there was and is room for further improvement.

The region's utilities were handicapped at the end of World War II by a larger than average proportion of old boilers and generators. There was much ground to be made up. As the New England utilities continue their expansion and modernization plans, it appears that the gap ought to narrow still farther. But so long as the price of fuel remains substantially higher in the region it will be impossible for the production expenses of steam plants to reach equality with those in the country as a whole. *Since steam plants will almost certainly provide a rising proportion of the region's electric power, regardless of how the region's undeveloped hydroelectric power is utilized, it appears that full equalization of power-production costs and power rates between New England and the country as a whole will be impossible unless a cheaper fuel becomes available.*

Even hydroelectric power is more expensive to generate in New England than in the United States as a whole. In both areas hydroelectric plants provide about one-fourth of electric generation by privately owned utili-

Table 5–13. *Characteristics of Major Steam Electric Plants in New England and the United States, 1947 and 1950**

	1947			1950		
	NEW ENGLAND	UNITED STATES	PER CENT DIFFERENCE N.E. FROM U.S.	NEW ENGLAND	UNITED STATES	PER CENT DIFFERENCE N.E. FROM U.S.
Number of operating employees per 100,000,000 kw-h. generated	31	22	+41	25	19	+31
Plant factor (per cent of actual to capacity generation)	51	61	−16	55	60	−8
Btu required per kw-h. generated	15,650	14,640	+7	13,630	13,220	+3
Price of fuel in cents per million Btu:						
Coal	33.0	23.6	+40	35.4	27.2	+30
Oil	33.4	33.0	+1	32.6	30.7	+6
TOTAL, ALL FUELS†	33.1	22.5	+47	33.6	25.0	+34

* In 1947 the plants covered generated 67% of the utility steam power in New England and 73% in the United States. In 1950 the corresponding proportions were 81% for New England and 91% for the United States.
† For the United States, 11% of fuel consumed in 1947 was gas at an average price of 9.1 cents per million Btu, and 17% was gas in 1950 at an average price of 12.1 cents per million Btu. The New England steam plants did not use gas as a fuel in either year.
Source: Compiled from Federal Power Commission data

ties. In 1947 the average production expenses of New England plants were .13 cents per kilowatt-hour, 43% greater than the national average of .09 cents. The low operating expenses of hydroelectric plants are more or less offset by higher carrying charges of depreciation and interest. New hydroelectric installations have been limited in their contribution to reducing the cost of producing power in New England during recent years because of recent high construction and land-damage costs in much of the region, and their rather small proportion of its total power capacity and production. In the following section we consider the possibilities for their making a greater contribution in the future.

The Future Electric Power Needs of New England and How They Should Be Met

Electric power sales to ultimate consumers by New England utilities increased from 6,737,000,000 kw-h. in 1939 to 16,004,000,000 kw-h. in 1952, or approximately 138%. In the same interval, the installed generating capacity of the region's utilities grew from 2,645,000 to 4,674,000 kw., an increase of 76%. The trends of electric power sales and capacity continue to move steadily upward with no saturation point yet in sight. To meet the power needs of the future through increased capacity is a continuing long-range problem. Constant planning is required to acquire sites, and to construct the necessary plants and lines, so that generation and other facilities will be ready when needed. In this planning, the interrelationships between steam and hydroelectric expansions present acute problems which require skillful handling.

Future Requirements. In 1952 the peak load of the New England utilities was 3,871,896 kw. Their capability was 4,408,849 kw., indicating a reserve of 13.8%. According to estimates of the Planning Committee of the Electric Coordinating Council of New England, peak load will rise to about 4,650,000 kw. in 1956. The expansion programs of the region's utilities are expected to provide a capability under adverse hydroelectric conditions of about 5,475,000 kw. in that year, which will provide an 18% reserve. Since the planned expansion will come into operation somewhat irregularly, the reserve ratio will vary from year to year, but it is not expected to fall below 11% at any time.

Looking farther ahead, the Electric Coordinating Council estimates that by 1970 the peak load in New England will be between 6,878,000 and 8,647,000 kw., representing an increase of 78% to 124% over the 1952 peak.[16] To meet that demand, capability would have to rise by 1970 to between 7,910,000 and 9,944,000 kw. In addition to the expansion of capacity, some of the region's older generating equipment will undoubtedly have to be replaced. *Even without any replacement, by 1970 New England will*

16. *Power Supply and Load for New England—Past, Present and Future,* Boston, 1952.

require from 3,400,000 to 5,400,000 of new generating capacity, roughly doubling the total capacity of the region in 1952.[17] The total may be even higher if large industrial concerns continue to shift from producing their own power to purchasing what they need from the utilities because of lower costs, as they have been doing during recent years.

While the precise amount of new power capacity required by New England in 1970 cannot be determined with any accuracy, it is large. To meet the needs will require flexibility in planning to meet changing conditions more than a few years in advance, yet the broader outlines of future power requirements will not change too much through the years.

Expansion of Hydroelectric Capacity. The potentialities for further water-power development in New England have been the focus of considerable controversy during past years. There is still much public misunderstanding about the opportunities for hydroelectric expansion, the possible effects of increased hydroelectric development on generating and transmission costs, and hence on electric rates in the region. In addition, there has been a conflict of opinion between those who believe that development of hydroelectric power should be solely by privately owned utilities and those who believe that the Federal Government should undertake large power developments in New England.

At the beginning of 1953 the New England utilities operated hydroelectric plants with a name-plate rating of 997,000 kw., 21% of the total capacity of all their plants. How much more hydroelectric capacity can be added to the total? Three recent efforts to determine the undeveloped potential differ widely, primarily because they rest on different assumptions and procedures.[18] The range is as follows:

STUDY BY	UNDEVELOPED POTENTIAL	BASIS OF ESTIMATE
Federal Power Commission	3,119,000 kw.	Primarily water flows and river profiles, apparently no consideration of engineering or economic feasibility; including 220,000 kw. from Passamaquoddy
Providence Journal-Bulletin	1,085,000 kw.	Engineering feasibility; excluding Passamaquoddy

17. The Federal Power Commission, in its *Power Market Survey: Power Requirements in the Northeastern Region* (New York, 1951), estimated that the peak load in New England would be 5,860,000 kw. by 1970. This load would require a total capability of about 6,635,000 kw. It appears that the FPC estimates are too conservative, in view of the rate of growth of power use.

18. Federal Power Commission, *Power Market Survey: New Hampshire, Vermont, Massachusetts, Connecticut, and Rhode Island*, New York, 1949; George H. Arris, *Providence Journal-Bulletin*, "New England Water Power—Myth or Fact?" December 1949; New England Council, Power Survey Committee, *Power in New England*, Boston, 1948.

STUDY BY	UNDEVELOPED POTENTIAL	BASIS OF ESTIMATE
New England Council, Power Survey Committee	500,000 kw.	Economic feasibility on the basis of private financing if and when it can be worked into the load; including 80,000 kw. of dual flood-control and power projects and excluding Passamaquoddy

In view of the differences among these estimates, it is important to consider the appropriate goal for hydroelectric development. Water power should be developed if it will provide the needed power more cheaply than steam generation, bearing in mind that hydroelectric power is subject to variations in dependability in accordance with stream flows. Cost evaluations must include land damages and the expense of moving highways, bridges, and other facilities, as well as construction costs. Moreover, the geographical location of hydroelectric sites is an important consideration, for transmission expenses and power losses must be added to production costs. All sources agree that a large proportion of New England's undeveloped potential is in Maine, mostly in northern Maine, where distance from present load centers is an important drawback to near-term development. Finally, for proper balance in the power system, each kilowatt of new hydroelectric capacity normally requires about three kilowatts of steam capacity to "firm it up." Hydroelectric developments, particularly in states like Maine or Vermont, which are already primarily dependent on water power, have to be balanced against the need for further steam-plant expansion.

Without attempting to pass judgment on the engineering appraisals, it seems fair to say that under private financing and ownership the amount of new hydroelectric capacity in the region that can be economically added to the private utility systems of New England by 1970 is no more than 15% of the total expansion that will be needed during that period, and it is probably less than 10%. The declining proportion of hydroelectric to total capacity will undoubtedly continue in New England, as in the country as a whole.

This does not mean that the new hydroelectric power is unimportant, however. Where it is economically feasible, it should be aggressively developed. The power companies should also cooperate to the utmost in building power loads in areas close to undeveloped potentials as well as in efforts to improve transmission and construction techniques. Further economies in construction and transmission may well convert some potentials from engineering to economic feasibility.

Public development of some power potential in New England by the Federal Government has been proposed by some persons as a substitute for private initiative. Lower costs, if achieved, would rest primarily on lower capital and tax expenses. *By distributing some of the cost to other parts of the country through general taxation, and by the different types of accounting employed for federal power projects, the bookkeeping costs of such projects would undoubtedly be lower than costs for private development, and a somewhat larger potential would appear to be economically feasible. Even so, the total would be only a small proportion of need during the next two decades.*

Public power projects raise other problems. So long as private utilities are willing to undertake needed developments, there seems to be no reason for federal intervention. As we shall see shortly, the possibility of rate reductions through public power projects in New England is not great enough to override other considerations. The burden of proof to demonstrate the benefits of public power in New England rests on its advocates, and those benefits have not been clearly demonstrated.

It is tempting to call on contributions from taxpayers in other parts of the country to help defray the cost of hydroelectric expansion in New England, as New Englanders have been called upon to do for other regions, but it is hard to justify such a policy unless there are evident benefits to the nation as a whole. The New England river valleys are different from those in the Far West and Southeast, where systematic large-scale power and other developments have been undertaken by the Federal Government. The rivers of southern New England, in particular, are already rather highly developed for power, and other water and land uses in the area limit the economy of further development. The region as a whole is already highly developed industrially and is not handicapped by unavailability of power.

Opportunities for industrial development based on power development are limited largely to Maine. Even in that state the rivers and their potentialities are small compared to those developed by the Federal Government in other parts of the country, and many other location factors affect the speed with which an industrial power demand could be built up to absorb the larger supply. Maine's power rates are at present generally lower than those in the rest of New England, and the Fernald Act has kept Maine's water power at home, yet its industrial development has not been appreciably accelerated by its power-cost advantage. Even the Tennessee Valley area, according to the National Planning Association's Committee of the South, has not shown a more rapid rate of industrial development than that of surrounding states, despite TVA's undoubted contributions to the area.[19]

19. Calvin B. Hoover and Benjamin U. Ratchford, *Economic Resources and Policies of the South* (New York, Macmillan, 1951), p. 242.

While the topography and geography of New England will not permit major valley developments of the Tennessee and Columbia River variety, there is, nevertheless, a role which government should play in the water-resource development of New England. The combination of flood control and power development provides an opportunity for joint public-private projects such as the Waterbury dam on the Winooski River in Vermont and similar joint projects which have been studied by Army engineers in the past. Some sites and dam systems which are uneconomic for power alone may be economical on a multipurpose basis. Where such opportunities exist, they should be undertaken, preferably on a partnership basis. If undertaken solely by the government, the power should be sold to utilities on an equitable basis for distribution.

Two specific proposals for hydroelectric development deserve special mention, the Passamaquoddy tidal basin and the St. Lawrence rapids. Passamaquoddy has been talked about for decades as a possible power site, but it is still uncertain how much the development would cost. Even the tests to determine economic feasibility would be expensive. Moreover, there is at present no local market for the amount of power that Passamaquoddy could produce, and use of long-distance transmission to other load centers might be more expensive than other ways of getting the power. *There is no doubt that the economical development of Passamaquoddy power is at best a long-term possibility, dependent on construction costs, alternative sources of power, transmission expenses, and load growth. Until adequate engineering data are available, feasibility cannot even be determined.* It would seem desirable for the interested federal agencies and utilities, if any, to conduct joint engineering studies to complete the collection of necessary basic information. These data should be reappraised periodically in the light of changing technological and economic conditions until the project becomes economically feasible, if it ever does.

The development of the St. Lawrence rapids is a different matter. It is agreed that this is feasible in terms of both engineering and economics. While it lies outside New England, its situation on an international river has both complicated its development and offered some possibility that a portion of its output might go to western New England. A number of competing proposals for development by the Federal Government, Canada, and New York State have slowed down action. *It seems clear that the power development should be undertaken. Federal construction should not be necessary except as a final alternative.* Any portion of St. Lawrence power allocated to New England would be but a small proportion of the region's needs during coming years. Even if as much as 25% of the estimated 568,000 kw. of firm power on the American side of the project were made available to the region, which is probably more than New England would receive, it would have little effect on the long-run supply program for the region. Nevertheless, it would be worth having and could be fitted into the general expansion of power supply in the region.

Finally, it is desirable to evaluate in a general way what effect the further expansion of hydroelectric capacity would have on the level of power rates in New England. Many persons glibly refer to all hydroelectric power as "cheap power." It is not necessarily cheap in New England; some of it is very expensive. At best, some of the undeveloped sites might be *somewhat* cheaper than alternative steam plants.

The future power needs of New England are so great that the addition of all the hydroelectric capacity that is likely to come on the line by 1970 would make scarcely a ripple in the region's over-all power-rate situation. If 500,000 kw. of hydroelectric capacity were added in New England by 1970 out of a total increase of 4,300,000 kw., and if the output of these 500,000 kw. was completely expense free—no operating expenses, no transmission or distribution expenses, no capital charges, no taxes, no anything—it would offer at most a 6% reduction in the region's power rates. Obviously, the power would not be expense free, whether developed by private or public sources. The actual contribution of hydroelectric power to the future of rates in New England must necessarily be considerably less. *Hydro can contribute, to be sure, and it should be pushed along as fast as is economical. Water-power developments can be of special importance in particular communities. But anyone who advocates hydroelectric power as a panacea for New England's higher than average power rates is guilty of a cruel deception.*

Expansion of Steam Capacity. It is apparent that steam power must provide all but a small proportion of the region's growth in power capacity during the next dozen or more years, whatever the standards of hydroelectric development. *The trend toward construction of steam plants at tidewater, where water deliveries of oil and coal can minimize transportation costs for fuels, will probably continue until the economical use of nuclear fuels frees the plants from fuel-transportation considerations. The expandable plant, designed for the construction of additional generating units as demand rises, may well become increasingly important.*

Even with conventional combustion fuels, it is clear from the changes between 1947 and 1950 that the region's costs of producing power and its power rates can decline in relation to those in the rest of the country. It is also plain that New England must rely primarily on steam plants for future capacity expansion and cost and rate reduction. The opportunities for improvement were far from exhausted in 1950.

One major approach is installation of the most efficient new equipment for expansion purposes. In past decades the average generating efficiency of New England utilities fell behind the national average level of efficiency. Since the end of World War II the utilities have been making rapid strides to catch up. There would seem to be every opportunity to continue the progress and forge ahead of much of the rest of the country in plant efficiency. Improvements in generating facilities reduce unit labor, maintenance, and other expenses, as well as fuel expenses.

No matter what the region's utilities do to reduce expenses, however, their higher fuel prices stand as a major obstacle to cost and rate equality between New England and the country as a whole. Transportation charges have kept coal prices in New England far above those in all other regions. Even if the pipeline movement of powdered coal or some other major change in transportation methods should become practicable, some portion of the coal disadvantage will persist.

Fuel oil prices in New England are not much higher than those in the other parts of the country where steam plants burn oil, and oil provides a substitute for coal in the region as the relative prices of the two fuels vary. But oil in New England is much more expensive than the lowest price fuels available to steam plants in most other areas. The efforts of American petroleum and coal interests to restrict the importation of foreign oil would further penalize New England, since the region obtains a substantial portion of its petroleum requirements from the Carribbean area. The region's interest would be best served by a reduction in import restrictions.

While natural gas has entered New England, it is not generally available for electric generation, and it is questionable whether much will become available for some time to come.

Within the last few years a possibility much more promising than any other alternative for equalization of New England's power rates with those in the rest of the country has changed from a visionary idea to a near-term opportunity. The substitution of nuclear fuels for combustion fuels seems to be far closer to reality than was generally expected just a short time ago. Teams of utilities and manufacturers have been working on the problem, along with the Atomic Energy Commission, and at least one major company believes it will be ready to begin construction of a nuclear-fueled power plant within a few years.

The conventional boiler of a steam plant would be replaced by a nuclear reactor and specialized heat exchanger to produce steam for turning the generator. Higher capital charges could be more than offset by low or negligible fuel expenses, especially if the plant were a dual-purpose plant for the production of power and plutonium for sale on a guaranteed price basis to the Federal Government. Even without the production and sale of plutonium, it appears quite likely that small advances beyond present knowledge could reduce the costs of nuclear power below those of the best conventional steam plants.

New England is singularly well suited to the substitution of nuclear for combustion fuels. It has much to gain from the general applicability of atomic power, and it is attractive as the location of the first or one of the first such plants. Its qualifications for the location of an early plant of this type are well known and appreciated by companies active in the development. All groups in the region should strongly support the development of nuclear power as the brightest opportunity for reductions in electric power rates and costs.

SUMMARY AND CONCLUSIONS

This report has considered the varied but related problems of water use, fuels, and electric power in New England. The region is well supplied by nature with water, but it is entirely dependent on other regions of the United States and foreign countries for its mineral fuels. These conditions have had an important bearing on New England's electric power situation.

Plentiful supplies of high-quality water are an important industrial asset to New England, and long-range planning of municipal supplies has put most New England cities and towns in an enviable position to meet their future water needs. Substantial precipitation normally well distributed throughout the year has minimized the need for agricultural irrigation. While there are occasional local inadequacies of water supply, they can and should be corrected by local action.

The high natural quality of many New England streams and rivers has been impaired, sometimes seriously, by years of abuse from the discharge of municipal and industrial wastes. The coastal sections of rivers in southern New England have been particularly affected, though rivers in northern New England have also experienced considerable pollution. Some progress has been made in improving the situation, but more is needed. All New England states except Maine are members of the New England Interstate Water Pollution Control Commission. Its long-range program for the classification of present conditions and desirable standards of future use, in cooperation with state agencies, can go far in maximizing the effective use of the region's rivers for recreational, industrial, navigational, and other purposes. Maine should join the commission, and all states, municipalities, industries, and other private groups should cooperate in the effort, each with due consideration of the interests of the others. Where private groups and municipal governments are unable to solve local pollution problems, it is the responsibility of the state governments to determine and secure the most desirable action.

While it is impossible to obtain absolute protection against both flash floods and general floods throughout the region, further flood protection on many New England rivers and streams would have a favorable ratio of benefits to costs. Existing flood control installations have already proved their worth, and further dam systems on both main streams and their tributaries should be constructed. Warning systems on some rivers could also be improved.

The dependence of New England on imported fuels causes higher than average fuel prices in the region. The region has a strong interest in the availability of foreign sources of oil as one way of holding down its cost disadvantage. Import restrictions on foreign petroleum and its products should not be tightened. New England also has a strong interest in improvements and cost reductions in the extraction and transportation of mineral fuels, as well as in the efficiency of their use. Major fuel users bear the responsibility for minimizing their fuel costs through modernization of equipment.

The New England power supply is adequate and dependable in meeting present needs. While this feature of the situation is advantageous to users, the rate structure, on the average, is higher than those in most competing states. Higher than average rates represent a small but sometimes important competitive disadvantage for manufacturers, and have represented a slight handicap to industrial growth in the region. High fuel prices are a major factor in the excess of rates, but other elements of expense controllable in the region have contributed to it. Progress during recent years in expense reduction has been encouraging, but further improvement is both desirable and possible.

By 1970 there will have to be an approximate doubling of generating capacity to meet New England's power needs. All but a small proportion of the expansion will have to be steam plants. While in absolute terms there is considerable undeveloped hydroelectric power which can be economically developed during coming years, it is small in proportion to the total need and can have only a relatively minor effect on the region's power supply or rates.

Further improvements in the efficiency of steam-plant generation in the region offer a much greater opportunity for further reducing the New England power-rate differential. Fuel prices present a major obstacle, but the rapid progress in nuclear power development gives hope that New England can look forward eventually to eliminating its power-cost disadvantage. New England is well suited to nuclear power development and should participate actively in it, including the possibility of providing the location for the first commercial plant of this type. New England's power problem of the future depends for its answer more on steam plants than on further hydroelectric development, though increased hydroelectric power naturally has a part to play.

In further improving the region's electric situation, continued integration through intrasystem and intersystem interconnections and exchange of energy is desirable. Maine's Fernald Act, which prohibits the export of almost all hydroelectric power from the state, should be repealed as the final major step in the further integration of New England's power facilities.

SELECTED REFERENCES

1. Arris, George H., "New England Water Power—Myth or Fact?" *Providence Journal-Bulletin,* December 1949.
2. Edison Electric Institute, *Statistical Bulletin,* New York, *Annual.*
3. Electric Coordinating Council of New England, *Power Supply and Load for New England—Past, Present and Future,* Boston, 1952.
4. Federal Power Commission, *Power Market Survey: New Hampshire, Vermont, Massachusetts, Connecticut, and Rhode Island,* New York, 1949.
5. ——— *Power Market Survey: Power Requirements in the Northeastern Region,* New York, 1951.
6. ——— *Statistics of Electric Utilities in the United States,* Washington, *Annual.*
7. ——— *Steam-Electric Plant Construction Cost and Annual Production Expenses,* Washington, *Annual.*
8. Federal Reserve Bank of Boston, "Industrial Power Costs in New England," *Monthly Review,* June 1950.
9. ——— "New England Manufacturing—Its Future Prospects," *Monthly Review,* September 1949.
10. Hoover, Calvin B., and Ratchford, Benjamin U., *Economic Resources and Policies of the South,* New York, Macmillan, 1951.
11. McCloud, Leland W., *Comparative Costs of Competitive Fuels,* West Virginia University Business and Economic Studies (Vol. *1,* No. 4), June 1951.
12. New England Council, Power Survey Committee, *Power in New England,* Boston, 1948.
13. U.S. Public Health Service, Federal Security Agency, *New England Drainage Basins,* Washington, 1951.

6

New England's Vacation Business

Drafted by Ray S. Kelley, Jr., under the direction of Arthur A. Bright, Jr.

New England's climate and topography are natural resources of the region, just as much as its forests, minerals, ocean fisheries, agricultural land, and water. In fact, the geography of New England is the basis of one of the region's more important economic activities—the vacation business.

While most of the other natural resources are extracted, processed, and transported to the user, the natural assets of the vacation business are permanent and immovable. The vacationist himself has to come to the mountains or the lakes or the seashore, and he has to pay part of the cost of his vacation before he reaches his destination. The enticements of other vacation areas make competition keen and challenge the ability of New England's vacation business to make the most of its assets.

This report sketches briefly the importance of the vacation business to New England, the nature of the region's vacation resources, both natural and man-made, and the kinds of resources that appeal to vacationists. Finally, it considers some of the major problems of the vacation business in New England and offers some suggestions for ways in which the business might be strengthened.

THE IMPORTANCE OF THE VACATION BUSINESS TO NEW ENGLAND

New England entertains about 6,500,000 vacationers a year from all sections of the United States, as well as a large number from Canada and other foreign countries. These vacationers, of whom around two-thirds are New Englanders, spend close to 70,000,000 vacation days within the region each year, which amounts to about 8% of the total United States vacation business. The estimates of their total expenditures in 1952 vary considerably and range up to $1 billion.[1] On the basis of a somewhat more conservative figure of $800,000,000, and assuming that two-thirds of the amount was spent by New Englanders themselves, there was still an influx of about $270,000,000 from outside the region. Probably New Englanders vacationing outside the region spent around $175,000,000 in other areas. New England's net vacation receipts in 1952, therefore, may be estimated at roughly $100,000,000.

1. There are no precise figures for total vacation expenditures. Much depends on the way they are defined. In any event, New England's vacation business receipts are large.

The vacation business is of special significance to the economies of the three states of northern New England. Scores of their communities rely principally upon the vacationist for economic support. Table 6–1 presents estimates of the vacation business done in each of the New England states during 1950. While Massachusetts attracted more vacation business than any of the other five, receipts in northern New England as a whole equaled those in the much more populous and highly developed southern states. The interstate differences in relative importance of the vacation business appear strikingly in the last two columns of the table.

Table 6–1. Estimated Vacation Business in the New England States, 1950

STATE	VACATION BUSINESS AS PER CENT OF NEW ENGLAND TOTAL	VACATION BUSINESS AS PER CENT OF TOTAL STATE INCOME PAYMENTS	VACATION BUSINESS PER CAPITA AS PER CENT OF NEW ENGLAND PER CAPITA
Maine	21	13	212
New Hampshire	18	19	326
Vermont	11	17	275
Massachusetts	37	3	74
Rhode Island	4	2	44
Connecticut	9	2	42
NEW ENGLAND	100	5	100

Source: Adapted from compilation by New Hampshire State Planning and Development Commission

Many groups benefit from New England's importance as a vacation center. Public lodging places—hotels, tourist homes, and cabin groups—receive roughly 25% of vacationists' expenditures in the region. Transportation expenses absorb another 20% or so. A great number of amusement parks, theaters, gasoline stations, and gift shops owe their existence to vacationists. Even the barbers, grocers, druggists, and sports shop operators in scores of New England communities derive a large part of their income from persons on vacations. According to *Printer's Ink,* retail stores received about 25% of the vacationist's dollar in 1951, and another 27% went for meals in restaurants. The breakdown of the 25% to retail stores is revealing. Nearly 11% went for clothes, over 4% for sporting goods, cameras, and other equipment, nearly 5% for gifts and souvenirs, and over 5% for food and beverages.

An important source of municipal income in many communities throughout New England, especially in Maine, New Hampshire, and Vermont, is property taxes on summer homes and other seasonal properties. Vacationists also contribute to state incomes by the payment of cigarette, gasoline, beer, and liquor taxes. The New Hampshire State Planning and Development Commission estimates that 5% of vacation expenditures in its state reach the state and local governments as tax payments. Fishing and hunting licenses are an additional source of state income. Probably as many as 500,000 hunting and fishing licenses are sold annually throughout New England, a sizable percentage of which are purchased by nonresident vacationers. All these payments help support community and state governments. The vacationist is an important person to attract into the region. Directly or indirectly, a large proportion of New Englanders benefits from his expenditures.

Employment in the vacation business is difficult to measure because of the seasonality of employment and the large number of family workers. A partial inventory of employment in public lodging places made by the New England Council in 1945 placed the figure at 42,000, excluding proprietors and their families. Sixty thousand seems a reasonable total estimate for 1945, and employment has undoubtedly increased considerably since that year. Thousands more are employed in other business catering to the vacationist.

NEW ENGLAND'S ENDOWMENTS AS A VACATION CENTER

Numerous characteristics make New England a desirable place for Americans and foreigners to spend their vacations. Nature has been benevolent to the region, and its historical significance has been great. *The topography of New England is a natural vacation asset of the utmost importance*—as varied and as interesting as the people. The thousands of miles of coast line, bordering every state but Vermont—which has the 120-mile-long Lake Champlain on its western border—offer an infinite variety of beach and harbor, cape and island. Inland are Maine's Blue Mountains, the Vermont Green Mountains, New Hampshire's White Mountains, the Massachusetts Berkshire Hills, and Connecticut's Litchfield Hills. There are 141 mountain peaks over 3,000 feet, 58 peaks over 4,000 feet, and 16 peaks over 5,000 feet. There are over 3,000 lakes and large ponds, and countless rivers and brooks. Almost everywhere forests blanket the land. Thirty-one million acres of pine and maple, hemlock and birch, spruce and oak, hickory and beech provide shelter for wild life, shade for campers, and beauty for all. No comparable area in the country has so large a percentage of forested land as New England.

New England's summer weather is generally highly favorable to the vacationer, but each well-defined season has its own attractions. The weather is exceptionally variable, however. The passage of high- and low-pressure areas across the continent shifts the prevailing winds, so that a cold blast from the North Atlantic and a warm draft from the Gulf Stream on the south may follow each other relatively closely. Prolonged cold or hot spells are rare, despite the heat record for July 1952.

In general, New England's climate may be classed as moderate. Winter temperatures average about 30°, approximately 70°. Rainfall averages about 45 inches a year and is normally distributed fairly evenly over the twelve months. Snowfall averages 60 inches and is much greater in the mountains, where it provides the attraction for ski enthusiasts. Average snowfalls in most of the Green and White Mountain areas are over 100 inches annually. Ocean temperatures are influenced by two great ocean rivers, the Gulf Stream and the Labrador current. The waters south of Cape Cod are usually quite warm in the summer, while those off Maine are somewhat cooler. For the region as a whole, the land masses are warmer than the ocean in the summer, but much cooler in the winter.

A large proportion of vacationists rank climate high in deciding where to take their vacations. New England's moderate summer climate and pollen-free mountain air appeal to many of them. As we shall show later, however, vacation promoters fail to stress the region's advantages of climate sufficiently in most of their advertisements. The autumn, spring, and winter seasons of New England have a potential appeal to a great many vacationists, but at present relatively little vacation business is done in the region except in summer. While there are distinct state variations, for New England as a whole over 80% of the vacation business is concentrated in the months of July and August. This means that fixed costs on most vacation lodging places have to be paid largely from receipts during just two months. The opportunities of the other three seasons are still underexploited. Such attractions as autumn hunting and hiking, winter skiing, and spring fishing, if more actively promoted, might attract many additional customers.

New England is also a mecca for sightseers. Few regions have such a large number of historic spots. While some have been allowed to run down, many have been kept up and attract thousands of visitors each year. For example, in 1951 the Bunker Hill monument had 200,000 visitors, the House of Seven Gables attracted 55,000 people, and the Bennington Monument over 17,000. Crowds of 30,000 and 74,000 visited the Old State House in Boston and Paul Revere's house. Of course, it would be mere fantasy to suppose that all, or even a majority, of such visitors came to New England merely to visit historic buildings and sites, but history does influence some in making up their vacation itineraries.

In addition to its topography, climate, and history, New England attracts many vacationists for cultural reasons. There are the Berkshire Festivals, summer schools, artists' colonies, summer theaters, and many similar activities. Students who have attended New England's schools during the winter often remain in the region during their school vacations or return after they have graduated. Some of them are solely vacationers, but others add to their incomes by acting as counselors at the children's summer camps scattered throughout the region.

One of the most important advantages the New England vacation business has is its location. It is close to the concentrated populations of New York and New Jersey, which have always been an important source of patronage for New England's vacation areas. New England draws them partly because of its location, partly through its own attractions, and partly because the resorts in the vicinity of the Middle Atlantic population centers do not have sufficient attractions or capacity to handle the demand.

Naturally, New England's varied vacation attractions also appeal to most of its own large population. Their vacation expenditures are extremely valuable to the region as a whole, in spite of being slightly less, because of proximity, than those of the average nonresident vacationer.

New England is also near a rich Canadian market. Quebec is growing rapidly, and no city of comparable size on the North American continent is keeping pace with Montreal. As the Canadian population and its income increase, New England may get considerably more vacation business from this source.

There was a large increase in Canadian vacationists during the summer of 1952, even though little was done to promote their coming. While most of the Canadians have been going to Maine and New Hampshire seashore resorts, all parts of the region have noted increases in the number of Canadian visitors. Nearly 40% of the total business at Hampton Beach, New Hampshire, was Canadian during the summer of 1952, and Gloucester reported that its Canadian business for the same period was 50 to 75% above the 1951 figure. This increase was partly the result of Canada's improved dollar exchange position, but largely because restrictions on money leaving Canada have been removed. *The opportunities for New England to attract more Canadian vacation business are very great.*

Another possible advantage New England has over many rival areas is its "old home appeal." Many people come back because they once lived here, their relatives still do, or some forebear came from here. Many of the cities and towns are well located for vacations. About half the vacationers in the United States stay with friends and relatives while on vacation, but the proportion may be higher in New England.

The New England transportation system is better than those in many other parts of the country. While some of the highways and roads need improvement, most of them are surfaced, and they form a close network throughout the vacation areas. *Improved or additional highways leading into New England from the New York area, however, would undoubtedly draw in additional vacation business, especially week-end business, from New York City and northern New Jersey.* In 1950 there were about 77,000 miles of rural roads in New England, of which 82% were surfaced. Air service is excellent, with over 200 commercial airports in the region. Air taxis serve 35 New England communities and resort areas. The railroad network includes about 6,500 miles of road, and bus service reaches almost every point. The railroads have catered to the vacationist by running "specials." For example, one railroad runs a series of ski trains and other specials, such as sugar-party trains and foliage specials, which help attract tourists in the off-season.

New England has numerous and varied facilities for vacationists. In 1947, the latest year for which fairly complete data are available, there were 1,339 resort hotels, 6,910 tourist homes and cabin groups, 716 boys' and girls' camps, and more than 165,000 seasonal dwellings. Over a third of the resort hotels were in Maine in 1947, while New Hampshire had 361, and Massachusetts

220. Connecticut ranked fourth with 100, followed by Vermont and Rhode Island. Maine also led in the number of tourist homes and cabins, followed by Massachusetts, New Hampshire, and Vermont. Massachusetts had the most boys' and girls' camps of any New England state, followed closely by Maine and New Hampshire. (See Table 6–2.)

Since 1947 there has been a marked increase in the number of vacation properties, especially of tourist homes, cabin groups and motels, and small inns and hotels. Vermont is the only state that conducts an annual inventory of vacation lodging places, though New Hampshire is currently completing a detailed inventory for the year 1952. The partial evidence available indicates that the value of vacation property has increased as much as 64% in the Lakes Region of New Hampshire, for example, and that the number of seasonal residences has risen considerably in Vermont and New Hampshire. *It would be highly desirable for the other New England states or a region-wide group to survey their vacation facilities regularly in order to determine trends and local conditions promptly.*

The vacation business of New England is handicapped, however, by the age of many of its lodging places. The principal reason for the high average age of lodgings is that New England contains some of the oldest resort areas in the country. Age itself is not a disadvantage, of course, if facilities are modern, but altogether too many New England public lodging places lack adequate facilities. Less than 20% of the region's resort hotels are under 20 years of age, and almost 40% are over 50 years old.

Table 6–2. New England's Vacation Lodging Places and Summer Camps, 1947[a]

STATE	TOTAL CAPACITY	HOTELS[b]		GUEST HOUSES AND CABINS		BOYS' AND GIRLS' CAMPS[c]	
		NUMBER	CAPACITY	NUMBER	CAPACITY	NUMBER	CAPACITY
Maine	85,815	482	28,774	2,780	39,418	196	17,623
New Hampshire	70,457	361	25,582	1,293	30,243	177	14,632
Vermont	24,626	96	6,594	681	11,743	83	6,289
Massachusetts	61,757	229	19,703	1,302	23,386	198	18,668
Rhode Island[e]	9,480	71	4,329	286	5,151	d	d
Connecticut[e]	25,229	100	8,598	568	10,232	62	6,399
NEW ENGLAND	277,364	1,339	93,580	6,910	120,173	716[d]	63,611[d]

a. Establishments doing more than 50% vacation business, based on New England vacation business inventory for 1946–47.   b. Includes cottage resorts with central dining facilities, adult camps, and sporting camps.   c. 1945.   d. No data for Rhode Island.   e. Estimated.
Sources: New England Council, *New England Vacation Business Inventory, 1945*, Boston, 1948; and Federal Reserve Bank of Boston

The public lodging facilities in New England were valued at $99,000,000 in 1945. The most recent separate valuation of seasonal dwellings for all New England was the $394,000,000 estimate in 1930. The total guest capacity of the public lodging places in 1947 was 277,364. The figure had probably increased about 25% by 1952, primarily because of a large increase in the number of cabin groups. By far the leading state in guest capacity was Maine, with about

31% of the New England total. Massachusetts and New Hampshire had about 22 and 25% of the region's guest capacity, respectively, and both Vermont and Connecticut had 9%. Rhode Island had relatively little guest capacity in 1947.

The vacation industry is noted for its large number of small businesses. The average guest capacity of New England resort hotels is 70, while the average tourist home or cabin group can accommodate only 17 visitors. Besides the lodging places and camps, there are thousands of restaurants, gift shops, and gasoline stations which cater to the tourist. This large number of small businesses presents serious management problems, which handicap the industry as a whole. Entry is easy because of the relatively low initial investment, and the mortality rate is quite high. The rapid turnover has resulted in a poor credit rating for the entire industry and has made it difficult for many capable operators to obtain capital for needed repairs, improvements, or expansion. We shall discuss these problems in more detail further on.

THE VACATIONER IN NEW ENGLAND

Will New England maintain its relative position in the country's vacation business? Could it increase its share? The vacation operators of the region will be in a stronger competitive position if they know the precise characteristics of their market and adapt their facilities and operations to cater as much as possible to the vacationer's demands. In no business is it more important to bear in mind the old maxim that the customer is always right. In this section we shall try to answer a few questions about vacationers. In the last section we shall suggest some major points in a program that should help New England attract more of them.

Here are some of the questions: What types of person take vacations? How many people now come to New England for vacations? Why do they come? How much do they spend? What do they spend it on? Where do they stay? These questions must be answered before we can know the vacationer and what he wants. Many of the tentative answers have to be based on sketchy or relatively old data. *New Englanders have not learned enough about their tourist customers. Some of the state development commissions, the New England Council, and the Federal Reserve Bank of Boston have made studies, but much more research is needed by public and private agencies before an integrated and detailed program can be worked out for increasing the region's share of the country's vacation business.*

Much of the information contained in this report is based on studies made by groups outside New England—the Curtis and Crowell-Collier publishing companies. And those studies were for the United States as a whole, not just for New England. Other information is from studies made over twenty years ago with the support of the New England Council, and from a more recent study by the Vermont Development Commission. The gaps in knowledge are serious. It is difficult to conduct the business effectively without knowing exactly what the potential customer desires and what his background is. State and other public groups cannot be expected to do all the work. *The vacation businessmen themselves should greatly increase their joint efforts to learn more about the market for their services.*

Number and Type of Vacationers

The vacation business is expanding rapidly throughout the country, and it will almost certainly continue to expand. The rising standard of living, the spread of paid vacations, and the increasing percentage of older people in the population all help to stimulate the expansion. During 1951, 51% of American families took a vacation, which was slightly less than the 54% of 1950. In each year about 21% of families took two or more vacations. The average number of persons on a vacation trip was 2.3, and these persons averaged almost 11 days per trip. As might be expected, urban families were more frequent vacationers. Nearly three-fifths of the urban families took vacations, but less than one-half the rural families left home for a vacation.

A large percentage of families in the upper income groups took vacations. As Table 6–3 indicates, more than three-fourths of the families with incomes over $7,500 took a vacation, while only 36 or 37% of those with incomes less than $2,000 did so.

Season of Vacations

While in the United States about half the vacations are taken in July and August, 80% of New England's vacation business is done, as we have seen, in those months. New England has remained largely a summer-resort area,

Table 6–3. Per Cent of United States Families Taking Vacation Trips, by Income Groups, 1950 and 51

	PER CENT TAKING VACATIONS	
INCOME GROUP	1950	1951
Under $2,000	36.3	36.9
$2,000–$2,999	49.6	44.5
$3,000–$4,999	58.2	54.9
$5,000–$7,499	70.5	66.8
$7,500 and over	78.7	80.1
TOTAL	54.2	51.3

Source: The Vacation Travel Market of the United States, Curtis Publishing Company, 1951 and 1952

though there has been some effort during recent years to develop more business in other months through promotion of skiing, foliage tours, hunting, and fishing.

New England's vacation lodging places do some commercial and boarding business in the off-season, so the seasonal fluctuations in their total business are not as pronounced as those in the vacation business alone. Only 65% of the lodging place business is in July and August. (See Table 6–4.) Nevertheless, the seasonality is still very great. Vermont, the state that has done the most off-season promotion, experiences considerable seasonality, but it is significantly below that of the New England average. Only 55% of its business is done in July and August. Nine per cent comes in the winter months of December, January, and February, compared with an average of 4% for New England as a whole. Vermont also does 7% of its business in October. Off-season promotion apparently pays.

Table 6–4. Percentage of Vacation Lodging Business Done in Each Month in New England: 1946–48 Average* (in per cent)

STATE	JAN.	FEB.	MAR.	APR.	MAY	JUNE	JULY	AUG.	SEPT.	OCT.	NOV.	DEC.
NEW ENGLAND	1.22	1.71	1.05	1.28	3.22	8.94	29.72	34.31	11.72	4.41	1.39	1.03
Maine	.28	.41	.25	.95	3.96	8.97	32.05	35.80	11.29	3.89	1.80	.35
New Hampshire	2.07	2.72	1.34	1.70	2.15	6.44	29.13	35.70	11.14	4.79	1.19	1.63
Vermont	2.39	4.15	1.95	1.13	3.54	8.17	24.52	30.21	12.68	7.32	1.87	2.07
Massachusetts†	1.19	1.59	1.38	1.35	3.19	11.01	29.18	32.73	12.21	4.07	1.11	.99
Rhode Island	.48	.63	.55	.75	2.71	10.74	32.14	35.59	12.49	2.96	.53	.43
Connecticut	1.31	1.57	1.47	1.46	3.53	10.50	29.21	33.21	12.14	3.55	1.06	.99

* Vacation lodging business includes hotels, tourist homes, and motor courts. Estimates based on Vacation Business Index of the Federal Reserve Bank of Boston and the Inventory on Vacation Accommodations of the New England Council.
† Except Suffolk County.
Source: The New England Economy, Report to the President by the Committee on the New England Economy of the Council of Economic Advisers, Washington (July 1951), p. 198

Source of Patronage

Table 6–5 shows the home regions of Americans who took vacations in New England during 1950. The data were derived from two publishing company surveys made in that year. While the surveys disagree in some details, their general findings are similar. Roughly two-thirds of the region's vacationists were New Englanders themselves. A large part of the remaining business came from the adjacent Middle Atlantic states of New York, New Jersey, and Pennsylvania, and other significant sources were the South Atlantic and East North Central regions. More recent and more complete figures would undoubtedly show a significant amount of Canadian business, especially from Quebec to the seashore resorts. The importance of a region as a source of New England vacation business typically decreases with distance.

In both New England and the rest of the country, about four-fifths of vacationers travel by automobile, though the percentage may be higher in the northern New England states. For example, during the eight years prior to World War II 87% of Vermont's vacation visitors used automobiles, ac-

cording to a survey conducted by the Vermont Development Commission. A
fairly large percentage use the railroads, however, as Table 6–6 shows. Vacationers coming to New England were more inclined in 1950 to travel by rail

Table 6–5. Residence of Americans Who Took Vacations in New England, 1950
(in per cent)

HOME REGION	CURTIS SURVEY*	CROWELL-COLLIER SURVEY†
New England	66.7‡	66.7
Middle Atlantic	20.8	16.2
East North Central	4.4	3.6
West North Central	.9	1.8
South Atlantic	5.9	7.2
East South Central	.1	—
West South Central	.7	4.5
Mountain	.3	—
Pacific	.4	—

* Curtis Publishing Company, op. cit. (figures partly estimated).   † The American Magazine Sixth Annual Travelogue,
Crowell-Collier Publishing Company, 1951.   ‡ Estimated.

than those going to other regions of the country, while the reverse was true
of busses. Although the proportion that traveled by air was fairly small, the
New England figure exceeded that for the rest of the nation.

Table 6–6. How Vacationists Traveled, United States and
New England, 1950

| TYPE | PER CENT OF ALL TRIPS* | |
	IN UNITED STATES	IN NEW ENGLAND
Automobile	81.9	80.9
Railroad (Pullman)	3.6	3.1
Railroad (coach)	13.6	19.1
Bus	12.1	7.4
Air line	3.1	3.7
Ship and boat	1.9	1.5
Other	1.9	.7

* Totals exceed 100% because some people used more than
one method of transportation.
Source: Curtis Publishing Company, op. cit.

Vacation Appeals

What does the vacationer seek when he leaves home on a trip? We have
pointed out some of New England's characteristics which appeal to vacationers, such as shoreline, mountains, climate, cultural activities, and historic
spots. Which appeal most to the vacationer? Inadequate knowledge on that
score handicaps both effective advertising and the sound planning of new
facilities.

Unfortunately, there has been little systematic study of what appeals to
vacationers. *The most recent New England-wide study on vacation appeals*

was made in 1930 by Lawrence W. Chidester, then at Tufts College. The study was conducted with the aid of the New England Council.[2]

Chidester found that the most important vacation appeal was "natural surroundings." Of the 566 respondents to his questionnaire, 465 ranked that appeal fifth or better out of ten possible choices. What type of "natural sur-

Table 6–7. Scenic Attractions Preferred by New England
Vacationists, 1930

TYPE	PER CENT WHO PREFERRED*
Mountains and lakes	39.8
Mountains	20.3
Mountains and seashore	15.1
Seashore	10.6
Lakes	5.7
Mountains, seashore, and lakes	5.3
Lakes and seashore	2.9
TOTAL	100.0

* Details do not add to total due to rounding.
Source: Lawrence W. Chidester, "New England's Recreational Appeals" (unpublished), 1930

roundings"? The responses Chidester got indicated that nearly 40% of those replying preferred a combination of mountains and lakes, 20% preferred mountains, and 15% preferred mountains and seashore. (See Table 6–7.) Clearly New England's mountains were its outstanding topographical at-

Table 6–8. Ranking of Vacation Appeals by
566 New England Vacationists, 1930

APPEAL	NUMBER OF TIMES EACH APPEAL APPEARED IN THE FIRST FIVE MENTIONS
Natural surroundings	465
Good food	408
Healthful climate	353
Reasonable rates	329
Quiet, comfort, and rest	267
Modern conveniences	252
Sports	217
Courtesy and service	201
Historic places	167
Social activities	42

Source: Ibid.

traction at that time. The lapse of 22 years, however, makes it important to reappraise that situation and determine any changes in consumer tastes.

In addition to "natural surroundings," other appeals that ranked high were "good food," "healthful climate," "reasonable rates," and "quiet, comfort,

2. A study of the vacation preferences of Vermont visitors was made by the Vermont Development Commission, however, for the years 1938–41. The results, while not directly comparable, were strikingly similar to the Chidester study and the Crowell-Collier Publishing Company survey. See H. H. Chadwick, *Millions for Vermont,* Vermont Development Commission (Montpelier, 1944), pp. 21–22.

and rest." Least important were "historic places" and "social activities." Table 6–8 presents the comparative ranking of the ten appeals.

There is no recent study for New England comparable to Chidester's, but the Crowell-Collier Publishing Company's survey of 1950 attempted to determine tourist appeals in the United States as a whole. The company listed a number of possible appeals and asked, "Which *two* of these factors are most important to you in planning where to spend your vacation?" The results are significant in the light of Chidester's earlier study.

While some of the appeals listed in the 1950 study were different from the Chidester list, many were similar. In 1950 "reasonable rates" was rated the most important, instead of fourth as in 1930. (See Table 6–9.) "Relaxation" was second in 1950, while in 1930 "quiet, comfort and rest" had ranked fifth. "Beautiful scenery" ranked third in 1950, while "natural surroundings" ranked first in the Chidester study. Low on the list in 1950 as in 1930 was "social activities."

Table 6–9. Ranking of Vacation Appeals by
United States Vacationists, 1950

APPEAL	PER CENT OF PERSONS SURVEYED CITING APPEAL AS ONE OF TWO MOST IMPORTANT
Reasonable rates	46
Relaxation	45
Beautiful scenery	37
Climate	20
Friendly people	19
Recreational facilities	14
Social activities	6
Other	7

Source: Crowell-Collier Publishing Company, *op. cit.*

It is always dangerous to compare two unlike studies and try to recognize trends from them. Nevertheless, with other information as a guide, these two studies suggest a few possible trends. Reasonable rates apparently have now become the most important general appeal to tourists. This may be because more young people and more persons in the lower income groups are taking vacations. To these groups, the problem of rates appears to be foremost. Relaxation, while it was always important, seems to appeal more to the vacationer today.

In both the 1930 and the 1950 studies, it appears from the low rank of sports, recreational facilities, social activities, and historic places that the vacationist wants to be left pretty much alone. He takes a trip primarily for a change of scenery and for relaxation, not to celebrate or to get an education in history. Resort areas should not become "rest homes," and social activities and sports should be available for those who rate such appeals high, as well as for those who use them only rarely but like to feel that they are around.

Historic places should also be maintained. *It appears, however, that historical and social assets should not be stressed unduly in promoting the New England vacation business as a whole.*

In addition to the analysis of appeals outlined above, Chidester also asked outsiders who had shown a prior interest in New England the following question: "Were you first interested in New England because of family connections in this section, or because you yourself lived here at one time?" Nearly 24% of those who replied answered "yes," an indication of the importance of "old New England connections" as an appeal to outsiders. Another of Chidester's questions was "What influence did or would road conditions in New England have on your decision to visit or tour this section?" The answers pointed up the importance of good roads to the region's vacation business, for 50.7% stated "very much," 27.7% said "much," 15.4% said "little," and only 7.2% replied "none." This was in 1930; good roads are probably even more important now, since such a large percentage of tourists travel by automobile.

Expenditures and Types of Lodging Used

Another topic on which only limited information is available is the level of expenditures by vacationists. In 1950, however, the Recreation Division of the Massachusetts Development and Industrial Commission released the results of a survey of vacationists' expenditures in Massachusetts during 1949. According to the study, the average vacationer in Massachusetts spent $10.58 a day. The average hotel guest spent $13.27, while guests at the other types of lodging places spent as follows: cabins, $9.88; tourist homes, $9.80; rented cottages, $8.57; friends and relatives, $8.21; other lodgings (trailers, tents, boats, etc.), $7.60. Those were total daily expenditures, not just for lodgings alone. While the figures applied only to Massachusetts, they were probably fairly close to the New England averages in 1949.

The type of lodging used apparently depends heavily on the income of the vacationist and on whether he is en route or has arrived at his destination. The Curtis Publishing Company found that during the year 1951 almost 60% of American families who took vacations stayed at least one night at a cabin or motel while en route (Table 6–10). There was a sharp increase in the percentage of families which used this type of lodging over that in previous years. More than 36% of the families stopped off at hotels or inns in 1951, a slightly lower percentage than during the two preceding seasons. While these are national figures, as are those in the next few tables, they probably provide a rough indication of the New England situation as well. It is obvious, however, that additional information of this type is needed for the New England area.

At their destinations, more than half of the nation's vacationing families stayed with friends and relatives at least part of the time during the last few years. (See Table 6–11). Hotels and inns and vacation cottages were the most frequently used types of lodging.

Table 6–10. Types of Vacation Lodging Used en Route in the United States, 1948–51*
(in per cent)

LODGING USED	TRAVEL YEAR 1948–49	TRAVEL YEAR 1949–50	CALENDAR YEAR 1951
Hotel and inn	37.9	41.4	36.2
Cabin and motel	40.5	51.5	59.3
Tourist home	11.1	13.4	11.0
Camp out	5.0	4.5	4.2
Trailer coach	1.2	1.0	1.3
Friends and relatives	35.9	28.7	29.8
Not reported	—	4.4	3.8

* Totals exceed 100% because in many instances more than one type of lodging was used on a trip.
Source: Curtis Publishing Company, op. cit.

The average number of nights spent by the nation's vacationists at each type of lodging in 1951, both en route and at destination, are shown in Table 6–12. The average was naturally lower en route, since most vacationists still prefer to spend the greater amount of time in one place rather than traveling. The recent trend, however, seems to be toward more mobility and shorter stays at each place. The average number of nights spent "at destination" in

Table 6–11. Types of Vacation Lodging Used at Destination
in the United States, 1948–1951*
(in per cent)

LODGING USED	TRAVEL YEAR 1948–49	TRAVEL YEAR 1949–50	CALENDAR YEAR 1951
Hotel and inn	25.8	22.7	24.9
Cabin and motel	9.2	7.5	9.9
Tourist home	4.1	4.4	4.1
Vacation cottage	16.9	13.4	11.2
Camp out	4.6	3.7	4.0
Trailer coach	.7	2.5	1.5
Friends and relatives	46.2	51.2	50.9
Not reported	—	2.6	2.1

* Totals exceed 100% because in many instances more than one type of lodging was used on a trip.
Source: Idem

1951 ranged from 11.6 for vacation cottages to 4.8 for cabins and motels.

The higher the income group, the greater the percentage of families using hotels and inns both en route and at their vacation destinations. (See Tables 6–13 and 6–14.) The middle-income groups were the largest users of cabins and motels in 1950, and the lower income groups turned more frequently to other types of accommodation. All groups, however, used each type of lodging quite extensively.

Such measurements as these are needed for the New England vacationist on a continuing basis. While national data are better than none, there are probably many ways in which the pattern varies within the region, as well as between New England and the United States as a whole. To guide the actions and policies of vacation business operators and promotional agencies, up-to-date information is vital.

Table 6–12. Average Number of Nights Spent at Each Type of Lodging by United States Tourists, 1951

TYPE OF LODGING	EN ROUTE	AT DESTINATION
Hotel and inn	2.5	5.6
Cabin and motel	3.8	4.8
Tourist home	2.1	8.4
Vacation cottage (rented or owned)	—	11.6
Camp out	3.1	8.1
Trailer coach	6.6	6.5

Source: Idem

Table 6–13. Per Cent of United States Vacationing Families Using Various Types of Lodgings While en Route, by Income Groups, 1950

	PER CENT USING		
INCOME GROUP	HOTELS AND INNS	CABINS AND MOTELS	OTHER LODGINGS
Under $2,000	25.0	32.9	42.1
$2,000–$2,999	24.7	30.5	44.8
$3,000–$4,999	26.8	38.1	35.1
$5,000–$7,499	31.9	34.7	33.4
$7,500–$9,999	28.7	39.6	31.7
$10,000 and over	37.1	35.8	27.1

Source: Idem

Table 6–14. Per Cent of United States Vacationing Families Using Various Types of Lodgings at Destination, by Income Groups, 1950

	PER CENT USING		
INCOME GROUP	HOTELS AND INNS	CABINS AND MOTELS	OTHER LODGINGS
Under $2,000	13.5	5.2	81.3
$2,000–$2,999	16.6	5.3	78.1
$3,000–$4,999	16.6	7.3	76.1
$5,000–$7,499	27.3	9.3	63.4
$7,500–$9,999	29.3	8.0	62.7
$10,000 and over	40.4	6.0	53.6

Source: Idem

Summary

This section has summarized the principal available information about the interests and other characteristics of the vacationer. It was concerned not only with finding out about the average vacationer but, more important, with determining the variations among vacationers. To attract larger amounts of vacation expenditures, operators and promoters must know these characteristics. *Knowledge about the New England vacationer is still extremely limited. To complete this picture, and to keep it up to date, much more study is needed by regional groups such as the New England Council, by state or local groups such as planning and development commissions or area development associations, and by trade associations of the vacation industry.*

The lack of considerable important information makes it difficult to plan a sound developmental program in detail. Nevertheless, certain major problems of the New England vacation business stand out, and New England has to move ahead with its planning even though not all the facts are in. As more data become available, the plans can be progressively refined and improved.

Any broad program for region-wide improvement of the vacation business should give particular attention to these problems: (1) the present inadequacy of promotions, (2) the sharp seasonal pattern of business, (3) the need for improved facilities, (4) the shortcomings of many vacation business managements, and (5) the need for specific changes in operating policies. We discuss these problems in the next section and offer some suggestions for improvement.

A PROGRAM FOR STRENGTHENING THE NEW ENGLAND VACATION BUSINESS

More Effective Promotion

Probably the most important element in a program to strength the New England vacation business is enlarged and improved publicity and advertising. In the past, promotion has been carried on by a large number of groups, operating independently, principally by the state development commissions, transportation companies, chambers of commerce, regional associations such as the New England Council, privately supported state publicity bureaus, and tourist-lodging trade associations. Of course, there is some promotion by individual resorts and lodging places, but the small operators are not in a position to carry out wide-scale advertising on an individual basis.

Since the benefits of increased vacation business are more widely distributed throughout a state than increases in many other kinds of business, it is logical for the citizens of the various states to help promote this business to some extent through state-financed advertising campaigns. State promotion should complement promotion by private groups and local agencies, but it should not replace it. There has been an increasing tendency to think in terms of state support when there is a need for expanded promotion expenditures. State promotion, it can be argued, permits operation on a larger scale than most private promotion and thus benefits from the economies of large-scale operation. On the other hand, large-scale promotion by the trade itself could also obtain cost benefits. While it is difficult for the small tourist lodging places to advertise effectively, their collective capacity is large.

The issue is really not *whether* both public and private groups should promote vacation business but *how* the effort should be divided. Obviously, the lodging place operators, transportation agencies, stores, and restaurants should carry on most of the total effort, since they reap the largest portion of the direct benefits. Moreover, too much state promotion smacks of subsidization, and the New England vacation business should be improved rather than subsidized. Nevertheless, the difficulties in organizing the multitude of small operators into an effective promotional group are very great. *It would appear that the larger operators should work more closely with the transportation agencies and interested organizations in a large, coordinated, sustained promotional campaign, and that the effort by each state government should be tailored to supplement the private activities.*

The New England state governments are at present spending somewhat more than $500,000 a year for tourist and vacation travel promotion. That is more than 10% of the total for all state governments throughout the country. But more than half the regional total is spent by Maine. The figures in Table 6–15 indicate that the expenditures of the other New England states have not been high in relation to their vacation business receipts or in relation to expenditures by some other leading vacation states. While the California state government spends nothing on vacation travel promotion, various cities and counties in the state do extensive advertising and promotion for this purpose. This practice is not followed in New England.

In most of the New England states, an increase in state promotion of the vacation business would seem to be in order, providing the private agencies do their part.

Total promotional expenditures by development groups apparently lag in New England. According to a 1951 study by the Curtis Publishing Company, private area and community organizations in California and Florida spent $1,006,000 and $903,000 respectively for vacation promotion in that year. Area and community organizations in Maine spent about $240,000, including $160,000 for the Maine Publicity Bureau alone; but those in the remaining New England states totaled only about $120,000, including $30,000 expended by the New England Council.

It is interesting to compare the expenditures of some specific groups in various states. For example, in 1951, according to the Curtis survey, the White Mountains Region Association spent $5,000 to attract tourists and vacationers. The Atlantic City Department of Public Relations spent $240,000 for the same purpose. The Nantucket Publicity Bureau had a promotion budget of $5,500 in 1951, while the Sea Island (Georgia) Company used $20,500 to attract tourists. The largest area or community promotional budget reported for New England, other than the Maine Publicity Bureau, was that of the Cape Cod Chamber of Commerce, which spent $20,000 in 1951. The All-year Club of Southern California, Ltd., had a budget of $465,000; the Redwood Empire Association spent $125,000; the San Diego–California Club, spent $82,600; and the Miami Beach Chamber of Commerce spent $270,000. *The advertising budgets of New England's private promotional groups obviously could be enlarged.*

Table 6–15. Expenditures by New England and Other
State Governments for Tourist and Vacation Travel
Promotion, 1951–52

STATE	TOTAL EXPENDITURE
Maine	$260,000
New Hampshire*	64,837
Vermont	41,875
Massachusetts*	126,470†
Rhode Island	25,000
Connecticut	10,000‡
NEW ENGLAND TOTAL	$528,182
New York	608,000†
Florida	384,000
New Mexico	341,410
California	none
UNITED STATES TOTAL	$4,937,978

* For 1950–51.   † An undesignated part was used
to promote agriculture and industry. ‡ Estimated.
Source: Idem, August 1951 (except for Connecticut)

A substantial part of the vacation advertising of New England is carried on by the region's transportation companies. A recent estimate placed the annual promotional expenditures by railroad, air line, bus, and automobile rental companies at more than $1,000,000 a year. *Naturally the transportation companies are direct beneficiaries of increased vacation travel, but it seems clear that some of the other direct beneficiaries, including many of the operators themselves and their promotional organizations, are not doing relatively as much to promote their common goal.*

Of course, the amount of money spent on advertising is not the only criterion for evaluating promotion campaigns. More important, in the last analysis, is the effectiveness of the promotion. The analyst should give a great deal of attention to "how" as well as to "how much" in promotion work. The mere fact that there is so little information about the New England vacationer indicates that not enough research has been undertaken to determine the most effective manner of promoting the vacation business. Moreover, publicity through news stories can be just as valuable as advertising and other paid promotion.

While we believe that private and local groups should increase their tourist promotion budgets considerably, it seems clear that even the present New England promotional budgets could be more effective. Is New England's promotion effectively designed? In his 1930 study Chidester found that vacation advertisements tended to emphasize most those attractions with the lowest relative appeal to the vacationer, such as "sports." Chidester analyzed 261 vacation advertisements of all sizes and description which were placed

*Table 6–16. Appeals Used in 261 Newspaper
Advertisements by the New England
Vacation Industry, 1930*

APPEAL	NUMBER OF ADVERTISEMENTS*
Sports	172
Natural surroundings	143
Excellent food	136
Modern conveniences	85
Social activities	54
Reasonable rates	33
Quiet, comfort, and rest	29
Courtesy and service	20
Healthful climate	9
Historic places	0

* Total exceeds 261 because some advertisements used more than one "appeal."
Source: Chidester, *op. cit.*

by the New England vacation industry in selected Boston and New York papers. The results of the analysis are shown in Table 6–16. Those findings, when compared with Table 6–8, indicate that the advertisers did not emphasize the attractions in proportion to their appeal to the customer. The stress on "sports" was far out of line, and the stress on "social activities" was

*Table 6–17. Appeals Used in 261 Newspaper
and Magazine Advertisements by the New
England Vacation Industry, June 1952*

APPEAL	NUMBER OF ADVERTISEMENTS*
Natural surroundings	153
Sports	143
Excellent food	118
Reasonable rates	110
Modern conveniences	65
Social activities	58
Quiet, comfort, and rest	35
Healthful climate	14
Courtesy and service	12
Historic places	4

* Total exceeds 261 because some advertisements used more than one "appeal."
Source: Boston Sunday *Herald*, June 15, 1952,
and *Holiday* magazine, June 1952

also too high. On the other hand, "healthful climate" and "reasonable rates" were apparently not featured enough.

To determine if the New England vacation industry had changed its emphasis, the Committee of New England made a similar study in June 1952. The results are shown in Table 6–17. The 1952 analysis shows an increased emphasis on "natural surroundings" and "reasonable rates" in advertising, but there is apparently still too much emphasis on "sports" and "social activities." Also, there still seems to be too little stress on "reasonable rates," "quiet, comfort, and rest," and "healthful climate."

Another limitation of most of the advertisements was their failure to mention New England as a region. There are some important advantages in promoting New England as a whole, rather than the individual states, to build up consumer recognition and acceptance of one "product" rather than six. Each state would benefit, since the region is so compact. According to the New England Council, tourist visitors to the region spend their money in an average of 4.3 of the six states.

In recognition of the mutual interest of the six states, the New England Council has sponsored a program of interstate cooperation in a large-scale New England promotional campaign throughout the nation, on the theme, "While you're in New England . . . see *all* New England." State agencies, trade and regional associations, transportation agencies, and others are all supporting the effort. The program calls for an annual additional expenditure of $500,000 a year for three years, with an ultimate goal of $1,500,000 each year. That effort is designed to increase New England's share of the nation's vacation business.

It has been suggested that the $500,000 minimum budget be raised by state donations of $250,000 and industry donations of $250,000. The money would be spent by a committee working with the New England Council for space advertising, publicity releases, travel posters, one or more full-color sound movies, and a quarterly magazine on New England. *We endorse the Council's general plan of cooperation between the states and the industry, although we believe that the industry's ratio of donations should be more than 50%. We also believe that part of the money should be spent for continuing research on the New England vacationer and the appeals that are most effective in attracting him.*

Extending the Season

Another major problem of the New England vacation industry is that of extending the vacation season. As we have pointed out, the industry faces a serious operating disadvantage because of the sharp seasonal demand for vacation facilities. The extreme seasonality means that a large percentage of the tourist facilities in New England must cover all fixed costs during a very short period. To remain profitable, either rates in New England must be higher than in regions where the seasonal business is not so sharp, or facilities cannot be as expensive as elsewhere—or both. Rates in New England apparently are not significantly out of line with those in other regions, but the lodgings on the average are apt to be less impressive. Even a partial solu-

CHART 6–1

Number of Seasonal Vacation Establishments Open* in New England, by Months, 1945 (exclusive of all-year establishments)

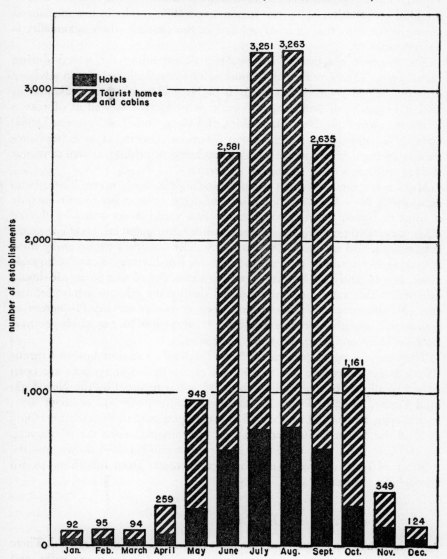

* Months open ten days or more. Partial coverage only. Some seasonal establishments failed to report.

Source: New England Council, *New England Vacation Business Inventory, 1945*

tion to the seasonality problem would be a great help to the operators in financing needed capital improvements.

In addition to its effects on financing, seasonality of business causes a seasonal labor problem that can be troublesome both to the operator and to the local community. Moreover, seasonal operation results in less specialized management than that in other sections of the country where seasonality is less pronounced.

The industry has tackled the problem of extending the season during recent years. The New England Council, for example, largely in an advisory capacity, helped promote fall business in New Hampshire in 1951, and in 1952 it helped push "sugaring-off" business in March, as well as off-season business in Vermont, New Hampshire, and Cape Cod. The Vermont Development Commission and the Greater Vermont Association have been promoting spring fishing and fall hunting and horseback riding, as well as winter skiing, apparently with significant success.

Much more such off-season promotion should be undertaken. There is no reason why New England should be considered by so many tourists as only a summer resort, when the region has fine vacation opportunities during other seasons. Many New Englanders consider spring and fall New England's best seasons, and it is probable that many more outsiders would enjoy these seasons if they could be tempted to try them. Furthermore, since "reasonable rates" is apparently the leading appeal to a majority of vacationers, it should be stressed that rates are much reduced during the off-season months, and that this does not imply fewer attractions or poorer service. *Promotion of fall, winter, and spring vacations should be an integral part of all cooperative, state, or other campaigns promoting the area.*

The sharp seasonal pattern of New England's vacation business means that a large percentage of the resorts and tourist lodging places are open only a small part of the year. Of the 1,263 hotels reported by the New England Council in its 1945 vacation business inventory, only 512, or about 40%, stayed open all year. More than 45% were open only in the summer. Only 35% of the tourist homes and cabin groups remained open the whole year, and 64% of them were open only in the summer. Chart 6–1 shows how the number of open seasonal establishments fluctuates from month to month throughout the year.

Improvements in Facilities

We have already pointed out that most New England hotels are old. There has been little new construction of large resort hotels for many years, and many of the old ones have been abandoned or destroyed by fire. To a great extent the declining relative importance of hotels is a result of the changing desires of the vacationist and the high cost of new construction. New construction has generally been cabin groups, motor courts, and smaller inns and hotels, to cater to the automobile tourist of limited means. Future construction should be based on careful study of trends in the desires of vacationists, in their methods of transportation, and in their expenditure patterns.

A large percentage of the region's guest rooms of all types, however, lack modern creature comforts. Less than 45% of the hotel rooms in 1945 had private baths. Only about 5% of the tourist-home guest rooms had private baths. Moreover, only about one-third of New England's cabins had private baths, less than half had toilets and running water, and only slightly over half had heat. Figures are not available for other United States regions, but it seems likely that New England compares unfavorably with its chief competitors. *There is an urgent need for improvement in facilities and modernization by many existing establishments.*

In spite of the short season, a large number of both modern lodging places and modernized older establishments have been operating profitably throughout New England. It can be done, therefore, and the short season and high costs are not a sufficient excuse for inadequacies. *It would appear that many of the poor facilities could be improved profitably if the management was of sufficiently high caliber.*

The relatively low cost of entry into the tourist business encourages many poorly managed concerns to enter the business each year. A large proportion of them are gradually forced out of business, but their places are too often taken by other poorly managed concerns. The mortality rate is relatively high. Under such conditions, the shortcomings in facilities tend to be perpetuated. To break out of that situation and make the improvements that the industry needs, there must be considerable new investment by able operators. Naturally, success in promoting the entire New England vacation business and in extending the season will assist greatly in the improvement of facilities, by encouraging both enterprisers and lenders.

In addition to the quality of the lodgings, however, the vacationist is often influenced by the availability and adequacy of public recreational facilities, such as beaches and state parks. The touring visitor to New England does not have access to the private beaches that line the region's coast line. New Hampshire has provided modern self-supporting beach facilities on its short coast. The other states have some public beaches, but they are often overcrowded and inadequate, especially in Massachusetts. State-owned beaches can be financially independent and can add to the enjoyment of the residents of a state, as well as of the out-of-state tourists. *A carefully worked out program of public beach development would be desirable for all five of the New England states which border the ocean. Moreover, each state should also reappraise the adequacy of its state parks and other inland recreational facilities.* They can be self-supporting, as New Hampshire has proved, and they can also provide an extra attraction for the visiting vacationer.

Improvements in Management and Operations

The poorly managed concern hurts the whole vacation industry in at least two major ways. First, by providing poor service and facilities to the customer it is a source of "bad will" for the industry. Tourists who are disappointed with the treatment they receive may not return to New England. Secondly, the high mortality rate gives the industry a poor credit rating with banks and other lenders. As a result, even well-established profitable concerns may find it more difficult to obtain loans for needed improvements.

In a free enterprise system it is usually not sound policy to erect artificial barriers to free entry into any business. Such barriers tend to undermine competition and may eventually result in stagnation. It seems unwise, therefore, to build up artificial barriers against entry into the vacation business. What can be done to prevent the destructive effects of easy entry?

A suitable management-education program would be of great assistance in solving this problem. At the outset, it should be made clear to prospective entrants that catering to the tourist is not an easy job. It requires hard work, specialized knowledge, good management, and a natural aptitude for getting along with people. Too many new vacation business operators underestimate the demands of the business.

The operator of a small establishment cannot afford a great deal of hired help, and must carry most of the burden himself. He must have a sound knowledge of the business and be prepared to work long hours. He must not only be a good organizer but be able to handle finances quickly and efficiently to meet payrolls, taxes, insurance, interest, and other operating costs promptly. He must understand how to take care of depreciation and obsolescence reserves. He must be able to do simple repair work and small carpentry and painting jobs. He must insist on cleanliness within and outside his establishment. Most important, he must enjoy people. Tourists away from home want to escape the drudgery of work. They insist on being catered to, and, since they are paying for the service, they should be. The job is not one for an older person or for a person who cannot devote a great deal of his time to it.

The small operator who has had no previous experience in the business may find himself seriously handicapped unless he realizes what he is up against and prepares himself adequately in advance. *An educational program which pointed out the nature and problems of the business to the prospective entrant might well winnow out many who are not suited for it, to the advantage of other entrants and of the New England vacation industry as a whole.* This educational process is a job for the industry itself, as well as for regional and area associations and other groups. While the facts should be widely disseminated, an excellent point of concentration is the banks. Most vacation business operators seek bank loans or banker advice. To the extent that the bankers of the region understand the qualifications for a good tourist lodging place operator, they can both encourage and aid the promising prospect and discourage many of those unlikely to succeed.

The second element of an education program would be to provide more management aids to those already in the tourist or resort business and to those definitely planning to enter. Such a program should make available comprehensive and detailed information on financing the business, accounting and bookkeeping procedures, repair work, recreational facilities, menus and food preparation, methods of determining rates, advertising, landscaping, and a host of other items.

Pamphlets or manuals on the various subjects can cover most of the general problems of the small operators. The United States Department of Commerce has published a number of pamphlets to aid the operators of small businesses, including one on *Establishing and Operating a Year-round Motor Court.* The booklet contains no magic formula for success but it does offer many sound suggestions on operating procedure, and it points out some of the problems in the business. Many other pamphlets and manuals are available from a variety of sources on topics of importance to the vacation business operator. The industry itself might benefit considerably from a close scrutiny of all available instructional literature, from the preparation of a complete course of study and reference material, and from the extensive distribution of that material to its members.

Vacation operators in New England now have one management aid that their competitors in other areas have not had. The Federal Reserve Bank of Boston initiated the industry's first Vacation Business Index in 1947. Through reports from hundreds of individual operators, the bank compiles monthly indexes of guest nights, receipts, and advance reservations for the various types of vacation establishments. The indexes help the individual operators to gauge their own situations in relation to those of their competitors and to take quick action when it is needed. The success of the Index in New England has led to its imitation in several other parts of the country. *The New England Vacation Business Index should receive continued strong support from the industry.*

In addition to published information, however, to complete the educational task would require ready access by the operators to competent advisers for the solution of special operating problems. At present, many operators undoubtedly receive assistance from their fellow operators, suppliers, trade associations, bankers, or other sources. Those more or less casual sources have not been enough. *A more widespread program of vacation operator counseling would be desirable.*

Who should handle such an educational program? There have been suggestions that a vacation operator training program and counseling service become part of the work of state agricultural schools and extension services. Michigan State College has had such a program for a number of years, and its tourist and resort series of circulars have been both interesting and helpful. Perhaps this method is the best way to handle such a program. We should prefer, however, to see the industry itself carry on the activities, either through a trade association or through some other privately sponsored group. It seems fairest that the operators should pay the costs of services from which they benefit so directly. The fees would not need to be large; even the smallest operator should be in a position to subscribe.

CONCLUSIONS

The New England vacation industry is of great importance to the entire region, as well as to the operators of the vacation establishments themselves. In view of the growing competition from other vacation areas, it is important that the industry extend, intensify, and improve its efforts to solve its problems and strengthen its position.

A detailed prescription for the business is complicated by the inadequacy of data about many of its phases. There is far too little information available about the New England vacationist himself, his desires, and how best to attract him. We strongly urge the region's developmental agencies and vacation trade associations to step up their research into these matters, in order to increase the efficiency of their promotional and other work.

On the basis of existing information, however, it would appear that the following approaches offer the best prospects for strengthening New England's vacation business. Some of them are already firmly entrenched in the thinking of those actively engaged in the development of the industry.

1. Increased advertising and promotion of New England by the region's private development agencies and local organizations, and, where appropriate, by the state governments.

2. Increased cooperation among the states and private organizations in the joint vacation promotion of New England as a whole.

3. Changes in the emphasis of advertising appeals to coincide more closely with the ranking of attractions by the vacationists themselves.

4. Special attention in promotion, and in the planning of facilities and operations, to the urgent need for extending New England's vacation season.

5. Continuing adaptation of the region's vacation facilities to the changing pattern of vacationists' desires and characteristics.

6. Modernization and improvement of a great many existing establishments.

7. Greater education of prospective entrants to the business by trade associations, banks, development organizations, and others, to help raise the average level of new operators and increase their prospects of success.

8. Greater provision of management aids to operators of vacation establishments, in the form both of printed pamphlets and manuals and of

counseling service, preferably by the industry itself through its trade associations or by area-development groups.

9. Greater research to learn more about the vacationer, as well as about the business itself. An up-to-date New England-wide inventory of facilities would be a step in the right direction, but much more than that is needed.

The people of New England can also be of service to the vacation industry. They should recognize its importance to the region and to themselves. They should treat the visiting tourist as they like to be treated when they are on vacation in other parts of the country. The visitor who returns is the one who is made to feel at home. It is important to New England's future prosperity that the visitors return.

SELECTED REFERENCES

1. Chidester, Lawrence W., "The Importance of Recreation as a Land Use in New England," *Journal of Land and Public Utilities Economics,* May 1934.
2. —— "Selling New England Scientifically" (unpublished), Tufts College, 1930.
3. —— "New England's Recreational Appeals" (unpublished), Tufts College, 1930.
4. Crowell-Collier Publishing Company, *The American Magazine Sixth Annual Travelogue,* New York, 1951.
5. Curtis Publishing Company, *The Vacation Travel Market of the United States,* Nationwide Survey No. 2, Philadelphia, 1951, and No. 3, 1952.
6. —— *Tourist and Vacation Advertising Expenditures by States, Areas, and Communities in 1951,* Philadelphia, 1951.
7. —— *Supplemental Report of Promotional Expenditures by State Governments,* Philadelphia, 1951.
8. Federal Reserve Bank of Boston, *Monthly Review.*
9. Massachusetts Development and Industrial Commission, *Massachusetts Vacation Survey,* Boston 1950.
10. New England Council, *New England Vacation Business Inventory, 1945,* Pt. 1 "Overnight Accommodations for New England Vacation Visitors," Boston, 1948.
11. New Hampshire State Planning and Development Commission, *Recreation Property in the Lakes Region, 1945–1952,* Concord, February 1953.
12. U.S. Department of Commerce, *Establishing and Operating a Year-round Motor Court,* Industrial (Small Business) Series, No. 50, Washington, 1946.
13. G. H. Ladd, *1949 Vacation Business Survey of Cabins, Hotels, and Tourist Homes,* Vermont Development Commission, Montpelier, 1950.
14. H. H. Chadwick, *Millions for Vermont,* Vermont Development Commission, Montpelier, 1944.

7

The People of New England and Their Employment

Drafted by William H. Miernyk under the direction
of Arthur A. Bright, Jr.

INTRODUCTION

There is a close interdependence between the economic health of a region and the characteristics of its people. This is universally true. The relationship between the people and the economic state of New England is perhaps closer than that in any other section of the United States. The region is not richly endowed with natural resources. It is located in a corner of the nation; it is faced with relatively high transportation costs. Yet New England is a major manufacturing region with a dense concentration of population and a high level of per capita income.

Unlike many other regions, New England cannot rely heavily on the fabrication of indigenous materials for sale in national and international markets. Most raw materials and all mineral fuels must be brought to its people. With their hands and brains they must convert them into products that can compete with those made in other regions and nations.

New England's major resource is its people. This report examines and evaluates some of their outstanding features. It also provides the basic introduction to later discussions of unemployment problems, wage rates, and labor-management relations.[1]

An inventory and appraisal of the human resources of New England is an integral part of any economic analysis of the region. How old is the average resident of New England? How many years of school has he completed? What facilities are available to protect his health and to provide education for his children? How many New Englanders have been migrating to other regions, and how many people have moved to New England in search of jobs?

How many people in New England are foreign-born? Are they less mobile than native New Englanders? Do they tend to remain in a community when job opportunities no longer exist? Do they have equality of economic opportunity with those whose foreign antecedents go back several generations? Many of these questions about the foreign-born are difficult to answer. There is a notable absence of factual data about them, yet such facts are of considerable importance in appraising how well the people of the region have developed their full potentialities. This report can provide

1. See our reports on "Employment Fluctuations in New England" (No. 8), "Wages in New England" (No. 9), and "Labor-Management Relations in New England" (No. 10).

only an introduction to this topic. It is a fertile field for much further sociological research.

Related to the discussion of New England's population is an analysis of
the region's labor force. How many people in New England are at work or
actively seeking work? Is there relatively more or less unemployment in
New England than in other regions? How do those who are employed
make their living? What changes have occurred in the occupational distribution of the region's labor force during the last few decades? What are
the consequences and future implications of these changes?

These are a few of the questions with which this report is concerned.

NEW ENGLAND'S POPULATION

More than 9,300,000 people live in the six New England states. One of
every 16 residents of the United States is a New Englander. Over half the
people of New England live in Massachusetts, and half of the Massachusetts residents live in the Boston metropolitan area. (See Table 7–1 for
population totals by states.)

Urban-rural, Age, and Sex Distributions

About three-fourths of all New Englanders live in urban places, a considerably larger proportion than in the nation as a whole. As might be
expected, the urban concentration is particularly large in southern New
England, but even in New Hampshire and Maine more than half the

Table 7–1. Total Population and Urban-rural Distribution, United States
and the New England States, 1940–50

STATE	TOTAL POPULATION 1940	TOTAL POPULATION 1950	PER CENT OF NEW ENGLAND 1940	PER CENT OF NEW ENGLAND 1950	PER CENT IN-CREASE, 1940–50	Urban-rural distribution, 1950 URBAN	Urban-rural distribution, 1950 RURAL	PER CENT OF STATE URBAN	PER CENT OF STATE RURAL
Maine	847,226	913,744	10.0	9.8	7.8	472,000	441,774	51.7	48.3
New Hampshire	491,524	533,242	5.8	5.7	8.5	306,806	226,436	57.5	42.5
Vermont	359,231	377,747	4.3	4.1	5.2	137,612	240,135	36.4	63.6
Massachusetts	4,316,721	4,690,514	51.2	50.4	8.7	3,959,239	731,275	84.4	15.6
Rhode Island	713,346	791,896	8.5	8.5	11.0	667,212	124,684	84.3	15.7
Connecticut	1,709,242	2,007,280	20.2	21.5	17.4	1,558,642	448,638	77.6	22.4
NEW ENGLAND	8,437,290	9,314,423	100.0	100.0	10.4	7,101,511	2,212,942	76.2	23.8
UNITED STATES	131,669,275	150,697,000	—	—	14.5	96,028,000	54,669,000	63.7	36.3

Source: Bureau of the Census, U.S. Department of Commerce

population is urban. Between 1940 and 1950, however, there was an increase
in the proportion of rural residents in New England. The rural population
rose relative to the urban population in all the states except Maine and
Vermont. This shift did not represent a "back to the farm" movement, of

course, but it was an indication that more families have been locating their homes outside congested urban areas.[2]

In the country as a whole there were approximately 50.6 persons for every square mile of land in 1950. In New England the population density was 147.4 persons per square mile. There is considerable variation within the region, however, as Table 7–2 indicates. Southern New England is far more densely peopled than the three northern states. Maine, which accounts for nearly half the land area of New England, has less than 10% of the region's population. Rhode Island, on the other hand, covers less than 2% of the region's land area and has 8.5% of its population.

Table 7–2. Population Density, United States and the New England States, 1950

STATE	SQUARE MILES OF LAND AREA	POPULATION	POPULATION PER SQUARE MILE
Maine	31,040	913,744	29.4
New Hampshire	9,024	533,242	59.1
Vermont	9,278	377,747	40.7
Massachusetts	7,907	4,690,514	593.2
Rhode Island	1,058	791,896	748.5
Connecticut	4,899	2,007,280	409.7
NEW ENGLAND	63,206	9,314,423	147.4
UNITED STATES	2,197,128	150,697,000	50.6

Source: U.S. Department of Commerce, *Statistical Abstract of the United States, 1950*

The heavy concentration of population in New England has important economic implications. The region contains a large labor force and a sizable market for consumers' goods. On the other hand, jobs must be provided for a large number of workers within a small area, and the southern part of the region faces many special problems arising out of its congestion.

The average New Englander is slightly older than the average resident of the nation, and the ratio of female to male residents in New England is somewhat higher than the national average. Chart 7–1 shows the age and sex distribution of the people of New England compared with the nation as a whole. While New England has a larger than national proportion of elderly residents, it also has a smaller than national proportion of residents less than 15 years of age. Accordingly, *a larger than average percentage of New Englanders is in the productive age brackets.*

The distribution is not uniform among all New England states, however. Both the median age and the ratio of females to males is highest in Massachusetts.[3] Vermont has the lowest median age of any New England state. Table 7–3 presents the median age and the sex division by states, and Chart 7–2 shows the differences in distribution between northern and southern

2. The urban-rural distribution of population in 1940 and 1950 may be only roughly compared because of a change in census definitions between the two census years.
3. The median is an average that exceeds half the values and is exceeded by half.

CHART 7-1

Age and Sex Distribution of Population, United States and New England, 1950

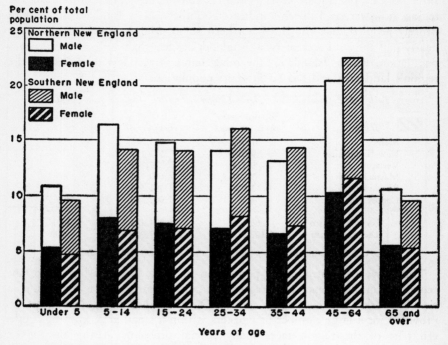

Source: Bureau of the Census, U.S. Department of Commerce

Table 7-3. Median Age and Sex Distribution, United States and the New England States, 1950

STATE	Median age (in years)			Sex distribution (per cent)	
	TOTAL POPULATION	MALE	FEMALE	MALE	FEMALE
Maine	30.2	29.7	30.6	49.7	50.3
New Hampshire	32.3	31.6	33.0	49.2	50.8
Vermont	30.1	29.6	30.7	49.7	50.3
Massachusetts	32.8	32.0	33.5	48.9	51.1
Rhode Island	31.8	30.6	33.0	49.3	50.7
Connecticut	32.7	32.2	33.1	49.2	50.8
NEW ENGLAND	32.3	31.6	32.9	49.1	50.9
UNITED STATES	30.1	29.9	30.4	49.5	50.5

Source: Bureau of the Census, U.S. Department of Commerce

CHART 7-2

Age and Sex Distribution of Population, Northern and Southern
New England, 1950

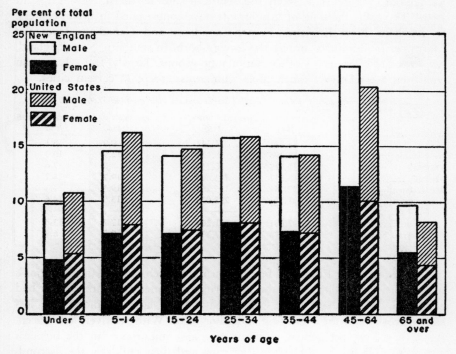

Source: *Idem*

New England. *The northern states have relatively more inhabitants in the
less productive age groups under 15 years of age and 65 or more. These differences provide a partial explanation of the lower per capita incomes in
the three northern states than in Massachusetts, Rhode Island, and Connecticut.*

The Foreign-born Population

New England has a larger proportion of foreign-born residents than any
other region of the United States. As in the country at large, however, the
region's foreign-born population has been declining both in absolute and
relative terms. The low level of immigration and the death of many older
immigrants, coupled with a rising domestic birth rate, sharply reduced the
proportion of foreign-born residents in the total population between 1940

and 1950. Table 7–4 shows the nature of the change during the decade of the 1940's. The New England proportion is still far above that of the nation as a whole.

Table 7–4 also indicates the substantial differences in proportions of foreign-born residents between the southern and northern New England states. Typically, the bulk of immigrants have congregated in urban centers. In northern New England, French-Canadians and Canadians from the Maritimes predominate among the foreign-born. In southern New England, however, immigrants of other nationality groups, largely from European countries, are relatively much more numerous, except in certain cities.

Table 7–4. Foreign-born Population, United States and the New England States, 1940–50

STATE	NUMBER OF FOREIGN-BORN		PER CENT OF TOTAL POPULATION	
	1940	1950	1940	1950
Maine	83,641	74,342	9.9	8.1
New Hampshire	68,296	58,134	13.9	10.9
Vermont	31,727	28,753	8.8	7.6
Massachusetts	848,852	713,699	19.7	15.2
Rhode Island	137,784	113,264	19.3	14.3
Connecticut	321,731	293,073	18.8	14.6
NEW ENGLAND	1,492,031	1,281,265	17.7	13.8
UNITED STATES	11,594,896	10,347,395	8.8	6.9

Source: Ibid.

As a group, New England's foreign-born are much older than the region's native-born population, since the great rush of American immigration had ended by 1920. These older people have been largely among the less skilled workers in the New England labor force. With relatively few exceptions, they have not gained positions of major importance in the business community. It has been claimed that they and their children, the "second-generation" Americans, have been discriminated against in the personnel policies of New England businesses and in the admission policies of the region's academic institutions. The problem of "ethnic minorities" is complicated, for it hinges on a complex of economic, educational, and sociological relationships. Adequate data are not available for a definitive answer to this question, but on the basis of fragmentary evidence a broad generalization may be made.

It appears that there have been substantial improvements in equality of opportunity during recent years, but it would seem that there is room for much further progress. Until every New Englander has an opportunity to develop his abilities to their full potentialities and to put them to work in the most productive fashion, the region is wasting part of its most valuable asset and depriving some of its citizens of their maximum economic and social well-being.

Recent Population Trends

As the population of the United States has increased, the center of population has shifted westward. The rate of population growth during recent decades has been greatest in the South and West. The increase in the South

Table 7–5. Net Gain or Loss through Internal Migration, New England States, 1920–50
(in thousands)

STATE	1920–30	1930–40	1940–50
Maine	−57	−1	−16
New Hampshire	−25	+13	+5
Vermont	−29	−19	−15
Massachusetts	-182	−67	+55
Rhode Island	−20	+1	+1
Connecticut	−1	+53	+128
NEW ENGLAND	−314	−20	+158

Source: 1920–30: Adapted from C. W. Thornwaite, Internal Migration in the United States, Philadelphia, University of Pennsylvania Press, 1934
1930–40: H. S. Shryock, "Internal Migrations and the War," Journal of the American Statistical Association, March 1943
1940–50: Bureau of the Census, U.S. Department of Commerce, "Provisional Intercensal Estimates of the Population of Regions, Divisions and States," Series P–25, No. 47, March 9, 1951

has been due largely to a high birth rate, while the rapid growth of population in the West has resulted from a combination of a relatively high birth rate and westward migration. New England, like other older and more thickly settled areas, has continued to show growth. Between 1940 and 1950

Table 7–6. Net Change in Population of the New England States, 1940–50
(in thousands)

STATE	NATURAL INCREASE	NET MIGRATION	NET LOSS TO ARMED FORCES	NET CHANGE
Maine	+94	−16	−11	+67
New Hampshire	+43	+5	−8	+40
Vermont	+39	−15	−4	+20
Massachusetts	+356	+55	−58	+353
Rhode Island	+70	+1	−6	+65
Connecticut	+187	+128	−22	+293
NEW ENGLAND	+788	+158	−109	+837

Note: Details may not add to totals because of rounding.
Source: Bureau of the Census, U.S. Department of Commerce, "Provisional Intercensal Estimates of the Population of Regions, Divisions and States," Series P–25, No. 47, March 9, 1951

the population of New England increased by 10.4%. This compares with an increase of 14.5% in the nation as a whole.

The rate of increase in the population of an area depends upon its natural rate of growth and the extent of in- or out-migration. New England's birth rate has been slightly below the national average, and its death rate slightly above. This has been largely a result of the age distribution of the region's population.

Trends in internal migration generally reflect changing economic conditions. From 1920 to 1940 fewer people moved into New England than out. The migration of the cotton-textile industry during this period, which was not offset by an equivalent flow of new industry into the region, meant declining job opportunities in the region's factories. Many New Englanders went elsewhere in search of employment. From 1940 to 1950, however, the trend was reversed. The natural rate of increase during this period was augmented by a net in-migration. The course of net migration for each New England state during the last three decades is given in Table 7–5.

Each New England state experienced a net out-migration in the 1920's, when there was a precipitous decline in employment in the cotton-textile industry. Since 1930 the trend has been mixed. Maine and Vermont have continued to show a net out-migration, which is fairly typical of states with a relatively large rural population. Connecticut had a net in-migration between 1930 and 1940, but it was not enough to offset in the regional totals the relatively large out-migration from Massachusetts. *After 1940 New England experienced a new in-migration, with the majority of in-migrants moving to Connecticut. The expansion of metal-working industries, in particular, attracted job seekers to Connecticut. The more moderate movements into New Hampshire, Massachusetts, and Rhode Island reflected some stabilizing in textile employment plus some growth in durable-goods manufacturing and other economic activities in those states.*

A more complete record of population growth in New England during the last decade is given in Table 7–6. In order to arrive at the net growth in the region's civilian population, a correction is made for the net transfers of New England residents to the armed forces. The region's civilian population grew by 837,000 persons between 1940 and 1950.

Long-run Population Growth

The long-run growth rate of New England's population has closely paralleled that of the nation, but at a somewhat lower level. By 1900 the *rate* of growth was declining in both the region and the nation, though the total population was rising steadily. In northern New England the rate began to increase again by 1920, though it was well below the level in the rest of New England. In southern New England and the nation as a whole the rate continued to decline irregularly throughout the depression years, but it turned upward again after 1940. These trends are illustrated by Chart 7–3, which shows the percentage changes in population from decade to decade since 1880.

Future Population Growth

What can we expect for the future? Will New England's population continue to grow? Will the net in-migration again turn into a net out-migration? It is always hazardous to make predictions. But *projections* can be made, based upon specific sets of assumptions. One projection based on past

CHART 7–3

Rates of Population Growth, United States and New England, 1880–1950

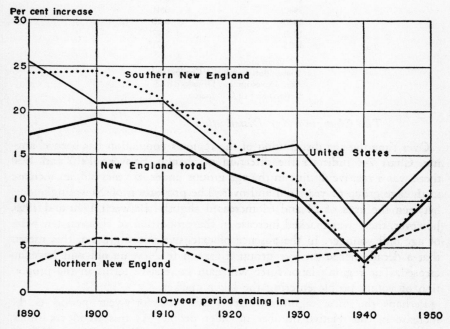

Source: *Idem*, adjusted by Department of Research and Statistics, Federal Reserve Bank of Boston

growth trends places New England's population in 1960 at approximately 10,100,000 persons, compared to 9,300,000 in 1950. By 1975, it is estimated, the region may have nearly 11,000,000 residents.[4] The actual course of population growth in the region will depend largely on economic, medical, and sociological developments during the next few decades.

4. The 1960 projection was made by the Bureau of the Census. The 1975 projection was made by the Area Development Division of the Department of Commerce. Both projections are based on the so-called "medium series," which is based on a moderate set of assumptions about birth rates and death rates.

Even if the population of New England continues to grow as expected in absolute terms, New Englanders will probably constitute a smaller share of the nation's population in the future because of faster growth in other less highly developed regions. This trend is to be expected and is in accordance with normal growth patterns of unevenly developed nations. The long-run trend, including future projections, is shown in Table 7–7.

Table 7–7. New England Population as Per Cent
of the United States, 1900–75

YEAR	PER CENT
1900	7.36
1910	7.12
1920	7.00
1930	6.65
1940	6.41
1950	6.20
1960	5.97ᵃ
1975	5.71*

* Estimated.
Source: Bureau of the Census and
Area Development Division, U.S.
Department of Commerce

The Changing Age Distribution

Over time the age distribution of the region's population has been changing. Chart 7–4 indicates the direction of change. Between 1910 and 1950 there was a relative decline in the age groups under 25 years old, an increase in the age group 65 years old and over. The proportion of New Englanders between the ages of 24 and 64 increased slightly. Between 1940 and 1950, however, there was marked increase in the proportion of children ten years of age and younger. In the absence of extensive out-migration, this means that a decade hence the age group from ten to 24 years old will have increased. The region's labor force will gain in relative terms in the proportion of young people entering the labor market.

Perhaps the most significant trend over the forty-year period is the increase in the relative number of older people. As this trend continues, an increasing proportion of the adult population will be withdrawn from the labor force. This raises some important questions: Will the continued aging of New England's population mean more pressure for pension plans? Will the region be able to provide jobs for those workers over 65 who are not yet ready to retire? Older workers are less inclined to migrate in search of jobs than younger workers. Either they must be able to find work or to continue at their jobs past the age of 65, or the economy must be ready to provide for them through industrial pension plans or realistic retirement benefits under social security programs. New England is already paying heavily for its older population through higher than average welfare expenditures by state and local governments.

If we make the assumption that many workers do not wish to retire when they reach the age of 65, which seems to be true, compulsory retirement programs at that age will tend to idle an increasing proportion of New England's population. The region will not be using its labor force to maximum advantage. It will lose the potential output which the older

CHART 7-4

The Changing Age Distribution of New England's Population, 1910-50

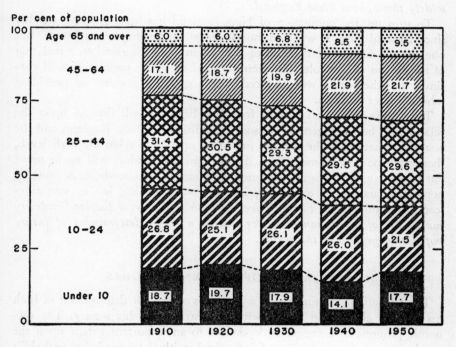

Source: *Idem, Census of Population,* 1910-50

workers are capable of producing, while they continue to consume. Moreover, many retired workers find it extremely difficult to make the human adjustments involved in retirement. *It would seem desirable to raise the compulsory retirement age, providing the worker is physically and mentally able to continue at work.*[5]

Another, though limited, approach to the problem of older workers can

5. This is not a plea for raising the voluntary retirement age. If a worker wishes to retire when he reaches the age of 65, he should be able to do so. See *Three Monographs Prepared for a Conference on the Retirement of Older Workers,* National Social Welfare Assembly, especially Monograph 3.

help bridge the gap between the present retirement age and any future increase. The deliberate recruitment of forcibly retired workers by businesses scattered throughout the region can aid the older individuals, community and state governments, and the businesses themselves. One experiment in this direction is Sunset Industries, Inc., which has employed older workers at standard wage rates to produce woodworking products in Eastport, Maine, and aprons in Boston, Massachusetts. The labor supply for such enterprises is plentiful, and there are many other products which would be appropriate for the physical abilities of older workers. *We hope that the movement to employ retired individuals will spread much more widely throughout New England.*

To sum up, the population of New England has been growing steadily since colonial days. It will continue to grow in the immediate future. But one should not expect the rate of growth in New England to equal that of the nation as a whole. The trend toward an aging population will continue, and the region will be faced with a growing problem of providing jobs for older workers.

The future migration pattern for New England will depend upon the relationship between general economic conditions in New England and the rest of the nation. If the region's industries operate at relatively high levels, there may be new in-migration; if not, New Englanders will again move out of the region in search of economic opportunities elsewhere. A growing population means an expanding market, but declining job opportunities lead to out-migration. *The effectiveness with which New England industry makes use of its human resources will be a major determinant of future population growth in the region.*

THE EDUCATION OF NEW ENGLANDERS

The educational attainment of a person is one major determinant of both his earning ability and his capacity to contribute to his society. The economic progress of a region is dependent to an important extent upon the steady increase in availability of individuals with the knowledge and skills necessary to continue and improve the production of necessary goods and services. While there is some worker mobility among different parts of the country, any area must depend largely upon its own people and its own educational system for manpower.

Average Years of School Completed

It is not possible to compare the knowledge of large groups of people directly, but the number of years of formal education received provides an indirect measure. Educational achievement varies from state to state. In Massachusetts, which has the highest New England record, the average person 25 years of age or older had completed 10.9 years of school in 1950. The comparable figures for the other states of the region ranged downward to Rhode Island's average of 9.3 years of school completed (Table 7–8). The table also shows the variations by place of residence. Typically, farm residents have lower averages of school years completed than the nonfarm population. Averages for other selected states are included, for comparative purposes.

On the whole, the level of educational achievement in the New England states compares favorably with that in other regions which resemble New England in terms of population, income, and industrial composition. The level is somewhat higher in the Far West, but that excess is at least partly due to the age distribution of the region's population. A few decades ago many more persons dropped out of school at a relatively early age than is true today. This tends to pull down the average number of school years completed in a region with a substantial proportion of older residents. *In view of the age distribution of the New England population and the high proportion of foreign-born, New England's record of school years completed seems to be good.*

Table 7–8. *Median School Years Completed by Residents* of New England and Other Selected States, 1950*

STATE	STATE MEDIAN	BY PLACE OF RESIDENCE		
		URBAN	RURAL NONFARM	RURAL FARM
NEW ENGLAND				
Maine	10.2	10.4	10.2	9.5
New Hampshire	9.8	9.6	10.3	9.8
Vermont	10.0	10.8	9.9	8.9
Massachusetts	10.9	10.8	11.1	10.1
Rhode Island	9.3	9.3	9.6	8.8
Connecticut	9.8	9.7	10.8	8.9
OTHER SELECTED STATES				
New York	9.6	9.6	9.9	8.9
Ohio	9.9	10.2	9.3	8.8
South Carolina	7.6	8.9	7.3	6.3
Tennessee	8.4	9.3	8.2	7.6
Colorado	11.6	12.0	10.1	9.1
California	10.9	11.8	9.4	8.9

* Persons 25 years old and over.
Source: Bureau of the Census, U.S. Department of Commerce (based on 20% sample)

The Support of Public Education

How well are the people of New England providing for the education of their children? How good are the public school systems of the region? It is not easy to devise a statistical measure of the effort of a community to support its school system. Nor is it easy to measure the "efficiency" of a school system.

The Council of State Governments, which has made extensive studies of these problems, believes that "the best single measure of the *effort* made by a state is the percentage of the incomes of the people of the state which is allocated to public schools." [6] This is a measure of the relative sacrifice made by the people to support public education. During the school year 1947–48 the states were ranked from a high of 3.6% in New Mexico to a low of 1.4% in Illinois. Massachusetts and Connecticut ranked just above Illinois, and the other New England states were farther up in the ranking.

The percentage of personal income spent on education may be the best measure of a state's *effort* to support education, but it is clearly not the best measure of *results*. Educational achievement in New Mexico is below

Table 7–9. *Expenditure per Pupil in Average Daily Attendance and Average Annual Teachers' Salaries, New England States and Other Selected States, 1947–48*

STATE	AVERAGE EXPENDITURE PER PUPIL*	RANK IN UNITED STATES	AVERAGE ANNUAL TEACHERS' SALARIES†	RANK IN UNITED STATES
UNITED STATES	$179.43	—	$2,440	—
NEW ENGLAND STATES				
Maine	133.04	39	2,000	38
New Hampshire	187.15	25	2,294	28
Vermont	166.90	31	2,062	35
Massachusetts	213.98	11	2,960	10
Rhode Island	220.69	7	3,085	6
Connecticut	217.44	8	3,067	8
OTHER SELECTED STATES				
New York	256.90	1	3,450	1
Illinois	223.19	6	2,780	16
New Mexico	186.49	26	2,958	11
Mississippi	71.42	48	1,293	48

* Office of Education, Federal Security Agency, *Statistics of State School Systems*, 1950, p. 21.
† Council of State Governments, *The Forty-eight State School Systems*, p. 207.

the national average, for example, while the achievement in Illinois, Massachusetts, and Connecticut is above the national average. Moreover, those states which spend a large proportion of personal income on education are generally the less densely populated states with relatively low per capita incomes. Two-thirds of the states which were above the median in the per cent of personal incomes spent on education had per capita incomes below the national average. The ten states which showed the lowest percentages of personal incomes spent on public education had per capita incomes above the national average.

It does not follow, of course, that the states which spend smaller proportions of their incomes on public education are necessarily slighting the education of their children. In general, such states are the wealthier states

6. *The Forty-eight State School Systems* (1949), p. 17. The italics are supplied. The Council of State Governments is a joint governmental agency established and supported by the states.

which are able to maintain high educational standards with relatively less effort. While the southern New England states rank low in the proportion of personal incomes spent on education, for example, their absolute levels of expenditures per pupil are high relative to the national average. Table 7-9 shows the amounts expended per pupil in public schools in New England and other selected states during the school year 1947–48. Again, there is a distinct contrast between the situations in the southern and northern states of the region, though the New Hampshire expenditures per pupil were also above the national average.

Table 7-10. Rejection Rates for Mental and Educational Deficiency under the Selective Service Act, New England States and Other Regions, 1940–44

AREA	REJECTION RATE PER THOUSAND EXAMINED	
	NONNEGRO	NEGRO
NEW ENGLAND	16	65
Maine	20	*
New Hampshire	20	*
Vermont	21	*
Massachusetts	15	47
Rhode Island	15	32
Connecticut	14	96
OTHER REGIONS		
Middle Atlantic	11	67
Southeast	52	202
Southwest	54	107
Central	12	61
Northwest	13	40
Far West	9	50

* Fewer than 100 Negroes in sample.
Source: Data provided by Conservation of Human Resources Project, Columbia University

To a substantial extent, expenditures per pupil depend upon the average level of teachers' salaries, as can be seen from the almost parallel rankings in Table 7-9. In general, however, states with relatively high expenditures per pupil also have better physical plants than those which spend less per pupil. Connecticut ranked eighth among the states in expenditures per pupil, and 65% of its school buildings were judged to be "satisfactory" during the school year 1951–52. In Maine, which ranked 39th in expenditures, only 21% of all public school buildings were considered to be in satisfactory condition.[7]

A high rate of expenditures on public education does not by itself prove that the educational system of a region is a good one, but it does show something about attempts to maintain a good instructional staff and to provide necessary physical facilities. The Selective Service rejection rate for

7. At the time of this writing, information on school facilities was available for only these two New England states. See Office of Education, Federal Security Agency, School Facilities Survey, First Progress Report, 1952.

educational and mental deficiencies provides an additional rough indicator of the effectiveness of a region's educational system in terms of the lower limit of educational achievement. Table 7–10 shows the rejection rate for New England men called up under the Selective Service Act between October 1940 and December 1944. For comparative purposes the rates for other regions are also shown.

New England's record of rejections for educational and mental deficiencies was fairly similar to that for other areas which resemble it in population characteristics, level of educational achievement, and related measures. It was slightly higher than that in some other regions, however, even in the southern New England states. As might be expected, the rejection rate in Maine, New Hampshire, and Vermont was above that in the rest of the region. *While these rates indicate that less than 2% of New England's inductees were rejected for educational or mental deficiencies, it appears that there is still some room to improve even the minimum educational opportunity for the region's youth.*

From the evidence at hand it seems that New England's educational needs are greatest in rural areas and in certain cities where economic distress has followed industrial unemployment. *Undoubtedly, low incomes and economic necessity are the principal causes of inadequate educational expenditures and substandard averages of educational attainment where they exist in various parts of New England.* Improvements in the basic economic strength of such communities would permit the raising of their educational standards, which in turn would aid in further economic improvement in future years. The educational problems of such areas are closely intertwined, therefore, with their fundamental economic needs and opportunities.

Nonpublic Secondary Schools

While a detailed discussion of private schools is outside the scope of this report, it should be noted that private schools are somewhat more important in New England than in the nation at large. With 6.2% of the nation's population, New England had 13.2% of the private secondary schools in the country in 1947–48. Twenty per cent of all secondary-school students in New England are being educated in nonpublic schools. In the United States as a whole, about 9% of all secondary-school students are enrolled in private secondary schools.[8]

Most of New England's nonpublic secondary schools are affiliated with religious bodies. Of the 404 nonpublic secondary schools in New England, during 1947–48, 217 (54%) were Catholic parochial schools. Some of the others were affiliated with other religious groups.

8. Office of Education, Federal Security Agency, *Statistics of Nonpublic Secondary Schools, 1947–1948* (1950), p. 6.

The region's relatively greater dependence on private schools, which is especially true in southern New England, has important implications for public educational expenditures. *If the New England proportion of private school education were the same as that in the rest of the country, the region's public schools would have to educate a larger number of pupils.* Total expenditures would have to be higher, expenditures per pupil would have to be lower, or both. *On the other hand, the substantial number of private secondary schools that draw in students from other parts of the country provides an important source of income for many towns scattered throughout New England.*

State and Federal Aid to Education

The source of funds for the support of public education has an important bearing on the local financial burden of maintaining the school system. If large quantities of funds for educational purposes flow in from outside an area, the need for local financing is reduced. If small quantities of funds flow in for these purposes, local resources must carry the burden.

In New England, the public school systems are supported predominantly by local governments and local tax collections. (See Table 7–11.) More than 91% of New Hampshire's school money comes from local taxes, the highest proportion of any state in the nation. The other states in the region also rank high in this respect.

Since most New England communities rely largely for revenue on property taxation, school expenditures have an important bearing on property tax rates. Obsolete systems of taxation, rising needs for educational expenditures, and slower than national growth of taxable property have held

Table 7–11. Per Cent of School Money from Local Taxes,
New England States, 1949–50

STATE	PER CENT	RANK IN U.S.
Maine	70.0	12
New Hampshire	91.1	1
Vermont	66.7	14
Massachusetts	80.7	3
Rhode Island	79.4	6
Connecticut	75.8	8

Source: Farm Bureau News (July-August, 1952), p. 5

the local burden of education at rather high levels in many towns and cities throughout the region. To some extent, earmarked or general distributions of state-collected revenues to New England cities and towns have held down the rise in local tax rates, but the pressure has been strongly upward. Many states in other regions make much greater use of direct state aid for education. Financing is thus spread more broadly over a larger tax base.

Recent proposals for general revision of state tax systems, as for example in Massachusetts, have had to pay special attention to the financial needs and resources of communities and their financial relations with the state. *It would appear desirable for the New England states, especially New Hampshire, Massachusetts, and Rhode Island, to reduce somewhat the dependence of their school systems on local tax collections and to integrate better their state and local taxation and expenditures.*[9]

A further source of financial aid for public education is the Federal Government. It operates various types of aid programs related to public education which, in effect, redistribute the burden of educational support among areas and population groups. New England participates in these aid programs, of course, though they represent but a small proportion of total public educational expenditures within the states. Most federal disbursements to state and local governments for educational purposes are made on the basis of land area, total or school-age population, per capita income, or some combination of them. Some distributions are made with the requirement that funds be matched by state or local governments.

Public schools in New England, as well as some private schools, receive federal aid under the national school-lunch program. This is one of the largest educational distributions by the Federal Government and is the principal one directly to the states, which are required to match the money part of the federal grants. Table 7–12 shows the distributions to New England states under this program during the 1950 fiscal year. The distribution of funds to New England was somewhat under the region's 5.7% of the nation's school-age population, and the value of food distributed within the region was relatively even smaller.

Most of the other educational grants of the Federal Government are for specialized purposes, often for higher education. The participation of New England in the more important of them is summarized in Table 7–13. The region's portion of total federal disbursements for these four purposes is almost as large as its share of the school-age population. There is considerable variation from program to program, however. The land grant colleges received more than 10% of the corresponding total during the 1949 fiscal year, but the six states received less than 2% of the surplus property transferred to educational institutions. The figures for vocational education and vocational rehabilitation were closer to the population ratio, though the latter was also below the expected figure.

Federal funds expended for the vocational rehabilitation and education of veterans under the G. I. Bill of Rights are not included in the table. They are distributed directly to educational institutions. In the fiscal year 1950 these payments amounted to $758,000,000 in the United States. About 5.6% of this total, $42,800,000, went to New England colleges and schools.

Despite the importance of federal disbursements for certain specialized educational activities, it is evident that they provide little support for local

9. See our report, "State and Local Taxation and Expenditures in New England" (No. 16).

elementary or secondary education. Under the existing arrangements, local governments must depend almost entirely on their own state's resources for public education. This makes even more evident the need for allocating the costs of education wisely between local and state governments.

Table 7–12. *Federal Aid under the National School-Lunch Program, New England States, Fiscal Year 1950*
(thousands of dollars)

STATE	SCHOOL-AGE POPULATION (PER CENT OF U.S.)	FUNDS		FOOD		TOTAL	
		AMOUNT	PER CENT OF U.S.	AMOUNT	PER CENT OF U.S.	AMOUNT	PER CENT OF U.S.
Maine	0.65	$ 372	0.6 ·	$ 200	0.4	$ 572	0.5
New Hampshire	0.35	233	0.4	143	0.3	376	0.3
Vermont	0.27	174	0.3	167	0.3	341	0.3
Massachusetts	2.82	1,377	2.2	706	1.3	2,083	1.8
Rhode Island	0.44	220	0.4	124	0.2	343	0.3
Connecticut	1.15	533	0.9	189	0.4	722	0.6
NEW ENGLAND	5.67	$2,909	4.7	$1,529	2.8	$4,437	3.8
UNITED STATES	100.0	62,060	100.0	53,809	100.0	115,869	100.0

Note: Details may not add to totals because of rounding.
Source: House Committee on Education and Labor, *Federal Educational Activities and Educational Issues before Congress*, prepared by Charles A. Quattlebaum, Library of Congress, Washington, December 1951

Table 7–13. *Federal Funds Allotted for Four Major Educational Programs,*
New England States, Fiscal Year 1949

STATE	FUNDS ALLOTTED		PER CENT OF UNITED STATES TOTAL			
	AMOUNT	PER CENT OF U.S.	TO LAND GRANT COLLEGES	VOCATIONAL EDUCATION*	VOCATIONAL REHABILITATION	TRANSFER OF SURPLUS PROPERTY
Maine	$415,289	0.7	1.58	0.70	0.53	.26
New Hampshire	282,952	0.5	1.50	.62	.21	.10
Vermont	326,867	0.6	1.47	.62	.46	.05
Massachusetts	874,679	1.5	2.37	2.07	1.04	1.01
Rhode Island	408,725	0.7	1.55	.67	.47	.17
Connecticut	714,010	1.3	1.78	1.04	1.84	.29
NEW ENGLAND	$3,022.522	5.3	10.26	5.71	4.54	1.89

Note: Details may not add to totals because of rounding.
* Below college level.
Source: Office of Education, Federal Security Agency, *Federal Government Funds for Education*, Bulletin No. 3 (1950), p. 9, and Council of State Governments, *The Forty-eight State School Systems* (1949), p. 175

Vocational Education

As a highly industrialized area, New England depends heavily for employment and income on its manufacturing plants. The region requires a steady flow of vocationally trained individuals for replacement and for industrial growth. In-plant and on-the-job training are satisfactory for many occupational categories, but the individuals trained by vocational schools are an important addition to the skilled manpower of the region.

While New England contains 5.7% of the nation's school-age population and about 9.5% of its manufacturing employment, only about 3.5% of all students attending federally aided vocational classes in the United States in 1950 were in New England.[10] Table 7–14 shows the distribution of enrollment in such classes among the New England states. In each state the proportion of students was less than the percentage of school-age population.

Despite this relatively low enrollment ratio of 3.5%, approximately 6.5% of total expenditures on vocational education in the nation were made in the region. In each New England state, expenditures per student in federally aided vocational classes were above the national average. The regional average of $68.36 per student in 1950 was almost double the national average of $38.38. (See Chart 7–5.) In Rhode Island the average expenditure was $76.71 per student, and in Massachusetts $74.35.

Table 7–14. Enrollment in Federally Aided Vocational Classes,
New England States, 1950

STATE	NUMBER OF STUDENTS	PER CENT OF U.S.
Maine	7,674	.21
New Hampshire	6,235	.19
Vermont	5,222	.16
Massachusetts	66,453	1.98
Rhode Island	3,435	.10
Connecticut	28,676	.85
NEW ENGLAND	117,695	3.49

Source: Office of Education, Federal Security Agency, Digest of Annual Reports of State Boards for Vocational Education (1950), p. 88

There was considerable variation in the sources of funds to support vocational education among the various states. Nearly half of Rhode Island's expenditures came from the Federal Government, while Massachusetts received only 11% from this source. In Connecticut the state government carried the greatest part of the burden of vocational education; this state also had the lowest New England average for expenditures per student. In Massachusetts, which ranked second in terms of expenditure per student, the cost of vocational education was shared almost equally by the state and local governments. In the other four states, the state share was much lower than that of the local governments.

The wide variations in the relative amounts of federal funds received by the New England states do not indicate discrimination against some states. Federal funds are granted to states for vocational education below the col-

10. No comprehensive information is available on vocational education activities which do not come under the federal aid program.

lege level under the Smith-Hughes Act of 1917. Grants are distributed for agricultural training on the basis of the distribution of the nation's rural population and for industrial and home-economics training on the basis of urban population distribution. The George-Barden Act of 1946 provides for supplemental appropriations, again on the basis of population distribution. Present laws require that the states must at least match the federal funds they receive. Individual states can, of course, contribute more than a matching share, as Chart 7-5 shows. The wide diversity in population density and rural-urban distribution from state to state, as well as the variation in extensiveness of vocational education, are bound to produce differences in federal participation.

CHART 7-5

Expenditures per Student in Federally Aided Vocational Classes,
United States and the New England States, 1950 *

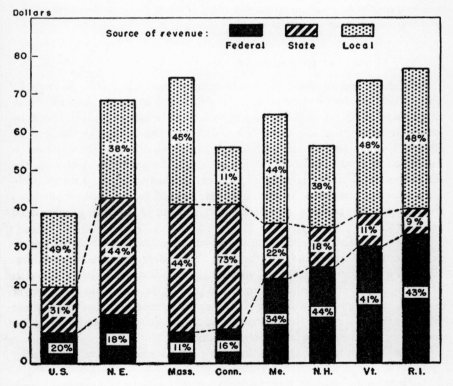

* The height of each bar shows the *total expenditure* per student, in 1950. Each bar is divided to show the *relative* contribution of federal, state, and local governments.
Source: Office of Education, Federal Security Agency, *Digest of Annual Reports of State Boards for Vocational Education,* 1950

The region's relatively small enrollment in vocational education classes compared to population and industrial distribution suggests that New England is not adequately providing for the training of the skilled workers which its industries require. The Department of Education of the State of Rhode Island has recently completed a comprehensive survey of vocational education facilities in that state which concludes that "a much more comprehensive program of vocational education is needed and warranted in Rhode Island." [11] Other surveys of vocational education in New England reach substantially the same conclusion with respect to the states of Massachusetts and Connecticut.[12] The vocational education facilities and activities of the region should be tailored to fit the requirements of industry and trade. *Not only must replacement workers be provided, but the attractiveness of New England to prospective employers will be enhanced if they can count upon the vocational schools to furnish them with well-trained craftsmen. More extensive vocational education is both a need and an opportunity for New England. The quality of the present vocational education appears to be above average, but there is room for improvement as well as for a larger scale of activities.*

Vocational Rehabilitation

Satisfactory use of the labor force requires that all possible persons be able to hold productive jobs. It is important to minimize the human wastes of physical disability and handicaps by adequate safety measures and by returning to employment those individuals who are injured or disabled by illness. During periods of high employment vocational rehabilitation is facilitated by ready availability of job openings. As unemployment rises, the difficulties of placing rehabilitated workers intensify and the human problems continue unabated. In communities plagued by unemployment even during general business prosperity the difficulties impeding vocational rehabilitation are greater.

In New England each state has a separate division devoted exclusively to rehabilitation of the blind. Furthermore, each state department of education has a division or bureau of vocational rehabilitation. It is the function of this agency to investigate and return to productive employment, wherever possible, all eligible disabled or handicapped persons, exclusive of those with visual handicaps, who otherwise would be dependent upon the community or private resources for their support.

Typical rehabilitation services include medical examinations, counseling

11. Rhode Island State Department of Education, *Improving Vocational Education in Rhode Island* (1950), p. 29.

12. William L. Stoddard, "Public Education for Labor Skills," *Harvard Business Review,* May 1951, and Industrial Development Reports, *The Industrial Education Facilities of New England,* a survey for the Lincoln and Therese Filene Foundation, Boston, 1951.

and guidance, physical restoration, training, and job placement. The division of vocational rehabilitation arranges for training by trade or vocational schools, for on-the-job training in factories or commercial establishments, or for correspondence instruction. After a rehabilitant has been replaced on a job, the division follows up the placement to make sure that the worker is adapted to his new job and that the worker and employer are satisfied.

Table 7–15 presents a brief summary of the activities of state vocational rehabilitation agencies in New England during the fiscal year 1950. The total active roll includes cases in various stages of rehabilitation. The most significant figure is that showing the rehabilitants returned to employment. They are persons who became able to maintain themselves and their families, where they might otherwise have remained public charges.

Vocational rehabilitation is one type of social service which results in an immediate monetary return to the community. For example, during the 1950 fiscal year 570 persons were successfully rehabilitated in Massachusetts. Their average cost of rehabilitation was $191.83.[13] On the average, this group of persons earned $3.90 per week prior to rehabilitation. After completing the program, the group averaged $33.07 per week in wages. The return to the community is obvious. Even more important, however, is the increased self-respect of the individual worker who is no longer dependent upon charity but who has become a self-supporting member of the community.

Vocational rehabilitation is a joint federal-state program. The Federal Government matches state funds spent on actual rehabilitation services. Beginning in 1943 the Federal Government was supposed to assume all costs of administration, though in recent years it has not done so. Since 1950 rehabilitation agencies have been subject to nondeficiency legislation. That is, a deficit incurred in any year is not covered by the Federal Government.

The present method of financing vocational rehabilitation is excessively rigid and is not adapted to meet changing needs. Each division of vocational rehabilitation must prepare a budget in advance of the next fiscal year without knowing the demand for its services or how much it can count on from the Federal Government. Furthermore, there is a tendency among state governments to match the federal grants and to make no additional expenditures.

Congress has criticized the states for this attitude. It is the position of Congress that the state and local communities stand to gain most from successful rehabilitation programs and that they should add to the federal

13. This is the average "case-service" cost for the 570 rehabilitants. The program may have been spread over several years, so this figure does not represent the average cost of rehabilitation during the fiscal year. Since many cases are only investigated, and since some are closed without successful rehabilitation, the *average* cost of the program per rehabilitant in Massachusetts was approximately $460 during the fiscal year 1950, about the same as the national average.

grant whatever is necessary to ensure a completely effective program, rather than simply matching federal funds dollar for dollar.

A better method of financing this program would be for each division of vocational rehabilitation to draw up its budget on the basis of case-load estimates and staff requirements. Each state should then provide the necessary amount of funds and treat the amount received from the Federal Government as revenue. There should also be more flexibility in the budget. If the case load during a fiscal year is greater than that anticipated, the division of vocational rehabilitation should be permitted to draw further funds from the state treasury. On the other hand, if there is a surplus in any fiscal year it should be applied to the next year's budget.

Table 7–15. Vocational Rehabilitation in the New England States, Fiscal Year Ended June 30, 1952

	REFERRALS	TOTAL ACTIVE ROLL	REHABILITANTS RETURNED TO EMPLOYMENT
Maine			
General	1215	544	225
Blind	105	59	29
New Hampshire			
General	533	250	96
Blind	30	34	16
Vermont			
General	604	327	164
Blind	66	52	17
Massachusetts			
General	3843	1448	705
Blind	1	1	—
Rhode Island			
General	928	710	305
Blind	54	141	24
Connecticut			
General	2268	2235	1143
Blind	170	109	47

Note: Not all referrals become active cases. Each case is investigated, but some persons do not receive rehabilitation services because the individual is found to be ineligible; the case is handled by some other agency; the disability is aggravated; or for some other reason the case is closed without positive action by the division of vocational rehabilitation.

Source: U.S. Department of Health, Education, and Welfare, Regional Office of Vocational Rehabilitation

The record of the New England vocational rehabilitation agencies seems to be good. Perhaps it could be improved if the states adopted more flexible financing methods. *We agree with the viewpoint of Congress that the states stand to gain most from the rehabilitation of handicapped persons and that state appropriations should be determined by local needs rather than by the amount of federal contributions.*

THE HEALTH OF NEW ENGLANDERS

The health of an area's population affects its vitality and productivity. It affects the standard of living and happiness of the population. High health standards are important to the economic and social progress of any area. There are many possible ways to measure the health status of New Englanders. Each individual measure can reveal only one facet of the situation, but in combination they can paint a fairly complete picture.

The incidence of communicable diseases is an erratic measure of health which requires careful qualification in use. The incidence of certain diseases is low in New England in comparison with some other parts of the country, for example, malaria and typhoid fever. On the other hand, the incidence of such diseases as pneumonia and other respiratory infections is relatively high. For the most part, climatic differences account for the differences in incidence. The variations in frequency of various types of diseases do show the nature of the health problems that an area faces, however. The prevalence in New England of respiratory diseases, especially the common cold, represents a serious drain on the efficiency of the labor force.

The discovery and application of better methods for preventing colds would produce a major increase in the productivity of the region, both directly and indirectly through the reduction of secondary infections. Advances in preventive medicine for the other diseases most common in New England would naturally offer similar benefits. Extensive research on these problems is under way, much of it in New England institutions. Financial support of such research by large employers in the region would be in their own interests and would also represent a distinct contribution to the entire region and nation.

Mortality rates for selected causes are another type of measure, though they too provide only an indirect reflection of a region's health status. The age distribution of population has an important bearing on mortality rates regardless of the general health level. In addition, however, some diseases strike concentrated populations most heavily, and the rural-urban distribution of population has an influence on death rates. The heavy urbanization of New England underscores the region's special interest in further progress in the prevention and cure of "urban" diseases.

The recent mortality record in New England is about what would be expected in view of the region's population characteristics. Except for those diseases which typically strike older persons and those that accompany urbanization, the mortality rates for selected causes in New England are below the national average. The region's death rates from childhood diseases, respiratory diseases, diseases of pregnancy, and other diseases not generally associated with any given age bracket are low. The rates of death caused by cancer, heart disease, arteriosclerosis, and other diseases of the older age groups are higher in the region than in the nation.[14] There is considerable variation in death rates from state to state in New England, of course, but the variations within the region are not as large as those among regions.

The state of health of a region's population is conditioned by climatic and other external conditions. It is also greatly affected, however, by the availability of medical services and the ability to pay for them. On both counts New England is in a favorable position. Per capita incomes in New England have long been above the national average. In 1952 the average income in New England was $1,749 for each person, in comparison with $1,639 in the nation.

New England has a larger proportion of medical personnel than its portion of the nation's population. In 1949, for example, the region contained 6.3% of the nation's population and 7.7% of the nation's doctors. The state distribution is given in Table 7–16. In each state of the region except Maine the proportion of physicians exceeded that of population.

Table 7–16. Distribution of Population and Physicians in the
New England States, 1949

| STATE | PER CENT OF UNITED STATES | |
	CIVILIAN POPULATION	ALL PHYSICIANS
Maine	.61	.55
New Hampshire	.35	.42
Vermont	.25	.27
Massachusetts	3.22	4.33
Rhode Island	.53	.56
Connecticut	1.36	1.59
NEW ENGLAND	6.32	7.72

Source: U.S. Department of Commerce, Survey of Current Business, July 1951

New England also has a larger than average share of the nation's public health nurses. New England cities accounted for about 7.4% of the nation's urban population in 1950, while in 1949 more than 13% of all urban nurses doing public health work were in the region. Although the difference is smaller in New England's rural communities, the geographical distribution of nurses doing rural public health work is similarly favorable to the region. Table 7–17 shows the distribution of population and of public health nurses for the New England states.

The favorable health record of New Englanders is without doubt partly due to the relatively large number of public health nurses in the region. By checking the spread of contagious diseases and by other preventive

14. Public Health Service, Federal Security Agency, Deaths and Death Rates for Selected Causes, 31, No. 4 (Washington), 48–53.

measures, public health nursing can lower the incidence of various diseases and contribute to a healthier population.

The extent to which residents of New England make use of hospitalization insurance programs is an indicator of the use made of health facilities

Table 7–17. Distribution of Public Health Nurses in the New England States, 1949

| | PER CENT OF UNITED STATES | | PER CENT OF UNITED STATES | |
| | URBAN POPULATION | URBAN NURSES DOING PUBLIC HEALTH WORK | RURAL POPULATION | RURAL NURSES DOING PUBLIC HEALTH WORK |
STATE	1950	1949	1950	1949
Maine	.49	.41	.81	1.17
New Hampshire	.32	.48	.41	.91
Vermont	.14	.14	.44	.59
Massachusetts	4.12	7.25	1.34	2.55
Rhode Island	.69	1.55	.23	.28
Connecticut	1.62	3.35	.82	1.35
NEW ENGLAND	7.38	13.18	4.05	6.85

Sources: Bureau of the Census, U.S. Department of Commerce, *United States Census of Population, 1950.* Nurses: Public Health Service, Federal Security Agency

in the region. In 1948 more than two-thirds of all residents of Rhode Island were covered by Blue Cross insurance policies, the highest proportion of any state in the nation.[15] In Maine only about one-fourth of the population was so covered, but Maine still ranked 15th among the 48 states. The other New England states fell in between, as is indicated by Table 7–18.

Table 7–18. Percentage of Population Enrolled in Blue Cross Programs in the New England States, 1948

STATE	PER CENT OF POPULATION ENROLLED	RANK IN UNITED STATES
Maine	23.6	15
New Hampshire	26.0*	12
Vermont	26.0*	12
Massachusetts	41.4	3
Rhode Island	67.4	1
Connecticut	35.6	6

* New Hampshire and Vermont are served jointly by one plan which has enrolled 26% of the aggregate population of the two states.
Source: Federal Security Agency, *The Nation's Health,* September 1948

In general, the average resident of New England appears to be better provided for, in terms of health personnel, than the average resident of the United States. The ratio of doctors and public health nurses to population in the region is well above the national average. Prepaid health insurance

15. Rhode Island has also pioneered in providing cash-sickness compensation for covered workers. The state program is financed by employee contributions. Benefits ranging from $52.00 to $650.00 are paid over a period extending up to 26 weeks.

is more widely used in the region than in the nation. Except for diseases associated with older people, the death rates for selected causes in New England are relatively low.

Despite the larger than average proportion of doctors in the region, individual New Englanders spend less for the services of physicians than the national average. Only in the low-income southeastern states does the average resident spend less for physicians' fees than the typical New England resident. Since the per capita income of the New England region is above the national average, physicians' fees represent an even smaller proportion of personal incomes in the region in relation to the ratios for other regions. Only in Vermont, with its lower than average income per person, was the average expenditure in 1949 (1.17% of income) more than the national average (1.16% of income).[16]

This situation provides New England residents with better than average health protection at less than average expense to themselves, a singularly fortunate condition. On the other hand, it means lower incomes for doctors in the region. The average gross income of nonsalaried physicians in New England was below that in any other region in 1949. Much the same situation existed also for dentists.

The relatively greater supply of doctors is one factor in their lower incomes in New England. The geographical imbalance persists primarily because of the pre-eminence of certain New England universities and hospitals as training and research centers for doctors and nurses. The outstanding skills of some New England doctors and hospitals attract patients from the rest of the nation and, indeed, the rest of the world. Attractive living conditions in the region also encourage the continuation of the relatively high ratio of doctors to population, even at the cost of some sacrifice in their incomes in comparison with doctors in some other areas.

All this does not mean, however, that the medical and health needs of the region have been completely satisfied. The fact that New England has a relatively good health record should not be accepted with complacency. The record shows what proper preventive measures and excellent health facilities can accomplish, but it should also serve as a stimulus to the people of the region to correct those deficiencies that still exist.

A recent survey shows that the ratio of acceptable hospital beds to population in New England is below the national average. With the exception of two of the low-income southern regions, all other parts of the country have higher ratios in this respect. Many existing hospital beds in the region have been classified as "nonacceptable" on the grounds that they constitute fire or health hazards or are obsolete in construction. *If New Englanders are to maintain their relatively favorable health record, they*

16. U.S. Department of Commerce, *Survey of Current Business,* "Incomes of Physicians, 1929–49" (July 1951), p. 19.

will have to support a major program to replace outmoded or obsolete hospitals and to provide for growing needs.

There are obviously other needed improvements in the health status of New Englanders. It would be desirable for larger proportions of the residents in each state to be covered by health insurance programs. Many business concerns could well expand the health services provided their employees. Better control and prevention of communicable diseases and of the diseases of old age offer much to the prosperity and happiness of the region's people. Continued research by private and public groups and close cooperation among all interested parties are necessary.

THE NEW ENGLAND LABOR FORCE

The "labor force" is defined as the number of persons 14 years of age or older at work or actively seeking work. The total labor force in New England numbered approximately 3,962,000 persons in April 1950. Of that total, about 173,000 individuals were active members of the armed services and the remaining 3,789,000 constituted the civilian labor force.

The size of the labor force may fluctuate widely and rapidly as changing conditions affect the employment desires of individuals. The end of each school year brings new entrants into the labor market, some temporarily and some permanently. Housewives often enter the labor market when the family needs additional funds and withdraw when the family's fortunes are improved. Older workers retire, and some women leave the labor force to be married or to have families. When economic conditions dictate, the size of the labor force can expand rather rapidly. Conversely, changed economic conditions may cause the labor force to shrink by making it unnecessary for housewives or other "second workers" in a family to seek employment.

As the population of a region grows, the labor force also grows, but over time the internal composition of the labor force changes. An increase in the average age of the people of a region produces, for example, an increase in the number of older workers in the labor force. Because the labor force is always changing, it is easiest to describe as of a given point of time. The best cross-section views can be obtained from the decennial census of population. It is possible to make estimates, however, of the average or "normal" size of some of the components of the labor force for intercensal periods.

An examination of the labor force must also consider long-run changes, for they are intimately associated with other fundamental changes in an economy. For example, there has been a long-term shift in the nation's labor force from the primary (extractive) occupations of agriculture, forestry, fishing, and mining to the secondary (fabricating) occupations of manufacturing and construction, and to the tertiary (service) occupations which include transportation, communication, trade, finance, and similar activities. The shifts in New England's labor force have been similar in many respects to those in the nation as a whole, but differences in economic development have also led to important variations.

Changes from 1940 to 1950

A comparison between the census data for 1940 and 1950 shows the recent changes in the composition of New England's civilian labor force, including the varying rates of expansion and contraction among the different industrial classifications. Table 7–19 presents these figures and shows also how New England's proportion of the national total in each category has changed.

Table 7–19. Civilian Labor Force in New England, by Industrial Classification, 1940 and 1950

	NEW ENGLAND				
	NUMBER† (THOUSANDS)			PER CENT OF UNITED STATES	
INDUSTRIAL CLASSIFICATION			PER CENT CHANGE		
	1940	1950	1940 to 1950	1940	1950
TOTAL CIVILIAN LABOR FORCE	3,602	3,789	+5.2	6.86	6.45
Employed	3,047	3,542	+16.2	6.79	6.34
Unemployed	555	247	−55.5	7.28	8.54
EMPLOYED CIVILIAN LABOR FORCE					
*Primary industries**	171	172	+0.6	1.82	2.08
Agriculture	149	141	−5.4	1.78	1.97
Fisheries	18	25	+38.9	14.40	14.71
Mining	4	6	+50.0	0.56	0.62
Secondary industries	1,312	1,535	+17.0	9.72	8.30
Manufacturing†	1,170	1,358	+16.2	11.07	9.62
Durable goods	483	618	+28.0	9.44	8.40
Nondurable goods	662	729	+10.1	12.55	11.10
Not specified	25	11	−56.0	13.66	6.01
Construction	142	177	+24.6	6.91	5.09
Tertiary industries	1,564	1,835	+17.3	6.85	6.12
Service	715	750	+4.9	7.07	6.23
Wholesale and retail trade	519	666	+28.3	6.88	6.41
Transportation, communication and other public utilities	179	209	+16.8	5.79	4.91
All other industries	151	210	+39.1	7.18	6.38

* Forestry employment is included in "all other industries."
† The figures in Table 7–19 relate to the census month of April for both 1940 and 1950. The figures for manufacturing employment, in particular, are lower than *annual average* manufacturing employment, which was estimated to be 1,433,000 in 1950.
Note: Details may not add to totals because of rounding.
Source: Bureau of the Census, U.S. Department of Commerce, and U.S. Fish and Wildlife Service

New England had a smaller share of the nation's civilian labor force in 1950 than it had had ten years earlier, despite the addition of more than 180,000 workers during the period. The labor-force growth was outstripped by expansion in other parts of the country. Employment in New England grew by 495,000 workers, however, and unemployment fell from 555,000 to

247,000 persons. Again, the nation's 62% drop in unemployment exceeded the New England drop of 55%, and in 1950 the region's proportion of unemployment was greater than it had been in 1940. In each year New England's proportion of unemployed exceeded its proportion of the labor force.

CHART 7–6

Distribution of Employed Labor Force by Industry, New England and the United States, 1940 and 1950

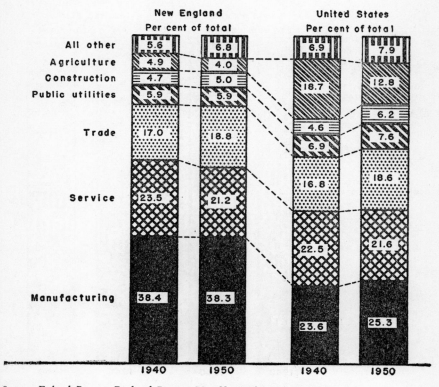

Source: Federal Reserve Bank of Boston, *Monthly Review,* March 1952

In both the secondary and tertiary categories, which provide New England with all but 5% of its employment opportunities, the region's 17% rate of job expansion was less than the corresponding 37% and 31% rates for the nation as a whole. Accordingly, the New England proportion of the national total in each category declined somewhat. On the other hand, the New England increase in fishing and mining employment offset the decrease in agricultural employment, while in the country as a whole there was a substantial drop in total employment by the extractive industries. The region's share of primary employment rose slightly.[17]

Apart from the more rapid rise in the labor force and in employment in most major categories outside New England, which was to be expected, there were other important changes in the distribution of the New England

CHART 7–7

Distribution of Employed Labor Force by Occupation, New England and the United States, 1940 and 1950

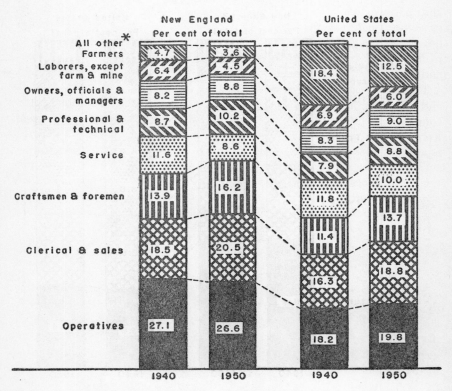

* New England, 1940 = 0.9, 1950 = 1.0; United States, 1940 = 0.8, 1950 = 1.4
Source: Ibid.

17. This assumes no compensating decline in employment in forestry. It is virtually impossible to make accurate estimates of employment in forestry as such. Because of the high degree of seasonality and because many workers in forestry are not covered by unemployment compensation, neither the Bureau of the Census nor the Bureau of Labor Statistics makes separate estimates of forestry employment. Since employment in the industry group "lumber and lumber products, except furniture" showed an increase of approximately 60% in New England between 1939 and 1947, however, it is safe to assume that there was some increase in employment in forestry as such during this period.

labor force during the decade from 1940 to 1950. The proportion of workers employed in manufacturing was almost the same in each year, but there was a distinct shift from the production of nondurable goods to durable goods because of their different rates of expansion. Although New England was still below the national proportion of durable-goods employment, the gap narrowed considerably.

While the over-all composition of the New England economy was changing somewhat, that of the nation as a whole was subject to even greater alteration. The national economy moved closed to that of the region in its basic characteristics. (See Chart 7–6.) Manufacturing rose in relative importance and agriculture dropped. In most other categories the regional and national patterns were already fairly similar. Accompanying the structural changes there was also a narrowing of the differences in occupational groupings. (See Chart 7–7.) The larger proportion of manufacturing in New England still requires a larger proportion of operatives, craftsmen, and foremen in the region, however.

The recent changes in employment composition in both New England and the nation as a whole have important implications for the region's future competitive position. Growing industrialization in underdeveloped regions has provided increasing competition for New England's older industries, especially for some branches of the textile group. That pressure, in turn, has encouraged the shift to durable-goods production and to growing specialization in all types of manufacturing industries. *The ability of New England producers to meet competition from other parts of the country should grow as the transition in structure continues, if it is accompanied by progressive business and governmental policies.*

Age and Sex Composition

Women make up a larger proportion of New England's labor force than they do in other regions. Also, there are relatively more workers, both men and women, in the older age groups in New England. Chart 7–8 shows the distribution of the region's labor force in 1950, by age and sex. In every age group but one the proportion of women was greater in New England than in the nation. The age groups 45 years old and over were relatively larger in New England. As was mentioned earlier, the provision of jobs for older workers is a more pressing problem in New England than in most other regions.

The Postwar Labor Force

The preceding discussion applies only to two census years. Since there are no intercensal estimates of the number of proprietors, self-employed persons, and domestic servants, it is not possible to study the short-term behavior of the total labor force. Estimates available for the other categories, however, permit a more detailed examination of many types of change in the labor force.[18]

Agriculture. There were actually more people at work on farms in New England than the number reported in the 1950 census of population. Some

CHART 7–8

Composition of Labor Force by Age and Sex, New England
and the United States, 1950

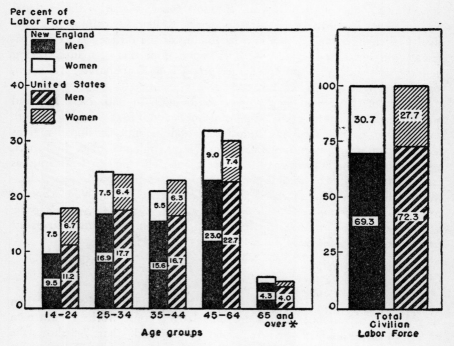

* Per cent of women: New England, 1.2%; United States, 0.9%.
Source: Ibid.

children under 14 years of age and some part-time farm workers who spend more time in nonagricultural than in agricultural employment are also engaged in farm work. Although such workers are not counted as part of the agricultural labor force by the Bureau of the Census, they are included in the monthly estimates by the Bureau of Agricultural Economics of all persons working on farms.[19]

18. For a discussion of seasonal and cyclical fluctuations in employment in the region, see our report, "Employment Fluctuations in New England" (No. 8).

19. Since the BAE survey includes some workers who are reported as employed in non-agricultural occupations by the Bureau of the Census, one cannot add the estimated agricultural labor force to the nonagricultural labor force without double counting.

During the five-year period 1945–49 an average of 232,000 persons worked on farms in New England. Approximately 169,000 were family workers, and 63,000 were hired.[20] There were fluctuations around this average, of course, for seasonal and other reasons. During this period there were continuing shortages of farm workers. Shortages were most serious on

CHART 7–9

New England Nonextractive Employment by Industrial
Classification, 1945–49*
(in thousands)

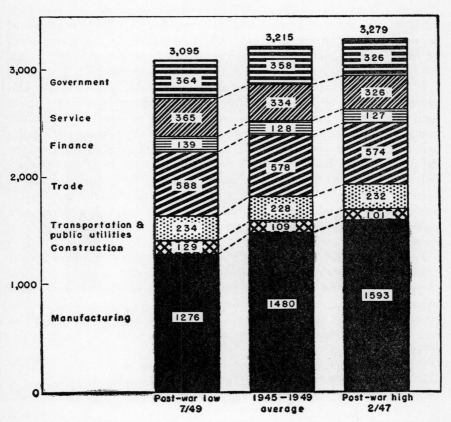

* Excluding proprietors, self-employed persons, domestic servants, unpaid family workers, and members of the armed forces.
Source: Bureau of Labor Statistics, U.S. Department of Labor

20. Bureau of Agriculture Economics, U.S. Department of Agriculture, *Farm Labor.* Unpaid family workers must work at least 15 hours per week to be included in the BAE survey.

dairy farms, but they also affected areas devoted to cranberries, tobacco, potatoes, apples, and truck farms. To meet these shortages, farm workers from Canada, Puerto Rico, and Jamaica were imported. In addition, for certain types of seasonal jobs, temporary workers were recruited in New England.

Fisheries. There has been relatively little fluctuation in the number of workers employed by the New England fishing industry in recent years. Since 1947 it has averaged approximately 25,000 workers, exclusive of processors and others working in shore establishments.

Nonextractive Industries. Although New England's share of the nation's total employment in the secondary industries of mining, manufacturing, and construction decreased between 1940 and 1950, the region still accounted for 8.3% of the nation's employment in these fields. The New England economy is based on manufacturing. Chart 7–9 shows the five-year average of employment in the nonextractive industries from 1945 to 1949. In addition, the postwar high and the postwar low are shown.

It is apparent that the greatest amount of "stretch" in the region's employed labor force is in manufacturing. The difference between the postwar high and postwar low of manufacturing employment was 367,000 workers, much more than the 184,000 change in the total employment during the period. There was also some variation in construction employment during the postwar years, but it was much smaller in amount. All of the "service" industries displayed a remarkable stability during the postwar period. *It is clear that the basic economic strength of the New England economy is due to its high proportion of manufacturing employment, but the region's major economic problems are also caused by the wide fluctuations in such employment.*

The Unemployed. There are wide variations in employment from month to month and from year to year. At best, only estimates of regional unemployment can be made. According to our estimate, however, about 259,000 workers in New England were without work, on the average, during the period 1945–49.[21] This period included years of high-level employment, as well as years during which unemployment was a serious problem in the region.

While it is not possible to determine exactly what proportion of the postwar labor force in New England has been unemployed, because of the unavailability of data for some types of employment, it is possible to compare unemployment estimates for New England with those for the nation as a whole in 1940 and 1950:

21. This estimate was built up from separate estimates made for local labor market areas in New England by the division of employment security in each state. Such estimates are not made, however, for each local area. To arrive at an aggregate estimate for the region, we related all available unemployment estimates to known unemployment compensation claims. The ratio derived was used to inflate monthly unemployment compensation claims figures, which are available for each local area. A correction was made to allow for seasonal variations.

In 1940 there was a fairly high level of unemployment in the United States, while 1950 was characterized by relatively "full" employment. In both years the rate of unemployment in New England was higher than that in the nation as a whole. Furthermore, the spread between the regional and national ratios was greater in 1950 than in 1940.[22] *It is evident that in these two years, at least, New England was not using its human resources as effectively as the nation as a whole.*

Table 7–20. *Unemployed Workers as Per Cent of Total Labor Force*

	1940	1950
New England	15.4	6.1
United States	14.5	4.8

Source: Bureau of the Census, U.S. Department of Commerce

Long-run Shifts in the Labor Force

In 1899 about 15% of New England's total population was employed in manufacturing. In 1950 the proportion so employed was slightly smaller, but compared to the nation as a whole New England was still a region in which employment was heavily concentrated in manufacturing. Table 7–21 shows the trend of manufacturing employment in relation to population in the region and the nation during the last half-century.

Table 7–21. *Manufacturing Employment in Relation to Population, New England and the United States, 1899–1950*

	1899	1919	1929	1933	1939	1947	1950
New England	15.3%	18.4%	13.5%	9.7%	11.2%	13.8%	14.9%
United States	6.1	8.1	6.9	4.6	6.0	8.3	9.4

Source: Ibid.

Between the end of World War I and 1950, New England's dependence upon manufacturing as a source of employment decreased in both absolute and relative terms. In 1919 there were 1,505,000 manufacturing workers in New England. By 1950 this number had dropped to 1,358,000, and it had been substantially lower during the decade of the 30's. In the nation as a whole, 9,939,800 workers were employed in manufacturing in 1919 compared to 14,110,000 in 1950. During the 31-year period, manufacturing employment in the United States increased 41.9%, while it decreased 9.8% in New England. Since 1950, manufacturing employment in the region has climbed above the 1919 figure again, but factory employment in the nation has risen still higher.

Outside New England the long-term increase in manufacturing employ-

22. This report is concerned only with the magnitude of unemployment in New England, since the unemployed are part of the region's labor force. The problems of unemployment are considered in detail in "Employment Fluctuations in New England," No. 8 in the Committee's report series.

ment was accompanied by a sustained reduction of employment in the primary industries of agriculture, forestry, fishing, and mining. The national increase in the tertiary industries such as transportation, communication, trade, service, and public utilities was relatively even greater than that in manufacturing. There was a shift from the primary industries to both the secondary industries of manufacturing and construction and the group of tertiary industries.

Within New England, there was a relatively small employment reduction in the primary industries after 1900, since agriculture was already a small part of total employment. The long-term pattern of growth of the tertiary occupations in New England, nevertheless, was quite similar to that for the nation as a whole. That growth was accompanied by a substantial relative decrease in manufacturing as a share of total employment.

What is the significance of these shifts in employment patterns in the nation and New England? Although there has been a large absolute increase of manufacturing employment in the United States, the relative share of the labor force engaged in manufacturing has risen appreciably only in recent years. Technological progress in manufacturing has permitted a tremendous expansion of production during the last three decades with little change in the share of the nation's labor force. The tertiary sector has been able to increase relative to other sectors, with the decrease concentrated in primary employment.

In New England, on the other hand, the expansion of tertiary employment has necessarily been primarily at the expense of manufacturing employment, although some of the shift has resulted from technological change which has reduced manufacturing man-hour requirements relative to output. Even though the past shift from manufacturing to services was a necessary accompaniment to a rising standard of living, any extensive continuation of the trend would probably be an unhealthy sign for the region. Because of its resource base, New England is primarily a manufacturing region. It must continue to be, if income levels in the region are to be maintained. Most of New England's tertiary employment is directly dependent upon the prosperity of manufacturing in the region.

We cannot regard with equanimity any further large relative decrease in manufacturing employment in New England. It is possible that there will be a gradual and slight relative decrease in the future as the result of continued technological progress, which might reduce the proportion of the labor force required to turn out an increasing quantity of goods. But such a change, which is a sign of economic health, should not be confused with an induced shift from manufacturing employment to tertiary occupations resulting from the inability of manufacturers in New England to operate in the face of increased competitive pressure from other regions.

This section of the report has described briefly the labor force of New England and has considered some of the long-term changes in its composition. What factors and pressures have been responsible for these changes? An answer to this question requires an examination of the region's resource base; its transportation system and relative transportation costs; federal, state, and local policies dealing with taxes, labor standards, and labor relations; the capital and credit structure of the region; the ability and resourcefulness of New England management; and the many other forces which influence the rate and direction of growth of the various regional economies of the United States. These topics are examined in other reports of the Committee of New England.

CONCLUSIONS

This discussion of the people of New England and their employment has described important population characteristics that affect their ability to make a living. It has also shown how the region's labor force is occupied. From this discussion it is clear that the New England population and labor force are different in several significant ways from those of the country as a whole:

1. New England's population is growing at a less rapid rate than that of the nation as a whole.

2. New England is one of the most densely populated areas of the United States, especially the three southern states of the region.

3. The age distribution of New Englanders is more heavily weighted in the older brackets.

4. New England has a much larger than average proportion of foreign-born residents, even though the proportion has been declining steadily since 1910.

5. The average New Englander has completed more years of school than the average resident of the United States.

6. The New England health record is better than the national average, and the region is better supplied with doctors and nurses.

7. As a result of the age distribution and the larger proportion of working women, New England's labor force is larger in relation to its population than is true for the country as a whole.

8. The region has a much smaller than average proportion of its labor force engaged in agriculture, fishing, forestry, and mining.

9. It still has a much larger proportion engaged in manufacturing and construction, despite a relative decrease in their importance during recent decades.

10. The relative importance of durable-goods employment in New England has increased while that of nondurable goods has decreased.

11. The unemployment rate in New England has been higher than that in the nation.

These characteristics, in general, provide New England with a large and able labor force of high productivity. They are the basis for the region's above-average per capita income and its high average standard of living.

At the same time, unemployment rates and other indications make it clear that the region is not making the best possible use of its most valuable resource—its people. Manufacturing is the principal economic support for the region, and further reductions in the proportion of the labor force engaged in manufacturing cannot be viewed with equanimity.

The region and its people can benefit from many types of action to increase the efficiency with which the region's human resources are used. This report contains some suggestions for desirable types of action, though its topical limitations require postponement to other reports of a great many other equally desirable proposals. These are some of the recommendations included in this report:

1. Vocational education in the region should be considerably enlarged and strengthened. This type of training is of unusual significance to an area like New England which depends so heavily on manufacturing and is undergoing a major transition in industrial structure.

2. Vocational rehabilitation by the states should be continued and extended to add to the productive capacity of the regional economy as well as to aid the affected workers.

3. The compulsory retirement age should be raised, providing the worker is physically and mentally able to continue to work. Also the movement to employ retired individuals in New England business and industry should be much more extensive.

4. There should be further improvement in educational and employment opportunities in the region, until every New Englander has the opportunity to develop his abilities to their full potentialities and to put them to work in the most productive fashion.

5. The minimum educational opportunity for the region's youth is in need of still further improvement.

6. There is need for further advances in the prevention and cure of communicable diseases, such as respiratory infections, that sap the productivity of the New England labor force. Industrial support of medical research and health programs is in the interest of both employers and the entire population.

7. There is need for a major program of hospital building to replace outmoded or obsolete buildings and to provide for growing health needs.

8. It would be desirable for larger proportions of the residents in each state to be covered by health insurance programs, even though the New England states are already among the national leaders in this respect.

SELECTED REFERENCES

1. Council of State Governments, *The Forty-eight State School Systems*, 1949.
2. Federal Reserve Bank of Boston, "The New England Labor Force," *Monthly Review*, March 1952.
3. Federal Security Agency, *The Nation's Health*, September 1948.
4. Federal Security Agency, Office of Education, *Digest of Annual Reports of State Boards for Vocational Education*, 1950.
5. —— *Federal Government Funds for Education*, Bulletin No. 3, 1950.
6. —— *Statistics of Nonpublic Secondary Schools, 1947–1948*, 1950.
7. —— *Statistics of State School Systems*, 1950.
8. Industrial Development Reports, *The Industrial Education Facilities of New England*, a survey for the Lincoln and Therese Filene Foundation, Boston 1951.
9. National Social Welfare Assembly, *Three Monographs Prepared for a Conference on the Retirement of Older Workers*.
10. Rhode Island State Department of Education, *Improving Vocational Education in Rhode Island*, 1950.
11. Shryock, H. S., "Internal Migration and the War," *Journal of the American Statistical Association*, March 1943.
12. Thornwaite, C. W., *Internal Migration in the United States*, Philadelphia, University of Pennsylvania Press, 1934.
13. U.S. Department of Agriculture, Bureau of Agricultural Economics, *Farm Labor*, 1945–49.
14. U.S. Department of Commerce, Bureau of the Census, *Census of Population*, 1950.
15. —— "Provisional Intercensal Estimates of the Population of Regions, Divisions and States," Series P–25, No. 47, March 9, 1951.
16. —— *Trends in Location of Industry and Population*, April 1951.
17. *Survey of Current Business*, "Incomes of Physicians, 1929–49," July 1951.
18. U.S. Department of Labor, Bureau of Labor Statistics, *Nonagricultural Employment by States*, 1943–47 and 1947–49.

8

Employment Fluctuations in New England

*Drafted by William H. Miernyk under the direction
of Arthur A. Bright, Jr.*

INTRODUCTION

During recent years parts of New England have had serious unemployment problems. The problems have been attacked in many ways, but they still exist. In this report we are primarily concerned with the record of employed fluctuations in New England since World War II, with the causes of unemployment in the region, and with its effects on the workers, their communities, and the region as a whole. From our analysis of these topics we have also drawn certain conclusions about desirable future actions in combatting the region's unemployment problems.

In an economy which is regulated by the market mechanism, there are always some unemployed workers. In the United States the rapid expansion of economic activity during the 19th century kept unemployment to a minimum. There were, of course, cycles of economic activity which led at times to widespread and serious unemployment, but there was no problem of chronic unemployment. Until the 1930's the problem of unemployment received little systematic attention. It was not until 1930 that the census of population included a count of the unemployed workers in the nation's labor force.

The unemployed worker, whatever the cause or duration of his unemployment, represents a drain on the community. During his period of unemployment he does not add to production, but he and his family continue to consume. Unemployment is both a business cost and a social cost. Under the American system of social security, the unemployed worker receives unemployment compensation for a stated period. A high level of unemployment means heavy expenditures for unemployment compensation. If unemployment-compensation payments continue to run at a high rate, the tax levied on the employer to support the program is also high.

The unemployment of workers who are capable of productive work also is costly to the individual. He and his family must curtail their standard of living, use up their savings, go into debt, or receive financial help from their governments. Protracted unemployment may rob a worker of his skills, and it will almost certainly cost him his self-respect. It may also embitter him toward a political and economic system which apparently has no use for his services. The loss of his job is of concern to the individual worker. It is also of serious concern to his employer, to his community in general, and to all who are interested in maintaining the economic health of a region or a nation.

In recent years there has been considerable emphasis on employment and unemployment at the national level. Total employment and unemployment in the nation are regularly reported in the press. For intelligent formulation of policies, it is necessary for Congress and others to know the facts about national employment and unemployment. Highly aggregated totals and averages are not enough, however. It is possible for employment in the nation to be at a high level, while in certain industries unemployment is widespread and persistent. The demand for automobiles may be high at a given time, for example, which might lead to labor shortages in Detroit and other automotive centers. At the same time, however, the demand for shoes and textile products may be low, and the communities in which those industries are localized may be experiencing widespread local unemployment. Relative to the national labor force, the unemployment may not be regarded as serious. To the region and communities concerned, it may spell the difference between prosperity or depression.

It is little comfort to a worsted weaver in Lawrence, Massachusetts, a shoe worker in Manchester, New Hampshire, or a jewelry worker in Providence, Rhode Island, to hear that employment in the nation is running at record levels, if he has been out of a job for months and has no immediate prospects of returning to productive employment. Nor is the grocer, the clothing retailer, or the furniture salesman reassured by reading about high levels of employment in the nation, when he can see the workers of his community walking the streets because their mill or factory has closed.

National trends are reflected in regional trends, of course, and the reverse is also true. There is an interdependence among the regional economies that comprise our national economy, and this same interdependence extends to the world economy as well. But as is true in all regions, New England has some unique employment problems.

CAUSES AND EFFECTS OF NEW ENGLAND'S
SHORT-TERM UNEMPLOYMENT

If an individual worker is out of work he is "unemployed." But is he out of work because he voluntarily left his old employment in an attempt to better himself? Is he temporarily laid off because of a seasonal letdown in the demand for his services? Does he know that he will be called back to his bench or machine in a few days or a few weeks? Has he become unemployed because of the vagaries of the business cycle? Has a machine taken over the task he formerly performed by hand? Is he out of work because his employer has liquidated or moved away? Is there some other reason for his enforced idleness?

Basically there are two kinds of unemployment. One involves the lack of a *job,* but in the other the worker is temporarily out of *work.* A worker out of a job must find new employment, but another worker may be temporarily laid off because of a seasonal slump in employment in his industry or for a wide variety of other reasons.

In each case the individual is not working, but the *cause* of his unemployment is different, and so is its *effect.* We cannot state precisely how much of New England's total unemployment is due to various causes, since the extent of each varies continually. We can examine the types of unemployment in some detail, however, and attempt to find out which kinds of unemployment in the region are most serious, which are tied most closely to national conditions, which kinds are more uniquely New England problems, and which are subject to some control. In this section of the report we limit our attention to short-term unemployment.

Frictional Unemployment

In a free labor market there are always some workers *temporarily* unemployed. A worker dissatisfied with his present job may not be able to transfer directly to a more satisfactory one. He may voluntarily leave his present employment in order to devote full time to searching for the job he wants. His unemployment is voluntary, to be sure, but he is still unemployed. A large volume of unemployment of this kind does not necessarily mean that the economy as a whole is in a weakened condition. When other job opportunities are plentiful, a worker is more willing to quit his present job if he is not satisfied with it. On the other hand, this "frictional" unemployment may last longer during a period of recession, when other jobs are scarcer.

Frictional unemployment exists because all workers do not have perfect knowledge about alternative job opportunities and because most workers are not completely mobile between jobs. Similarly, the fact that some employers are not aware that satisfactory workers are available to fill some job vacancies contributes to frictional unemployment. For every frictionally unemployed worker there exists a job somewhere, but the worker and the job are not brought together. A shift in jobs often requires a period of hunting, and sometimes retraining. It is impossible to estimate accurately the actual extent of frictional unemployment at any one time, but it certainly accounts for only a small fraction of total unemployment. It is always present to some degree, however, and it is one reason why we can never achieve "full" employment, in the sense that every person who wants work is employed at any moment of time.

Other Kinds of Temporary Unemployment

Not all temporary unemployment is "frictional." Some workers may be temporarily idled when a plant closes down for a short time to retool for model changes. Such workers are "laid off" for a few weeks, and they feel certain that when the plant begins to operate again they will be called back to their old jobs. But they are eligible for unemployment compensation and are included in the statistics of the unemployed.

Other workers may be temporarily unemployed when their plants close for a few days or weeks for repairs or modernization, or because of a temporary shortage of materials, or for any of a host of other possible causes. The common characteristic of all such unemployment is that it is temporary.

Part of this kind of unemployment is beyond the control of the individual employer or any other agency, but part of it is subject to at least some control. The coordination of model changes and routine maintenance or repairs with vacation periods can minimize the unemployment they produce. Adequate fire protection can help guard against losses to both employees and employers as a result of major fire damage. Careful planning of material requirements can reduce the disruptions of shortages, though shortages caused by extended strikes in other industries are beyond the control of the consuming industries.

To reduce the disrupting effects of material shortages caused by strikes, better policies and action are needed to limit the duration of strikes in basic industries, particularly steel and bituminous coal. The steel strike during the summer of 1952, for example, caused considerable unemployment in other industries in New England and the rest of the country. This problem is a national problem, of course, but New England shares the national interest in it. We discuss the effects of industry-wide strikes on the regional economy in "Labor-Management Relations in New England" (report series, No. 10).

Regardless of the best future efforts of those who are in a position to control these short-period causes of unemployment, however, one should not be surprised if there are many thousands of workers drawing unemployment-compensation benefits in the region even when employment is at a high level. When conditions in the regional labor market are particularly tight, as during a war or defense period, these types of unemployment may decline but they never disappear.

Seasonal Unemployment

Many types of economic activity are seasonal, and they also produce short-term unemployment. Agriculture is perhaps the outstanding example. During the winter months, farm work is slow. Agricultural employment begins to rise in the spring, and it reaches a peak during the fall harvest season. Chart 8–1 shows average monthly employment on farms in New England for the period 1945 through 1949. The five-year monthly averages are based on surveys conducted by the Bureau of Agricultural Economics of the United States Department of Agriculture.[1] An average of about 230,000 persons was employed on New England farms during the postwar

CHART 8–1

Seasonal Employment on New England Farms, 1945–49,
Monthly Averages
(thousands of workers)

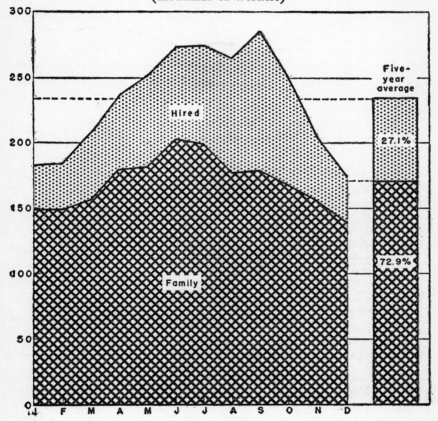

Source: Department of Agriculture, Bureau of Agricultural Economics, *Farm Labor,* monthly releases

1. The total number of farm workers shown exceeds that reported by the Bureau of the Census, since the census reports only farm workers 14 years of age and older who are not also employed in some nonagricultural pursuit. The figures in Chart 8–1, therefore, are maximum estimates of farm employment in New England.

years, but the average employment rose to a peak of approximately 285,000 in September and then fell to about 175,000 in December, the low month.

The average number of hired farm workers varied from a low of about 35,000 to a high of approximately 105,000. In a typical postwar year, therefore, the number of hired farm workers increased by about 70,000 between January and September. During the winter months many of these workers

CHART 8–2

Seasonal Fluctuations in Nonagricultural Employment and Insured Unemployment in New England, 1947–51, Monthly Averages
(thousands of employees)

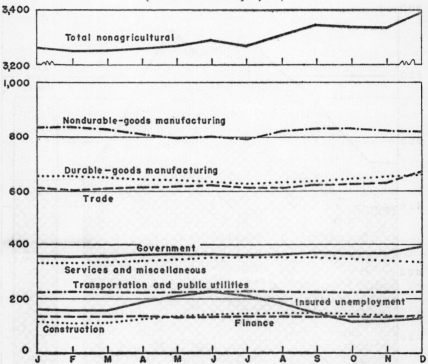

Source: Basic data provided by Department of Labor, Bureau of Labor Statistics, and Bureau of Employment Security

had to find temporary employment in other occupations, or they became unemployed. Unemployed agricultural workers do not show up in the monthly unemployment statistics based upon unemployment-compensation returns, since they are not covered by unemployment insurance. They are included in estimates of unemployment made by the Bureau of the Census based on sample studies.

Some types of nonagricultural employment are also quite seasonal. One outstanding example in New England is offered by the region's shoe industry. Typically, shoe production consists of two semiannual "runs," with two peaks of output each year. The first peak of employment comes in March or April, the second in September or October. Since the New England shoe industry employs about 85,000 workers, on the average, its seasonal fluctuations have a substantial impact upon the total seasonal employment pattern of the region, though of course the effects are felt most in those communities where the shoe industry is heavily concentrated.

The nondurable-goods industries as a whole show more seasonal fluctuation than the durable-goods industries in New England. The averages plotted in Chart 8-2 show seasonal variation in the major employment groups other than agriculture. In the nondurable-manufacturing industries, maximum average employment from 1947 to 1951 reached nearly 840,000 workers, and the average minimum during the year was about 796,000. There was an average difference of more than 40,000 from peak to trough. The high points of employment in the nondurable-goods industries come in the spring and fall, and the low point is in July.

The shoe industry is a major contributor to that pattern, but other nondurable-goods industries are also subject to seasonal swings. There is a slight seasonal dip during the summer months in New England's textile, apparel, and rubber industries. On the other hand, the food and food-processing industries show a slight seasonal increase beginning in June, which helps to offset to some extent the seasonal decline in the other soft-goods industries.

Employment in the durable-goods industries during the period 1947–51 typically reached a peak in December, though the low point also came in July. The difference between the highest and lowest monthly averages was about 33,000 workers. The durable-goods industries, which employ somewhat fewer workers in New England than the nondurable-goods industries, are subject to less seasonal fluctuation in employment, both absolutely and relatively. The pattern of seasonal employment in the durable-goods industries is a smooth one, with a gradual descent to a low point in July and a gradual rise to a peak in December.

Turning to the nonmanufacturing industries, we find considerable variation in seasonal patterns. New England construction employment shows a marked dip during the winter months and a rise in the spring, and it holds fairly steady throughout the remainder of the year. Employment in wholesale and retail trade increases gradually from January to November, with a small decline in the summer. There is a sharp increase in December, however, when department stores and others augment their regular staffs with temporary employees to help handle the Christmas trade.

Employment in transportation and public utilities and in finance shows virtually no seasonal change throughout the year. The service and miscellaneous industries, however, typically experience some increase in employment during the summer months. That expansion is largely attributable to the employment in hotels, summer resorts, and similar establishments, which operate only during the summer season or which add temporary employees at that time.

Government employment in New England, which includes federal, state, and local jobs, is relatively steady throughout the year, except for a sharp increase in December. The end-of-the-year increase undoubtedly results primarily from temporary employment at post offices during the Christmas rush, although it may also reflect temporary employment in other government activities.

The combined seasonal employment pattern of the separate nonagricultural groups in New England is different from that of any of the individual groups, though it follows the outlines of the trade and government categories more closely than any of the others. From January until June the decline in manufacturing employment is offset by increasing employment in trade, service, and construction activity. There is a sharp dip in July, when manufacturing employment reaches its low for the year, but employment rises rapidly to a fall plateau and a December peak. This increase is due to the composite effects of rising employment in manufacturing, trade, and government throughout the latter half of the year. After the month of December, there is typically a substantial letdown, and the seasonal pattern repeats itself in the following year.

Insured Unemployment

Five-year monthly averages of *insured unemployment* in New England based on the period June 1946 through May 1951 are also shown in Chart 8–2. We must emphasize that these averages consistently understate the actual extent of unemployment. Agricultural workers and domestic employees are not included under the unemployment-insurance program, nor are new entrants to the labor force who have not yet found jobs. In addition, some unemployed workers exhaust their benefits before returning to work. Though they remain unemployed, their names are removed from the unemployment-compensation rolls.

Part of the typical increase in insured unemployment in April is attributable to administrative procedures rather than to an actual increase in unemployment itself. During the period covered by Chart 8–2 most of the New England states started their benefit year in April. Workers who were unemployed in earlier months, but who had exhausted their benefit rights for the preceding year, again became eligible to receive unemployment compensation and were counted once more among the insured unemployed. But the large increase in the number of workers receiving unemployment compensation from March through June is primarily a reflection of the seasonal decline in manufacturing employment during those months. The decline in insured unemployment from June to October is explained for the most part by the rise in manufacturing employment during these months.

Although manufacturing employment in the region is less than employment in the other nonagricultural activities, the manufacturing industries account for most of the insured unemployment and dominate its seasonal fluctuations. It may seem paradoxical that there is an increase in both insured unemployment and total nonagricultural employment from November through December. Most of the "extra" employment in trade and government in December is temporary, however. Housewives, students, and others not regularly attached to the labor force take jobs for a few weeks during the Christmas rush. There are, of course, persons seeking part-time or temporary employment throughout the year. And there is a demand for such workers at all times. There is a constant movement of part-time and temporary workers into and out of the labor force, but there is a heavy concentration of such employment during the Christmas season. Many of these workers are employed for only a week or two and do not become eligible for unemployment compensation. They do not, therefore, cause a rise in insured unemployment during January or February of the following year. The increase in insured unemployment from November to December is caused by the seasonal employment decline in nondurable-goods manufacturing, in service occupations, and in construction activity.

If a region or state is heavily dependent upon a single or several highly seasonal industries, the recurring unemployment in those industries may constitute a serious problem. The periodic surges in unemployment will cause a substantial drain on unemployment-compensation funds year after year. Even in the absence of large cyclical unemployment, it may require a high unemployment-insurance tax rate to prevent the depletion of the fund.

The seasonality of shoe production, textile production, construction, and some other major insured sources of employment in New England does create steady drains on the unemployment-compensation funds of some of the states. This is especially true in the soft-goods states—Maine, New Hampshire, Massachusetts, and Rhode Island. Even if seasonality can be reduced to some extent, there is bound to be an important volume of seasonal unemployment at most times in addition to the frictional unemployment and that resulting from other short-term causes. The seasonal unemployment will undoubtedly continue to be largest in the summer months.

From the point of view of total employment, however, seasonal unemployment is not a serious problem in New England. Seasonal swings in manufacturing are partly offset by different seasonal patterns in other lines of employment. As manufacturing activity falls during the spring and summer months, employment is increasing in agriculture, trade, and the construction industries. When farm work and construction jobs begin their seasonal downturn in the fall, manufacturing employment is increasing again. This does not mean that workers move easily from manufacturing jobs to farm or construction work, nor does it mean that seasonally unemployed farm and construction workers can readily find factory jobs during the winter.

Unfortunately, little is known about the extent of the movement of workers from one seasonal occupation to another in New England. There is undoubtedly some mobility of this kind, but the important point is that the seasonal patterns in different industries tend to offset one another. The fluctuations in total employment are less than they would be if the regional economy were less diversified.

It is impossible to state exactly how much of insured unemployment is a consequence of seasonal unemployment. Other short-term causes were probably responsible for part of the 115,000 difference between the July and October averages shown in Chart 8–2, but even in October there is a minor amount of seasonal unemployment in some of the smaller industries. It seems fair to assume, nevertheless, that the average peak of seasonal non-agricultural unemployment in the region during the five-year period did not exceed 115,000 workers. Large though that number is in absolute terms, it amounts to only about 3% of the region's labor force. Also, seasonally unemployed workers are generally out of work for only a few weeks or at most a few months at a time, and during most of the year the proportion is much smaller. Moreover, many of the seasonal workers are employed for only part of the year by choice. They are often "extra" workers in a family, who work during the peak seasons to supplement family incomes but who do not want full-time jobs.

On the other hand, seasonal unemployment should not be accepted with complacency as something about which nothing can be done. To some degree, the present amount of seasonal unemployment may be reducible for individual manufacturers. Some of the industries which experience most seasonality produce to order rather than for stock. There are often good reasons for this type of production, however, particularly in industries manufacturing highly styled products. One cannot expect a manufacturer to expose himself to a major risk of large inventory losses, solely to de-seasonalize his production. To do so may mean bankruptcy of the firm, and this is a much less desirable prospect than a continuation of some seasonal unemployment, since it would result in a permanent loss of the jobs offered by this firm. Other manufacturers can perhaps reduce the seasonality of their employment by diversification of their product lines to include more products with offsetting seasonal patterns.

There may be a better means of reducing seasonal unemployment by dovetailing the seasonal jobs with different employers, especially in fairly diversified communities. During a seasonal decline in one industry, some workers may be reluctant to accept temporary employment of some other kind, partly in fear that they will not be called back to their regular jobs when there is work for them again. They may feel that it is safer and easier to accept unemployment compensation than to risk the prospect of losing their regular employment. It is also probable that many workers do not know of alternative opportunities for temporary employment, and therefore do not take other temporary jobs, even though they are willing to do so.

If workers could be kept better informed of temporary jobs that might be available during periods of seasonal layoff, and if they could be assured that acceptance of such temporary employment would in no way jeopardize their steady jobs, the average level of seasonal unemployment in New England might be lowered somewhat.

Local offices of the Division of Employment Security can, and in some cases do, keep workers informed of temporary employment opportunities, but such activities could be stepped up and made a larger part of regular employment policy. Unions and employers could contribute to such a program by letting the worker know that neither his union status nor his job security would be placed in jeopardy if he accepted employment outside his trade while temporarily laid off because of a seasonal decline.

CYCLICAL EMPLOYMENT AND UNEMPLOYMENT IN NEW ENGLAND

Seasonal unemployment recurs from year to year. It is fairly certain that there will be some increase in unemployment in the region during the spring and summer of each year, and another upsurge beginning in October or November. In other seasons of the year unemployment-compensation claims fall off as seasonally unemployed workers are called back to their jobs. There is another type of periodic unemployment, however, which is less regular but more serious when it occurs. Many types of economic activity are *cyclical* in nature. There are periods of high-level employment followed by periods of widespread unemployment. The extent and duration of unemployment resulting from cyclical forces are less predictable than seasonal unemployment.

In general, manufacturing and construction employment are more subject to cyclical variation than nonmanufacturing employment. Within the manufacturing category there are different cycles in the durable and nondurable-goods sectors and in the individual industries. Employment in the hard-goods industries typically is subject to wider swings than employment in the soft-goods industries. Cycles of employment and unemployment in the nondurables also tend to be of shorter duration. During the last several years, we have heard more about unemployed shoe, textile, and apparel workers in New England than about unemployment in the region's steel mills, machine shops, and electrical-equipment factories. Because of the greater intensity of cyclical swings in the production of durable goods, however, whenever unemployment spreads through the durable-goods industries, the impact upon the regional economy is likely to be greater than that caused by the more frequent recessions in the soft-goods industries.

We have plotted New England's employment in industrial and nonindustrial occupations from 1943 through 1951 in Chart 8–3. Unfortunately, data are not available to show employment in durable- and nondurable-goods manufacturing separately for this period, nor are comparable figures

CHART 8–3

Cyclical Fluctuations in Nonagricultural Employment in New England, 1943–51, and Insured Unemployment, 1946–51, Annual Averages (thousands of employees)

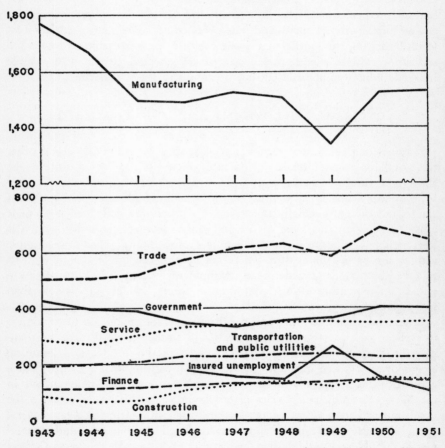

Source: Basic data provided by Department of Labor, Bureau of Labor Statistics, and Bureau of Employment Security

available for earlier years. Annual averages were used to eliminate, as far as possible, the influence of seasonal swings in employment. Chart 8–3 also shows the annual averages of insured unemployment for the postwar period. Again we add the qualification that *insured unemployment provides a record of only those workers covered by the system, and it understates the actual level of unemployment at any one time.*

Even during the short span of years pictured in the chart, there were several different sets of economic conditions. The wartime economy operated under unusual conditions of labor shortage, and in most of the war years the level of unemployment was very low. The decline in manufacturing employment from 1943 to 1945 was a decline from the feverish level of war production to the more "normal" level of manufacturing employment in a peacetime or even a defense economy. The further abrupt drop of 160,000 manufacturing workers between 1948 and 1949, however, represented a cyclical slump due to changes in market conditions.

The downturn of manufacturing and government employment that started in 1943 was partly cushioned by rising employment in trade and service occupations. The cyclical downturn of manufacturing employment in 1949, however, carried with it a recession in wholesale and retail trade and a small decline in construction activity. That was a genuine recession, not at all the same as the previous readjustment from the wartime economy. Another indication of its nature was the sharp upward bulge in insured unemployment, which increased by about 120,000 from 1948 to 1949. Unemployment would have increased even more had it not been for an increase in government employment and the relative strength of the service occupations, transportation and utilities, and finance.

Chart 8–3 shows clearly that *manufacturing employment has been the most volatile of all types of employment in New England during the postwar period.* A sharp recession in manufacturing employment generally also has secondary effects upon employment in some nonmanufacturing activities, especially trade and construction. Under favorable conditions such as those after the war, however, a decline in manufacturing employment can be cushioned to some extent by rising employment in other occupations. At other times, increasing employment in manufacturing can be reinforced by rising employment in other sectors of the regional economy.

The recovery in manufacturing employment between 1949 and 1950 was intensified by the nation's return to a defense economy after the outbreak of the Korean war. The rise in New England's total manufacturing activity after 1950 was retarded somewhat, however, by a new recession in the shoe and textile industries. The decline of employment in the nondurable-goods sector during 1951 was accompanied by a dip in trade, although employment in other activities held firm.

Increased manufacturing employment sent the rate of insured unemployment plummeting between 1949 and 1950. It continued to fall between

1950 and 1951, though at a much slower rate. After 1951 trends were mixed. Employment in the durable-goods sector has held steady or increased, but employment in nondurable-goods industries remained at a fairly low level through the first half of 1952.

The Industrial Composition of New England and Cyclical Unemployment

During the past three decades, the structure of New England's manufacturing economy has been gradually changing. In 1919 about 37% of the region's manufacturing employment was in the durable-goods sector, while the comparable figure for the nation as a whole was about 48%. By 1947, however, 44% of New England's manufacturing workers were employed by factories making durable goods, and the national ratio had increased to 51%. Compared to the entire nation, there has been a greater shift of manufacturing employment from the nondurables to the durables within New England. What does this imply for the stability of employment in the region?

In the past, fluctuations of employment and unemployment in New England's textile, shoe, and similar nondurable-goods industries have not been as great as those in the machinery, fabricated metal, and similar durable-goods industries. *As employment in the manufacture of nondurable goods shrinks in relative importance, the region may become subject to wider cyclical swings in total employment and unemployment. The downturns can hurt more, and the upturns can come more suddenly and proceed more rapidly.*

The New England economy was relatively stable compared to the nation as a whole. The recession of 1921, for example, was short but severe. In only one New England state, Connecticut, did employment decline as rapidly as in the nation as a whole. Connecticut was at that time, and still is, the state with the highest proportion of employment in durable-goods manufacturing in New England. We should also point out, however, that the recovery was more rapid in the nation than it was in New England. During the other recessions and depressions of the interwar period, New England continued to show greater relative stability.

But relative stability of employment is not a virtue in itself. The ideal goal is relative stability of employment at a high level in those industries which generate the greatest amounts of income per worker. There is some "best industry-mix" which would give the region the protection of the relative stability of nondurable-goods employment, as well as the growth and higher incomes that are associated with employment in many of the durable-goods industries. While that "best" structure is hard to determine precisely, under the general economic conditions which have prevailed since World War II and which appear likely for the near future, *a continuation of the shift to durables in New England seems desirable. But the shift should be brought about by growth in the durable-goods sector while minimizing losses in nondurables.*

The adjustment is just as important for individual states and communities as it is for the region as a whole. Unbalance in either direction is risky. *We join with others in recommending that communities heavily dependent for employment on the textile or shoe industries work actively to increase their diversification, and we also recommend the same kind of effort in communities heavily dependent on any other industry. In the enthusiasm for the growth of the durable-goods industries in New England, however, one should not forget the contribution to employment stability which the nondurable-goods industries can make.*

Each cycle of economic activity is unique in some respects, although there are always some similarities from cycle to cycle. Cyclical employment and unemployment in New England are closely tied to employment conditions outside the region. The level of employment in New England depends in part upon the level of business activity in the nation, and in part on international economic relations. Since the nation's economy is so closely knit, the cyclical swings of the region generally follow those of the rest of the country, though there are always some differences in timing and magnitude.

The ramifications of some world-wide economic developments are less universal in the United States, despite the general relationship. New England benefited unusually from the sustained world-wide demand for American nondurable goods after World War I, for example, but it suffered after World War II. During the interwar period, the structure of the world economy changed considerably. The production of shoes, textiles, and similar nondurable consumers' goods expanded abroad. The competition for world markets became keener. That expansion was halted temporarily by World War II, but after the war foreign textile producers, in particular, staged a rapid comeback. As a result, by 1950 there was a world-wide recession in textile production and employment, which led to a rise in cyclical unemployment in New England. These events may have a lasting impact upon the economy of New England by narrowing the market for some of its products. The changed outlook may "cut the top off the employment cycle" in the New England textile industries. While the long-term effect may be to help stabilize employment in the region's textile industries, whatever improved stability results will probably be at a lower level.

In general, the durable-goods industries of New England are higher wage industries than the nondurable-goods industries, and they are less susceptible to seasonal unemployment. In the immediate future, the stability of employment in the hard-goods industries will depend heavily upon the course of international events. As long as the nation remains in a state of preparedness for war or on a partial war footing, the demand for most types of durables will remain at a high level. This will tend to carry employment in many other regional activities along with it. New England cannot afford not to build up its durable-goods production while the opportunity exists, even though in the process its over-all employment stability becomes somewhat less.

Seasonal and Cyclical Unemployment Combined

Seasonal and cyclical forces may tend to counteract one another or they may act to reinforce each other. If a seasonal decline in employment coincides with a cyclical expansion, the amount of seasonal unemployment is minimized. But if the economy is in the downward phase of a cyclical

CHART 8–4

Insured Unemployment in New England, June 1946–March 1952
(thousands of individuals)

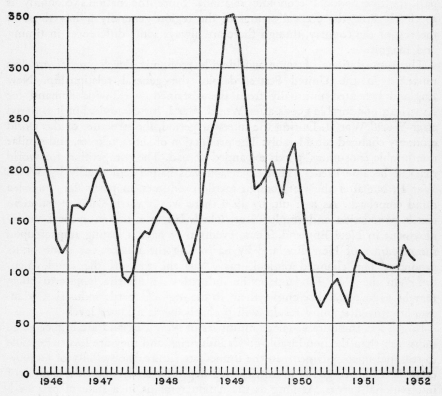

Source: Department of Labor, Bureau of Employment Security

movement, the problems of seasonal unemployment are intensified. One indication of the joint movements of seasonal and cyclical unemployment is given in Chart 8–4, which shows insured unemployment from June 1946 through March 1952. While other sources of unemployment influenced the level of insurance claims and to some extent their movements, the seasonal and cyclical fluctuations dominated the rise and fall during that period.

The swings in unemployment in 1947 and 1948 were relatively mild compared to those in 1949. Typically, seasonal unemployment in New England begins to decline in July, and by September it has about reached the March level again. In 1949, however, the seasonal pickup in employment which began in July was strongly reinforced by a cyclical upturn, and insured unemployment declined sharply until October. There was the usual seasonal increase in unemployment in October, but it was much smaller than it had been during the three preceding years. In 1950 and 1951 the expected seasonal increases in unemployment were tempered somewhat by the continued climb of employment in the durable-goods industries. But the textile recession of 1951 kept the level of unemployment from falling sharply in July of that year. The increase in cyclical unemployment almost offset the usual seasonal decline in 1951.

In summary, the foregoing charts and discussion show that there are several major forces which produce changed levels of unemployment in New England. None of the types of unemployment which we have considered so far is unique to the region. All parts of the country have their seasonal industries, and their individual cyclical patterns all fit into the same general pattern, despite the variations in timing, intensity, and duration.

It is the interaction of many forces which determines the fluctuations of employment in New England, as is always true. Seasonal unemployment considered alone is not a critical problem in New England, nor is unemployment caused by other temporary conditions. Nevertheless, *reductions in seasonal unemployment by improved dovetailing of the various kinds of seasonal jobs would benefit the region by reducing the unproductive time of its workers, by increasing workers' incomes, and by reducing the drains on state unemployment-compensation funds.*

There is little reason to expect a rapid growth of total employment in New England's nondurable-goods industries. Although there may be increased employment in some of them, others will probably experience declines, especially those which are experiencing employment declines in the nation as a whole. Prospects for increased employment are greater in the durables, which also offer less seasonal variation. So long as defense spending remains at high levels, total employment in New England will probably be buoyed up, as it will be in the nation as a whole. In the long run, as the region continues its shift from nondurable-goods production to the manufacture of durable goods, it will undoubtedly become increasingly susceptible to wider swings in employment and unemployment. At the same time, it will probably improve its opportunities for growth. Those generalizations apply particularly to Massachusetts and Rhode Island, and also to New Hampshire and Maine. Connecticut and Vermont already approximate the national proportion of durable-goods manufacturing, but there is no reason why these states, too, should not increase their proportion of this type of manufacturing.

CHRONIC OR PERSISTENT UNEMPLOYMENT

Historically, New England has been a shoe and textile manufacturing center. It still is, although the relative importance of the shoe and textile industries has been declining for decades. Despite the relative decline, there are many communities in New England which depend primarily upon shoe factories and textile mills for employment. The level of unemployment in most of these communities has been high since the end of World War II.

During the war, when almost all industries were operating close to capacity, there was no persistent unemployment in New England. On the contrary, there were serious labor shortages in many manufacturing communities in the region, as was true in other parts of the nation. After the end of the war, however, some of the woolen and worsted mills in New England began to close their doors, as many cotton mills had done after World War I. Some simply closed, and others migrated to the South. The relocation of shoe factories also resumed, even though many factories just moved from one state to another within the region. Until 1947 the liquidations and removals were checked to some extent by the high level of production needed to satisfy postwar consumer demand. Then total textile demand fell off, and even those mills which remained in business operated well below peak capacity. Since that year, community after community in New England has been plagued by what may be called "chronic" unemployment.

We have found that there is a rather close correlation between the level of chronic unemployment in manufacturing communities in the region and the degree to which they depend upon the shoe and textile industries for employment.[2] In those Massachusetts communities where more than 50% of the labor force covered by unemployment insurance was employed by the shoe and textile industries, the level of persistent unemployment during the postwar period averaged about 20% of the covered labor force. More than 10% of the covered workers were chronically unemployed in seven of the 11 communities where dependence upon shoes and textiles

2. By "chronic" or "persistent" unemployment we mean that unemployment which remains after accounting for seasonal and cyclical unemployment. For a more complete definition and a detailed report of our findings, see our Staff Memorandum No. 2, *Chronic Unemployment in New England from 1947 to 1951*, May 1952.

was more than 30%. In those Massachusetts communities with less than 10% of the covered labor force employed in shoe factories and textile mills, however, the level of persistent unemployment was only about 6%. While 20% represents a seriously high degree of persistent unemployment, 6% would seem to be a tolerable level. Actually, some of these workers may well have been frictionally unemployed.

Connecticut's situation was more favorable than that of Massachusetts. Only four of the 13 important labor-market areas in that state had more than 30% of the covered labor force engaged in the production of shoes and textiles. In three of them, the level of persistent unemployment was a little more than 10%, and the figure for the fourth community was only 6%. Concentration in the textile and shoe industries was below 20% in all the other Connecticut labor-market areas, and there was a fairly low level of persistent unemployment in all but one of them. It appears that Connecticut has been less seriously affected by the problem of chronic unemployment than the other New England states. It also has the least concentration in shoes and textiles.

Each labor-market area in Rhode Island had at least 20% of its covered labor force employed in textile mills during the postwar period. There were no shoe factories in the state. In two communities, workers in textile mills accounted for nearly 60% of the covered labor force. In four of the five Rhode Island labor-market areas, at least 10% of the labor force was chronically unemployed. Rhode Island is the least diversified of all New England states, and its heavy dependence upon a single industry means that the state is hit hard when textiles are in one of their recurrent slumps.

In seven of New Hampshire's ten labor-market areas, more than 20% of the covered labor force was in shoe or textile employment. In all seven, the level of chronic unemployment was above 10%. Four of Vermont's eight most important labor-market areas depended upon the textile industries for more than 10% of local employment. In three of those areas the rate of persistent unemployment was 10% or greater. Similarly in Maine, three of the four communities with more than 30% of the covered labor force employed in making shoes and textiles had an unemployment rate in excess of 10%.

When we combine the figures for the six separate states into one composite whole, we find that their patterns fit together rather closely. As the average dependence upon shoes and textiles in New England manufacturing communities increased by intervals of 10% during the postwar years, their average level of persistent unemployment increased by approximately 1.5 percentage points. These relationships are summarized in Chart 8–5.

The existence of chronic unemployment in a community does not necessarily mean that the same individuals are continuously without work. In some cases, the available work in a local labor-market area is shared by the workers of the community. Under a system of "staggered" employment,

one worker is employed a certain number of weeks, and then he is replaced by another for approximately the same period. During his period
of unemployment, the worker receives unemployment compensation. Even
if he works six months or less a year, his annual income is greater than it
would be if he had to depend upon earned income alone. Where staggered
employment is regularly practiced, as in Lawrence, Massachusetts, there

CHART 8–5

Relationship between Unemployment and Concentration in Shoe and
Textile Employment; New England, 1947–51[a]

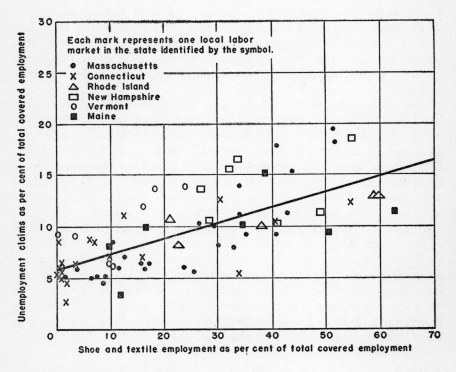

Shoe and textile employment as per cent of total covered employment

[a] Five-year averages of April data.
Source: Data provided by the Employment Security Divisions of the six New England states

are more workers attached to factories than the factories can continuously
employ even if they are operating at full capacity.[3] Under those conditions,
there is a steady drain on unemployment-compensation funds and often a
high tax rate on the employer to compensate for the depletion.

3. See "Job Rotation in Lawrence," in *A Report on Unemployment Compensation Benefit
Costs in Massachusetts,* Massachusetts Division of Employment Security, August 1950, Monograph 5, pp. 217–245.

"Staggered" employment and high rates of chronic unemployment have had serious effects on the unemployment-compensation reserve funds of Massachusetts and Rhode Island. At the end of 1950 reserves in the nation as a whole amounted to 8.6% of taxable wages. In Rhode Island reserves were only 4.2%, and in Massachusetts the fund was down to but 2.7% of taxable wages. Rhode Island and Massachusetts were at the bottom of the list of states in their reserve ratios. *Studies made by the Division of Employment Security indicate that the low level of reserves in these New England states was not due to their more liberal compensation provisions, but rather to their higher rates of insured unemployment. The heavy drains on unemployment-compensation funds pulled down the reserves and forced up tax rates.*

The system of staggered employment in New England had its origin in the worsted industry of Lawrence. Employers in that area welcomed the plan, since it assured them a full force of trained workers during periods of peak production. The practice has spread, however, to other communities, states, and industries. It is prevalent in the textile and jewelry industries of Rhode Island,[4] and some plants in other Rhode Island industries have also adopted it.

In part, staggered employment or "job rotation" has resulted from *technological* unemployment; that is, unemployment caused by the displacement of workers by new and more productive machines. But the principal cause has been the liquidation of textile mills or their migration to other regions. If the management of a textile mill determines to close or relocate, it tends to let its plant and equipment run down. Some day, when the industry is caught in a slump, the mill closes its doors permanently. A new mill may be built, but it is built in another region. Many of the mill's workers may be left stranded. Some of them, especially the younger, unmarried ones, may migrate. But most of them do not. Those workers who are married and have family responsibilities, the older workers in particular, are tied to their community by friendships, church, union, and other ties. They do not pack up and move to a new and strange community even as readily as the mill can close its doors and open up again at a new location. The result has been a substantial flow of workers into the group which is chronically unemployed.

It is the existence of this pool of persistently unemployed workers, more than anything else, which has been responsible for the higher average level of unemployment in New England than in the nation during recent years. In any industrialized region there is frictional, seasonal, cyclical, and technological unemployment. New England has its share of these kinds of unemployment, as do other regions. In addition, however, New England is faced with the problem of persistent unemployment, and this is more

4. *Benefit Financing and Solvency of the Employment Security Fund in Rhode Island,* Rhode Island Department of Employment Security (1951), pp. 50–61.

uniquely a New England problem. The major attack upon the problem of unemployment in New England must be against chronic unemployment.

It is evident that *there are only two major paths to the solution of the problem of chronic unemployment, though they are not mutually exclusive. One is to bring new jobs to the workers; the other is to move the unemployed or partially employed workers to new jobs.* Of the two, the former is the more attractive from a regional, community, and individual point of view. But a number of questions arise. Can former textile and shoe workers be readily transferred to other occupations in new industries? Can the skills that those workers have acquired be transferred to new occupations? Does the availability of a supply of workers with previous factory experience attract new manufacturing plants to the communities in which chronic unemployment has been prevalent? These are questions about which there has been relatively little factual information. We shall try, however, to provide some tentative answers.

What Happens to Workers When a Mill or Factory Closes?

The ease with which workers in a mill or factory find new jobs, after the liquidation or migration of the plant, depends on the circumstances surrounding its closing. General economic conditions in the nation and the region, the age of the workers, the skills they possess, the ratio of male to female workers, the number and kinds of other local employers, and a host of other varying factors determine whether or not the transition to new employment is easy. In attempting to throw some light upon the general problem, the research staff of the Committee of New England made an analysis of three mill liquidations and the subsequent employment history of their former workers.[5]

Although the three cases are not sufficient for broad generalizations, we found that *even under relatively favorable circumstances the transfer of workers to new jobs is not easy.* In the case of a New Hampshire woolen and worsted mill which was liquidated in the last quarter of 1948, 67% of the mill's work force were known to have found new jobs in covered employment within the state by the end of the second quarter of 1950. On the average, they found new jobs only after 20 weeks of compensated unemployment. Also, the average worker earned considerably less in his new job than he did while employed by the textile mill, partly because many of the new jobs offered less continuous employment than the old. There was also a downgrading of skills. Only 40% of the workers who had been classified as skilled operatives in the mill were able to find new skilled jobs.

5. The results are reported in detail in *Inter-Industry Mobility of Workers and the Transfer of Worker Skills in New England,* our Staff Memorandum No. 5, Pt. 1, June 1952. The analysis was based upon data provided by the New Hampshire Division of Employment Security and the Employment Security Division of the Connecticut Department of Labor.

Few of those who did retain their skilled ratings were able to take jobs outside the textile industries; most of them found employment in other textile mills in the state. In general, there was a fairly high degree of movement from the textile industry to other manufacturing industries and to nonmanufacturing occupations. But the transition was obviously an induced one. It was made at the expense of the workers' accumulated skills and incomes, which also means at the expense of the *community's* income, and only after several months of unemployment.

In the case of a New Hampshire shoe factory which went out of operation in the third quarter of 1949, the results were somewhat different. Sixty-eight per cent of the displaced shoe workers were able to find new jobs in the same industry in the same community, and 87% obtained covered employment in the state by the end of the first quarter of 1951. There was less downgrading of skills and a smaller drop in quarterly earnings. Eighty-eight per cent of the skilled workers obtained new skilled jobs. While there was some movement to other industrial and nonindustrial occupations, interindustrial mobility was smaller, since more alternative job opportunities were available locally in other shoe factories. Even in this case, however, the transfer from old jobs to new ones was not smooth. The average worker was unemployed for 18 weeks before he found a new job, and some workers were out of work for a much longer period.

In both New Hampshire cases, a number of workers withdrew completely from the labor force after losing their old jobs. The proportion of withdrawals was higher for the textile mill (13%) than for the shoe factory (9%), probably because there was less opportunity for alternative employment. Most of those who left the labor force were older workers, many of them women past 60 years of age. Some younger married women also withdrew from the local labor force, as did some younger men who apparently entered military service or moved to another state in search of employment.

In the third case, another woolen and worsted mill, we do not have complete information for all the plant's workers, but we do have data for a large sample of those who found new jobs within ten weeks. This Connecticut mill closed in 1951, when employment in the area was rising. Eighty-two per cent of the 437 workers in the sample found new jobs outside the textile industry, but again there was a substantial downgrading of skills. Only half of the skilled and semiskilled workers remained in those classifications after they had found new jobs. In the Connecticut case the transition was apparently somewhat easier, since the Connecticut Division of Employment Security made special efforts to place them in available jobs on the basis of aptitude tests. There is no information, however, about the workers not included in the sample. Some of them may have joined the ranks of the chronically unemployed, and some may have withdrawn from the labor force entirely. Also, there is no information on the earnings of this group of workers before and after the transition, though there is a presumption that the lower skill classifications were accompanied by somewhat lower earnings.

The results of these three case studies show that there was considerable mobility of workers from one industry to another but little actual transferability of their skills. Even the interindustry mobility of the workers depended heavily upon the availability of other jobs in the same industry. One should distinguish between actual or observed transferability of skills and potential transferability. *It may be that a more careful analysis of the skill characteristics of the displaced textile and shoe workers and of the skill requirements of other jobs would permit a greater degree of transfer of skill levels. We recommend that the employment security agencies study this problem intensively and give special attention to it in aiding displaced workers to find new employment.*

We cannot generalize too broadly from the findings of the three case studies alone, but others who have studied this problem have come to essentially the same conclusions as our own. Professors Myers and Shultz of the Massachusetts Institute of Technology, for example, made a study of a New England community in which a large textile mill had been liquidated. They concluded that "Only a few of the workers who found new jobs were able to better themselves. More frequently they were forced to take less skilled work than they had in the mill, with correspondingly lower earnings . . . nearly 40% of all the laid-off workers (employed and unemployed) liked their former mill jobs well enough to say that if they had their choice they would still take the mill job . . ." [6]

Job displacement as a result of the liquidation or migration of a mill or factory is particularly hard on the older worker. If a worker past 50 years of age can continue at his present work, he may have many years of productive and remunerative employment left to him. If he loses his job, most employers will be reluctant to hire him. He may be barred from continuous productive work at a relatively early age, and he may be forced to accept such casual employment as comes his way or to withdraw from the labor force entirely. In the latter event, he must be supported by his family or the community.

New England cannot gloss over the problems raised by the liquidation of many of its textile mills or their migration to other regions, or even the less serious problem of the *intra*regional movement of some of our shoe factories. Because total New England employment in certain other industries, particularly electrical equipment and electronics, has been expanding in recent years, there has been a tendency for some individuals to adopt an "all is well" attitude. If more workers are finding jobs in the growing industries than are losing jobs in the declining industries, we are asked, how can anyone say that New England has an employment problem? They

6. Charles A. Myers and George P. Shultz, *The Dynamics of a Labor Market* (New York, Prentice-Hall, 1951), p. 43.

also point out that average weekly wages in the expanding industries are higher than those in the contracting industries although this is not always true of hourly earnings.

All this is well and good. It is indeed fortunate for the regional economy as a whole that many new plants are being located in New England and that many old ones are expanding. Enthusiasm for the region's growing industries is understandable. New plants should be encouraged to locate in the region and should be welcomed. A substantial proportion of them fill gaps left by liquidated textile and shoe plants. But the new plants have not yet solved the problem for all the specific communities affected, despite strenuous efforts by many local and state organizations. A large task remains. Despite the fact that there is some mobility of workers from the declining to the expanding industries, the transitional problem remains. How many of those who find new employment in the expanding industries are workers who have lost their jobs in the declining ones? Are the new plants hiring older workers or are they turning primarily to new entrants to the labor market?

New England Labor and the Location of New Manufacturing Plants

We can provide some answer to the question, "Are the new manufacturing plants in New England locating here because they can get workers with previous factory experience, especially former textile or shoe workers?" The research staff of the Committee of New England surveyed the experience of 23 newly established manufacturing plants in the region.[7] Most of those new establishments are located in areas where employment in textile mills or shoe factories has been declining. As in our case studies of liquidated mills, we wanted to find out how much the training workers received in their old jobs helped them to adapt to tasks in other industries.

The 23 plants surveyed employed a total of 8,618 workers at the beginning of 1952. Almost 31% of those for whom previous employment experience was reported had worked in shoe factories or textile mills. Another 55% had had previous experience in some other occupation. Only 14% were without previous job experience. These proportions indicate again that workers can and do shift from one industry to another, when employment opportunities are available to them.

The new plants covered a broad range of industries, including plastics, precision castings, electrical equipment, electronics, drugs and medicines, optical instruments, paper, and others. How well were these plants able to apply the skills of the former shoe and textile workers to their new jobs? The 23 companies reported a total of 1,068 skilled workers. Only two of these had backgrounds in shoes or textiles. Of 3,643 workers classified as

7. The detailed results are presented in Staff Memorandum No. 5, Pt. 2.

semiskilled by the surveyed plants, 27 had worked in shoe factories or textile mills. In total, only about 2% of the former skilled and semiskilled shoe and textile workers had been able to transfer their skill levels directly to their new jobs.

It is evident that the skills of unemployed shoe and textile workers do not in themselves provide an inducement for a manufacturer to locate a plant in New England. But the availability of a labor supply with previous factory experience and with the industrial discipline which it produces does attract some types of manufacturing plants to a community where such a supply of labor is available.

According to the respondents in our survey, plants which manufacture heavy durable goods pay less attention to the problems of labor supply in selecting a location than those which specialize in lightweight durable goods. The former pay relatively more attention to transportation costs. The producers of light nondurable goods also said that they were not particularly influenced by the availability of experienced labor in making their decisions to locate in New England. *The most likely industrial prospects for New England, then, so far as absorbing the region's surplus labor is concerned, are those companies which produce the lighter durable goods.*

There is much other evidence that many manufacturing plants have located in New England during recent years because of the availability of the desired type of labor in the region. In some cases, companies have stated that it was trained labor, or labor that could be easily retrained, which led them to choose a New England location. The Hammel-Dahl Company of Warwick, Rhode Island, chose that community because of the availability of skilled precision workers. The Cornish Wire Company located a branch plant at Rutland, Vermont, because there was an ample supply of experienced labor in that vicinity. Three months after its new site was selected, the Cornish plant was turning out finished products, despite the fact that each worker had to be trained to his new job.[8] The Raytheon Corporation, one of the nation's most rapidly expanding electronics producers, located a new plant at Quincy, Massachusetts. One of the prime considerations was the availability of the kind of workers which this company required for its precision operations. More recently, Raytheon opened another plant at Brockton, Massachusetts, a community in which declining shoe employment has created a labor surplus.

These few examples could be multiplied at length. Have enough new plants come into New England or grown within the region, however, to absorb the surplus workers of those communities in which the level of unemployment has remained high since the end of World War II? Not yet. It is true that each new manufacturing plant in New England helps to absorb part of the region's surplus labor force. It is also true that not

8. For other examples see "Yankee Labor Key to New Industries," *The New England News Letter,* New England Council (June 1952), p. 7.

enough of the new plants have settled in communities plagued by chronic unemployment to solve their problems, although in many instances they have helped alleviate what would otherwise have been critical situations.

Since the specific skills of textile and shoe workers are generally not directly transferable to other industries, the attractiveness of those workers and their earning power can be enhanced if they learn new skills. The interindustry mobility of workers without so much downgrading would undoubtedly be increased if better facilities were available for retraining, particularly for the skills in greatest demand by the growing industries. Most New England states have extensive vocational education facilities, but they are designed, in the main, to teach craft and trade skills to younger persons who have not yet entered the labor market. The idea of retraining workers is not a new one, but it is difficult to translate into practice on a large scale. Part of the difficulty is that such a program is expensive, and it raises the question, "Who is going to pay the bill?" Obviously the displaced worker cannot, and the employer will not if he can obtain workers without the trouble and expense of training them.

The idea of public education, including vocational training, is deeply ingrained in our thinking in this country. But the idea of *retraining* adult workers at public expense is at present less accepted. Yet there is no logical difference between educating a young person before he or she enters the labor market and retraining a worker who has had previous work experience. *In fact, the urgency for retraining and its importance to both the community and the worker may be greater than that for training new workers. It would seem feasible to encourage the retraining of workers while they are drawing unemployment compensation.* The local community and the state should be able to bear the cost of retraining, with perhaps some assistance from the Federal Government under its present program of grants-in-aid to encourage vocational education. Essentially, we recommend that adult workers be given the same opportunity to acquire new skills that are now offered to youngsters of school age. Over time, such a program should be self-liquidating.

The local community might agree to underwrite the cost of retraining workers for a new plant after the decision has been made to locate a plant in the area. Since there is usually some time lag between the decision to locate a plant and the actual opening of the plant, this time could be used as a retraining period. Specialized skills could be provided for new plants coming into the community. Otherwise such plants might have to import skilled workers even though the community is a surplus labor area. Also, retraining should increase the mobility of some workers, and where the level of persistent unemployment is high some workers should be induced to migrate to other areas where job opportunities are more plentiful.

The effectiveness of the industrial development efforts of the cities and towns most seriously affected by persistent unemployment has varied greatly. Even some of the best have made only limited headway in their struggle as new textile or shoe closings have intensified the problem. So long as additional textile plants or shoe factories are closing down or moving out of the region, the goal of eliminating chronic unemployment is a retreating one. In addition to encouraging new manufacturing plants in other industries to locate in New England, therefore, every effort should be made to keep the existing textile mills and shoe factories and to help them operate efficiently at their present locations in the region. Each type of action eases the transition.

Because the decline in textile employment in New England has been accompanied by growth in other industries, some persons have advanced the view that the loss of textile jobs is of no great concern to the region. Others have expressed the view that it is inevitable that mills remaining in the region must depart. The president of a large woolen and worsted corporation recently stated that in ten years there will be no woolen and worsted mills left in New England. Whatever the motives for making such statements, they have a disturbing psychological effect upon the region's textile industry and upon the region as a whole. Those manufacturers who are making a sincere effort to continue competitive operations in the region feel that their industry has been cast in the role of an unwanted child. The morale of millworkers, who are naturally concerned about their future job security, suffers from such off-the-cuff remarks about the unfavorable outlook for New England's textile mills. While it is almost certain that *some* more mills will fail or leave,[9] particularly in the woolen and worsted industry, the migration should not be heralded either as inevitable for the whole industry or as something that is desirable for New England.

The "many advantages" which other regions offer to the textile industries are frequently mentioned in the perennial debates about why some of the mills have been and are leaving New England. These "many advantages" usually boil down to one: low-cost labor—although in some cases employers believe it an advantage to locate in a region where there is less likelihood that their mill will be organized or where they can escape their present union commitments. Textile labor costs are not solely dependent on what happens within the region, of course, since the actions and policies of competitors elsewhere and of the Federal Government play an important role. But to do their part in working out the problems of labor cost in New England's textile mills, unions and management must operate in a favorable local climate. The contribution of the textile industries to the regional economy and the problems that will be created by the departure of more mills must be universally recognized. The least that the New England public and its local and state governments can do is to provide understanding cooperation for those most intimately connected with the textile

9. The reasoning behind this conclusion is given in *The Textile Industries of New England,* our Staff Memorandum No. 10, August 1952.

industries in working toward the solution of their problems. In addition, they can help resolve the problem by intensifying their efforts to encourage the location and growth of plants that will provide alternative job opportunities to displaced workers.

The first part of a two-pronged attack upon the problem of chronic unemployment, then, involves (1) conservation of the maximum number of textile and shoe jobs; (2) encouragement for the growth of those new industries which can most readily use part of New England's surplus labor supply. This includes encouragement of the growth of new establishments *within* the region, as well as efforts to attract new firms and branch plants from outside. But will that always be enough? In some communities it will probably not.

The Migration of Workers

The principal textile and shoe centers of New England, where most of the region's chronic employment is centered, appear often on the United States Department of Labor's list of "surplus-labor areas." Typically, the New England labor-market areas account for a far larger proportion of the nation's cities on the list than their number in relation to the national total. It is highly unlikely that enough new industries can be attracted to all those centers to end their chronic unemployment. It may be necessary to encourage some of the workers in such communities to move elsewhere.

The Geographical Immobility of Workers. There is little factual information available about the movement of workers from one community to another or from one region to another. The fact that there is a high level of persistent unemployment in a number of New England communities, while there are shortages of labor in other states, suggests that most workers do not migrate easily. All case studies of New England mill closings and unemployment experience support that conclusion. *As another phase of the attack on the problem of chronic unemployment, some of the region's stranded textile and shoe workers should be encouraged to migrate to other areas where there is a promise of more steady employment.*

There is no doubt that the most desirable solution to the problem of chronic unemployment in New England is to bring new jobs to the workers, to the fullest extent possible. The experience of recent years indicates that that approach is not enough in some key communities. While new manufacturers are being encouraged to locate or expand in such communities, some of their surplus workers in the area should be *encouraged* to go elsewhere, if they can better themselves by doing so. Of course, this is not a suggestion which will be popularly received. There is always the hope in a "depressed" community that better times lie ahead.

In small communities, where one or two substantial new employers can ease the situation, such hopes are often justified. In larger cities, where the problem is of greater magnitude and often of longer standing, such hopes may be illusory. State and local development agencies have made notable accomplishments in Manchester, Nashua, and a few other textile and shoe cities. Private operators who have taken over and subdivided large old mills in those cities have done exceedingly well in filling them with new small companies. Yet the same cities are still among the first to appear on national lists of surplus-labor areas during any downturn in business activity.

In their desire to attract new employers, state and local development agencies should also continue, by discouraging internal migration, to guard against simply transferring the problems of chronic unemployment from one local community in the region to another. While the interest of such organizations is of necessity concentrated on their own areas, they should keep the broader regional interest in mind.

The most satisfactory guides for the developmental programs of state and local agencies are well known by most such agencies in New England. Action must rest on a sound understanding of the *real* advantages which a community can offer specific types of manufacturing plants and the *real advantages which the plants can offer* the community. If it is economically sound for a manufacturing plant to locate in New England rather than elsewhere, then the community, the region, and the nation will all gain by its location in New England. If a community has the right kind and quantity of trained labor, managerial talent, research facilities, and other factors which will enable a manufacturing plant to operate there as efficiently or more efficiently than it can operate elsewhere, then every effort should be made to assist the plant in settling there. Unsound or artificial inducements, such as major tax concessions, often harm a community more than they help it. Such attractions, held out as bait, offer only transitory advantages to a plant and tend to attract "fly-by-night" enterprises. New England agencies, as a whole, have rightly avoided the use of those devices.

Similarly, if there are economically compelling reasons for a plant to move out of New England, the region may not gain much by attempting to retain the plant indefinitely, even though the unemployment problem is intensified by its leaving. In such instances, while efforts should be made to improve the competitive position of the plant, sound forward planning by the community is better than relying solely on defensive measures. We should, in brief, evaluate the long-run consequences of employment policies as well as their immediate effects. Temporary expedients may only put off the day of reckoning.

Among such expedients have been the attempts to channel defense orders to communities in New England classified by the Department of Labor as areas with a "substantial labor surplus." The established policy of the Federal Government has been to place defense orders for most soft goods on the basis of low bids. In some cases, such as orders for shoes, federal agencies have ruled that defense contracts can be negotiated if there are equally low bids from two areas. Under these circumstances, the order can be placed where there is the greatest surplus of labor. Such contracts are of limited magnitude, and it is evident that New England cannot even count upon defense spending as a whole to solve its problems of unemployment. From a long-run point of view it may be undesirable to subsidize marginal manufacturing plants under the artificial stimulus of defense spending, if such plants cannot be expected to continue profitable operations in the future on the basis of civilian demand. Where unfavorable competitive positions are likely to persist indefinitely, the time to make the industrial adjustment is when general business activity is high. If, on the other hand, military expenditures are to remain at a high level for an indefinite period, it will be necessary for New England manufacturers to obtain their share of government contracts.

New England manufacturers should be permitted to compete with manufacturers located elsewhere for Federal Government contracts on the basis of equal minimum wage rates, as presently provided by the Walsh-Healey Public Contracts Act. Minimum wages in the textile industries should be increased by order of the Secretary of Labor to conform to the intent of the law.[10] Beyond this, we do not believe that further concessions are justified.

If it is unlikely that surplus labor can be completely absorbed by new manufacturing plants, and if other expedients do not offer strong hope of reducing our level of chronic unemployment, we must return to the possibility of induced migration as a means of reducing the more or less permanent oversupply of workers in certain communities. A policy of induced migration may well be most difficult to implement. Will the local community take the initiative in establishing such a policy? In a sense, this might be regarded as an admission of defeat. It is more typical for community leaders to hope that the depressed industries will experience better times in the future. Furthermore, some local industrialists may not be averse to having a "loose" labor market, on the assumption that this will tend to keep their own labor costs from rising.

The state governments could do more to encourage interstate mobility, and some state departments of employment security have attempted to shift workers from areas of labor surplus to other places where jobs are more available. In general, however, the emphasis has been on placing workers in new jobs close to the communities in which they live, so that they can commute to work and continue to live in their old community. An example is the encouragement offered to workers in Brockton, where employment in the shoe industry has been declining, to commute to Boston and other nearby communities. This has not included efforts to have the worker *move* from Brockton.

A program designed to increase the geographical mobility of workers will require increased cooperation among state and federal agencies, under the

10. This topic is discussed further in our report on "Wages in New England" (No. 9).

existing employment security program. *The federal, state, and local divisions of employment security could cooperate to induce workers to move from areas of labor surplus to areas of labor shortage,* with the emphasis on *inducement,* since such a program must be a voluntary one. In deserving cases, and under careful rules of eligibility, financial assistance would be in order to help a family move. Such assistance should be given, of course, only if the worker is employable elsewhere and can produce evidence that he is financially unable, but otherwise willing, to make the move. The costs of such a program would probably be more than offset by savings in unemployment-compensation and welfare costs. Cooperation between employment and housing agencies would also be required, since one deterrent to mobility is the worker's inability to find housing to fit his needs and budget, even if he knows that he can find a job elsewhere.

We should not rely completely upon government activities to induce worker mobility. *Closer cooperation between private employers and the public employment service should also lead to the movement of some workers. Employers in tight labor markets could list their jobs in surplus labor areas. Such job recruitment is not new in the case of skilled workers. Perhaps it could be expanded to include semiskilled workers with factory experience. Finally, we know too little about the causes of worker immobility, and we recommend further study to discover those causes.*

Employing the Older Worker. There will always be workers, however, particularly the older ones, who will be unwilling to move. Even a well-developed program of induced migration cannot be regarded as the final step in solving the problem of chronic unemployment. There is also need for a complete revision of attitudes toward the hiring of older workers. The "older worker" may be 35 or 60 years of age, depending upon general conditions in the labor market. At present, there is a definite bias against hiring older workers, regardless of where the line is drawn at any one time.

New England is already a region with a higher than average proportion of older workers, and the problem of maintaining employment for them will increase with time. It is not enough to pass a law, as some states have done, to prevent employers from asking the age of a prospective employee. Though the intent of such laws is laudable, it cannot prevent employers from discriminating against the older worker. A positive approach is needed. Trade associations, unions, community organizations, and any other agency interested in the future economic, social, and political health of the region should take an interest and actively participate in a program designed to encourage the hiring of competent older workers. There is no satisfactory way of forcing the employer to hire such individuals, and indeed there should not be, but unfair bias against the hiring of older workers where it exists can and should be broken down. *We do not recommend that older workers be hired on the basis of age alone. But we do recommend that employers give honest consideration to the qualifications of older workers, and where workers can meet the qualifications that age not be a bar to their employment.*

There is also a need for more objective studies of the ability, stability, and productiveness of older workers compared to younger persons in the labor force. There are many kinds of jobs, both in manufacturing and nonmanufacturing activities, which the older worker can do as well as his younger counterpart. Employers need more complete knowledge about those kinds of work. The older and less mobile worker in the region must be utilized to his best capacities if the region is to make the most effective use of its labor force.

Reducing Chronic Unemployment

The attack upon the problem of chronic unemployment must be an unremitting one. It should not stop when economic conditions are generally favorable. Although the final objective is to bring the number of jobs and the number of workers in the region more nearly into line, there is no single simple means by which it can be accomplished. To summarize, *we recommend the following major policies:*

1. *Continued efforts to attract new manufacturing plants,* including branch plants, where the in-migration of such plants can be economically justified.

2. *The encouragement of industrial growth from within the region.* Sound enterprises which can absorb part of the region's surplus labor should be provided with an environment that will encourage their growth.[11]

3. *Development of an environment favorable to the solution of problems faced by the region's textile industries.* Every effort should be made to retain in the region those mills and factories that are capable of continued economic operations in the region.

4. *Encouragement of retraining for workers during their periods of enforced idleness,* with emphasis on the development of those skills which the region's growing industries need.

5. *Encouragement of the out-migration of part of the surplus labor supply in those communities in which the problem of chronic unemployment is most serious and least promising of solution.*

6. *Modification in employers' attitudes toward the hiring of older workers.* In the future, there will be more workers in the older age groups than there have been in the past. If those workers are not permitted and encouraged to support themselves, they will have to be supported by the community.

11. See our report on "New England's Financial Resources and Their Use" (No. 11).

CONCLUSIONS

New England's principal employment problem is that of reducing the level of chronic unemployment. A solution to that problem would also minimize the unfavorable effects of staggered employment, or job sharing. Even if New England is successful in reducing chronic unemployment to a tolerable level, however, there will continue to be unemployment in the region. Seasonal and cyclical unemployment may be expected to recur, and in view of the changing structure of the region's manufacturing economy, it will probably experience wider cyclical swings in the future.

Cyclical unemployment in New England is largely due to the *interde-pendence* of economic activities among the various regions of the country. Acting alone, the people of New England cannot combat cyclical unemploy-ment effectively. There is need for continuous improvement in a national policy whose object is to smooth out the recurrent booms and recessions which create alternate periods of labor shortage and widespread unemploy-ment. New Englanders should take a more active part in shaping federal anticyclical policies, both to protect their own self-interests and to contribute toward the national goal of relative stability of employment in an expanding economy.

Within the region, we should try to minimize the number of seasonally unemployed workers by encouraging workers to accept temporary employ-ment when they are laid off from their regular jobs, and perhaps by more product diversification within individual plants. The disruptions in employ-ment from other temporary causes can also be minimized, among other ways, by care in scheduling repairs, material requirements, model changes, and the introduction of new equipment.

New England should set its goals high in working to reduce unemploy-ment. The success with which the region makes use of its greatest natural endowment—the workers of New England—will be measured by the extent to which they can be fully and productively employed. That success will also affect the incomes and standards of living of most New Englanders.

SELECTED REFERENCES

1. Connecticut State Employment Service, *Labor Market Letter* (monthly).
2. Maine Employment Security Commission, *Labor Market Newsletter* (monthly).
3. Massachusetts Division of Employment Security, *Employment Trends* (monthly).
4. ——— *A Report on Unemployment Compensation Benefit Costs in Massachusetts*, prepared under the direction of Walter Galenson, August 1950.
5. New Hampshire Division of Employment Security, *Employment and Unemploy-ment in New Hampshire* (monthly).
6. Rhode Island Department of Labor, monthly releases on employment and unem-ployment.

7. ——— Benefit Financing and Solvency of the Employment Security Fund in
    Rhode Island, 1951.
8. U.S. Department of Agriculture, Bureau of Agricultural Economics, Farm Labor
    (monthly).
9. U.S. Department of Labor, Bureau of Employment Security, The Labor Market
    and Employment Security (monthly). Employment Security Review (monthly).
10. ——— Bureau of Labor Statistics, Nonagricultural Employment by State, 1943–50.
11. Vermont Unemployment Compensation Commission, Vermont Labor Market
    (monthly).

Statement by Committee Member

THE REPORT on "Employment Fluctuations in New England" presents several necessary planks in a positive employment program. It urges maintenance of the region's textile and shoe industries and encouragement of industrial expansion, particularly of the durable-goods industries. We approve of suggestions to encourage retraining adult workers and the scrapping of hiring prejudices against older persons. Workers should be aided in outmigration from communities in which chronic unemployment exists.

The report unfolds the difficulties of persons who have lost their jobs because of closed plants, but it does not, as it should, make this a number one responsibility of the New England community. Creating new jobs is one challenge; getting displaced persons jobs in the new industries is an equally important responsibility.

Displaced workers who find jobs in new plants usually earn less money. Many new plants are exploiting local clusters of unemployment to establish low wage schedules. Moreover, they are rejecting older applicants for employment.

The report properly urges local communities to discourage fly-by-night operators who want to locate in their confines. It calls for retraining. But it fails to outline an adequate program to meet the problems of the large numbers of displaced older persons. Employers in the region must accept the responsibility of engineering their jobs for the profitable employment of older persons, who can be trained for new jobs as successfully as younger persons if the training methods are adapted to their needs. Industry's responsibility is not discharged until it employs all persons desirous of work. The system of free enterprise has not met its challenge until it opens jobs for all.

A number of proposals such as the dovetailing of seasonal employments, training and aid to migrants require community action. Unfortunately, few public employment offices have tripartite advisory agencies on which labor and management are represented, to help in the realization of such desirable objectives. The community organizations are often dominated by business and exclusively concerned with business problems and are, therefore, unprepared to deal with the workers' needs in the community. Labor must participate in all community planning activities.

Federal preference in the award of government contracts to the New England textile industry must remain a fundamental part of all industrial programs for the region. It is not an expedient. It is an important permanent aid to mills and workers to help overcome the subsidies and preferences enjoyed by mill owners in other areas. These advantages tend to create unfair competitive conditions and should be offset by preferential contract allocation to New England.

Unfortunately, the southern industrialists have successfully used their political influence to prevent a multiple price system which would enable mills to get contracts at higher than competitive bid prices. Mills have recently sent in bids at below cost levels in order to employ idle equipment, thereby weakening the position of the legitimate producers. Government contracts must not be used to destroy wage standards. In such periods it is important for governmental authorities to award contracts at prices commensurate with the costs of production of mills needing the work to maintain their work forces. Should these mills be forced to close, their employees will be dispersed, their capacities destroyed, and many employees will be doomed to the human scrap heap. The ultimate public cost will be much higher than that represented by the differential price. Moreover, the award of contracts on such a basis will provide the public and the employees with a clear challenge to prod individual managements into more efficient operation and modernization of their businesses. Too many enterprises have been permitted to languish because neither employees nor community had knowledge of the condition of the concern until the plant had closed.

We believe that the profits of liquidation should be taxed—specifically to finance the rehabilitation of the local economy and displaced individuals.

We believe that a manufacturer must "expose himself" to major risks in the operation of a business in order to assure regular annual employment. Management has shirked its responsibility. Workers are demanding that management assume this obligation. To the extent that it fails to do so, earnings must be maintained through a guaranteed annual wage.

Several additional observations are pertinent. First, the job rotation system in the woolen and worsted industry originated from its highly seasonal character and has been extended by the huge displacement of manpower following technological changes. The durable-goods industries which are producing consumer goods are assuming many seasonal characteristics commonly found in the nondurable-goods industries. Finally, the steel strike of 1952 as well as the bituminous coal strikes have had a minimum of impact in New England or the rest of the country. It is completely foreign to the spirit of our system of industrial relations to invoke action which will limit the workers' right to strike.

VICTOR J. CANZANO

9

Wages in New England

*Drafted by William H. Miernyk under the direction
of Arthur A. Bright, Jr.*

INTRODUCTION

New England is a region of higher than average incomes, but in general
it is not a high-wage area. The average wage level is below that of the other
states in the industrial Northeast, and also below that on the Pacific coast.
On the other hand, it is above that of any of the southern regions.

Since the geographical distribution of different economic activities varies
considerably, New England is a high-wage area for some industries and a
low-wage area for others. This is why some plants in New England have
been attracted by the lower wages of other regions, while other plants
have evidently been attracted to New England by the availability of reliable
and efficient workmen at wages somewhat lower than those paid in other
industrialized regions.

At the same time, some of New England's relatively low-wage industries
do not necessarily operate in the region just because wages are low. Other
economic factors, such as nearness to markets, may have more influence upon
their competitive position than the wages they pay. In each industry, a complex of factors affects New England's competitive position, and wages are
only one element of varying importance. We have a situation in which high
wages in some New England industries may be an important competitive
disadvantage, while low wages in other industries may not be a decisive
competitive advantage.

As part of total costs, the wage bill an employer pays has a bearing upon
his competitive position and his ability to provide stable employment for his
workers. But wages are not only a cost. Wages and the other payments he
receives for his services constitute the *income* of the New England worker.
That income is translated into expenditures and income for others. While
the employer wants to hold his costs of production to a minimum, the worker
is anxious to receive as much income as he can. This does not mean that the
two objectives are in basic conflict. Higher wages mean increased purchasing
power. And high wages do not necessarily produce high labor costs. If high
wages are accompanied by a high rate of output per man-hour, wages may
be high and costs may be low. *The ideal goal for New England is a higher*

than average wage level accompanied by a higher than average rate of output per man-hour.

It is obvious that particular wages are "high" or "low" only in comparison with some other wages. To the New England employer in one industry, wages may be high compared to those paid by his competitor in another region. The same wages may be low, however, when compared to those of workers in other industries in New England.

In considering costs to the employer and returns to the worker, we cannot consider only wage rates or hourly earnings. Vacation and holiday payments, contributions to pension plans and retirement funds, premium pay for second and third shifts, and other "fringe benefits" constitute an increasingly important part of the employer's labor cost. Naturally these payments are also part of the worker's income, either present or future.

These introductory observations indicate that there is no simple "wage problem" in New England. Careful analysis is required before we can arrive at definite conclusions about the effects of New England's wage levels upon the region's economic health.

Finally, what forces influence the level of earnings in New England? What government policies affect wages in the region? It is not enough to know what wage levels are; we should also know what control the region as a whole has over its wage policies. The influence of unions upon wages and labor costs in New England is examined in another of the Committee's reports.[1] Here, however, we shall consider the effect of state and federal policies upon wage levels and incomes in New England, and the effect of those policies upon the competitive position of New England industry. *Whether or not existing federal wage policies should be modified depends upon the effects that such modifications would have on the total economy of the nation. But New England has a definite stake in guarding against sectionalist policies inspired by other regions that might injure the competitive position of the region's producers and the employment and incomes of its workers.*

SOURCES OF INCOME IN NEW ENGLAND

Per capita incomes in New England are higher than the national average. There is a marked division, however, within the region. The inhabitants of the three southern New England states have incomes well above the national average, and the Connecticut figure is one of the highest in the nation. In Maine, New Hampshire, and Vermont, on the other hand, the income per person is considerably less than the national average. Table 9–1 presents the 1951 figures for each of the New England states, as well as the regional and national averages.

1. No. 10, "Labor-Management Relations in New England."

What are the principal sources of income in New England? Table 9–2 shows the distribution of income payments by source in 1951. The inhabitants

Table 9–1. Per Capita Income Payments in New England
and the United States, 1951

AREA	PER CAPITA INCOME	PER CENT OF UNITED STATES
United States	$1,584	100.0%
New England	1,715	108.3
Maine	1,298	81.9
New Hampshire	1,444	91.2
Vermont	1,322	83.5
Massachusetts	1,738	109.7
Rhode Island	1,691	106.8
Connecticut	1,999	126.2

Source: U.S. Department of Commerce, Survey of Current Business, August 1952

of all New England states but Maine and Vermont receive a greater share of their total incomes in the form of wages and salaries than the residents of the average state in the nation. How can that be true, when New England is not a high-wage region? More of New England's workers obtain their incomes by working for others. Agriculture is relatively less important in every state in the region except Vermont than it is in the nation as a whole, and manufacturing is relatively more important. This is reflected in the lower proportion of income received in the region by proprietors, and the different shares of proprietors' income in northern and southern New England.

Table 9–2. Sources of Income in New England and the United States, 1951
(type of payment as per cent of total)

AREA	WAGES AND SALARIES	PROPRIETORS' INCOME	PROPERTY INCOME	OTHER
United States	66.9%	16.8%	10.6%	5.6%
New England	71.1	9.5	13.2	6.7
Maine	65.9	12.7	14.5	6.9
New Hampshire	68.7	12.3	12.3	6.7
Vermont	63.9	16.4	13.6	6.1
Massachusetts	72.0	8.6	12.7	6.7
Rhode Island	70.8	8.8	12.8	7.6
Connecticut	72.4	9.2	14.1	4.3

Note: Percentages may not add to 100 because of rounding.
Source: Ibid.

In addition, the proportion of the people of New England in the labor force is larger than in the South or West. In part, this is due to the age distribution of the region's population. Relatively more New Englanders are in the employable age groups. Also, as appears to be true in other highly industrialized regions, there is a higher than average proportion of families in New England with more than one wage earner.

WAGES AND HOURLY EARNINGS

Regional averages of wages and incomes are useful for making broad generalizations, but they conceal the variations within a region. Tables 9–1 and 9–2 show that there are substantial variations in both the average levels and sources of income from state to state within New England. One should also examine the extent and direction of intraregional variations in wages or hourly earnings.

Even state averages may be too inclusive, since there are substantial differences in wages among communities. In our attempts to assemble the wage picture for New England, we have analyzed the available wage information for particular occupations on a local labor-market basis. The size of a local labor market varies with its industrial composition and the ease with which its workers can commute to their jobs. A local labor market may be a city, a metropolitan area, or several cities located close to one another. There are some occupations for which wage information is available only on a statewide basis. In such cases it is not possible to measure intrastate variations, but we can still make state-to-state comparisons.

Wages in Agriculture

New England has fewer agricultural workers than any other major census region in the United States. During the postwar period, nevertheless, farms

Table 9–3. *Agricultural Wages in New England and Other Regions, October 1, 1951*

REGION	AVERAGE HOURLY WAGE RATES*	AVERAGE DAILY WAGE RATES*	AVERAGE MONTHLY WAGES†
NEW ENGLAND	$0.96	$7.40	$112.00
Middle Atlantic	.93	7.10	109.00
East North Central	.93	6.90	111.00
West North Central	.94	7.60	117.00
South Atlantic	.58	4.65	n.a.
East South Central	.52	3.95	n.a.
West South Central	.64	5.40	n.a.
Mountain	.90	7.50	144.00
Pacific	1.02	n.a.	162.00

Note: n.a. indicates data were not available.
* Without board or room.
† With board and room.
Source: U.S. Department of Agriculture, Bureau of Agricultural Economics, *Farm Labor*, October 10, 1951

in New England employed about 60,000 hired workers, on the average, in addition to approximately 170,000 family workers. While agricultural employment is a relatively small part of the region's total employment, incomes of agricultural laborers constitute a part of the region's total income which one cannot ignore.

How do farm wages in New England compare with those in the rest of the country? Average monthly, hourly, and daily wages for the nine census regions are given in Table 9–3. Hourly and daily wages do not include board and room, but monthly averages are for those workers who receive board and room in addition to their money wage. We have used wages as of October 1, 1951, for purposes of comparison. By October the peak of seasonal employment has passed, but more than the annual average number of hired workers are still employed.

Among the nine regions, New England ranks second in hourly wages, fourth in monthly wages, and probably fourth in daily wages. Only the Pacific region has a higher hourly average. Hourly wages probably provide the most significant comparisons for farm labor, since daily and monthly wages are influenced by the number of hours worked and other factors. In general, agricultural wages in New England are fairly high.

Table 9–4. *Agricultural Wages in the New England States and Other Selected States, October 1, 1951*

STATE	AVERAGE HOURLY WAGE RATES*	AVERAGE DAILY WAGE RATES*	AVERAGE MONTHLY WAGES†
New England	$0.96	$7.40	$112.00
Maine	.90	7.00	99.00
New Hampshire	.97	7.50	115.00
Vermont	.97	7.10	114.00
Massachusetts	1.01	7.80	120.00
Rhode Island	1.00	7.80	122.00
Connecticut	1.00	7.70	122.00
Other States			
New York	.99	7.60	113.00
Illinois	.94	7.20	122.00
Kansas	.99	8.20	119.00
South Carolina	.46	2.95	n.a.
Mississippi	.50	3.70	n.a.
Texas	.67	5.80	n.a.
Colorado	.89	7.60	136.00
Washington	1.11	n.a.	180.00

Note: n.a. indicates data were not available.
* Without board or room.
† With board and room.
Source: Ibid.

Table 9–4 shows the variations in average agricultural wages among the six New England states. For purposes of comparison, one state from each of the nation's other regions is also included. The differences within New England in average hourly wages are not large, except in Maine, where hourly earnings are from 7 to 11 cents below those paid by farmers in the other five states. But 21 states in the rest of the country have lower hourly rates than Maine. Only seven states in the nation have higher hourly rates than those paid in Massachusetts.

In part, the level of farm wages is influenced by the availability of alternative employment opportunities. In the populous and highly industrialized southern New England states, agricultural wages are high. They are somewhat lower in the three northern states, where there is relatively less factory employment and more farm work. *The New England farm worker is well paid compared to his counterpart in most other regions. Though he does not receive the highest agricultural wages in the nation, he is well up toward the top.*

Wages in Manufacturing Industry

Manufacturing wages are of considerably greater relative importance as a source of income in New England than are agricultural wages. New England is one of the most heavily industrialized regions in the nation. Approximately one-third of the region's income is derived directly from manufacturing activity, and manufacturing accounts for another third or more indirectly.

New England's manufacturing wages do not rank as high as its agricultural wages. A comparison of regional wage levels made in 1946 by the Bureau of Labor Statistics of the United States Department of Labor showed that New England had average wages above the national average in 14 of 27 selected manufacturing industries and below the national average in 13. For the seven metalworking industries studied, New England showed wage levels below the national average in five. Five of the six industries in the paper and allied products group had lower wages in New England than in the nation. But of five selected textile industries, four showed wages in New England above the national average. The only textile industry in New England which had lower than average wages was the full-fashioned hosiery industry, and this industry employs only a small number of workers in New England.

We can tell more about how New England's manufacturing wages compare with those in other regions by studying averages for smaller areas. It would be desirable to compare wages in all industries by local labor-market areas. The basic data are not available for making such comparisons for all industries, but it is possible to make them for some of the region's most important industries.

The Bureau of Labor Statistics has made a series of wage studies, by industry and labor-market area, for the postwar period. These studies present hourly earnings data without over-all summaries or interpretation. We have computed weighted averages of hourly earnings for all the industries studied, by local labor markets, to reduce the information provided by the bureau to summary measures. In addition, we have made estimates of the level of vacation and holiday payments wherever possible, again by local labor-market areas. While the Bureau of Labor Statistics studies do not cover all production centers for each industry, they covered most of the important ones and provide a fairly good indication of geographical variations.

The hourly earnings figures discussed in the next few pages are weighted averages and must be interpreted carefully, as is true of all averages. The averages are undoubtedly influenced to some extent by differences among areas in the sizes of plants and companies and by differences in product specialization among regions. They may also be influenced by differences in the proportions of women in the labor force in the various regions, and by different methods of wage payment. For example, incentive wages may be more common in some regions than others. At the same time, the figures have the virtues of averages. They permit us to present a summary picture of the relative wage level in each industry and area. Moreover, some of the area differences in the characteristics of plants may tend to offset one another.

Tables 9–5 and 9–6 present the highest and lowest average hourly earnings and annual vacation and holiday payments in selected manufacturing industries, by labor-market areas, for both New England and the rest of the country.[2] They show the nature of the intraregional variations, as well as those between New England and other parts of the United States. The differences in some industries are greater within the region. Moreover, the tables show that wage payments in the durable-goods industries are typically higher than those in the nondurables.

The geographical variations do not form a consistent and clear-cut pattern in many instances. *Within New England, it appears that Hartford is generally a higher wage area than the rest of the region, and Providence and northern New England are generally lower wage areas. There are some exceptions to even those characterizations, however, and such centers as Boston and Worcester are not consistently either high- or low-wage areas in relation to the rest of the region.* There are similar problems in generalizing about variations in the rest of the country, though wages in the South are typically lower than those elsewhere.

The following sections discuss in some detail the geographical wage patterns for a few of New England's major industries. In each industry our concern is with major production centers, not individual plants.

The Shoe and Leather Industries. New England is often spoken of as a high-wage region for the production of shoes. This does not seem to be an accurate characterization. *There is a wide variation in average hourly earnings among the region's numerous shoe-producing centers. Some are fairly high-wage areas, and some fairly low wage. New England as a whole does not appear to be a particularly high-wage region for shoe manufacturing.*

The situation varies somewhat among the different branches of the indus-

2. The complete results of the industry wage analysis, and a discussion of the methods of calculation, are presented in our Staff Memorandum No. 9, *Wages and Supplementary Payments in Selected New England Industries,* July 1952.

Table 9-5. Straight-time Hourly Earnings in Selected Manufacturing Industries during Recent Years, by Labor-market Areas

INDUSTRY AND YEAR	NEW ENGLAND		OUTSIDE NEW ENGLAND	
	HIGHEST AVERAGE HOURLY EARNINGS	LOWEST AVERAGE HOURLY EARNINGS	HIGHEST AVERAGE HOURLY EARNINGS	LOWEST AVERAGE HOURLY EARNINGS
Nondurable goods				
Leather (1947)	Boston $1.31	Lowell $1.17	Gloversville, N. Y. $1.41	All South $0.83
Men's shoes (1950)	Brockton 1.43	Worcester 1.37	Wisconsin 1.46	Wisconsin 1.46
Women's shoes (1950)	Boston 1.52	New Hampshire 1.32	New York City 2.01	Missouri 1.25
Cotton textiles (1950)	Northern N.E. 1.19	Fall River 1.18	Greenville, S. C. 1.10	Statesville, N. C. 1.05
Synthetic textiles (1950)	Southern N.E. 1.23	Northern N.E. 1.19	Allentown, Pa. 1.23	Charlotte, N. C. 1.09
Woolen and worsteds (1950)	Lawrence 1.40	Northern N.E. 1.30	All South 1.14	Charlotte, N. C. 1.14
Dyeing and finishing (1946)	New Bedford .94	Connecticut .88	New York City 1.08	All South .74
Knit outerwear (1946)	Lowell .86	Boston .85	New York City 1.18	Charlotte, N. C. .85
Knit underwear (1946)	Boston .83	Boston .83	Philadelphia .92	Chicago .74
Paint and varnish (1951)	Boston 1.39	Boston 1.39	San Francisco 1.70	Louisville 1.31
Durable goods				
Machinery (1951)	Worcester 1.65	Providence 1.48	Seattle 1.97	Dallas 1.41
Machine tools (1949)	Hartford 1.49	Providence 1.41	Detroit 1.87	Chicago 1.54
Ferrous foundries (1951)	Hartford 1.81	Boston 1.66	Milwaukee 2.00	Birmingham 1.26
Nonferrous foundries (1951)	Hartford 1.49	Springfield 1.46	San Francisco 1.85	Philadelphia 1.42

Note: Dates in parentheses indicate year to which wage averages applied. Where the same location is shown as both highest and lowest, data were not available for other areas.

Source: Staff Memorandum No. 9

Table 9-6. Average Annual Vacation and Holiday Payments in Selected Manufacturing Industries during Recent Years, by Labor-market Areas

INDUSTRY AND YEAR	NEW ENGLAND				OUTSIDE NEW ENGLAND			
	HIGHEST PAYMENT		LOWEST PAYMENT		HIGHEST PAYMENT		LOWEST PAYMENT	
Nondurable goods								
Men's shoes (1950)	Brockton	$125	Worcester	$103	Illinois	$172	Illinois	$172
Women's shoes (1950)	Boston	121	Worcester	102	New York	256	Missouri	150
Cotton textiles (1950)	Northern N.E.	105	Rhode Island	100	N.W. Georgia	98	Charlotte	47
Synthetic textiles (1950)	Southern N.E.	114	Northern N.E.	107	Allentown	125	Greenville, S. C.	73
Woolen and worsteds (1950)	Rhode Island	157	Northern N.E.	122	All South	111	All South	111
Paint and varnish (1951)	Boston	180	Boston	180	San Francisco	227	Baltimore	121
Durable goods								
Machinery (1951)	Bridgeport	245	Providence	198	New York City	241	Atlanta	114
Machine tools (1951)	Hartford	216	Hartford	216	Cleveland	253	Detroit	213
Ferrous foundries (1951)	Hartford	236	Boston	226	San Francisco	230	Birmingham	69
Nonferrous foundries (1951)	Springfield	221	Boston	159	San Francisco	252	Philadelphia	164

Note: Dates in parentheses indicate year for which vacation and holiday payments have been calculated. Where the same location is shown as highest and lowest only one average could be calculated.
Source: Ibid.

try. The most recent information available, for 1950, shows that average hourly earnings at Brockton, Massachusetts, were slightly below those in the state of Illinois. Both of these areas are major producers of men's shoes. In addition, average annual vacation and holiday payments in Illinois were $47 above similar payments in Brockton, a difference of 37%. Average hourly earnings in men's-shoe factories in the Worcester area were below those for Brockton, as was true of vacation and holiday payments. The higher price and quality of Brockton shoes probably accounted for a large part of the excess of the Brockton earnings figure over that for Worcester. Though the number of observations is small, hourly earnings in the major men's-shoe centers in Massachusetts were slightly below those in other men's-shoe centers outside New England where approximately the same grade of shoe is made.

Information is available for a larger number of production centers for women's shoes, and there is greater dispersion both within and among regions. In New England, Boston had the highest level of hourly earnings and vacation and holiday payments in 1950. The New England range in hourly earnings was from $1.32 in southeastern New Hampshire to $1.52 in Boston. Vacation and holiday payments varied from $102 annually at Worcester to $121 at Boston. In New York, however, hourly earnings averaged $2.01, and average vacation and holiday payments amounted to $256.50 a year. Hourly earnings in St. Louis were lower than those at Boston or Haverhill, but they were above the level in all other New England women's-shoe centers. The four labor-market areas studied outside New England showed higher annual vacation and holiday payments than were found in any of the six areas studied within the region.

Comparative data on hourly earnings in the leather industry are available for a single year only. In 1947, the typical leather worker in the Boston area received $1.31 an hour, compared to $1.17 in Lowell, Massachusetts. Average earnings at Gloversville, New York, came to $1.41 an hour. Of the 14 labor-market areas studied in five regions, Boston ranked second and Lowell was in sixth place. The necessary data for making estimates of the cost of vacation and holiday payments in the leather industry are not available.

In the shoe industry, in particular, some of the differences in earnings from one area to another are due to differences in product specialization. This may also be true of the leather industry. Earnings in the women's-shoe industry in New England are usually lower than those in the men's-shoe branch. Where high-grade shoes are produced, the level of wages is generally above that in areas which specialize in the production of cheaper shoes. Such differences are not revealed by a regional average.

Until the mid-twenties the New England shoe industry was losing ground relative to other regions. Since then, however, it has about held its own. Shoe factories have continued to move out of high-wage areas to lower wage areas, but most of them have remained in New England. Maine and New Hampshire have gained at the expense of Massachusetts. Since wages in other regions have increased more rapidly than those in northern New England, shoe manufacturers in recent decades have not been induced to move out of the region, although their movements within the region show that the attraction of low-cost labor is still strong for some of them. The behavior of the shoe industries in recent decades confirms our conclusions about the level of wages in New England's shoe factories.

The Textile Industries. New England has also been characterized as a high-wage area for the textile industries. This *is* an accurate characterization. In 1950 there was an average differential of 13 cents an hour between cotton mills in northern New England and mills in Charlotte, North Carolina, which is an important competing production center.[3] The average differential between the Fall River–New Bedford area in New England and three other important cotton-manufacturing areas outside the region was 8 cents an hour. Vacation and holiday payments were consistently higher in New England than in the South, although these payments also varied among different locations.

Comparing annual vacation and holiday payments in northern New England to Charlotte, for example, we find an absolute difference of $57 and a relative difference of more than 100%. Between Connecticut and northwest Georgia, the difference in average vacation and holiday payments was only $2.65 a year, less than 2%. New England's cotton manufacturers are not equally handicapped by "interregional differentials," but while the size of the differential varies with the areas selected for comparison, it is consistently in favor of the South.

More recent information on a *regional* basis for the cotton-textile industry is contained in a Bureau of Labor Statistics release dated May 28, 1952. In March 1952 New England mills producing carded yarn or fabric paid average wages of $1.36 an hour, while those producing combed yarn or fabric averaged $1.39 an hour. In the Southeast the averages were $1.17 and $1.16, respectively. The differentials of 19 and 23 cents an hour were substantially wider than they had been in 1950. Between New England and the Southwest, the differential in March 1952 was even greater. Mills producing carded yarn or fabric in the Southwest averaged $1.03 an hour, compared to New England's average of $1.36. Arbitrated wage cuts of 6 to 8.5 cents an hour in many New England cotton mills during the summer of 1952 reduced the spread somewhat, but even after the reductions there was still a substantial interregional difference. *Wages in the New England cotton-textile industry are clearly higher than those in the South. The relatively small variation within New England is explained by the fact that most of the mills in this region are under union contract, and this has led to considerable uniformity*

3. Some union spokesmen distinguish between a "difference" in wages, based on plant averages of hourly earnings, and a "differential" which contrasts the general level of wages among plants or areas. What we have called a *differential* they would call a *difference*. This is a matter of terminology, however, and we believe the term as we use it will be readily understood.

*of wage rates in New England. In the South only a small fraction of the mills
are organized. The unorganized southern mills are able to set their rates according
to the prevailing local levels.*

In mills producing rayon, nylon, and other synthetic fabrics, average
hourly earnings in 1950 varied from a low of $1.09 at Charlotte, North
Carolina, to a high of $1.23 an hour in southern New England and in the
Allentown-Bethlehem area of Pennsylvania. The average wage in northern
New England was $1.19, 4 cents an hour below that in the three southern
New England states. In other areas in the South, however, earnings averaged
$1.16 or $1.17 an hour. The differential in hourly earnings between western
Virginia and northern New England was only 2 to 3 cents. Annual vacation
and holiday payments averaged $107 in northern New England and $114 in
southern New England. In the South, vacation and holiday payments ranged
from $73 at Greenville, South Carolina, to $103 in western Virginia. In the
Allentown-Bethlehem area, vacation and holiday payments averaged $125
annually, higher than similar payments in New England.

As was true in cotton textiles, there was a widening of the differential in
synthetic fabrics after 1950. Regional averages for March 1952 showed that in
New England average hourly earnings had advanced to $1.39, while in the
Southeast hourly earnings were $1.20. Wage cuts during the summer of
1952 narrowed the spread somewhat, but it was still larger than it had been
in 1950. In neither 1950 nor 1952 was the differential in hourly earnings between
New England and competing southern areas producing synthetic
fabrics as great as that in the cotton-textile industry. There was undoubtedly
considerable dispersion around the regional averages in 1952, as there had
been two years earlier.

*The woolen and worsted industry showed a larger absolute differential in
average hourly earnings between New England and the South than any of
the other textile industries.* Only one southern average is available for 1950,
when southern woolen and worsted mills were paying $1.14 an hour. In
northern New England, average hourly earnings were $1.30, the low for the
region. At Lawrence, Massachusetts, average earnings were $1.40. The differential
between New England and the South ranged from 16 to 26 cents an
hour in 1950. Annual vacation and holiday payments averaged $111 in the
South and ranged from a low of $122 in northern New England to a high
of $157 in Rhode Island. Wage movements since 1950 suggest that the differential
in hourly earnings, and probably also in vacation and holiday payments,
had been widened by 1952.

*New England is clearly a high-wage area for the textile industries, despite
the fact that the earnings of most New England textile workers are lower
than those of many workers in other manufacturing industries in the region.
The geographical differences have been reflected in a gradual migration of
many textile mills from New England to the South; first in the cotton-goods
industry and more recently in the woolen and worsted industry.*

Machinery and Machine Tools. In the production of a wide variety of machinery, the average hourly earnings in New England ranged from a low of $1.48 at Providence to a high of $1.65 at Worcester during December 1951. Annual vacation and holiday payments were $198 at Providence and ranged up to $245 at Bridgeport, Connecticut, in January 1951. Bridgeport had the highest vacation and holiday payments of the 21 labor-market areas in all regions for which we have such information. On the other hand, Worcester ranked only seventh among the 11 areas for which hourly earnings are available, and Worcester paid the top wage in New England. Approximately the same situation existed for the machine tool industry. Hourly earnings were generally lower in New England than in most other areas, but vacation and holiday payments were fairly high. *On balance, it appears that in the combined machinery and machine-tool industries New England is a relatively low-wage area in comparison with other regions. But workers in those industries in New England obtain somewhat more liberal vacation and holiday payments. They also receive somewhat higher average wages than those in the nondurable goods industries.*

Foundries. During the postwar period hourly earnings in New England's ferrous foundries have been below those in most areas outside the region. In 1951 average earnings at Boston were $1.66 an hour, lower than the average in any major area outside the South. Hartford foundries paid an average of $1.81, however, and ranked seventh among the 25 areas for which comparable information is available.

In the nonferrous foundries, only the Philadelphia-Camden area showed average hourly earnings lower than those in New England. Hourly earnings in the Springfield-Holyoke area of Massachusetts ranked in ninth place among the 11 areas studied, although vacation and holiday payments ranked second. Again it appears to be true that while hourly earnings are relatively low in New England's nonferrous foundries, the region's workers receive somewhat more liberal vacation and holiday payments than workers in most other regions.

The Over-all Pattern of Manufacturing Wages in New England.

As a broad generalization, it is true that many of New England's non-textile industries pay somewhat lower wages than the same industries in other highly industrialized regions. On balance, New England's industrial wages seem to be fairly close to the national average. There are important variations, however, both within and among regions in the levels of both hourly earnings and vacation and holiday payments. Except for textiles, there is no clear-cut interregional wage differential. There are some locations in New England which pay lower than average wages, and there are others where the level of wages in the labor-market area is above the average for the industry.

These conclusions are in agreement with many other statements that have been made about wage levels in New England. They also jibe with the evaluations of manufacturers in the region. Roughly half of the 663 companies which participated in a study conducted by the Federal Reserve Bank of Boston in 1949 stated that the wages they paid had little effect on their competitive positions in relation to producers outside the region. The other half were almost evenly divided between those who claimed important competitive advantages and those who claimed important competitive disadvantages.

In this report, however, we have presented somewhat more than the usual wage details about a few of the region's important industries to emphasize the extent of the internal variation. In one important case, we believe that the usual public statements require important modification. New England as a whole is not a high-wage region for the shoe industries. Within New England, there are both high-wage and low-wage areas. Manufacturers who have decided to relocate their shoe factories because they felt that their wage scales were too high have not had to leave New England to find lower cost labor.

It is not a new discovery that New England is a high-wage area for the textile industries. Again, we wish to stress the direction and extent of variations *within* New England. It is typical to discuss interregional wage differentials in the textile industry. But the fact that *intra*regional differentials exist, as well, indicates that not all textile manufacturers in New England operate under the competitive handicap that is suggested by region-wide averages. On the other hand, regional averages understate the actual wage differentials with which some textile manufacturers are faced.

Finally, there is a tendency for vacation and holiday payments in New England to rank somewhat higher than hourly earnings, in comparison with other regions. For fringe-benefit payments, too, there is variation from area to area within regions, so that in many cases it is difficult to make a single, summary statement about hourly earnings and fringe-benefit payments combined. If we knew the average number of hours worked a year in each industry and in each local labor-market area, it would be possible to translate the annual vacation and holiday payments into hourly earnings. In the absence of such knowledge it would be misleading to combine the two figures, even though failure to do so makes it more difficult to generalize.

Earnings in Nonproduction Occupations

The Bureau of Labor Statistics has recently completed a survey of hourly earnings in a number of nonproduction occupations in 28 major cities located in all regions of the United States. This survey cuts across industry lines. It affords a ready comparison of the position of three New England cities in relation to the other 25 cities studied. The necessary data to make comparisons of vacation and holiday payments were not included in the study.

Maintenance and Power Plant Jobs. Table 9–7 shows average hourly earnings in three key New England cities for selected maintenance and power plant jobs in all types of establishments. In addition to the earnings figures,

Table 9-7. *Average Straight-time Hourly Earnings in Maintenance and Power Plant Jobs, 1951–52**
(for 3 New England and 25 other major cities)

OCCUPATION	HOURLY EARNINGS AND RANK†						HIGH-EARNINGS CITY		LOW-EARNINGS CITY	
	HARTFORD		PROVIDENCE		WORCESTER		CITY	AMOUNT	CITY	AMOUNT
Carpenters, maintenance	$1.77	21	$1.66	23	$1.68	22	San Francisco	$2.18	New Orleans	$1.53
Electricians, maintenance	1.82	24	1.69	26	1.79	25	Detroit	2.16	Okla. City	1.61
Engineers, stationary	1.76	18	1.79	16	1.73	21	Newark	2.17	Okla. City	1.59
Firemen, stationary boiler	1.43	21	1.42	23	1.48	20	Detroit	1.84	Memphis	1.11
Helpers, trades, maintenance	1.42	21	1.38	23	1.49	20	Houston	1.71	Memphis	1.08
Machinists, maintenance	1.79	24	1.65	27	1.83	23	Detroit	2.18	Scranton	1.60
Mechanics, maintenance	1.79	19	1.66	26	1.76	24	Detroit	2.15	New Orleans	1.55
Oilers	1.39	22	1.36	24	1.49	18	Detroit	1.79	Scranton	1.21
Painters, maintenance	1.62	22	1.48	26	1.55	25	San Francisco	2.08	New Orleans	1.39
Tool-and-die makers‡	1.96	19	1.79	27	1.82	24	San Francisco	2.37	Okla. City	1.74

* Male workers only.

† Rank among 28 cities throughout the country.

‡ Does not include tool-and-die makers in job shops.

Source: U.S. Department of Labor, Bureau of Labor Statistics, "Average Earnings for Selected Occupations Studied on a Cross-industry Basis, 28 Selected Areas, September 1951–March 1952," special release, May 29, 1952.

the table presents the rank of each city among the 28 studied throughout the nation. The selection of cities in New England is excellent since, in general, Hartford is one of the region's highest wage cities, Providence is a relatively low-wage city, and Worcester is fairly representative of those that fall in between. We have also included the high- and low-wage cities for the nation, in order to give the reader some idea of the range of average hourly earnings and the place which New England cities occupy within that range. The survey covered the period from September 1951 to March 1952.

The highest rank of any of the three New England cities in maintenance and power plant jobs was the 16th-place ranking of stationary engineers in Providence. At the same time, the average earnings of tool-and-die makers in Providence were in 27th place, just above Oklahoma City. The wages of maintenance electricians, machinists, mechanics, and painters in Providence also ranked near the bottom of the 28 cities, and none of the other occupations ranked higher than 23rd place. Hartford ranked above Providence in all but one occupation, but its highest rank was 18th place for stationary engineers. The earnings of oilers in Worcester ranked in 18th place. All other wages ranked below this level.

Table 9–7 makes it clear that in the skilled, nonproduction crafts New England is a relatively low-wage area. In most cases either San Francisco or Detroit paid the top wage, while with few exceptions the low-wage cities are located in the South.

Office, Professional, and Technical Jobs. Table 9–8 presents a similar comparison of the weekly earnings of office, professional, and technical workers in the same 28 cities. *Unlike New England's average wages in maintenance and power plant jobs, which consistently clustered near the bottom, there was more dispersion for some types of office workers. On the average, nevertheless, New England is a low-wage area for the white collar occupations.*

Class B typists and secretaries at Hartford had average weekly earnings that were exceeded in only four cities throughout the country. Except for key-punch operators, Hartford ranked in 18th place or higher in all the occupations studied. Again Providence showed a strong tendency toward the bottom end of the wage rankings. In only one occupation, class A file clerks, did Providence rank above 20th place. For three of the selected occupations, Providence ranked just above the lowest wage city among the 28 studied. There was more dispersion in Worcester's rankings, but not so much as for Hartford. Except for class A filing clerks, office, professional, and technical personnel in Worcester were not well paid relative to their counterparts in other sections of the country. Detroit and San Francisco again lead in weekly wages for these selected classes of workers, and with few exceptions a southern city is at the bottom of the scale.

Table 9–8. Average Straight-time Weekly Earnings in Office, Professional, and Technical Jobs, 1951–52*
(for 3 New England and 25 other major cities)

OCCUPATION	WEEKLY EARNINGS AND RANK†			HIGH-EARNINGS CITY		LOW-EARNINGS CITY	
	HARTFORD	PROVIDENCE	WORCESTER	CITY	AMOUNT	CITY	AMOUNT
Bookkeepers, hand	$56.50 15	$53.00 24	$56.00 17	Detroit	$69.50	New Orleans	$51.50
Comptometer operators	47.00 11	42.00 27	43.00 25	Detroit	56.50	Okla. City	43.00
Draftsmen (men)	77.50 18	72.00 24	73.50 23	Detroit	98.50	Memphis	65.50
Draftsmen, junior (men)	60.50 18	58.00 22	58.50 20	Detroit	72.50	Richmond	48.00
File clerks, class A	45.00 16	44.50 17	50.00 6	San Francisco	53.00	Okla. City	38.00
File clerks, class B	37.00 14	34.00 24	36.00 20	San Francisco	43.00	Okla. City	33.00
Key-punch operators	42.00 23	40.00 24	43.00 20	Detroit	53.50	Richmond	40.00
Nurses (registered)	61.00 9	55.50 23	57.00 22	Norfolk	70.50	New Orleans	52.50
Office girls	36.00 16	34.50 20	37.00 14	San Francisco	45.00	New Orleans	30.50
Secretaries	62.00 5	52.00 27	55.50 19	New York	65.00	Scranton	47.50
Stenographers, general	48.00 15	43.00 27	45.00 25	Detroit	57.50	Scranton	41.00
Switchboard operators	45.50 14	41.00 21	42.00 20	San Francisco	52.50	Memphis	36.00
Typists, class A	50.00 7	43.50 22	48.00 12	Detroit	55.00	Salt Lake	39.50
Typists, class B	42.50 5	37.00 24	39.00 18	San Francisco	47.00	New Orleans	35.00

* Women workers unless otherwise specified.
† Rank among 28 cities throughout the country.
Source: Ibid.

Evaluation of New England's Wage Position

New England's agricultural workers are fairly well paid compared to those in other regions. But agriculture in New England is a smaller part of total economic activity than in the rest of the country, and manufacturing is of more than average relative importance. In those manufacturing industries for which information is available, New England is not a high-wage region, except for textiles, where there is a differential in hourly earnings and partial fringe-benefit payments that consistently favors southern manufacturers. In a broad range of office, professional, and technical occupations, New England appears to be a genuinely low-wage area.

What is the significance of the over-all wage picture in New England? The relatively high wages in the region's textile industries have been a primary reason for the migration of many mills to low-wage areas. Do low wages in other industries and occupations attract new enterprises to New England? *Certain types of manufacturing plants have been coming to New England because they can obtain the kinds of workers they want at relatively lower wages than they would have to pay in other highly industrialized regions.* In fact, it is a little surprising that there have not been more of them, in view of the tight labor supply in some areas and the availability of workers in New England. Not all low-wage industries in New England, nevertheless, can be expected to grow simply because of their low wages.

If a manufacturer is interested in low wages alone, he will prefer to locate in the South. Compared to the South, New England is still a high-wage area for nearly all industries. Where a manufacturer is looking for something more than the lowest wage labor, as he often is, and where there are no unsatisfied special requirements which might keep him from coming to New England, the fact that wages are *relatively lower* in New England than in other comparable industrial regions can be an important attraction. What are some possible examples?

The electronics and electrical-equipment industries have been growing rapidly in New England. In November 1951 hourly earnings in the radio, television, and related products industry in New England averaged $1.16 an hour, compared to a national average of $1.36.[4] This substantial differential helps explain why the electronics industry has been growing more rapidly in New England than elsewhere. Certain types of precision-casting plants, some producers of plastics, manufacturers of small machine parts, precision tools or instruments, and various other types of manufacturing enterprise which make light, high-valued products have been expanding in New England in recent years partly because of the availability of the kind of work-

4. U.S. Department of Labor, Bureau of Labor Statistics, *Wage Structure Radio, Television, and Related Products,* Series 2, No. 84 (November 1951), p. 4.

ers such plants require at lower wages than are paid in neighboring industrial regions.[5]

There is evidence that certain types of garment-manufacturing plants have been migrating to New England, attracted by the availability of an adequate supply of labor at relatively low wages. In this industry one should compare New England's wages primarily with those in the New York City area rather than in the South. There is an advantage in being located fairly close to the New York market, but at the same time the wage scale in New England is lower than that in the other old, established garment centers.

Too much should not be expected from the garment industry, however, when one is considering the sound future growth of New England manufacturing. Where garment manufacturers have located to take advantage of a supply of displaced textile workers, for example, there has been a substitution of one relatively low-wage industry for another. Some garment manufacturing firms are less stable than the textile mills they have replaced. The stable garment manufacturer who intends to sink his roots into a new community and to operate on a long-term basis should be encouraged and assisted as much as the manufacturer in any other field. But the "fly-by-night," who is taking advantage of a temporary boom in the garment business, may be no great asset to a community. We do not suggest that artificial barriers be erected against entrance of such manufacturers into any community. The region's "depressed" communities do better, however, when they concentrate upon attracting more stable industries with higher wage levels and greater promise of continued operations. Local stability of employment at relatively high wages is the best deterrent to the "overnight" operator who promises little to the long-run development of a community.

Some types of manufacturing plants serve local areas, and they cannot be expected to locate in New England simply because of a favorable wage structure. For such establishments as ferrous foundries, for example, the size and future prospects of the local market are the major considerations. Low wages are not a particular geographical advantage in such cases, because other economic factors outweigh their importance. There are many other types of economic activity which are noncompetitive from region to region, and for them interregional wage comparisons mean little.

Any attempt to assess the influence of relatively low wages in many New England industries and occupations upon the future economic growth of the region must proceed on an industry-by-industry basis. Low wages in some New England industries will not attract new plants to the region, nor will high wages in some others cause them to migrate elsewhere. In each case the importance of labor costs as a percentage of the total cost of production must

5. For further details see the discussion of *Inter-industry Mobility of Workers and the Transfer of Worker Skills in New England* in our Staff Memorandum No. 5, June 1952, Pt. 2. See also New England Council, *New England News Letter*, May 1952 and June 1952.

be considered, as well as the market area to be served by the industry and comparative data for other cost elements.

Quite apart from the effects of New England's wage structure on future industrial development, wage rates can have an important bearing on the costs and competitive strength of existing manufacturers in the region. *Clearly, where a New England manufacturer pays lower wages than his competitors elsewhere, he has a potential operating advantage that can help offset any costs that are higher in New England. Since in some industries labor costs are about one-third of total manufacturing cost, they far overshadow such cost elements as power, state and local taxation, and even transportation.* As we have noted, New England manufacturers as a whole consider that they are in an essentially neutral competitive position with regard to the wage rates that they pay. The ones who point to a competitive disadvantage are concentrated, for the most part, in the textile industries. In most other industries, therefore, New England's present industrial-wage structure offers a positive competitive advantage or at least no handicap. This situation is an important element in the success of many employers in the region.

On the other hand, one should always remember that low wages are an obstacle to a region's economic progress to the extent that they mean lower income levels and purchasing power. *An increasing standard of living for New England's people is the principal economic goal of the region and the major criterion by which its progress should be measured.* While New England's per capita income is still 8% above the national average, that excess is not as great as it was 20 years ago.

PRODUCTIVITY AND LABOR COST

It is apparent that relatively high wages are not a competitive disadvantage to a manufacturer if they are offset by relatively high labor productivity. Nor are relatively low wages a competitive advantage to a manufacturer if they are accompanied by a low level of productivity. Labor cost per unit of output is the important thing, and labor cost depends on how efficiently workers' time is used, as well as on wage rates.

The direct measurement of labor productivity is a difficult, if not an impossible, task. To compare the personal labor productivity of two workers in two different plants—much less two regions—all other conditions would have to be exactly the same, a condition which is never achieved. It is possible, however, to measure changes in *output per man-hour* and to make comparisons among different regions for a few selected industries. Information is available for only a few industries to compare absolute man-hour requirements. For others, it is only possible to compare changes from some common base year.

Though productivity is measured in terms of the number of man-hours required to produce a unit of output, it is not labor productivity alone which leads to changes in man-hour requirements. Labor productivity may remain constant, but improved machinery may produce a sharp drop in man-hour requirements. Interference with the regularity of production due to seasonal changes in demand may cause man-hour requirements per unit of output to rise. Changes in design or quality often change man-hour requirements without any change in basic labor productivity, and there are many other possible causes for the same effect. In brief, man-hour requirements are the resultant of a complex of causes, many of which lie in the province of management. They are a general measuring rod, and one should not attempt to relate all changes in productivity to changes in worker effort or skill.

Despite these limitations, indexes of output per man-hour are useful indicators of *over-all* changes in the efficiency with which the workers' time is used in an industry.[6] They help to indicate the relationship between wage payments and labor cost. We shall present the highlights of available evidence for a few important industries in New England and then offer some general conclusions about productivity in the region.

Shoes and Leather

New England manufactures both men's and women's shoes in large quantities. In each branch of the industry, man-hour requirements per unit of output fell sharply during World War II and increased again afterward. During the war, there was a more stable demand for shoes, a reduction in style changes, and a shortage of labor. These factors temporarily eliminated seasonal fluctuations, and the more regular production that followed led to a substantial drop in man-hour requirements.

Man-hour requirements dropped more sharply in New England than in other regions, since the New England producers had previously been more subject to seasonal fluctuations. In general, New England's shoe factories produce less for stock and more "to order" than competitors in most other parts of the United States. The availability of a pool of skilled shoe workers in this region was also a definite factor contributing to the region's favorable productivity record during the war years.

On the other hand, after the sustained demand for shoes fell off following the end of the war, the New England shoe industry returned to the prewar pattern of seasonal production and, in women's shoes, more frequent style changes. As a result, man-hour requirements tended to rise more rapidly than in other shoe-manufacturing regions. For the entire period from 1939 to 1950, however, the record for New England's producers of men's shoes was better than that for men's-shoe producers in the nation as a whole and in the major competing area of the Middle West. The record for women's

6. For a more complete discussion of the problem and for additional details about man-hour requirements in certain industries, see our Staff Memorandum No. 13, *Output per Man-hour in Selected New England Industries,* June 1953.

shoes in New England was better than the national average, though it was not quite as good as for some competing areas.

Some shoe manufacturers in New England have stated that one of their greatest assets is the availability of a supply of skilled shoe workers. Since craftsmanship counts for more in this industry than in many other manufacturing industries, this is an important advantage, especially when the demand for shoes expands suddenly. In general, New England's shoe manufacturers seem to feel that their workers are at least as efficient as those in other regions, and some believe that they are more productive. They would probably all agree, however, that external conditions such as the regularization of production during the war have the greatest influence on relative changes in man-hour requirements in the New England shoe industry.

In the leather industry, New England has had a favorable productivity record since 1939, the base year from which changes are measured by the Bureau of Labor Statistics. The trend in man-hour requirements per unit of output has been downward, and the New England record is better than that of all other regions except the Middle Atlantic states. A number of factors were responsible for this relatively favorable showing. Plant modernization, a low level of labor turnover, less absenteeism than is found in some other regions, a more complete utilization of plant capacity, and probably some additional factors all combined to lower man-hour requirements in New England's leather industry. The stability of the labor force in the region was probably one of the more important factors. Unlike the record for the shoe industry, man-hour requirements in the production of leather in New England have been fairly stable since 1943, indicating that the conditions which led to higher productivity were more permanent than those which affected the shoe industry.

Electrical Equipment

The problems of making interregional comparisons of output per man-hour are compounded when we turn from those industries which manufacture a few similar products to the more complex industries, such as the electrical-equipment industry. The Bureau of Labor Statistics has made an effort, however, to achieve comparability by including only plants of about the same size in its regional studies and by limiting comparisons to key products.

New England's record of output per man-hour in this industry group is an excellent one. Man-hour requirements in the region were fairly stable between 1939 and 1945. They rose sharply in other regions, however, until 1944 or 1945. Since 1945 there has been a decline in man-hour requirements in all regions.

The favorable wartime record in New England, compared to other regions, was apparently also due in part to the greater stability of the region's labor force. There was less turnover and less absenteeism. The low turnover meant that fewer workers had to be trained, and it always takes some time for a new worker to reach his peak level of efficiency. The postwar decline in man-hour requirements, in which the New England industry shared, resulted largely from technological improvements. Better plant layout, newer equipment, fewer raw-material shortages, and continued good labor performance led to greater over-all efficiency in New England's electrical-equipment factories.

General Industrial Equipment

This "industry" is another complex one which produces a wide variety of products. Again, however, care has been taken to select comparable plants in different regions for study. New England's record of declining man-hour requirements in the production of industrial equipment during the past decade is more favorable than that of any other region. In part, this has resulted from specialization in the production of those types of equipment which have benefited most from technological improvements since the end of World War II. Favorable size of plant, more efficient machinery, and improved plant layout were all factors in the region's excellent showing. There is also presumptive evidence that the region's workers are doing at least as good a job as those in other regions.

Textiles

We should add some final remarks about productivity in the region's textile industries, which presents some special problems. No interregional productivity studies have yet been made for the textile industries. The types of products made by textile mills lend themselves fairly readily to the measurement of output per man-hour. It would be desirable to have such studies, in order to throw some objective light upon the perennial controversy over textile machine assignments. Some persons claim that smaller machine assignments in New England mills lead to lower rates of output per man-hour and to higher costs per unit of output; some state that the differences are more apparent than real because of differences in types of products, machinery, and other conditions; and others reply that, though machine assignments may be smaller in New England mills, the quality of output in the region is higher and the proportion of "seconds" is smaller.

This issue deals with the number of machines an individual operator tends. *Although a few New England textile manufacturers have expressed satisfaction with their present job assignments, many others feel that their workers could handle more machines without a corresponding increase in effort, particularly when new and more productive machines are installed to replace outmoded equipment.* The reluctance of textile workers to accept larger machine assignments stems largely from their fear of unemployment. Since chronic unemployment of former textile workers is common in many New

England communities, this fear is understandable. Equally understandable, however, is the desire of management to increase output per man-hour.

Obviously the machine assignment problem in New England textile mills would be aided substantially by a reduction in the extent of persistent unemployment in communities where the mills are located. If textile workers could feel that those who are displaced by the introduction of new machinery will be able to obtain other jobs with a minimum of difficulty, they will be less reluctant to accept larger assignments. More objective information on output per man-hour and comparative job assignments on comparable machines, fabrics, qualities, and other conditions is also necessary for the textile industries. Better information of these sorts would not put an end to the controversy but it could help narrow the area of disagreement and provide a stronger base from which unions and management could realistically negotiate changes in machine assignments in the future.

There is no simple formula that can provide a satisfactory job assignment in every given situation. The problem of machine assignments can be solved only within each mill, but there should be adequate recognition of the competitive importance of interregional comparability, as well as of the unique aspects of each particular situation. The continued existence of New England's textile industry is as important to the workers and their unions as it is to the millowners. The workers would be the greatest ultimate losers if real machine assignment handicaps provided the final impetus for a mill to liquidate or migrate. *Any final solution must come from negotiations between mill managements and the representatives of their workers. A broad and understanding approach by each side is vital for its successful resolution.*[7]

Conclusions on Productivity and Labor Cost

There is relatively little information upon which to base definite conclusions about labor productivity in New England as compared with other regions. *Wherever interregional comparisons have been made, New England has a favorable record of improvements in output per man-hour. How much of this can be attributed to New England workers remains an open question. In no case has it been possible to isolate quantitatively the contribution of labor to the increased productivity of specific industries. But there is a strong presumption that New England workers are at least as efficient as those in other regions, and there are undoubtedly many cases where they are more efficient.*

The survey made in 1949 by the Federal Reserve Bank of Boston, to which we previously referred, gives some indication of how New England management feels about its workers. Only 25% of the 663 participants reported that they felt their wage rates were an important competitive advantage to them,

7. Various aspects of the work-load problem are discussed in more detail in our Staff Memorandum No. 10, *The Textile Industries of New England,* August 1952.

but 57% stated that the *character* of their labor force was an important competitive advantage. This suggests strongly that New England manufacturers are even more satisfied with the attitudes of their workers and their ability to produce than they are with wage scales, which we have seen are not relatively high except for textiles. Many commentators on New England have stressed the higher than average character of the region's labor force and the constructive attitudes of the region's workers toward their jobs. This is an important asset for the region and its employers.

To what extent is high labor efficiency the result of "harder work" (in the sense of expending more energy per unit of output), of a more reliable labor force with a low turnover rate, or of greater inherent ability of the workers? Within the borders of the United States it is doubtful that there are significant variations in the workers' inherent ability. Under comparable conditions of education and training, workers in one state seem to be about as capable as those in another. In the productivity studies made by the Bureau of Labor Statistics, however, there is a recurrent suggestion that *a low rate of job turnover has a favorable influence on output per man-hour. The rate at which New England workers transfer from one job to another seems to be low compared to other regions.*[8] *Thus, a labor force which can be relied upon to stay on the job is undoubtedly an important factor in New England's favorable productivity record in recent years.*

We recognize that it takes both good management and reliable, efficient workmen to achieve savings in man-hour requirements, but management must be counted on most for further reductions in the number of man-hours required to make a unit of product. Such reductions require continuous technical alertness. It is necessary for management to keep abreast or ahead of technological developments in other areas, to make steady improvements in plant layout and process flows, and to search unremittingly for better raw materials, production processes, and products.

There are only a few ways to reduce labor costs. One is to cut wages, but the most that can be expected from this method is temporary relief. Another more permanent way is to reduce the "labor content" of the production process by substituting newer and better tools and machines for hand processes. This means a permanent reduction in the amount of labor time required to make a unit of output. The return to the worker need not fall, and can rise, while costs of production decline. The latter method is, of course, the ideal situation. Higher worker incomes mean higher community incomes. Lower man-hour requirements mean lower labor costs. *A proper blending of rising wages and falling man-hour requirements will strengthen the competitive position of New England's manufacturers, while at the same time the income position of the region will be improved.*

There is no simple way to achieve the ideal situation. There are always stresses and strains and transitional problems. The twin goals should be

8. See our Staff Memorandum No. 13.

higher incomes and lower costs. The two are not incompatible, but it requires understanding, patience, and foresight to make progress toward them concurrently.

WAGE AND EMPLOYMENT LEGISLATION

A number of state and federal laws have a bearing upon the level of wages in New England and upon other payments which are part of the employer's labor cost and the worker's income.[9] These are the laws which are designed to protect the minimum standards of the worker. We shall examine the more important ones in this section and evaluate some of the changes which have been suggested, especially as they relate to the New England economy.

The Fair Labor Standards Act of 1938

This law, popularly known as the "wages and hours" law, is administered by the secretary of labor through the Wages and Hours Division of the Department of Labor. The act sets minimum wages, overtime provisions, and child-labor standards for industries engaged in interstate commerce. The basic standards provided by the act, as the result of amendments effective January 1950, are as follows:

1. A minimum wage of 75 cents an hour in all covered industries. Special exceptions are made for Puerto Rico and the Virgin Islands.

2. Time and one-half pay for overtime after 40 hours in any given work week, unless specific exemptions are provided.

3. A minimum age of 16 years for general employment, 18 years for hazardous occupations, and 14 years for certain occupations outside of school hours.

Subminimum rates can be paid under special conditions to learners, messengers, apprentices, and handicapped workers. The phrase "workers engaged in interstate commerce," which determines who is and who is not covered by the act, is interpreted broadly to include virtually all workers not engaged in strictly local activities.

The philosophy of the act is one of providing a floor below which workers' wage standards cannot fall, as the title of the law implies. Demands have been made from time to time to use the law to "take labor out of competition." Such demands are usually initiated by unions, but they often find the support of employers in relatively high-wage areas. *We do not subscribe to the notion that the Fair Labor Standards Act should be used to narrow interregional wage differentials. From a purely practical point of view, we do not think that successive increases of the minimum wage could permanently equalize either labor costs or wage rates among regions.*

9. Legislation dealing with labor-management relations is discussed in our Report No. 10, "Labor-Management Relations in New England."

If the statutory minimum were raised to the prevailing minimum of high-wage areas, there might be a temporary equalization of wage rates, though not necessarily of labor costs. It would be unrealistic to expect such equalization to last, both because of the varying geographical pressure of economic forces and the varying geographical activities of trade unions. Unions would be impelled to press for higher wages in formerly high-wage areas, and labor shortages in particular areas would re-create geographical differentials. Moreover, the whole price and market system might be affected. At the same time, the unions' most effective argument for organizing the unorganized workers in presently low-wage areas would be destroyed.

Furthermore, it would be undesirable to legislate equal money wages, even if it were possible. Differences in costs of living among regions and among communities of varying sizes make the purchasing power of equal wages different. While it is probably a desirable ultimate goal for the nation to have equal *real wages* for the same work, regardless of location, such an equalization should come through the operation of economic forces, including trade union activities, as the nation continues its development.

This argument should not be construed as opposition to raising the minimum, as general economic conditions warrant and as old minima become progressively obsolete. There are always some employers so situated that they could and would pay subminimum wage rates in the absence of such legislation. The purpose of the law is to ensure that those employers pay a guaranteed minimum where workers, because of ignorance or inertia, are unable to achieve such wage conditions for themselves. *We believe that the law should remain an instrument of protection against subminimum standards and that collective bargaining and the normal competition for workers' services should determine wages above the minimum level.*

The law does not have much direct bearing on New England's wages as a whole, since it is aimed at protecting the workers of individual employers from subminimum wage rates. New England does share, however, in the national interest in a sound policy for statutory minimum wages.

The Walsh-Healey Public Contracts Act

This federal law sets basic wage standards for work done on United States Government contracts in excess of $10,000. Under the act, the secretary of labor is authorized to determine prevailing minimum wages *in an industry* on the basis of standards specifically provided in the act. Typically, the minimum wage to be established is determined after public hearings of all interested parties. Once established, the minimum rate or more must be paid to all workers except office, custodial, and professional employees.

The Walsh-Healey Act was amended during the summer of 1952, and the present status of the law is uncertain. An amendment introduced by Senator J. William Fulbright, of Arkansas, now requires judicial review of all wage determinations made by the secretary of labor, as well as a review of all his "orders, rules, and interpretations." Although one amendment was defeated which would have exempted government purchases of "standard items available on the open market" from the provisions of the act, as was a second which would have provided for the determination of minimum wages for each industry in each "city, town, or village or other civil sub-division," instead of on the usual industry-wide basis, the amendment that did pass has thrown the basic intent of the law open to question. Spokesmen for some southern states claim that the original intent of the law was to provide for individual minima for each local area. Representatives of industry in higher wage areas insist that the law was intended to provide an industry-wide minimum.

This issue will now have to be settled in the courts, and it may take two years or more before the slow-moving judicial process can carry it to the Supreme Court. Until a final decision is handed down, it is unlikely that present minima, most of which have been made obsolete by inflation, will be revised upward. Even if some minima were raised, they would still have to receive judicial approval. There would be a considerable time lag between the determination of the new minimum by the secretary of labor and the time it became effective. *In the interest of administrative effectiveness of the Walsh-Healey Act, the Fulbright amendment should be repealed.*

Under uniform industry-wide minima, no employer is discriminated against. But if the law were amended or judicial review were to require the determination of separate minima for each labor-market area, the government would be committed to a policy of systematic discrimination against high-wage areas. In the case of New England, this would mean discrimination against the region's textile industries. Where an industry in one region is in direct competition for sales to the Federal Government with the same industry in other regions, we believe that uniform industry-wide minima should apply. *We favor upward revision of industry minima if the old determinations are rendered obsolete by inflation. If the law is to protect the workers on government contracts from substandard wages, the legal minimum should be close to the lower limit of the average rates paid by the vast majority of employers in an industry.*

We have taken a position in opposition to the use of the Fair Labor Standards Act as a device to replace collective bargaining in wage determination. We feel that it should continue to be used as a protective device against the payment of subminimum wages. Similarly, we feel that the Walsh-Healey Act should continue to protect the minimum standards of workers. In all cases in the past, the industry-wide minima have been well below the average level of wages in all regions.

In our evaluation of federal minimum-wage legislation, we have tried to avoid a sectionalist point of view and arrive at our conclusions on the basis of national interest. We feel that our position with respect to the Walsh-

Healey Act is consistent with this objective. It would be a fallacy to believe that all manufacturers in low-wage areas are interested in paying substandard wages, and the few that are probably cause as much concern to their nearby competitors as they do to competitors in other regions. Relatively few New England manufacturers would be affected by upward revisions that have been proposed for some minima.

The Walsh-Healey Act is one of a series of laws designed to protect minimum standards for workers. It should continue to fulfill that purpose rather than be used as a means of furthering interregional competition.

State Minimum-wage Laws

Massachusetts passed the first minimum-wage law in 1912. Today, all New England states except Vermont have similar legislation. Originally, the state minimum-wage laws applied only to women workers. Since 1939, however, Connecticut, Rhode Island, Massachusetts, and New Hampshire have amended their laws to include men.

There are two general types of state minimum-wage laws. One sets a statutory minimum, as does the Federal Fair Labor Standards Act, and the other issues "wage orders," generally for an industry or a specific occupational group. Connecticut, Massachusetts, and New Hampshire have laws that combine the statutory and wage-order provisions. Maine and Rhode Island make use of wage orders alone. The typical state minimum-wage law excludes agricultural workers and domestic servants from coverage.

In general, the state minimum-wage laws are designed to provide the same kind of protection to *local* workers, such as those employed in hotels, restaurants, laundries, and similar establishments, that is afforded to workers in industries engaged in interstate commerce by the Fair Labor Standards Act.

State minimum-wage laws cannot be regarded as a competitive disadvantage to a business enterprise, unless the enterprise serves a market in two or more states. High wages are a competitive disadvantage only if there are low-wage employers who are selling in the same market. In the production of shoes, textiles, clothing, and other products sold in national markets, high wages may be a significant competitive disadvantage unless they are offset by equally high rates of output per man-hour or advantages in other cost elements or operating conditions. But the laundry operator in Boston is not in competition with the laundry operator in Atlanta, Georgia. Any comparison of their respective wage levels, while it may show that standards for workers differ in the two locations, tells us nothing about the competitive position of either of them. Moreover, the state minima, like the national minima, do not affect the wage rates of most businesses but only prevent certain employers from paying substandard rates. *The adequacy of any particular state minimum-wage law or its administration depends on whether, in fact, it does protect intrastate workers from substandard wages.*

State Unemployment-insurance Laws

Under the American system of federal-state unemployment compensation, no two state laws are exactly alike. They differ in extent of coverage, benefit provisions, duration of benefits, eligibility qualifications, and in other significant respects. All New England states exclude agricultural workers, domestic servants, and employees of nonprofit organizations from coverage by their unemployment-insurance laws. In Massachusetts, all other establishments employing one or more workers for a period of 13 weeks are covered. In Maine and Vermont, establishments employing eight or more workers for a period of 20 weeks are covered. Coverage in the other New England states ranges in between.

Table 9–9. Unemployment-benefit Provisions in New England and Selected States in Other Regions, 1952

	WEEKLY BENEFIT AMOUNT FOR TOTAL UNEMPLOYMENT		MAXIMUM TOTAL BENEFITS PAYABLE
STATE	MINIMUM	MAXIMUM	IN BENEFIT YEAR
NEW ENGLAND			
Maine	$ 7.00	$25.00	$500.00
New Hampshire	7.00	28.00	728.00
Vermont	6.00	25.00	500.00
Massachusetts	7.00	25.00†	575.00†
Rhode Island	10.00	25.00	650.00
Connecticut	8.00	36.00*	936.00*
OTHER STATES			
New York	10.00	30.00	780.00
Pennsylvania	10.00	30.00	780.00
Michigan	6.00	35.00	700.00
Mississippi	3.00	20.00	320.00
North Carolina	7.00	30.00	780.00
Tennessee	5.00	22.00	484.00

* Includes maximum additional allowance for dependents. Without dependents, the weekly maximum in Connecticut is $24 and the yearly maximum is $624.

† Maximum including additional allowance for dependents not shown, since this depends upon the average weekly wage and the number of dependents in each case.

Source: U.S. Department of Labor, Bureau of Employment Security, *Comparison of State Unemployment Insurance Laws* (1952), pp. 44–45

Each state in New England has an initial waiting period of one week after unemployment begins before a worker is eligible to draw benefits. The ranges of weekly benefit payments and total benefits payable in a single benefit year are given in Table 9–9.

In part, total benefits payable within a benefit year depend upon the number of compensable weeks. In Maine and Vermont, workers may receive compensation for 20 weeks, in Massachusetts for 23 weeks, and in the other three New England states for 26 weeks. Compensable weeks in the other selected states in Table 9–9 range from 16 in Mississippi to 26 in New York, Pennsylvania, and North Carolina.

Connecticut and Massachusetts provide additional allowances for dependents. In Connecticut the allowance is $3 a week for each dependent up to four, with the additional allowance limited to one-half the weekly benefit allowance. Massachusetts pays $2 a week but does not limit the number of dependents. The augmented benefit, however, cannot be more than the average weekly wage of the recipient. Nine states outside New England also provide allowances for dependents.

In general, the New England states have somewhat more liberal unemployment compensation laws than many other states, especially those which are still in the process of becoming industrialized. On the other hand, the New England laws are generally about in line with those in other industrialized states. Because of its special dependency allowances, the benefit scale in Massachusetts is somewhat higher than the stated maximum would suggest, but it is not as high as some critics claim. The average weekly benefit payment in Massachusetts during 1951 was $23.71. That figure was second among the states, exceeded only by Michigan's $27.03 average. But the national average was $21.63, not far below the Massachusetts figure, and there were a number of other state averages clustered near that of Massachusetts.

It is not a fair statement to say that the high unemployment-compensation taxes in New England, and especially in Massachusetts and Rhode Island, are the result of the liberal benefit provisions of their laws. The size of their benefit payments cannot account for the depletion of the state funds and the forced elimination of merit rating in those two states. It has been pointed out repeatedly by the administrators of the state laws, as well as by informed persons in the regional office of the Division of Employment Security, that the high cost of unemployment compensation in New England is due primarily to the higher than average level of unemployment in this region. *As we have pointed out elsewhere, there has been a high level of persistent or chronic unemployment in New England, especially in the states where textile and shoe production are heavily concentrated. So long as this remains true it is likely that there will be a continuous drain on the unemployment-compensation funds.*[10]

The end of merit rating in Rhode Island and Massachusetts was also precipitated in part by their failure to build up adequate reserve funds during World War II, when unemployment was low. Their accumulated funds were not sufficient to meet the pressure from the postwar textile recession, and the reserves of these two states have been the lowest of all states in proportion to taxable wages during the last few years. *In view of the competitive problems in some of New England's industries, and especially textiles, it would seem*

10. See our report on "Employment Fluctuations in New England" (No. 8) and *Chronic Unemployment in New England from 1947 to 1951*, Staff Memorandum No. 2, May 1952.

desirable to build up the reserve funds as rapidly as possible with the goal of reducing unemployment-compensation tax rates. Action on proposals for any further increases in benefits should be approached most cautiously until the tax rates have been reduced.

Workmen's-compensation Laws

There is considerable variation in workmen's-compensation laws in New England, as there is for unemployment insurance. Payments for permanent total disability in 1950 ranged from 50% of average wages in Connecticut to 66⅔% in Maine, Massachusetts, and New Hampshire. The maximum weekly payment for the New England states varied in that year from a low of $24 in Maine to a high of $32 in Connecticut, compared to averages of $29 in eight important northern industrial states and $24 for 11 southern states. Massachusetts is the only New England state which makes such payments for life, but New York, Ohio, and many other states also permit lifetime payments. Massachusetts is also the only New England state which permits additional payments above the minima referred to above for dependents, though eight other states in the rest of the country provide similar dependency allowances.[11]

Payments for partial disability and payments to widows and children in death cases roughly follow the interstate pattern of total disability payments. The average payment in the New England states is somewhat higher than the average in the South, but it is about on a par with similar payments in other industrialized states in the North. *The legal protection which the workmen's-compensation system provides workers in the various New England states, therefore, is approximately in line with that in comparable industrial states outside the region, though there are state-to-state variations in all regions. Massachusetts stands out as one of the more liberal states in this respect, but it is impossible to rank the states exactly because of the great number of variations among the laws.*

It is similarly difficult to determine exactly how the operation of the workmen's-compensation system affects employers in the various states, through the insurance rates which they pay. There are differences in factory operations, in hazards, in the relative frequency of accidents, and in other conditions which affect rates. Rates vary from industry to industry, and the effects on all industries within a given state are not uniform. *Nevertheless, it appears that average insurance rates are somewhat higher in Rhode Island and Massachusetts than in many other northern states, while those in Connecticut and New Hampshire are somewhat lower. Though these payments are but a small fraction of the total manufacturing costs, they naturally*

---

11. For further details see Frank T. deVyver, "Labor Factors in the Industrial Development of the South," *Southern Economic Journal* (October 1951), p. 197; and U.S. Department of Labor, Bureau of Labor Standards, *State Workmen's Compensation Laws*, 1950.

have some effect on the competitive positions of the employers who pay the bills.

It is sometimes contended that lax administration of workmen's-compensation laws leads to fraudulent claims, and that this in turn increases the cost of a workmen's-compensation program. There is no doubt that fraudulent claims are made, in the New England states as well as elsewhere. There are no objective data available, however, for comparing the administration of these laws in the New England states with that in all other states. *We can only repeat the injunction that the best guarantee against the misuse of legislation designed to protect the worker is sound administration of the laws. Wherever the laws themselves are vague and confusing, they should be clarified.* The surest way to weaken seriously the protection of workers' standards is to tolerate misuse of the laws. Labor unions, in particular, should guard against the abuse of workmen's-compensation programs by their members and others.

The most certain way to reduce the costs of workmen's compensation is to reduce the incidence of industrial accidents. Safety precautions and the proper training and cooperation of employees are the best kind of insurance.

Cash-sickness Compensation Laws

Rhode Island was the first state to initiate a statewide disability system when it passed its "Cash-sickness Compensation" law in April 1942. The only other states which had cash-sickness programs under state law at the beginning of 1953 were New York, New Jersey, and California. The Rhode Island law provides for payments to covered workers during a period of sickness or injury Weekly benefits range from a minimum of $10 to a maximum of $25 for a period extending up to 26 weeks. Maximum total benefits payable to an individual amount to $650.

The Rhode Island program is financed by a 1% tax on the wages of all covered workers. Members of religious sects who depend upon spiritual healing may be exempted from paying the tax upon request. *There is widespread misconception that the Rhode Island program is jointly financed by employers and workers. The law specifically provides that the contributions be made entirely by the worker.*[12] Thus the worker is guaranteed minimum protection from lost time due to illness or accident, but the law does not directly raise labor costs to Rhode Island employers, and it appears doubtful that much of the cost is carried over into higher wage rates.

Cash-sickness legislation has been proposed at various times in Connecticut, New Hampshire, and Massachusetts. The proposed laws did not follow the Rhode Island model. Instead, they would have levied a tax on both employer

12. See Rhode Island Department of Employment Security, *Preliminary Report on Financing Cash-sickness Compensation in Rhode Island,* February 1951; and Nathan Sinai, *An Analysis of Rhode Island Cash-sickness Compensation, idem* (1950), p. 23.

and employee. At the middle of 1953, however, Rhode Island remained the only New England state with a cash-sickness law on the books.

Evaluation of State Labor Legislation

In general, state labor legislation in New England is more liberal from the worker's point of view than that in the less highly industrialized southern states. Comparisons of New England's laws with those in other northern industrial states show much less difference, although Massachusetts and Rhode Island are typically among the leaders.

Perhaps there has been too much stress upon the "liberality" of New England labor legislation as a factor in raising costs. The principal item of cost among the programs is the unemployment-compensation tax. This is high in some of the New England states far more because of their higher unemployment experience than because of the more liberal benefits. *To reduce the cost of unemployment compensation in such states, it is most important to reduce the average level of unemployment. It would seem that the most effective way in which those individuals and groups who are concerned about the level of such taxes could contribute to achieving reductions would be through aiding in the industrial redevelopment of communities plagued by chronic unemployment.*

Furthermore, the importance of other types of state labor legislation as cost-raising factors may sometimes have been overemphasized in terms of their relative importance to employers. How important are these items of cost as a percentage of the total cost of producing and distributing the products of this region? Compared to differentials among areas in the costs of labor, power, fuel, and transportation, differences among states in the cost of such social legislation as workmen's compensation are usually quite small. Repeated references to New England's "advanced" social legislation may, in fact, have made it harder to hold down such costs by discouraging prospects from considering this region as a likely location for a manufacturing plant. *At the same time employers, who are asked to contribute to the cost of social legislation, have both the obligation and the right to insist upon high standards in the administration of these benefit programs. Their responsibility also requires strict adherence to high standards in their own relationship with the programs.*

A SUGGESTED WAGE POLICY FOR NEW ENGLAND

Every New Englander will undoubtedly agree that a desirable goal for the region is higher per capita real incomes. A necessary corollary objective is a high level of wages in the six New England states. Wages and salaries accounted for about 71% of personal income payments in New England in 1951. The fact that *wages are income* is sometimes lost sight of in the emphasis on the cost of labor in New England. This does not mean, of course, that an arbitrary wage increase will ensure higher incomes. But the goal of New England should be to achieve that combination of jobs which will lead to the highest possible income per person consistent with a high and stable level of employment.

The gradual change which has been taking place in New England's industrial structure should contribute to a higher wage and income level. Some of the manufacturing plants which have departed for other regions paid fairly low wages. Some that have started operations in New England during recent years pay higher than average wages. It will require more than the growth of new industry alone in New England, however, to raise the level of wages and incomes in this region sufficiently.

A major part of a program designed to raise wages and the general level of incomes in New England is to increase output per worker. When such a proposal is made, some persons seem to interpret it as meaning that the worker should somehow "work harder." That interpretation presumes, first, that the individual worker has a great deal of control over his daily output, and second, that workers in general have a tendency to restrict output deliberately in order to maintain employment in their respective trades. In most cases, neither of these assumptions is true. We do not deny the existence of feather-bedding practices in some industries, nor do we condone them. There are also special problems faced by some New England industries in adjusting machine assignments. In general, however, the individual worker is part of a larger production process, and he must maintain the pace set by the process itself. Indeed, technological progress has made it possible for the modern worker to turn out far more goods with a smaller expenditure of effort than did his predecessor a few decades ago.

Further increases in productivity will come not by exhortations to the worker to work harder but through new technological developments and improved efficiency in using workers' time. New and better machines and plant methods, and new products and processes, are the keys to rising wages and incomes in New England. Naturally, the worker must make his contribution, both as an individual and through his union. It is desirable, wherever possible, to tap the worker's accumulated knowledge and ingenuity through a compensated suggestion system for improvements in plant operations. But in the last analysis, the worker has less control over output per man-hour than the plant manager.

The New England textile industries are faced with a special problem, since they stand almost alone as high-wage industries in the region. While the textile worker's hourly wage rate is above that of his counterpart in other regions, his earnings are well below those of workers in some other New England industries. In textiles, too, the long-range objective should be to maintain or increase earnings while driving down costs. These objectives are not incompatible, if output per man-hour can be increased. The surest method of increasing output per man-hour is to pioneer in technological developments.

The wage cuts granted by arbitrators in the cotton and rayon industry during the summer of 1952 have been recognized as temporary expedients and not as a permanent solution to the textile-wage problem. It is impossible to isolate the effects of the wage cuts on employment. Following the cuts there was a rather sharp pickup in employment in a number of the region's cotton and rayon mills. Market conditions, of course, were also important. Even in the absence of wage cuts there would have been some increase in employment, and if market conditions had become worse employment would have continued to fall off. It was a combination of the wage cuts and improved market conditions which led to the rise in employment.

As the textile industries enter the upward phase of another cycle, some of the pressure on costs will be relieved. Possibly wages in other regions will rise as conditions improve, and differentials between New England and the other regions will be narrowed. In future textile crises, however, the labor-cost differential may become a critical issue again. Those firms which have decreased the labor content of their production processes are the ones which will be hurt least, and the same will be true for their employees. A reduction in the relative importance of labor cost is the surest way to minimize the relative importance of those wage differentials that persist. In the process of adjustment, some firms will probably fall by the wayside, as is true in any competitive industry. The tendency will be, however, to cut out the weak spots in what must be the strong fabric of New England industry.[13]

Some may object that in recommending cooperative efforts to reduce costs while keeping earnings high we are avoiding real issues. We do not think so. High earnings and high incomes are inseparable, and the two stem from rising productivity. New England as a region will do well to take a lesson from the book of some of its successful manufacturers.

A large thriving shoe manufacturer in New England has informed us that his wage rates are the highest in the nation for his particular type of shoes. He produced figures to show that his rates are well above the regional average. The statement was not made as a complaint, but as a point of pride. Although wages are high in this company, unit labor costs are not. Every effort has been made to reduce man-hour requirements so that labor has benefited from higher earnings and management has gained from falling costs. In the shoe industry, much machinery is obtained on lease, and there is a tendency for the same type of machinery to be used in all factories. This alone makes it difficult for a shoe firm to operate in the face of large wage differentials. By tightening up efficiency all along the line and specializing in

13. We do not mean to minimize the importance of the short-run problems which currently beset the textile industries. For a more complete discussion, see our Staff Memorandum No. 10, *The Textile Industries of New England,* August 1952; and *Report on the New England Textile Industry,* by Committee Appointed by the Conference of the New England Governors, 1952.

quality products with a fairly stable demand, this company has been able to do more than survive at its present location; it has operated profitably.

We recognize that there are differences in managerial ability, in labor-management relations, in product specialization, and in a host of other variables that influence the competitive position of an individual company. There are successful and unsuccessful firms in every industry, and we do not pretend to suggest the "right" wage policy for each of the region's important industries. *For the region as a whole, we inevitably return to the conclusion that New England should strive to be a region of both high wages and low labor costs, with high labor productivity as the means by which the twin goals can be achieved.*

Accompanying this general wage policy for New England, several specific actions relating to wages and labor costs are desirable. A few of the suggestions offered in this report are:

1. The Fair Labor Standards Act should remain an instrument of protection against subminimum wage standards, and it should not be used as a substitute for collective bargaining and other economic forces in forcing the elimination of interregional wage differentials.

2. Minimum wage determinations under the Walsh-Healey Public Contracts Act should be revised upward where the old minima have become obsolete. The amendment which requires judicial review of all wage determinations should be repealed.

3. The reserve funds of the state unemployment-compensation programs, especially in Massachusetts and Rhode Island, should be built up as rapidly as possible in order to reduce the unemployment-compensation tax rates.

4. State workmen's-compensation legislation should be re-examined and clarified. Sound administration of the workmen's compensation laws, with the cooperation of both employers and unions, is the best protection against their misuse.

5. Reduction in the costs of social legislation designed to protect the worker can be achieved most effectively and equitably by reducing the incidence of the risks themselves, especially unemployment.

SELECTED REFERENCES

1. Rhode Island Department of Employment Security:
   Preliminary Report on Financing Cash-sickness Compensation in Rhode Island, February 1951.
   An Analysis of Rhode Island Cash-sickness Compensation, prepared by Nathan Sinai, 1950.
2. U.S. Department of Agriculture, Bureau of Agricultural Economics, *Farm Labor* (monthly).
3. U.S. Department of Labor, Bureau of Employment Security, *Comparison of State Unemployment Insurance Laws as of December 1952.*

4. U.S. Department of Labor, Bureau of Labor Standards:
    Federal Labor Laws and Agencies, August 1950.
    State Workmen's Compensation Laws, September 1950.
5. U.S. Department of Labor, Bureau of Labor Statistics, *Current Wage Developments*
    (monthly).
6. —— *Community Wage Surveys* (OWR–23)
    Cotton Textiles
    Ferrous Foundries
    Industrial Chemicals
    Knit Underwear
    Leather
    Machinery
    Machine Tools and Accessories
    Men's Goodyear Welt Shoes
    Non-ferrous Foundries
    Paint and Varnishes
    Rayon, Nylon, and Silk
    Rubber
    Women's Cement Process Shoes
    Woolen and Worsted Textiles
7. —— *Trends in Output per Man-hour*
    Dress Shirts, March 1948, May 1950
    Electrical Equipment and Supplies, April 1950
    Electrical Appliances, April 1950
    Footwear, March 1948, May 1950, October 1950
    Industrial Equipment, April 1948, April 1950
    Selected Types of Leather, March 1950
8. —— *Trends in Wage Differentials, 1907–1947.*

10

Labor-Management Relations in New England

*Drafted by William H. Miernyk under the direction
of Arthur A. Bright, Jr.*

INTRODUCTION

The relationship between management and New England's most important
resource, its labor force, is one of the key determinants of the productiveness
of the regional economy. Good labor relations in a company, by enhancing
the company's productiveness, will increase returns to both workers and
management. Poor labor relations, on the other hand, may be reflected in
reduced output, deterioration of workmanship, and lower returns to worker
and employer alike. Similarly, for the regional economy as a whole, good
labor relations will make the region more productive, and a poor relationship between workers and management will have the opposite effect.

The labor news that makes headlines deals with industrial strife. A strike
or the threat of a strike, the loss of production and incomes due to strikes,
or violence when it occurs are usually given prominent coverage in the daily
press. Less public attention is focused on industrial peace and the fruits of
good labor-management relations. But it is the latter which leads to rising
output and incomes.

The rise of trade unions in America has brought about a revolution in
the relationship between workers and industrial management. New England is an old industrial region where trade unionism has deep historical
roots. In the past, good labor relations in a mill or factory depended primarily on the intelligence and understanding of management. Today the
intelligence and understanding of the elected representatives of employees
also bear upon the kind of labor-management relations to be found in any
company where the workers have organized for purposes of collective bargaining.

Those interested in labor-management relations in New England will
want to know the answers to a number of questions. How extensively are
the workers of New England organized, compared with those in other
regions? What has been the region's strike record in recent years? How
have government policies affected labor-management relations in New England? What positive accomplishments have been made by New England
unions and management in creating and preserving industrial peace? How
much control do New England labor leaders have over labor-management
relations in the region, and to what extent must they follow the policies
of national union leaders? And finally, recognizing that there is no magic

formula which will guarantee good labor-management relations in the myriad of situations in which New England workers and employers find themselves, what is the essence of a sound program of labor-management relations for the region?

NEW ENGLAND'S TRADE UNIONS

The Extent of Trade Unionism in New England

Although local unions know fairly accurately the number of members they have at any one time, there is no system of continuous reporting which would permit accurate estimates of union membership to be kept current. In Table 10–1 we present our estimates of union membership in the New

Table 10–1. Estimated Union Membership in New England, 1951

STATE	UNION MEMBERSHIP* NUMBER (THOUSANDS)	PER CENT OF TOTAL	NONAGRICULTURAL EMPLOYMENT† NUMBER (THOUSANDS)	PER CENT OF TOTAL	UNION MEMBERSHIP AS PER CENT OF NON-AGRICULTURAL EMPLOYMENT
Maine	79	7.7	265.9	7.7	29.7
New Hampshire	40	3.9	171.7	5.0	23.3
Vermont	23	2.2	99.5	2.9	23.1
Massachusetts	598	58.5	1,800.9	52.1	33.2
Rhode Island	97	9.5	296.5	8.6	32.7
Connecticut	186	18.2	820.6	23.7	22.7
NEW ENGLAND	1,023	100.0	3,455.11	100.0	29.6
UNITED STATES	13,600		46,401		29.3

* Excluding Railroad Brotherhoods.
† Annual averages provided by U.S. Department of Labor, Bureau of Employment Security.
Source: Commonwealth of Massachusetts, Department of Labor and Industries, Forty-seventh Directory of Labor Organizations in Massachusetts, 1951, adjusted by Committee of New England. Basic data for all other states were provided by the A.F. of L., State Federation of Labor, C.I.O State Industrial Union Councils, and by independent unions.

England states, exclusive of the Railroad Brotherhoods. The figures for Massachusetts were obtained from the Massachusetts Department of Labor and Industries; the others were collected by the Committee of New England from state offices of the A.F. of L. and the C.I.O., and from the region's larger independent unions. *We estimate that there are about one million union members in New England, and that the proportion of the region's workers who are unionized is about the same as that in the country as a whole.*

For purposes of comparison we have related estimated union membership to total nonagricultural employment. The New England union membership of 29.7% of nonagricultural employment is only slightly above the

29.3% average of the United States.[1] But Table 10–1 shows that there is considerable variation from state to state. Rhode Island, with union membership of 32.7%, and Massachusetts, with 33.2%, are more extensively organized than the average state in the nation; the remaining four New England states are less extensively organized. Connecticut, with 22.7%, and Vermont, with 23.1% have the smallest proportion of unionization.

We should repeat that these are *estimates* of union membership. Nevertheless, they are probably not grossly in error. They check rather closely with the only other independent estimate of union membership that we have been able to find. We have not been able to clarify union membership by industry, but in New England the most heavily organized industries appear to be the textile group, the metal and machinery trades, the building trades, the clothing and garment trades, the footwear industries, the paper industry, trucking, and printing. A substantial proportion of workers in other industries are, of course, union members.

In New England, as in the nation as a whole, most union members are affiliated with the two large federations. We estimate that there are about four A.F. of L. members in New England for every three members affiliated with the C.I.O. It is more difficult to estimate the relative size of independent unions in New England. There are several fairly large independent unions in the region, but we conservatively estimate that more than 80% of all union members in New England are in the A.F. of L. or C.I.O.

Work Stoppages in New England

A region's strike record may be used as a rough barometer of the state of its industrial relations. A strike represents a failure of labor and management to resolve differences of opinion peacefully. It is a resort to a test of economic strength. Strikes may or may not settle differences of opinion, but they are evidence of a breakdown in the machinery of industrial relations.

New England's recent strike record is summarized in Table 10–2. On the whole, it is a favorable one. In the periods both before World War II and after it New England had a smaller proportion of workers involved in work stoppages than its proportion of the nation's nonagricultural labor force. The same was true of the proportion of man-days idle due to strikes. Furthermore, the postwar record shows some improvement over the prewar record. New England has about 7.5% of the nation's nonagricultural labor force. In the prewar period covered by Table 10–2 New England accounted for 5.6% of the number of workers involved in work stoppages in the nation. In the postwar period it accounted for only 3.2%. *In terms of man-days idle, which is the most meaningful measure when considering the*

1. To achieve maximum comparability, the Railroad Brotherhoods have been excluded from the figure for national union membership.

impact of strikes on production and incomes in the region, New England accounted for 4.9% of the nation's total in the prewar period and 4.2% in the postwar period.

The records for the individual states are also given in Table 10–2. In each state the absolute number of workers involved in strikes, as well as the absolute number of man-days idle due to work stoppages, increased between the two periods shown in the table. But in each state the *proportion* of the nation's workers involved in strikes and the proportion of man-days idle due to strikes either declined or remained the same. Relative to the nation as a whole, New England's strike record improved.

Table 10–2. *Work Stoppages in New England, 1935–39 and 1947–51*

STATE	NONAGRI-CULTURAL LABOR FORCE AS PER CENT OF UNITED STATES, 1951	WORK STOPPAGES						MAN-DAYS IDLE			
		NUMBER		WORKERS INVOLVED							
				NUMBER*		PER CENT OF U.S.		NUMBER*		PER CENT OF U.S.	
		1935–39	1947–51	1935–39	1947–51	1935–39	1947–51	1935–39	1947–51	1935–39	1947–51
Maine	0.6	10	16	2.3	3.4	0.2	0.1	57.7	41.7	0.3	0.1
New Hampshire	0.4	8	18	3.9	4.0	0.4	0.2	18.5	49.0	0.1	0.1
Vermont	0.2	4	6	1.2	1.1	0.1	†	27.9	30.3	0.2	0.1
Massachusetts	3.9	147	153	33.1	45.8	2.9	1.9	434.0	879.2	2.6	2.4
Rhode Island	0.6	36	28	10.0	8.1	0.9	0.3	124.2	237.7	0.7	0.7
Connecticut	1.8	53	63	11.8	17.1	1.1	0.7	165.7	279.6	1.0	0.8
NEW ENGLAND	7.5	258	284	62.3	79.5	5.6	3.2	828.0	1,517.5	4.9	4.2

* In thousands.
† Less than 0.05%.
Source: U.S. Department of Labor, Bureau of Labor Statistics.

In most New England industries collective bargaining was carried on without resort to strikes. Issues were settled over the bargaining table or by the decisions of impartial arbitrators. Some of the man-days lost were due to industry-wide or nationwide strikes. National unions and national corporations cut across regional lines, and national union and management policies will affect to some extent the strike record of any region. When we consider these influences on the behavior of New England's leaders, *the recent history of collective bargaining in the region is a favorable one.*

We should expect relatively fewer strikes in New England than in some other sections of the United States where unions are still struggling to establish themselves as accepted institutions. *The relatively favorable strike record in New England is due in a large part to the maturity of its labor relations.* Where the union has been accepted by the community there will be fewer strikes. The two parties will not struggle over the basic issue of whether or not the union has a legitimate interest in such matters as wages, hours, working conditions, and fringe-benefit payments, but will deal with concrete issues. Over time the area of disagreement, even over more specific issues, is narrowed. The relationship between the two parties is spelled out in the labor-management agreement. During the life of the agreement disputes may arise, but these are settled through the established grievance procedure, which in many cases calls for final determination of disputed issues by the decision of an impartial arbitrator if the two parties are unable to settle the issue short of this step. The content of agreements also changes over time as precedent is established for the peaceful handling of matters that formerly led to disputes. Finally, a region's strike record will be influenced to some extent by the quality of its union leadership.

The Quality of Unions in New England

Much has been written about the quality of management in New England. And New Englanders are justly proud of the pioneering efforts of some of the region's outstanding businessmen. They have equal reason to be proud of their unions and union leaders. For the most part unions in New England are stable, responsible and democratic. Many union leaders in the region play an important part in civic and community affairs.

New England labor leaders are generally aware of the roles played by unions in our modern, complex society. They see the need for educational programs designed for the rank-and-file members and for the general public as well. The Massachusetts Federation of Labor has sponsored scholarship contests for secondary-school students. Under this program thousands of students, and their teachers as well, have added to their knowledge about trade unions in the United States.

The unions are also concerned about the development of trained and responsible union leaders. Each year, for example, the Massachusetts Federation of Labor has offered on a competitive basis two trade union fellowships at Harvard. New England labor is trying to offer the same opportunities to its leaders and potential leaders that business is giving to its executives. The C.I.O. and some of the independent unions are engaged in similar programs to educate their membership and to provide for the training of union executives.

How does New England business feel about its workers, and the union representatives with whom management must deal? In a survey conducted by the Federal Reserve Bank of Boston in 1949, 663 New England manufacturers listed various locational advantages and disadvantages in this region. Of this group 57% stated that they felt the character of the labor force was an important regional advantage, while only 8% stated that they were at a disadvantage compared with other regions. Nearly half of the manufacturers surveyed stated that their relations with labor constituted neither an advantage or disadvantage; but of the remainder 31% listed relations with labor as an important advantage, only 8% stated that their labor relations constituted a disadvantage, and the other 12% did not answer the question. Labor relations were cited as an advantage 3.6 times as often as they were cited as a disadvantage. While such evidence cannot be regarded as conclusive it is suggestive. Very few factors were cited more often than the character of the labor force and relations with labor as locational advantages in New England.

The quality of labor leadership in New England is further revealed by the content of collective bargaining agreements in the region. Although national union policy will determine contract provisions in some cases, there are other agreements which take local conditions into consideration. In the discussion that follows we wish to call attention in particular to the contract provisions dealing with technological change.

THE PROVISIONS OF LABOR-MANAGEMENT AGREEMENTS IN NEW ENGLAND MANUFACTURING INDUSTRY

There is no uniform pattern of provisions in labor-management agreements. Because basic conditions differ widely from industry to industry, we should expect to find differences in the collective bargaining agreements that gradually evolve in each industry. In an attempt to obtain a summary picture of the agreements that have developed in New England, we made an intensive study of 253 labor-management agreements between manufacturing firms employing 300 or more workers, and various trade unions. Provisions studied include those dealing with union security, wage and supplementary payments, and technological change. These are the provisions which are most likely to lead to disputes, and an absence of disputes over them is indicative of sound and workable labor relations.[2]

As of June 1952 there were about 1,500,000 manufacturing workers in New England. The Boston office of the Bureau of Labor Statistics had on file labor-management agreements covering 693,000, or 46%, of these workers. Our sample of agreements covered approximately 357,000 workers, or about 52% of those covered by agreements in the Bureau of Labor Statistics file. Industry coverage varied from a low of 22% of the region's textile industries to 59% of all workers employed in New England's electrical machinery industry. Since our sample is restricted to firms employing 300 or more workers, it is biased toward the larger firms. We found certain patterns of provisions within the various industries, and variations from union to union, but there was no discernible relationship between the various provisions and the size of firms. *It appears that the industry to which a firm belongs and the union with which it deals will determine the provisions of its labor-management agreement rather than the size of the firm.*[3]

2. For detailed discussion of these and other contract provisions see Staff Memorandum No. 11, *The Provisions of Union-Management Contracts in New England Industry,* December 1952.

3. For a further discussion of the composition of our sample and the degree to which it is representative of New England manufacturing establishments covered by union agreements, see *ibid.*

Union Security Provisions

Under the Taft-Hartley Act the closed shop is illegal, and the maximum degree of union security that can be achieved today is the union shop. There are various types of union shop agreements, but essentially each aims to bring all of the workers in a bargaining unit into the union. The opposite extreme to a union shop provision is the contract which makes no provision for union security. The union is recognized, but there is no provision that workers must join it within a stated period after they are employed. Fifty-two per cent of all contracts, covering 45% of the workers in our sample, have some form of union shop provision.

About half of all those workers in our sample who are affiliated with A.F. of L. unions come under a union shop agreement. A smaller proportion of workers in C.I.O. and independent unions enjoy the maximum degree of union security permissible today. The extent of union shop provisions and the relative number of workers covered, by union affiliations, are given in Table 10–3. Fewer than half the workers covered by our study operate under union shop contracts.

The relative extent of union shop agreements in four selected New England industries is given in Table 10–4. The paper industry shows the high-

Table 10–3. *Percentage of Contracts and Workers Covered by Union Shop Clauses in 253 New England Agreements, by Union Affiliation*

UNION AFFILIATION	PER CENT OF CONTRACTS	PER CENT OF WORKERS COVERED
A.F. of L.	58	52
C.I.O.	53	42
Independent unions	38	40
TOTAL	52	45

Source: Staff Memorandum No. 11

est proportion of union shop agreements, with 88% of sample workers operating under union shop agreements. The nonelectrical machinery industry, on the other hand, had only 22% of sample workers covered by a union shop provision. In the textile industries, the Textile Workers Union of America (C.I.O.) had a larger proportion of workers covered by union shop agreements than either the United Textile Workers of America (A.F. of L.) or the independent unions. But in the paper industry, where nearly all workers in A.F. of L. unions were under union shop contracts, a negligible proportion of C.I.O. workers were so covered. In the leather industries, which include producers of shoes and other leather products, all of the C.I.O. contracts we studied carried a union shop provision, as did a majority of the contracts with other unions.[4]

4. The four industries for which special tabulations have been prepared were represented by 133 agreements in our survey. Those four industries were selected because: (1) they are

It would be erroneous to use the number of union shop provisions as a measure of the strength of the respective unions in the industries analyzed. Some unions, for a variety of reasons, have pushed more aggressively for union shop provisions than others. Furthermore, the A.F. of L. contracts may not cover the same branches of the industry that are covered by C.I.O. contracts. This may account for some of the differences observed in Table 10–4 and subsequent tables which compare contract provisions in A.F. of L., C.I.O., and independent unions.

Table 10–4. Union Shop Agreements in a Sample of Selected New England Industries
(Percentage of contracts and workers covered)

UNION AFFILIATION	TEXTILES		PAPER		LEATHER		NONELECTRICAL MACHINERY	
	CON-TRACTS	WORKERS COVERED	CON-TRACTS	WORKERS COVERED	CON-TRACTS	WORKERS COVERED	CON-TRACTS	WORKERS COVERED
A.F. of L.	67	64	83	89	75	74	31	25
C.I.O.	76	87	9	5	100	100	29	20
Independents	33	36	—	—	60	61	33	24
TOTAL	69	78	82	88	72	79	30	22

Source: Ibid.

Fringe-benefit Provisions

During World War II the pressure of unions for higher wages was restrained by the imposition of wage ceilings as part of the nation's anti-inflationary program. As a result there was increased pressure for various types of fringe-benefit payments, such as added vacation and holiday pay, premium pay for Saturday and Sunday work, shift differentials, health, welfare, and pension provisions. Such provisions were allowed by the War Labor Board in lieu of wage increases. Today, therefore, straight-time hourly earnings do not accurately reflect labor costs to the employer or returns to the worker. Elsewhere we have presented estimates of the amount of vacation and holiday payments in New England industry compared to the same payments in other regions.[5] *In the textile industries, vacation and holiday payments in New England are higher than similar payments in the South, but are about equal to those in the Middle Atlantic States. In all other industries studied by us, such payments were about equal to or less than the national average.*

Shift Differentials. About 80% of all manufacturing workers covered by our sample of 253 union agreements received premium pay for second or third shifts. Premium rates range from 4 to 15 cents an hour. Typically the

---

important sources of employment in New England, and (2) the samples of contracts in these industries were judged to be especially representative of all contracts in each industry. Similar information is given for all New England industries in the Committee of New England's memorandum, *op. cit.*

5. Staff Memorandum No. 9, *Wages and Supplementary Payments in Selected New England Industries,* July 1952, and "Wages in New England," Report Series No. 9.

third shift rate is higher than the second shift rate. Some contracts call for premium pay based on the rate of average hourly earnings. Such provisions range from 5% to 11% of hourly earnings, with the higher rates again being applied to the third shift.

Premium Pay for Saturday and Sunday Work. The Fair Labor Standards Act provides for time-and-one-half pay for overtime after 40 hours in a work week. But some contracts call for premium pay for Saturday work "as such," i.e., regardless of the hours worked during the week, while others merely go along with the Fair Labor Standards Act. Eighty-five per cent of all sample contracts call for premium pay for Sunday work, usually at a double-time rate. These contracts cover 83% of the workers in our sample.

Holiday Payments. Fifty-three per cent of the workers included in the sample are paid for six holidays annually, 27% are paid for seven, and 7% of all workers in our sample receive pay for eight or more holidays a year. According to a nationwide study of contracts made by the Bureau of Labor Statistics in 1949, these provisions are fairly typical of the average contract in the United States.

Paid Vacations. Forty-three per cent of the manufacturing workers in our sample receive a maximum of two weeks of paid vacation after periods of service ranging from one to five years. Thirty-five per cent are entitled to three weeks of paid vacation after they have accumulated from 10 to 20 years of service. In the nation as a whole, about 60% of all agreements provide for two-week paid vacations. In New England only 48% have such a provision. But while 33% of all agreements in New England grant three weeks of vacation pay, only 30% in the nation as a whole have such a provision. In all cases, the length of vacations is tied to length of service provisions.

Health, Welfare, and Pension Provisions. About 60% of the sample of New England contracts have some form of health and welfare provision, but only 13% have a pension program spelled out in the contract. Another 25% of workers in the sample operate under contracts which have neither health and welfare nor pension provisions.

About 9% of the workers in our sample have health and welfare programs financed by joint contributions of labor and management. Thirty-four per cent of the workers are covered by contracts which call for a noncontributory health and welfare program, i.e., one financed entirely by the employer. In the remaining agreements the method of financing cannot be fully determined from the agreement.

The extent of supplementary pay provisions in selected New England industries is summarized in Table 10-5. There is considerable variation from industry to industry. In the textile and machinery industries a majority of the organized workers receive double-time pay for Sunday work. Some contracts call for double-time pay for Sunday work, regardless of the number of days worked during the week. Others specify that double-time will be paid only if Sunday is the seventh work day. Except under unusual conditions, however, it is not common for workers to be asked to work a seven-day week.

A negligible proportion of the region's paper workers receive seven or more paid holidays a year. But nearly all are entitled to three weeks of paid vacation after accumulating a specified number of years of service. Few textile workers receive either of these supplementary payments, but more than 90% of them are covered by a health and welfare clause in their contracts. There is less variation among these industries in the extent to which health and welfare provisions are granted than is true of the other types of selected fringe-benefit payments.

Table 10–5. Supplementary Pay Provisions in a Sample of Selected New England Industries
(Percentage of contracts and workers covered in sample)

INDUSTRY	DOUBLE-TIME PAY FOR SUNDAY WORK*		SEVEN OR MORE PAID HOLIDAYS YEARLY		THREE WEEKS OR MORE OF PAID VACATION YEARLY†		HEALTH AND WELFARE PROVISIONS	
	CON-TRACTS	WORKERS COVERED	CON-TRACTS	WORKERS COVERED	CON-TRACTS	WORKERS COVERED	CON-TRACTS	WORKERS COVERED
Textiles	80	82	28	15	2	1	91	93
Paper	52	45	—	—	87	94	57	66
Leather	33	33	22	21	33	19	61	77
Nonelectrical machinery	91	96	63	59	39	34	70	63

* About one-third of the clauses provided for double-time for "Sunday as such," the remainder applied to Sunday as the seventh consecutive working day.
† After periods of service extending from 10 to 20 years.
Source: Ibid.

This selected sample of industries and provisions reveals the difficulty of making a general statement about the extent to which New England's manufacturing workers have been granted fringe benefits. When we ignore the industry breakdown, it appears that fringe benefits granted to the organized workers in our sample roughly parallel the same benefits received by organized workers in the nation as a whole. But the industry breakdown is important. When we hear that New England organized labor receives more paid holidays than workers in other regions we know that this does not apply to the region's paper workers. Similarly, liberal vacation provisions, while granted to most paper workers, do not apply to the textile industries of the region.

Provisions Relating to Technological Change

What effects do trade unions in New England have upon the rate of technological change? Do unions encourage or discourage the introduction of new processes? Unions regard it as one of their duties to protect, insofar as they are able, the jobs of their numbers. They feel that the worker should have a voice in such matters as the introduction of new machines which might displace part of a plant's labor force. There is a wide range of attitudes toward technological change, however, and we will examine some that are representative.

Pledges of Union-Management Cooperation. Some contracts embody a clause in which the union specifically states that it will cooperate with management in improving the over-all efficiency of the plant. The importance of such provisions should not be minimized. They indicate a recognition of the need for continued improvement in productivity, and the union has pledged itself to further such improvement.

Thirty-two per cent of the workers in the sample are covered by contracts which pledge them to cooperate with management in improving the efficiency of their respective concerns. The extent of such pledges in four important New England industries is given in Table 10–6.

Table 10–6. Pledges of Cooperation in a Sample of Selected New England Industries
(Percentage of contracts and workers covered in sample)

INDUSTRY	PER CENT OF CONTRACTS	PER CENT OF WORKERS COVERED
Textiles	32	27
Paper	65	48
Leather	33	22
Nonelectrical machinery	69	63

Source: Ibid.

Though the machinery industry leads in making pledges of cooperation, it may come as a surprise to some that 27% of the region's textile workers are covered by agreements which go beyond the acceptance of technological change and pledge the workers to cooperate with management in making such changes. At the same time, however, nearly half of the paper workers and 63% of all workers in the nonelectrical machinery industry in our sample were covered by contracts pledging them to cooperate in making technological improvements. Of the selected industries, the leather industry, with only 22% of workers in the sample covered by a provision pledging cooperation, showed the least amount of positive union participation in encouraging technological improvements.

Specific Provisions Dealing with Technological Change. While some agreements do not pledge the cooperation of the worker to encourage technological change, they recognize management's right to make necessary changes. Forty-nine per cent of the contracts in our sample state that it is management's prerogative to introduce new machinery or processes or to make other technological changes. *These contracts cover 36% of the workers in the sample. Only 4% of the contracts studied have a provision which limits management's right to make any desired change in the production process. But we find that these contracts are concentrated in a few industries.*

In the textile industries, for example, 41% of all agreements examined, which cover 33% of the workers included in the sample, state unequivocally that it is management's right to regulate the production process. Twenty-two per cent of the textile contracts, covering 34% of the textile workers in the sample, explicitly provide for a trial period for the new operation, after which the union may file grievances about factors such as work assignments, rates of pay, and other conditions of the job. In general, these contracts specify that management is free to introduce work assignments for a trial period. At the end of the trial period the union may file a grievance. Provision is made for such grievances to eventuate in arbitration, however, and the decision of the arbitrator is final and binding.

Perhaps some will wonder why the union has any voice in the matter of technological change at all. The union does not object to technological change as such, but it does object to the unemployment that such change sometimes creates. Thus if new machinery is installed in a mill, the union may wish to negotiate the number of machines its workers will tend in an attempt to protest the jobs of the workers in the mill. This is part of the often discussed but little understood work-load problem in New England's textile industries.[6]

The remaining textile contracts (37% of the total), which cover 33% of the textile workers in our sample, do not explicitly mention the matter of technological change. Presumably in these remaining cases management is free to introduce new machinery or processes without negotiating with the union.

The extent to which contract provisions covering union participation in technological change have retarded the modernization of some of New England's textile mills is a controversial question. Some of New England's most modern and progressive textile mills operate under such contracts. They have replaced outmoded equipment as rapidly as finances permitted, and carried on negotiations with the union afterward. But some mills may have been reluctant to install new machinery for a trial period, since they would prefer to know beforehand that they could make larger machine assignments than were permitted on the old equipment.

It is significant, however, that only one-third of all textile workers in our sample are covered by contracts which require negotiations with the union before adjustments to technological change can be made. Unions in other industries, as well as in textiles, reserve the right to negotiate wage rates and work loads after new machinery has been introduced.

Rates and Work Loads on Jobs Affected by Technological Change. One-half of the contracts studied, which cover 61% of the sample of workers, provide for settling disputes about rates and work loads by means of the grievance machinery. Usually this means that management sets the rate or determines the machine assignment, and if the workers protest they may file a grievance. If the grievance cannot be settled by consultation between

6. This problem is discussed in the Committee's Staff Memorandum No. 10, *The Textile Industries of New England*, August 1952.

representatives of labor and management, it typically becomes a matter for arbitration. The decision of the arbitrator is accepted as final and binding upon the two parties.

Forty-seven per cent of all contracts in the sample, which cover 34% of the workers, have no provision for dealing with rate setting or work-load determination during the life of a contract. Presumably in these cases all such matters are either negotiated when a new agreement is being considered or settled by unilateral management decisions.

The remaining contracts (3%), which cover 5% of the workers, provide for joint determination of rates by negotiation during the life of the contract. In these cases, however, the decision is not subject to arbitration. In the event of a deadlock a strike could result, or the parties might carry over the dispute to the next contract negotiation.

The distribution of contract provisions to settle work-load or wage-rate matters by means of the grievance process, or by joint negotiation, in a sample of four of New England's important industries is summarized in Table 10–7.

Table 10–7. Wage-Rate and Work-Load Disputes Settled by the Grievance Process
as Joint Negotiation, in a Sample of Contracts in Selected
New England Industries
(Percentage of contracts and workers covered in sample)

INDUSTRY	PER CENT OF CONTRACTS	PER CENT OF WORKERS COVERED
Textiles	65	75
Paper	9	5
Leather	67	81
Nonelectrical machinery	59	80

Source: Ibid.

Outside the textile industries most of the contract provisions deal with wage rates rather than work loads. In the textile contracts, however, both wage-rate and work-load provisions are covered. A larger proportion of leather and machinery workers are covered by contracts which call for settling rate disputes during the life of a contract by means of the grievance procedure than is true of the textile industries, but there are no provisions dealing with work loads as such. It is regrettable that similar studies have not been made for contracts on a nationwide basis. No comparison with similar provisions in other regions can be made.

Minimizing the Effects of Technological Change. Contract provisions designed to minimize the impact of technological change upon the worker are of two general types. One calls for some form of severance or dismissal pay. The other provides for transfer of workers, displaced from their old jobs by the adoption of a new process or the introduction of a new machine, to another job, usually with no change in pay. Evidently few contracts in New England have such provisions. Eighty-seven per cent of the contracts studied, covering 91% of the workers in the sample, have no clause dealing with a worker's displacement from his job by technological change.[7] Most of the workers who are covered by a provision dealing with the effects of technological change are members of independent unions.

In textiles, 29% of all contracts covering 9% of the workers in the sample provided that a displaced worker had the right to learn new equipment at his old rate of pay. In the leather industry 16% of the contracts, covering 15% of the workers in the sample, gave preference to displaced workers on new jobs. Six per cent of the workers in the leather industry were covered by a provision that senior workers would be transferred to new machinery at the rate of pay decided upon for the new job.

Summary of Contract Provisions

Space limitations prevent a complete analysis of all contract provisions in all of New England's industries here. We have been able to select only a few provisions for brief discussion.[8] But even from this brief analysis some definite conclusions stand out.

The union shop is somewhat less prevalent in New England than in the nation. Considered in the aggregate, fringe-benefit provisions embodied in New England contracts are about the same as similar provisions in contracts throughout the nation as a whole, but there is considerable variation from industry to industry. One industry may have a large proportion of its workers covered by a clause which grants a large number of paid holidays a year but limits vacation pay. Others have liberal vacation provisions but grant few paid holidays. *No summary statement about fringe-benefit provisions applies equally to all industries.*

About one-third of New England's textile workers are covered by contracts which call for union review of work assignments after a technological change. There are few such provisions in other industries. About 60% of the organized workers in our sample, however, are covered by contracts which call for union participation in rate setting after a technological change has been made. Only 9% of the workers in our sample work under a contract which makes specific provisions for minimizing the impact of technological change, either by granting the displaced worker severance

7. In some contracts, however, this may be covered by the seniority provision. Mr. Solomon Barkin, research director of the TWUA, has pointed out to us that in March 1951 his union negotiated an agreement covering about 16,000 workers which includes a provision for "technological displacement compensation." This agreement was not included in our sample. Its inclusion would have meant that substantially more than 9% of the sample workers were covered by a severance or dismissal pay clause. It remains true, however, that most New England agreements do not contain such provisions.

8. In our special study of contract provisions in New England, we have made a statistical summary of all important provisions for all of New England's major industry groups. These are presented in Staff Memorandum No. 11.

pay or by providing for his transfer to another job, generally at his old rate of earnings.[9]

In general, trade union leaders do not think in regional terms. They do not try to obtain one set of conditions for their workers in New England and another set for their workers located elsewhere. They strive for maximum gains in all regions, but regional differences sometimes appear because a union may be stronger in one region than in another. As a matter of policy, union leaders attempt to eliminate or narrow such interregional differences. But as a matter of fact the failure of unions to organize substantial segments of industries in other regions tends to perpetuate such differences.

A vast majority of all contracts in New England either pledge the union's cooperation to assist management in making technological improvements or specifically state that it is management's prerogative to make such improvements. As a broad generalization, unions have not negotiated more fringe-benefit provisions in this region than they have in other industrial regions where the extent of union organization is comparable to that in New England. We recognize, however, that there are exceptions to such sweeping conclusions, and we have tried to point some of them out in the discussion above.[10]

UNIONS AND THE LAW

Federal Legislation Affecting Labor Relations

Labor-management relations are subject to numerous pressures, and the process of collective bargaining is carried on within a legal framework. The growth of trade unionism in America received a tremendous impetus with the passage of the National Labor Relations Act in 1935. This law, better known as the Wagner Act, imposed new rules of conduct upon industrial management, including the requirement that management bargain in good faith with the elected representatives of workers. Other laws, such as the Norris-LaGuardia Act, which restricted the use of injunctions granted by federal courts, had a direct bearing upon the collective bargaining process. The influence of these laws has been adequately discussed in many books and articles dealing with the recent history of labor relations in the United States, and we limit our attention to the revisions of the National Labor Relations Act embodied in the Labor Management Relations Act of 1947, the Taft-Hartley law.

Many discussions of the Taft-Hartley Act have been clouded by emotionalism and partisanship. The law has become a political issue and is rarely

9. See, however, footnote 7.

10. For estimates of the average cost of vacation and holding payments for selected industries in New England see Staff Memorandum No. 9.

judged solely on its merits or lack of them. Competent, impartial students of labor relations have concluded that it is neither a slave labor law, as some have charged, nor an ideal code for guiding the conduct of the two parties in collective bargaining. It is important to examine the experience of unions in New England under the law.

Table 10–8 gives the results of collective bargaining elections by region for the period 1948–52.[11] Collective bargaining elections are held to determine which union, if any, is to be the bargaining agent of the workers in a plant or other bargaining unit. The request for an election may be made by an employee, a group of employees (usually acting through a union), or an employer who has been approached by union representatives who claim they represent a majority of workers in the bargaining unit. The National

Table 10–8. Results of Collective Bargaining Elections by Region, 1948–52

| | VALID VOTES CAST* | | PER CENT OF VALID VOTES CAST | | | |
REGION	NUMBER	PER CENT OF U.S.	A.F. OF L. UNIONS	C.I.O. UNIONS	INDE-PENDENT UNIONS	NO UNIONS
New England	67,589	11.9	20.6	38.5	19.7	21.2
Middle Atlantic	141,072	24.7	22.5	34.0	25.4	18.1
East North Central	141,453	24.8	22.3	37.8	17.6	22.3
West North Central	38,824	6.8	33.0	30.3	15.3	21.4
South Atlantic	58,956	10.3	19.1	34.5	11.8	34.6
East South Central	28,034	4.9	27.6	33.4	11.3	27.7
West South Central	32,590	5.7	29.9	31.3	10.5	28.3
Mountain	10,439	1.8	36.0	20.3	17.6	26.1
Pacific	52,004	9.1	39.0	23.4	17.6	20.0
CONTINENTAL UNITED STATES	570,961	100.0	25.0	33.9	18.3	22.8

* Five-year averages, 1948–52.
Source: National Labor Relations Board, Annual Report, 1948 through 1952

Labor Relations Board investigates and decides if an election is called for.

New England, with approximately 7.5% of the nation's nonagricultural workers, accounted for 11.9% of the valid votes cast in collective bargaining elections in the United States during the period 1948–52. Of these votes, 21.2% were for "no union." More than 38% of the votes cast in New England were for C.I.O. unions. A.F. of L. unions received the second largest number of votes, and independent unions ranked in third place. Only two regions, the Middle Atlantic and the Pacific, had a smaller percentage of no-union votes than New England during this period. It is significant that the three southern regions showed the largest percentage of such votes.[12]

11. Changes in the method of reporting the results of elections make impossible a direct statistical comparison, by regions, with an earlier period.

12. We should point out that in collective bargaining elections there is not always a choice between alternative unions or no union. The choice may be between a single union and no union.

There was considerable variation in the results of collective bargaining elections within New England, as Table 10–9 shows. Union successes were greatest in Massachusetts, followed by Connecticut and Rhode Island in that order. The proportion of no-union votes in the three northern New England states was far above the national average. Except in Maine, where the A.F. of L. obtained the largest percentage of votes, the C.I.O. shows larger percentages than the A.F. of L. or independent unions.

The results of collective bargaining elections must be interpreted with caution. A large number of no-union votes clearly indicates that unions are

Table 10–9. *Results of Collective Bargaining Elections in the New England States, 1948–52*

PER CENT OF VALID VOTES CAST*

STATE	A.F. OF L. UNIONS	C.I.O. UNIONS	INDEPENDENT UNIONS	NO UNIONS
Maine	29.0	20.4	15.0	35.6
New Hampshire	27.2	32.9	4.4	35.5
Vermont	17.5	28.7	14.2	39.6
Massachusetts	19.3	39.8	25.6	15.3
Rhode Island	17.8	40.2	13.6	28.4
Connecticut	21.4	41.3	12.9	24.4

* Five-year average, 1948–52.
Source: Ibid.

not meeting with success in their organizational efforts. A small percentage of no-union votes indicates that unions are being successful either in organizing new plants or in *retaining recognition in plants that have already been organized*. But a small percentage of no-union votes need not mean that union membership is growing. It may mean that rival unions are attempting to win members from each other. The fact that New England accounted for a large proportion of the valid votes cast in collective bargaining elections in 1951 is indicative of a high degree of union activity, but it does not necessarily mean that union membership is growing more rapidly in New England than elsewhere.

New England also had 455 union shop authorization polls in 1951 and accounted for 5.8% of all valid votes cast in such elections in the United States. Such elections are of historical interest only. Prior to the end of the fiscal year 1951, if a union desired to request a union shop clause, a referendum by secret ballot was required under the Taft-Hartley Act. About 98% of all such elections were won by the unions, and in the first amendment to the Taft-Hartley Act since its enactment in 1947 the union shop poll requirement was abolished.[13] This is a welcome amendment to the law. The union shop poll requirement was time-consuming and expensive to administer, and in view of the vote record it was a pointless requirement. Unions overwhelmingly won union shop referenda, and the decision to abolish them was a sensible one.

13. See National Labor Relations Board, *Annual Report, 1951* (Washington, 1952), *16*, 136–7, 318 ff.

The impact of federal labor legislation upon union activity is not necessarily the same in all regions. *Judged by their success in collective bargaining elections, unions in New England do not appear to have been handicapped by existing federal labor legislation.* But union leaders in New England have joined with those in other regions in claiming that the Taft-Hartley Act is inimical to their welfare. Some union spokesmen feel that their efforts to organize the substantial nonunion segment of the region's labor force have been hampered by the "free speech" clause of the Taft-Hartley Act.[14] Others claim that the law has had indirect effects upon labor relations in some New England industries.

The inability of unions to organize workers in the South, it is claimed, has perpetuated interregional differences in labor costs, and these differences influence the bargaining relationship between labor and management in New England. Unions in the New England textile industries, for example, have been unable to press for wage increases—and at times have accepted arbitrated wage cuts—because nonunion mills in the South refused to follow the lead of northern mills in setting wages after the unsuccessful southern textile strike of April 1951.[15]

It is undoubtedly true that the Taft-Hartley Act has had some effect upon the organizing activities of unions in the South. But it would be erroneous to conclude that the Taft-Hartley Act was *entirely* responsible for the failure of the southern organizing campaign launched by unions after World War II. The fact that unions have continued to meet with success in other regions, where the principle of trade unionism is more widely accepted by the community, indicates that other forces are at work to encourage or discourage the growth of trade union membership in various areas of the United States.

This should not be interpreted as a plea for the status quo in federal labor legislation. Our labor laws should be adaptable to changing needs and conditions. There is little doubt that some changes will be made in the Taft-Hartley Act. It *is* doubtful, however, that any law can be drawn up that will be completely acceptable to the extremists in either labor or management groups. Where collective bargaining is widely accepted, as it is in New England, it is unlikely that moderate changes in federal labor legislation will have much influence on the relationships between labor and management in general.

State Labor Laws in New England

On the whole, the state labor laws of New England reflect the general acceptance by the community of the principal of trade unionism. The labor

14. On this, compare the views of the Committee on the New England Economy, U.S. Government Printing Office, *The New England Economy,* July 1951.

15. For a more complete discussion see Staff Memorandum No. 10.

laws of the three southern New England states, in particular, may be classified as "protective" for unions.[16] Some states in other regions, notably the South, have laws which are restrictive on union activity. On the whole the labor laws of New England cannot generally be regarded as restrictive on union activity, although there are definite restrictions against the intimidation of workers by their employers. Employers cannot ask their employees to refrain from joining unions. The use of injunctions in labor disputes is prohibited or restricted. *In general, state labor legislation in New England has been designed to protect the organizational activities of unions in industries engaged in intrastate activities and to foster the collective bargaining process once unions have been recognized.*[17]

Good labor-management relations cannot be created by laws alone. It is true that mediation and conciliation services can be set up to encourage the voluntary settlement of disputed issues. And good labor relations will be fostered by a legal system which imposes at least a minimum obligation on both labor and management. Thus the kind of relations that evolve between the two parties in a state will be gradually reflected in the laws of that state. There are in New England some employers who have resisted the principle of collective bargaining. They continue to regard the elected representatives of their workers as intruders. But in the main employers in New England have accepted unions in principle as well as in practice. The community as a whole has accepted a set of laws which recognize the legitimate aspirations of workers and which encourage the collective bargaining process and the voluntary settlement of labor-management disputes.

LABOR-MANAGEMENT RELATIONS

Local and National Collective Bargaining

Much of the collective bargaining in New England is conducted on an area or regional basis. Shoe workers and cotton-rayon textile workers, for example, usually negotiate contracts with employers in a given area of the region. But in some more geographically dispersed industries multi-employer bargaining is on the increase. The national union has long been the center of power of the American trade union movement, and as an increasing proportion of such industries as steel, automobiles, electrical machinery, and others have been organized, bargaining has been conducted at the national level. Strikes, when they are called, are often industry wide. As a result, the Federal Government has taken a more active part in labor-

16. Frank T. deVyver, "Labor Factors in the Industrial Development of the South," *Southern Economic Journal* (October 1951), *17*, 201–2.

17. See *General Laws of Massachusetts,* Chapter 149, Sections 19–20, and State of Connecticut, *Labor Laws,* Sections 7408–9, for some typical provisions.

management relations, especially where the health and safety of the nation might be placed in jeopardy by an extended strike.[18]

One result of industry-wide bargaining is to narrow the area of control which New Englanders have over their labor-management relations. When a national union calls a strike, New England locals must adhere to national policy. There is, however, no reason to doubt that New England labor leaders are generally in accord with national union policy.

One suggested approach to the problem of industry-wide strikes is that which would "return collective bargaining to the local level." Usually such proposals would require bargaining to be restricted to individual companies and local unions.[19]

Laws designed to restrict collective bargaining to the local level would be essentially unworkable. The laws that have been proposed are based on a misconception of the structure of modern industrial society. Even if we were to assume that this approach were desirable, it is doubtful that it could be translated into practice. Such proposals as those contained in the Gwinn-Fisher and Lucas bills, for example, leave too many questions unanswered. Would the national union be abolished? Would it be illegal for two or more local unions in the same industry to call a strike at the same time? Would the same apply to two or more employers? Would unions be prohibited from presenting the same set of demands to different employers? Who would determine when local unions were in collusion? How would such determination be made?

Basically, laws designed to reduce the national union to impotency are poorly concealed attacks on the institution of trade unionism as it has developed in the United States. Attacking the institution of trade unionism as such does not encourage responsible union behavior. The problem of nationwide strikes would not be eliminated by requiring local collective bargaining. Under our present system of communications each local union or local employer would know what other local unions were doing. Under a system of free collective bargaining we could not prohibit one local from following the behavior of other locals even in the absence of centralized union decision making.

Federal policies which will minimize the impact of the industry-wide strike on the national economy should be welcomed by New Englanders as by everyone else in the nation. But it may be that the best policy is one which will require less, not more, government intervention in the collective bargaining process. Where the area of disagreement between labor and

18. One should always distinguish clearly between a strike which might jeopardize the health or safety of the people of the United States and a strike which merely causes some inconvenience. Much popular discussion of industry-wide strikes fails to make this distinction.

19. The most recent proposals along this line are contained in H. R. 7697 and H. R. 7698, submitted to Congress on May 1, 1952 by Representatives Ralph W. Gwinn of New York and O. C. Fisher of Texas, and H. R. 2545 introduced in the 83d Congress by Representative Wingate H. Lucas of Texas.

management can be narrowed by voluntary means, the resulting gains are more likely to be permanent.

Where the national health or safety would truly be jeopardized by an industry-wide strike, government action, including temporary seizure and continued operation of the industry, may be necessary. Even in such cases the two parties should be encouraged to arrive at an eventual settlement by voluntary means. Where this can be done the likelihood of another strike over the same issues at some future time will be reduced.

In spite of the influence of industry-wide strikes, New England's recent strike record is a good one. But statistics alone cannot tell the story of labor-management relations in the region. Statistics can tell us that there are relatively fewer strikes in New England than in some other regions, but they cannot tell us *why* this is true. We have already indicated that the maturity of labor-management relations in New England is partly responsible for its favorable strike record. The composition of New England industry is also a contributing factor. For example, there are no coal mines in the region to be affected by strikes in this industry. But these are broad generalizations, and we will have to turn to specific cases to get at basic causes.

The Causes of Industrial Peace

Four of the National Planning Association's case studies on The Causes of Industrial Peace under Collective Bargaining deal with New England firms and the unions with which they have agreements. The results are reported in detail in the series mentioned above.[20] We summarize their findings briefly because we believe they are duplicated in other collective bargaining situations in New England. The following are typical of the causes which were given credit for outstandingly good labor-management relations in these and the other cases studied:[21]

1. Management has fully accepted the principle of collective bargaining and the institution of trade unionism.

2. The unions fully accept private ownership and operation of the industry.

3. The unions are strong, responsible, and democratic.

4. There is mutual trust between unions and management.

20. Douglas McGregor and Joseph N. Scanlon, *The Dewey and Almy Chemical Company and the International Chemical Workers Union,* Case Study No. 3; Charles A. Myers and George P. Shultz, *Nashua Gummed and Coated Paper Company and Seven AFL Unions,* Case Study No. 7; George P. Shultz and Robert P. Crisara, *The Lapointe Machine Tool Company and United Steelworkers of America,* Case Study No. 10; and George S. Paul, *American Velvet Company and Textile Workers Union of America,* Case Study No. 11, National Planning Association, Causes of Industrial Peace under Collective Bargaining series, Washington, September 1948–.

21. *Ibid.*

5. The company does not interfere in the unions' internal affairs nor does it seek to alienate the workers' allegiance to their union.

6. There are no serious ideological incompatibilities.

7. Neither party has adopted a legalistic approach to the problems of collective bargaining.

8. Collective bargaining negotiations are "problem centered." They deal with concrete problems, not abstract principles.

9. There are effective two-way communication channels between the management and the union.

10. There is widespread union-management consultation.

Where these conditions have been met, good labor-management relations are almost bound to follow. But it would be erroneous to imply that such relationships exist between all New England companies and the unions with which they bargain. Labor-management relationships in New England run the entire gamut from firms such as those mentioned above, who have established a sound, workable relationship, to those which continue to regard the union as an intruder even though they may reluctantly recognize it. They recognize the union because the alternative is protracted and costly labor strife.

Some New England firms have pioneered in developing advanced methods of industrial relations. *The region needs more firms of the exceptional type in which management goes out of its way to develop effective cooperation with the work force.* There is probably no single plan that can be applied to every labor-management situation because basic economic conditions differ from industry to industry and even from firm to firm within the same industry. In many cases, however, management is inclined to blame the union for all of its labor problems. But it takes two parties to make a labor dispute or to create a bad labor-management situation.

In several of the cases discussed in the Causes of Industrial Peace series, labor-management relations had reached a low ebb. Then management reviewed its situation and decided to adopt a new approach. In most cases the management felt it was experimenting, but the situation was so bad there was little or nothing to lose. In these cases the results were successful, probably beyond the original expectations of workers or employers. Now they are held up as models for others to emulate.

If there is a lack of harmonious relations in a firm perhaps a little self-examination is needed. Is management doing all it can to improve communications between the workers, or their representatives, and themselves? Has it solicited suggestions from the workers? Or even more basically, has it recognized that workers are human beings and wish to be treated as such? There are many ways whereby productivity in a plant can be increased by the development of effective labor-management cooperation. If an intelligent method of sharing the gains from increased productivity can be devised the resulting advantages to the firm are obvious.

A satisfied work force, in which the workers feel a sense of participation, can lead to direct savings in production costs. If the rate of turnover is reduced, cost savings will follow. Employee suggestions can improve efficiency in many ways. Absenteeism, tardiness, and defective or shoddy workmanship can all be reduced by eliciting worker cooperation, especially if the worker knows that he stands to gain from the reduction in costs and increases in productivity.

In many cases management may not be aware that its relations with labor could stand improvement. We urge New England management to take stock of its present relations with the work force. And we recommend a careful study of the cases reported in the Causes of Industrial Peace series. These cover firms in a wide variety of industries and localities. They may contain clues to the solution of problems now troubling the managements of some New England firms. If over-all labor-management relations in New England can be improved, the region's competitive position will be strengthened; workers and management alike will benefit from lower production costs and increases in productivity.

In considering the role played by the trade union in achieving labor peace, we must distinguish between union *recognition* and union *acceptance.* Union recognition, where a majority of the workers in a bargaining unit have voted to be represented by a union, is required by law. But union acceptance is something that can only grow from within. *In the final analysis, good labor relations cannot be legislated. Good labor relations must evolve through the development of mutual trust, respect, and responsibility.*

A large proportion of the industrial workers in New England and in other regions of the nation have indicated their preference for collective bargaining through trade unions, but there are examples of good labor relations in the absence of a union. And there are cases where the union has been recognized but not accepted. Where unions have been truly recognized and accepted, we usually find labor peace and the results which labor peace engenders. In the cases of recognition without real acceptance, the two parties engage in endless recrimination and frequently resort to tests of economic strength to settle issues which could easily be resolved over the bargaining table if the basic condition of union acceptance were achieved.

Labor Relations under Profit-sharing Plans

One device adopted by some managements, to achieve labor peace and to provide incentives for workers to increase their productivity by sharing in the resulting gains, is some form of profit-sharing plan. Profit-sharing programs operate with or without union participation. About 32% of the profit-sharing plans reported in the most recent issue of the *Profit*

Sharing Manual are operated by companies which have recognized unions, and, in view of the good relationship that exists in these cases, have accepted the union.[22] A total of 41 New England companies were members of the Council of Profit Sharing Industries in 1951. The geographic distribution of New England memberships is shown in Table 10-10.

Table 10-10. New England Memberships in the Council of Profit Sharing Industries, 1951

STATE	NUMBER OF FIRMS
Connecticut	17
Massachusetts	20
Rhode Island	2
New Hampshire	2
	—
NEW ENGLAND	41

Source: Council of Profit Sharing Industries, *Revised Profit Sharing Manual,* 1951

Profit sharing is not, of course, a foolproof method of achieving industrial peace and sound labor-management relations. Some companies try it and later discard their programs. In the main, however, those who participate in profit-sharing programs become enthusiasts. Where such programs work, they seem to work well. The number of firms adopting profit-sharing plans is growing, but they are still a small minority in both New England and the nation.

Programs of union-management cooperation must be instituted from within the firm. They must have the wholehearted support of both labor and management to be successful.[23] We make no predictions about the future of profit sharing and other programs of labor-management cooperation—such as the "Scanlon Plan" for increasing the returns to workers by increasing productivity—in New England.[24] *But profit sharing and other forms of labor-management cooperation have made their contribution to sound, workable labor-management relations in a number of New England firms.* There is no single avenue to labor peace and increased productivity. What will work well with one company or one union may not work at all in other situations. But in all situations labor and management should work toward the twin goals of labor peace and rising productivity with all the participants in the production process sharing in the gains. Whatever furthers this goal furthers the economic development of New England.

22. Council of Profit Sharing Industries, *Revised Profit Sharing Manual,* 1951. Not all companies with profit-sharing plans are members of the Council, so that no accurate estimate of the total number of such plans in operation in the United States can be made.

23. For an example of a successful profit-sharing plan in New England see George S. Paul, *American Velvet Company and Textile Workers Union of America, op. cit.*

24. For a discussion of a case where the Scanlon Plan is employed see George P. Shultz and Robert P. Crisara, *The Lapointe Machine Tool Company and United Steelworkers of America, op. cit.*

CONCLUSIONS AND RECOMMENDATIONS

1. The proportion of workers who are union members is about the same in New England as it is in the nation as a whole. Massachusetts and Rhode Island, however, are more heavily organized than the average state in the nation.

2. New England has had a favorable strike record in recent years; with 7.5% of the nation's nonagricultural workers it accounted for 4.2% of man-days lost due to strikes over the period 1947–51. In part this is a reflection of mature labor-management relations, and in part it is due to the industrial structure of the region.

3. It is difficult to generalize broadly about fringe-benefit payments. In some industries, such as the paper industry, New England unions have won liberal vacation provisions but relatively few holidays. In others, such as nonelectrical machinery, the reverse is true. In general, however, it appears that fringe-benefit provisions in New England labor-management agreements roughly parallel those in the remainder of the country.

4. Few contracts in this region have provisions that could be regarded as restrictive on technological change. Our study of a large sample of New England agreements which provide for union review of work assignments indicated that, except for approximately one-third of the textile contracts, few had provisions that restrict management's right to make whatever changes it desires. A substantial number of New England contracts pledge the cooperation of the union in furthering technological improvements. About 60% of the workers in our sample study were covered by agreements which provided that the union participate in setting new wage rates after a technological change had been made.

5. The strength of unions in New England does not appear to have been impaired by the passage of the Taft-Hartley Act. Unions, however, stand for the repeal of the law since they claim that it has retarded their organizational activities in other regions, and therefore has indirectly influenced labor relations in New England. It is unlikely that small changes in the law will materially influence the future course of labor-management relations in New England.

6. While recognizing that in some cases there are advantages in local negotiations, we are opposed to proposed legislation which would limit the scope of collective bargaining to the local level. The laws as proposed thus far would be essentially unworkable in a modern industrial society. Rather than leading to more industrial peace and better labor-management relations they might lead to a deterioration of the sound relationships that have evolved in many industries.

7. Most state labor laws in the region are essentially protective for unions. While a few state laws, especially in northern New England, cannot be

regarded as protective, none can be considered generally restrictive on union activity.

8. Mature labor-management relations in New England are the result of long experience with collective bargaining. The region has a long history of successful labor-management relations under trade unionism which, in many instances, predates the Wagner Act. Labor laws and labor relations in New England are the product of a mature industrial society. There are cases where labor relations are far from good, but in the main New England has in recent years enjoyed a high degree of labor peace based upon the development of mutual respect and confidence between the two parties in collective bargaining.

9. There are cases in New England where exceptionally poor labor-management relations have been radically altered when the two parties saw that it was to their mutual advantage to adopt a plan that would increase productivity with all concerned sharing in the gains. Some of these have been discussed in the preceding pages. Where there is still need for improvement in labor-management relations, we urge the companies and unions involved to study these cases. They may well serve as a guide for the development of a plan which will lead to an amicable settlement of existing differences. If present areas of disagreement can be gradually narrowed, New England will look forward to further improvement in its already good record of labor-management relations.

SELECTED REFERENCES

1. Commonwealth of Massachusetts, *Annual Report on the Statistics of Labor,* Vol. *78,* Pt. 1, 1951.
2. ———— "Labor Laws," Chapters 5, 23, 149, and 167 of the *General Laws of Massachusetts.*
3. Council of Profit Sharing Industries, *Revised Profit Sharing Manual,* 1951.
4. National Labor Relations Board, *Annual Report,* 1948 through 1952.
5. National Planning Association, Causes of Industrial Peace under Collective Bargaining series, Washington, September 1948–.

   McGregor, Douglas, and Scanlon, Joseph N., *The Dewey and Almy Chemical Company and the International Chemical Workers Union,* Case Study No. 3.

   Myers, Charles A., and Shultz, George P., *Nashua Gummed and Coated Paper Company and Seven AFL Unions,* Case Study No. 7.

   Paul, George S., *American Velvet Company and Textile Workers Union of America,* Case Study No. 11.

   Shultz, George P., and Crisara, Robert P., *The Lapointe Machine Tool Company and United Steelworkers of America,* Case Study No. 10.
6. State of Connecticut, *Labor Laws* (revised to July 1, 1949).
7. U.S. Department of Labor, "Mobilizing Labor for Defense," *Labor Yearbook,* Vol. *1.*
8. ———— Bureau of Labor Statistics, "Analysis of Work Stoppages," *Annual Reports,* 1935–39 and 1947–51.

Dissenting Opinion by Committee Member

The report properly presents the relatively mature state of union-management relations in New England. But there are individual companies which still campaign actively against workers joining unions, thereby utilizing their economic power to reinforce their announced distaste for collective bargaining. They are singular in New England but common in such regions as the South. Trade unionists have urged the repeal of those sections of the Taft-Hartley Act which have unloosened this economic power to frighten workers from freely joining unions. The present members of the National Labor Relations Board are broadening the opportunities for employers to engage in such anti-union intimidation. This condition must be corrected if we are not to plunge back into the days before the Wagner Act when the right to union membership could only be established through strike action.

While union-management relations at the plant level are relatively stable in the area, employers, particularly in the textile industry, are not generally prepared to consider with unions common industrial problems. Such cooperative relations found in other regions are still foreign to the pattern of collective bargaining in New England. As a result it has been impossible to obtain joint consideration by the textile employers of proposals for improving the competitive position of mills.

The authors of the report labored under the handicap of trying to summarize conditions of employment and policy attitudes in terms of the provisions in union agreements. It is a well-known fact that benefits frequently exceed those actually recorded in contracts.

As for the attitudes toward job changes, the report tends to judge them in terms of the specific contract sections dealing with the subject. A fairer appraisal would relate the general grievance provision as well to these changes, since in most industries grievance procedures prove sufficient to allow for the solution of such questions as they affect complements of men, production rates, and assignments. To provide for more complex situations such as are found in the textile industry, the contracts in the latter case deal separately with routine, technological and other types of job changes. As a result the simplified analysis contained in the report inadequately covers the subject since it focuses solely on the technological changes. The writer believes that the methods evolved in the textile industry result in a balanced accommodation of interests without interfering with technological and managerial advances.

VICTOR J. CANZANO

11

The Financial Resources of
New England and Their Use

*Drafted by Edward K. Smith under the direction
of Arthur A. Bright, Jr.*

INTRODUCTION

New England possesses large financial resources that are available for the use
of its citizens and business enterprises. The resources stem primarily from
the region's highly developed financial institutions and from its above-
average personal incomes and savings. As in most areas, however, there are
charges that the availability of capital and credit in New England is inadequate for the economic development of the region and that the operation of
its financial system is discouraging to investment. There are also hot denials
of these charges.

In this report we shall summarize and appraise the financial resources of
New England and their use, in an effort to determine which of the various
conflicting claims are valid. In addition, we shall try to place the problem of
regional investment in the wider context of national financial policy, especially
in relation to new and small firms. Most of the problem areas in New England's financial markets are not limited to this region but are nationwide.

New England has pioneered in the past in the development of such great
financial institutions as insurance companies, savings banks, and mutual investment funds. It is in the front ranks at present in establishing venture-
capital institutions and industrial development corporations. In the future, it
should continue to be a leader in developing new kinds of organizations and
procedures to cope with the problems of saving and investment in a dynamic
economy, both for its own welfare as it meets the problems of an older industrial economy in transition and for the national good.

This report considers the resources and operations of both private and
governmental institutions for capital and credit, their uses and limitations,
and some possible changes in their operations. Institutional and legal barriers
in the money market are discussed briefly, as are proposed changes designed
to increase the effectiveness of saver-investor relationships. Among the more
important changes which have been suggested, those designed to improve the
long-term credit and equity position of smaller businesses are given special
attention, including the proposals for a capital bank and changes in federal
tax laws. We are not, however, exclusively concerned with small business.
All businesses, whatever their size, have their financial requirements, and
they are all important to New England's future.

We have approached the financial problems of New England within the framework of the present banking and financial system. A consideration of proposals for far-reaching changes in the structure of the nation's banking system would be beyond the scope of this report, regardless of their merits. The recommendations advanced here are for actions which we feel are desirable and possible and which can be approached at least in part on a regional basis.

FINANCIAL RESOURCES IN NEW ENGLAND

Institutional Resources

New England contains an unusually large number and variety of financial institutions. It is one of the regions in the United States best supplied with banks. At the end of 1950 New England had 518 commercial banks, 342 mutual savings institutions, 279 cooperative banks and building and loan associations, 56 federal savings and loan institutions, and 13 other types of financial institutions, in addition to numerous credit unions and small loan companies. While these are concentrated most heavily in the more populous southern states of the region, the northern states are also well covered.

Some of the largest insurance companies in the nation have their headquarters in New England, and the region's investment trusts and mutual funds include the largest. These institutions draw funds into the area from all over the country. In every New England state there are local and state industrial foundations or development corporations which provide funds for industrial development. As in all well-developed industrial areas, the normal channels of trade credit and other special types of credit institutions are used extensively.

These private institutions constitute a vast reservoir of funds available for the region's economic development. They cover virtually the entire range of types of credit and investment, as well as every variation in geographical scope from the local community to the entire nation. Some idea of the size of these resources is given in Table 11–1 for certain major types of financial institutions. New England's proportion of the nation's financial assets is far larger than its proportion of population or income for every one of the listed categories except commercial banks: the heavy concentration of deposits in New York City and the greater use of savings institutions in New England inevitably pull down the New England proportion of commercial bank deposits. In addition to their services to industry, agriculture, and other types of economic activity, the financial institutions are of considerable direct economic importance to New England. They employ more persons in the region than several of the important manufacturing industries. An estimate by the Federal Reserve Bank of Boston placed employment by New England's financial institutions in 1946 at nearly 70,000. Boston has been traditionally known as one of the nation's important banking and insurance centers, while

Connecticut, Massachusetts, and Vermont have long been considered "insurance" states.

Table 11–1. *Financial Resources of Selected Types of Institutions in New England and the United States, 1951 (in billions of dollars)*

	NEW ENGLAND	UNITED STATES	NEW ENGLAND PER CENT OF UNITED STATES
Commercial banks	$ 8.8	$164.8	5.4
Savings institutions	7.8	39.3	20.0
Insurance companies:			
Life	13.8	68.3	20.0
Other	2.9	16.7	17.2
Investment trusts	1.5	4.1	36.0
TOTAL	$34.8	$293.2	12.0

Sources: Federal Deposit Insurance Corporation, Home Loan Bank Board, *Spectator Year Book,* and estimates by the Committee of New England and Federal Reserve Bank of Boston

New England is not, of course, the financial center of the nation. New York holds that distinction. But New England's great resources can make a significant contribution to its future prosperity, *providing* the extent and quality of investment opportunities in New England can put the available funds to work there. New England's greatest financial problem at present is not the possibility of a capital and credit shortage, but rather the underutilization of available funds. There is evidence that there has been a significant financial outflow in the past. Where they exist, shortages of funds are usually restricted to certain kinds of borrowers. Such shortages are more likely to be national than regional problems. We shall discuss these specific problems later.

Individual Resources

In addition to the resources of financial institutions in an area, the savings of its citizens are available for investment. To be sure, most individual savings flow into savings and checking accounts in banks, insurance, savings bonds, or other financial institutions. The recent tendency has been toward greater security of investment, and the bulk of personal savings are not directly invested by the savers themselves. The amounts which are available to financial institutions depend heavily, however, on the levels of income and savings in the area. Moreover, direct investment by individuals remains a major source of financing for new and small businesses.

Personal Income. New England's per capita income is above the national average, as it has always been. The relative excess is not so great as it was before World War II, however, and there are important variations within the region.

Table 11–2 shows both the relative levels of per capita income in the New England states and in other regions, and the changes that have occurred since

1929. In all areas there have been large increases in absolute amounts since 1940. The national figure rose from $575 per person in that year to $1,584 in 1951. The New England increase over the same period was from $724 to $1,715. New England held most of its absolute advantage, but its percentage excess shrank sharply.

Table 11–2. *Differentials in Per Capita Income Payments, New England States and Other Regions, 1929–51 (per cent of national per capita income)*

	1929	1940	1945	1948	1951
NEW ENGLAND	123	126	110	106	108
Maine	83	87	88	86	82
New Hampshire	96	98	94	92	91
Vermont	88	91	87	87	83
Massachusetts	132	133	112	106	110
Rhode Island	125	125	111	105	107
Connecticut	135	144	125	120	126
Middle East	136	131	120	116	115
Southeast	51	56	67	67	68
Southwest	68	70	80	82	86
Central	106	105	105	110	108
Northwest	79	79	96	103	95
Far West	127	130	120	115	118

Source: U.S. Department of Commerce, Office of Business Economics

The big changes occurred during the war years, when there was major readjustment in the national economy. The industrial states of New England, the Middle East, and the Far West did not move ahead as fast as the agricultural areas and the newly industrialized states. In general, the low-income regions improved their position, while the high-income areas lost ground. There has been a substantial leveling effect on the geographical distribution of income. While these changes affect the financial resources of a region but slowly, the changes wrought by the war may reduce somewhat New England's long-term advantages over most other regions in the future availability of capital and credit.

The relative downward movement for New England's per capita income stopped in 1948. There was some recovery of position in the region's three southern states by 1951. The three northern states, which had maintained their positions fairly well since 1929, however, lost some ground after 1948. It is apparent that whatever advantage New England retains in its individual financial resources depends most heavily on the continuance of above-average incomes in Connecticut, Massachusetts and Rhode Island.

There were many reasons for New England's rate of growth in per capita income during the war years being slower than the national rate. For the most part, they stemmed from the economic structure of the region and the specific effects of wartime changes. The same forces produced similar declines in relative per capita income in some other regions, as well as relative increases in still others. We may sketch briefly the salient features of the change:

1. New England is predominantly a manufacturing area, and manufacturing is a producer of high income. The region's proportion of income drawn from manufacturing is far higher than the national percentage (see Table 11-3). In 1951 each of the six states in the region received a higher proportion of income payments from manufacturing than did the nation as a whole. New England did not have as much opportunity to shift its resources into manufacturing during World War II, however, as did some other regions. Their gains indicated rather that they were catching up with New England than that New England was falling behind.

Table 11–3. Sources of Income Payments, United States and New England States, 1940 and 1951
(per cent of total income payments)

STATE	AGRICUL-TURE		GOVERN-MENT		MANUFAC-TURING		TRADE AND SERVICE		ALL OTHER	
	1940	1951	1940	1951	1940	1951	1940	1951	1940	1951
UNITED STATES	7.2	7.6	14.5	15.3	20.3	23.9	25.5	25.9	32.5	27.3
NEW ENGLAND	2.0	1.7	13.7	14.8	26.7	32.6	23.4	24.4	34.2	26.5
Maine	6.0	3.7	16.0	17.1	23.3	28.0	23.5	23.7	31.2	27.5
New Hampshire	2.7	3.0	14.8	15.9	26.8	32.5	23.4	24.8	32.3	23.8
Vermont	10.4	9.2	13.8	14.1	18.8	25.2	23.4	24.0	33.6	27.5
Massachusetts	1.1	1.0	14.9	16.3	23.8	30.2	24.7	25.7	35.5	26.8
Rhode Island	.8	.6	15.3	17.1	30.6	34.7	21.8	23.3	31.5	24.3
Connecticut	2.0	1.6	9.5	10.0	34.0	39.2	21.2	22.3	33.3	26.9

Source: Department of Commerce, Office of Business Economics

2. Except for Vermont, the New England states draw a smaller proportion of their income from agriculture than does the United States as a whole. Agriculture showed a large relative increase in income during the war period. That expansion aided the three northern states in the region to maintain their position in per capita income until the end of the war. The farm states and regions in the rest of the country benefited considerably from the more favorable income position of agriculture.

3. The specific combination of industries in New England did not lend itself to keeping pace with the national increase in per capita income. There was not the expansion in finance, insurance, and real estate, for example, that there was in the production of chemicals and primary metals. The region's heavy concentration in textiles and shoes tended to slow the rate of expansion. In general, New England had below-average employment in those industries which experienced the largest gains in income, and above-average employment in those which had the smallest gains in income.

4. There was a higher wartime rate of capital investment in low-income regions than in the old high-income regions such as New England. In part this was because of a deliberate effort to spread production facilities around the country in order to maximize national security and take better advantage of the nation's human and natural resources. In part it was the result of the differential income changes to which it also contributed.

5. New England derives a larger proportion of its income from property

than any other region, and property income increased relatively less than that from any other source. Property income has declined considerably in its relative importance, both to the nation and to New England, as interest rates have fallen, rents have been held down by government controls, and dividends have constituted a smaller proportion than usual of corporate earnings.

In view of these basic conditions it is not surprising that New England's per capita income has risen less since 1940 than that in any other region. The region's higher than average income is still solidly based upon its manufacturing industry, however, and it should continue to retain most or all of its present advantage.

The impact of New England's changed position in per capita income on the capital and credit structure of the region is not easy to describe precisely. As we have noted, part of the region's income advantage over most other regions has been lost but part still remains. Presumably the geographical relationships in per capita income after taxes are essentially the same as those for income before taxes. Inevitably, the supply of savings in other regions has increased relatively faster than in New England. Those savings simplify the capital and credit problems in the rapidly developing parts of the country to some extent, but New England has maintained its absolute advantage in both income and accumulated stock of capital. Moreover, changes in income are not the only element in the adequacy of a financial system. Changes in investment opportunities and the demand for funds are also important, as are the institutional arrangements for channeling available funds into profitable uses. All things considered, it would appear that the broad economic changes of recent years have not decreased the supply of funds relative to demand in New England and that the region's financial system has maintained its strength.

A final point deserves mention in connection with the relationship between incomes and investable funds. The distribution of income among income classes is an important determinant of savings. The largest part of nonbusiness savings which become available for direct investment comes from the upper-income groups. In New England, Massachusetts, Connecticut, and Rhode Island have relatively more individuals in the high-income brackets than most other states. In 1945, for example, 0.49% of the total individual federal income tax returns had adjusted gross incomes of $20,000 or more. The comparable percentages for the New England states were Connecticut .60, Massachusetts .56, Rhode Island .55, Maine .29, New Hampshire .28, and Vermont .27. In addition, New England had 13% of the taxable fiduciary returns (for estates and trusts) during that year, with 12.7% of the income declared under those returns. New Englanders received 15.9% of the nation's fiduciary income from dividends and interest in 1945.

The census estimates of income distribution in 1950 have not been completed at this writing for all the New England states. Of the ten most populous states, however, Massachusetts ranks sixth in median income for all families and unrelated individuals. Its income distribution in the upper and lower brackets is favorable to savings, for it ranks sixth highest in the percentage of families with incomes over $5,000 and sixth lowest in the percentage of families with incomes under $2,000. Connecticut and Rhode Island should also compare favorably with the wealthier states when the census study is completed.

Liquid Savings. New England's generally higher than average incomes and its favorable income distribution have contributed in the past to a large volume of personal savings in the region. The same conditions continue to offer a favorable savings outlook for New England. Personal savings have increased greatly in all parts of the country during the past decade, though the peak in savings was reached during the war years.

New England has shared in the recent national increase in personal savings and has, in fact, far outstripped the nation as a whole in its accumulated per capita savings. Table 11–4 summarizes the cumulative New England and United States records for the principal types of liquid savings during recent years. By the end of 1950 New Englanders had personal liquid savings of more than $17 billion. Their per capita total for these categories was almost 50% larger than the comparable national figure. They have maintained their absolute advantage in current savings over the residents of the rest of the country, though the recent rate of increase has been somewhat smaller in New England because of the region's higher starting point. The tabulation does not include, however, additional liquid savings available in the form of cash, deposits in credit unions and the like, for which data are not available.

Table 11–4. Accumulated Per Capita Personal Savings, by Type, New England and the United States, 1948–51 (estimates as of December 31)

TYPE OF SAVING	1948		1950		1951	
	NEW ENGLAND	UNITED STATES	NEW ENGLAND	UNITED STATES	NEW ENGLAND	UNITED STATES
Mutual savings deposits	$582	$126	$592	$132	$609	$136
U. S. savings bonds	469	362	503	381	504	375
Life insurance equities	382	323	415	355	432	372
Commercial bank time deposits	213	246	203	241	205	249
Savings and loan shares	107	75	123	92	135	105
Postal savings deposits	9	23	8	19	8	18
TOTALS*	$1,762	$1,154	$1,844	$1,221	$1,893	$1,254

* Details may not add to totals due to rounding.
Source: Federal Reserve Bank of Boston

The most popular form of liquid savings in New England is mutual savings bank deposits. In the rest of the United States federal savings bonds are the leading choice. Both savings bonds and life insurance equities are relatively more important in the rest of the country than in New England, though the per capita amounts are higher in New England. The New England preference for savings deposits in savings banks rather than commercial banks is in part due to their higher interest rates and in part to historical influence and tradition.

The record of personal savings, of course, is closely related to the record of per capita incomes and the resources of financial institutions. Each is really just one part of the same thing. In each respect, however, New England rates well in comparison with the country as a whole. The momentum of many decades of high industrial activity and financial strength is serving the region well during its present period of transition.

Stock Ownership. Stock ownership is another important part element in the financial resources of a region. Whether stocks are held by individuals or organizations, they are indicative of accumulated wealth and of money potentially available for new investment.

A recent Brookings Institution study estimates that New England has 11.8% of the nation's shareholders and 9.2% of the number of shares of common and preferred stocks of publicly held companies.[1] Despite its position as eighth in population among the nation's nine census regions, New England is third in number of shareholders and fifth in number of shares. Massachusetts is fifth among the 48 states in both respects, and Connecticut also ranks high. The concentration of equity ownership and other financial resources in the other northeastern states provides an important potential addition to New England's own large reservoir of investable funds.

Governmental Resources

In addition to the financial resources of private institutions and individuals in the region, New England like other regions has access to various governmental programs of direct loans or loan guarantees. While many of the loan programs are restricted to agriculture and residential building, some other programs have been instituted to increase the effectiveness of financial institutions. Our concern here is with sources of credit for businesses.

The most important business-loan programs authorized by the Federal Government are those of the Reconstruction Finance Corporation and the Federal Reserve banks. The Veterans' Administration also conducts a program of business loans to veterans. It is only a small part of the total business lending under federal programs, however. The VA loans are usually equipment loans to small owner-operated businesses.

By far the largest governmental lender to business is the Reconstruction Finance Corporation. It was initially established in 1932, and its scope and authority were greatly expanded during the thirties. Its resources are limited

1. Lewis H. Kimmel, *Share Ownership in the United States,* Brookings Institution (Washington, 1952), p. 80. These figures have been adjusted for beneficial owners, i.e., shares registered in the names of nominees, brokers, and dealers have been credited to the state of the owner of the equity.

only by Congress, and they are, of course, available to New England businesses that are unable to obtain financing from private sources. The R.F.C. authorized business loans in excess of $164,000,000 in New England during the period January 1948 through March 1952. That amount was about 5.2% of the comparable United States total of new loan authorizations. Regional totals are not available for the entire period of R.F.C. operations. As of March 1952 more than $25,500,000 in R.F.C. loans was outstanding in New England.[2]

The Federal Reserve banks were given authority by Congress in 1934 to make or guarantee direct loans to businesses as working capital under Section 13(b) of the Federal Reserve Act. The banks initially loaned Treasury money, but since 1947 new loans have been made directly by the banks from their own funds. The majority of 13(b) lending was done before 1940. Since 1937 lending by the Federal Reserve banks to business has tapered off. The experience in New England has been the same in this respect as in the nation. Under Section 13(b) the Federal Reserve Bank of Boston approved loans totaling more than $23,000,000 during the period 1934–51. That amount was about 3.4% of such loans approved in the United States.

THE OPERATION OF TRADITIONAL SOURCES OF CAPITAL AND CREDIT IN NEW ENGLAND

While it is evident that New England has great financial resources at hand, their mere presence is not in itself sufficient evidence of the satisfactory operation of the region's financial system. Several important questions must be answered. Can New England businessmen get the money they need? Are some types of businesses better able to get funds than others? Is the demand for money within the region sufficient to use that share of resources which would normally be available? Are there institutional and legal barriers to the most effective operation of the financial system? In this and the following sections we shall try to answer these questions.

Short-term Loans

Adequacy of capital and credit is an elusive concept. The various demands for money must be separated to avoid confusion. First of all one must distinguish between the demands for equity capital and for loans. Many of the complaints of inadequate credit arise from businessmen, especially those owning small businesses, who really need permanent capital but are unable or unwilling to obtain money through equity financing. In addition, there are always the problems associated with attempting to borrow short-term funds for long-term uses.

2. From a special tabulation for the Committee of New England, by the Reports Division, Office of the Controller, Reconstruction Finance Corporation, Washington, July 1952.

On the whole, it appears that the short-term credit requirements of business are being met satisfactorily in New England. In all the studies of New England small-business finance, a relatively small proportion of companies expresses dissatisfaction with short-term sources of credit or reports an inability to obtain needed short-term funds. Moreover, the complaints of would-be borrowers do not take into consideration whether the credit is "deserved." Typically, though not always, the claims of inadequacy come from companies with poor profit records or some other indication of greater than average credit risk.

A questionnaire survey conducted by the Committee of New England among the members of the Smaller Business Association of New England early in 1952 indicated that 94% of the companies which tried to raise short-term funds outside the company after 1945 were able to obtain all or part of the funds they sought.[3] Most of them received all that they asked for. The commercial banks were overwhelmingly the major source of such credit.

Twenty per cent of the Smaller Business Association respondents expressed the opinion that the customary sources of short-term credit were not meeting the needs of New England small business adequately, but the percentage was sharply higher for the companies that had not been able to obtain all funds sought, and lower for those whose personal needs had been satisfied. In general, a small businessman's own borrowing experience strongly colors his attitude toward the financial system, and his profit record strongly affects his borrowing experience.

A similar study in the Pioneer Valley area of Western Massachusetts in 1950 produced essentially the same conclusions.[4] Only six of the 92 companies interviewed reported unsatisfied requirements for short-term loans, and all of them had poor financial records. Another survey of credit needs by the National Association of Manufacturers in 1950 showed the same general situation with respect to unsatisfied credit needs. That study, which is the only one permitting comparisons between New England and the rest of the country, indicated that the availability of credit in New England has been somewhat greater than in the nation as a whole.[5]

All these studies, as well as other available evidence, indicate that the inability to obtain short-term credit is a special problem rather than a general one. There is no doubt that some small companies which "deserve" credit are unable to obtain it, though such cases are relatively few. The best

3. For full details on the findings from the answers of 156 companies, see our Staff Memorandum No. 6, *The Financing of Small Business in New England: Opinions of Members of the Smaller Business Association of New England,* July 1952.

4. Federal Reserve Bank of Boston, "The Financial Needs of Small Manufacturers in Pioneer Valley," *Monthly Review,* March 1951.

5. For details on the New England–United States findings for all topics covered by the study, see Staff Memorandum No. 7, *The Financing of Small Business in New England: Findings of the National Association of Manufacturers,* August 1952.

approach to reducing the number still further would appear to be through greater lender-borrower understanding and cooperation on a local or state-wide basis.

Some small-business borrowers do not understand the responsibility of banks to their depositors and the nature of bank lending. They do not know what a bank requires in the way of information about a firm and its principals, or how to present their case for a loan. Some bankers, on the other hand, do not fully recognize their responsibility to the community and their key role in local economic progress. They may approach lending in a mechanical fashion, not probing beneath the superficial appearances. They may be prejudiced against new ventures and not take the trouble to investigate an application fully. Where such situations exist, there is bound to be conflict. One of the changes desired by small businessmen in the lending policies of financial institutions, as found in the Committee's survey of small-business financing, is a "greater recognition of the intangibles" in the borrower-lender relationship and less reliance on the more mechanical means of determining credit worthiness. This is, for the most part, a problem of "understanding."

It would seem desirable for the various state bankers' associations and clearinghouses in New England to take the initiative in bringing together groups of bankers and small businessmen in "clinics" for mutual education and strengthened relations. It would also appear worthwhile for the banks to check periodically on their past lending judgment by examining the subsequent experience of the applicants to whom loans were refused.

We have stressed small business in this consideration of short-term loans, since most large firms find it easier to obtain adequate credit of this type. The larger firms usually are better established, have smoother working arrangements with their banks and suppliers, and often have sounder capitalization. For them short-term credit is rarely an important problem.

Long-term Credit and Equity Financing

It is in the long-term credit and equity-capital financing that the major problems arise for the new and small firms. As it is essential to New England's prosperity and growth that new and small businesses be encouraged, this topic is the central one in considering the adequacy of New England's financial system. Availability of funds is, of course, only one phase of small-business success, and it is far less important than the quality of small-business management. Nevertheless, the improved mobilization of funds for small business is one approach to improving the position of small business in the region.[6]

Large and well-established firms, especially those that are "national"

6. See our report No. 14, "New England's Industrial Management," for a discussion of small-business management problems in New England.

companies, are not now experiencing any important shortage of funds of any type. The large company usually has well-established lines of credit, is able to borrow from large city banks or insurance companies, and can sell new stock and bond issues. Its credit from suppliers is generally more than sufficient. In addition, it normally has substantial funds available from its earnings and depreciation allowances, and it may not have to go to the money market at all. Indeed, the major financing problem of the typical large business is not *whether* it can get funds but *which* of many alternative forms of fund raising it should use to minimize costs.

The average small firm is in a quite different position. While it may have short-term credit arrangements with a local bank and established credit arrangements with suppliers, its ability to obtain long-term credit and capital is often severely restricted. It can rarely, if ever, resort to bond issues. Few investors, other than relatives or personal friends of the principals, are normally willing to purchase its stock or buy a partnership interest.[7] The public flotation of securities is also expensive. It may be difficult for the business to accumulate funds internally, because its profits are typically small and often erratic. Long-term loans from banks and other financial institutions may be difficult to obtain partly because of legal or other restrictions, partly because of risk, and partly because smaller loans may not be profitable.

For the new firm each of these difficulties is multiplied in intensity. It may earn no profits for several years, and its depreciation reserves build up slowly. The risky nature of investment, especially in the more competitive industries, makes equity financing unusually difficult. As a substitute for equity funds, the new companies generally turn to long-term credit. Those concerns which are based on the production of a new product may meet special resistance from lenders because of the untested market.

It is little wonder, then, that small firms are the ones which complain most of unsatisfied needs for long-term credit. All studies on the subject show a relatively larger proportion of companies reporting unsatisfied needs for long-term or permanent capital than for short-term loans. While such claims are still made by only a minority of companies, they are frequent enough to merit serious consideration.

Among members of the Smaller Business Association of New England who responded in our survey, for example, 15% of those who tried to obtain long-term credit after 1945 reported that they were unsuccessful in raising any of the funds desired, and others obtained only part of what they tried to get. Many had to try several sources before they were successful. Twenty-one per cent of those who sought additional equity funds failed to raise any of the money. Among the 92 small manufacturers interviewed in the Pioneer Valley, 11 reported an unsatisfied need for long-term credit, and six stated that they had been unable to obtain the additional equity funds they required. The

7. As the differential between income and capital-gains taxation increases, however, investors become more willing to risk their funds in new enterprises.

respondents to the N.A.M. survey, and especially the smallest firms, also mentioned term loans most frequently in specifying the nature of their unsatisfied financial needs.

Forty-three per cent of all participants in the Smaller Business Association study, however, expressed the opinion that the customary sources of long-term credit were not adequately meeting the needs of small business in the region. There is clearly a lack of meeting of the minds between many small businesses and the financial institutions regarding the role of the latter in providing long-term credit. The principal changes in lending procedures proposed by the small businessmen are "more long-term loans" and "greater liberality." Yet more than two-thirds of the companies in the Smaller Business Association survey which had tried to obtain long-term loans from either banks or insurance companies had obtained all or part of the funds they sought. *A greater mutual understanding of this problem, as well as of short-term lending, could also emerge from closer banker-borrower relations.*

The question of liberality of lending policies is of some importance, naturally, and we shall discuss it in a later section. But the difficulty is more deep-seated. It has resulted primarily from several basic changes in conditions affecting the money markets during recent years, of which these are probably the most important:

1. Relatively less direct investment by individuals and relatively more institutional investment.
2. Higher individual and corporation income taxes.
3. Rapid capital expansion and growth in output since 1939.
4. A large accumulated need for capital replacement and modernization.
5. A steadily rising price level.

These are national problems, not just problems for New England. While there are always opportunities for existing organizations to improve their effectiveness, *any solution of the long-term capital problem for small business must be broader than simply to make changes in the lending policies of banks and other traditional financial institutions.* We shall return to this topic shortly for a more complete discussion. First, it seems desirable to consider the nature of the demands for long-term credit that have helped to produce this situation.

Investment Needs and Opportunities

It is impossible to state precisely how much new investment is needed each year in New England, or by how much actual investment in the region has fallen short of the "need." It is possible, however, to consider the broad national need in general terms and relate it to the economic situation in New England. It is also possible to highlight the particular kinds of investment required in New England to increase the strength of the regional economy.

Total investment demand must be related to the nation's rate of growth, to the level of employment, and to other economic and noneconomic variables. There is no agreement on what constitutes the proper investment demand for a given period. Past trends in durable-equipment investment, however, give a clue to what may be needed in the future. Though deviations from the trend have been large during the depression and postwar years, an average increase of 3% a year in real investment (corrected for price-level changes) appears to be the national growth rate. Thus, total investment requirements for replacement and growth over the period 1949–59 will be about two and one-half times those of the 1920's.[8] Outlays in recent years have been above those necessary for a continuation of the secular trend, but the deferred replacement of the depression and war years and the great growth of population and income suggest continuing high levels of investment expenditure for many years to come.

It is not to be expected that New England will exactly follow the national rate of capital growth, any more than it has in past decades. Starting from a higher level of industrial development and population density, the New England rate will naturally be somewhat lower than that for the newer and less developed regions. Nevertheless, continued population growth in the region and technological advances call for steadily expanding productive service and distributive capacity in the region and the replacement and modernization of existing capacity.

The complaints of many small businesses in New England about inadequacies of long-term credit have arisen from this situation. The small companies have had a difficult time financing expansion and replacement from internal sources and have found themselves in a money market not oriented to providing long-term or equity funds for small business in the quantities desired during recent years. Demands for capital funds by small business are likely to remain relatively high in the region so long as the basic conditions which produced the present situation continue.

In addition to capital equipment, New England's investment needs are large in the construction of new industrial plants. Because the average age of the region's industry is greater than that in many other parts of the country, its factories and other industrial buildings are more in need of modernization or replacement. One-seventh of the 663 respondents in a 1949 survey by the Federal Reserve Bank of Boston expressed the opinion that their plant buildings put them at a disadvantage in competing with producers outside the region.[9] While that proportion is fairly small, the matter of adequacy of plant is subject to control by man, which is not so true of various other important competitive disadvantages in New England.

8. Joint Committee on the Economic Report, *Factors Affecting Volume and Stability of Private Investment,* Senate Document No. 232, Washington, 1950.

9. Federal Reserve Bank of Boston, "New England Manufacturing—Its Future Prospects," *Monthly Review,* September 1949.

Despite their extensive expenditures on new plant and equipment in New England during recent years, the manufacturers of the region as a whole have apparently not improved their capital position in relation to the rest of the country. For example, the 1947 Census of Manufactures indicated that in that year New England's total investment in manufacturing equipment per production worker was 25% below the United States average, and New England's expenditures per worker for new plant were nearly 50% below the United States average. No other region had lower percentages. The rapidly growing Southwest, on the other hand, had comparable figures of 79% and 208% above the United States average.

While similar data are not available for other postwar years, it is unlikely that the situation has been very different more recently. Over the period 1939–49 New England had only 4.8% of the nation's private construction. Since 1939 New England's share of construction has been decreasing. Non-residential construction per capita fell from 113% of the United States average in 1939 to 76% in 1949. The greatest change in New England's position has come since the end of the war.[10]

The principal cause of New England's relatively poor showing in capital expenditures has been the more rapid industrial expansion elsewhere. Even though such differentials in growth are to be expected, they increase the urgency for the region's manufacturers to replace existing plant and equipment that are no longer competitive. *New capital investment in New England must be larger if the region is to maintain or increase its competitive strength.*

Future capital requirements pose a major challenge to New England's financial system, especially in relation to the small firms. If their capital expenditures in recent years have been restricted by shortages of long-term or permanent funds, as seems sometimes to have been the case, the interests of the whole region require a more adequate channeling of funds into long-term investment. The need will continue great if the region's relative position is to be maintained and if new firms are to be encouraged.

Since the New England economy rests heavily upon a base of manufacturing activity, plant and equipment investment in manufacturing are of major importance to the future economic health of the region. A large demand for capital funds will probably come from the rapidly growing electrical and electronic, machinery, and related industries. Of equal importance, however, is investment in other industries, such as textiles, where intensified competition from other regions puts a premium on plant efficiency. The large old multistoried buildings which once epitomized New England's position as a premier manufacturing area are still useful for some purposes if they have been or can be acquired at low cost. Their usefulness is less than it used to be, however, and they are no longer a claim to leadership but only a reminder of it.

10. See U. S. Department of Commerce, *Regional Trends in the United States Economy* (Washington, 1951), Tables 39, 40, 41, 42.

In addition to the needs for new plant and equipment for manufacturing, New England needs and will continue to need new long-term investment in forestry, the vacation business, and in other industries based upon natural resources, as well as in transportation, power, gas, and other service industries. While the extent of the investment required will depend on changes in technology and many other factors, the substantial size of the need is clear.

Limitations to New Investment

There is little doubt that the financial resources of New England are large enough to satisfy present and probable future demands for funds. The economic growth of the region, the increased level of real personal income which has taken place since the great depression of the thirties, and the great growth in insurance companies and investment trusts are factors favorable to the region's development. There are several limiting factors, however, which pose important problems in marshaling the region's financial resources to meet the needs.

Investor Outlook. A major element in the limitation of long-term investment in new or small companies, in particular, is the attitude of investors. While the savings of New Englanders are sufficient to meet all likely requirements, whether or not these savings will flow toward the creation of private capital in the region depends to a considerable extent on the desires of investors and on their appraisals of investment opportunities. The desire for security of principal has been an important attribute of the modern investor, despite the rising price level in recent years. The increasing diversion of funds toward the less risky types of investment hinders the financing of new and growing small enterprises.

Every reasonable incentive, economic, legal, and political, should be given to the region's investors to encourage their long-term investment in New England enterprises. The matter of taxation is naturally of major importance. Income taxes drain off large quantities of funds that would otherwise be available for risk-taking investment. Moreover, the combination of high corporate and individual income tax rates tends to weaken the incentive to make risky investments, for a high rate of earning can become a low rate of return after taxation. The Federal Government's financial needs during the present defense period clearly must be met, but the present tax system may be seriously affecting the long-term growth of real income in the nation. While this danger is well known, its avoidance depends far more on sober analysis of the complex economic relationships involved than on impassioned pleas for tax reduction without consideration for the type, timing, and effects of the reductions.

Investor attitudes also reflect public opinion about economic conditions and opportunities. An optimistic outlook is a necessity, if savers are to place funds in the hands of entrepreneurs. Other areas of the nation are at present growing at a much more rapid rate than New England. If the prospective rates of return on certain investments are high in other regions, it is to be expected that some money will flow from New England toward those areas. That situation should not prejudice the investor against New England, however, for there is a broad variation in the attractiveness of investment opportunities in any area. It appears that the attitude of New Englanders toward their own economy is often overly pessimistic, based on unjustified generalization drawn from particular events highlighted in press reports. Noneconomic barriers should not be erected to halt the outflow of investment, but at the same time noneconomic factors should not be allowed to encourage it. *There is a great need for better public understanding of the strengths of the New England economy and the opportunities for profitable investment which the region offers.*

In brief, while there may be few direct restrictions on individuals in their investment decisions, it is obvious that considerations of security, taxation, yield, and knowledge of the market strongly influence the direction of their investments. Individuals acting in corporate capacities are influenced in their investment decisions not only by factors pertinent to the particular industry but also by their individual prejudices, outlooks, and attitudes. *Thus it is important to New England that the individuals who make the investment decisions, both as suppliers and as demanders of funds, should be well informed and as free as possible from popular prejudices which hinder investment in the area.*

Individual Saving. The changing patterns of individual savings during recent decades have also acted as a limitation to direct long-term investment in small enterprises by individuals. This development, of course, is largely an outgrowth of investor attitudes and the greater desire for security. The experience of many individuals with losses during the depression of the thirties had a strong psychological effect, and apparently that influence has hung on for more than a decade. The desire is primarily for security of principal and dollar income rather than security of real income, despite the inflation of the last dozen years. The Federal Reserve Board's 1951 survey of consumer finances confirms this observation. In early 1951 nearly seven of every ten consumers with incomes of $3,000 or more preferred investment assets of fixed dollar value. Assets of fluctuating money value, such as common stocks and real estate, became more popular as incomes increased, but they were still minority choices. The main reasons stated for holding assets of fixed value were safety and liquidity. For savings bonds, the additional factors of yield and patriotism were prominantly mentioned. In the case of real estate and stocks, yield was the most important attraction. Strangely enough, not many investors in real estate and stocks expressed preferences for these assets as inflationary hedges. Apparently, the principal reason for not investing in assets of fluctuating value was unfamiliarity with them. More recent surveys do indicate some change, however, in favor of real estate and stocks.

The growth of savings and investment through institutional channels has been a major phenomenon of recent decades. At present life insurance equities and the ownership of government bonds account for more than half the major types of accumulated liquid savings by individuals. Individual bank deposits of all types have declined gradually in relative importance since 1930, though of course they are also channels for institutional investment. The greatest decline in relative importance, however, has apparently been in direct investments by individuals in productive enterprise.

Institutional Barriers. In view of the growing concentration of investable funds in financial institutions, it is especially important to note how legal and other restrictions affect their investment and lending operations. Insurance companies, banks, and other traditional types of organizations operate under state or federal laws which place restrictions on certain types of investment. Moreover, custom and tradition in financial institutions often act as deterrents to changes in investment policies, even where legal restrictions are removed. To the extent that such limitations in New England conflict with the region's needs for investment, funds are encouraged to flow to other areas. We cannot make an exhaustive analysis of all such limitations but we can point out a few.

If savings banks could place more of their funds in equities, they might find higher rates of return available within the region. Their customary emphasis has been on first mortgages, government bonds, bank stocks, and the like. Savings banks in Massachusetts, Connecticut, Rhode Island, and Vermont cannot invest in equities other than bank stocks. New York, on the other hand, does not allow savings banks to invest in bank equities, but has recently passed a law to permit investment in other stocks and the establishment of an investment company for the purchase of stocks. The demands for liquidity and security do not seem to be great enough to necessitate savings banks to being as restricted as they are at present, both by law and by tradition. Past experience has shown that the mutual savings banks as a group have not made full use of new lending powers which have been granted to them,[11] however, and there is no assurance that more liberal laws would overcome such conservatism. Nevertheless, outmoded legal restrictions serve no useful purpose and should be relaxed to permit greater participation in meeting capital requirements by those institutions willing to depart from past practice.

Insurance companies provide another example of savings flowing preponderantly into less risky investment channels. Government bonds and mortgages, most of which were on noncommercial properties, accounted for

---

11. Cf. John Lintner, *Mutual Savings Banks in the Savings and Mortgage Markets,* Harvard University, Graduate School of Business Administration (1948), Pt. 2.

more than half the assets of life insurance companies in 1950 and for nearly half in 1951. Very few states prohibit insurance companies from investing in equities, but all of them set definite limits on the amounts which can be purchased. The equities held are usually those of old and well-established companies.

Table 11–5. The Distribution of Assets of United States Life Insurance Companies, 1921–51 (in percentage)

YEAR	U.S. GOV'T SECURITIES	ALL OTHER GOV'T BONDS	SECURITIES OF BUSINESS	MORT-GAGES	REAL ESTATE	OTHER	TOTAL
1921	10.6	8.5	24.5	35.2	2.3	18.7	100
1929	2.0	5.9	28.0	41.7	2.7	19.7	100
1939	18.4	8.0	28.9	19.4	7.3	18.0	100
1945	45.9	4.4	24.7	14.8	1.9	8.3	100
1950	21.0	4.1	39.7	25.1	2.2	7.9	100
1951	16.1	3.9	41.3	28.3	2.4	8.0	100

Source: Institute of Life Insurance

The conservatism of insurance company investment is assured by law, but even when the laws are relaxed the companies seem reluctant to take advantage of the change, as the recent New York experience indicates.[12] Insurance company investments in industrial and public utility bonds are very large (31.4% of assets in 1950), but such investments are rarely made in new or small companies.

It has been estimated that in New England 45% of the wealth is in fiduciary hands such as trustees, trust companies, investment companies, insurance companies, savings banks, colleges, and other educational institutions, foundations, etc.[13] For the United States as a whole, estimates of the amounts held in personal trusts by trust institutions and individual fiduciaries alone run from $37 to $100 billion.[14] When the amounts in pension funds, endowments, agency and custodian accounts, and similar fiduciary holdings are added, the total is immense. Most of these monies cannot be invested in new companies by law or are not so invested by custom. Those states which have a legal-list rule restrict investments to the "blue-chip" stocks and the better bonds, unless the trustees are specifically allowed greater discretion. Other states regulate the investments under the "prudent-man" rule. In either case there is little likelihood that any but the larger and older businesses may benefit from the use of these funds.

Investment companies, especially of the "open-end" type, have been growing rapidly. Mutual investment companies had total net assets of $401,000,000 in 1941, and by 1951 their assets had increased to over $3 billion. The

12. New York companies were permitted limited investment in common stocks after March 1951. See "Life Insurance News Data, March 12, 1952," Institute of Life Insurance, New York.

13. Merrill Griswold, Testimony before the Joint Committee on the Economic Report, Hearings, Volume and Stability of Private Investment (Washington, 1950), Pt. 2, p. 447.

14. Ibid., p. 455. Cf. Gilbert T. Stephenson, "Trust Business in the United States," The Trust Bulletin, April 1948.

Boston-domiciled open-end companies comprise over 40% of the industry, as measured by net assets. While many individuals who never before owned stock in American industry now participate indirectly by their purchases of shares in these investment companies, the investment companies must confine their operations to trading existing or new issues of the better stocks. They also tend to stress the selling end of their business more than the investing end, and this works against new ventures.

Commercial banks, long a major source of short-term funds for all types of businesses, have fairly recently extended their operations to include long-term lending. *The greater use of term loans has served as a partial substitute for equity capital and is one way in which the banks can and have aided in the problem of capital for small business.* The continued complaints of small businesses about inadequacies of long-term credit suggest, however, that no reasonable increase in liberality of long-term lending by the banks would meet the claimed needs. Moreover, the commercial banks as a whole are not equipped to lend large amounts by this method. Bank practice and banking law tend to restrict such lending.

Long-term loans are not easily given to new or small firms, for the security of such loans depends largely on the assets and prospective earnings of the business. The small firms most in need of long-term financing are usually the least able to furnish adequate security. While the better established firms may take advantage of such loans, the banks are genuinely restricted in their ability to lend large sums in this form.

The frequent charge made by banks that bank examiners "will not permit" a bank to make many long-term loans seems to be an exaggeration, but there is little doubt that it is necessary to exercise much more care in making long-term loans than in extending short-term credit. Many banks hesitate to encourage such borrowing. Furthermore, only the large banks can engage in any significant volume of such loans, and most banks are small. Thus, most long-term lending is done by the larger banks in the major money centers to the larger and better established businesses.

An increase in the capitalization of commercial banks would help to make more long-term lending possible. In the last analysis, however, such borrowing is often only a substitute for an increased equity investment in a firm. While it is desirable for commercial banks to help fill the breach, and some further expansion in term lending would probably be desirable, a *very* large increase in the use of term loans by banks is not necessarily the best solution to the long-term capital problem, from the point of view of either borrower or lender. A more fundamental solution is required.

With due recognition of the special situations faced by various types of financial institutions, it seems evident that both institutional and legal restrictions hamper and/or prevent equity investment in new and growing business, and that funds are increasingly being placed in the hands of institutions which are most restricted. The increasing recourse to long-term

debt rather than equity financing is evidence of this trend, although its de-
velopment is also partly a symptom of the tax benefits of debt financing. It
would seem highly desirable for the financial institutions to examine care-
fully the restrictive laws to which they are subject in the various states. They
should themselves take the initiative in pressing for modifications, where
they are desirable and in accord with the responsibilities of the institutions,
to permit them to adapt their operations better to the changed needs of the
business community. All financial institutions should also examine their own
investment policies continuously from the point of view of service to the
community, as well as in terms of their own position.

NEW PRIVATE INSTITUTIONS AND TECHNIQUES
FOR MEETING CAPITAL REQUIREMENTS

The problem of channeling more long-term and equity funds into new
investment has been recognized by many observers, and there have been a
number of positive approaches to its solution. Some of those approaches have
been through the development of new lending techniques by traditional
types of organizations. Others have been through the growth of new kinds
of institutions. Each offers assistance in overcoming the difficulties which
hinder the flow of funds to business. While our special concern is with new
or small and growing firms, the more extensive use of these new methods
can also be helpful to many larger and better established businesses. In this
section we discuss briefly some of the principal examples of new kinds of
organizations and techniques which are in operation or which have been
proposed. Term loans by banks, which belong in this category, were considered in the preceding section.

Venture-capital Organizations

The most direct approach to the equity-capital problem is through organizations specifically designed to provide venture capital. There are only a
few such organizations in the United States, and most of them are but a few
years old. Most of them are also "private" organizations, based upon the
wealth of an individual or family. The two New England venture-capital
organizations are located in Boston. In addition to their present and future
value to the region, they are models that might well be duplicated elsewhere
to the benefit of the entire nation.

The American Research and Development Corporation is perhaps the
boldest experiment in providing venture capital. The Massachusetts corporation was organized in 1946 to aid the financing of new companies based on
new products which show technological promise. It advances either equity
funds or credit, as required, and works closely with the companies in which
it invests to help assure their success.

The corporation is a risk-taking organization, and its own outstanding stock of 300,000 shares is publicly held. A closed-end type of investment company, it provides an excellent indirect way for an investor to furnish capital funds to a diversified group of new companies. That diversification and the corporation's careful investigation of new propositions reduce the risk to individual investors. Some of its investments have proved unsound but most of them have been successful. Some failures are to be expected, of course, if the corporation is to fulfill its risk-taking function properly.

At the end of 1952 American Research and Development had outstanding $4,610,501 in investments in 25 companies. After the gradual build-up of its early years, the corporation itself has become a profitable organization. Its future appears to be promising, with prospects of substantial capital gains as well as dividends and interest income.

The importance of such an organization is great, even though the number of its investments is fairly small. Its financial and managerial assistance are important to the genesis and growth of new types of products and to the expansion of employment in industries which offer much to the region. While American Research and Development invests in promising ventures wherever they are located, its location in the heart of the region's research center has redounded to New England's advantage.

American Research and Development is highly selective in its investments, however, for it limits its interest to genuinely new products based on research. From the hundreds of inquiries and applications, only a few are accepted. The aid goes to those most promising both for the corporation and for the nation's economic progress, but other new and small companies in need of similar types of funds are not covered by its operations.

The other New England organization of this type is New Enterprises, Inc. It operates in a somewhat different fashion, although it too is concerned primarily with new companies based on technological advances. New Enterprises acts as an investigatory and screening agency, which passes on its recommendations to a group of associated individual investors for investment as they see fit. Its contributions to the region, as well as to its more limited group of investors, are similar to those of the American Research and Development Corporation.

The experience of these new institutions indicates that investment in risky ventures can be profitable as well as helpful when the companies are carefully selected and aided during the difficult first years. *The continued growth and contribution of venture-capital organizations to the equity-capital problem are both desirable and probable.*

Industrial Development Corporations

Two other types of organization have been growing in importance in New England as devices for reducing the unsatisfied needs of business for long-term capital. Through their operations, local industrial foundations and state-wide development credit corporations help meet the long-term capital problem while working toward their principal objectives of industrial development.

Industrial foundations are not new, but their greatest expansion has been since World War II. Their principal function is to attract new manufacturing establishments to a community by offering new or existing plant space on a lease or sale basis.[15] Firms unable to build or buy plants from their own funds are aided to expand without the need for new equity funds. Since rentals are usually applied toward the purchase of the plant, the tenant eventually pays for and owns it.

By the middle of 1952 there were 36 active local industrial development corporations in New England. Rhode Island was the only state in the region which had none in operation, although one was in process of formation. Sponsored by private individuals or organizations such as chambers of commerce, most of these community corporations were organized to help diversify manufacturing or to induce new manufacturers to locate in communities which had suffered unemployment because of discontinued businesses. Many of the local development corporations are willing to erect buildings to a manufacturer's specifications, and they carry on a wide range of other activities.

The operations of local industrial foundations are typically financed by the sale of stock to local citizens and businesses. The investment is generally made as a contribution to civic improvement rather than for profit. Nevertheless, most foundations have made profits or at least broken even. Such local organizations as these may provide that extra stimulus needed to induce a firm to locate in a given community, and in so doing they both take advantage of and help to reduce the unsatisfied demand for long-term and equity capital.

A newer type of state-wide development corporation has been pioneered in New England since the end of the war. It has the same general objective of encouraging industrial growth, though its geographical scope is broader. Those so far in operation stress direct loans rather than plant construction or leasing. The state corporations do occasionally cooperate in financing the projects of local industrial foundations, however, and they sometimes take capital stock in a borrower's company as part of their lending terms.

The Maine Development Credit Corporation was the first of its kind, and it has served as a model for similar organizations in other states.[16] The Maine Corporation was chartered in 1949 by special act of the state legislature,

15. For a detailed discussion of the operations of industrial foundations in New England, see Federal Reserve Bank of Boston, "New England Industrial Development Corporations," *Monthly Review*, June 1952.

16. See Federal Reserve Bank of Boston, "The Development Credit Corporation of Maine," *Monthly Review*, January 1951.

upon the initiative of banking and other leaders in the state. It started with a small capital base of $50,000, subscribed by individuals and businesses, and by the beginning of 1951 had built up a borrowing potential of approximately $550,000 from the 38 banks and other financial institutions which had joined it as members. The cooperating financial institutions agree on call to loan the Development Credit Corporation up to 2.5% of their capital and surplus or equivalent, as the funds are needed.

The Maine Corporation does not compete with banks; it supplements their activities and cooperates with them. Where possible, it attempts to place loans with banks rather than take them itself.

The Maine organization has only a small paid staff. For screening and evaluating applications, it has to utilize extensively the talents and knowledge of its large board of directors and its member institutions, as well as of other individuals in all parts of the state. It is only through these unpaid services that it can minimize its operating expenses while giving each application thorough consideration.

Since only risky loans come to its attention, careful analysis and selection of applicants are necessary. During its first two years of operation the corporation had small losses, but as the volume of loans increased its operations passed the break-even point. Its screening had also turned up a still larger number of loans which member organizations were willing to make, even though they had previously been refused credit by banks or other financial institutions. That experience indicates that the usual credit examinations by banks are sometimes too limited to determine the credit worthiness of loan applicants, and that the Development Credit Corporation does in fact aid in reducing the unsatisfied demand for capital funds in Maine, both directly and indirectly.

New Hampshire has set up a similar state-wide development corporation patterned on the Maine plan, although its charter permits the public flotation of its own securities to raise funds, as well as subscriptions by its members. Rhode Island has recently organized a comparable organization with even broader powers. Vermont and Connecticut are well advanced in their planning for development corporations, and there have also been proposals for such an institution in Massachusetts.

The situations in Rhode Island and Massachusetts have been complicated by competition between proponents of the Maine system and advocates of state-financed corporations. Since the cooperation and support of banks are necessary to the success of this type of venture, it is important for them to take the initiative in forming development corporations. Organization and operation by the state governments themselves would be an alternative, though probably not the best, in view of the always present danger of political intervention in the operation of such an institution.

The long-term and venture capital which local industrial foundations and state-wide development corporations can make available, in addition to the sale, lease, and construction of plants, is valuable in meeting the needs of many businesses for long-term or permanent investment, in helping to establish new businesses in the region, and in raising the level of employment. To be effective, however, these institutions need adequate financing themselves, their leadership must be dynamic, and political pressures must be scrupulously avoided. Tax avoidance should not be relied on as an attraction. Firms which depend on tax concessions or loopholes to become competitive are rarely desirable risks for a community or state.

State development corporations and local industrial foundations are not cure-alls. Much more must be done to attract new industry or to stimulate its indigenous growth. Perhaps one of the more important functions which such agencies can perform is to help show prospective manufacturers that the community or state is vitally interested in their welfare. To dispel the instinctive fears or antagonisms which some businessmen have toward any government helps to develop the healthy optimism that is necessary for investment. The monetary and employment value of such an intangible is large.

Leasing Arrangements

During recent years there has been an increasing use of "sale and lease-back" arrangements, in New England as well as in the rest of the country, as a method of improving the financial position of business firms. Many manufacturing, retail, and other concerns have sold their buildings to insurance companies, educational institutions, or other investors and continued to occupy them as tenants. Such an arrangement frees for working purposes capital formerly tied up in expensive plant, and reduces the firm's current tax liability. Under appropriate arrangements, the entire rental payment is a deductible expense. Insurance companies also frequently finance the construction of new factories, stores, office buildings, and other capital facilities that are built to the order of particular companies and then leased to them. Often a leasing arrangement can produce considerable savings over conventional borrowing methods.

The leasing of capital equipment by suppliers is not new, of course, but the extension to leasing major buildings by financial institutions and the "sale and lease-back" combination are fairly recent innovations. While large corporations are the principal users of the technique, it is also adaptable to growing small concerns of high standing. *Leasing arrangements by insurance companies and similar investors can make an important contribution to the long-term capital problem of small businesses.* Industrial foundations make extensive use of the attractions of leasing in their operations, of course, but they restrict their activities to limited areas. Large insurance companies and similar investors are in a position to provide for the long-term capital needs of a company, no matter where it is located.

When corporate income taxes are high, as at present, the leasing method is especially attractive. It must be used cautiously, for a major decrease in federal income taxation could eliminate many of the advantages which this arrangement possesses. Regardless of tax savings, however, it will continue to provide a way for many firms to reduce their need for additional long-term credit or equity investment.

Bank Pools

There has been some experimentation by banks in pooling their resources informally to spread the risk of making questionable loans. The bank pool is a loose method of accomplishing part of what a development credit corporation is designed to do. It is designed to encourage a more liberal lending policy to help meet the credit needs of companies which are otherwise unable to obtain funds.

Pooling arrangements have been tried in Connecticut, Rhode Island, and Massachusetts, as well as in other parts of the country. They usually have only limited success. Typically, the pool falls apart or the volume of loans is so small that little good is accomplished. Two factors militate against the effective operation of such pools: (1) if a loan is risky, most members are not anxious to venture their funds and they usually find it difficult to agree on the share which each will take; and (2) if a loan is promising, one bank usually wants to take the entire loan. Without a separate organization to make the loan decisions and a firm formula for sharing the risks, it is almost impossible to prevent a pool from breaking down.

Better results are usually obtained by the use of correspondents to share the risk of questionable loans. Two parties can agree more easily than several. Typically, a large bank takes part of the risk for a small bank, which services the loan. While such arrangements permit a small bank to make larger and more risky loans than it could if it had to bear the full risk, they fail, because of their informal nature and the limited experience of smaller banks, to provide a continuing or generally available source of credit to all firms in an area which could benefit from it.

A few large banks and insurance companies have announced their willingness to take up to 90% of any loan made and serviced by a small bank. The small banks have been slow to take advantage of the opportunity, but this development appears highly desirable and worthy of greater use. New England institutions could well emulate this practice. City banks could do more to help their country correspondents by enhancing the prestige of the smaller banks and building confidence in them. This should help remove some of the fears of the small bank that it might later lose business to the large bank.

Both the pools and the correspondent relationships are directed primarily to the usual short-term loans, though they do not necessarily rule out longer term credit. They are indications of the growing cooperation within the banking system in helping the more risky enterprises to obtain loans. Nevertheless, they are of only minor importance in solving the more serious problems of getting long-term and equity investment into new and small firms.

Capital Banks

Each of the kinds of organization or financing techniques mentioned above has made some contribution to the more effective operation of the financial system of New England and the rest of the nation. In combination with the traditional types of financing, they provide an enormous quantity and variety of capital and credit resources. Yet there are still strong indications of unsatisfied needs for long-term credit and equity funds, especially by small businessmen.

Many plans have been advanced for new types of institutions and new procedures to increase the flow of equity or long-term capital to small businesses. The most frequent proposals are for capital banks, loan-insurance systems, and mutual development corporations. The first two types are usually conceived as public or semipublic in nature, the last as wholly private.

The capital-bank proposal is central to the question of desirability of new institutions. Opinion is divided as to the need for and effects of capital banks. Even among the small businesses which stand to profit most there is considerable difference of opinion. The Smaller Business Association of New England is officially on record as supporting the establishment of capital banks, and it has tried to educate its members about the functions of such institutions. Yet in the Committee's survey of the association's members only 10% of the respondents stated that they personally felt a need for a capital bank for long-term credit, as compared with the 36% who stated that there should be some new kind of organization to provide long-term credit.[17] Thirteen per cent reported a need for a new organization to provide equity funds, but they were vague about what type it should be. These percentages are far from overwhelming, yet the minorities are large enough to deserve careful consideration. Only a minority of firms is expected to take advantage of any new institution, but that group may make a considerable difference in the economic life of an area.

The typical capital-bank proposal contemplates a regional bank in each Federal Reserve district. Their capital would come from the Federal Government or the Federal Reserve banks, and eventually from private individuals and financial institutions, though some proposals envisage the banks as counterparts of the Federal Reserve banks. The Federal Government's role would be to charter the institutions, to make or provide for the original subscription of capital (to be repaid as private subscriptions increased), and to insure that the banks would be taxed on a conduit basis rather than as separate institutions.

17. See our Staff Memorandum No. 6.

The capital banks would both loan for long terms and purchase equities. While they would not restrict themselves to dealing with small business, special attention would be directed toward this group. They would consider applicants only if they had failed to obtain needed funds from other sources. They might also carry on a loan-guarantee program in addition to their lending and investing operations.

A new system of this sort, if established, would presumably be given broad enough powers to develop new procedures to meet changing situations, and its charter might specifically direct it to cooperate with monetary and Treasury authorities in minimizing cyclical fluctuations. It would emphasize the new and growing enterprises and leave the "rescue" type of loan to the Reconstruction Finance Corporation and other special programs. Superior management and highly skilled staff personnel would be necessary for its success.

An example of a successful institution of this sort is the Industrial Development Bank of Canada, which was created by Parliament in 1944 with a paid-in capital of $25,000,000 subscribed by the Bank of Canada. The I.D.B. supplements the activities of the regular banks by medium or long-term lending for the acquisition of plant and equipment by industrial enterprises otherwise unable to finance these assets at a reasonable cost. The bank may also underwrite stock or bond issues of corporations. As of September 1951, it had authorized 945 loans, investments, and guarantees in the amount of $69,900,000 and had outstanding $29,400,000 of such loans, investments, and guarantees. It has been profitable every year since operations began. The typical borrower is a small industrial enterprise; 66% of the authorizations are for less than $50,000 each. While some commercial banks opposed its establishment, they have generally come to believe that its activities aid the growth of small firms and help them become better customers for short-term bank lending.

The desirability of such a system in New England and the rest of the United States depends on the use that would be made of it and on its contribution to the creation of income and employment. Every new type of financial institution for providing long-term or equity capital has so far attracted a number of worthy applicants. It appears that the same would be true of capital banks, though the actual extent of their use could be determined only by an initial experiment in some one region. In Canada, for example, approximately half of all applications have been accepted, though preliminary screening may have discouraged the obviously undesirable applicants.

The need for capital banks in New England appears to be less than in the country as a whole, because of the region's present well-organized financial system and the existence of some new specialized organizations, such as the development credit corporations and the venture-capital organizations. Nevertheless, the changes in both supply of long-term and equity capital and demand for it have been so great that the capital-bank idea has much to com-

mend it in providing a broad and generally accessible source of such capital in the region. Furthermore, a regional capital bank could have a much larger capitalization and could draw a wider range of talent than the smaller institutions.

If the basic conditions which have caused the "capital shortage" persist, as appears likely, it is almost inevitable that some such system will eventually come into existence on a national scale. The special new organizations and techniques, useful as they are, leave out many areas and types of companies. It would be highly desirable for the banks and other existing financial institutions to take the initiative themselves in setting up a region-wide or nation-wide complementary program of this type within the framework of the private financial system rather than leaving action to the federal or state governments.

A well-financed and aggressive development credit corporation in each New England state might well make the usual concept of a capital bank unnecessary in the region, however, if its powers and activities included equity investment. The separate state institutions could be linked together through a small regional organization which would serve as a discount, guaranteeing, and service agency. It would not be correct to say that a regional development corporation system is the only alternative to a capital bank, for there are other possible arrangements that could be employed. Yet it does seem clear that the choice lies with the existing financial institutions. If they do not collectively solve or greatly reduce the magnitude of the problem themselves, government is likely to take matters into its own hands, as has happened so many times before.

Other Considerations

In this report we have emphasized the availability of long-term and equity funds to new, small, and growing businesses. We realize fully that far more than money is necessary to make a small business successful. Management is the key element in survival and ability to make a profit. Inadequacy of financing rarely causes failure but it may prevent growth and the creation of new jobs. The financial system has an important function in aiding that growth, both by adapting its techniques and methods to meet changing conditions and by creating new institutions specifically designed to fill new kinds of needs.

It is obvious that the principal role of the Federal Government in ensuring the adequate flow of capital into business enterprise, large and small, is in adapting its tax structure to maximize that flow, with due regard for its other responsibilities and goals. The operations of the Reconstruction Finance Corporation and other federal lending agencies, important though they may be, are of considerably less importance than the federal tax laws. Without amplification at this point,[18] *we suggest that the Federal Government could materially aid in solving the problem of capital if it would radically alter its adherence to the present rigid and arbitrary depreciation allowances under the corporate income tax laws, eliminate the "double taxation" of dividends, allow newly formed businesses a longer period to carry over losses, adjust the rates of taxation to favor (but not overfavor) smaller businesses, reduce or at least refrain from increasing the rate on the taxation of capital gains, and eliminate the tax exemption of state and local bonds. The taxation of inheritances and its effects on closely held corporations should be thoroughly reviewed.* There are other tax loopholes which are causing increasing distortions in the economy; they too should be closed. Changes such as these could provide an important additional stimulus to productive new investment and the nation's growth.

THE OPERATION OF FEDERAL SOURCES OF CAPITAL AND CREDIT

The Federal Government has established many credit agencies, and their facilities are available to New England as well as to other parts of the country. Special agencies make loans to farmers, to homeowners, to veterans, and to businesses. Other federal actions have increased the effectiveness and stability of the nation's financial structure and its operation by the establishment of the Federal Reserve System and the Securities and Exchange Commission.

The role of government in loans to business, with which we are concerned in this section, has increased greatly since the depression of the thirties. Depression and war have provided the impetus for government entry into direct- or indirect-lending operations. All such present operations developed out of specific needs or pressures, either as rescue operations or to encourage production expansion and minimize economic dislocation during war periods. An appraisal of their operations is, for the most part, separate from the consideration of needs for long-term and equity capital by new or small businesses.

While each of the programs has made a distinct contribution to business and many New England businesses owe their present existence to help received from the Reconstruction Finance Corporation and the Federal Reserve's 13(b) program during the thirties, only the R.F.C. has continued as an important and active lending agency during peacetime. Most of the others have been temporary or have declined in use as the need for them has declined. In this section we shall discuss briefly the operations of the R.F.C., the 13(b) loans of the Federal Reserve System, and certain of the more important war-financing programs.

18. See our report No. 16, "New England's Financial Relations with the Federal Government," for a discussion of the effects of present taxation.

The Reconstruction Finance Corporation

The R.F.C. began its operations as a rescue agency at the beginning of the depression of the thirties. Its functions grew, and it gradually assumed an important position in the nation's financial system. In its usual business lending, which is just one of its many functions, it serves as a last resort for firms that are unable to obtain loans from ordinary sources. To the extent that it makes term-loans, it contributes to the supply of long-term capital for risky ventures, but it does not make equity investments.

A comparison of the recent business-lending operations by the R.F.C. in New England and in the country as a whole reveals some important differences. The Office of the Controller of the R.F.C. has prepared a special comparative summary of the record in New England and the United States for the latest years.[19] Geographical data are not available, however, for the entire period of R.F.C. lending.

At the end of March 1952 New England borrowers had 3% of the number and 5% of the dollar total of R.F.C. loans outstanding. For both New England and the United States the larger loans dominate the dollar totals (see Table 11–6), but the percentage of larger loans (over $200,000) was greater in New England than in the United States as a whole.

Table 11–6. Size Distribution of R.F.C. Business Loans Outstanding, March 31, 1952, New England and the United States (per cent of dollar totals advanced by the R.F.C.)

SIZE	NEW ENGLAND	UNITED STATES	NEW ENGLAND PER CENT OF U.S.
Under $5,000	0.2	0.3	4
$5,001–10,000	0.5	1	2
$10,001–25,000	2	4	2
$25,001–50,000	5	8	3
$50,001–100,000	10	13	4
$100,001–200,000	14	8	9
$200,001–500,000	19	12	8
$500,001–1,000,000	14	8	9
Over $1,000,000	36	46	4
TOTAL	100	100	5

Source: Office of the Controller, R.F.C.

From 1945 through the first quarter of 1952 around 50% of the number of loan authorizations in New England were for loans of $25,000 and under. These loans accounted for only 2% of the region's dollar total. Only 5% of the number of authorizations in New England were for loans of over $500,-000, yet they accounted for 66% of the money amount of authorizations made. The comparable figures for the United States were 58% and 6%, respectively, for the small loans, and 2% and 54% for the large loans. The distribution of

19. These tabulations were made available to the Committee of New England through the courtesy of Harry A. McDonald, administrator of the R.F.C.

loan applications by size in New England, on the other hand, was quite similar to that for the nation.

Comparative data for applications, authorizations, and rejections of loans are not available for the longer period 1945–52 but are available for the period January 1949–March 1952. During this period (see Table 11–7) a larger per-

Table 11–7. Size Distribution of R.F.C. Business Loan Applications, Authorizations, and Declines,* New England and the United States, January 1, 1949 through March 31, 1952 (in thousands)

SIZE	APPLICATIONS		AUTHORIZATIONS		DECLINES	
	NEW ENGLAND	UNITED STATES	NEW ENGLAND	UNITED STATES	NEW ENGLAND	UNITED STATES
$25,000 and under	$ 5,869	$ 161,893	$ 1,567	$ 56,284	$ 3,270	$ 56,575
$25,001–100,000	28,505	570,587	8,344	206,175	12,880	197,973
$100,001–500,000	59,103	741,347	20,158	223,830	23,495	289,553
$500,001 and over	217,770	4,164,423	86,598	850,619	18,242	1,353,962
TOTAL	$311,247	$5,638,250	$116,667	$1,336,908	$57,887	$1,898,063
PER CENT †						
$25,000 and under	2	3	1	4	6	3
$25,001–100,000	9	10	7	15	22	10
$100,001–500,000	19	13	17	17	41	15
$500,000 and over	70	74	74	64	32	71
TOTAL	100	100	100	100	100	100

* R.F.C. amounts exclude amounts loaned directly by banks.
† Details may not add to totals due to rounding.
Source: Office of the Controller, R.F.C.

centage of the smaller loans was granted in the United States than in New England. Forty-four per cent of the applications for loans under $25,000 were accepted and authorized in the United States while only 31% of similar applicants were granted loans in New England. The reverse situation applied for the loans over $500,000, for in this category only 33% of applicants were granted loans in the United States while 52% were accepted in New England. In dollar terms, New Englanders received 27% of the small loans requested and 40% of the large loans. In the United States 35% of the dollar amount of small-loan applications were approved but only 20% of the large loans.

Withdrawals of applications affected the acceptance ratios, but the principal reason for New England's different pattern of loan authorizations was the ratio of loan rejections. For loans of $25,000 and under, the New England agency declined 53% of all applications, as opposed to a 38% rejection rate for the nation. For the large loans the rejection rate for New England was significantly lower than that for the nation as a whole. Table 11–8 shows how the percentages of rejected applications changed as the size categories increased.

The explanation of these differences presumably lies either in the character of the loans sought and quality of the applicants or in some differences between the operations of the New England office of the R.F.C. and those of other offices. Whatever the principal reason, it appears that the typical small businessmen who turn to the R.F.C. for small loans are less likely to receive approval in New England than elsewhere. The reverse appears true for loans to larger businesses. The evidence supports two possible conclusions. First, it may be that in their short-term-lending operations commercial banks and other sources of credit in New England do a better than average job of screen-

Table 11–8. Size Distribution of R.F.C. Business Loans Declined as a Percentage of Applications, New England and the United States, January 1, 1949 through March 31, 1952

| | PER CENT OF NUMBER | | PER CENT OF AMOUNT | |
SIZE	NEW ENGLAND	UNITED STATES	NEW ENGLAND	UNITED STATES
$25,000 and under	52.5	38.0	55.7	34.9
$25,001–100,000	47.0	36.1	45.2	34.7
$100,001–500,000	41.0	39.0	39.7	39.0
$500,001–1,000,000	33.3	37.2	34.0	34.0
Over $1,000,000	14.3	28.6	5.0	32.3
ALL	46.6	37.2	18.6	33.6

Source: Office of the Controller, R.F.C.

ing small-business loans and that only the riskiest loan applications reach the R.F.C. The committee's study of small-business financing in New England also found a relatively low percentage of small-loan acceptances by the R.F.C. in comparison with other sources.[20] On the other hand, it would seem that New England's banks and other financial institutions are not lending to large borrowers as readily as those in other regions of the country. Apparently, the quality of the larger borrowers who turn to the R.F.C. for loans is higher in New England. Many of them seek longer term loans, often for the financing of permanent assets.

An alternative explanation involves the assumption that the quality of both short-term and long-term loan applicants to the R.F.C. in New England is not significantly different from that in the rest of the nation. If that assumption is correct, R.F.C. policy in New England discriminates against small borrowers and favors large borrowers to a greater degree than in the rest of the nation.

It appears that the R.F.C. is making an important contribution to the financing of many middle-sized companies in New England, including the extension of some long-term credit. The operation of its business-lending program appears to have been of less than average assistance to small businesses in the region, despite the large number of small loans authorized. Since only the poorest credit risks reach the R.F.C., usually after prior rejection by a bank, that agency has continued to function largely as a "rescue" agency, so far as small business is concerned.

20. See our Staff Memorandum No. 6, pp. 13–14.

Section 13(b) Loans by Federal Reserve Banks

Another emergency loan program born during the depression was the 13(b) lending to business by the Federal Reserve banks. Authorized in 1934 by an amendment to the Federal Reserve Act, the 12 Federal Reserve banks were permitted to make direct loans or to guarantee loans to companies which were unable to obtain credit through normal channels.

The amendment and accompanying regulation by the Board of Governors of the Federal Reserve System were deliberately worded to provide each Reserve bank considerable freedom of action. The five-year loan limit was restrictive, however, and most of the smaller loans made under Section 13(b) by the Federal Reserve Bank of Boston had terms of about one year. The larger loans often ran five years and in a number of cases renewals were granted beyond the original term. Interest rates ranged from $2\frac{1}{2}$ to 6%, depending on the size and type of the loan, its term, the security offered, and other considerations.

The period of greatest activity under the program was during the depression and recovery years 1934–39. During those years the Boston Reserve Bank acted on 505 applications in the amount of $29,497,612. It made loans to 128 firms for a total of $13,605,000. The major reasons for the 321 rejections of loan requests (the remaining 56 were withdrawn) were inadequate management, insufficient security, unsatisfactory financial condition, or poor business prospects. As the program progressed, the ratio of acceptances to rejections rose. By 1939 over 43% of new applications were accepted. Rejections of the loans under $25,000 were more numerous than for any other group, both absolutely and relatively.

The Boston Reserve Bank did not actively push its lending operations under Section 13(b). It encouraged the commercial banks of the district to make the loans themselves or to participate with the Reserve Bank. The desire to have local banks participate in the loans seems to have been greater in the Boston district than in most other districts. Direct commitments of the Boston bank were lower than the national rate of 44% from 1934 to 1939, and after the first few years almost all of Boston's 13(b) loans were participations. Over the entire period from 1934 to 1952 the Boston bank handled 3.1% of the dollar amounts and 5.2% of the number of loans made under the program. Most other Reserve banks exceeded this percentage.

After 1939 direct lending by the Federal Reserve banks fell off sharply. Increased activity by the R.F.C. was partially responsible, but the principal reason for the declining use of the program was the defense and war boom. The need for short-term lending dropped off, and new demands for emergency wartime financing were handled in other ways. Although the program is still in existence, the Boston Reserve Bank has received relatively few applications for 13(b) loans since 1940, and the latest commitment under the authority was made in 1949.

The 13(b) program should be continued largely on a stand-by basis, as it is now. It cannot be of much help to the new or growing small firm which seeks funds for expansion. During periods of economic stress, however, it can make a contribution to established businesses which need working capital when the regular credit sources are unwilling to take the risks involved.

Emergency Defense and Wartime Financing

The urgent need for expanded military production following the outbreak of World War II and the Korean war brought expanded requirements for financing capital expansion and for working capital. The private financial institutions expanded their loans and investments greatly in response to both types of needs. Many special situations arose, however, which required special financing arrangements by the Federal Government. Investment in specialized plant facilities that were not readily convertible to peacetime production, expansion of capacity beyond expected peacetime demand, increase in required output beyond a firm's proven ability to produce—these and other situations could not be handled in the normal way.

A great many devices were evolved for meeting those peculiar needs. The federal guarantee of working-capital loans made by commercial banks, direct long-term capital lending through the R.F.C., advance payments and loans by the military procurement agencies, income tax concessions to encourage capital expansion, and other programs came into existence during World War II. They were dropped when the first emergency was past and revived with some modification in 1950 or later. In this section we discuss a few of the programs of special interest or importance.

Besides the question of the effectiveness of wartime financing in aiding New England's contribution to military production, its effects on the region's economic trends are also important. During World War II New England manufacturers received 9.1% of the military procurement contracts awarded in the United States. At the beginning of the defense period after the outbreak of the Korean war an even larger percentage of total military procurement and construction was placed in New England, though the proportion then tapered off and amounted to 8.5% for the entire period from July 1950 through March 1952. During World War II, however, New England's total investment in new plant and equipment was only 5.3% of the nation's. The region's proportion of plant expansion during the current defense period has been even lower, on the basis of available data.[21] While it was to be expected that New England's expansion of productive capacity would be less than that in most other regions, it appears that the emergency methods of financing capital investment contributed in part to the region's lag.

Accelerated Amortization for Tax Purposes. During the present defense

21. See Defense Production Administration, *Defense Programs (supplement); Federal Aids for Facilities Expansion,* Washington, September 10, 1951.

period Congressional action has permitted investors in defense or defense-supporting plants and equipment to amortize a large part of their cost for tax purposes over a period of five years, instead of over the longer periods usually required by the Bureau of Internal Revenue. There was a comparable program during World War II. Approval of the accelerated amortization at present requires the issuance of a "certificate of necessity" by the Defense Production Administration. The program grants short-term tax concessions to those whose investment increases the military-production capacity of the nation. While the certificate-of-necessity arrangement does not involve federal lending, it is nonetheless of material temporary financial assistance to the companies whose capital investments are approved.

As of August 27, 1952, New England firms had been granted 1,021 certificates for $591,000,000 in new plant and equipment, excluding the lapsed certificate for the New England steel mill. That amount was approximately 2.5% of the comparable total for the United States. Excluding transportation and electric utilities, the New England figure was an even lower percentage of the national total. These figures were far lower than the region's portion of industrial capacity and its contribution to defense production.

For a variety of reasons the certificate-of-necessity windfall has been of greater assistance to other regions than to New England. For one thing, the industrial structure of the region does not lend itself as readily to such expansion as does that in other regions. The production of primary metals, especially steel and aluminum, and certain other key items which have been of major importance in the expansion programs is of relatively less importance in New England than elsewhere.

Producers of textiles, shoes, and other industries which are of special importance to New England have been almost entirely absent from the list of recipients of certificates of necessity. In general, there is "overcapacity" in the textile industries. Some certificates have been issued for the construction or equipment of textile plants but almost all of them have gone to southern plants. In other industries where certificates have been granted despite available existing capacity, New England has not been an important beneficiary. Moreover, there is little doubt that much of the capital expansion covered by certificates of necessity had been planned before accelerated amortization became available. A large part of the expansion of electric power capacity, for example, would have taken place in the absence of these provisions. Eligibility has been interpreted broadly, and that liberality has aided other regions more than New England. The recent additional requirement of approval under the industrial dispersal program may also mitigate against New England. While the objective is dispersal of industry within an area, the denser existing concentration of industry in New England makes it somewhat harder to comply with that requirement. Dispersal of industry is important, of course, to the nation's security, but it should be recognized that whatever effect it has on New England will be to reduce its rate of growth relative to that of the rest of the country.

The regional effects of the program of accelerated amortization are clear, especially in conjunction with the industrial dispersal program. They accelerate the capital expansion of other areas relative to that in New England, and they accentuate the differences that would exist under more normal conditions. The newer industrial areas have been presented with a windfall. From the tax point of view this windfall may not persist, but the economic effects flowing from these changes will not disappear. The greater addition to new plant and equipment in other areas helps to place New Englanders, businessmen and workers alike, in a poorer competitive position for future production. In addition, it places the smaller firms, which are much less able to take advantage of the rapid write-offs, in a poorer position with respect to their larger competitors. *The program is of some importance as an incentive to investment in needed plant capacity, but it is unfortunate that it has had these differential effects.*

The V-loan Program. Both World War II and the present period of expanded military production created a need of many manufacturers for expanded working capital to finance their military contracts. A loan-guarantee program was designed to assist the private financial system to meet those special needs without requiring the banks to take the full risk. Under federal statutes and Regulation V of the Federal Reserve System, the Federal Reserve banks have acted as fiscal agents for the Army, Navy, Air Force, and other guaranteeing agencies of the Federal Government.

Under the system, guarantees of working-capital loans by private institutions to finance procurement contracts may range from 50 to 100%. The term of the loan is usually limited to the time required for completion of the contract. Interest rates may not exceed 5%, and the lender pays a graduated guarantee fee from his interest income for the protection against total loss.

During World War II about $10.3 billion in authorized loans was guaranteed in the United States under the program. Losses were only about $6,000,000 and were more than covered by reserves from the guarantee fees. V-loan authorizations in the New England district were large, though specific figures are not publicly available. The program was revived in 1950 and is again contributing to the financing of military production. A substantial proportion of the $1,868,000,000 of authorized loans under the program at the end of June 1952 has not been put to use. Information on the regional use of V-loans during the present period has not been released by the Board of Governors of the Federal Reserve System, but the program is active in the New England district as well as in the rest of the country.

Section 302 Loans. Direct loans to firms engaged in defense production may be made through the R.F.C. under Section 302 of the Defense Production Act of 1950. These loans are primarily for the expansion of production capacity for basic materials. They may be granted for essential projects when financing is not available from private sources on "reasonable terms." Typically, the R.F.C. participates in the loans with private lenders. Again, the arrangement is a special one to meet an emergency need, though the economic effects of the capacity expansion will persist after the program is terminated.

At the end of November 1951, $188,000,000 in loans under this program had been approved, though less than this amount had been disbursed. R.F.C. participation in the total of approved loans at that time ran to over $63,000,-000. The R.F.C. may also make loans on its own authority for defense purposes under the defense D-loan program. As of May 1951, $86,900,000 in such loans had been granted. Figures are not available for New England's participation in these programs, but it appears to have been small.

The Small Defense Plants Administration. Under Section 714 of the Defense Production Act the Small Defense Plants Administration may recommend loans to the R.F.C. These loans may be made for defense purposes to small businesses for the acquisition of plant, equipment, or materials, or for research and development work. They are granted only when the necessary funds are not available elsewhere. Altogether, $100,000,000 is available at any one time under the program.

As of April 1952, the S.D.P.A. and the R.F.C. had approved 30 loans to small firms totaling $2,600,000. Two loans which totaled $125,000 were approved for Connecticut firms. Eleven of the loans, however, were made under authorities other than Section 714. Thus 19 loans had actually been authorized under Section 714 for a total amount of $1,300,000 out of the 458 applications for $206,000,000 which had been received at that time. Only 42 loan applications had been rejected, and the rest were still pending.

The S.D.P.A. certified loans appear to be a promising, though restricted, governmental source of both long- and short-term funds for small firms which are taking part in the defense program and are hampered by limited funds from making their maximum contribution. The program is too new to judge its effects, but it would appear to be a worthwhile counterbalance to the other defense-loan programs which have helped the larger firms far more than the smaller ones.

Conclusions on Defense and Wartime Financing.

The federal financing programs during periods of large military production are designed principally to aid those defense contractors who cannot obtain the necessary financing at reasonable rates through normal channels. These programs, several of which we have discussed briefly in this section, are important and necessary temporary supplements to the regular financial system. Most of the special financing arrangements can be used much more effectively by large firms, however, than by small ones.

While all businesses are affected to some extent by the changes which large military procurement creates, small businesses are especially vulnerable. If they produce products for civilian use, they may be greatly restricted in availability of critical materials. Military procurement agencies tend to place the bulk of prime contracts with large firms. Small companies which have highly specialized plants may not be able to adapt them easily to government work.

These small firms which produce highly specialized products associated with military needs find themselves in a very favorable position, however, and New England is fortunate in the number of such companies located in the region. During times like the present they have an excellent opportunity to grow and to develop product lines with major peacetime applications. *It is to the long-term advantage of New England's financial institutions, as well as of the region as a whole, that small firms have access to the money needed for their expansion during defense periods. To the fullest extent that they can, the banks and other financial institutions of the region should provide these funds themselves. Where the risk is too great to bear alone, the financial institutions should assist actively in aiding the firms to obtain the funds through the appropriate emergency program of the Federal Government.*

During World War II the emergency financing programs were relatively less used in New England than in most other parts of the United States. The same appears to be true during the present defense period. In large part this is a result of the industrial composition of New England and the lesser need for such aids in the region. It may also be partly a result of the relatively greater availability of funds for such purposes from normal sources in the region. In any event, the existence of programs of this sort is desirable to help maximize the productive contributions of all firms, wherever they are located. The low loss ratios under such programs in the past also help to show that risks in such lending are not necessarily as great as a superficial examination might suggest.

CONCLUSIONS ON NEW ENGLAND'S FINANCIAL SYSTEM

It is evident that New England has a large and well-organized financial system with ample resources to meet the needs of business in the region. The size of the resources is due in great part to the above-average incomes of New Englanders and their higher than average personal savings. Institutional wealth in the region is an additional major source of financial strength, and the resources of governmental lending agencies provide an important supplement to business financing, particularly during emergencies of depression and war.

In the operation of its financial system the limited available evidence indicates that New England's financial institutions more nearly meet the needs of business firms than those in the country as a whole. Nevertheless, there appear still to be some inadequacies, and the most significant comparison for New England is between its present and its potential position. While short-term credit needs are in general met satisfactorily, there is need for better borrower-lender understanding on a local basis.

Institutional and legal traditions and requirements, in combination with fundamental changes in the money markets, have widened the gap between the demand for long-term credit and equity investment and the available supplies of such funds. New England shares in this problem, though it is a national rather than a regional situation. In fact, New Englanders have been leaders in the development of new financial institutions and techniques to meet these capital requirements. Venture-capital organizations, local industrial foundations, statewide development credit corporations, and the greater use of term loans are all important devices which have been pioneered or used in New England. Unless they are developed to their full potentials, however, the continuation of the new set of market conditions may require the creation of a new type of capital bank.

In this report we have stressed the availability of the kinds of funds needed to meet the needs of business, and we have stressed small businesses, for which the problems are usually greatest. We wish to emphasize, however, that we do not conceive financial aids as any cure-all for small-business problems. No matter how liberal a lending or investing institution may be, short of accepting all applications, some businessmen will always find it difficult to obtain the funds they want and think they need. There is always a line of credit evaluation below which applicants will be refused.

Even if *all* the money demands of small businesses were satisfied, not all could be successful. It is impossible for every small firm to become large and powerful, or even profitable, because competitive forces intervene. Successful businesses result far more from good management than from endless supplies of funds. Most business failures are due to poor management, not lack of funds. While growth must be accompanied by more funds, whether externally or internally obtained, these are not the sole conditions of progress.

The most encouraging climate for business in New England can exist only when employment in the nation is high. Even the best organized financial system in the region cannot function well and make its proper contribution if the national economy is unstable. Implicit in our discussion of New England's financial resources and their use has been the assumption of need for financial policies, both private and governmental, which encourage investment at the proper times and discourage it at other times. Policies to dampen cyclical fluctuations and preserve high-level employment and income are not just the province of public officials.

Federal actions, nevertheless, are a critical element in the stability of the national economy. Federal tax collections, disbursements, and debt management are naturally of the utmost importance. In addition, the monetary policies of the Federal Reserve System have a broad influence over the entire national economy. Treasury actions in handling the national debt affect the money markets in many ways. The activities of government agencies have elevated federal credit and fiscal policies to an importance much greater than that of twenty years ago. Federal acceptance of much of the responsibility for economic stability is no longer in the realm of theory—it is a fact.

Neither the smugness of many of the well-financed large firms nor the exaggerated cries of some small firms should be allowed to detract from the more important goal of high-level economic stability in the nation. If the country's economy is healthy and stable, the New England economy is bound to benefit. It is within this context that any changes in the region's financial framework should be conceived. Changes and improvements in New England's financial system must be accompanied by changes in tax, banking, and insurance regulations, if the capital and credit structure is to be fully effective.

The various detailed improvements which we have suggested in this report cannot in themselves, however, create the demand for investment essential to New England's growth and prosperity. The whole economic and political complex determines that demand. Excellent financial arrangements can help, but they do not automatically provide the favorable outlook necessary to the creation of new investment.

SELECTED REFERENCES

1. Board of Governors of the Federal Reserve System, *Survey of Consumer Finances,* Washington, 1948–52.
2. Butters, J. K., and Lintner, J., *Effect of Federal Taxes on Growing Enterprises,* Harvard University, Graduate School of Business Administration, Boston, 1945.
3. Dirks, F. C., and Hopkins, E. J., *Private Capital Requirements,* Board of Governors, Federal Reserve System, Postwar Economic Studies, No. 5, Washington, 1946.
4. Federal Reserve Bank of Boston, *Monthly Review* (Boston): "Institutional Investors," October 1948; "Broader Investment Channels for Life Insurance Companies," November 1949; "The Development Credit Corporation of Maine," January 1951; "The Financial Needs of Small Manufacturers in Pioneer Valley," March 1951; "New England Industrial Development Corporations," June 1952.
5. Kimmel, Lewis H., *Share Ownership in the United States,* Brookings Institution, Washington, 1952.
6. Litterer, Oscar F., *Where Does Small Business Obtain Its Capital?* Federal Reserve Bank of Minneapolis, 1949.
7. U. S. Bureau of the Census, *1950 Current Population Reports* and *Preliminary Reports,* Series P–60, No. 9; PC–7, Nos. 2 and 5; PC–6, No. 3.
8. U. S. Congress, Joint Committee on the Economic Report: *Factors Affecting Volume and Stability of Private Investment,* 81st Congress, 2d Session, 1950; *Monetary Policy and the Management of the Public Debt,* 81st Congress, 2d Session, 1952; *Volume and Stability of Private Investment,* Hearings, 81st Congress, 2d Session, 1950.
9. U. S. Congress, Committee on Expenditures in the Executive Departments, Subcommittee Hearings, *Inquiry into the Policies, Procedure, and Program Involving Granting of Certificates of Necessity and Defense Loans,* 82d Congress, 1st Session, 1951.

10. U. S. Department of Commerce, *Regional Trends in the United States Economy* (Supplement to *Survey of Current Business*), 1951.

11. U. S. Senate, Committee on Banking and Currency, *Small Business Act of 1950,* Pt. 1, 81st Congress, 2d Session, 1950; *R.F.C. Administrative Policy,* Hearings, 82d Congress, 1st Session, 1951; *R.F.C. Act Amendment of 1951,* Hearings, 82d Congress, 1st Session, 1951.

12. U. S. Senate, Committee on Finance, *Adjustment of the Basis of Property for Depreciation, Obsolescence, Amortization and Depletion,* Hearings on H.R. 3168, 82d Congress, 2d Session, 1952.

13. U. S. Senate, Select Committee on Small Business, *Tax Problems of Small Business,* Pt. 1, Hearings, 82d Congress, 2d Session, 1952, Annual Report, 1952.

Dissenting Opinion by Committee Member

THE REPORT lists many institutional difficulties in the way of stimulating capital investment and financing of enterprises, and recounts the several experimental efforts for more financing of new types of concerns. The major recommendation is for the "creation of a new type of capital bank."

The report, sensitive to the fact that it is addressing the financial interests, conciliates them with the conclusion that "limited available evidence indicates that New England's financial institutions more nearly meet the needs of business firms than those in the country as a whole." This conclusion is not borne out by the report, or by the essential facts of the New England economy which prompted the organization of the present Committee of New England. Complacency with the general outlines of the present organization of financial resources and their modes of operation has no place in a region needing to reconstruct its industrial and physical structure. The region's financial system "may have maintained its strength" but it has not served the regional economy.

Several facts tellingly related by the present report conflict with the feeling of restraint, which has stifled bolder and more venturesome proposals. First, new concerns and employment opportunities are needed in the region, and these have not arisen at the rate experienced elsewhere. Second, funds are most highly concentrated in this area in conservative, nonventuresome savings institutions. Third, capital and funds have been exported in large volume from New England to other regions, though the capital had been earned in it. Fourth, the possessors of funds have had no confidence in the region in which they have earned their monies. Fifth, investment policies have been conservative.

The surveys used in this report to determine the unsatisfied needs of small business examined the attitude of the businessmen who survived the troublesome period of getting started. No information is provided about the role of our financial institutions in accelerating the demise of unsuccessful ventures. These are legion, as figures on business mortality confirm. This experience cannot be waived aside as being merely the record of the unworthy. The financial institutions no doubt played their part in producing this high mortality rate. Nor has this survey examined the many charges publicly made that the Boston banking interests have deliberately discouraged investments in New England and promoted emigration of capital to other regions. These banking organizations are mobile, have organized branches in other regions, and have developed those investment opportunities. Nor has the investigation dealt with the effect of the high concentration of financial resources in two large Boston banking interests upon the process of financing business in New England. The new ethnic groups which have peopled New England during the last 50 years have made little progress in this region's financial fraternity. Significantly these people have had less opportunity and encouragement to initiate and develop new manufacturing enterprises.

The report does not deal with the problem of business financing with the boldness required to plan for the expansion of a growing economy in the process of reconstructing its structure and increasing opportunities. New England requires a rate of new investment above the average national rate to strengthen the older industries. To be satisfied with less than a full-employment economy, and retreat to the vague objective of "a high-level economy," reflects the prevailing caution in the business fraternity rather than the constructive imagination of the independent scholar, using the people's well-being as the point of departure.

Accompanying these restraints manifoldly disclosed in the report are the usual demands for changes in federal tax policy demanded by businessmen, phrased somewhat more modestly as behooves more circumspect writing. Rather than stressing the obligation of the administrators of American wealth, the report suggests concessions and privileges to entice them to perform their routine function. We are all sharing the burdens of high governmental costs, and the nation is expanding its industrial and economic structure at an impressive rate. One is therefore unjustified in arguing for a shift in the tax burden from business to other groups on the assumption that investment is being discouraged. Moreover, the report does not establish any relation between these recommendations and the region's investment problems.

We take exception to the recommendations for changing the practices on depreciation allowances, eliminating the tax on dividends, extending the period for carrying over losses, and lowering the taxes on capital gains. We favor the elimination of tax exemptions on state and local bonds, of tax concessions or other privileges to subsidies, and the closing of tax loopholes.

We wish to join the writers in emphasizing that a major problem in the expansion of industrial opportunities is the combined tasks of development and financing. This challenge the financial institutions have hardly met. In rebuilding an economy the period of reorganization, research, and experimentation can be shortened through the cooperative endeavors of the citizenry. Reliance on individual isolated undertakings, encouraged or more often discouraged by the conservatism of our financial institutions, is inadequate, too haphazard, and too obsolete a procedure for handling a challenge so vital to the well-being of millions of people. To define this problem of financing as a technical issue of making funds available to a group or individual who initiates an enterprise is to conceive of it in proportions unsuited to their needs. Financing and development must be merged with careful research and planning. Such a body must be developed by the citizenry of

New England, dedicated to its growth and expansion and advance rather than to each individual's immediate self-interest. We should not be shy about utilizing federal, financial, and other facilities to help this region.

The responsibilities of the administrators of wealth to rebuild the economy, the industries and areas from which they secured their riches, are neglected and overlooked. A system of private enterprise demands that the administrators of our economy recognize their first duty is to those who shared in creating it. This sense of regional responsibility has been lacking in part because the major financial interests have lost their local ties with the people of New England.

We endorse the proposal for state and regional capital banks associated with a regional developmental agency dedicated to farsighted planning and works rather than to advertising and attracting fly-by-night manufacturers preying on stranded labor groups.

VICTOR J. CANZANO

12

Freight Rates and New England's Competitive Position

Drafted by William H. Miernyk under the direction of Arthur A. Bright, Jr.

INTRODUCTION

New England's economic existence depends on transportation. Its manufacturing industries, on which much of the region relies for income and employment, are based largely on raw materials brought in from the rest of the United States or from foreign countries. Its manufactured products are sold in national markets. Almost all fuels are "imported" into the region. There is a large two-way flow of agricultural products.

New England's location in the northeastern corner of the United States conditions its transportation costs. While it is contiguous to the populous Middle Atlantic region, which is the nation's richest market, many of its producers face competitive transportation-cost disadvantages in reaching more distant markets. The typical New England manufacturer has competitors located between his factory and every part of the national market outside the Northeast. In a poll of 663 New England manufacturers conducted by the Federal Reserve Bank of Boston in 1949, a third of the respondents expressed the opinion that they were operating under an important competitive transportation-cost handicap.

The importance of transportation costs varies from industry to industry, of course. The competitive position of manufacturers who use heavy or bulky raw materials or large quantities of fuel, or who make heavy products of low value, is materially affected by the cost of transportation. Those who use light raw materials and little fuel, or whose products are light in relation to value, are less affected. Nevertheless, most New England manufacturers are concerned, to a greater or lesser degree, with the freight bills they must pay in comparison with those of their competitors outside the region.

This report appraises the freight-rate situation of New England and the effects of rates upon the competitive position of the region's producers.[1] We have stressed railroad freight rates, since New England's most important commodity trade with other areas is by rail. The geographical relationships of railroad freight rates in the United States are of considerable significance to the present position and future development of the New England economy.

1. A companion report, "New England's Transportation System and Its Use" (No. 13), contains a discussion of New England's transportation facilities, and a discussion of the problems of the transportation agencies and related topics.

Railroad rates are complex. An evaluation of their structure, relationships, and effects on New England requires a consideration of some rather technical topics, even if in highly simplified form. In view of the important recent changes in geographical railroad freight-rate relationships and the possibility of future changes, it is desirable to preface the discussion of the present situation by a brief description of the evolution of freight rates in the United States.

The report also contains discussions of motor and ocean freight rates as they affect New England. Together with the railroads, these media of transportation carry most of New England's inbound and outbound commodities and finished products. Air freight, though growing rapidly, is still only a minor factor in the region's transportation of goods. Except for natural gas, which has but recently entered New England, and a petroleum pipeline from Maine to Canada, the region's pipelines operate as local distribution facilities for petroleum products. The report does not cover pipeline rates, but it does contain a short consideration of parcel post rates. While each of these "minor" methods of shipping goods is important to some segments of the region's economy, they are far overshadowed by the "major" methods of rail, truck, and water.

RAILROAD FREIGHT RATES IN NEW ENGLAND

The Development of Freight-rate Regulation

Historically, the railroad freight-rate structure of the United States developed along regional lines. This was a natural corollary of the growth of the United States by regions. During the last century rail lines were gradually extended from one region to another as the need arose. The result is the intricate network of railroad lines that now blankets the country. Even more complex, however, was the structure of freight rates and freight classifications that evolved.[2]

There had been some regulation of rate making since colonial times, but it was not until 1887 that freight-rate regulation came under federal jurisdiction. In that year the Act to Regulate Commerce was passed. In 1920 the name of the law was changed to the Interstate Commerce Act. This law, as variously amended, still guides transportation policy in the United States today.[3] It is administered by the Interstate Commerce Commission, an 11-man body appointed by the president of the United States.

Before 1940 the Interstate Commerce Act did not mention freight-rate dis-

2. A freight *rate* is the charge applied to an article per unit of weight and distance. A freight *classification* determines which of a number of rates is to be applied.

3. For a complete analysis of the Act to Regulate Commerce through its most recent amendment, the Reed-Bulwinkle Act, see Frank M. Cushman, *Manual of Transportation Law*, Dallas, Transportation Press, 1951.

crimination among regions. The original intent of the law was to protect the individual shipper from being discriminated against by a railroad. Since its establishment in 1887, however, the commission has interpreted the act to be in opposition to interregional discrimination as well. This was made explicit in an amendment made by the Transportation Act in 1940 which included the words "region, district and territory" in the injunction against discrimination. In addition, section 3 of the Interstate Commerce Act, as amended by Section 5 (b) of the Transportation Act of 1940, directed the commission to investigate the existing freight-rate structure with a view to the removal of any unjust or discriminatory rates it might find.[4] The commission had already launched an investigation out of which grew its prescription of a new uniform rate system. The order became effective in 1952. An understanding of that order requires first a brief review of the nation's railroad rate structure.

The Freight-rate System of the United States

The United States is divided into five major freight-rate territories. Within some territories there is further subdivision into zones. (See Map 12–1.) Until May 1952 each territory had its own structure of freight rates, and different freight classifications applied from one territory to another. Both the level of rates and their progression with distance differed among territories. Since May 30, 1952, however, there has been a single system of freight classification that applies to all territories, with the exception of Mountain-Pacific territory. Eventually it will apply throughout the nation. Territorial division has been retained only for the purpose of rate publication.

Basically there are three generic types of freight rates—class rates, rates derived from exception ratings, and commodity rates. The class rates apply to general categories of freight, while the commodity rates cover specific products. The basic class rate in each territory is the first-class rate. Other class rates are set at some specific percentage of first class. Many articles that would normally move under class rates are granted rates derived from exception ratings, and exception ratings may vary from one territory to another.

The class-rate system was designed to accommodate the wide variety of articles shipped by rail. Articles that are relatively light in weight and high in value, and which are not excessively bulky, are shipped under first-class rates. Articles that are heavier or more bulky in relation to their value are assigned to lower classes. But thousands of items move by rail, and it would be impossible to design an all-inclusive system of rate classes. The use of exception ratings has given the system a degree of flexibility which it otherwise would not have had.

As a rough generalization, about 85% by *weight* of all rail freight is moved

4. *Class Rate Investigation, 1939,* Docket No. 28300, and *Consolidated Freight Classification,* Docket No. 28310, 262 I.C.C. 688–689.

under rates other than class rates. The relative importance of class, exception, and commodity rates varies from territory to territory, however. Many of the raw materials and all of the coal shipped into New England move under commodity rates. The high-valued, fabricated products that go from New England to other regions are usually shipped under class or exception rates, although some move under commodity rates.

Exceptions are made by rate territory and they are granted for various reasons, one of which has been to permit railroads to meet motor-truck competition. Most exceptions were formerly designated as *column* rates.

MAP 12-1

Railroad Freight-Rate Territories and Zones of the United States

Source: Board of Investigation and Research, Interstate Commerce Commission

Some column rates were a specified percentage of first-class rates. Articles listed in "column 10" moved at 10% of the first-class rate; those in "column 20" at 20%, and so on. Articles that formerly moved under column rates are now combined into new classes. Column rates as such are no longer used. Other types of exception rates are used, however, and they are arrived at by a more complicated process.

In certain zones of some territories, special additions to rates are authorized. Such additions are referred to as *arbitraries*. Arbitraries are prescribed for lines that make primarily short hauls or for lines that are financially weak. The average freight haul on New England railroads is about 133 miles, compared to a United States average of about 230 miles.[5] Arbitraries applied to New England rates prior to May 30, 1952, raised New England rates to about 105% of Eastern or Official territory rates in Zone A (southern New England) and to 115% of the Official scale in Zone B (northern New England).

Commodity rates are published for specific commodities moving between two specified points. Each rate applies to one commodity only, and usually the rate applies only to a movement in one direction. It is impossible to generalize about commodity rates except to state that they are "constructed on no consistent basis." [6] This does not mean that commodity rate making is guided by caprice. It does mean that the wide variation in the specifications and economic characteristics of commodities requires separate rate determinations for each one. Heavy or bulky products such as coal, lumber, livestock, wool, cotton, and many others are shipped exclusively under commodity rates. In addition, however, many fabricated items which move in large and steady volume also carry commodity rates.

Under the old system of freight rates, the determination of class rates for shipments between territories was extremely complex. The principle generally followed was to achieve a "blend" of the class rate which applied in each territory, approximately in proportion to the distances of the shipment within the respective territories. In view of the complexity of freight-rate determination under a system of territorial freight rates, it is no wonder that there was a lack of uniformity.

There were, and still are, many pressures at work in the making of freight rates. "Each rate structure is the product of the policies of rate-making officials of the railroads, with whom initiative in rate making rests, modified by the pressures of shippers' groups seeking rates which would be advantageous to their interests, and modified further by the policies of State and Federal regulatory authorities." [7]

Increasingly, the Interstate Commerce Commission has played a more direct role in rate making, although the commission has not actually initiated rates. It has the authority to do so, but in practice the carriers have initiated rates. It was the commission, however, not the railroads or shippers, which initiated the *investigation* that led to the new class-rate structure now in effect. It is true that the commission was responding to the pressure of railroads and shippers in some regions when it initiated its study, but it was by a ruling of the commission, later sustained by the Supreme Court, that the new system of rate making was introduced. What problems were to be corrected by the new structure of rates and classifications?

5. William J. Cunningham, "Transportation and Its Relation to the New England Economy," *Bulletin of the American Academy of Arts and Sciences* (February 1948), p. 6.

6. *Summary Report on Study of Interterritorial Freight Rates,* 78th Congress, 1st Session, House Document No. 145, p. 13.

7. *Ibid.,* p. 3.

The Railroad Freight-rate "Problem"

Before the advent of federal regulation of railroad rates, the rate on any particular article shipped was determined by railroad rate officials. Both the revenue needs of the carriers and the ability of the shipper to pay established rates were considered. New England was the first region in the United States to become industrialized. Since the region lacks many types of natural resources, its original rate structure was developed to facilitate the flow of raw materials and coal into New England and the movement of fabricated products to markets in other regions. Both commodity rates to New England and class rates from it were relatively low.

During the early period of railroad development in the United States, it is obvious that New England enjoyed a freight-rate advantage. The rate structure at that time was also to the general economic advantage of other regions, which could ship their raw materials to New England cheaply and obtain fabricated products from this region at relatively low freight rates.

Gradually the situation changed. New York, Pennsylvania, Michigan, and other states in the northeastern quadrant of the United States became more industrialized. New England lost much of its earlier freight-rate advantage, because producers in the Middle Atlantic and East North Central regions were located closer to the inland and southern markets that all industrial producers were trying to serve. Still later, the South and West began to emerge from their status as producers of raw materials and fuels. Factories sprang up in those regions, and their owners wished to compete in national markets with manufacturers located in the older industrial areas. The cry of "freight-rate discrimination" was first raised shortly after the Civil War, although a systematic attack on the freight-rate structure did not develop until about the time of World War I. Then it was claimed that the system of freight rates which had evolved during the earlier era no longer applied and that discriminatory freight rates were perpetuating the concentration of industry in the Northeast and retarding the economic development of the South and West.

From the outset the Interstate Commerce Commission was sympathetic to the view that the old system of class rates was discriminatory. Over the past 35 years there has been a gradual narrowing of class-rate differentials. Beginning with the "15% case" in 1917, which increased rates in Official territory by 15% while leaving those in all other territories unchanged, there were other rate increases of unequal percentages which gradually narrowed the gap between class rates in Official territory and rates in all other territories.

It is extremely difficult to measure accurately the average level of freight rates, even when the examination is limited to class rates. According to estimates of the Interstate Commerce Commission, as indicated in Table 12–1, the average of class rates narrowed substantially among the various territories between 1943 and 1950, and there had already been considerable narrowing before 1943. Like all averages, however, these indexes do not show the variations in interterritorial comparisons of individual rates.

The gradually disappearing spread among the indexes for the various territories was not enough to satisfy the critics of the old freight-rate structure. They continued to demand a complete revision of the entire system of class rates. It was in response to this demand that the Interstate Commerce Commission launched its investigation in 1939.

Commodity rates were not included in the demand for revision, even though they carry a much larger proportion of railroad tonnage than class rates. Although there are no averages of commodity rates which would permit comparisons among territories, it appears that most commodity rates in the Southern territory, for example, were closer to Official territory rates than were Southern class rates, and in many cases were lower than Official territory commodity rates. The large number of exception rates, however, came under the class-rate investigation.

Table 12–1. Indexes of First-class Railroad Rates, by Territories,*
1943 and 1950 (for distances up to 1,000 miles)

TERRITORY OR ZONE	AVERAGE OF FIRST-CLASS RATES	
	1943	1950
Eastern (or Official)	100	100
Southern	139	108
Western trunk-line		
Zone I	128	100
Zone II	146	107
Zone III	161	117
Southwestern	161	117

* Excluding the Mountain-Pacific territory, for which data were not available for 1950.
Source: Interstate Commerce Commission, Summary Report on Study of Interterritorial Freight Rates, p. 4, and 281 I.C.C. 229

The Consolidated Rate Investigation of 1939 and the Consolidated Freight Classification

A Unified Freight Classification. Prior to May 30, 1952, there were three systems of freight *classification* in the United States. One applied to Official territory, one to Southern territory, and the third to all remaining territories shown in Map 12–1.

The proponents of complete revision of the rate structure argued that the three systems of classification contributed to the allegedly discriminatory freight rates borne by shippers in the South and West. They advocated a single, uniform system of freight classification to be applicable throughout the country. Among the groups which favored a new classification were the

Southern Governors' Conference, the Tennessee Valley Authority, the American Farm Bureau Federation, various transportation regulatory bodies in the western and southwestern states, various motor-carrier interests, and associations of shippers in the southern, southwestern, and western trunk-line territories.

Opponents of complete revision, which included spokesmen for New England shipper and carrier interests, pointed to the wide diversity in transportation conditions from one territory to another. They argued that the old freight classifications were tailored to fit the needs of each territory, and that complete revision would upset established relationships with detrimental effects upon the revenues of carriers in Official territory.

After hearing the evidence and conducting its own investigation, the Interstate Commerce Commission ruled that the system of three freight classifications was unjust and discriminatory. It ordered into effect "Uniform Freight Classification No. 1" as of May 30, 1952.

The new classification will apply throughout the United States.[8] There are now 31 basic freight classes, compared to a maximum of 12 (in Southern territory) under the old multiple-classification system. Some articles that formerly moved under column ratings have been combined into new classes. The number of exception ratings has been reduced. Some observers believe that the commission's eventual goal is a single system of class rates which will minimize the number of exception ratings by including most of them in the augmented system of class rates.

A Unified Class-rate Structure. The Class-rate Investigation of 1939 also undertook to determine whether or not the old *rate* structure was "unjust, unreasonable, unduly prejudicial, unduly preferential, or otherwise unlawful, and to make such findings and order or orders as may be proper." [9]

Again, spokesmen for the southern and western states advocated complete revision of the rate structure, while opposition to sweeping changes came largely from Official territory. Nevertheless, the controversy over revision of the freight-rate structure was not strictly a "North versus South" affair. Although the Southern Governors' Conference favored a thorough revision, some southern industrial interests were aligned with the opponents of such a move. They contended that while a revision might indeed result in lower class rates for the South, lower class rates might react unfavorably on the revenue of southern carriers and force commodity rates upward. The Southern States Industrial Council favored an adjustment in rates through established methods without changing the basic structure of the entire system.

8. It now applies everywhere except Mountain-Pacific territory where new tariffs to accompany the classification have not yet been published. Most shipments from New England and other states along the Atlantic coast move under separate *transcontinental rates* to points west of the Rocky Mountains. Such shipments may move from any point along the Atlantic coast to any point along the Pacific coast at identical rates, although there are cases where uniform rates apply only within regions.

9. 262 I.C.C. 513.

The Southeast Shippers Conference and the New Orleans Joint Traffic Bureau also opposed uniformity in the entire class-rate structure. Although sectionalism played a part, the controversy was not entirely a sectional one.

The issue was between those who wanted a sweeping revision of the freight-rate system and those who favored the elimination of discriminatory rates where they were found, through recognized channels. Those who advocated complete revision argued that the old rate structure permitted shippers in Official territory to penetrate the "natural" market areas of shippers in other regions. In some cases, they constructed maps which showed "natural" market areas in terms of distance only. Actual market areas that could be served on the basis of existing freight rates were then compared to the areas that could be served under a unified rate system. On this basis, they alleged that the old system of freight rates acted as a protective tariff to the established industrial regions and tended to perpetuate a geographical distribution of industry that no longer conformed to the distribution of population, natural resources, and other factors which normally determine the location of manufacturing plants.

Some opponents of complete revision again warned that a new system of rates would upset established relationships among freight-rate territories and that this would have a detrimental effect upon the revenues of carriers in Official territory. A more forceful argument was that a unified rate structure ignores the fact that transportation conditions vary widely from one territory to another. The composition of traffic is not the same in all territories. In one there may be small movements of low-grade commodities which are shipped at relatively low rates and large movements of high-grade commodities shipped at higher rates. In another these conditions may be essentially reversed. In one territory there may be more inbound than outbound freight, which means that empty cars must be moved in one direction. The average length of haul varies from territory to territory. The cost of operations is not the same in all territories. In brief, opponents of complete revision argued that in the absence of uniform *conditions* in all territories, a uniform system of freight rates as well as of freight classifications was unrealistic.

Those who argued in this vein did not object to making changes in rates that were necessary to eliminate discrimination. They held that the old rate structure was the result of years of investigation and effort by the Interstate Commerce Commission, shippers, and railroads to adjust rates to meet the changing needs of commerce. They urged the commission to "make haste slowly."

The advocates of revision stated that discriminatory rates had retarded the industrial development of the South and West. In reply, the opponents of complete uniformity pointed to the more rapid industrialization of those regions than the rest of the country in recent years and argued that this was not consistent with the allegation that freight rates were unduly hampering their economic growth.

The commission ultimately ruled that the structure of class rates at issue was unjust and unreasonable and violated the Interstate Commerce Act.[10] It ordered the establishment of a uniform scale of class rates based only on distance in all territories covered by the investigation. The decision was challenged and taken to the Supreme Court, which sustained the commission's ruling. The twin goals of a uniform freight classification and a unified class-rate system, toward which the commission had been moving since its inception in 1887, were finally achieved. At midnight May 30, 1952, after twelve years of investigation, hearings, and study by transportation experts, the new system of classification and class rates went into effect. In practice, however, there was no sudden change in rates. It would take several years before the thousands of class rates and exception ratings under the old system could be revised to fit into the new.

The Impact of the New Classification and Rate Structure on the New England Economy

The objective of the new system was to replace the bewildering diversity of rate tariffs, schedules, exceptions, and interterritorial rates by a highly simplified structure. The theory that lies behind it requires equality of rates for any given kind of freight of the same weight which moves the same distance, regardless of the origin or destination of the shipment. Complete installation of the system would permit the quick determination of a rate, once the classification, weight, and distance were known. Freight-rate territories would no longer have meaning, though they might be retained, as they have been thus far, to simplify the publication of rate schedules. Most arbitraries based on short hauls or higher costs have already been eliminated or are scheduled to be eliminated, though some will be continued where the I.C.C. feels that conditions warrant their application.

What effect will this general revision have on the New England economy? The total effect will not be felt for several years, unless and until the transition is complete. *The specific effects on any particular freight rate or any particular shipper may vary widely from the effects on other rates or shippers, in view of the complexity and diversity of the former rates and the individual patterns of distribution and competition of each shipper. In general, however, it appears that rates will be lower than they were formerly in the South and West, relative to those in New England and the rest of the Northeast. The removal of the 5 and 15% arbitraries in southern and northern New England will reduce some rates on shipments within the region, but it will not affect rates on shipments outside New England which did not formerly carry an arbitrary.*

The kinds of changes that may be anticipated are easier to visualize when

10. 262 I.C.C. 701.

viewed against the background of actual railroad charges prior to May 30, 1952. Railroad charges for the shipment of goods depend in part on classifications and rates, but they also depend on the distances between the points of origination and termination. It is the combination of rates and distances which determines how far a shipper can reach into national markets before he suffers a transportation disadvantage in relation to his competitors.

Table 12–2. Railroad Charges* for Finished Cotton Piece Goods, May 15, 1952

TO THESE SELECTED MARKET CITIES	FROM THESE PRODUCTION AND DISTRIBUTION CITIES					
	AUGUSTA, ME.	LEWISTON, ME.	NASHUA, N.H.	FALL RIVER, MASS.	CHARLOTTE, N.C.	GREENVILLE, S.C.
Montreal, Canada	$2.29	$2.18	$2.18	$2.40	$2.90	$2.97
Toronto, Canada	3.23	3.13	2.94	3.06	2.91	3.18
Boston, Mass.	1.09	1.00	†	†	1.91	2.00
Harlem River, N.Y.	1.49	1.43	1.10	1.09	1.75	1.82
New York, N.Y.	1.53	1.52	1.22	1.15	1.75	1.82
Pittsburgh, Pa.	2.09	1.91	1.76	1.76	1.72	1.98
Cleveland, Ohio	2.06	1.80	1.69	1.69	1.89	1.98
Cincinnati, Ohio	1.78	1.78	1.78	1.78	1.55	1.51
Baltimore, Md.	1.77	1.74	1.43	1.41	1.49	1.64
Chicago, Ill.	1.84	1.84	1.84	1.84	2.06	2.06
Minneapolis, Minn.	3.27	3.10	3.05	3.05	2.64	2.67
St. Louis, Mo.	2.09	2.09	2.09	2.09	2.06	2.06
Kansas City, Mo.	3.44	3.27	3.18	3.18	2.54	2.48
Raleigh, N.C.	2.16	1.91	1.78	1.78	0.92	1.14
Nashville, Tenn.	2.78	2.53	2.44	2.44	1.53	1.43
Atlanta, Ga.	2.56	2.31	2.23	2.23	1.06	0.93
New Orleans, La.	3.16	2.91	2.82	2.82	1.84	1.71
Dallas, Texas	4.79	4.62	4.52	4.52	2.86	2.70
Denver, Colo.	5.09	4.92	4.82	4.82	3.70	3.64
Salt Lake City, Utah	5.71	5.71	5.71	5.71	5.61	5.61
Seattle, Wash.	5.71	5.71	5.71	5.71	5.61	5.61
San Francisco, Cal.	5.71	5.71	5.71	5.71	5.61	5.61
Los Angeles, Cal.	5.71	5.71	5.71	5.71	5.61	5.61

* Charge per 100 lbs. from selected production and distribution centers to selected markets, by rail, in less-than-carload lots.
† No railroad rate quoted.
Source: Staff Memorandum No. 3

To test the proposition that the old rate system favored New England shippers over their competitors in other regions, the Committee of New England undertook an analysis of point-to-point railroad charges for 26 products and commodities of special importance to the New England economy. With the cooperation of the New York, New Haven, and Hartford Railroad and other railroads throughout the country, we compiled and analyzed 1,440 freight charges paid by New England shippers or purchasers and their competitors outside the region. The freight charges were based on rates as of May 15, 1952, and included all increases granted to that date.[11]

The patterns of all 26 cases were quite similar. In general, they showed that *regardless of the interterritorial rate differentials, New England manufacturers rarely had a significant transportation-cost advantage over their competitors. The geographical distribution of leading production or distribution centers and major consuming centers dominated the competitive situation. In most instances, competitors in the Middle Atlantic or East North Central states stood between New England producers and the national sources of supply or national markets.* Where the principal competing production centers were not distant, New England's "natural" market occasionally extended beyond the typical limits of the region itself and southeastern New York.

Table 12–2 illustrates the type of comparison made. It shows charges from four New York and two southern centers of cotton-goods production to major markets throughout the United States and Canada. The heavy underline indicates the production center with the lowest freight charge to each of the listed markets. The light underline indicates the second lowest charge in each case. In shipping cotton piece goods, Fall River, Massachusetts, had a transportation-cost advantage in the Middle Atlantic and most of the North

Table 12–3. Railroad Charges* for Machinery, NOIBN†, May 15, 1952

	FROM THESE PRODUCTION AND DISTRIBUTION CITIES					
TO THESE SELECTED MARKET CITIES	BOSTON, MASS.	BRIDGE- PORT, CONN.	PROVI- DENCE, R.I.	CINCIN- NATI, OHIO	CHICAGO, ILL.	CHATTA- NOOGA, TENN.
Harlem River, N.Y.	$1.64	$0.98	$1.53	$2.83	$3.14	$2.92
New York, N.Y.	1.79	1.22	1.64	2.83	3.14	2.92
Philadelphia, Pa.	1.90	1.44	1.80	2.63	3.02	2.78
Nashville, Tenn.	3.41	3.41	3.41	1.78	2.06	1.31
Columbia, S.C.	2.79	2.78	2.78	2.47	3.08	2.01
Little Rock, Ark.	4.50	4.33	4.50	2.89	2.89	2.56
Kansas City, Mo.	4.30	4.15	4.30	2.54	2.12	3.21
Denver, Colo.	5.83	5.71	5.83	4.46	4.08	4.97

* Charge per 100 lbs. from selected production and distribution centers to selected markets, by rail, in less-than-carload lots.
† Not otherwise indexed by name.
Source: Ibid.

Central regions, compared to Charlotte, North Carolina, or Greenville, South Carolina. But southern production centers had an advantage in all markets located closer to them, and they had a favorable transcontinental rate compared to New England, based on their distance advantage.

Table 12–3 shows the results of a similar comparison for shipments of a broad class of machinery. Bridgeport, Connecticut, could reach the New

11. The results are reported in detail in our Staff Memorandum No. 3, *Railroad Transportation Charges to New England and Competing Shippers*, June 1952.

York and Philadelphia markets more cheaply than shippers located in the Middle West or the South. This is to be expected, since Bridgeport is on the doorstep of New York and not far from Philadelphia. Producers in each of the selected centers shown in the table appear to have had a well-defined area of freight-cost advantage, based primarily on distance.

Even though distance was the principal factor in determining the areas of competitive advantage for shippers of the various products, there were significant variations in charges per mile for shipments between the various cities. Table 12–4 presents an example of the kind of situation that existed for many products. It shows actual charges, mileages, and charges per mile, from one northern and one southern cotton-textile center for the shipment of cotton piece goods to major markets throughout the country. The pattern is a characteristic one. For long hauls, the charge per mile was generally much less than for short hauls. Moreover, the charge per mile was generally very high for shipments to more or less protected markets (e.g., Nashua to Montreal and Toronto, or Greenville to Atlanta) and very low to highly competitive markets (e.g., Boston to Chicago, St. Louis, New Orleans, and the West coast).

The charges per mile were lower from Nashua than from Greenville to 13 of the 22 selected markets. They were lower from Greenville to seven of the cities and the same for the other two. For every market listed except Chicago, the actual charge was lower from the closer point of shipment, but the charge from Nashua to Chicago was lower despite its greater distance. The table is worth studying carefully as an indication of the kind of change in rates a shift to an exclusively mileage basis would have. For many markets, the rate relationship of May 15, 1952, would be essentially unchanged. For others, the position of the Nashua shipper would be improved. And for others, such as the important Chicago market, the Nashua shipper would be adversely affected.

The net effect on the Nashua shipper would depend on his geographical pattern of distribution and on the location of his competitors. One manufacturer who sold extensively in Chicago might be seriously affected, while another who sold largely in New York might be materially aided. *To determine the final effects of the new principle of rate determination for any particular company, therefore, requires a careful analysis of its rate charges and those of its competitors. Each New England shipper would be well advised to examine the cost and competitive implications of the new rate policy himself, even in advance of any move to change his particular rates, and he should take the initiative himself in making known the effects on his competitive position.*

A shift to a mileage basis for all exception ratings and commodity rates, as well as class rates, would tend to reduce the competitive ability of shippers farthest removed from the various markets. Under the old system of rate making, lower rates per mile for the longer shipments assisted the distant

shippers in penetrating national markets, even though their rates remained
higher than those of closer shippers. That is, their freight-rate disadvantage
was smaller than it would have been on the basis of distance alone. This was
of special importance to New England shippers, since their geographical
location has put them at a disadvantage in the shipment of finished goods to
most parts of the country.

Table 12-4. Railroad Charges per Mile for Finished Cotton Piece Goods from Nashua, N.H., and
Greenville, S.C., to Selected Markets, May 15, 1952

	CHARGE PER 100 LB.,* FROM		MILEAGE FROM		CHARGE PER 100 LB. PER MILE, FROM	
TO	NASHUA	GREENVILLE	NASHUA	GREENVILLE	NASHUA	GREENVILLE
Montreal, Can.	$2.18	$2.97	287	1,094	.76¢	.27¢
Toronto, Can.	2.94	3.18	412	974	.71	.33
New York, N.Y.	1.22	1.82	256	714	.48	.25
Pittsburgh, Pa.	1.76	1.98	647	724	.27	.27
Cleveland, O.	1.69	1.98	634	704	.27	.28
Cincinnati, O.	1.78	1.51	873	510	.20	.30
Baltimore, Md.	1.43	1.64	439	533	.33	.31
Chicago, Ill.	1.84	2.06	955	786	.19	.26
Minneapolis, Minn.	3.05	2.67	1,241	1,181	.25	.23
St. Louis, Mo.	2.09	2.06	1,156	756	.18	.27
Kansas City, Mo.	3.18	2.48	1,376	1,029	.23	.24
Raleigh, N.C.	1.78	1.14	741	264	.24	.43
Nashville, Tenn.	2.44	1.43	1,168	440	.21	.33
Atlanta, Ga.	2.23	.93	1,104	155	.20	.60
New Orleans, La.	2.82	1.71	1,582	645	.18	.27
Dallas, Tex.	4.52	2.70	1,809	992	.25	.27
Denver, Colo.	4.82	3.64	1,988	1,580	.24	.23
Salt Lake City, Utah	5.71	5.61	2,444	2,136	.23	.26
Seattle, Wash.	5.71	5.61	2,951	2,936	.19	.19
San Francisco, Cal.	5.71	5.61	3,066	2,792	.19	.20
Los Angeles, Cal.	5.71	5.61	3,201	2,430	.18	.23

* Shipped in less-than-carload lots.
Source: Derived from Table 12-2

*While the new system will not affect all New England producers uni-
formly, as we have noted, on balance it appears that the unfavorable effects
on the region will be considerably greater than the favorable effects.* If the
newer parts of the country continue to grow more rapidly than the Northeast, as appears likely, New England producers will find that their transportation charges make it progressively more difficult to reach the growing
share of the market outside the Northeast. Geography is the principal factor
in the change, but the steady movement toward rate equality has intensified
the trend.

Freight charges are only one element of cost, of course, and their relative
importance varies from industry to industry.[12] In general, industries which
use heavy, low-valued, raw materials will feel the effects of the new freight-
rate relationships most strongly. Some of the region's growing industries,

12. For an approximation of the relative importance of freight charges as a percentage of
the value of selected products, see *ibid.,* p. 6.

such as electrical and electronics equipment, plastics, pharmaceutical, precision metal products, and others, which produce relatively light and high-valued goods, will feel the effects much less. For all which are affected, however, relatively higher freight charges mean one more item that has to be offset by some other advantage if output and employment are to be maintained.

Despite the fact that New England's shippers will probably be adversely affected over time by the new system of rates, as they have been by past adjustments, are uniformity of freight classifications and rates desirable for the best interests of the nation? Presumably, this is the criterion which guides those responsible for regulating freight rates, as it should be. There is no simple answer to this question. It depends on the complicated set of effects on industrial growth, employment, allocation of resources, and the financial strength of the railroads in the various parts of the country. *Nevertheless, changed freight-rate relationships may injure one part of the country more than they help others. The change in freight rates can provide an extra impetus to the growth of an industry in one area and to its decline in another. If alternative job opportunites in the area which experiences the loss are less productive, the nation may suffer a net loss.*

This possibility is of special importance to New England, where several branches of the textile industry, in particular, have been hard pressed by their competitors. The new rate structure, if carried to its logical extreme, will tend to encourage in a small way the future growth of textile and other manufacturing industries in the South, and it will apparently add to the difficulties of textile producers and certain other "exporters" in New England. Even if the magnitude of the effect is not great, it would be one more element for the region to overcome in its industrial development efforts. To the extent that it added to the problem of persistent unemployment in New England's textile towns, both New England and the nation might lose.

Actually, the effects of the new class-rate structure may be controlled to a considerable extent by the way it is administered. If sufficient flexibility is retained to permit exceptions where they are justified from the point of view of the shipper and the carrier, the new system may not seriously upset existing competitive relationships among producers in different territories. But if the Interstate Commerce Commission insists upon adhering rigidly to a narrow formula of rate determination, it may mean a loss of employment in some of the region's industries, and it may retard the long-run growth of manufacturing in New England.

We recommend that during the transition the Interstate Commerce Commission give careful study to the long-run effects of the changed relationships which will result from the new system. In general, we subscribe to the principle that freight rates should be dependent largely upon weight, value, and distance, but it seems clear that there are many cases where departure from this principle is desirable. We urge that exceptions be granted, where they can be justified, even if they add to the complexity of the rate system. New England producers should not receive favored treatment, but shippers and carriers in all areas should have an opportunity to present their cases for exceptions, and their arguments should be realistically appraised. The new theory of rate determination is based on the implicit assumption that transportation conditions are everywhere the same. Failure to conform to that abstract theory should not be adequate grounds for refusal to grant exception rates.

MOTOR FREIGHT RATES IN NEW ENGLAND

Motor Freight-rate Determination

Motor freight rates for common carriers are determined on an entirely different basis in New England from that in all other regions of the United States. Outside New England, motor freight rates follow the pattern established by rail rates. For shipments *within* New England, there is a separate schedule of motor rates.[13] New England rates are based on the carriers' calculations of costs, and each truck haul is expected to be compensatory. The rate of each haul, no matter how short, is supposed to cover the costs of the haul. Outside New England this is not necessarily true. A trucker may lose on some short hauls, but he expects to offset those losses by longer hauls. As is true of other forms of transportation, the cost of shipping by truck does not increase in direct proportion to distance.

Motor carriers outside New England follow a national freight classification. New England has its own classification. An attempt has been made to fit all articles and commodities shipped by truck in New England into five broad classes on the basis of density. Where there are sound reasons for departing from this principle, however, there is sufficient flexibility in the system to permit such departure. The value of an article may result in a modification of the classification. If the article is of relatively high value, for example, it may be upgraded to a higher class than would be appropriate on the basis of its density.

Unusual fragility may also lead to departure from the normal classification. Articles that are easily broken in transit require more careful handling. On the basis of density, such an article may fall into the third or fourth class. The necessity for greater care in loading, packing, and unloading may move the article into first class. Some commodities may impregnate other articles in the same shipment. Fish oil is an example. The classification of such commodities may also depart from the density basis.

Both the different rate-making system and the different classification sys-

13. For rate-making purposes, New England includes all territory lying east of the Hudson River and south of United States highway 7. It includes part of New Jersey and such major cities in New York as Schenectady, Albany, and New York City.

tem arose out of differences between the patterns of hauls within and outside New England. The average motor haul in New England is shorter than the national average. In general, costs are higher and truck rates within New England are higher per mile than rates in other regions. Some articles that are shipped at first-class truck rates in territories outside New England move at second- or third-class rates in New England. But there are cases where the second-class rate in New England is higher than the first-class rate in other regions.

It should be emphasized that New England motor rates govern only shipments *within* the region. All interterritorial shipments are governed by the rate *outside* New England, whether the shipment originates or terminates in New England. The New England shipper does not operate under a discriminatory rate structure on his interterritorial shipments. Only for shipments in New England does the shipper pay a higher rate per mile than his counterpart in other regions. We should emphasize that this is differential pricing and not discrimination, in technical transportation parlance.

The mechanics of motor freight rate making are roughly analogous to the steps followed in arriving at railroad rates. Each individual carrier in New England decides upon his own rates. They are filed with the New England Motor Rate Bureau, if the carrier is a member of the bureau, or directly with the Interstate Commerce Commission if the carrier is a nonmember. The bureau files rates with the commission for its members. All new rates are posted at the commission's Washington office, where representatives of the various bureaus and carriers have an opportunity to review them. If there is no protest, the rates become effective 30 days after they are filed. If there is a protest, the commission may order adjustments to bring the new rates in line with prevailing rates. This procedure tends to equalize rates among carriers.[14]

Though there is supposed to be no discrimination among shippers, the highly complex system of motor freight rates that results from this method of rate determination makes the system a difficult one to police. Unlike the railroads, where there are relatively few carriers, there are thousands of independent motor carriers to be regulated.

Are there any compensating advantages to New England shippers to offset their higher motor freight rates for shipments within the region? For some shippers there are, for others there are not. The rate system in New England has been designed to produce approximately the same return per trailer load, irrespective of the class of freight being shipped. Most carriers are relatively indifferent about the kinds of freight they carry. New England shippers of low-class freight have little difficulty in obtaining carriers to move their goods. Outside New England, however, carriers realize a higher return on high-class freight than they do on low. As a result, the carriers tend to "shop around" for the more attractive shipments, and shippers of low-class freight frequently have difficulty in getting their goods moved. *For intraregional*

14. The commission also has the right to determine rates ex parte, i.e., on its own initiative.

*shipments, the shippers of lower classes of freight within New England
have the advantage of better service than they might have under a different
system of rate making. But at the same time they pay more for the service
than they would if the New England system followed the national procedure.*

Rail versus Truck Rates

Within a rather broad range, railroads and motor trucks are in competition with one another. Yet each form of transportation has a distinct competitive advantage for some types of shipments. Railroads are generally the most economical carriers of heavy and bulky commodities over long distances. Trucks have the advantage of greater flexibility in pickup, delivery, and scheduling. Each type of transportation is necessary to the functioning and development of the New England economy. Public policy should encourage both and favor neither over the other. Competition between the two media spurs each to improve its service and lower its costs. The shipper and the consumer both stand to gain.

There are some instances where the two types of transportation service dovetail neatly into one another. For example, in recent years motor trailers have been shipped by rail in New England. At their rail destination, the trailers are unloaded and attached to tractors to complete their journey. The economies of mass rail shipment are realized on part of the trip, and the flexibility of the truck shipment is still achieved for the remainder of the combined rail-truck trip. *Such cooperative ventures are desirable, and they are a healthy sign that the two media of transportation can learn to live and work together.*

Under the railroad system of rate making there are generally only two volume categories. Articles shipped in less-than-carload lots move at one rate. The same articles shipped in carload lots move at another. For each type of shipment, the rate is quoted per 100 pounds. The same *rate* applies whether 100 or several hundred pounds are shipped, provided the weight of the shipment does not move it from the less-than-carload to the carload class.[15]

This is not true of truck shipments within New England, however. Within each of the five basic classes of motor freight there are *five or six* weight categories. A rate is quoted (in terms of 100 pounds) for each breakdown. As the weight of the shipment increases, the rate per 100 pounds falls. This makes it difficult to compare motor and rail rates directly, unless one knows the weight of all shipments. But the fact that motor rates fall as the weight of a shipment increases is significant, since it contradicts the popularly held

15. For some commodities, minimum weights are quoted. Even for a less-than-carload lot, therefore, this minimum must be reached to take advantage of the quoted rate. Below the minimum another higher rate applies. This exception to the rule applies to only a limited number of commodities such as wool and steel sheets or steel plates.

notion that small shipments always move more cheaply by truck while large shipments always cost less to ship by rail. *There are cases where it is cheaper to ship 100 pounds by rail than by truck, just as there are cases where it is cheaper to ship one ton by truck than by rail.*

Table 12–5 presents New England motor freight rates from Boston to New York for the five commodity classifications, with the rate shown for each weight breakdown. Representative commodities are indicated in the various classes for illustrative purposes. It is evident that the rate per 100 pounds

Table 12–5. Motor Freight Rates from Boston to New York, March 26, 1952

CLASS	TYPICAL COMMODITIES	WEIGHT BREAKDOWN (POUNDS)	RATE IN DOLLARS (PER 100 POUNDS)
First	Plastic products, toys, television sets	0– 249	$5.80
		250–1399	5.34
		1400–2699	4.65
		2700–4499	4.27
		4500–over	3.03
Second	Clothing	0– 399	3.08
		400–2399	2.74
		2400–4799	2.36
		4800–8499	2.10
		8500–over	1.53
Third	Shoes	0– 649	2.07
		650–3799	1.77
		3800–7999	1.48
		8000–14499	1.24
		14500–over	.94
Fourth	Paper envelopes	0– 899	1.63
		900–5299	1.35
		5300–10699	1.11
		10700–19999	.93
		20000–over	.69
Fifth	Cotton piece goods	0– 999	1.34
		1000–5999	1.06
		6000–11999	.84
		12000–19999	.75
		20000–27999	.58
		28000–over	.52

Source: New England Motor Rate Bureau, Inc., Tariff 3D, Class Rates Tariff MF I.C.C., No. A 113

falls rather sharply within each class as the weight of the shipment increases.

Under the motor freight rates in effect during 1952, it cost $1.34 to ship 100 pounds of cotton piece goods from Boston to New York. By rail, the rate as of May 15, 1952, was $1.22 per 100 pounds. If the shipment weighed 1,000 pounds, the motor rate dropped to $1.06 per 100 pounds, and the total charge for the shipment was $10.60. The rail rate remained the same for each 100 pounds, however, and the total charge for the rail shipment was $12.20.

There are only three weight breakdowns for shipments between New England and the Middle Atlantic territory. Table 12–6 shows the 1952 rates for shipments to Philadelphia and Baltimore for the first three classes of commodities. Although a direct comparison is not possible because of the different weight breakdowns, the differences in rates *within* New England and *between* New England and points outside the region are obvious from a comparison of Tables 12–5 and 12–6. The higher rates in New England territory stand out in sharp contrast to the interterritorial rates. A shipment of first-class freight from Boston to New York, a distance of 188 airline miles, cost $5.34 per 100 pounds for shipments up to 1,400 pounds. A first-class shipment from Boston to Baltimore, 358 airline miles, cost $2.26 per 100 pounds for shipments up to 2,000 pounds. One would have expected the longer shipment to cost more, but the "all New England" shipment costs more than twice as much as the Middle Atlantic shipment of twice the distance.

Table 12–6. Motor Freight Rates from Boston to Philadelphia and Baltimore, March 26, 1952

WEIGHT BREAKDOWN (POUNDS)	FIRST CLASS* (RATE PER 100 LBS.)		SECOND CLASS† (RATE PER 100 LBS.)		THIRD CLASS‡ (RATE PER 100 LBS.)	
	TO PHILADELPHIA	TO BALTIMORE	TO PHILADELPHIA	TO BALTIMORE	TO PHILADELPHIA	TO BALTIMORE
0–1999	$2.03	$2.26	$1.78	$1.98	$1.53	$1.69
2000–5999	1.80	2.03	1.55	1.75	1.30	1.46
6000–over	1.67	1.90	1.42	1.62	1.17	1.33

* Includes such commodities as clothing.   † Includes such commodities as books.   ‡ Iron and steel plate or sheet and various kinds of castings are typical of commodities in this class.
Source: Middle Atlantic States Motor Carriers Conference, Inc., Tariff 20G, Class Rates Tariff I.C.C. A 420

Long-haul shipments from New England correspond more closely to railroad rates. Beyond the East Central territory there are no weight breakdowns.[16] Shipments to the South and West move according to the class rate only, with no downward progression as the weight of the shipment increases. In those markets New England shippers pay higher transportation costs than their competitors primarily because of the greater distance of shipment. So far as competitors in the Middle Atlantic states are concerned, this handicap is greatest in markets closest to New England, and it diminishes in markets more distantly located.

Table 12–7 compares the cost of shipping first- and second-class freight from Boston and New York to two selected midwestern markets. For shipments of first-class products (up to 2,000 pounds) from Boston or New York to Cleveland, the New York shipper has an advantage of 12 cents per 100 pounds over the Boston shipper; but for shipments to Chicago, this advantage is reduced to 3 cents per 100 pounds. West of Chicago this differential is narrowed further and eventually eliminated. The differentials for second-class products are virtually the same as for first-class shipments. As the length of the haul increases, motor freight differentials between shippers located fairly close together become negligible or disappear.

16. For shipments to and from East Central territory there are two weight breakdowns.

Sometimes the New England manufacturer using motor freight is at a rate disadvantage even within New England. Many shippers outside New England, such as those located at Philadelphia and Baltimore, can ship into Connecticut at a lower rate than manufacturers in New Hampshire or northern Massachusetts. For example, on January 15, 1953, it cost $2.51 to ship 100 pounds of wool knit sweaters from Manchester, New Hampshire, to New Haven, Connecticut. In New England, wool knit sweaters move under second-class rates. Despite the fact that such sweaters are shipped under first-

Table 12-7. First- and Second-class Motor Freight Rates from Boston and
New York to Selected Midwestern Markets, March 26, 1952*

	FIRST-CLASS (RATE PER 100 LBS.)		SECOND-CLASS (RATE PER 100 LBS.)	
TO	FROM BOSTON	FROM NEW YORK	FROM BOSTON	FROM NEW YORK
Cleveland	$2.76	$2.64	$2.38	$2.27
Chicago	3.42	3.39	2.94	2.91

* For shipments of 0 to 1999 lbs.
Source: Eastern Central Motor Carriers Association, Class Rate Tariff, 14 I, I.C.C. A 84

class rates in Middle Atlantic territory, a 100-pound shipment from Philadelphia to New Haven cost the shipper only $1.67. To consider a second example, television sets move under first-class rates in New England and would be shipped at a rate of $4.73 for the first 100 pounds from Manchester to New Haven. A similar shipment from Philadelphia to New Haven would cost the shipper $2.09, although television sets move at 125% of first-class rates in Middle Atlantic territory.

How Will the New System of Rail Rates Affect New England's Motor Freight Rates?

Since motor freight rates outside New England have followed rail rates rather closely in the past, it is likely that most motor rates will change in the same direction and by approximately the same amount as any changes that occur in railroad rates outside the region. Interterritorial motor freight shipments, both to and from New England, will continue to be based on the outside rates. Accordingly, *the changes in interterritorial truck rates will probably show the same mixed effects indicated for rail rates, but on balance the effects will probably be disadvantageous to New England shippers as a whole.*

Motor freight rates within New England have not been tied to rail rates, however, and it is uncertain how they may be affected by the new system of rail rates. *If intraterritory rates are not appreciably changed, the relationship between rates in the New England territory and in the rest of the country would be altered. This might react to the disadvantage of New England shippers for movements within the New England territory.*

If, for example, shippers to the south of New York should be granted lower motor rates as a result of the rail-rate change, while New England motor rates remained the same, some New England users of truck transportation would have higher *relative* rates than they had in the past for shipments to New York or other points within the New England territory. Whether or not a change in relationships would force motor rates in New England down depends upon the responsiveness of the carriers to changes in the demand for their services. If the changed relationship resulted in a lower volume of freight to such important markets as New York, New England motor freight rates might be forced down to re-establish the old relationship.

Can New England Carriers Justify Their Higher Intraterritorial Rates?

If the cost of operating common carriers in New England is higher than it is elsewhere, somewhat higher rates in this territory would seem to be justified. It is accepted that short hauls are more costly per mile than long hauls, because the longer the haul the greater the number of miles over which overhead and terminal costs are spread. Since the average intra-New England haul is short, it would appear that the "average" New England rate should be higher than that in the rest of the nation.

There is an important question, however, whether the New England rates are higher than is necessary to compensate for the extra costs. Are the rates so high that inefficient trucking firms can continue in business? If that is the case, the more efficient carriers are making unusually large profits and the region's shippers are handicapped in serving their own territory. Data are not available for a definite answer to this question, but so long as each trailer load of freight must pay its own way, the New England motor rate system provides a potential umbrella for the inefficient operator and a prop to the level of rates.

There does not appear to us to be enough flexibility in New England's motor freight rate system. It would seem to be logical for New England carriers to average out their costs over all shipments, as carriers do in other parts of the country. Even though the intraterritorial level of rates would probably remain above the national level, it might well drop somewhat in the process. At the same time, however, the practice of "shopping around" for high-class freight would have to be discouraged since this tends to discriminate against the shipper of low-class freight. While returns to the trucking operators must be high enough to encourage them to provide first-class service, the rates cannot be so high that they decrease the competitive strength of the shippers on whom the trucking firms depend for their livelihood.

The high-cost New England carriers might be driven out of business by an over-all lowering of rates. If this should happen, the low-cost carriers would be in a position to expand their operations. The reduction in numbers might permit cost savings as a result of the "economies of scale" usually associated with large-scale enterprises. There is a growing tendency in the West for the trucking business to gravitate to fewer and larger enterprises. In New England, and much of the rest of the East, trucking firms are smaller and there are many more of them. While large numbers of firms are typical of highly competitive industries, from which the consumer is supposed to benefit, many small firms are often less efficient than a smaller number of larger firms.

If New England is to have a motor freight rate structure that balances the interests of both the region's common carriers and shippers, the motor freight system would seem to require an intensive reappraisal. Under present conditions, some large shippers have met the problem of high freight charges in New England by establishing their own fleet of trucks. Others have entered into contracts with trucking firms for the full-time use of trucks. Private and contract carriers are playing an increasingly important role in the motor freight industry. This movement puts pressure on and limits the market of common carriers. In itself, it may help to eliminate the inefficient carriers and force the rest to bring their rates more nearly into line with rates in other regions. This process is slow, however, and it is not a substitute for a thorough examination and revision of the present rate structure.

The Regulation of Motor Freight Rates

While railroads in this country have been under federal regulation since 1887, the trucking industry, which first became a competitive threat to the railroads in the 1920's, has been regulated only since the passage of the Motor Carrier Act of 1935. This act was brought about by pressure from some large truck lines as well as from the railroads.

It is difficult to evaluate the effectiveness of motor freight rate regulation. With thousands of individual firms to cover, the ability of the Interstate Commerce Commission to police motor rates is limited. If the trend toward fewer and larger trucking firms continues, the problem of regulation may be simplified to some extent. The large company is usually more impersonal than the small firm. It may be less willing to grant special concessions to its "best" customers. More important, however, the job of regulating rates will be simplified if the regulatory agencies have fewer individual concerns to deal with.

Few persons today doubt the necessity of freight-rate regulation, though there is room for debate about the proper kind of regulation. *Since efficient railroads and efficient trucking firms are both essential to New England's and the nation's future progress, rate regulation should not favor one medium of transportation over the other. But rates for one medium should not simply follow rates for the other. Each type of transportation should compete on the basis of costs as well as service in that range of commodities and distances for which it has a competitive advantage. Regulation should be directed continuously to ensuring that this objective is pursued above all others in the establishment of rates.*

PARCEL POST RATES AND NEW ENGLAND

Many distributors and some manufacturers use parcel post as a major method of shipping merchandise. This type of shipment is especially appropriate for the distribution of small articles of relatively high value to scattered points. It is the basis of thousands of mail-order businesses, ranging in size from Sears Roebuck down to small household business sidelines.

Parcel post is the least expensive way to ship small packages, but compared to shipments by private carrier, parcel post service is often slow and inconvenient. Formerly, packages weighing up to 70 pounds and not exceeding 100 inches in combined length and girth could be shipped anywhere in the United States by parcel post. Since January 1, 1952, however, the following regulations apply:

1. *For shipments originating and terminating at first-class post offices.* Shipments within the "local zone" (zones 1 and 2) up to 150 miles may weigh up to 40 pounds and be up to 72 inches in length and girth combined. For shipments over 150 miles, the weight is limited to 20 pounds while the combined length and girth may be up to 72 inches.

2. *For shipments originating at first-class post offices but terminating at second-, third-, or fourth-class post offices,* the old regulations still apply, i.e. the package may weigh as much as 70 pounds, and be up to 100 inches in length and girth combined. This is true regardless of the length of the shipment. The same regulations apply to shipments originating at second-, third-, or fourth-class post offices but terminating at a first-class post office, and to all shipments *among* second-, third-, and fourth-class post offices.

Evidently, the purpose of the revision is to shift parcel post shipments away from the busy first-class post offices, but not to disturb the old arrangements in second-, third-, and fourth-class post offices.[17]

Because of its geographical location New England is at a transportation disadvantage in reaching most domestic markets where the freight charge varies by zones based on distance, as it does for parcel post. The most advantageous location for a concern which plans to ship packages by parcel post in any quantity is approximately in the center of the United States. It is no accident that the headquarters of the large mail-order houses are located in the vicinity of Chicago.

The new parcel post regulations should not have much effect on the New

17. For further details see Frank M. Cushman, *Transportation for Management* (New York, Prentice-Hall, 1953), chaps. 2 and 3; and *United States Official Postal Guide,* Pt. 1, July 1953.

England economy. There are few distributors in the region who shipped large parcels to other parts of the country by parcel post. Other forms of transportation are available for them even though at somewhat higher rates.

Legislation has been proposed in Congress which would restore the old parcel post regulations, but other bills have been introduced to limit further the weight and size of packages eligible for shipment by this medium. *We believe that the old regulations should not be restored, and there are strong arguments in favor of further limitation.* Parcel post is a form of subsidized freight, and it adds to the burden of the postal system. The system should be retained for the convenience of individuals and for those concerns which make small sales by mail. But in general it should not be a substitute for direct shipments by air, rail, or truck.

OCEAN FREIGHT RATES IN NEW ENGLAND

Historically it was foreign trade that made New England the first workshop of America. Inbound shipments of raw materials and foodstuffs and outbound shipments of fabricated products resulted in a steady flow of ships into and out of the New England ports. Over the years, however, ports in other regions have expanded more rapidly than those in New England. New York was the first to surpass the Port of Boston in the volume of imports and exports. Since the turn of the century, Philadelphia, Baltimore, and other ports have forged ahead of Boston.

In general, these developments were to be expected. The growth of population in the South and West and the increasing industrialization of other regions gradually created many new important market centers away from Boston. They were closer to New York or other ports to the south of New England. It was easier and less costly to lengthen the ocean haul in order to minimize overland transportation.

In part, however, New England's smaller share of the nation's ocean trade, and of export trade in particular, has resulted from an unusual freight-rate situation. At one time New England was able to capitalize on its location advantage. Ocean rates from the Port of Boston to Liverpool, for example, were lower than the rates from New York, Baltimore, or Philadelphia. But many years ago ocean rates to foreign ports were equalized from all ports in the North Atlantic Conference, which extends from Portland, Maine, to Hampton Roads, Virginia.

While export and import ocean rates were equalized to all North Atlantic ports, export and import *rail* rates were not equalized. As one transportation authority wrote: "The situation is one in which the Interstate Commerce Commission with respect to rail rates gives weight to relative distance while with respect to ocean rates the distance factor is ignored. Boston suffers by the higher rate inland to the port and is denied any advantage in its shorter ocean distance to Europe." [18] It is well known that New England ports are one or two days closer to Europe and various other ports of the world than are other ports on the Atlantic coast. But since it is cheaper to ship from inland points through the ports of Baltimore or Philadelphia than through the Port of Boston, much of the export traffic is diverted to the former, even though the ocean voyage is a longer one.

The Interstate Commerce Commission has no jurisdiction over ocean rates. It does, however, regulate export and import rail rates. Ocean rates for common carriers are formally under the jurisdiction of the Federal Maritime Board, but in practice this agency has little to do with rate determination or regulation. Ocean rates are set by "conferences" of the carriers themselves. There are between 50 and 60 conferences in the United States, made up of operators who ply between ports within a particular geographical area. The members of each conference follow the established rates. A few independent lines usually quote rates below conference rates, but the vast majority of carriers are conference members. Most individual lines prefer to remain within the conference in order to avoid costly and destructive rate wars.

The various conferences operate within "ranges" of ports. Within each range all ocean rates to particular destinations are identical, though they may differ from range to range. As we have noted, the North Atlantic range extends from Portland, Maine, to Hampton Roads, Virginia. The South Atlantic range includes all ports south of Hampton Roads to the tip of Florida. The Gulf ports make up a third range. In general, rates in the South Atlantic and Gulf ranges are about equal to those in the North Atlantic range.

The principal rate problem facing the New England ports today is the lower "export" rail rates from inland production and distribution centers to the ports of Baltimore and Philadelphia. For at least 75 years the ports of New York and Boston have had rail rate parity. The effect of the favorable rail rates to Philadelphia and Baltimore has been to funnel increased shipments of grain and other "bottom cargo" through those ports rather than through New York or Boston. For most commodities, it is more important to a shipper to save on his freight bill than to save a day's time on his ocean haul. With little bottom cargo to offer the shipping lines, there has been a significant reduction in Boston's shipping services. Exports from the Port of Boston declined steadily over a long period. In 1952 the volume of foreign imports through the Port of Boston was about six times the volume of foreign exports.

The first major break in the rate situation came on December 3, 1951, when the United States Supreme Court upheld the decision of a lower court that grain rates from Buffalo to all North Atlantic ports should be equalized. For the first time in 47 years, *both* rail and ocean rates were equalized on shipments of at least one type of commodity. A later decision by the Interstate

18. Cunningham, "Transportation and Its Relation to the New England Economy," *op. cit.*, p. 8.

Commerce Commission resulted in an order that railroads could not cut export grain rates to Philadelphia and Baltimore and that rail rates on grain must be equal to all North Atlantic ports. This decision is being contested by the ports of Philadelphia and Baltimore, but there is little reason to expect that it will be reversed.

What will the equalization of railroad grain rates to all North Atlantic ports mean to New England? It may appear that we are giving undue emphasis to rates on one type of commodity. But if Boston can offer more bottom cargo to the ocean lines, the total volume of export trade flowing through the port should increase considerably, and grain is the only bottom cargo available to Boston at present. During recent years, more than three-fourths of all New England-made foreign exports have been shipped through the Port of New York. If there are more regular export shipments from Boston, fewer New England shipments will go through New York. Furthermore, more inland shipments may be routed through the Port of Boston. Where the ocean rates are equal from all North Atlantic ports and Boston service is improved, some shippers may be more interested in the faster trip from Boston to Liverpool, Amsterdam, and other North European ports.

Perhaps the most important effect of the grain decision, however, is the precedent which it may establish in later cases. If ocean rates are to remain equalized, there seems to be no justification for differentials in export and import rail rates. If transportation regulatory agencies and the courts believe that rail differentials on other items should remain, then the New England ports should be permitted to benefit from their distance advantage and lower their ocean rates accordingly. The position adopted by some persons that it is unjust to deny ports to the south of New England the benefit of their shorter distance to inland sources and markets is entirely at variance with their insistence upon continued equalization of ocean rates. We do not see how the courts can accept such arguments. The net effect of the present trend should be a gradual increase in export traffic through the ports of New England.

CONCLUSIONS

The freight-rate system of the United States has been undergoing almost continuous change since the beginning of comprehensive regulation in 1887. New England's freight rates are now in the midst of a period of transition, resulting from a complete revision of the railroad freight classification and rate structure and important changes in the relationship between ocean and rail rates.

The effects of the new system of rail rates upon the future development of the New England economy will depend heavily upon the way the system is administered. We believe that in making the adjustment from the old to the new system the commission should proceed cautiously. If there are sound reasons for granting exceptions to the new rate structure, they should be granted. The revenue needs of carriers and the competitive position of shippers should not be completely subordinated to a desire to achieve simplicity in the rate system. Differences in transportation conditions, the composition of traffic, and the industrial composition of various regions indicate the need for exceptions to a rigid formula for rate determination. The commission should recognize that the resources of the nation, including human resources, are not equally distributed over a flat plane. So long as there are real economic differences from region to region, the need for exception ratings will remain.

The recent decision on export grain rates should result in a greater flow of export traffic through the ports of New England. Since those responsible for making ocean freight rates have not recognized the distance factor, it is logical to have equalized export and import rail rates as well. If in the future the Interstate Commerce Commission should insist upon restoring rail-rate differentials to ports south of New England because of their favored geographical relationship to inland sources and markets, the system of equalized ocean rates should be discarded. If New England should again be penalized for its greater distance from inland markets, it should be permitted to profit by its closer location to the ports of northern Europe and other parts of the world.

We believe that the motor freight-rate system in New England is in need of a complete re-examination. We cannot pass final judgment on the present rates, but the higher rates paid by New England shippers within the region are a competitive disadvantage to them, especially in the New York market. If the higher rates can be fully justified by higher costs, little relief can be expected unless the rates have been set so high as to protect inefficient operators. It is likely that costs in New England would be higher under the most efficient system of motor transport, because of the preponderance of short hauls. Nevertheless, a more efficient system of motor transport could be expected to lower rates somewhat relative to those in other regions.

Transportation costs to New England shippers and purchasers will remain relatively high under any system of nondiscriminatory freight rates, because of the geographic location and characteristics of the region and the distribution of population and business units within the region, which results in many short hauls. New Englanders cannot expect favored treatment. They can and should expect equitable treatment. The dislocating effects of a rigid system of rate making should be minimized. Abstract principles of rate determination are desirable, and indeed necessary, but real life seldom lends itself to the strict application of abstract principles. We recommend that in administering the new system of railroad rates the Interstate Commerce Commission give greater recognition to the differences among the various regions than it did in the hearings that preceded its decision to make a complete and sweeping revision of the freight-rate structure of the United States.

SELECTED REFERENCES

1. Cunningham, William J., "Transportation and Its Relation to the New England Economy," *Bulletin of the American Academy of Arts and Sciences,* February 1948, pp. 6–8.
2. Cushman, Frank M., *Manual of Transportation Law,* Dallas, Transportation Press, 1951.
3. Interstate Commerce Commission, *Report on Interterritorial Freight Rates,* 78th Congress, 1st Session, House Document No. 303.
4. ———— *Class Rate Investigation, 1939,* Docket No. 28300, and *Consolidated Freight Classification,* Docket No. 28310, 262 I.C.C.
5. ———— *Summary Report on Study of Interterritorial Freight Rates,* 78th Congress, 1st Session, House Document No. 145.
6. University of Georgia, School of Business Administration, *Proceedings of the First Annual Southeastern Transportation Clinic,* December 10, 1952.
7. Sullivan, Austin P., "The Port of Boston," *Monthly Review,* Federal Reserve Bank of Boston, February 1950.
8. Tennessee Valley Authority, *Regionalized Freight Rates: Barrier to National Productiveness,* 78th Congress, 1st Session, House Document No. 137.
9. U.S. Senate, Senate Committee on Interstate and Foreign Commerce, *Domestic Land and Water Transportation,* 82d Congress, 1st Session, Senate Report No. 1039.

13

The New England Transportation System and Its Use

Drafted by Robert A. Nelson under the direction of George H. Ellis

INTRODUCTION

The function of transportation is to overcome the barriers to production and distribution imposed by distance. Historical improvements in the means of transport have resulted in the tendency toward centralization of production at points of lowest cost. As distance has been conquered other factors of cost, such as land fertility and labor characteristics, have become more decisive in industrial location. A lowering of the level of transport costs relative to other production costs favors the distant producer. It enables him more fully to utilize whatever cost advantages he may have over competitors closer to the market. Conversely, of course, a rise in transport cost favors the near producer and encourages industrial decentralization.

New England finds itself today more remote from United States raw material sources than in the past and on the periphery of the national market. In the 19th century the advent of canals and railroads favored development of the extractive industries—agriculture and mining—at more productive points. More recently the slow westward gravitation of the industrial and consumer markets has had an unfavorable impact on New England producers. The level of transport cost in relation to other production costs is vital to New England. Rising transportation costs can effectively strangle New England's access to markets; lower transportation costs can extend those markets.

In the postwar period New England has seen the effect of rising transport costs forcefully demonstrated. General rate increases have been percentage increases; for example, all rates increased by 10%. As a result, if two producers compete in the market from different distances, the more distant is subjected to the larger transportation cost increase.

Producer A——— $1.00 + 10\% = $1.10

Producer B——————————————→ Market
$1.50 + 10\% = $1.65

B selling in competition with *A* finds his costs of shipping to the market increased 15 cents as compared to *A's* 10-cent increase. If materials used must first be shipped in from the direction of the market, as is frequently true, then the more distant producer *B* may find his cost of materials has also increased due to the rise in rates.

This type of rate increase, prevalent after the war, has been to New England's disadvantage. It is justified by the carriers on grounds of practicality. A simple percentage increase applied to all rates eliminates the immediate necessity of reprinting tariffs (rate schedules). That percentage increases are an unsettling factor in competitive price adjustments is undoubted. Whether they can be justified on theoretical cost grounds is uncertain. In any case the carriers in the exercise of managerial prerogatives have resorted to this type of increase and the regulatory authorities have given assent.

There are two ways of coping with rising transport costs. One is to persuade carriers to ignore cost relationships. This can be done by rate equalization as, for example, in export rates from inland points through several of the Atlantic coast ports. Much can be done along those lines in the short run to preserve competitive positions.[1] *A second and more rewarding approach is to stimulate and encourage transport innovations leading to permanent cost reductions. Much can be done by the region in this direction. Better roads, airports, research programs, wise and fair regulations are all means by which New England can encourage the better transportation vital to its economic existence.*

This study is concerned with the second approach—that is, consideration of the long-run adequacy of New England transportation facilities and steps that may be taken to improve them. We shall discuss in turn each of the basic media of transport—rail, motor, water, air, and pipeline—comment on their performance, and where appropriate offer recommendations for their better use. Emphasis will be placed on the transport of goods rather than people. Conditions of passenger transport are more routine, and show less variance from one region of the country to another. However, where passenger volume and revenue affect freight costs, as in the case of the railroads, attention will be given to both.

Relative Importance of Transportation Agencies in New England

The relative importance in New England of the different agencies of transportation has not been accurately determined for lack of statistical information. However, the Interstate Commerce Commission annually makes an estimate of the breakdown of intercity freight ton miles by agency in the United States.[2] The Commission's figures indicate that in 1952 railroads carried 57.7% and motor carriers 13.0% of intercity freight ton miles. Oil pipelines accounted for 14.8% and water transport for 14.4% of the total. The share of trucks in New England is probably higher than the

1. See our report No. 12, "Freight Rates and New England's Competitive Position."
2. The ton mile is the most commonly used measure of transportation. It represents the movement of one ton of freight one mile.

national figure. In a limited study of motor transportation made under the auspices of the Federal Reserve Bank of Boston in 1950, it was estimated that 29% of tonnage to and from New England went by truck. This figure, it should be noted, is for tons rather than ton miles. We estimate that motor carriers are responsible for 25% to 40% of the intercity freight ton miles performed in New England, including both intraregional and interregional shipments.

TRANSPORT FACILITIES IN NEW ENGLAND

Railroads

Much of the movement of freight in New England today is by motor carrier. However, railroads are still the prime means of transporting cargo overland *into* and *out of* New England. Thus, New England's most important rail routes are those which connect with other regions.

The New York, New Haven, and Hartford serves as the single rail route through southern New England, with a virtual monopoly over rail transport in southern Massachusetts, Rhode Island, and Connecticut. There are two main lines to the west—the Boston and Albany division of the New York Central, which runs from Boston through Worcester to Albany, and the Boston and Maine which has its main line from Boston through Fitchburg to Troy and Mechanicville, New York. Despite its name, the Boston and Maine's lines are largely in northern Massachusetts and New Hampshire. They run through southern Maine to Portland, throughout New Hampshire, and up the Connecticut River Valley to Wells River below the Canadian border, connecting there with the Canadian Pacific Railroad.

Two railroads, the Maine Central and the Bangor and Aroostook, lie almost entirely in the state of Maine, serving the area north of Portland and connecting with other roads to the south, west, and the Canadian roads to the north.

The two large Canadian roads, the Canadian National and the Canadian Pacific, have lines in northern New England. The Canadian National, through its ownership of the Central Vermont Railway, has a route across Vermont and down the Connecticut River valley to Amherst, Massachusetts, and thence to New London, Connecticut. It also has a line across southern Maine to Portland.

The Rutland Railway operates north and south on the western side of Vermont, acting largely as an interchange road between the Canadian railroads and New England and New York roads.

Railroads constitute a smaller segment of the New England economy than is the case for railroads in the country as a whole. Statistics reveal that while New England has 6.1% of the population and contributes 8.3%

of the value added by manufacture of United States production, New England railroad percentages are noticeably smaller. Operating revenues of New England carriers have averaged slightly over 3% of the total railroad operating revenues in the United States. New England's compact area, only 2.1% of the United States, affects operating revenue by reducing the average length of haul and also stimulates more competition from alternate carriers. The position of railroads in the region's economy is a reflection of the relatively higher value of goods transported to, from, and within New England compared to the rest of the country. Since freight charges are not directly proportional to commodity value, transport costs are a smaller proportion of total production cost in New England. It may also be true that a larger share of New England transportation is carried by other than rail carrier.

Table 13-1. Miles of Class I Railroads Operated in New England during 1952

Bangor and Aroostook	569
Boston and Albany	360
Boston and Maine	1,679
Canadian National	172
Canadian Pacific	
Maine	234
Vermont	90
Central Vermont	422
Maine Central	945
New York, New Haven, and Hartford	1,765
Rutland	407
TOTAL	6,573

Source: Annual Reports of Railroads for 1952, and I.C.C., *Statistics of Railways in the United States, 1950*

Operations of New England Railroads

It has long been maintained that the operational costs of New England railroads have been higher than average for the country. The Interstate Commerce Commission has given recognition to that fact on several occasions, viz., in approving zone rate levels higher than the Official Territory class-rate level, and in granting a larger share in the division of joint rates. Insofar as the New England roads are concerned, there is little doubt that New England shippers pay a higher level of charges than do shippers in most of the rest of the country.

In the past, higher costs and higher charges have been attributed to unfavorable operating conditions. Cited as being unfavorable are the shorter average haul possible in New England, the low density of traffic, the unbalance of traffic, and the cost of fuel. These conditions, of course, vary from one road to another. Unquestionably they play a significant part in the higher costs of New England roads.

Shorter Average Haul. The average haul of the New England roads is shorter than the average for all roads in the United States. Inasmuch as terminal costs are calculated to be 50% to 60% of total rail operating cost, the shorter average haul results in a higher ton-mile cost because of the fewer miles over which costs can be spread. For shipments within New England where the New England carrier bears both terminal costs, the higher ton-mile cost is a cause for higher rates. However, for shipments to and from New England where the length of haul may be closer to the national average, the higher ton-mile cost in New England does not justify a higher freight charge for the whole movement. The New England

Table 13–2. *Average Revenue per Ton Mile, 1951*

	IN CENTS	N.E. ROADS AS A PERCENTAGE OF ALL DISTRICTS
ALL DISTRICTS OF UNITED STATES	1.34	100
NEW ENGLAND REGION	2.18	163
Bangor and Aroostook	2.74	205
Boston and Maine	2.10	157
Canadian National	1.63	122
Canadian Pacific lines in Maine	1.28	96
Canadian Pacific lines in Vermont	1.34	100
Central Vermont	1.62	121
Maine Central	2.24	167
New York, New Haven, and Hartford	2.39	178
Rutland	1.88	140

Source: I.C.C., *Comparative Statement of Railway Operating Statistics, 1951 and 1950, Individual Class I Steam Railways*

carrier is entitled to a relatively larger share in the division of the charge between carriers to compensate for his shorter line haul and his terminal cost. At the present time it appears that New England roads in general receive a favorable proportion of rate divisions. Thus, interregional rates do not constitute a burden upon regional rates.

Low Density of Traffic. Higher costs due to low density of traffic *may be caused* by higher than average charges impeding the development of new traffic. Railroads have been quite conservative in their willingness to try reducing rates to stimulate traffic. The competitive situation today with highway carriers has tended to eliminate any possibility of higher rates impeding the development of new traffic. In some cases the New England railroads and their connections have reduced the rates on manufactured articles going to and from New England to achieve a mile-for-mile rate parity for New England producers in comparison with their non-New England competitors. New England railroad managements today generally believe that freight rates are as high as they can go, and present thinking is toward more realistic and competitive rate making.

Empty Car Mileage. It has been stated that five loaded freight cars move into New England for every two which leave fully loaded.[3] Thus, it is alleged, the cost of moving empty freight cars back to their point of origin constitutes a heavy burden on New England carriers. The facts indicate that New England roads are not much worse off than the average of all roads in the United States. In 1951 all railroads in the United States had freight cars loaded for 66% of their total freight car mileage. In that year the Boston and Maine averaged 71.2% and the New York, New Haven, and Hartford 69.3%. The Bangor and Aroostook had less success, with 55%; the Maine Central averaged 63.2%. Thus, the two major roads in New England were able to fill their freight cars oftener than the national average. (See Table 13-3.)

Table 13-3. Percentage of Loaded Freight Car Miles to Total Freight Car Miles, 1951

	PER CENT	RATIO OF EACH N.E. ROAD TO ALL RAILROADS
ALL DISTRICTS OF UNITED STATES	66.0	
Bangor and Aroostook	55.0	83.3
Boston and Maine	71.2	107.8
Canadian National	61.7	93.5
Canadian Pacific in Maine	72.9	110.5
Canadian Pacific in Vermont	70.4	106.7
Central Vermont	69.2	104.8
Maine Central	63.2	95.8
New York, New Haven, and Hartford	69.3	105.0
Rutland	75.8	114.8

Source: I.C.C., *ibid.*

Fuel Cost. For many years New England roads labored under a disadvantage compared with other eastern roads, with respect to fuel costs. New England has no indigenous supply of coal, and consequently must import it from other regions. When diesel locomotives were adopted, the New England railroads' relative cost position improved. Diesel fuel comes largely from the southwest and abroad, and must be brought in by all eastern roads. Since tankers are the cheapest means of transporting petroleum, consuming points near tidewater have an advantage. New England roads currently are able to obtain fuel at a cost only slightly above the average cost for all carriers in the United States. (See Table 13-4.)

Indices of Performance. The Interstate Commerce Commission annually publishes statistics for individual Class I railroads in the United States. One section of these statistics is devoted to what the I.C.C. labels "freight and passenger train performance." These figures should not be considered as measurements of efficiency because figures higher than the national average are partially the result of the factors enumerated above; but we may obtain some insight into the problems of New England railroads by perusing them.

3. See our Staff Memorandum No. 1, *Origins and Destinations of New England's Rail Traffic, 1949,* March 1952.

Statistics indicating freight and passenger train performance are measurements of the degree of utilization. Utilization is extremely important in railroad operation because of the high proportion of total cost which is fixed or semifixed. Additional loaded freight cars can be hauled with relatively small additional cost. The figure for gross and net ton miles per freight train mile measures the degree of utilization of the tractive power involved in the movement of a freight train. Train miles per train hour, road miles per locomotive day, car miles per freight car day are measurements of the utilization of the way and structure as well as equipment. Net ton miles per freight car day and per cent serviceable of locomotives and freight cars show the utilization of available equipment. (See Table 13–5.)

Table 13–4. Cost of Locomotive Fuel to New England Railroads, 1951

	COST PER TON OF COAL (DOLLARS)	PER CENT OF U.S. AVERAGE FOR COAL	DIESEL FUEL PER GALLON (CENTS)	PER CENT OF U.S. AVERAGE FOR DIESEL FUEL
ALL DISTRICTS	5.28		9.79	
Eastern district	5.59		10.42	
Great Lakes region	5.66		10.42	
Central Eastern region	5.35		10.47	
Southern district	5.24		9.95	
Western district	4.65		9.35	
NEW ENGLAND REGION	8.81		10.19	
Bangor and Aroostook	12.08	228.8	11.96	122.2
Boston and Maine	8.38	156.8	9.47	96.7
Canadian National	10.47	198.3	—	—
Canadian Pacific in Maine	9.56	181.1	—	—
Canadian Pacific in Vermont	9.36	177.3	14.28	145.9
Central Vermont	8.55	161.9	11.66	119.1
Maine Central	9.58	181.4	9.72	99.3
New York, New Haven, and Hartford	8.03	152.0	10.50	107.3
Rutland	8.78	166.3	10.42	106.4

Source: I.C.C., ibid.

The performance of New England roads according to these measures is not as good as the average of all roads in the United States. A distinction should be made between New England roads and Canadian-owned New England roads. The Canadian roads achieve a higher level of utilization because they are bridge carriers and haul freight almost exclusively. If we rule out the Canadian-owned lines, we find the New England roads below average in most cases. The Bangor and Aroostook, Boston and Maine, Maine Central, and New York, New Haven, and Hartford lag behind in measurements of utilization. In Table 13–5 we see that in only six cases out of 32 did any one of the New England roads exceed the average for all roads in the United States. The Bangor and Aroostook in no case had a figure above the national average. The Boston and Maine had

Table 13-5. Freight Train Performance of New England and United States Railroads, 1951

	GROSS TON MILES PER TRAIN MILE	NET TON MILES PER TRAIN MILE	TRAIN MILES PER TRAIN HOUR FREIGHT	GROSS TON MILES PER TRAIN HOUR FREIGHT	SERVICEABLE FREIGHT CARS AS PER CENT OF THOSE ON LINE	ALL ROAD MILES PER LOCOMOTIVE DAY FREIGHT	CAR MILES PER FREIGHT CAR DAY ALL FREIGHT CARS	NET TON MILES PER FREIGHT CAR DAY
ALL DISTRICTS	2,774	1,301	17.0	46,424	95.3	92.0	45.0	980
Eastern district	2,830	1,362	15.4	42,773	93.8	88.2	33.8	763
Southern district	2,790	1,396	16.8	46,407	96.0	83.4	48.7	1,154
Western district	2,790	1,216	18.3	49,344	96.6	99.9	55.3	1,124
NEW ENGLAND REGION	2,111	906	15.5	32,490	97.2	88.5	38.3	719
Bangor and Aroostook	1,577	561	15.7	24,681	95.0	51.5	27.5	403
Boston and Maine	2,410	1,034	15.9	38,192	97.7	100.9	46.4	880
Canadian National	1,056	442	17.2	17,077	97.4	80.1	20.4	356
Canadian Pacific in Maine	1,428	636	19.3	27,353	98.1	69.0	108.1	2,182
Canadian Pacific in Vermont	1,615	668	15.6	25,021	98.4	90.0	54.3	954
Central Vermont	1,788	748	14.1	25,117	91.9	81.8	61.7	1,106
Maine Central	1,864	778	14.6	27,204	96.4	70.7	35.6	636
New York, New Haven, and Hartford	2,424	1,071	14.9	36,136	97.6	115.6	31.3	608
Rutland	1,384	637	15.0	20,628	91.9	68.5	33.9	719
				(Per cent New England of United States)				
ALL DISTRICTS	100.0	100.0	100.0	100.0	100.0	100.0	100.0	100.0
Eastern district	102.0	104.7	90.6	92.1	98.4	95.9	75.1	77.9
Southern district	101.6	107.3	98.8	100.0	100.7	90.7	108.2	117.8
Western district	101.6	93.5	107.6	106.3	101.4	108.6	122.9	114.7
NEW ENGLAND REGION	76.1	69.6	91.2	70.0	102.0	96.2	85.1	73.4
Bangor and Aroostook	57.8	43.1	92.4	53.2	99.7	56.0	61.1	41.1
Boston and Maine	86.9	79.5	93.5	82.3	102.5	109.7	103.1	89.8
Canadian National	38.1	34.0	101.2	36.8	102.2	87.1	45.3	36.3
Canadian Pacific in Maine	51.5	48.9	113.5	58.9	102.9	75.0	240.2	222.7
Canadian Pacific in Vermont	58.2	51.3	91.8	53.9	103.3	97.8	120.7	97.3
Central Vermont	64.5	57.5	82.9	54.1	96.4	88.9	137.1	112.9
Maine Central	67.2	59.8	85.9	58.6	101.2	76.8	79.1	64.9
New York, New Haven, and Hartford	87.4	82.3	87.6	77.8	102.4	125.7	69.6	62.0
Rutland	49.9	49.0	88.2	44.4	96.4	74.5	75.3	73.4

Source: I.C.C., ibid.

three, the New York, New Haven, and Hartford had two, and the Maine Central one.

These statistics, taken without qualification, might be regarded as evidence that not only is the physical performance of New England railroads inferior to that of other railroads but the management is inefficient. Such a conclusion, however, would not recognize the fact that the statistical averages quoted here are more the result of the burden of operating handicaps and peculiar traffic characteristics than of the degree of operating efficiency. Obviously the lower degree of equipment and train utilization in New England means higher ton-mile costs and higher freight rates. The degree in which operating and traffic handicaps can be reduced by management, and lower costs translated into lower freight rates, is quite uncertain. The possibilities, however, present a challenge.

New England Railroads

This section is devoted to consideration of each of the railroads in New England from the point of view of its financial position, traffic, and other aspects of operation. Financial well-being of the railroads is intimately associated with the general economic picture in New England.

Bangor and Aroostook. The Bangor and Aroostook Railroad operates about 600 miles of road in the northern part of Maine. (See Map 13–1.) Its main line extends from Searsport on the coast northerly to Van Buren on the Canadian border. Branch lines run north and south roughly paralleling the main line. Its principal connections are with the Maine Central at Northern Maine Junction near Bangor, the Canadian Pacific at Greenville and Brownville Junction, and the Canadian National at St. Leonard in New Brunswick, Canada.

This railroad depends for a large proportion of its revenue upon the movement of Maine potatoes. In 1951 this constituted 21.7% of freight tonnage and contributed 33.4% of freight revenue. In 1952 the traffic of potatoes contributed 41 cents to every dollar of freight revenue received by the railroad. Other important sources of traffic are newsprint paper, which contributed 11%, and pulpwood which contributed 12.5% of freight revenue in 1952. Dependence upon potato traffic and the danger of losing it to motor carriers induced the railroad in April 1949 and July 1950 to make several reductions in freight rates on potatoes. The road also began a program of improvement of facilities and services to potato shippers. Additional refrigerator cars and insulated boxcars were placed in service to meet the needs of the potato growers.

The Bangor and Aroostook's operation is relatively stable through the business cycle because of the nature of its traffic. Historically, raw material production, especially of agricultural products, has not fluctuated as much as industrial production. The Bangor and Aroostook has less to fear from a

decline in national production than from a loss in traffic to motor carrier
competition. If the present level of service can be maintained at competitive
rates, this railroad is likely to remain solvent and continue to meet the needs
of the area which it serves.

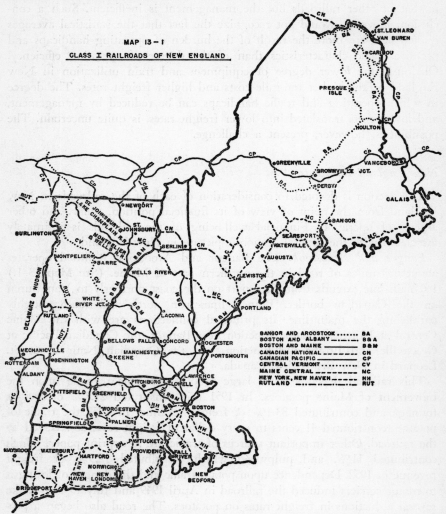

MAP 13-1

CLASS I RAILROADS OF NEW ENGLAND

According to general financial practice, the capitalization of the Bangor
and Aroostook is not as favorable as might be desired: 58% debt and 42%
stock. However, income available for fixed charges in 1952 was 2.61 times
actual fixed charges.[4] In 1951 the figure was 2.19. Also, the railroad had

4. Security analysts generally feel that a railroad ought to earn its fixed charges at least
twice in order to achieve a margin of safety.

accumulated a surplus which in 1952 made the relation between equity and debt 56–44, a sound situation provided the earned surplus is retained in the corporation.

Boston and Maine Railroad. The Boston and Maine operates 1,679 miles in central and northern Massachusetts, southeastern Maine, all of New Hampshire, and small amounts of mileage in Vermont and New York. Its important terminals are Portland, Maine; White River Junction, Vermont; Boston, Worcester, Springfield, Massachusetts; and Mechanicville, New York. The main freight line runs between Boston and the Troy-Mechanicville-Schenectady area. Much of the rail traffic entering or leaving northern New England moves over this line.

Connections with other roads provide 90% of the tonnage carried. The road participates in the heavy movement of raw materials into New England and shares in the movement of agricultural products, potatoes, and pulp and paper products, originating on its own line as well as on the Bangor and Aroostook and the Maine Central.

The Boston and Maine is especially susceptible to competition from motor carriers for the high-class freight which originates in its territory. Manufactured goods tend to be shipped in smaller lots with greater diversity of destination and less regularity of movement than raw materials. This type of traffic, which generally bears higher rates and demands good service, is appropriate for motor carriers. The fact that a large volume of raw materials is brought into New England via the Boston and Maine and leaves as manufactured goods presents a problem in empty car movement. Moreover, at certain seasons the Bangor and Aroostook and the Maine Central need extra cars to haul potatoes and pulpwood, thereby requiring the Boston and Maine and the Canadian roads to haul in empty cars.

Passenger service constitutes a problem for the Boston and Maine. On a basis of fully allocated expenses, passenger costs exceeded passenger revenues by about 45% in 1952. Even expenses directly attributable to passenger service exceeded passenger revenues by about 11%. This burden of passenger service on freight service is part of the explanation why the railroad is not inclined to make any additional investment in passenger equipment beyond what is provided for by depreciation allowances.

Much of the passenger deficit is due to commutation service. The Boston and Maine, like some other railroads in the United States, faces a difficult problem with respect to commutation traffic. The railroads must deal on matters of rates and services with state regulatory agencies which are in many cases under political pressure to maintain depressed commutation rates.[5] At times, the roads have been forced to continue passenger service on

5. In 1952 coach passengers in the United States paid an average of 2.53 cents, commutation passengers an average of 1.87 cents.

lines where revenues have not covered even direct expenses. Public service companies cannot and do not expect revenues to cover fully allocated costs on all segments of their service. However, from the point of view of equity to the owners of railroad property, and all users of rail service, the carrier should be permitted to discontinue a unit of service for which revenues do not cover direct costs. Funds which otherwise could be used for the improvement of service are devoted to a subsidy of commuters on those lines.

The railroads and the state regulatory agencies have a public obligation to provide the most efficient, low-cost commutation service possible. The regulatory agencies should not impose burdens upon the railroads which result in a general deterioration of service. The railroads, on the other hand, should investigate fully all possibilities for reducing the operational costs of commuter service.

A railroad may find direct unit costs using old equipment (of little salable value) to be less than full unit costs using new equipment, and thereby justify continued use of the old equipment. However, such a policy does not consider the general disaffection of commutation passengers and their ill will toward the carrier, which will in the long run reflect on total passenger and freight activity. Some railroads have found that single diesel-propelled cars are a partial solution to the problem of passenger service. These "Budd" cars are already widely used on the Boston and Maine.

The Boston and Maine's capitalization has imposed a burden on its attempts to improve operating efficiency. During the 1930's the road managed to avoid insolvency and bankruptcy although laboring under a relatively heavy burden of debt. In 1940, under a voluntary plan of exchange, maturities were postponed and a rearranged debt structure was set up consisting of income bonds as well as fixed interest-bearing bonds. The total amount of debt under this plan was reduced by redemption of $26,000,000 of bonds.

In 1952 the Boston and Maine earned its fixed and contingent charges 1.03 times out of income available for that purpose. In 1951 the figure was 1.01. This means that the railroad has had very little money after meeting capital charges to use for additions and improvements to the operating property. During a period of rising prices, depreciation reserves have been insufficient for that purpose. Fortunately, through purchase and conditional sale arrangements, the road has been able to obtain additions to rolling stock (locomotives, freight, and passenger cars). However, funds have not been available for improvements in way and structure.

The Boston and Maine was able to reduce its funded debt, other than equipment obligations, by approximately $45,000,000 between 1939 and 1952. Annual fixed charges were reduced from $3,788,000 in 1946 to $3,055,000 in 1951. Between 1939 and 1951 interest charges were reduced approximately 41.7%. These reductions indicate a healthier financial situation for the road.

If they are continued, more income should become available for improvement of service.

New York, New Haven, and Hartford Railroad Company. The New York, New Haven, and Hartford Railroad operates about 1,765 miles of road in Connecticut, Rhode Island, southern Massachusetts, and southeastern New York. The main line runs between Boston and Harlem River, New York, with passenger connections into Grand Central Station, Manhattan. An important freight branch extends from the New Haven area to Maybrook, New York, where connection is made with railroads going west.

Traffic is largely made up of manufactures (63.9% in 1951). Of traffic tonnage *originating* on the New Haven, manufactures amounted to 82.6% in 1951. The heavy proportion of manufactures has made the operating revenues extremely vulnerable to fluctuations in business activity and to competition from motor carriers. From 1946 to 1951 New Haven freight tonnage declined from 29,627,000 to 24,777,000. Much of the lost tonnage passed to motor carriers.

The New Haven has attempted to cope with this problem by cooperation with motor carriers. Since the war truck trailers have been transported by flatcar between New York, New Haven, Springfield, Providence, and Boston. In 1952, 34,620 trailers were handled producing a revenue of $1,358,-970—an increase of 11,727 trailers and $478,978 over 1951. There are plans to obtain more flatcars and eventually to extend this service to New Jersey terminals.

The New Haven is to be commended for pioneering in the transport of truck trailers by rail. Opposition has appeared from motor transport unions but so far has been overcome. In the interest of better service at lower cost, this service could perhaps be adopted to advantage by other New England roads.

The New Haven obtains a high percentage of its revenues from passenger traffic. Its percentage of passenger revenues to total operating revenues was 31.62% in 1952 compared to the national figure of 8.94%. Almost alone among Class I roads in the United States, the New Haven shows revenue covering fully allocated expenses for passenger operation. The road has made a concerted effort to maintain and improve passenger service. It adopted "Budd" diesel-powered cars, which can be operated independently or together. Forty of these cars were acquired or on order as of August 1953. Also, to improve passenger service, the New Haven opened a passenger station on its Boston–New York line at Route 128 in Canton, Massachusetts. The management believes that passenger terminals of the future may be located outside of downtown metropolitan areas to provide greater accessibility for motor vehicles.

The New Haven was forced into bankruptcy in 1935. The road was operated by trustees until 1947, when it emerged from reorganization proceedings. Annual fixed charges were reduced to about one-half of their former figure. Since 1947 the New Haven has made strenuous efforts to reduce its funded debt, and by December 31, 1951, the figure was $164,631,000 compared to $194,938,000 at the end of 1947. However, debt capital still constitutes a heavy burden. In 1952 fixed and contingent charges were earned 1.63 times out of income available for that purpose.

Maine Central Railroad Company. The Maine Central Railroad operates about 945 miles of road mostly in Maine, with some mileage in the states of New Hampshire and Vermont. The company has two main lines with terminals at Portland. One line leads northeast from Portland to Vanceboro on the Canadian border, the other from Portland northwest to St. Johnsbury, Vermont. Freight is interchanged with the Boston and Maine, Canadian National, Bangor and Aroostook, and Canadian Pacific railroads. The Maine Central's traffic pattern is fairly balanced between raw materials and manufactured products. Paper, pulpwood, and potatoes are the largest items of traffic. About 60% of the Maine Central's tonnage originates with other carriers.

Passenger service does not produce much revenue (less than 10% in 1952) for the Maine Central. The road had, by the end of 1952, dieselized all its regular operations, freight and passenger.

The Maine Central has been able to maintain a relatively sound financial position even during times of business depression. In 1952 and 1953 the company demonstrated its credit by the sale of about $18,500,000 of mortgage bonds on reasonably good terms. The purpose of the bond issue was to obtain funds to meet maturing debt. In 1952 the company earned its fixed charges 2.73 times out of income available for that purpose.

Rutland Railway Corporation. The Rutland Railway Corporation operates about 400 miles of line in western Vermont and eastern New York states. Its main lines run north and south in western Vermont, connecting White Creek, New York, and Bellows Falls, Vermont, with Burlington and Alburg on Lake Champlain. An important branch runs from Alburg westerly to Ogdensburg, New York. The Rutland interchanges with the New York Central, Boston and Albany, Boston and Maine, Central Vermont, and the Canadian Pacific.

The transport of milk has declined on the Rutland over the past 25 years with the general transition in New England agriculture. It has not been replaced by traffic of other kinds. Pulpwood constitutes the only traffic which seems to be increasing and offers possibility of offsetting declining revenues. The Rutland meets competition from other larger railroads—the Delaware and Hudson, Boston and Maine, Central Vermont—and is generally at a disadvantage because of its smaller size and poorer connections. Over 80% of traffic is received from connecting lines. The Rutland has also suffered severely from the competition of motor carriers.

The road has had a dismal earnings record over the past 20 years. Several times in the 1930's earnings failed to meet fixed charges. The Rutland remained in trusteeship until 1950. A reorganization completed in 1950 provided for the replacement of all funded debt with capital stock; thus the company has relatively small fixed charges to meet annually. Despite this the Rutland in 1951 showed a sizable deficit.

During 1951 the management took drastic steps to reduce operating expenses. Old equipment was sold and replaced by diesel locomotives. The company also abandoned several unprofitable operations and made plans to abandon others. However, the future of the Rutland Railway is not bright. It is perhaps not an essential road since much of its traffic potential can be provided by other rail carriers.[6]

Central Vermont Railway, Inc. The Central Vermont is wholly owned by the Canadian National Railways, but the railroad is operated separately.

This railroad consists of a main line with several short branches from St. Johns, Quebec, down through St. Albans, Vermont, to White River Junction and on down to New London, Connecticut. Total mileage operated amounts to about 422, all but about 28 miles being in New England.

The Central Vermont Railway is an important interchange road for the manufacturing areas of central and southern New England with the Midwest and with Canada. Its traffic is made up generally of raw materials moving down from Canada, foodstuffs and manufactured articles from the West to New England, and manufactured articles from New England to Canada and the Midwest. On paper, the Central Vermont Railway has been a poor financial holding from the Canadian National. However, its value to its parent lies not in the annual profit or loss shown but in the traffic which is turned over to the Canadian National. The income statement of the Central Vermont Railway has shown losses consistently over the postwar years, so that by 1951 the accumulated deficit amounted to over half the book value of the assets. This is not of great significance, however, since all of the debt is owed to the parent company.

Canadian National Railways Lines in New England.[7] The Canadian National Railways also operates in its own name an important line from the Canadian border across New Hampshire and Maine to Portland. The railroad owns a large grain elevator at Portland.

Canadian Pacific Railway Company Lines in Maine and Vermont. The Canadian Pacific Railway operates two separate lines in Maine and Vermont. The Vermont line comes down from Montreal across the border to St. Johnsbury and Wells River. The Canadian Pacific in Maine bisects the state from east to west leading from Sherbrooke, Quebec to St. John, New Brunswick.

6. Since a strike in July 1953 passengers have not been carried on the Rutland, and substantial improvement in net operating revenue has been evident since that time. In January 1954 the Vermont Public Service Commission was studying the situation to determine to what extent, if any, it would order the Rutland to resume passenger service.

7. Popularly known as the Grand Trunk Railroad.

Boston and Albany Railroad Company (*New York Central System*). The Boston and Albany Railroad retains its name although its operation has been integrated into the New York Central System and it does not report separately to the Interstate Commerce Commission. The New York Central operates about 360 miles of road in New England, which are known as the Boston and Albany lines. The main line, with several short branches, extends between Boston and Albany through Worcester, Springfield, and Pittsfield, Massachusetts.

The New York Central encountered difficult economic problems in the postwar years due to declining traffic and higher costs. Shortly after the war the road decided to dieselize, and at present the Boston and Albany lines are operated entirely with diesel locomotives. The New York Central System also, to overcome mounting passenger deficits, has installed self-propelled diesel "Bee-Liner" cars. These efforts to reduce costs have met with considerable success.

Other Railroads in New England. Besides the separate corporate entities whose property is leased to the major railroads in New England, there are several independent roads operating a very small amount of mileage. These are the Barre and Chelsea Railroad Company in Vermont, 48 miles; the Belfast and Moosehead Lake Railroad Company owned by the city of Belfast, Maine, 33 miles; the Grafton and Upton Railroad Company, Massachusetts, owned by Draper Corporation, 15 miles; St. Johnsbury and Lamoille County Railroad, Vermont, 96 miles; Sanford and Eastern Railroad Corporation, Maine, 47 miles; and Clarendon and Pittsford Railroad Company owned by the Vermont Marble Company, 19 miles. Also unique in its operation is the Mount Washington Cog Railway.

Conclusions

Many persons believe that the railroad industry is a declining one. It has been alleged that railroad management has lost its vitality and talent for innovation and is unwilling to break out of established patterns. The inability of the railroads to provide their investors with comfortable returns is the chief evidence cited to support these beliefs.

Perhaps some of these contentions have a basis in fact. However, the railroads provide more transportation service to the New England economy today than they did before World War II. It is true that their share of the nation's total transportation activity has fallen. Nevertheless, railroad ton miles and passenger miles are at or near record highs that surpass all but the war years.

Railroad management has succeeded in shaking off much of the conservatism which has characterized its activities in the past, especially in the 1930's. In the years since World War II a large portion of the rolling stock has been modernized—in particular locomotives, which are now largely diesel. Passenger cars have generally been brought up to improved standards of comfort and convenience. Freight cars have been increasingly standardized and designed for greater efficiency. In general, the railroads have demonstrated a determination to keep pace with the rest of the economy.

The situation is perhaps not as satisfactory in New England as it is elsewhere. Increased demands on the New England railroads have not been as great as elsewhere in the country, so that a comparable expansion of facilities has not been needed. Furthermore, transportation conditions in New England have encouraged motor transportation to a greater degree than in other regions where bulk commodities move over longer distances. As Table 13–7 shows, some New England roads have lagged behind with respect to improvements.

Table 13–6. New England Class I Railroads

REVENUE FREIGHT TON MILES

1926–30	9,373,568,000	1941–45	12,954,313,000
1931–35	6,128,371,000	1946–50	11,003,444,000
1936–40	6,887,879,000	1951	11,068,358,000

PASSENGER MILES

1926–30	2,604,964,000	1941–45	4,269,010,000
1931–35	1,501,876,000	1946–50	3,195,867,000
1936–40	1,949,443,000	1951	n.a.

n.a. means figures are not available. Figures are averaged for each period.
Source: I.C.C., *Comparative Statement of Railway Operating Statistics, 1951 and 1950, Individual Class I Steam Railways* and *Statistics of Railways in the United States*

In some cases railroads are controlled by groups which have neither an awareness nor interest in the region in which the road may be located. These circumstances have sometimes resulted in conflicts of interest, particularly with regard to service and improvements. The long interruptions in the payment of railroad corporate dividends and the uncertainty of the railroad industry's future have made rail management cautious about reinvesting large sums of money in railroad property. Many railroad investors believe that rail capital should be retrieved as quickly as possible and transferred to other industries. While this may be a wise policy for investors, it is not calculated to improve railroad service. *On the other hand, railroad management interested in and willing to cooperate with the region in which it is located can contribute significantly to the regional economy.* A good example is the evident attempt of the Bangor and Aroostook to meet the needs of potato growers along its lines. Rate adjustments and improvements in service brought benefits to both parties. Another example is the New Haven Railroad's efforts to improve commuter service along its lines.

The cooperation should be bilateral. The region should provide the conditions and atmosphere conducive to the improvement of railroad service. It should refrain from restrictive and damaging action directed against the railroads.

Table 13-7. *Comparisons of Gross Capital Expenditures, New England and United States Railroads, 1946–52*

	EXPENDITURES PER MILE OF ROAD OPERATED			EXPENDITURES PER DOLLAR OF OPERATING REVENUE		
	EQUIPMENT	ROAD AND STRUCTURE	TOTAL	EQUIPMENT	ROAD AND STRUCTURE	TOTAL
ALL RAILROADS IN UNITED STATES	$24,703	$10,134	$34,837	$00.0854	$00.0350	$00.1204
Bangor and Aroostook	21,819	6,336	28,155	.15	.0435	.1935
Boston and Albany*		9,285			.0263	
Boston and Maine	17,151	9,748	26,899	.049	.0278	.0761
Maine Central	13,004	5,831	18,834	.0741	.0338	.1079
New York, New Haven, and Hartford	40,489	13,563	54,052	.0660	.0221	.0881
Rutland	5,973	951	6,941	.0607	.0096	.0633

* Equipment supplied by New York Central System.
Source: "Transportation," *Moody's Manual of Investments,* and Annual Reports of Railroads, 1952

To a large extent, railroad regulation is in the hands of the federal authorities. In that respect the region can do little more than recommend fair and impartial treatment. There are matters, however, in which the states can take specific action to encourage a healthier economic outlook on the part of rail management.

The following are general recommendations for revision of public policy at the federal and state level with respect to railroads. These recommendations are directed at the general tone of regulation rather than to its detail.

FEDERAL:

1. Greater cognizance should be given to the strong element of competition existing in the transportation field today. Rail management should be permitted more discretion to adjust rates to changing economic circumstances. Preservation of the discrimination provisions of the Interstate Commerce Act would probably be sufficient to protect the shipper against exploitation.
2. The carriers should be afforded greater latitude to decide upon abandonment of service. They should not be required to provide service for revenue less than out-of-pocket cost.

STATE:

1. The carriers should be granted more discretion to determine intrastate rates provided they are kept nondiscriminatory. At the state level this applies particularly to passenger rates.
2. Regulation at the state level should not require carriers to provide service for less than out-of-pocket cost. More discretion should be given to the carriers in matters of service abandonment.

Motor Transportation

By a combined tonnage and distance measure, railroads are the most important means of transport in the United States. But more tonnage is moved by motor carriers than by all other forms of transportation, although the great proportion of tonnage moved by motor carriers is over short distances. It is likely that for hauls of 150 miles or less the motor carrier is the dominant form of transportation.[8] In all probability trucks handle most of the intra-New England trade and important parts of shipments between New England and other regions.

Unfortunately, we cannot discuss with statistical precision the place of motor transport within the New England regional economy. A great deal of motor transportation is private or exempt from regulation, and statistics are nowhere formally reported. Also, many motor carriers entering New England are not domiciled there and therefore do not report as New

8. Frank M. Cushman, associate professor at Northeastern University, estimates that the motor carrier is the dominant form of transportation for hauls of 400 miles or less.

England carriers. Finally, some carriers domiciled in New England and reporting statistics as New England carriers operate outside of New England as well as within.

New England has approximately 400,000 registered motor trucks, of which about 65,000 are operated by "for-hire" carriers. The for-hire carriers include all those who sell transportation service. For purposes of regulation, they are segregated into the categories of interstate and intrastate carriers, common and contract, regulated and exempt carriers. Interstate for-hire carriers, with the exception of those whose business is the transport of agricultural products, fish, and newspapers, are regulated by the Interstate Commerce Commission. The regulation of intrastate for-hire carriers varies from state to state. Regulation by authorities in Massachusetts is comprehensive and complete. Regulation of carriers of property in Vermont, New Hampshire, and Maine is considerably less comprehensive.

Among the interstate for-hire carriers of property domiciled in New England are approximately 2,300 common carriers and 250 contract carriers.[9] Of the 2,300 about 175 had revenues in excess of $200,000 in 1952 and received the Interstate Commerce Commission designation of Class I carrier. It must be recognized that carriers domiciled in New England may do much of their business in other states and conversely carriers domiciled in other states may operate largely in New England. About 185 interstate Class I common carriers conduct more than half of their business in New England.

The motor transport industry offers a striking contrast to railroads. The economic characteristics of the two industries, in strenuous competition with each other, differ greatly. The railroad industry is large scale, the motor carrier industry small scale. The railroads have most of the characteristics of monopoly, which they fail to attain chiefly because of the competition of motor carriers. The small scale of the motor carrier industry results in intense competitive activity. The 2,200 Class I motor carriers in the United States do less than half of the business done by the industry. The 131 Class I railroads in the United States receive 99% of the railroads' revenue. The typical firm in motor transport is small compared to the typical railroad.

The chief reason for the divergent cost structures of the two industries relates to the right of way. The railroads build, own, and maintain the routes over which they operate. Motor carriers operate over the public highway. If motor carriers had to bear the investment cost and maintenance of the highways, their operating characteristics would be more like the railroads. Although motor carriers contribute to the cost of highway building by payment of registration fees and gasoline taxes, fixed charges for highway construction are underwritten by the public through governmental agencies.

9. Common carriers offer their services to the general public. Contract carriers restrict their service to a limited number of shippers with whom they have contacts, usually running over a period of time.

The basic economic characteristic of motor transport is flexibility. Adaptability gives the motor carrier its advantages over rail transport. On an average ton-mile basis, motor carrier costs are three to four times rail costs. For specific segments of traffic, however, motor carriers can beat rail costs. The traffic in which motor carriers have an advantage includes shipments of less than carload quantities, shipments originating or terminating away from railroad sidings, and commodities needing special handling and attention. At one time, motor carrier operations were circumscribed by the economic length of haul. This is still true but to a lesser extent than in the past.

Operations of New England Motor Carriers

In view of the broad range and variety of firms in the industry, it is difficult to generalize about the level of performance of the New England motor carriers. It might be presumed that the existence of strenuous competition would act to bring about a maximum efficiency of operation. There are several factors, however, which tend to prevent this result. The most important of these is regulation. Passage by Congress of the Motor Carrier Act of 1935 imposed upon the motor carrier industry a pattern of regulation similar to that which had long been applied to railroads. Congress gave little recognition to the fact that controls applied to a monopolistic industry might be fundamentally inappropriate for an industry characterized by a high degree of competition.

Entry into the interstate motor carrier industry is limited. The federal Motor Carrier Act requires every common carrier seeking new routes to meet the test of public convenience and necessity. The premise upon which such regulation is based is that if unlimited entry were permitted, the industry would tend to generate an excess capacity, as the railroads did, which would cause economic demoralization of the industry and consequent deterioration of service to the shipping public. On this supposition Congress froze the route structure of the industry in 1935 and placed upon the Interstate Commerce Commission the responsibility of revising it to meet changing needs. Expediency and the reluctance of the I.C.C. to probe into managerial functions have tended to result in preservation of the inefficient carrier as well as the efficient. Aggressive firms with the potential to expand are limited by their ability to obtain certificates from the I.C.C., or to buying out other carriers, with I.C.C. approval.

Another cause of inefficiency is the inflexibility of the route pattern. Carriers are often forced to operate on routes which for one reason or another have become obsolete in terms of traffic flow. The route pattern of 1935 is not necessarily the ideal one for 1953. To meet this problem the I.C.C. has revised motor carrier certificates and permitted consolidations. However, despite the I.C.C.'s recognition and concern, irrationalities still exist in the route structure.

The realization by the motor carrier industry of greater efficiency through large-scale installations is impeded by the intenseness of competition. No single carrier can obtain either the funds or the volume to bring about a consolidation of terminal facilities. The ultra-individualism of the carriers precludes cooperation in activities of this nature. Perhaps this is a legitimate sphere of activity for government, especially if such things as terminal planning are carried on in conjunction with highway planning. At present there is disagreement within the industry about the desirability of public motor carrier terminals. Large carriers which have built their own terminals are averse to losing their investment and competitive advantage. Their boycott of public terminals would probably make the terminals unprofitable during the first years of their operation.

The above-mentioned conditions in the trucking industry are national in scope, as, of course, is federal regulation. But there is reason to believe that New England motor carriers, like New England railroads, operate at a cost level above the average of the country. Why this should be so is not completely clear, although various explanations have been advanced. Apart from current costs of equipment, labor, taxes, fuel, and so on, there are circumstances of terrain, climate, and traffic flow which allegedly result in higher costs to New England carriers. To what degree these conditions increase the costs as compared to those of carriers in the rest of the country is problematical. The average length of haul in New England is shorter than the national average. (See Table 13–8.) On the other hand, the density of traffic in New England is greater than in much of the rest of the country. To maintain that the shorter average haul in New England is responsible for the higher level of costs is to ignore the cost structure of the motor carrier industry. Motor carrier costs, unlike those for railroads, bear a close relationship to distance traveled. Thus a shorter average haul should not result in any appreciable increment in cost per mile. Table 13–8 indicates that the average haul in New England is considerably less than in any other region, and the average revenue per intercity ton mile is 40% higher than in any other region.

Probably we should seek some other cause for the difference between the New England average cost and the national average. There is reason to believe that the industry is excessively atomized in New England. This stems from the fact that the industry was pretty well developed in New England by the time of the passage of the Motor Carrier Act of 1935, and the pattern of routes and carriers was already laid down. The scale of the industry was smaller then than it is today. As the motor carrier industry developed in other parts of the country, it was able to adjust with greater facility to changing economic conditions. Many New England carriers are too small to obtain economies of large-scale operations. This development is by and large not the fault of the carriers but rather of the regulatory agencies whose perception and response to changing economic conditions is slow, and who are hampered by the terms of legislation under which they function. If economic forces were less hampered by government control it is likely that New England would have a more efficient motor transport system. Table 13–8 also shows the comparatively small size of the New England motor carrier in terms of revenue and average load.

Table 13–8. Comparative Trucking Statistics for United States, by Region, 1950

	AVERAGE HAUL (MILES)	AVERAGE LOAD (TONS)	AVERAGE REVENUE PER INTERCITY TON MILE	AVERAGE REVENUE PER CARRIER	AVERAGE REVENUE PER INTERCITY TON*
UNITED STATES	235	9.0	5.0¢	$1,459,728	$11.38
NEW ENGLAND	133	7.5	8.1	824,082	10.00
Middle Atlantic	181	9.3	5.6	1,156,235	9.57
Central	258	8.7	4.9	1,936,196	12.06
Southern	300	9.0	4.6	1,530,668	14.10
Northwestern	176	9.1	5.5	1,359,304	9.44
Midwestern	279	9.3	4.4	1,552,761	13.07
Southwestern	235	7.0	5.6	1,409,147	12.17
Rocky Mountain	405	10.2	4.2	1,757,080	16.39
Pacific	222	12.1	4.4	1,369,403	9.44

* 1951 figures. The average revenue per intercity ton of New England carriers is lower than the national average primarily because of the shorter haul in New England.
Source: American Trucking Association, American Trucking Trends, Washington, 1952

Regulation of Motor Carriers

The Motor Carrier Act of 1935 stipulated that common and contract carriers operating on June 1 and July 1, 1935, respectively, should receive certificates and permits without having to make a showing of public convenience and necessity or, in the case of contract carriers, public interest. This priority status was called "grandfather rights." Thus, the I.C.C. was given authority to regulate a motor transport network in existence as of 1935, whether the structure of routes was rational and efficient or not.

The I.C.C. has had the problem in recent years of constructing a sound and efficient motor transport system to fit changing circumstances and yet not infringe upon the preferred position of the holders of grandfather rights. Many anomalies have appeared which it has been powerless to overcome. There are many cases of route duplication, roundabout routing, and too narrow certification. The I.C.C. is not permitted to revise or remake the pattern of the original routes to any degree in order to bring about greater efficiency. It was also enjoined by Congress to "preserve competition," a requirement which has sometimes led to the preservation of smaller, weaker carriers at the expense of greater efficiency.

The result of this regulatory policy promulgated by Congress has been to impede the natural economic development of the industry. Grandfather rights plus the injunction to preserve competition have fragmented the industry to an extent greater than necessary to maintain a competitive situation. It has not been able to adjust to changing circumstances, opportunities, and procedures. Excess capacity has appeared in some places and shortages in others. Probably a greater degree of carrier consolidation would have taken place if permitted by congressional policy. As equipment becomes heavier and terminal facilities more important the size of the most efficient firm in the motor carrier industry will increase. Regulatory policy that does not recognize that development becomes outmoded.

It is generally conceded even by members of the motor carrier industry that some small lot shipments are not sought and are even avoided by motor carriers because of their lower profitability. This is a symptom of a seller's market. If there were more competition among carriers, there would be greater inclination to solicit the business of small lot shippers who are particularly dependent upon common carrier service. In motor transportation the competitive stress is at the big shipper level where the alternatives of rail, private, and contract carriers are available. For the small occasional shipper, the motor transportation market is something less than competitive on the seller's side.

Although new carriers might provide better service to shippers, the Interstate Commerce Commission is under heavy pressure not to certify them since it would intensify competition. The I.C.C. is hesitant to certify new service which might become redundant in a period of declining business activity. Perhaps it would be wise to return to the market place the decision whether new firms will be allowed to start.

The crux of the argument against relaxation of regulation, aside from resulting hardship to higher cost firms, is that service to the shipper would suffer. It is maintained that unstable, irresponsible firms would undercut the established firms, and erratic, undependable service result. The experience of the early 1930's is invoked to support this view. However, the fact is disregarded that the early thirties were years of depression when many other industries were also characterized by price cutting. There is little reason to believe that less regulation at the present time would engulf the industry in competitive chaos. In any case safeguards such as rate publication and nondiscrimination provisions could be applied which would retain the salutary effects of competition and limit the harmful ones.

Highways

Adequate highways are absolutely essential for well-developed economic activity. The number of passenger miles annually traveled by private vehicles in the United States far exceeds the total passenger miles by all other forms of transportation. The I.C.C. estimates that in 1952 private vehicle passenger miles were about 85% of total intercity passenger miles.

Nearly everyone agrees that more and better highway systems are needed in the United States. Perhaps no better proof of this need exists than the great volume of traffic flowing on the few genuinely modern highways. The New Jersey Turnpike running between the New York City area and the Delaware River, completed in 1951, had by 1953 exceeded traffic figures expected for 1962. The problem of highway building is one of design and finance. Wise and proper planning can in the long run lessen the burden of financing.

The problems of highway design are of the following nature:

1. Highways intended for use by private passenger vehicles are less expensive to build than general purpose highways available for use by heavy trucks and trailers.

2. The states bear the primary responsibility for road building in the United States. Interstate traffic requires cooperation between states to coordinate the construction of through roads. Fortunately this cooperation is often present, although in some circumstances it has been lacking.

3. Improved intercity highways are of less value if cities themselves are permitted to constitute traffic bottlenecks. On the other hand, by-passing cities may result in business activity by-passing the city as well. Here again cooperation and coordination are necessary to relate highway and city planning.

Highway design is affected by financing methods. If private passenger vehicles pay most of the cost of highway construction, the highways should reasonably be tailored to the needs of such vehicles. If heavy motor carriers pay a large proportion of the costs, consideration should also be given to their needs. Ideally each type of user should pay in proportion to the cost incurred for that particular user. However, ascertaining the share of cost which can be allocated to each class of highway user is not a simple matter. There is not much agreement about the causes of highway deterioration. Some experts insist that most wear and tear is a function of the weather. Others maintain that axle loads beyond a certain weight multiply the damage done to the roads. The Western Association of Highway Officials is currently carrying on experiments to determine the causes of wear scientifically over a specific stretch of highway. However, final conclusions are not yet available and may not apply to another set of highway conditions.

Highway design of the future ought to consider that in some circumstances operation of both commercial and private passenger vehicles on the same highway may lessen the efficiency of both types of vehicles. The growth of motor transportation should not be hindered by limitations imposed by passenger vehicles. If motor carriers are willing to pay for specialized facilities for their exclusive use such as truck lanes, by-passes, and truck terminals, the states ought to cooperate in providing them.

Practical devices for accurately assessing highway cost against all types of users have still to be developed. The gasoline tax does not distinguish between degrees of user cost. That is, gasoline consumption is not entirely proportional to use in that it does not vary directly with the weight of the vehicle. Toll roads can be utilized for strategic locations but do not provide a general solution, and may in fact result in a more than due charge against the user. Various other expedients have been attempted such as the ton-mile tax which is based on the weight and length of haul. The ton-mile tax may be sound in theory, but it is also costly to the taxpaying concern. The expense of record keeping and collection frequently amounts to a large share of its total yield. Its application depends on individual users reporting mileage covered and tonnage carried. Several states have tried and abandoned the ton-mile tax as impractical.

New York and Oregon have experimented with a "truck mileage" tax. In New York a charge per mile is based on the gross maximum weight or the unladen weight, depending on whether the vehicle travels loaded or empty. The law requires the carriers to maintain extensive records of each trip of each vehicle. In New York the first full year of operation revealed a collection cost of 9.5% of revenues. In Oregon, with longer experience in administration and enforcement, collection costs were 5.3% of revenues in 1951.

The difficulties encountered in relating cost to use should not deter continued investigation and research along those lines. *If a proper coordination of transport facilities based on the "inherent advantages of each" is to be obtained, it is imperative that each carrier be called upon to contribute his full share of cost.*[10] Only in the special circumstance of the early developmental state of a transport facility is a drain upon the public purse justified.

It is quite apparent that the New England states cannot embark upon a program of user charges for highways if other states do not follow suit. If the New England motor carriers' costs were increased for this reason, New England shippers would have a further disadvantage in their competitive relationships with shippers in other states. Some form of interstate cooperation to set up reasonably uniform standards for the assessment of charges for use of the highways should be devised.

The existing highway mileage of New England shows up well statistically. The large majority of New England roads are paved; the national proportion is less than 50%. Table 13–9 shows mileage and type of surface of New England's roads.

Well-paved roads of archaic design do not constitute safe and adequate highways. The New England states have recognized the need for modern roads, but the cost of a modern expressway, usually over $500,000 per mile, has caused understandable hesitancy in meeting those needs. All of the states are currently engaged in building programs which should vastly improve the New England system. Massachusetts has spent or authorized

10. Transport Act of 1940.

the expenditure of $400,000,000 since 1949. Maine expects to spend $98,000,000 over a seven-year period to improve more than 1,300 miles of highways. Vermont has plans to improve its highways to the extent of $52,000,000 in the next ten years. The New Hampshire legislature in 1951 authorized an increase of one cent per gallon in the gasoline tax and an $8,000,000 bond issue. The 1953 legislature authorized a $5,000,000 bond issue all to be used for highway construction. Connecticut has announced a ten-year program of highway improvement estimated at $375,000,000 of which $184,000,000 will be financed by self-liquidating bonds.

Because of state autonomy over the highways, interstate motor transport is subject to various state highway and safety regulations, and unquestionably the efficient flow of motor transport is affected. The constitutional right of the states to impose these regulations is well established. A motor carrier regularly operating through several states must comply in many respects, such as length of vehicle unit, with the provisions of the most restrictive state. At present there is little agreement among the states as to the proper extent and restrictiveness of such regulation.

Although local highway conditions vary, greater uniformity of safety and other legislation applying to motor carriers could be achieved without endangering the public or the highways. Often the terms of the law reflect the demands of competing carriers more than they do the need to safeguard the highway. The problem is not acute in New England as compared to other parts of the country, particularly the Southeast. Variations exist, however, especially with respect to the load weight limits.

All the New England states impose a 50,000 pound limit on tractor semi-trailer combinations—the most commonly used unit—except Connecticut, which currently permits 60,000 pounds provided the combination utilizes at least four axles. The State of New York allows 63,000 pounds on four axles. Thus for the heavy flow of goods between southern New England and the New York area the load limit is quite liberal. Movements to and from Massachusetts, however, are limited to 50,000 pounds gross even though much of the movement may take place in Connecticut and New York.

With respect to motor carrier licenses and taxes, the New England states have achieved less uniformity. Registration fees range from a maximum of $180 in Massachusetts to a maximum of $500 in Vermont. Fees are collected from all carriers domiciled within the state as well as all carriers maintaining an intrastate business. Interstate carriers domiciled in states with reciprocity agreements may be granted exemption from paying registration fees in other states with similar agreements.

The present pattern of interstate reciprocity is unsatisfactory. States in general grant to other states that which is granted to them. Thus, a carrier operating between two states with different levels of charges for registration will (other things being equal) choose the state with the lowest level of

Table 13-9. Rural and Urban Highway Mileage in New England, 1951, classified by type of surface

	TOTAL MILEAGE			RURAL MILEAGE			URBAN MILEAGE		
	SURFACED	NONSURFACED	TOTAL	SURFACED	NONSURFACED	TOTAL	SURFACED	NONSURFACED	TOTAL
Maine	17,892	3,915	21,807	17,135	3,592	20,727	757	323	1,080
New Hampshire	9,991	3,615	13,604	8,917	3,602	12,519	1,074	11	1,085
Vermont	11,033	2,743	13,776	10,233	2,736	12,969	800	7	807
Massachusetts	23,083	1,098	24,181	16,745	1,050	17,795	6,338	48	6,338
Rhode Island	3,575	457	4,032	1,521	137	1,658	2,054	320	2,374
Connecticut	14,637	350	14,987	10,006	317	10,323	4,631	33	4,664
New England	80,211	12,178	92,387	64,557	11,434	75,991	15,654	742	16,348

Source: U.S. Department of Commerce, Bureau of Public Roads, Highway Statistics, 1951

charges for its domicile. The carrier then is free of registration charges in the other state provided a reciprocity agreement exists. In many cases the carrying on of intrastate business in one or more states makes such a choice impossible. Sometimes a state may conclude that the benefits of reciprocity are not equal to the loss of revenue in registration fees. Then all carriers regularly entering that state must pay the full registration fee.

Table 13–10. Approximate Maximum Fee for Registration in Six New England States, New York, and New Jersey

Maine	$350
New Hampshire	300
Vermont	500
Massachusetts	180
Rhode Island	300
Connecticut	250
New York	315
New Jersey	240

Source: American Trucking Association Bulletin Advisory Service

Motor carriers are also subject to taxes which differ from state to state such as mileage, ton-mile, and tonnage taxes. In most cases, the most onerous aspect of the tax is the record keeping entailed. A carrier may be required to keep a variety of records differing from state to state. For small or occasional operators detailed record keeping may amount to an undue burden.

The current New York State truck mileage tax requires that all tax-eligible property carriers keep accurate records of all movements within the state. All carriers operating within the state of Maine must record mileage and gasoline purchases and under certain circumstances pay a tax. The objective of this tax is to ensure that Maine receives gasoline tax revenue proportionate to the use of the highways.

Changing economic circumstances frequently cause problems that transcend the capabilities of existing political entities. Perhaps this is nowhere more clearly seen than in the regulation of transportation. Much of modern day transportation is interstate in nature. Economic regulation is by and large the function of two federal agencies, the Interstate Commerce Commission and the Civil Aeronautics Board. Nevertheless, much state regulation in the guise of control and care of highways has important economic impact. *To avoid a further gravitation of regulatory power to the Federal Government, a compromise line of action involving greater cooperation among states within regions should be explored.*

The device of interstate authorities has, of course, been used in the past, the notable example being the Port of New York Authority. *It might be possible for the New England states to organize a New England Highway and Motor Vehicle Authority which could work for greater uniformity of*

*highway construction and use. An alternative for the present is increased
emphasis upon cooperation among the states in drawing up legislation in
order to achieve some measure of uniformity.*

Taxes of the nature of the ton-mile tax may cause serious inconvenience
to motor transport if applied by each state without concern for or recognition
of action being taken in other states. Different levels of taxes disturb rate
levels on interstate traffic. For example, the I.C.C. has temporarily permitted
motor carriers to make a surcharge on that part of a shipment which moves
within New York State and is thereby subject to the New York State
truck mileage tax. Tariffs are already sufficiently complex to baffle many
shippers without introducing surcharges varying from state to state. The
concept of the ton-mile tax as an obligation of motor carriers for government services received may be sound, but its application should minimize
hindrance to the free flow of interstate commerce.

Conclusions and Recommendations

FEDERAL:

1. Regulation of motor carriers should be relaxed to admit more of the
stimulating effects of competition. Many of the complex problems of
regulation, such as the relations between regulated and unregulated carriers, would be avoided by lessening or removing regulatory distinctions
between carriers. An example of relaxation of regulation would be a certification requirement of "in the public interest" rather than the present one
demanding "required by public convenience and necessity." Legislation
should be rewritten to achieve more fully the benefits of competition, yet
safeguard against irresponsible practices.

STATE:

1. There should be greater correlation between federal and state regulation
of motor transportation. This would have the desirable result of encouraging greater uniformity of regulation among the states and also be
a step toward a national transportation policy.

2. In the interest of fair and impartial regulation the states should
investigate and experiment with means of accurately assessing against
direct users of public facilities such as highways most of the cost of their
construction and maintenance.

3. The states should take the responsibility for providing, in conjunction
with highway planning, freight and passenger terminals for motor transport. With so many small firms in the industry, cooperation in terminal
operations is desirable but difficult to obtain without some encouraging,
directing influence such as the state. Full cost should be met by users of
the terminal.

4. The New England states should cooperate in highway planning and
also in safety and tax legislation applying to motor vehicles. The flow of

interstate commerce should not be hampered by divers state vehicle requirements.

Air Transportation

Commercial aviation is still primarily occupied with passenger transport and probably will continue to be for some time to come. However, one may visualize the eventual emergence of airborne craft as primary agencies for the transport of goods. Because of its location on the periphery of the national economy, New England needs to be keenly interested in the growth of any new form of transportation. Transport improvements reduce the importance of distance as a cost factor. For certain types of goods air transport is even now improving the competitive position of some New England manufacturers.

In the pattern of world transport, New England is a highly strategic location. Boston is the natural western terminus of North Atlantic air routes. From Boston traffic splits off to the west and south. Boston undeniably has the potential to be one of the world's great air centers.

Air Service

Central and southern New England is well served by scheduled air lines. The four largest United States airlines—American, Eastern, United, and Trans-World—fly to and from Boston. Direct flights are available to every large city in the United States. (See Table 13–11.) The two big air freight carriers, the Flying Tigers and Slick, operate to Boston through southern New England.

Foreign air service is also excellent at Boston. Trans-World Airlines, Pan-American (United States carriers), Air France, and British Overseas Airways Corporation offer direct service to major points in South America, Africa, Asia, and Europe. Northeast and Trans-Canada connect Boston with eastern Canada.

If Logan Airport is to achieve its potential as an air center, more foreign carriers should be certified by the Civil Aeronautics Board to stop at Logan. At present Royal Dutch Airlines (KLM), Scandinavian Airlines System, Swissair, Sabena (Belgium), and other foreign carriers are not permitted to land at Boston. The reason is undoubtedly the desire to retain traffic advantages for United States carriers. All of the above carriers land at New York and, of course, if permitted only one point of entry would choose New York. However, this protection given to United States carriers destroys the natural advantage which Logan has over the airports at New York. Probably all of the foreign carriers on North Atlantic service would stop at Boston if permitted. They would bring additional activity to Logan and also stimulate United States carriers to provide better schedules.

The Civil Aeronautics Board has the power, subject to approval by the

president of the United States, to grant certification to foreign carriers to
include Logan on their North Atlantic flights. From the region's viewpoint, it is highly questionable whether Boston's potential should be
sacrificed to the advantage of certain United States carriers.

MAP 13-2

New England Airline Service Density Map
as of September 15, 1951

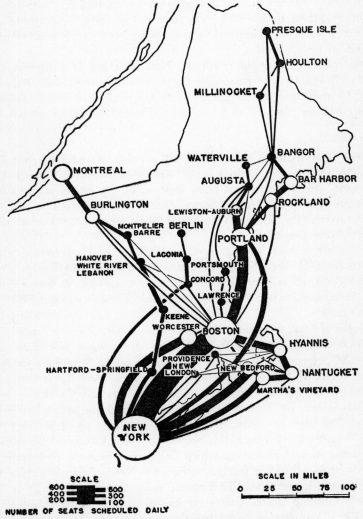

REPRODUCED WITH PERMISSION OF ROY R. ROADCAP & ASSOCIATES
COPYRIGHT 1952

Northeast Airlines provides an air service in northern New England which is essentially local. (See Map.) For four years Wiggins Airlines offered local air service through the central part of New England from Boston to Albany, including such points as Keene, Lawrence, North Adams, Pittsfield, Providence, Hartford, etc. The service was not well patronized and in 1952 the Civil Aeronautics Board refused to renew Wiggins' certificate. Although many regarded the action of the board as a blow to New England, it was probably justified considering that over 90% of Wiggins' revenue was derived from federal mail pay, most of it outright subsidy. The development of air transport hardly justifies such a drain on the public purse. The claim that local service airlines in other regions receive subsidy is no excuse for continuing an operation so expensive to the government as Wiggins.

The Wiggins service has been partially replaced by Mohawk Airlines which now serves Albany, Pittsfield, Springfield, Worcester, and Boston.

By and large, there is little that states or communities can do directly for airlines. Their control and promotion rest almost entirely with the Federal Government. However, communities and states can encourage air transport through the provision of airport facilities.

Awareness that good air service depends on adequate airports has not been lacking in New England. Portland, Boston, Worcester, Springfield, Providence, Hartford, Bridgeport, and New Haven all have airports capable of handling today's large commercial planes. Modern airports are in many cases too large to be supported only by direct users. Municipalities have been obliged to make large expenditures with an uncertain prospect of being repaid.

Public intervention for the building of airports has resulted in inconsistency of policy. During waves of enthusiasm about aviation large funds have been appropriated. In the ensuing ebb of interest, appropriations have sometimes been reduced to the point where simple maintenance of the airport investment has been endangered. To cope with this problem some political units have created independent self-sustaining airport organizations. Higher levels of traffic as well as better administration have helped make some of these new units successful.

Logan International Airport. Logan Airport is in East Boston, adjacent to Boston Harbor. Surrounded on three sides by water, it is undoubtedly one of the finest airports in the world. By virtue of its peninsular location it avoids the common operational hazards of airports surrounded by settled areas. It lies only 15 minutes from the downtown area by urban transit and even less by taxi or private car. *Without question, Logan Airport is one of New England's greatest transportation assets.*

Two thousand acres largely reclaimed from Boston Harbor permit room for three runways of over 7,000 feet and one runway of just over 10,000 feet, sufficient for any plane flying today. *The combination of runways and*

Table 13–11. Principal Airports of New England

AIRPORT	AIRLINE USER	NUMBER OF RUNWAYS	MAXIMUM LENGTH
Maine			
Lewiston-Auburn Airport	Northeast	3	4,500
Augusta State Airport	"	4	4,200
Dow Field, Bangor	"	2	7,000
Brunswick Naval Air Station	"	3	8,000
Caribou Municipal Airport	"	2	3,500
Deblois Airport	"	1	4,000
Dexter Municipal Airport	"	1	3,000
Eastport Airport	"	2	2,850
Houlton Airport	"	2	5,600
Millinocket Airport	"	2	5,000
Portland Airport	"	3	4,250
Presque Isle Airport	"	3	7,400
Robert L. LaFleur, Waterville	"	3	4,000
New Hampshire			
Concord Municipal Airport	Northeast	3	4,000
Dillion-Hopkins, Keene	"	2	4,000
Lebanon Municipal Airport	"	2	4,000
Grenier Air Force Base	"	3	7,000
Vermont			
Barre-Montpelier Muncipal Airport	Northeast	2	4,000
Burlington Municipal Airport	Colonial, Northeast	3	8,500
Rutland Municipal Airport	" "	2	4,000
Connecticut			
Bridgeport Municipal Airport	American, Northeast	3	4,750
Trumbull-Groton, New London Airport	Northeast	3	5,000
New Haven Municipal Airport	American, Eastern, Northeast	2	4,700
Bradley Field, Windsor Locks	American, Eastern, Northeast, United	3	6,700
Massachusetts			
Edward Lawrence Logan International Airport	Domestic: American, Eastern, Northeast, TWA, United, Mohawk; Foreign: TWA, British Overseas, Air France, Pan-American, Trans-Canada	4	10,022
Fitchburg Municipal Airport	Northeast	2	4,500
Barnstable Municipal, Hyannis	"	3	4,150
Lawrence Municipal Airport	"	3	4,000
Nantucket Memorial Airport	"	2	4,000
New Bedford Municipal Airport	"	2	5,000
Orange Memorial Airport	"	3	5,000
Pittsfield Municipal Airport	Northeast, Mohawk	1	3,500
Provincetown Municipal Airport	"	1	3,500
Martha's Vineyard Airport	"	3	4,000
Barnes Municipal Airport, Westfield	Mohawk	3	7,000
Worcester Municipal Airport	Northeast, Mohawk	3	5,500
Rhode Island			
Theodore F. Green Airport, Providence	American, Eastern, Northeast, United	4	5,450

Source: U.S. Department of Commerce, Civil Aeronautics Administration, Airport District Office, Boston

clear areas adjoining them will probably give Logan an important advantage in the use of jet transport. The airport has all the modern navigational facilities appropriate to its size.

Since World War II a new apron building has been erected which affords a maximum of convenience and facilities to passengers. Parking space is available close by. *Perhaps the only necessary additions to the airport in the near future are hangars which can be financed by long-term leases to the airlines.* The first of these hangars is currently under construction.

Airport Administration

In 1948 the General Court of Massachusetts set up an agency known as the State Airport Management Board to operate the state-owned Logan and Bedford airports. The Airport Management Board is responsible only to the governor and council. The unpaid board directs a full-time commissioner who has executive control over the airports. Board and commissioner have a considerable latitude of control over the activities of the airports. However, here as in the case of the Boston Port Authority, the legislature has kept a hold on the purse strings which has perhaps caused more grief than benefit. All income of the airports becomes general revenue of the state. Expenses are covered by appropriations. The basic difficulty with this system is that appropriations for the airport are not correlated to need but rather to the mood of the legislature regarding aviation. Thus, in 1953 an economy-minded legislature failed to provide adequate capital to complete necessary runway construction.

Good business practice suggests that the Airport Management Board should be held responsible for final results to the legislature, but should be permitted discretion at least within the range of its income. Emphasis should be placed on making the airports self-supporting enterprises, and the board should be given control of funds to carry out that objective.

Finances. The financial picture is a steadily improving one, partly because of better organization and management but mostly because civil aviation has begun to fulfill its postwar expectations. In 1951 revenues exceeded operating expenses for the first time. In 1952 net revenue covered the average annual interest cost of $200,000.

Regulation of Aviation. Since aviation in general transcends state borders, regulation must necessarily be largely federal. The Civil Aeronautics Board makes regulations which are enforced by the Civil Aeronautics Administration. Any aircraft utilizing a federal airway is subject to federal regulation. Since it is not possible to fly any great distance without entering a federal airway, practically all civil aviation is affected. Probably federal control is adequate for most problems, and state regulation is largely superfluous.

States are generally reluctant, however, to concede to the Federal Government any area where they have a claim to regulate. In many cases legislatures have been persuaded that aviation within the state needs regulation and have set up agencies for its accomplishment. Once such an agency is established, in order to justify its existence it must scurry about accruing activities which in many cases are already carried on by other agencies. To obtain more scope of activity, the state agencies have sought to have some federal regulation given to the states, thereby creating the danger of a fragmented and inconsistent pattern of regulation such as has afflicted surface carriers.

It is essential that the state legislatures recognize the limited nature and extent of regulation of civil aviation needed at the state level in order that air transport not be unnecessarily burdened with restrictions. Care should also be taken not to confuse regulatory policing functions with those of administration. The operation of an airport is a business and should be carried on according to business principles.

Use of Air Freight. A number of New England firms with competitive disadvantages in distribution to other parts of the country have found air freight a partial solution to their problems. One such firm contemplated establishing several regional warehouses to provide desired rapid service to customers. It discovered that, without adding to cost, use of over-night delivery by air freight transportation eliminated the necessity of decentralized warehousing. Service from a central point being preferred to that from regional warehouses, this company turned to air freight as a basic distribution method.

It should not be presumed that air freight offers a solution for all disadvantageously located firms. But shippers of high value specialty goods may find that air freight provides a better service, overcoming the disadvantage of a somewhat higher ton-mile cost.

The trend of air freight rates has been downward and undoubtedly will continue to be so. Aircraft handling methods and surface connecting means are being constantly improved. The result is that air freight volume has grown rapidly in recent years. The New England shipper may look forward to a consistently better possibility of utilizing air freight service.

Conclusions and Recommendations

FEDERAL:

1. If Logan is to be an "international" airport, foreign carriers flying to New York City should be permitted to stop at Boston. There is little question that these carriers would avail themselves of the opportunity.

2. Greater self-sufficiency should be imposed on the air transport industry. In return the intensity of regulation should be lessened to permit greater latitude to management initiative and responsibility.

STATE:

1. The states should provide coordination and encouragement to communities having or planning municipal airports. In some cases this may

require financial support from the state. It is important that airport development be sound, consistent, and geared to reality.

2. The functions of civil air regulation and airport operation should be delineated. The two functions are of a different and sometimes conflicting nature.

3. Airport operation should be placed on a business basis to the maximum extent possible. This involves granting to airport management a high degree of independence of legislative units. At the same time, airports should be required to achieve greater self-sufficiency.

Water Transport

Inland water transportation—river and lake—is of negligible commercial importance in New England, except for lumbering and pulpwood operations in northern New England. The region's rivers and lakes are generally too small to permit extensive commercial water traffic.[11]

Waterborne tonnage entering New England ports other than Portland, Boston, and Providence comes mainly from other parts of the United States and is mostly bulk shipments of fuels and chemicals. Foreign tonnage and general cargo enter or depart through the three main ports, which contain most of the public facilities for water transport. The United States Army Engineers listed 102 ports in New England in their 1951 report, but only three of these ports handled more than 5,000,000 tons of cargo that year. Boston with nearly 19,000,000 tons, Portland with 10,000,000, and Providence with 8,000,000 accounted for nearly two-thirds of the total waterborne tonnage handled by all New England ports in 1951. In the light of these facts our discussion of New England facilities for water transport will be limited to descriptions of the ports of Portland, Boston, and Providence.

Port Facilities

Port of Boston. Physical Features. The harbor of the Port of Boston is one of New England's greatest natural assets. Less than seven miles from open ocean, it provides easy access and yet a high degree of protection against rough weather. It comprises 47 square miles exclusive of islands and has a water frontage of over 140 miles.

For deep-water shipping there are three main channels of entrance from the sea to the deep-water anchorage of President Roads. In these the mean low-water depth varies from 40 feet in North Channel and 30 in South Channel to 27 in the Narrows. The depth of these channels is adequate for ships at present afloat. Also, there are a number of other channels to accommodate coastal and other vessels having less draft.

11. Lake Champlain is used extensively for canal traffic moving between New York, Albany, and Montreal.

Before World War II considerable general cargo tonnage entered New England from the coastal and intercoastal trade. The wartime sinking of the coastal fleet, and the stronger competition of rail and motor carriers, have discouraged new postwar investment in waterborne service. In 1939, 1,707,933 tons of general cargo from the coastal trade were handled at the Port of Boston. In 1953 the figure was 144,000 tons. It is evident that restoration of this coastal service through public investment would be quite costly.

From President Roads the Main Ship Channel extends to the mouths of the Mystic and Chelsea rivers and to Charlestown Bridge on the Charles River. This channel has been deepened since World War II to 40 feet so that the main commercial piers in the Port are now adjacent to 40-foot channels. Beyond this point channels of lesser depth extend up the Chelsea, Mystic, and Charles rivers. Also, Fort Point Channel extending southerly from the Main Ship Channel separates Boston from South Boston.

Responsibility for maintaining the physical accommodations of the harbor rests with the United States Army Corps of Engineers. At present the harbor facilities are adequate for most commercial needs, but channel deepening in the Mystic River, at the anchorage basin, President Roads, and in the Weymouth Fore River, would be desirable improvements.

Commercial Facilities. The Port of Boston has 259 piers or wharves amounting to 30 miles of berthing space. Many of these have rail connections and are in close proximity to storage warehouses. However, most of the 259 are private or government piers not available for general commercial use. Nine of the ten public piers are owned by the Commonwealth of Massachusetts and the other (Army Base) is owned by the United States. These ten contain 30 berths completed and three in process of construction. By location, the public piers divide into the South Boston, the Charlestown, and the East Boston terminals. The New York, New Haven, and Hartford, the Boston and Maine, and the Boston and Albany railroads serve these respective terminal areas. The South Boston terminals are most important for general cargo. The Army Base, Castle Island, and Commonwealth Pier No. 5 have 18 of the 26 covered berths in the Port.

Existing port facilities are more than adequate for the volume of tonnage currently being handled. The public piers have rail connections extending over their length, making possible direct loading between ship and freight car. The same type of direct transfer of cargo is also possible for trucks. The Port of Boston offers a cargo-handling arrangement which is unexcelled by any other port on the Atlantic coast. Especially does it have an advantage over the Port of New York, where lighter movements are necessary on almost all shipments.[12]

Although the Port of Boston has achieved a high level of physical

12. It has been the practice of the railroads in the Port of New York to absorb lighterage charges when a rail movement is involved.

facilities, it has been troubled by labor problems, which have made steamship companies reluctant to enter the port. In October 1951 an important step to achieve more peaceful labor relations was taken with the signing of an agreement between the International Longshoremen's Association and the Boston Shipping Association. This was the first wage contract to be negotiated since the middle 1930's. The agreement apparently conforms in most respects to that in force in the Port of New York. Its signing has not eliminated entirely the hostility and lack of cooperation between labor and management. Steamship operators who measure their costs by the day are hesitant about entering a port where delays may occur.

It is to be hoped that some of the results of the reform activity currently transpiring in the Port of New York may extend to Boston. Obviously, the workers themselves are not entirely to blame for abuses which have occurred in the Port. To some extent they have been victimized by a system which has resisted many attempts to change.

Shipping Services. The Port of Boston offers freight services on all world trade routes from Atlantic coast ports which the United States Maritime Commission designated as "essential" to American shipping. These routes extend to the following areas:

1. Australia and New Zealand
2. Canada and Maritime Provinces
3. Far East, Philippines, Hawaii
4. Pakistan, India, Persian Gulf
5. Mediterranean
6. West Indies and Mexico
7. Scandinavian ports
8. South America
9. South, East, and West Africa
10. United Kingdom and Ireland
11. Netherlands and continent
12. Coastwise and intercoastal

Over 80 steamship lines serve 50 countries and territories from the Port of Boston. Obviously the frequency of sailing to many destinations is relatively low, and often sailings are not immediately available because they depend on the volume of cargo. On the other hand, these 80 lines have evinced a willingness to increase service at the Port of Boston if due tonnage is forthcoming.

It is apparent from the tonnage statistics that tonnage moving *inward* through the port is more than ten times the tonnage *outward*. This peculiarity constitutes the major problem of the Port of Boston. If outward tonnage could be brought to parity with inward tonnage the position of the Port of Boston among the ports of the United States would be materially improved. (See Table 13-12.)

Much of the inward domestic tonnage comprises petroleum and coal, which move to New England largely by water. This bulk traffic has no balancing tonnage leaving the ·Port. *If steamship companies could be assured that the Port of Boston would provide adequate outbound cargo, including bulk hold-cargo, Boston would receive better service in the export trade.* At present the only bulk shipments moving outward from the Port consist of grain, a valuable but uncertain item of export. This commodity attracts ships to the Port which provide general cargo service as well. However, the rejuvenation of European agriculture makes it quite likely that a smaller volume of grain will be exported by the United States in the coming years.

Table 13–12. Ships and Tonnage Passing through the Port of Boston, 1948–52

YEAR	GENERAL CARGO	BULK CARRIERS	COLLIERS	TANKERS	TOTAL	TOTAL TONS OF 2,000 LBS.
1952	1,183	169	273	676	2,301	19,237,945
1951	1,237	189	274	620	2,320	18,976,880
1950	1,527	220	254	800	2,801	18,194,438
1949	1,329	206	268	762	2,565	15,363,529
1948	1,207	152	569	727	2,655	18,317,356

IMPORT AND EXPORT TRAFFIC

YEAR	IMPORTS	EXPORTS	TOTAL
1952	4,958,366	420,438	5,378,804
1951	5,300,446	436,730	5,537,166
1950	5,282,995	247,364	5,530,359
1949	2,361,341	414,857	3,776,198
1948	2,833,989	360,734	3,194,723

DOMESTIC TRAFFIC

YEAR	INWARD	OUTWARD	INTRAPORT	TOTAL
1952	11,575,250	694,458	1,589,433	13,859,141

Source: Port of Boston Commission

Port Administration. The Port of Boston Commission, a state agency, was created during 1953 by Chapter 608 of the General Laws of the Commonwealth of Massachusetts, superseding the Port of Boston Authority which had been set up in 1945. It consists of five members appointed by the governor with advice and consent of the council.

The commission is in administrative charge of the Port of Boston and is empowered, subject to approval by the governor and council, to make all necessary plans for the development of Boston Harbor. It has immediate charge of the lands, piers, and other structures and facilities in the Port owned by the Commonwealth, except lands under the control of the Metropolitan District Commission.

In 1945, when the Port Authority was set up, it was supposed that political involvements would be minimized. The Authority was given a large degree of autonomy over the activities of the Port. However, the legislature kept a hold on finances, which at times has threatened to strangle the Port. All income of the Port goes directly to the state treasury.

Funds must be appropriated annually to meet Port expenses. It is evident that managerial discretion is severely hampered by the legislature. No real autonomy exists when every decision involving expenditures is subjected to legislative approval.

The appointment of the five-man Board of Commissioners by the governor with approval of the governor's council has also been criticized. No standards of technical qualification were set up in the 1945 law. On this basis appointees with neither interest nor experience in port affairs might be chosen. This alleged shortcoming has been partially overcome by the Act of 1953 effective October 1, 1953. Under the new law the governor makes appointments from a slate of candidates advanced by 23 organizations concerned in one way or another with port matters. However, the governor is not required to limit his appointments to the slate advanced by the 23 organizations.

At the present time the administration of the Port still is not completely satisfactory to some groups with vital economic interest in the Port of Boston. *Logically the Port should be operated with the scope and latitude of managerial activity usually afforded to business enterprise. Much precedent exists among other ports throughout the country for an independent agency free to act in accord with commercial needs and circumstances.*

Port of Portland. The Port of Portland is the most northerly and easterly port of major importance on the Atlantic coast of the United States. The harbor lies three and one-half miles from the open ocean, with a waterfront of about eight and one-half miles. It is made up of three parts: Main Harbor containing the commercial piers, Fore River, and Back Cove. In the Main Harbor Channel and in part of the Fore River depth at mean low water is 35 feet, adequate for freight shipping.

The Port contains six public piers. Three are owned by the Canadian National Railroad, one by the State of Maine, and two by the Portland Terminal Company. The Portland Terminal Company is a subsidiary of the Maine Central Railroad and operates the terminal facilities for the Maine Central and the Boston and Maine. The most important facility at the Canadian National piers is the grain elevator with a capacity of 1,500,000 bushels. Two steamers can be loaded at a time at a rate of 12,000 bushels per hour per steamer. The Maine State Pier, 1,000 feet long, has berthing space for four ships and 140,000 square feet of cargo sheds for transit cargo. Tracks on one side of the pier permit direct handling of cargo between freight car and ships. All railroads entering Portland have access to the State Pier. At the westerly end of the Port are the wharves of the Portland Terminal Company with berth space for five ships. Each wharf has tracks permitting direct rail transfer to and from ships. Wharf No. 3 is specially equipped for handling bulk cargo, including scrap iron. Adequate storage space is available on the wharves.

Portland has no regularly scheduled foreign steamship services. However,

American and foreign lines ordinarily will call for cargo in lots of 500 tons or more.

The Maine Port Authority was created by a special act of the Maine legislature in 1929, as amended in 1941, 1945, and 1947. The general purpose of the Authority is "to acquire, construct, and operate piers and terminal facilities at the Port of Portland with all rights, privileges, and powers necessary therefor." It has charge of the Maine State Pier.

Officials of the Port consist of five directors, four of whom are appointed by the governor and one by the City of Portland. The Port Authority may, for a term not exceeding five years, lease or rent any real property owned by it, and may, for a period not exceeding five years, make contracts or agreements for carrying out its purposes, except that it shall not commit the Authority to spending a sum greater than $50,000 without the consent of the governor and council. No form of indebtedness issued or liabilities incurred by the Authority shall become an obligation of the State of Maine. The net income of the Port Authority may be used for improvements and extensions of the property of the Port Authority at the discretion of its directors.

Thus, the Port Authority of Maine has greater control over and discretion in the use of funds than does the Boston Port Authority. Perhaps most important, the revenue earned by the Port may be used for necessary improvements and additions without legislative action.

Port of Providence. The Port of Providence lies at the head of Narragansett Bay about 30 miles from open water. A 35-foot mean low-water channel permits ships to enter the main area of the port.

There are in the Port 25 private docks, a municipal dock, and a state pier, both available for public use. The Port offers full custom service, warehousing, bunkering, and all repairs short of drydocking. The Municipal Dock is a modern pier with storage and rail facilities at shipside. Mean low-water clearance is 30 feet. The State Pier is less used for ocean freight, clearance being 24 feet on one side and 23 feet on the other.

Ninety-eight per cent of the tonnage of cargoes received at the Port of Providence consists of coal and petroleum products. Since inward cargo is nine times outward cargo, it is clear that the Port of Providence is almost exclusively a depot for incoming petroleum and coal. General cargo movement is relatively insignificant, with the result that the Port has no regularly scheduled cargo services.

The Port of Providence has no centralized authority. The Municipal Pier is operated by the City Public Works Department and the State Pier by the Division of Rivers and Harbors of the state.

Recommendations. It is difficult to achieve a clear perspective about the place of New England ports, especially the Port of Boston, within the New England economy. Water transport is important as the figures show, but a preponderant share of the tonnage is bulk commodities. The facilities for transporting and unloading coal, petroleum, chemicals, and so on are largely private. Public facilities for water transportation are devoted to a minority of the traffic.

In recent years Massachusetts has made a strenuous but not entirely effective attempt to build up the Port of Boston. Recollections of Boston's days of maritime glory are invoked to stimulate public interest and willingness to invest public money in the Port. Extensive plans have been prepared for construction programs calculated to return Boston to a position of eminence among the nation's ports.

Over the optimism about the place of the Port of Boston in the New England economy lies the shadow of the St. Lawrence Seaway. The development of the Port depends on its continuance as a port for shipments to and from areas to the west of New England. Considering that southern New England is tributary to the Port of New York, New England volume alone probably will not support a large port at Boston. Port of Boston estimates indicate that the seaway might divert as much as 30% of the foreign traffic which now passes through Boston.

The adverse effect of the seaway on the Port of Boston does not constitute a conclusive argument against its construction. If Congress decides that the seaway is in the over-all national interest, New England's interest will be overridden. *However, Massachusetts and also Maine—with respect to Portland—need to recognize and prepare for the eventuality of the seaway. It is likely that much of the grain movement through Portland and Boston would cease. This would have the unfortunate result not only of reducing traffic volume but also of removing the essential bottom cargo which is so scarce at the Port of Boston.*

Existing facilities of New England ports appear to be adequate for the present volume of traffic. So far as further public construction at New England ports is concerned, the wise policy would appear to be to wait until the effects of the seaway and other developments may be discerned.

Pipelines

Petroleum pipelines play a relatively unimportant part in the New England economy. Most petroleum enters New England via tanker and is then distributed by motor carrier or rail to inland points. However, there are two petroleum products lines in southeastern New England. The Shell Oil Company owns a pipeline that originates near Fall River and runs north to Dedham. From Dedham one branch goes to Waltham and the other passes Boston and continues on to Lawrence. The other products line originates near Providence and goes by way of Worcester to Springfield. A spur from Springfield connects with Hartford.

The only large private pipelines in New England have little significance for the region's economy. They run between Portland, Maine, and the

Canadian border en route to Montreal. These two lines of 18 and 12 inch owned by the Portland Pipeline Corporation extend for 166 miles in New England, carrying crude petroleum to Canada.

The pipelines permit Canada to import crude petroleum throughout the year, and to avoid the 1,000-mile haul around and down the St. Lawrence River.

There is no evidence to indicate that additional pipelines are a pressing need for New England. Ocean tanker movements of petroleum are at a fraction of the cost of shipment by pipeline. Motor and rail carriers appear adequate for further distribution within New England.

THE USE OF NEW ENGLAND'S TRANSPORT FACILITIES

An intelligent appraisal of the adequacy and efficiency of New England's transport facilities should be related to the nature of their use. We should not be concerned about the shortcomings of facilities if they are in fact little used. Thus, an attempt has been made to analyze the flow of goods to and from New England and within New England.[13] From these statistics the volume and type of commodity movement is revealed. Conclusions may then be drawn as to where and what improvements should be made in New England's transportation system.

The lack of definitive statistics about some important aspects of motor transport impedes quantitative conclusions about the use of New England transportation facilities. It would be highly desirable to establish a procedure for reporting the statistical performance of New England motor transport. A knowledge of the growth and needs of motor transport is essential to the making of meaningful policy in respect to transportation.

Despite the lack of complete information, some conclusions can be developed based on rail and water carrier statistics. A distinction may be drawn between the flow of goods to and from New England and the flow within New England. In this study, interregional trade includes foreign trade as well as domestic. Interregional trade reflects New England's relation to other regions—that is, the kind and volume of goods which enter New England compared to the goods which are shipped out. Intraregional movements, which are most important in aggregate tonnage, indicate the structural pattern of trade within the six-state area.

The statistics are limited to rail and water for interregional and to rail for intraregional shipments. An exception is that the data on traffic between Canada and the United States include truck movements. The Interstate Commerce Commission, the Corps of Engineers, and the Bureau of the Cen-

13. See our Staff Memorandum No. 1, and No. 12, *New England's Trade with the Rest of the United States and with Foreign Countries.*

sus are the sources of information. In some cases, figures are estimated from samples and therefore may not be completely accurate.

The most striking characteristic of New England trade is that in almost every commodity category tonnages inbound exceed outbound. (See Table

Interregional and Foreign Trade

Table 13–13. Tonnages to and from New England by Rail and Water, 1949
(thousands of short tons)

	TOTAL OF ALL SHIPMENTS			TOTAL OF ALL SHIPMENTS		
	TO N.E.	FROM N.E.	NET TO N.E.	TO N.E.	FROM N.E.	NET TO N.E.
TOTAL	62,865	11,330	51,535	20,503	11,136	9,367
Domestic rail						
Manufactured products	7,900	4,390	3,510	7,900	4,390	3,510
Products of mines	9,480	760	8,720	424	744	−320
Products of agriculture	4,310	1,180	3,130	4,310	1,180	3,130
Products of forests	963	607	356	963	607	356
Animals and products	1,060	140	920	1,060	140	920
TOTAL	23,713	7,077	16,636	14,657	7,061	7,596
Domestic water						
Manufactured products	21,879	2,767	19,112	793	2,767	−1,974
Products of mines	8,879	462	8,417	397	46	351
Products of agriculture	102	19	83	102	19	83
Products of forests	247	2	245	247	2	245
Animals and products	48	25	23	48	25	23
TOTAL	31,155	3,275	27,880	1,587	2,859	−1,272
Foreign water						
Manufactured products	3,756	149	3,607	689	149	540
Products of mines	1,282	21	1,261	331	12	319
Products of agriculture	166	240	−74	166	240	−74
Products of forests	84	2	82	84	2	82
Animals and products	189	10	179	189	10	179
TOTAL	5,477	422	5,055	1,459	413	1,046
Foreign rail and truck*						
Manufactured products	754	266	488	754	266	488
Products of mines	464	104	360	464	87	377
Products of agriculture	369	41	328	369	41	328
Products of forests	894	131	763	894	131	763
Animals and products	39	14	25	39	14	25
TOTAL	2,520	556	1,964	2,520	539	1,981

* To Canada.
Source: I.C.C., Carload Waybill Analysis, 1949, and U.S. Bureau of the Census

13–13.) Approximately six tons of goods arrived in New England by rail and water for each ton sent out. Inbound rail tonnage was more than three times outgoing shipments. Tonnage receipts by domestic water carrier were more than nine times the tonnage shipped out. This situation, of course, has great impact on carrier operation in that empty conveyances must constantly be sent out of New England. The inbound traffic must bear most of the operational cost.

Further scrutiny of the 1949 figures indicates that the imbalance of in and out movements was greatest in the categories of manufactured products and products of mines. In both of these cases the heaviest tonnage was that of fuel and petroleum products. Crude petroleum and coal were considered products of mines. Refined petroleum was included with manufactures. Fuel comprised two-thirds of the incoming tonnage. By contrast only a very small amount of the outbound tonnage was fuel. Of the 21,800,000 tons of manufactured goods transported to New England via domestic water almost all were petroleum and petroleum products.

In the right panel of Table 13–13 New England tonnage figures are presented with the tonnage of fuel and petroleum products excluded. The disparity between receipts and shipments is seen to be reduced from 6 to 1 to less than 2 to 1. In the case of domestic water, it appears that New England ships out more manufactured goods (fuel excluded) than it brings in. When fuel is excluded from consideration, the in-out ratio is still unfavorable to New England. However, the much smaller net inflow can be more than compensated by heavier truck out-movements and/or the lower cubical density of the typical exports of New England. For example, although rail tonnage in is 3.3 times rail tonnage out, loaded incoming freight cars are 2.5 times the number of loaded outgoing freight cars.

The decisively unbalancing factor is fuel. The industrial activity and climate in New England require a high per capita fuel consumption. However, this state of affairs is not one which by itself must cause great concern. Throughout much of the United States and the rest of the world petroleum must be transported in. New England is relatively fortunate in that most of its fuel tonnage can be brought in by water for which the ton-mile cost is considerably lower than by rail or by pipeline.

A natural presumption in light of the above set of facts might be that New England should develop back haul traffic to fill the tankers, colliers, hopper and tank cars, and thus lessen the burden of cost on the main haul. This commendable course of action is greatly limited, however, by the specialized nature of the oil and coal conveyances. Tankers can take other liquid cargo after cleaning, but it is difficult to imagine a liquid product which New England could ship to the Gulf Coast. Colliers run between New England and Norfolk, Virginia. Bulk shipments which can be put on colliers destined for Norfolk are less than numerous.

Rail hopper cars are somewhat more adaptable to other uses such as carrying gravel, crushed rock, etc. However, many cars must be returned empty. Practical traffic for the return haul is not quickly and easily found.

Considering the above factors, it is difficult to conceive of a means whereby New England's imbalance of traffic can be materially lessened. The shipment of grain through the Port of Boston has been much encouraged to supply the out-cargo for freighters discharging at Boston. This solution applies to foreign water transport which by bulk is only about 8% of New England trade. Also, it creates for the railroads a problem of empty freight cars at the Port of Boston.

Origin and Destination of New England's Interregional and Foreign Trade

By weight, manufactured products accounted for over half of New England's receipts by rail and ship in 1949. (See Table 13–14.) About 87% of the manufactured products came from the rest of the United States. Of the remaining 13%, which were foreign shipments, large refined petroleum

Table 13–14. *Summary of Shipments by Rail and Water into New England, by Product Groups and Areas of Origin, by Weight, 1949*

AREA OF ORIGIN	MANUFAC- TURED PRODUCTS	PRODUCTS OF MINES	PRODUCTS OF AGRI- CULTURE	PRODUCTS OF FORESTS	ANIMALS AND PRODUCTS	TOTAL ALL PRODUCTS
Totals, all areas (thousands of short tons)	34,289	20,105	4,947	2,188	1,336	62,865
Per cent of total	54.5%	32.0%	7.9%	3.5%	2.1%	100.0%
Per cent of product group received from:						
All foreign countries	13.2%	8.7%	10.8%	44.9%	17.1%	12.7%
Canada†	2.3	3.4	7.5	44.4	6.7	4.6
Caribbean Islands	9.7	0.4	*	—	*	5.4
Northern area, E. & W. Coast, S. America	0.3	4.4	0.1	—	—	1.6
Northwest Europe area	0.3	0.2	*	*	0.1	0.2
Indian Ocean–S. China Sea area	0.2	*	0.8	*	0.3	0.2
Argentina	*	*	0.3	—	1.9	0.1
Brazil	*	*	0.8	0.1	0.2	0.1
Australia	*	*	*	—	2.8	0.1
Netherlands, Belgium	0.1	*	0.1	*	0.5	0.1
All other	0.2	0.2	1.1	0.3	4.6	0.4
U.S. rail shipments	23.0	47.2	87.1	44.8	79.3	37.7
U.S. coastal shipments	63.8	44.2	2.2	11.3	3.6	49.6
TOTAL	100.0%	100.0%	100.0%	100.0%	100.0%	100.0%

Note: Details may not add to totals because of rounding.
* Less than 0.05%.
† Includes truck shipments.
Source: Ibid.

shipments from the Caribbean Islands dominated with almost 10% of the total. Products of mines were almost a third of the inbound tonnage, and more than 90% of such receipts originated in the United States. The products of agriculture shipped into New England equaled about 8% of the total, and again almost 90% of that category came from elsewhere in the United States. Inbound shipments of forest products and animals and their products were comparatively small in weight, in proportion to the total. Almost all imports of forest products were from Canada.[14]

The commodities which were shipped out of New England destined for the rest of the United States and for foreign countries were not dominated by a few items, as was true of inbound shipments. Fifteen commodities represented 75% of the weight of New England's outbound rail and water shipments in 1949. Again petroleum and its products were the largest group, with over a fifth of the total weight. Other large items, in terms of weight, were paper and paper products, vegetables, iron and steel products, sand and gravel, chemicals, and machinery. The tonnage of outbound shipments was only about one-sixth of that which entered the region. Many of the shipments which left New England, such as petroleum products, coal and coke, and wheat, were reshipments.

Table 13–15. Summary of Shipments by Rail and Water out of New England, by Areas of Destination, by Weight, 1949

AREAS OF TERMINATION	MANUFAC-TURED PRODUCTS	PRODUCTS OF AGRI-CULTURE	PRODUCTS OF MINES	PRODUCTS OF FORESTS	ANIMALS AND PRODUCTS	TOTAL ALL PRODUCTS
Total, all areas	7,571	1,480	1,347	742	190	11,330
(thousands of short tons)						
Per cent of total	66.8%	13.1%	11.9%	6.5%	1.7%	100.0%
Per cent of product group shipped to:						
All foreign countries	5.5%	19.0%	9.3%	20.0%	12.8%	8.6%
Canada*	4.4	2.9	7.8	17.7	8.3	5.5
France	0.2	2.6	0.2	0.1	0.1	0.5
Germany	0.1	2.8	—†	—	0.5	0.5
United Kingdom	0.1	2.2	0.3	—†	1.5	0.4
Mediterranean Islands	—†	3.0	—†	—	0.3	0.4
Netherlands, Belgium	0.1	2.2	0.2	0.1	0.8	0.4
Italy	0.1	1.0	—†	—	0.8	0.2
Indian Ocean	0.2	—†	—†	0.1	0.4	0.1
All other	0.3	2.3	0.7	—†	0.2	0.6
U.S. rail shipments	58.0	79.7	56.4	81.8	73.8	62.5
U.S. coastal shipments	36.5	1.3	34.3	0.3	13.3	28.9
TOTAL	100.0%	100.0%	100.0%	100.0%	100.0%	100.0%

Note: Details may not add to totals because of rounding.
* Includes truck shipments.
† Less than 0.05%.
Source: Ibid.

Manufactured products represented two-thirds of the total weight of shipments in 1949 by rail and water from New England to the rest of the United States and abroad. (See Table 13–15.) About 95% of the shipments of manufactured goods went to other regions in this country. Products of agriculture and of mines accounted for another 25% of the total. Products of forests and of animals played only a small role in the region's outbound shipments. Foreign exports were a fairly small portion of tonnage shipments

14. See our Staff Memorandum No. 1 for an extended discussion of this topic.

Table 13–16. Rail Trade of the Individual New England States, by Product Groups, 1949

	INTRASTATE SHIPMENTS	SHIPMENTS TO STATE (−) FROM OTHER N.E. STATES	SHIPMENTS FROM STATE (+) TO OTHER N.E. STATES	NET SHIPMENTS TO OTHER N.E. STATES
Maine				
Manufactured products	670,100	350,800	742,900	392,100
Products of mines	742,800	60,200	108,400	48,200
Products of agriculture	115,400	54,800	92,900	38,100
Products of forests	998,500	30,500	233,700	203,200
Animals and products	—	2,300	3,200	900
TOTAL	2,526,800	498,600	1,181,100	682,500
New Hampshire				
Manufactured products	101,100	334,400	132,400	−202,000
Products of mines	26,000	253,300	—	−253,300
Products of agriculture	28,700	40,700	14,600	−26,100
Products of forests	45,800	204,700	122,500	−82,200
Animals and products	—	2,300	5,900	3,600
TOTAL	201,600	835,400	275,400	−560,000
Vermont				
Manufactured products	86,000	273,000	246,700	−26,300
Products of mines	11,400	185,300	146,800	−38,500
Products of agriculture	17,600	4,300	104,100	99,800
Products of forests	30,200	30,300	82,000	51,700
Animals and products	—	4,700	6,000	1,300
TOTAL	145,200	497,600	585,600	88,000
Massachusetts				
Manufactured products	663,300	1,003,600	638,500	−365,100
Products of mines	723,700	317,400	413,600	96,200
Products of agriculture	135,500	92,500	34,400	−58,100
Products of forests	20,800	135,000	41,100	−93,900
Animals and products	38,800	33,900	13,000	−20,900
TOTAL	1,582,100	1,582,400	1,140,600	−441,800
Rhode Island				
Manufactured products	22,300	83,700	386,200	302,500
Products of mines	14,200	43,000	179,600	136,600
Products of agriculture	—	18,900	700	−18,200
Products of forests	—	19,900	2,600	−17,300
Animals and products	—	500	3,000	2,500
TOTAL	36,500	166,000	572,100	406,100
Connecticut				
Manufactured products	243,300	300,600	199,400	−101,200
Products of mines	384,000	116,100	126,900	10,800
Products of agriculture	7,300	45,900	10,400	−35,500
Products of forests	1,800	69,000	7,500	−61,500
Animals and products	—	3,200	15,800	12,600
TOTAL	636,400	534,800	360,000	−174,800

* Estimates inflated from 1% sample.
Source: Ibid.

in each category except that of products of agriculture—where the trans-shipment of wheat from the rest of the country increased the percentage—and of forest products.[15]

Intraregional Traffic

It is for intra-New England transport that the lack of statistical information on motor transport is most serious. Probably at least 50% of the intra-regional tonnage is transported by truck, and the figure may in fact be much higher. The statistics available are exclusively for rail and are presented here with the recognition that they cannot be considered representative of actual tonnage flows in New England. Probably the most serious discrepancy is in manufactured products, which move largely by truck over distances up to 500 miles. However, there is some value in obtaining a picture of the flow of products by rail between the New England states. (See Table 13–16.)

Rail tonnage to and from New England in 1949 amounted to over 30,000,-000 tons as compared to just over 9,000,000 tons transported by rail within New England. This indicates that a great deal must have moved within New England by truck, since total tonnages for short distances are usually greater than for long.

Connecticut, Massachusetts, and New Hampshire received more tonnage than they shipped. The other three states were in the opposite position. Maine has a favorable balance of trade in every category. New Hampshire, on the other hand, had the largest deficit of the six states. Approximately half of this deficit stems from fuel which is transported by rail from tide-water points in the other New England states. Maine's tonnage outflow to some extent alleviates the acute New England problem of more loaded freight cars in than out. Table 13–16 presents the rail trade within the New England states by product groups for the year 1949.

Summary

From the statistics which have been presented the following summary statements may be made about New England's *rail and water trade* in 1949:

1. Almost 90% of the inflow of goods to New England came from the rest of the United States.
2. Sixty-five per cent of the inflow of goods was fuel, crude and refined petroleum, accounting for 42%, and coal and coke, accounting for 23%.
3. Over 90% of the outflow of goods from New England went to the rest of the United States.
4. Approximately 50% of all imports from foreign countries to New England were fuel.

15. See our Staff Memorandum No. 12 for a more extensive discussion of this topic.

5. Thirty-five per cent of all imports from foreign countries came from Canada. Most of this was not fuel.
6. Sixty per cent of all New England exports to foreign countries were sent to Canada; half of these were manufactured and miscellaneous goods.
7. Fifty per cent of the inbound tonnage arrived in New England by water carrier.
8. Thirty-four per cent of the outbound tonnage was shipped by water carrier.
9. Inbound rail and water tonnage was almost six times the outbound.
10. If fuel tonnages are excluded, inbound tonnage was less than twice the outbound.
11. Five loaded freight cars entered New England for every two loaded cars which left.
12. Rail tonnage *to and from* New England was over three times rail tonnage which moved within New England.

This survey of New England's use of transport facilities has pointed out several distinctive features that should be considered in making recommendations for the improvement of New England transportation. For example, the fact that a large proportion of the waterborne inbound tonnage (petroleum and coal) moves entirely via private carrier places this segment of traffic beyond either federal or state transport regulation. By and large its financing and organization lie in private hands. Public policy regarding taxes, labor relations, etc., will affect the private carriers favorably or adversely as it does other firms, but little can be done directly to foster the private carrier without discriminating against other private business activity.

Probably there are only limited possibilities of balancing the flow of trade by rail and water to New England. The imbalance is symptomatic of geographic specialization and specialization of transport facility, both of which contribute to lower cost of production. It is difficult to conceive of bulk cargoes being developed in New England which could utilize the back-haul space on tankers and colliers.

Rail traffic statistics rather conclusively demonstrate the declining importance of the railroads in intrastate traffic. *Public policy should permit the railroads to withdraw gradually from short-haul service. Along with the substitution of motor or rail for local movements, coordination of motor and rail on long hauls should be encouraged.* Eventually the railroads would become long-haul bulk carriers.

Canada is overwhelmingly New England's biggest partner in trade. The rapid growth of the Canadian economy suggests an increasing opportunity for New England's exports, and the desirability of good transport between the two areas. Further study should be made of the means by which this trade is carried on.

SUMMARY AND RECOMMENDATIONS

The government's role has historically been promotion and subsidy of transportation. Unfortunately, when the dictates of the free market are abandoned, criteria for judging how far the government should go in its developmental role are elusive and uncertain. Moreover, the subsidizing of a new form of transportation imposes a severe burden upon older forms of transportation. It can be argued that if the New England states would spend large amounts for building supermodern transport facilities industry would thereby be attracted to New England. Presumably the increased use would eventually justify the expenditure of those funds. On the other hand, it can be argued that the state's entry as a proprietor merely shifts cost from the shipper to the public with no resultant stimulation of transport activity.

This report has not attempted to evaluate the possibilities of public promotion of major undertakings. The objective has been to describe and appraise present transport facilities, and to make limited recommendations for improving their efficiency. Accordingly, no effort has been made to say that New England should have any given amount of new highways, airports, port facilities, or inland waterways.

It has been determined statistically that New England shippers pay more per ton mile of freight shipped by rail and truck than shippers in any other region of the United States. This higher level of charges stems from the higher operating costs of New England carriers. It is difficult, if not impossible, to determine the causes of the higher costs of operation. In any case, it is idle simply to berate the carriers. A more constructive approach is to create a condition which will stimulate them to achieve maximum effectiveness.

The function of competition as a spur to efficiency and public benefit has been too glibly and easily rejected in the transportation field. Today there are five types of transportation—rail, motor, water, air, and pipeline—which either do, or could, compete with each other in varying degrees. The shipper has more alternatives today for the shipment of his goods than ever. Nevertheless, to a great extent regulation prevents this potential competition from becoming actual. The more aggressive carrier is denied the reward for greater efficiency which should be his. While seeking to insure the public against monopolistic exploitation, regulation has the tendency to protect the inefficient carrier from his betters.

We have repeatedly recommended that government regulation of carriers be relaxed. This recommendation is premised on the belief that the public benefit resulting from increased competition will be significant and that the public can be protected by provisions prohibiting discriminatory actions.

Regulation is national in scope, so it is impossible for the New England states to take separate action in that respect. *However, the New England congressional delegation might well take the lead in developing a new national public policy in transportation.*

There are several measures which can be taken by state and local authorities to encourage and provide for better transportation. They have been mentioned earlier in the body of the report and may be summarized as follows:

1. Greater uniformity of motor vehicle registration, tax, weight, truck length, height, width, and other requirements should be legislated. Variations have the effect of unduly harassing the motor carrier operating in interstate commerce.

2. State regulatory agencies should not impose on carriers passenger service requirements which have the effect of burdening the movement of freight.

3. State public works agencies should improve the coordination of their planning and construction to the end of creating a more continuous and uniform net of good roads.

4. Increased efforts should be made to assess the cost of highways against users in proportion to their responsibility for cost. Also, separate facilities should be provided for particular classes of users if they are willing to pay for them. For example, a special highway truck lane should be paid for by truckers.

5. The states and municipalities should consider public motor transport terminal facilities, coordinated with highway and community planning.

6. Both airports and seaports should be insulated from irresponsible political pressures. To the maximum extent possible they should be forced to be self-sufficient.

7. We have strongly urged that the policing of civil aviation and the management of airports not be merged. Furthermore, we have suggested that a go-slow policy be adopted with respect to regulation of aviation at the state level.

8. If Logan is to become a truly international airport, all the foreign carriers on the North Atlantic route should be enabled to stop there as well as at Idlewild, New York. This involves action at the federal level by the United States Department of State and the Civil Aeronautics Board.

9. The New England states should sponsor or support research on the following topics in transportation:

   a. A system for the collection of statistics on the tonnage movement by motor transport in New England. This would include both for-hire and private carriage.

   b. A determination of user cost of the highways. The question of who causes the wear and tear of the highways could and should be more conclusively ascertained.

   c. A study of the need for and location of public or cooperative terminal facilities for motor transport.

    d. The possibility for greater coordination between road and rail, including the use of flatcars for the carriage of truck trailers.

SELECTED REFERENCES

1. Baker, George P., *Formation of the New England Railroad System,* Cambridge, Harvard University Press, 1937.
2. Cunningham, William J., "The Railroads of New England," *New England's Prospect: 1933,* ed. John K. Wright, American Geographical Society, Special Publication No. 16, New York, 1933.
3. Cushman, Frank M., *Transportation for Management,* New York, Prentice-Hall, 1953.
4. Interstate Commerce Commission, *Comparative Statement of Railway Operating Statistics, Individual Class I Steam Railways in the United States,* Statement No. 52200, Washington.
5. —— *Statistics of Class I Motor Carriers,* Statement No. 5030, Washington.
6. —— *Statistics of Railways in the United States,* Washington.
7. *Moody's Manual of Investments,* "Transportation," Moody's Investors' Service, New York, 1952.
8. Nicholson, Joseph, *Air Transportation,* New York, Wiley, 1951.
9. University of Wisconsin, "The Economic Basis of Public Policy for Motor Transport," *Land Economics,* August 1952.
10. U.S. Department of Agriculture, *Factors Affecting Freight Rates on Agricultural Commodities: The Railroad Passenger Deficit,* Production and Marketing Administration.
11. Westmeyer, Russell E., *Economics of Transportation,* New York, Prentice-Hall, 1952.

14

New England's Industrial Management

*Drafted by Alfred C. Neal on the basis of material
prepared by Arthur A. Bright, Jr.*

INTRODUCTION

A region like New England cannot depend for its prosperity upon the richness of its own natural resources or its overwhelmingly preferred market
position. It must of necessity depend more heavily upon the ingenuity
and skill of its people. As the late Edward Chase of Maine once said, a
people having disadvantages in location, fuel, and power must "work
longer, harder, be smarter, or work for less." This report on management
in New England deals essentially with whether the region's management
is enough "smarter" to eliminate the necessity for adopting the less pleasant
alternatives. Human capacities being reasonably well distributed geographically, there is a presumption at the outset that New England management is not likely to be smarter than management elsewhere. If, however,
it is not even equal to competitive management, its own shortcomings
impose unnecessary burdens upon others whose living is derived from the
region's economic activity. Therefore the adequacy of New England management to perform its functions is a concern not only of management or
of ownership but of all whose future depends to any important extent upon
the economy of the region—workers, retailers, bankers, professional people,
and many others.

This appraisal of management is limited to *industrial* management.[1] As
we have noted before, the region is predominantly industrial, with 44%
of its labor force engaged in manufacturing industry, a higher proportion
than that for any other region. When the tertiary employment dependent
upon manufacturing is taken into account, from 75% to 80% of New
England's employment and income must be dependent upon manufacturing
industry. Therefore an appraisal of industrial management will omit but
little that is significant to the economic base of the region.

What is management? It is first of all a function, the function of pro-
curing, directing, and coordinating the various materials, plants, machinery,
and people who make up a going business enterprise. We shall be concerned in this report with appraising the effectiveness with which the
management function is performed, not with valuating the executives.

1. New England's financial management is appraised, at least indirectly, in report No. 11,
"New England's Financial Resources and Their Use."

What standards should be used to appraise the management function? In dealing with this question, the point of view of the Committee of New England may differ somewhat from the goal that management has set for itself. Individual management executives may judge their own performance by some combination of the satisfaction they get out of the job, their earnings or those of their company, their ability to lead a quiet and well-rewarded life, and other standards. Our standard, in keeping with the purpose of our work, is management's contribution to the regional economy. Is management making its maximum contribution to regional employment and income? Is its contribution adequate to bring about the growth and expansion needed to provide jobs at good wages for the region's growing population? These two questions are obviously different; management's maximum contribution may still be inadequate to meet the region's requirements. If the best is not good enough, some New England people will have either to work harder and longer for less money or to migrate elsewhere. If management is not doing its best, then people will make the adjustments asked of them grudgingly or only when compelled by the stern discipline of unemployment that might otherwise have been avoided.

Our first question then is how good is New England's industrial management? We shall leave until later the question whether it is good enough, because the answer to the first question will help us to answer the second.

Effectiveness of management in performing the task expected of it by the region might be measured in several ways:

1. Management in New England could be compared with *management elsewhere:* (a) in terms of the profits it produces for the company, (b) in terms of various criteria of good management such as the application of scientific management principles, growth and stability of company activities, aggressiveness, and the like.

2. Management in New England could also be measured by comparing its practices with *standards of good management,* without reference to managements elsewhere. For example, a list of good management practices could be drawn up and a management could be rated in terms of the extent of its use of each "good" practice. In the second type of test it should be recognized, of course, that mere use of management "gadgets" considered to be good practice would not prove good management; rather, the use of specific practices would be considered only to be indicative of the philosophy, approach, and attitude of good management.

3. Finally, the two types of test might be validated, one against the other. Good management as measured by standards of excellence could be compared profitwise with poor or less good management. We have explored each of these approaches and have reached tentative conclusions about New England's industrial management in terms of each.

THE PROFITS TEST OF MANAGEMENT

There can be little doubt that one of the most important tests of management is its ability to produce an adequate and sustained level of profits for the company it serves. How much profit is adequate? In a competitive economy, adequacy can and should be measured against the standard of profits in closely competitive enterprises. We have applied this measure to New England's industrial management to the extent that the data for the years 1946 through 1949 permit.

Do New England manufacturers show as good a profit record as their non-New England competitors? The profit test of the quality of management was suggested by Stanley Balmer and explored by him and John Tomb, partner and associate respectively of the Boston office of McKinsey and Company, a highly regarded national firm of management consultants. It was later tested, so far as the data permitted, by a research worker of the Federal Reserve Bank of Boston.[2] This test was made in the following manner:

1. All firms having 250 employees or more in Hall's *Directory of New England Manufacturers* were listed, approximately 1,000 in all. Published statements were sought for each of these companies in the financial manuals. Statements for 140 were found.

2. Lists were sought of the closest competitors of each of the 140 firms which published their financial statements. In 44 cases this list was provided by the firms themselves. In 25 additional instances, because the firms did not answer an inquiry, it was necessary to discover closest competitors by references to persons familiar with the industry, by the answers given by similar non-New England firms, and by using other methods. Incomplete information, either of a financial nature or about competitors, limited the final comparison to 81 New England companies. Because not enough information was available in all cases to use each of these 81 companies separately, some of them were grouped, thereby limiting the comparison to 69 cases of New England firms or groups of firms for whom information was available both as to their own profitability and the profitability of their closest competitors outside the region. There were 149 separate non-New England firms used in the comparison with the 69 New England cases.

3. For each of these firms, whether New England or non-New England, profits data were secured for the years 1946 through 1949. (In a few cases the comparison was limited to 1947 through 1949 or 1946 through 1948 because data were lacking for the fourth year.) Financial data in the published statements were adjusted to put all firms on a before-tax basis so far

2. Ebenfield, Arthur A., "A Comparative Study of New England Industry with Its Non-New England Competition" (unpublished master's thesis), Brown University, October 1950.

as federal income taxes were concerned and to eliminate nonrecurring items, such as tax refunds, accelerated depreciation, extra-ordinary reserves such as the initial funding of a pension plan, etc.

The profit measure used for comparison was the average ratio of profits to sales for the years used, mainly 1946 through 1949. It was felt that this ratio would be less subject to erratic influences than the ratio of profits to net worth, but as an additional test the ratios of profits to sales were correlated to the ratios of profits to net worth. The correlation was close enough so that the results would not be changed by the use of the alternative ratio.

Reasonably comparable data compiled for 69 firm groups representing 81 New England firms and 149 non-New England firms yielded the following results:

1. In 46 of the 69 firm groups the non-New England competitors' average ratio of net profits to net sales was greater than the average for the New England firms or firm group. Because the data were not sufficiently precise, the difference was not considered to be significant if the ratios for the New England and competitor group were within 0.5 of each other.

2. In 19 of the 69 firm groups the average ratio for the New England firm was higher than that for its competitors.

3. In four cases the difference was of no apparent significance.

Statistical tests were made to determine whether differences in size of the New England and the non-New England firm affected the results, and there was found to be no significant effect on the profitability ratios because of difference in size alone. Other tests also indicated that differences in age were of no clear-cut influence on the results.

The data on profitability were also used to determine whether New England manufacturing firms were less profitable on the average than non-New England firms in the same industry. For this purpose the profits ratios computed by the National City Bank of New York in its *Monthly Letter* were compared with the profits ratios of 77 New England firms for which comparable data were available. The National City Bank's method of computing the ratio of profits to sales was employed on both sets of data before comparison, which was limited to the years 1947 through 1949 because data for 1946 were not available in the bank's compilation. An average ratio of profits to sales was computed for 12 classified industry groups for the New England branch of the industry and for the national industry. The 12 groups were woolen goods; cotton goods; silk and rayon; other textiles; pulp and paper; building, plumbing, etc., equipment; tires and rubber products; shoes and leather products; machinery; electrical equipment; radio and television; hardware and tools; and unclassified.

In eight out of the 12 industry groups the New England branch of the industry had a lower ratio of profits to sales for the three years than the industry as a whole. In but two cases, cotton goods and machinery, did

New England lead the national industry. In the case of cotton goods the favorable position is due mainly to the statistical accident that one very profitable firm in New England dominates the region's ratio. In two industry groups there was little difference between the New England and non-New England ratio of profits to sales.

The New England–national industry profits comparison was finally reduced to two average figures. A weighted average ratio of profits to sales for 1,029 firms in the National City Bank's sample was computed for the industry groups for which comparable data were available for New England firms. The average ratio of profits to sales for these industries was 7.1 for the three years. For 77 New England firms in the same industry groups the corresponding ratio of profits to sales was 5.7, or about 20% less.

While the tests just described are in many respects limited as to number of firms and subject to numerous qualifications, they indicate no superiority of profitability on the average of New England manufacturers as compared with their competition. Instead, they indicate the possibility that the average profitability of the New England manufacturers is substantially less than that of their non-New England competitors. Among the numerous exceptions to this conclusion one of the most surprising is in the cotton-goods industry.

In view of the limitations of the data, New England's poorer showing in the profit comparison should not be overstressed. It does suggest, however, a test which every good New England management should make for itself: How does profitability of our company compare in recent years with the profitability of our competitors, particularly those not in New England? The scarcity of published information on the profitability of New England manufacturers suggests also that it might be desirable for some properly equipped agency to undertake to compile regularly and on a current basis financial data obtained both from private and published sources which would enable New England manufacturers, their bankers, and their stockholders better to judge the earnings record of particular manufacturing companies.

The Test of "Excellent Management"

The use of profitability as a test of management leaves many questions unanswered. Even where several years' profits are averaged, companies following a pricing policy which in the long run might produce greater growth for the company and a higher financial reward for its owners might appear to be less profitable than others following a shortsighted policy. Similarly, everyone knows of cases where managements which have violated every important principle of good management have succeeded for a number of years in making perhaps quite extraordinary profits simply because they were carried on by the momentum of a going organization and were ruthless in their reduction of costs at the expense of the company's future. These and many other considerations would have to be taken into account in a comprehensive appraisal of management. The only attempt along these lines of which the Committee became aware was the work of the American Institute of Management.

The American Institute of Management was established in 1948 to study and appraise the management methods and problems of American business corporations. It has developed a numerical rating system which it applies to determine whether a company qualifies for the Institute's "excellent" rating. It makes no attempt to distinguish between degrees of excellence but merely uses its method to determine whether a company is excellently managed according to its criteria.

The Institute's rating system is based upon the answers to 301 questions about the company, grouped into ten categories with a maximum number of points assigned to each. The standard which warrants the application of the maximum number of points was set by the actual practice of a major company which the Institute believed to excel with respect to that particular category. The categories, the maximum number of points given for each category, and the company which serves as a yardstick are listed in Table 14–1.[3]

3. Inasmuch as the rating system employed by the American Institute of Management depends fundamentally upon the type of question that it asks, a description of the ten categories may be helpful at this point:

1. *Economic function* is concerned with the public significance of the company, the ultimate test of which is whether, if the company were to vanish overnight, the nation would be a true economic loser. By this criterion a steel producer is more important than the producer of tobacco or motion pictures, for example. Inasmuch as only 4% of the points were allocated to this factor, there seems little reason to raise the obvious questions about the subjective nature of the appraisals which might be applied when it is used to appraise a company's management.

2. *Corporate structure* deals generally with whether management is so well organized that policy can be carried out effectively throughout the organization; whether the decisions of the general executive body can be implemented; and whether the organization can effectively carry out its function to meet the growing needs of society. This category received 5% of the total number of points.

3. *Health and economic growth* is concerned with ability to earn profits in good years and bad, and with whether the earnings growth has arisen out of an enlargement of the company's own purposes and a rise in the social value of the corporation itself (6% of total points).

4. *Fairness to stockholders* means essentially what the proprietors of the company get out of their investment in it (7% of points).

5. *Research and development* questions deal with whether the company has kept abreast of all developments in its industry and whether, in addition, it has created new products, new methods, and thereby new markets which will sustain its earnings and enlarge them (7% of points).

6. *Directorate analysis* measures whether directors are attuned to change and whether they give encouragement to the ambitions and aggressiveness of younger management executives. Diversity of age, experience, and training on the board of directors is rated high. A board upon which the general public is represented is rated higher than a board from which the public is deliberately excluded (9% of points).

The companies studied by the American Institute of Management are primarily the larger corporations whose securities are publicly traded. At the time the Committee's analysis was made, in the early part of 1952, the Institute had examined 2,204 corporations by either interview or other intensive investigation. These constituted about two-thirds of the corporations whose securities are listed on any organized American stock exchange. The total also includes all insurance companies and banks with resources of more than $50,000,000. This study, like the profit study, is

Table 14–1. The Point System for the Rating of Business Management

CATEGORY	MAXIMUM RATING	COMPANY EMPLOYED AS YARDSTICK FOR EACH CATEGORY
Economic function	400	American Telephone & Telegraph Co.
Corporate structure	500	General Motors Corp.
Health and economic growth	600	U.S. Plywood Corp.
Fairness to stockholders	700	Pennsylvania Salt Manufacturing Co.
Research and development	700	Merck & Co.
Directorate analysis	900	General Foods Corp.
Fiscal policies	1,100	E. I. duPont de Nemours and Co.
Production efficiency	1,300	Standard Oil Co. (N.J.)
Sales vigor	1,400	The Grand Union Co.
Executive evaluation	2,400	Procter and Gamble Co.
TOTAL	10,000	

Source: The American Institute of Management

limited to companies which publish financial data, and it is further limited to the larger companies. It includes, however, so great a proportion of the nation's large companies that there seems little question of its being a reasonable sample of the bigger corporations.

As of January 1952, 298 of the 2,204 companies which had been studied were rated "excellently managed." The Committee of New England staff has had confidential use of the names of all companies studied and has classified each company according to its geographical location and industrial classification. The companies were separated into three geographical

---

7. *Fiscal policies* is concerned with all policies having to do with the disposition of the corporation's funds, including price policy, dividend policy, borrowings, and expansions (11%).

8. *Production efficiency* is evidenced by relative rate of growth of plant capacity as compared with competitors, relative wage level, the gearing of production schedules to general economic circumstances, the trend of production costs in relation to prices and wages, the nature of new equipment introduced, and labor-management relations and the way these are handled at all levels in the organization (13%).

9. *Sales vigor* deals with sales in relation to market potential, the way in which sales' objectives are geared to production efficiency, and the distribution of overhead costs (14%).

10. *Executive evaluation* is concerned with how men have obtained their positions— whether by merit or by nepotism—with their age, capacity to meet new challenges, judgment, specialized qualities to meet particular functions, and with whether the executive group operates as a team. The public-relations value of the executives is given weight in this category (24%).

For a more complete discussion of the rating system as a whole, see Jackson Martindell, *The Scientific Appraisal of Management.*

groups: (1) "New England companies," those with headquarters in New England and most or all of their operations within the region; (2) "national companies," those with headquarters outside New England but with one or more important plants or other major facilities within the region; and (3) "non-New England companies," those which do not have any major operation in New England. The industrial classification is a condensed form of that used by the Securities and Exchange Commission.

In the list of 2,204 companies there were 151 New England, 237 national and 1,816 non-New England companies. Table 14–2 presents the number

Table 14–2. Geographical Groupings of "Excellently Managed" Companies, by Industrial Classification, January 1952

INDUSTRIAL CLASSIFICATION	NO. OF COMPANIES STUDIED				NO. RATED "EXCELLENTLY MANAGED"				PER CENT RATED "EXCELLENTLY MANAGED"			
	N.E.	NAT'L	NON-N.E.	TOTAL	N.E.	NAT'L	NON-N.E.	TOTAL	N.E.	NAT'L	NON-N.E.	TOTAL
TOTAL, ALL GROUPS	151	237	1,816	2,204	22	81	195	298	15%	34%	11%	14%
MANUFACTURING	72	180	841	1,093	15	60	133	208	21%	33%	16%	19%
Nondurable-goods inds.	29	98	361	488	3	34	58	95	10%	35%	16%	19%
Textiles, apparel	15	14	43	72	1	5	4	10	7%	36%	9%	14%
Other nondur.	14	84	318	416	2	29	54	85	14	35	17	20
Durable-goods inds.	43	82	480	605	12	26	75	113	28%	32%	16%	19%
Elec., nonelec. mach.	17	21	113	151	4	11	28	43	24%	52%	25%	28%
Other durables	26	61	367	454	8	15	47	70	31	25	13	15
NONMANUFAC.	79	57	975	1,111	7	21	62	90	9%	37%	6%	8%
Insurance companies, banks	55	1	506	562	3	1	16	20	5%*	100%†	3%*	4%*
Other nonmanufac.	24	56	469	549	4	20	46	70	17	36	10	13

* See text explanation for the low level of these percentages.
† Only one company studied in this category.

of companies studied, the number excellently managed, and the percentage of excellently managed companies for each geographical classification broken down by major industry groups.

The low percentages of banks and insurance companies in the "New England" and "non-New England" categories rated in Table 14–2 as excellently managed will be noted. The banks and insurance companies represent a special situation unlike that of any of the other groups or companies included in the study. Their large number, the difficulty of securing information about many of them, the short time that the Institute has been in existence, and its initially greater emphasis upon other industrial categories made it impossible to study them all carefully enough to warrant any more inclusions at the beginning of 1952. Therefore we have made no use of the comparisons of nonmanufacturing companies.

Almost half the companies studied were in manufacturing, 72 of them New England companies. Of these, 15, or 21%, were considered excellently managed. This compares with 33% for the national manufacturing companies and 16% for the non-New England companies. However, the better showing of the New England manufacturing companies as compared to the non-New England companies may be attributed to the margin of superiority shown by the New England durable-goods manufacturers. Twenty-eight per cent of those studied in the durable-goods field in New England were rated excellently managed as against 16% of the non-New England companies and 32% for the national companies. *In the nondurable-goods industries only 10% of the New England companies were rated excellently managed as against 16% for the non-New England companies and 35% for the national companies.*

The number of companies was not large enough to permit significant comparisons for each individual manufacturing industry. However, the textile and apparel producers, as the largest group in the New England soft-goods industry, were separated from all other nondurables. The proportion of the textile and apparel industry rated as excellently managed is 7%, fairly close to the 9% so rated among the non-New England companies, but only a fraction of the 36% so rated among the national companies.

The lower than average rating of the nondurable-goods group—only 10% excellently managed against 28% of the durable-goods group—may not be explained entirely by poor management in New England as against good management in the non-New England companies. The explanation may lie in the tendency of the Institute's rating system to give a higher proportion of "excellently managed" ratings to larger than to smaller concerns. Both the New England and the non-New England textile companies are likely to be small in comparison with the larger corporations included in this analysis.

A test which eliminates a good deal of the difference due to size was made by taking only the 658 manufacturing corporations that are included in the list of the 1,000 largest manufacturing companies. In this list of 658 there were 50 New England companies, of which 18 were in the nondurable-goods industries and 32 in the durable-goods industries. In this test only 6% (one out of 18) of New England's nondurable-goods producers qualified as excellently managed, compared with 22% for the non-New England companies and 37% for the national companies. The per cent for New England was even lower than that when all nondurable-goods producers included in the study were used. New England's nondurable-goods manufacturers seem, therefore, to be the group which, on the average, shows up weakest in the management ratings. It should be noted that the region's large durable-goods producers show up even better when the comparison is limited to large companies.

The results for the 658 largest American manufacturing corporations are presented in Table 14-3.

The following conclusions appear to be justified on the basis of the study:

1. The proportion of the larger manufacturing companies rated "excellently managed" by the American Institute of Management is highest for national companies, second highest for New England companies, and lowest for non-New England companies. New England's showing depends heavily upon its well-managed durable-goods industries. While New England companies compare well when measured against their non-New England competition, that they have plenty of room for improvement is evidenced by their poorer showing against the national companies.

2. In the nondurable-goods industries the proportion of companies rated excellently managed is highest for the national companies, second highest

Table 14–3. Geographical Groupings of the 658 Largest American Manufacturing Corporations Studied and Rated by the American Institute of Management, January 1952

CLASSIFICATION OF COMPANIES	NEW ENGLAND	NATIONAL	NON-NEW ENGLAND	TOTAL
Number studied:	50	149	459	658
Nondurable-goods inds.	18	81	195	294
Durable-goods inds.	32	68	264	364
Number rated "excellently managed":	13	55	98	166
Nondurable-goods inds.	1	30	43	74
Durable-goods inds.	12	25	55	92
Per cent rated "excellently managed":	26%	37%	21%	25%
Nondurable-goods inds.	6%	37%	22%	25%
Durable-goods inds.	38%	37%	21%	25%

Source: American Institute of Management and the Federal Trade Commission

for the non-New England companies, and lowest for the New England companies. This is the only major industrial grouping in which the New England companies rate lower than the non-New England companies. If these findings are correct, the most serious management deficiencies in New England are to be found in its nondurable-goods industries, the most important of which have been declining for decades in the area.

3. The study does not provide direct evidence about the proportions of excellently managed companies among the smaller companies or among the larger ones whose securities are closely held, nor does it indicate the average ratings of management among those companies whose securities are not publicly traded.

A PILOT STUDY OF THE RELATIONSHIP BETWEEN CRITERIA OF GOOD MANAGEMENT AND PROFITABILITY

The test of good management in terms of profitability and in terms of criteria which have been discussed above suggests a third type of test which combines the two. This test was developed by McKinsey and Company, and a pilot study of this technique was conducted by that firm as a community service, without cost to the Committee of New England. The expense incurred in conducting the pilot study indicated that a study based on a larger sample of companies was beyond the financial ability of the Committee of New England to undertake. However, the technique developed by Mc-Kinsey and Company for use in the pilot study and the results of that study itself we believe make a significant contribution to knowledge on this subject.

The Committee of New England selected three pairs of manufacturing companies in New England in three different industries. One member of each pair had a considerably higher ratio of profits to sales during the years 1947 through 1949 than did the other member. The hypothesis to be tested

Table 14–4. Summary of Affirmative Answers to Questions about Management Practices.* Pilot Study of Six New England Manufacturers by McKinsey & Co. for the Committee of New England of the N.P.A.

COMPANY	TOTAL, ALL CATEGORIES	I ORGANI-ZATION	II PERSONNEL RELATIONS	III MARKET-ING	IV MANU-FACTURING	V FINANCE	VI CONTROLS	VII RESEARCH & DEV.†
			NUMBER OF APPLICABLE QUESTIONS					
Company 1	103	14	22	22	12	11	14	8
" 2	103	14	22	22	12	11	14	8
" 3	103	14	21	22	13	11	14	8
" 4	103	14	22	21	13	11	14	8
" 5	99	14	22	22	9	10	14	8
" 6	102	14	22	21	13	10	14	8
			NUMBER OF QUESTIONS ANSWERED "YES"					
Company 1	81	9	13	22	11	11	10	5
" 2	79	8	13	18	9	10	14	7
" 3	75	9	12	17	12	8	10	7
" 4	73	12	13	10	12	10	9	7
" 5	63	2	19	16	6	9	9	2
" 6	60	8	16	6	10	8	10	2
			PERCENTAGE OF APPLICABLE QUESTIONS ANSWERED "YES"					
Company 1	79%	64%	59%	100%	92%	100%	71%	63%
" 2	77	57	59	82	75	91	100	88
" 3	73	64	57	77	92	73	71	88
" 4	71	86	59	48	92	91	64	88
" 5	64	14	86	73	67	90	64	25
" 6	59	57	73	29	77	80	71	25

* All questions related to the years 1947–49.

† Answers to question No. 8 in the research and development group have been omitted from this summary, since most of the companies did not know the answer.

on these three pairs was that the companies having the higher profitability ratio would make more extensive use of the techniques recognized as being "good management" than would those having a lower profitability ratio. It was recognized that use of techniques alone did not automatically represent good management but that good management would be led to develop either the approved techniques or their equivalent in each field.

McKinsey and Company developed 103 questions about management techniques in seven different fields of an industrial company's operation. Because we believe that these questions might well become the basis for a preliminary self-audit by management, we are presenting them with the permission of McKinsey and Company as Appendix A.

A team of McKinsey specialists in the seven fields each spent a day with the appropriate executives of each of the six companies concerned in the pilot study. By supplementary questions and evaluation of responses the

McKinsey team determined whether the answer to each question would be yes or no, or whether the question was not applicable. The results of the survey are presented in Table 14–4.

The percentage of affirmative responses relating to management practices during 1947 through 1949, the years covered by the profitability comparison, varied from 79% for Company 1 to 59% for Company 6. Because of the small number of companies involved, no identification can be given without a possible breach of the confidence under which the answers were obtained.

How do the percentages of affirmative answers compare with the profit ranking for the period 1947–49? In two of the pairs the companies with the higher ratios of profits to sales for the years 1947 through 1949 answered "yes" to more of the questions about management practices than did the companies with the lower profit ratios. In the third pair the company with the lower profit ratio gave more "yes" answers. The field interviews, however, showed that the situation in that pair was unique, and we believe it does not invalidate the hypothesis which was being tested. In this pair the company with higher profitability but lower affirmative answers has been the beneficiary of the vitality, inspiration, and organizing ability of one man. As this man has grown older a change has become apparent within the company. It is adding new management techniques. It would appear likely either that it will pull up sharply in "yes" answers during the next five to ten years or that its profit ratio will fall off when the inspiring leadership of its present chief executive is gone.

The pilot study demonstrated that there was a large spread in "yes" answers not only among the companies in the pilot study but also among the various phases of the operations within the companies. It also disclosed that between the period 1947–49 and 1952, the year in which the survey was made, there had been a decided movement toward the use of more of the good management techniques. For example, for 1947–49 there was a spread between the high and the low companies in "yes" answers from 79% to 59%, or 20 percentage points. By 1952 this spread had been reduced to a difference between 79% and 63%, or to 16 percentage points. If all six companies adopted before the end of 1952 the techniques that they were contemplating, then the spread would be reduced to that between 83% and 70%, 13 percentage points. The fact that the less well managed companies are moving steadily toward the practices of the better managed companies indicates that the techniques used as criteria by McKinsey and Company in its survey are believed by the companies themselves to be worth adopting in the interest of better management.

We present the results of this pilot study in the interest of showing how an appraisal of management can be related to the relative profitability of a company, and in the hope that similar techniques will be used by managements as a basis for a preliminary self-examination. This might in turn lead to the selection and adoption of those techniques that would improve each company's performance.

Opinions of Consulting Engineers on New England Management

In the belief that it might shed further light on the quality of New England management as compared with that elsewhere, the research staff of the Committee of New England included a question on this subject in the survey mailed to all members of the Association of Consulting Management Engineers and to all members of the Association of Consulting Chemists and Chemical Engineers.[4]

The responses of the consulting firms were only opinions, it should be emphasized, but opinions based on broad experience. Each consulting firm works with a large number of clients, and those clients are usually well distributed geographically.

The management consultants who participated in the survey were on the whole fairly favorably impressed with New England management. The opinions they expressed are summarized in Table 14–5. Their comments

Table 14–5. New England's Industrial Management. General Appraisals by Responding Management Consultants

APPRAISAL	NUMBER OF CONSULTING FIRMS LOCATED IN*				AVERAGE N.E. PERCENTAGES OF TOTAL DOLLAR BILLINGS FOR ALL FIRMS IN EACH GROUP†	
	TOTAL	N.E.	MIDDLE ATLANTIC	ALL OTHER	ARITHMETIC AVERAGE	MEDIAN
Essentially equal to management elsewhere	13	3	9	1	24%	10%
Falls short of management elsewhere in various respects	7	0	4	3	5	5
Very low opinion	1	0	1	0	0	0
No appraisal given	6	0	3	3	3	2
TOTAL	27	3	!7	7	13.5%	6%

* Where firms have multiple offices, the location used for classification is that of the head office.
† For consulting services to United States manufacturers.

have been grouped into four categories although they were given by the respondents in their own words.

Almost two-thirds (13) of the 21 management consultants who expressed specific opinions about New England management felt it was essentially

4. For a fuller description of the survey, see the Committee of New England Staff Memorandum No. 4, *The Use of Professional Consultants by New England Industry and Consultants' Opinions about New England Management*, Arthur A. Bright, Jr., June 1952.

equal to management elsewhere. It should be noted, however, that no consulting management engineer unequivocally stated that New England management was better than that elsewhere. Where the consultants felt New England management as a whole to be deficient in some respect, the deficiency singled out was almost always excessive conservatism or lack of aggressiveness rather than adminstrative incompetence.

The attitudes of management consulting firms were inversely related to the distance of their headquarters from New England. All the consultants with headquarters in New England felt the region's management essentially equal to management elsewhere. Where opinions were expressed, those with headquarters in the Middle Atlantic states, however, voted only two to one that New England managements were equal, while of those in the Middle West only one out of four conceded equality. Apparently the closer the consultants were to New England manufacturers the higher their opinion of them.

The same general results were obtained with the chemical consultants, whose opinions are tabulated in Table 14–6.

Table 14–6. *Alertness of New England's Industrial Management in Product and Process Improvement. General Appraisals by Responding Chemical and Chemical Engineering Consultants*

| APPRAISAL | NUMBER OF CONSULTING FIRMS LOCATED IN | | | | AVERAGE N.E. PERCENTAGES OF TOTAL DOLLAR BILLINGS FOR ALL FIRMS IN EACH GROUP* | |
	TOTAL	N.E.	MIDDLE ATLANTIC	ALL OTHER	ARITHMETIC AVERAGE	MEDIAN
Essentially equal to management elsewhere	9	2	7	0	12%	5%
Falls short of management elsewhere in various respects	7	0	5	2	3	1
Very low opinion	0	0	0	0	—	—
No appraisal given	23	2	17	4	7.5	1
TOTAL	39	4	29	6	7.5%	2%

* For consulting services to United States manufacturers.

Some important differences should be noted, however. A much larger proportion of the chemical consultants than of the management engineers failed to express an opinion. Of those who did express an opinion, the ones who felt New England managements equal to those elsewhere outnumbered the others by only a small proportion—nine to seven. The appraisal again was higher the closer the consultant was to the region and the higher the proportion of business that he did within the region. No chemical consultant found New England management in general to be more alert than that elsewhere, and criticisms again revolved around caution and lack of aggressiveness rather than lack of competence.

The composite opinions of both management consultants and chemical consultants suggest that a sizable proportion of New England's industrial management compares favorably with that elsewhere, but a substantial minority of each group of consulting firms feels that there are enough overly conservative New England managements to pull the region's performance average below that in other parts of the country.

A SPECIAL PROBLEM OF MANAGEMENTS OF SMALL COMPANIES

The evidence presented so far has of necessity been limited for the most part to the larger companies. Lack of data has prevented the extension of the studies described above to the smaller companies. Because New England is an incubator of new manufacturing companies and because so many companies in the region are small, it is appropriate at this point to mention one problem peculiar to the smaller manufacturing company which bears heavily upon its aggressiveness and its willingness to expand.

Many a small or even medium-sized manufacturing company in New England is essentially the lengthened shadow of one man, who either established the company or brought a previously established small firm to its present state of prosperity. He has been able either to retain or to acquire for himself and his family, and sometimes for a few associates, all or most of the stock or other ownership interest in the company which he runs. As the owner-executive gets on in years, he is constantly faced with the problem of how to obtain liquidity to meet his estate inheritance taxes when he passes on. The stock or other ownership interest which he holds and which gives him control of the company he runs is unknown to the securities markets, or is subjected to such infrequent and small trading that the market has not established its true value. In situations of this type he must either maintain a highly liquid position both in his company and in his own personal finances or run the risk of embarrassing his heirs with financial problems at his death. Possibilities of expanding, of taking on new products, of research and development, the tapping of new markets—these are all risks which loom larger and larger in relation to the possible gains as the owner-executive grows older. In many cases lack of aggressiveness is the conscious or unconscious result of the peculiar financial situation confronting the older executive who owns all or a substantial portion of his own company. No study of New England's management would be complete without mentioning this problem and suggesting careful consideration of it both for the financial institutions which are now established and for those who are studying the establishment of new ones.

CONCLUSIONS

Is management making its maximum contribution to New England's employment and income? This question, with which we started the survey, must now be answered to the best of our ability in terms of the information we have obtained.

By the test of profitability, such data as we have been able to get not only indicate that on the average New England's industrial concerns are not earning as much as their principal competitors but raises doubt that the managements of most New England industries are equal to those elsewhere.

The test of New England management against standards of excellence corroborates the profitability test in that the proportion of New England's larger industrial companies rated excellently managed is less than the proportion of the national companies so rated. New England's management in the durable-goods industries, however, rates well in comparison with managements of both national and non-New England companies. New England's greatest source of management weakness appears to be in its traditional nondurable-goods manufacturing industries, especially in those lines which have been declining in the region for decades.

Many of New England's industrial companies must be considered to be excellently managed by any test. The generalizations given above do not apply to a large number of firms which consistently earn profits equal to or superior to those of their competitors, and which are models of excellence so far as their management practices are concerned. It would be invidious and unfair to name only a few examples in this connection, but it would be desirable to develop means of identifying New England's better managed companies so that they can be emulated by the less well managed.

Is the contribution that New England's management is making to the regional economy adequate to bring about the growth and expansion needed to provide jobs at good wages for the region's growing population? The findings so far presented would indicate that New England's industrial management could make considerable improvement in providing jobs for its people. The weaker performance of New England in the recession of 1948–49, in which most of its industries showed a larger decline in employment than did the national industries of which they were a part, together with the findings presented above, raises a serious question whether New England will be able in the years ahead to provide an adequate number of jobs at good wages for its people *unless its industrial management is improved.*

The fact that there is considerable room for improvement in management should be taken as a most hopeful finding of this study. If in the face of its industrial history, during which so many plants have closed and so many adjustments have been required, it were found to be a fact that New England's industrial management was generally of the highest level and showed little potential for improvement, then New England would have cause to be worried indeed. The existence of a large potential for improvement clearly points the way to the solution of many serious problems and provides the basis for a somewhat optimistic outlook for the future. The relationship of profitability to management practice which was shown to exist by this study points out one of the ways in which management can determine the scope of its own improvement. The opinions of consultants with respect to the aggressiveness of New England's industrial management, or lack of it, also indicate a way in which improvement can be made.

The shortcomings of management probably help to explain some of the other findings most often cited to demonstrate New England's decadence. About a seventh of New England's manufacturers have admitted that their plants were in such shape and are so located that they suffer a competitive disadvantage. There is in this state of affairs a potential for future improvement in earnings and for industrial growth.

New England's machine tools are older, on the average, than those in other parts of the country: 39% are over 20 years old as against 21% for the national average.[5] Of its metal-forming equipment, 34% is over 20 years old as against a national average of 28%; 17% of its other shop equipment is over 20 years old as against 11% for the national average. In these figures also is to be found the basis for substantial improvement and in that improvement the source of additional industrial growth and strengthening of competitive position.

That New England's industrial performance falls short of its potential is also demonstrated by the data on expenditures for new equipment. These expenditures are of vital importance because they provide the tools with which the industrial labor force works. New England being an older industrial area, it is logical to expect its plant expenditures per worker not to match those for the country as a whole or for rapidly growing areas that are building new plants. Equipment expenditures, however, reflect management decisions to keep up to date. In 1947, the latest year for which data are available, American manufacturers spent on the average $271 per worker for new equipment; New England manufacturers spent only $206. While differences in the structure of industry might be expected to account for some differences in expenditure per worker, a breakdown of these expenditures by industry indicates that most New England industries spent less than the national average per worker for new equipment. Table 14–7 shows that expenditures per worker for new equipment equaled or exceeded the national average only in the apparel, leather and leather products, fabricated metals, and miscellaneous industries—industries which, incidentally, have shown a good performance record.

Moreover, others among the older industrial states which are competitive with New England were spending more than New England's $206 for new plant and equipment. The average expenditure for new machinery and equipment in New Jersey was $286 per worker, in Pennsylvania $231, in Ohio $267, in Illinois $262, in Michigan $317; only New York in this group spent $194, close to the New England rate. The newer industrial states spent

5. *American Machinist* (November 3, 1949), pp. 138, 140.

substantially more than New England, as would be expected; Maryland $326, North Carolina $248, Georgia $224, Tennessee $268. In these figures, which reflect management decisions, there is ample scope for the improvement of New England's industrial performance. On the average, there seems to be little question that New England's management is not aggressive enough in replacing old equipment and installing new. Continuation of this trend will make New England progressively less competitive. A

Table 14–7. *Expenditures per Employee for New Machinery and Equipment in 1947,*
U.S. and New England
(selected industries)

	U.S.	NEW ENGLAND
Textiles	$213	$201
Apparel	57	81
Lumber and products	182	131
Furniture and fixtures	159	108
Paper and products	644	417
Rubber and products	304	259
Leather and products	61	68
Primary metals	328	235
Fabricated metals	203	219
Machinery (except electrical)	227	187
Electrical machinery	224	202
Transportation equipment	216	179
Instruments	175	126
Miscellaneous	162	167
AVERAGE, ALL INDUSTRIES	$271	$206

Source: Bureau of the Census, U.S. Department of Commerce, *Census of Manufactures*, 1947

carefully considered, stepped-up rate of replacement of machinery and equipment will go a long way toward making many New England factories more competitive than they now are.

One further conclusion emerging from our study and analysis of New England's industrial management, supported by the observations of professionals rather than by any formal survey, is a corollary to the lack of aggressiveness complained of by so many of the consulting engineers. The conclusion is that in many of New England's industries there is a well-developed tradition that "the shoemaker sticks to his own last." This was literally so in the case of infants', children's, and juveniles' shoes, the fastest growing branch of the shoe industry, which has been found to be only slightly represented in New England, although it now seems to be making up for lost time. It is also true in a figurative sense of a good many other New England industries, particularly in the nondurable-goods field. Management is conceived to be limited to the particular line of products with which it has been traditionally concerned. Management has not been looked upon as a profession with transfer value to other industrial fields. This tradition is best exemplified in the history of mill closings in the textile industry. The values of a going concern and of the management team were not recognized in most of the mill closings. If management found it could not make a satisfactory profit in the manufacture of the textile products for which the mill was designed and equipped, it closed down the mill. Little attempt was made to convert the going concern, the management team, and the physical plant to a different type of manufacturing. Yet the same plants in which textile manufacture was abandoned have generally been taken over by other manufacturing concerns under other managements, which lacked the management team and going concern relationships the original textile company had. Converting plant, management, and labor force to other industries by abandoning the plant is probably the most wasteful technique that could be used. While it may seem farfetched to most textile manufacturers to consider themselves capable of entering the metal-working or electrical machinery or other seemingly unrelated fields, it did not seem farfetched for the Firestone Tire and Rubber Company, for example, to undertake the management of a shell-loading plant in New Bedford, for the Vermont Marble Company to enter and stay in the metal-working field, or for General Mills to take on the production and distribution of a line of light household appliances. New England's future would look brighter if more managements broadened their horizons and adopted an aggressive entrepreneurial attitude more in keeping with their own ability and capacity. In this respect, shortcomings of New England management have been lack of aggressiveness and little imagination to meet changes by adaptation.

RECOMMENDATIONS

What Management Can Do

Throughout most of these reports on the New England economy there runs the theme that this is an economy in transition. It is sloughing off the old, taking on the new, particularly in its industrial structure. Basically the extent of, the need for, and the success of the transition depend now and will depend in the future on the decisions of manufacturing executives themselves. They are the most important single group in determining the future of the New England economy. They must look primarily to themselves and within themselves for those actions which are necessary to make the transition successful. They cannot rely upon government or any outside group to do their own job. The principal focus of their attention must be on making their own businesses run better by adapting policies, techniques, and operations to changing conditions and by developing and keeping a forward-looking attitude. The attitudes of management constitute one of the most important keys to New England's future. "Research-mindedness" in the broadest sense on the part of management is vital if New England is to maintain and to improve its industrial position.

Our first recommendation, therefore, is that every New England management carry on an intensive, continuous self-examination of all aspects of its own business. As one member of the Committee of New England Research Advisory Committee has well stated, "Management . . . is a continuing daily . . . concern with the worker, the work place, the materials, the tools, and the methods of doing work, a relationship of men and women individually and not in the mass . . . Competent management prevents discord, not fire-fighting it after it gets too bad to last."

Because the New England economy is and must be in transition from products, methods, and equipment that have become uncompetitive to those that provide a margin of competitive superiority, our next recommendation is that management should seek more aggressively for new products. In this connection, there is much to consider in the report by the Arthur D. Little Company to the Federal Reserve Bank of Boston, *A Survey of Industrial Opportunities in New England*. A few of the specific opportunities singled out by the A. D. Little study are listed here for convenience: (1) fabrication of aluminium and other light metals, especially titanium; (2) new types of power tools, particularly for household use; (3) new types of machinery, ranging from machinery for the production of miniature electronic components and specialized medical equipment to further development of electronic computing machines and other office equipment; (4) electronics, particularly miniature components, printed circuits, semiconductors, electronic instruments, and automation of manufacturing processes; (5) glass-fiber products; (6) pharmaceuticals and specialty chemicals; (7) paper printing plates, laminated building papers, food wrappers, and other paper specialities; (8) pulp molding; (9) materials, such as reinforced plastics and unplasticized polyvinyl chloride.

Many New England industrial managements should do more to improve their own production processes and equipment. We recommend that as a basic policy they invest all of their depreciation allowances in new equipment, and in addition invest something more for growth and improvement.

Any New England management that is uncertain whether it is doing the best job possible, or that has not given itself a thorough objective examination in recent years, would do well to adopt a research viewpoint and have its operation appraised to determine whether it is abreast of its competition. This line of action would appear to be a must for any company whose profit record over a reasonable period of years has fallen significantly short of that of its principal competitors.

As a corollary to the previous recommendation, every New England manufacturing concern would be well advised to examine the composition and qualifications of its board of directors and seek the benefits of a balanced board. Is the directorate well distributed as to age? Does it include people from outside the company? Does it have at least one director who is scientifically trained? Does it have a good balance between finance, production, sales, and other professional points of view? Boards of directors should be working boards and not window dressing.

Many a New England top management executive has been extremely critical of the treatment accorded his company by the local community and by his state government. It is one of the functions of good management to develop, or at least assist in developing, a community environment which is favorable to the operation of its business. Members of top management should devote some time and energy to community services, including those related to industrial development if the community needs industrial development. Farsighted management will also cooperate with educational institutions, not simply to secure technically trained people but also to help bring about a better understanding of the business and economic system within which private enterprise can make its maximum contribution. Managements that are doing the kind of job that needs to be done in the field of community relations will not let discriminatory tax systems develop or continue where they are harmful to those industries which provide the economic lifeblood of the community, the state, and the region.

What Government Officials Can Do

Government at all levels in New England has an obligation to work for conditions favorable to industrial prosperity and industrial growth. This obligation involves a structure and level of taxation which are not out of line with those in competing states or areas. It involves a kind and degree of legislation which protects the general interest without discriminating against the region's industry to the benefit of industry located elsewhere. It involves assistance to manufacturers and local communities in securing planning and zoning that provide scope for industrial operations. It includes a program of adequate and prompt information needed by established businesses and by those seeking to locate in the area.

Because New England is an incubator of new industrial firms, most of which are deficient in one way or another in management techniques, there is need for a program of management aids to small industry that small industry itself cannot pay for. This might take the form of a management extension program analogous to the agricultural extension programs that are well established in the New England states and elsewhere. This subject has been dealt with in the report on "Technical Research in New England."

What Others Can Do

The public in New England, as well as those whose business it is to inform the public, need a better understanding of the economy of the region.

This need was a basic motivating force in the organization of the Committee of New England and in the preparation of its reports. Generally New England people have taken their industry too much for granted. Industry has been predominant in the region for generations. Today's generation appreciates less than did its forebears what the requirements are for an expanding, high-level regional economy. New England has become so accustomed to successful enterprise that it no longer pays the honor it once did to those who have achieved industrial success. It does not value its industrial leaders and the contribution they can make as highly as do less industrialized areas which can see directly the improvement in their own standard of living from the establishment of new industry.

The state of affairs just described gives rise to a suggestion that some region-wide business organization like the New England Council establish a means of determining outstanding managements and giving recognition for excellence and improvement in management. Such a program might start on a modest scale and be limited to those aspects of management which are capable of being determined easily and objectively: for example, awards for low labor turnover, for the maximum proportion of business derived from new products, and the like.

There may be need for an institution in the field of finance to improve the marketability of the stock of small closely held companies. This might take the form of a small-business shares trust or some other appropriate institution designed to exchange the limited marketability of the closely held company stock for the broader marketability of a larger, more diversified company. We suggest that New England's financial leaders study and consider what might be done in this field to remove the inhibition to growth and expansion present in many closely held firms.

Finally, we commend the American Research and Development Corporation for its financial support of many new ventures, the work of the development credit corporations in the six New England states which are providing the financial means for expansion to many companies otherwise incapable of expanding, the work of the community industrial foundations which are providing factory space to new and growing concerns, and the regional, state, and area development programs conducted by the New England Council, the various states, chambers of commerce, regional associations, and others, all aimed at expanding the industrial base of the region. We strongly recommend continuation and expansion of all of these programs, most of which are entirely private and in keeping with the traditions of self-help of New England.

SELECTED REFERENCES

1. Balderston, C. Canby, and others, *Management of an Enterprise*, 2d ed. New York, Prentice-Hall, 1949.

2. Carroll, Philip, *How to Control Production Costs,* New York, McGraw-Hill, 1953.

3. Copeland, Melvin T., and Towl, Andrew, *The Board of Directors and Business Management,* Cambridge, Harvard University Press, 1947.

4. Dewing, A. S., *Financial Policy of Corporations,* 4th ed. New York, Ronald Press, 1941. 2 vols.

5. Drucker, Peter, *Concept of the Corporation,* New York, John Day, 1946.

6. Kehl, D., *Corporate Dividends,* New York, Ronald Press, 1941.

7. Mace, Myles, *The Board of Directors in Small Corporations,* Cambridge, Harvard University Press, 1948.

8. —— *The Growth and Development of Executives,* Cambridge, Harvard University Press, 1950.

9. Martindell, Jackson, *The Scientific Appraisal of Management,* New York, Harper, 1950.

10. Patton, Arch, "Incentive Compensation Develops Executives" (New York, Society for the Advancement of Management), *Advanced Management,* April 1952, pp. 7–10.

11. Rautenstrauch, Walter, and Villers, Raymond, *Economics of Industrial Management,* New York, Funk & Wagnalls, 1949.

12. Riegal, John W., *Executive Development,* Ann Arbor, University of Michigan Press, 1952.

13. Slichter, Sumner, *Union Policies and Industrial Management,* Washington, Brookings Institution, 1941.

14. Taylor, Frederick Winslow, *Principles of Scientific Management,* New York, Harper, 1911.

15. Tead, Ordway, *The Art of Administration,* New York, McGraw-Hill, 1951.

16. Tomb, John O., "Should Industry Move South?" *Harvard Business Review,* Sept., 1953, pp. 83–90.

17. Tosdal, Harry, *Salesmen's Compensation,* Cambridge, Harvard University Press, 1953. 2 vols.

APPENDIX

Criteria for Pilot Study of Management Techniques in Selected Companies for the Committee of New England

By McKinsey and Company

Contents

I. Criteria for Organization. II. Criteria for Personnel Relations. III. Criteria for Marketing. IV. Criteria for Manufacturing. V. Criteria for Finance. VI. Criteria for Controls. VII. Criteria for Product Research and Development.

Note: Respondents were asked to check as their answers "Yes," "No," or "Not Applicable."

I. CRITERIA FOR ORGANIZATION

1. Does the company have a formal plan of over-all organization showing the specific functions required for the achievement of company objectives?

2. Does the company's organizational plan distinguish clearly between "line" and "staff" functions?

3. Does the company develop and then reduce to writing the specific responsibilities, authorities, and relationships of its executives?

4. Does the company place upon one of its executives the responsibility of keeping the over-all organizational plan in tune with changing objectives and conditions?

5. Does the company follow a policy of balancing its board of directors with representative "outside" members?

6. Does the company refer major policy problems to board members with explanatory information in adequate time for consideration before action is taken by the board?

7. Does the company's plan of organization provide for an executive committee which is authorized to act on behalf of the board of directors?

8. Does the company have an organized program for training and developing its management personnel?

9. Does the company have any limitation on the hiring of immediate relatives?

10. Does the company maintain a policy of compulsory complete retirement?

11. Does the company follow a definite program for recruiting, training, and preparing junior executives for eventual assumption of greater responsibility?

12. Does the company make regular audits of management personnel at all levels to appraise availability of qualified personnel for future needs?

13. Does the company have a formal incentive compensation plan for its executive group?

14. Does the company have a formal plan for retirement compensation?

II. CRITERIA FOR PERSONNEL RELATIONS

1. Does the company have an organized and centralized personnel relations department?

2. Does the company's personnel director report directly to the chief executive officer?

3. Does the company use aptitude or dexterity tests to select nonmanagement personnel?

4. Does the company use aptitude, intelligence, or personality tests in selecting personnel for advancement to the management group?

5. Does the company have an employees' handbook or training manual to acquaint new personnel with company history, objectives, policies, and organization?

6. Does the company provide each employee with a clear and definite description of the job or position to which he is to be assigned?

7. Does the company have an organized orientation and training program for nonmanagement employees?

8. Does the company have an organized training program for foremen?

9. Does the company base its wage and salary rates upon an organized program of job evaluation?

10. Does the company publicize to its employees the pattern of progression from one job to another?

11. Does the company provide for periodic progress reviews with hourly paid employees?

12. Does the company provide for periodic progress reviews with salaried employees?

13. Does the company operate an organized employee suggestion system?

14. Does the company acquaint employees affected by changes in policies, organization, or procedures with these changes—and the reasons for them—before the changes take place?

15. Does the company have a formal grievance procedure?

16. Does the company use exit interviews for hourly paid employees?

17. Does the company use exit interviews for salaried employees?

18. Does the company encourage executives to participate actively in business, civic, or technical associations or societies?

19. Does the company have an organized safety program?

20. Does the company have an organized health or medical program?

21. Does the company have an organized program for promptly informing foremen or supervisors, before union stewards, of all management action or decisions affecting employees under their supervision?

22. Does the company have a formal program designed to develop and maintain satisfactory community relations?

III. CRITERIA FOR MARKETING

1. Does the company measure its growth within the industry by analyzing trends in its share of the total market potential for each product line?

2. Does the company locate and measure its sales opportunities by analyzing its share of the potential market by geographical areas?

3. Does the company regularly analyze its sales opportunities by type of customers?

4. Does the company determine its channels of distribution through studies of customer buying habits and service requirements?

5. Does the company determine the minimum size of order which it can profitably fill?

6. Does the company prepare an annual sales plan or sales budget which states anticipated company sales by products?

7. Does the company plan its sales for each territory?

8. Does the company plan its sales to each major customer?

9. Does the company have an organized procedure for determining the attitude of its customers toward the company, its products, service, pricing, and promotion?

10. Does the company have an organized procedure for market testing new products, new models, or new features?

11. Does the company study and periodically review the location of warehousing facilities from the point of view of customer service, transportation costs, and competitive conditions?

12. Does the company have an organized procedure for studying and evaluating the activities of competitors with respect to such elements as product quality, pricing, discounts, customer service, and sales promotion?

13. Does the company have a sound formal plan of organization for the field sales force?

14. Does the company establish equitable work loads for the territories covered by salesmen or distributors in terms of such factors as number and size of customers, service required, area covered, etc.?

15. Does the company set forth in writing a full description of the job of its field salesmen?

16. Does the company have an organized program for recruiting suitable candidates for its field sales force?

17. Does the company have a sales manual for the guidance of the field sales force?

18. Does the company have an organized program for training the members of the field sales force?

19. Does the company have an incentive compensation plan for salesmen?

20. Does the company have an organized program for planning and directing the activities of field salesmen?

21. Does the company establish definite objectives for its advertising program?

22. Does the company provide its salesmen with an up-to-date set of sales promotional material?

IV. CRITERIA FOR MANUFACTURING

1. Does the company establish standards of production on direct labor operations by time studies?

2. Does the company have an organized program to improve the methods of production?

3. Does the company have an organized procedure for planning and controlling production and inventories?

4. Does the company have an established procedure for controlling process or machine development costs?

5. Does the company follow an organized plan for machine replacement?

6. Does the company operate a wage incentive plan for direct labor?

7. Does the company operate an incentive plan for foremen?

8. Does the company have bills of material for each item manufactured?

9. Does the company provide written operating instructions covering each item manufactured?

10. Does the company use modern material-handling equipment?

11. Does the company have an organized program for controlling quality?

12. Does the company inspect all important purchased items against specifications upon receipt from vendors?

13. Does the company control quantity, maintenance, and usage of tools?

V. CRITERIA FOR FINANCE

1. Does the company determine and then program its cash needs in advance of each fiscal year?

2. Does the company avoid the permanent use of short-term borrowings in financing its over-all operations?

3. Does the company make studies, at least annually, to determine if it is adequately protected by insurance?

4. Does the company have a well-organized tax research program as a means of availing itself of all possible opportunities for tax savings?

5. Does the company have a well-organized and effective credit and collection procedure as a means of avoiding unnecessary losses from bad debts?

6. Does the company follow a policy of keeping its banking sources informed as to its plans, accomplishments, and problems in order to strengthen such relationships?

7. Does the company follow a policy of keeping its stockholders informed as to its plans, accomplishments, and problems?

8. Does the company's dividend policy give full consideration to future cash needs, in addition to current earnings, in establishing dividend rates on its common stock?

9. Does the company recognize the increasing cost of plant and equipment *replacements* by setting up additional depreciation reserves from current earnings?

10. Does the company's investment in *replacement* of plant and equipment over the last ten years substantially exceed its depreciation charges for the same period?

11. Does the company's method of inventory valuation provide for proper consideration of such conditions as raw material price reductions, slow-moving stocks, and obsolete goods?

VI. CRITERIA FOR CONTROLS

1. Does the company's plan of organization provide for the establishment of a single executive position with responsibility for all accounting and control methods and procedures?

2. Does the company's classification of accounts follow definite lines of executive accountability?

3. Does the company operate a cost-accounting procedure which develops accurate unit costs?

4. Does the company utilize standard costs as a means of providing a sound basis for control of operating costs and for profit improvement?

5. Does the company provide cost-control information periodically to executives at all levels of responsibility where appropriate corrective action can be taken?

6. Does the company classify its costs and expenses as between fixed and variable components?

7. Does the company analyze its break-even point data to see what policies are necessary in order to obtain the increasing profits available beyond the break-even point?

8. Does the company develop and use a budgetary control plan as a means of coordinating company operations, estimating future profits resulting therefrom, and then measuring the effectiveness of executive performance against planned results?

9. Does the company assign to one executive the responsibility to prepare, analyze, and interpret financial facts and figures, and to explain the significance of financial operating data to company management?

10. Does the company provide for periodic conferences of appropriate executives to discuss the reasons for variances from planned results?

11. Does the company make periodic studies to improve clerical methods and procedures, records, and executive reports?

12. Does the company conduct regular internal audits of its transactions to supplement the work of outside auditors?

13. Does the company obtain its monthly financial and operating statements reasonably soon after the close of each month?

14. Does the company maintain an up-to-date manual of detailed instructions covering clerical methods and procedures?

VII. CRITERIA FOR PRODUCT RESEARCH AND DEVELOPMENT

1. Does the company have an organized and centralized product research and development department?

2. Does the company's research director (or person with equivalent function) report directly to the chief executive officer?

3. Does the company have a well-defined research program for the improvement of existing products and the development of new products?

4. Does the company's research program attempt to develop products completely unrelated to the existing product line?

5. Does the staff of the research and development department include both men with engineering and men with scientific training?

6. Does the research and development department have freedom from responsibility for product control and testing?

7. Has the approximate sales volume traceable to the company's own new product development activities increased 10% or more since 1937?

8. Has the company's gross-profit margin increased 10% or more as the result of its new product development activities since 1937?

9. Does the company call upon outside assistance?

15

Technical Research in New England

Drafted by Arthur A. Bright, Jr.

INTRODUCTION

Technical progress is the fundamental source of most of man's material advancement. Through the findings of research and technology man can create new products that did not exist before; he can create or use new processes and materials to make better products; and he can make existing products more efficiently and reduce their cost. As Vannevar Bush has written,

> Advances in science when put to practical use mean more jobs, higher wages, shorter hours, more abundant crops, more leisure for recreation, for study, for learning how to live without the deadening drudgery which has been the burden of the common man for ages past. Advances in science will also bring higher standards of living, will lead to the prevention or cure of diseases, will promote conservation of our limited natural resources, and will assure means of defense against aggression.[1]

National interest in technical research as a method of achieving these ends has increased tremendously during recent decades. Total expenditures for research and development in the United States rose from about $65,000,000 in 1920 to $345,000,000 in 1940. They leaped upward during World War II and continued their rapid rise each year after the war. By 1952 the estimated total was more than $3,500,000,000.

The largest single factor in this increase was the Federal Government. Its research expenditure rose during the period from only about $15,000,000 to approximately $2 billion.[2] The increase in industrial research was almost as sharp, however, and universities and other types of institutions also greatly expanded their efforts. Since large portions of the federal appropriations for research and development went to industrial concerns and educational institutions, their combined research activities in 1952 were still almost three times as great as those in government laboratories.

Research and development have become a major type of economic activity. In 1951 they absorbed approximately 130,000 of the nation's scientists and engineers. More than half worked in industrial laboratories, and about one-fourth each worked in universities and nonprofit institutions or in govern-

1. Vannevar Bush, *Science—The Endless Frontier*, Report to the President by the Director of the Office of Scientific Research and Development (Washington, 1945), p. 5.
2. National Science Foundation, *Second Annual Report, 1951–52*, Washington.

ment laboratories. Since every professional research worker is supported by an average of more than one nonprofessional worker, the total national employment in research and development exceeded 300,000 individuals.

There are no signs that the increase in research and development has stopped. Both "basic" and "applied" research are moving ahead along a broad front. The interest of government in research continues great, of course, especially in relation to national defense and public health. Industry has increasingly recognized the opportunities for larger profits through research and development. The development of new, better, and cheaper products is a competitive aid that can keep a company ahead of its fellows. Great new industries have sprung from research, and there is no reason to doubt that other new industries will be created in the future. The horizons of research move ahead as fast as they are approached. In some large national companies more than half of total sales consist of products not made in 1940. The success stories of hundreds of new research-based companies have encouraged thousands of others to take up or expand their own research and development activities.

THE IMPORTANCE OF TECHNICAL RESEARCH TO NEW ENGLAND

The steady rise of research and development is of enormous importance to the New England economy. The citizens of the region share the interest of all persons in the fruits of technical progress, of course, but their dependence on research is even more immediate. New England's economic life depends largely on its manufacturing industries. As the most highly industrialized region of the country its economic future depends heavily on the ability of its manufacturers to maintain their sales, employment, and profits.

As an established industrial area New England has several important problems and handicaps, as well as several advantages. Some of its largest industries are the "old" industries, such as textiles and shoes. Their plants are frequently antiquated, and sometimes their equipment and methods of operation are outdated. These industries face keen competition from the newly industrialized regions, which often have significant competitive advantages as they begin their industrial build-up.

New England's location in the extreme northeastern corner of the United States presents several inherent difficulties in serving national markets, and most of these difficulties revolve about transportation costs. Domestic raw materials of many types must move in over long distances, and competitors are often closer to all markets outside the region itself. Fuel and power costs also reflect the higher transportation costs.

Faced by these and certain other cost disadvantages, many New England manufacturers have found that they can prosper by maintaining the superiority of their products. In a study conducted by the Federal Reserve Bank of

Boston in 1949,[3] manufacturers who claimed that they had outstripped their competitors during the preceding year attributed their success chiefly to superior products or better sales techniques. They rarely laid it to lower costs or prices. On the other hand, the companies that admitted they had not kept up with their competitors placed a large portion of the blame on their higher costs or prices. Manufacturing success in New England does not require lower costs, so long as the producer turns out a unique or superior product, but the producer who makes a standard product may find that his costs represent an important competitive handicap. Technical leadership in an industry can also lead to manufacturing economies which help to overcome whatever cost disadvantages are inherent in a particular geographical location.

As competition from other regions has increased, more and more New England manufacturers have adapted their products to changing conditions and have turned to opportunities in the "newer" fields. To a greater extent new companies and new plants in New England are making new products which have sprung from research. Many older companies have improved or diversified their products. Technical progress has aided the region to make necessary adjustments in industrial structure and at the same time has provided a source of dynamic expansion to keep pace with population growth. The plastics, electronic, and aircraft industries, for example, which a few decades ago barely existed, provided employment for about 140,000 workers in New England during 1952.

The successful efforts of a great many research-minded New England companies in a wide range of industries indicate how basic technical progress is to the region's industrial progress. Research and development lie behind the strong positions and large employment of such varied companies as United Aircraft Corporation, Foxboro Company (instruments), Dewey and Almy Chemical Company, Pitney-Bowes, Inc. (postage meters), Polaroid Corporation, Bates Manufacturing Company (cotton textiles), National Research Corporation (high-vacuum equipment), and the numerous branches of the General Electric Company and Westinghouse Electric Corporation in New England. There are scores of others. During the last few years a whole new generation of research-based enterprises has come into existence, frequently to exploit new scientific and engineering knowledge acquired during World War II. A large number of such companies, including High Voltage Engineering Corporation, Tracerlab, Inc., Baird Associates, Inc., Cambridge Corporation, Ionics, Inc., and Control Engineering Corporation, have settled and grown near their spawning ground in Cambridge, Massachusetts. More are coming into existence each year. Some fail and others fail to grow, but a select few succeed and expand. In expanding they provide more jobs and income for the people of the region.

3. "New England Manufacturers and Their Competition," *Monthly Review*, Federal Reserve Bank of Boston, August 1949.

The processes of transition and growth are far from finished in New England. Indeed, they can never be finished. The continued discovery and use of new technical knowledge are vital to the ability of New England producers to meet the challenge of producers in other, and often lower cost, regions. New England's manufacturers can no longer survive by making standard products and selling them in a standard fashion. They have moved far toward the development of unique and specialized products.

NEW ENGLAND'S RESEARCH FACILITIES

It is common for New Englanders to speak in glowing terms about the research facilities of the region. They are proud of their many leading university and college laboratories, industrial and consulting laboratories, and other research activities. It is important to appraise these facilities and their use in some detail, however, to determine how well New England measures up to the performance of other parts of the nation. Even more important, how well does New England live up to its own potentials in research activity?

There are several major types of research facilities. Each has its particular characteristics and presents its own special opportunities for technical progress. This portion of the report analyzes New England's research facilities, their number, activities, and some of the problems in their use. Six categories of research facilities are considered:

1. Industrial laboratories of individual companies.
2. Trade associations and industry-supported research.
3. Nonprofit research foundations and institutes.
4. Commercial consulting laboratories.
5. University and college laboratories.
6. Government laboratories.

Industries that result from technical progress tend to cluster about research centers, so it is important to study the geographic distribution of New England's research and development activities. For the most efficient further development of the region a fairly extensive scattering of research facilities is desirable. Each area stands to gain by concentrating its research efforts on products for which the area is best suited or which offer the greatest opportunity for its economic progress.

Industrial Laboratories

According to studies by the National Research Council, there were at least 2,820 industrial research laboratories in the United States in 1950 operated by individual manufacturing and nonmanufacturing concerns, exclusive of consulting firms and trade associations.[4] Of this total 311 were located in

4. National Research Council, *Research and Development Personnel in Industrial Laboratories, 1950,* Report to the National Scientific Register, Scientific Manpower Series, No. 1, Washington, 1951. The New England data in this section are from a special tabulation prepared by the National Research Council for the Committee of New England.

New England. The region's 11% of the nation's industrial laboratories compares favorably with its approximately 10% of total manufacturing employment.

The New England laboratories employed 5,433 professional workers and 8,973 supporting personnel, a total of more than 14,400 individuals. These figures represented only 8% of the nation's professional workers in similar laboratories, 10% of the supporting personnel, and 9% of the total personnel (see Table 15-1). On the average, the New England industrial research laboratories were smaller than those elsewhere in the country, especially in terms of the number of professional personnel. In both New England and the country as a whole, more than 80% of the laboratories had fewer than 20 professional employees. But there were more large laboratories in the rest of the country. New England housed only 18 of the nation's 231 laboratories with 50 or more professional workers, and it had only one of the 18 laboratories with 500 or more professional employees.

New England's largest industrial laboratory was that of the Pratt and Whitney Aircraft Division of the United Aircraft Corporation, at East Hartford, Connecticut. The high ratio of supporting to professional employees in Connecticut's aircraft laboratories explains New England's larger proportion of supporting than professional personnel in the national totals for each type.

Table 15-1. *Industrial Research Laboratories* and Personnel in New England and the United States, 1950*

	NEW ENGLAND	UNITED STATES	NEW ENGLAND AS PER CENT OF UNITED STATES
Number of laboratories	311	2,820	11
Number of employees:			
Professional personnel	5,433	65,936	8
Supporting personnel	8,973	89,383	10
TOTAL	14,406	155,319	9
Average number of employees per laboratory:			
Professional personnel	17	23	x
Supporting personnel	29	32	x
TOTAL	46	55	x

* Excludes commercial consulting laboratories and trade association laboratories.
Source: National Research Council

Industrial Distribution of Laboratories. Table 15-2 shows the distribution of industrial research laboratories and their professional personnel by industry groups for both New England and the United States. While most industries are represented in the New England listing, it is evident that there is much more activity in some industries than in others. Despite the small relative importance of New England's chemical industries in the region's total manufacturing activity, for example, chemicals account for more than 20% of the total professional personnel in the region's industrial laboratories. The aircraft, machinery, electrical and communications-equipment industries account for another 34% or more. Such important New England manu-

Table 15-2. *Industrial Research Laboratories* and Professional Personnel in New England and the United States, by Industry Groups, 1950*

	NUMBER OF LABORATORIES			NUMBER OF PROFESSIONAL PERSONNEL		
INDUSTRY GROUP	NEW ENGLAND	UNITED STATES	NEW ENGLAND AS PER CENT OF U.S.	NEW ENGLAND	UNITED STATES	NEW ENGLAND AS PER CENT OF U.S.
Manufacturing:						
Ordnance	2	13	15%	51	1,047	5%
Food products	12	205	6	47	2,895	2
Tobacco products	0	7	0	0	81	0
Textiles and apparel	24	84	29	190	785	24
Lumber and wood products	1	13	8	2	110	2
Furniture	1	10	10	4	47	9
Paper products	22	105	21	238	1,378	17
Printing and publishing	4	13	31	74	134	55
Chemicals	61	722	8	1,115	15,632	7
Industrial inorganic and organic	23	246	9	671	7,488	9
Drugs and medicines	8	167	5	54	3,313	2
Soaps, cleaners, and textile auxiliaries	10	56	18	210	1,069	20
Paints, varnishes, lacquers, and inorganic pigments	5	84	6	34	1,567	2
Other chemical products	15	169	9	146	2,195	7
Petroleum and coal products	3	103	3	10	6,577	†
Rubber products	12	51	24	236	1,891	12
Leather and leather products	2	12	17	28	76	37
Stone, clay, and glass products	6	101	6	103	1,259	8
Primary metal products	9	133	7	139	2,407	6
Fabricated metal products	7	106	7	78	1,093	7
Machinery (except electrical)	41	306	13	724	4,336	17
Electrical equipment	27	192	14	483	3,623	13
Communications equipment	16	154	10	214	9,726	2
Motor vehicles	2	67	3	22	2,399	1
Aircraft	4	42	10	849	4,679	18
Instruments	28	199	14	373	3,338	11
Miscellaneous manufacturing	12	52	23	81	413	20
TOTAL MANUFACTURING	296	2,690	11%	5,061	63,926	8%
Mining	0	33	0%	0	343	0%
Railroads	0	14	0	0	427	0
Utilities	4	16	25	74	351	21
Miscellaneous nonmanufacturing	11	67	16	298	889	34
TOTAL NONMANUFACTURING	15	130	12%	372	2,010	19%
TOTAL, ALL INDUSTRIAL	311	2,820	11%	5,433	65,936	8%

* Excludes commercial consulting laboratories and trade association laboratories.
† Less than 0.5%.
Source: National Research Council

facturing industries as food products, textiles, apparel, lumber and wood products, furniture, and leather and leather products employ more than 40% of the region's manufacturing workers, yet they have only about 5% of New England's professional workers in research laboratories.

The interindustry differences in New England's research activity are highlighted in Table 15-3, which compares total employment and professional research personnel for all industry groups. The first two columns of the table indicate that there is often no relation between the size of an industry and its research and development effort. Some industries, and particularly the older ones such as textiles, have in general been less research-minded than some of the smaller or newer industries. They have tended to rely much more heavily for technical progress on suppliers of materials and equipment than on their own efforts. *It is probably true that the characteristics and organization of some industries make it easier for them to conduct research and development activities, but the tremendous interindustry variations that exist at present do not seem satisfactory in view of the fact that research provides opportunities for all industries.*

The last two columns in the table provide a rough basis for comparing the aggregate research efforts of New England manufacturers with those in the country as a whole. Although the region's portion of total professional research personnel is less than its share of the nation's manufacturing employment, in several industry groups New England shows up fairly well. Interestingly enough, the best relative performance is sometimes in those industries whose absolute research performance is poorest, such as textiles and apparel, furniture, and leather and leather products. For these industries it is apparent that the small amount of research is a national phenomenon, not a local one, but the situation provides an opportunity for more New England producers to move ahead of their competitors. Competitive pressures make it imperative that they do so.

Research by New England's paper, chemicals, stone, clay, and glass, machinery, and transportation-equipment industries also show up fairly well. On the other hand, the region's ordnance, food, lumber, rubber, fabricated-metal, and electrical-equipment industries, among others, do not employ their "normal" shares of research workers. *So far as competitive position is concerned, comparison with research activity in other parts of the country is an even more significant indicator of the need for additional research and product development in many New England industries.*

It is also important to bear in mind that in 1950 there were still only about 300 industrial laboratories in New England, an average of one for each 70 or so manufacturing establishments. There has been a substantial increase in the number of industrial laboratories and industrial research workers since 1950, to be sure, and the engineers and production people of many companies carry on some research and development work without a formal research organization, but the general situation is still the same. While the bulk of the region's manufacturers are small and cannot afford to maintain separate laboratories, *there is still an enormous opportunity and need for expansion of industrial research in New England.*

Naturally the need is not solely a matter of more research, personnel, and dollars. The quality of research is just as important as the quantity. The research program of any individual company must be carefully integrated into its over-all objectives and operations, with close liaison between the research group and management. Emphasis should be placed on *more good research,* not just *more research.*

Table 15–3. Distribution of Employment and Professional Research Personnel*
in New England Manufacturing Industry, 1950

INDUSTRY GROUP	PER CENT OF NEW ENGLAND TOTAL		PER CENT OF UNITED STATES	
	MANUFAC- TURING EMPLOYMENT	PROFESSIONAL RESEARCH PERSONNEL	MANUFAC- TURING EMPLOYMENT	PROFESSIONAL RESEARCH PERSONNEL
ALL MANUFACTURING	100	100	10	8
Ordnance	1	1	53	5
Food products	5	1	4	2
Tobacco products	†	0	1	0
Textiles	19	4	21	24
Apparel	6		7	
Lumber and wood products	3	†	5	2
Furniture	1	†	6	9
Paper products	5	5	14	17
Printing and publishing	4	1	8	55
Chemicals	2	22	4	7
Petroleum and coal products	†	†	2	†
Rubber products	3	5	17	12
Leather and leather products	8	1	29	37
Stone, clay, and glass products	1	2	4	8
Primary metal products	4	3	5	6
Fabricated metal products	7	2	11	7
Machinery (except electrical)	11	14	12	17
Electrical equipment (including communication equipment)	7	14	13	5
Transportation equipment	4	17	4	12
Instruments	2	7	14	11
Miscellaneous manufacturing	7	2	12	20

Note: Details may not add to totals because of rounding.
* Excludes commercial consulting laboratory and trade association laboratory personnel.
† Less than 0.5%.
Source: National Research Council; U.S. Bureau of Labor Statistics

Geographical Distribution of Laboratories. An outstanding characteristic of the nation's industrial research laboratories is their geographical concentration. Eighty-four per cent of the laboratories and more than 90% of the personnel are located in 66 of the nation's metropolitan areas. New England's urban concentration of laboratories is not quite so great. Two-thirds of the region's laboratories and four-fifths of the laboratory personnel are in just nine metropolitan areas. The Boston area alone has close to a third of the regional total.

As Table 15–4 indicates, there are only 17 industrial research laboratories in the three northern New England states, and they employ but 3% of the professional laboratory personnel in the region. Most laboratory workers in those states are employed by paper manufacturers. Massachusetts and Connecticut combined account for 88% of the region's industrial laboratories and 94% of their professional employees. *Since research and development activities tend to create new employment, and since northern New England is in need of further industrial development and diversification, those states should work strenuously to attract and develop new technically oriented manufacturing establishments.*

Government Research and Development Contracts. Each year the Federal Government places several hundred million dollars in research and development contracts with industrial concerns, universities, and other private organizations.[5] More than half the total goes to industrial concerns. Such contracts, therefore, can be an important source of income and employment to many individual companies. In the course of fulfilling the contracts, most of which are military in nature, the contracting companies frequently develop equipment, processes, or information which they can use in their civilian business. Many small companies get their start through research and development work for the Federal Government.

Table 15–4. Industrial Research Laboratories* and Personnel in New England, by States, 1950

STATE	LABORATORIES		PROFESSIONAL PERSONNEL	
	NUMBER	PER CENT OF NEW ENGLAND	NUMBER	PER CENT OF NEW ENGLAND
NEW ENGLAND	311	100	5,433	100
Maine	8	3	112	2
New Hampshire	5	2	54	1
Vermont	4	1	11	†
Massachusetts	155	50	2,215	41
Rhode Island	22	7	164	3
Connecticut	117	38	2,877	53

Note: Details may not add to totals because of rounding.
* Excludes commercial consulting laboratories and trade association laboratories.
† Less than 0.5%.
Source: National Research Council

Data are not available to show accurately the extent of participation by New England's industrial laboratories in government research and development contracts. From the fragmentary information which can be obtained, however, *it appears that the region's manufacturers in total hold a relatively small proportion of the contracts of these types placed with manufacturers throughout the country.* To some extent, this situation is the result of the na-

5. Governmental research expenditures are discussed in greater detail in a later section of this report.

ture of New England industry. A larger than national proportion of the region's manufacturing employment is in the consumers goods industries, which naturally attract fewer research and development contracts. Also, much of New England's employment in the durable goods industries is by branch plants or subsidiaries of large national corporations which have their principal research laboratories in other parts of the country.

There are, of course, many individual examples of research for the Federal Government by individual New England companies. In 1951 the Atomic Energy Commission had contracts outstanding with more than 50 New England companies for $27,000,000. There were also large Defense Department contracts with the Electric Boat Company for the development of a hull for an atomic-powered submarine and with Pratt and Whitney for a nuclear-powered aircraft engine. There were numerous others. *But many more New England manufacturers could improve their long-run positions by seeking out research and development contracts for the Federal Government, even if the short-term profit aspects of those contracts are not great.*

Evaluation of Industrial Research in New England. It is difficult to generalize about so elusive a topic as the evaluation of industrial research activities in New England. Obviously the situation varies greatly from industry to industry and from company to company within each industry. The same is true of industry in the rest of the nation. Some of New England's weak spots, as well as some of its strong ones, stand out from the summary of laboratories and personnel by industry groups. On balance, it would appear that from an over-all statistical point of view *New England's industrial research and development efforts are a little below the United States standard. In the light of the uncertain balance between its locational advantages and disadvantages, this is not good enough for a region which is passing through an important transition in industrial structure.*

The extent of any company's research and development activities rests on decisions of its management. The whole topic of research and development is just one specialized aspect of industrial management.[6] *In New England the attitude of management toward research varies from company to company throughout the complete range of possibilities, from complete conviction to complete indifference.* In some companies research expenditures amount to more than half of total expenditures. Others maintain such expenditures at a small and more or less constant ratio to total sales. Still others are beginning to see the need for research and development activities but do not yet understand what is involved. For example, one New England manufacturer who cautiously inquired of a consultant what a research program would cost objected to the $10,000 salary suggested for a qualified research man, and then rationalized that he could afford $5,000 since the need would be for only six months.

---

6. See our report "New England's Industrial Management" (No. 14), for a broader discussion of this subject.

Other manufacturers are even more skeptical. The president of one large textile firm with plants in New England is reported to have said at his stockholders' meeting, in answer to a query about the company's research plans, that the company would not establish a large laboratory and undertake extensive research until it was convinced the effort was worthwhile and would pay off. And then there are some companies whose managements do not even think of research and development, since they have been getting along without it for a long time. There would be more such companies in New England, but many of them are no longer in business.

In deciding about the extent of research expenditures, management must realize that it is considering a long-term investment. Many companies feel that their research expenditures have been their *best* investment. A quick pay-out from research is possible, but when it happens it should be considered a windfall rather than a desired objective. Management should also realize that a large percentage of research projects necessarily fail and that it is the one successful project out of 20 or 30 or 50 which carries the entire effort. Several years are often required to transform even the successful research projects into increased profits. Patience and perseverance are essential to successful research operations. Stability and continuation of effort are imperative, and expenditures for the purpose should not be tied too closely to current sales. *A company's considered judgment of its long-term objectives should rule in establishing research budgets, rather than short-run considerations.*

Since it was impractical to try to appraise directly the attitudes of New England management toward research and development in comparison with those of their counterparts in other sections of the country, it has been necessary to approach the problem indirectly. Our findings on the subject are suggestive rather than conclusive. In addition to the statistical data already presented, however, they indicate that while the region is not lagging disastrously, as its critics sometimes charge, neither is it forging far ahead of other parts of the country, as some of its boosters claim.

Technical consultants are in a strategic position to observe and appraise the management attitudes of large numbers of companies. Most of them serve companies in many industries and in scattered geographical locations. While their appraisals are personal opinions, they rest on extensive experience and carry considerable weight. The Committee of New England drew on that experience by conducting a survey among the members of the Association of Consulting Chemists and Chemical Engineers. The objective was to determine if, in their judgment, there was a significant difference between the alertness of New England's industrial management in product and process improvement, as compared with the situation in the rest of the United States.[7]

7. For a full report of the findings see Staff Memorandum No. 4, *The Use of Professional Consultants by New England Industry and Consultants' Opinions about New England Management*, June 1952.

The opinions of the consultants varied, of course, depending on their individual experience in New England. Of those who were willing to give an opinion, a little more than half expressed the belief that the "technological alertness" of New England manufacturers, on the whole, is essentially equal to that of managements elsewhere. A little less than half felt that New England management falls short of management elsewhere in this respect. They stressed the cautious attitudes and lack of aggressiveness that they frequently encountered. There were no charges of incompetence.

It is of some importance to note that the appraisal of New England management was higher the closer the consultant's location to the region and the larger the proportion of his New England business to his total business. Nevertheless, lack of acquaintance seems to be only a partial explanation for the low reputation of New England management with some chemical consultants. While some of them intimated that they had observed a substantial improvement during recent decades, others apparently felt that there is ample room for further change in attitude.

A few of the comments by the chemical consultants are worthy of note:

> "Our experience leads us to believe that no valid generalization can be made on the technological alertness of management in one region as compared with another. The differences among companies are much more important than any general differences there may be between regions."

> "Our experience has been that it is entirely a matter of the attitude of individual concerns rather than of New England industry in general. From our contracts in New England as well as in other parts of the country, it is our impression that there is in New England as high a proportion of management alert to the value of products and process improvement as in other parts of the country. Certainly this is true of the *successful* New England concerns and the others do not last very long."

> "My opinion is not intended as criticism but merely as honest comment. It is my view that the majority of New England's management is not as alert to, or aware of, the continuous need for studying their products or processes for the purpose of improving them as management in many other parts of the country. I will say, however, that New England rates much higher in that connection than management in the South. It seems to me that the mental attitude on the part of New England's management is one to let well enough alone, not realizing that well enough may not be good enough tomorrow, or in fact, today. Of course, these are generalities, but nonetheless generalities based on multiple instances. But I did find that clients in New England easily see the advantages of research and development once they embark on even a small program."

On the whole, the evaluations seem encouraging, particularly in view of the accusations hurled at New Englanders during recent years. But New

England industry should leave no room for doubt that it is as alert to technical progress as industry elsewhere. The future course of technical activity in New England industry depends on the attitudes and initiative of the individual company managements. Their present and future decisions about research and development loom large as an influence on employment and income growth in the region.

Another indication of the attitude of management toward technological activity is the extent to which it takes advantage of locally available, technically trained personnel. To determine the extent to which the technical graduates and recipients of advanced technical degrees from New England colleges and universities were taking positions in the region, the Committee of New England conducted a survey among the placement officers of the colleges and universities. Although the coverage was not complete, the substantial similarity in findings for all reporting institutions strongly suggests that the results were indicative of the New England-wide situation.

For every college and university that reported, there was a net outflow of technically trained students. For example, in one group of seven widely separated colleges and universities in four New England states that reported in considerable detail, 2,163 students were awarded bachelor's degrees in technical fields from 1948 to 1950. Although 1,640 of them had lived in New England previously, only 1,043 of the 2,163 remained in New England after graduation, 853 to take jobs and 190 to do graduate work. There was a net outflow of 597 graduates (36%) to the rest of the country. The flow went most heavily to the Middle Atlantic, South Atlantic, and East North Central regions. This general pattern applied to state universities, technical institutes, and liberal arts colleges. It apparently existed for different groups of institutions, for which data were less complete. It also applied to students who received advanced degrees. The figures varied, but the direction of flow was the same.

The experience of the region's textile schools indicates the nature of the situation. One of them, for example, has had a continuous net outflow of its graduates to other parts of the country throughout this century. The outflow was especially great from 1920 to 1940, when about a third of the New England students went to other parts of the country after graduation, especially to New York, New Jersey, and Pennsylvania. During the 1940's, however, the net loss dropped to only 12%. *The interest of New England textile manufacturers in trained personnel has apparently increased during recent years, though not enough to check the drain entirely.*

In the last few years New England textile manufacturers have made only one-third of the requests for personnel at the placement bureau of the institution. The Middle Atlantic states were the source of 47%; the South accounted for but 7% of the balance. *Contrary to some charges, the proportion of graduates from New England's textile schools who go south has apparently not been rising significantly during recent decades.* Less complete data from the other textile schools support these conclusions.

It is widely recognized that the physical, cultural, and historical environment of Boston and other New England cities is attractive to many of the science and engineering students enrolled in the region's educational institutions who come from other states. They often remain in the area after graduation. It is not correct, however, to look on this phenomenon as a net gain for New England. On the basis of available information, for every non-New England student who remains in New England to work or study further, more than one student of New England origin leaves the region. The migration in each direction leavens the national culture, but New England tends to lose more than it gains.

This picture of the flow of technically trained personnel has a conceivable offset, of course. Students of New England origin attend educational institutions in other parts of the country, and they and their non-New England fellows might come to New England after graduation in sufficient numbers to compensate for the outflow from New England institutions. While we have no data to prove it, we believe that it is *extremely unlikely* that there is any such net return flow from this source. Rather, it would appear that there is a further net loss, for the same reason that there is a net outflow from the New England institutions—there are relatively more numerous and more attractive job opportunities for technical graduates in other parts of the country, in relation to the local supply of such graduates.

We were informed by several New England educational institutions that more of their technical graduates would like to remain in New England if they could obtain satisfactory employment, but that they were unwilling to make great financial sacrifices to do so. Quite apart from the number of job openings, salaries in New England are low. As an illustration, the median salary of Ph.D. scientists employed by private industry in New England in 1948 was lower than that in any other region of the country except the Mountain and Plains states.[8] Many New England companies are unable to compete for young engineers and other technical specialists with companies in other parts of the country because of their lower salary standards. Few of the giant companies which operate large research laboratories have their laboratories in New England, and few of the large New England companies conduct organized recruitment of new technical personnel. *It seems clear that New England industry is not yet taking full advantage of the rich resources of technical manpower available within the region. In view of the present shortage of engineering and technical personnel in the country, and the high probability that the shortage will become more acute during the next decade, it is important that New England industry should face the situation squarely.*

There is a real need in much of the region's industry to cultivate greater

8. See U.S. Bureau of Labor Statistics, *Employment, Education, and Earnings of American Men of Science*, Bulletin No. 1027, Washington, 1951.

research consciousness. This is largely a question of the attitudes of top management. It applies to the company's own research and development activities and the extent to which it takes advantage of available supplies of trained personnel. Merely doing as well as industry in the rest of the country is not enough. *Despite the many outstanding individual examples of research activity and technical alertness in the region and considerable improvement in recent years, New England industry as a whole is not yet doing as well as it should in these respects.*

Trade Association and Industry-supported Research

The individual members of an industry frequently join forces in research and development efforts where it is impractical or impossible for them to carry on such activities as individual firms.[9] There are many advantages in such joint efforts. They can provide research benefits to small companies that otherwise might be able to do little or no research themselves. They can minimize research costs by eliminating duplication of effort. And, of course, they lead to the same benefits as individual company research in lower manufacturing costs, improved materials and processes, better products, and new markets.

One approach to industry-wide research is through trade associations. According to the National Research Council, there were at least 31 trade association laboratories in the United States in 1950. They employed 264 professional workers and a slightly larger number of supporting personnel. The largest were the Underwriters Laboratories and the American Gas Association Testing Laboratories. While smaller, the others covered a wide range of industries from butter, baking, and meat to heating and ventilating, asphalt, chilled railroad car wheels, lithography, lumber, and Portland cement. None of the trade association laboratories is located in New England, though presumably many of their members are New England concerns. This is only slightly surprising, however, for most national trade associations are quartered in geographically central locations for the convenience of their members.

Another approach to industry-wide research is through trade association sponsorship of research projects at university, institute, and other laboratories, such as the National Bureau of Standards. A partial listing by the United States Department of Commerce for the year 1946 indicated that a substantial number of trade associations use this device. The Massachusetts Institute of Technology and Harvard University were the only New England institutions mentioned among nearly a hundred which were doing the work. Again, no New England trade associations and only one national association with

9. For a more complete discussion of this subject, see Gustav E. Larson, *Trade Association Industrial Research*, U.S. Department of Commerce, Industrial Series, No. 77, Washington, 1948.

headquarters in the region, the American Association of Textile Chemists and Colorists, were on the list.

A third approach to cooperative research is through the direct establishment of support for laboratories or institutes by members of an industry. While there are apparently fewer organizations of this type than trade association laboratories, the use of the device appears to be growing. There are, for example, institutes conducting research on gas, paper, textiles, plywood, and other products, supported in whole or in part by manufacturing members.

One organization of this general type is the Pulp and Paper Foundation formed in 1950 at the University of Maine with both company and individual members. It is concerned with the education of pulp and paper technologists, as well as with research on matters of interest to the pulp and paper industry. Though not restricted to New England members, it offers the New England paper industry an important supplement to the activities of the individual companies. A somewhat similar organization located in New England is the Northeastern Wood Utilization Council. It is similarly supported by companies and individuals as a nonprofit undertaking to aid in the utilization of low-grade wood and wood wastes. While its activities are principally educational, it also assists in applied research and investigations in this field. There is also the Worcester Foundation of Experimental Biology, which is partly supported by grants from the pharmaceutical industry.

These are the only industry-supported research organizations now operating in New England that have come to our attention. There are no such broadly supported research activities at present in the New England textile industries, despite the importance of textiles to the region. The two principal groups outside New England are the Textile Research Institute at Princeton, New Jersey, which is concerned primarily with basic research on wool, and the Institute of Textile Technology at Charlottesville, Virginia, which serves a fairly small group of members. *It would appear desirable for the textile manufacturers of New England to sponsor jointly, either through membership in a new institution or through their trade associations, fundamental research that would provide broad benefits to many of the region's firms.*

Other New England industries, particularly those that use indigenous New England materials or that consist largely of small companies, should also consider the desirability of establishing similar research institutes for the mutual benefit of their members. The seafood industry seems to be especially well suited to this kind of cooperative effort,[10] as do the jewelry, furniture, and other industries.

10. See our report on "The Fisheries of New England" (No. 2).

Nonprofit Research Foundations and Institutes

In addition to the national foundations and institutes that are supported by individual industries, there are several large, endowed, nonprofit research institutions and a hundred or more small ones. They provide research services to companies in a wide range of industries in addition to their extensive programs of fundamental research. Some of them are affiliated with educational institutions, though they usually operate more or less independently.

The name of the Mellon Institute of Industrial Research, Armour Research Foundation of the Illinois Institute of Technology, and Battelle Memorial Institute are well known. Each maintains a laboratory of several hundred technical and other workers and covers a tremendous range of research topics. A similar institution in Canada, the Ontario Research Foundation, has become an important supplement to the laboratories of individual concerns and universities in that country. Manufacturers sponsor much of the work of the foundations and institutes, often through fellowships, and obtain the benefits from it.

In addition to the older and larger ones, there are many newer nonprofit research institutions in the United States. The Midwest Research Institute, Southern Research Institute, and Southwest Research Institute, for example, were organized to meet regional needs and demands. There are numerous others, most of which concentrate their efforts on a limited number of research fields. For example, the Woods Hole Oceanographic Institution in Massachusetts conducts research in oceanography and marine aspects of biology, physics, geology, chemistry, and meteorology.

One of New England's new and promising research foundations affiliated with an educational institution is the Lowell Technological Institute Research Foundation. It was established in 1951 by the Massachusetts legislature, since the Lowell Technological Institute of Massachusetts is a state-operated school, but its board of directors consists of industrialists, educators, and a representative of organized labor. The foundation has been successful from the outset. It has operated on a contract basis with manufacturers and the Federal Government in the solution of research, development, and testing problems, and it has been self-supporting. It is meeting at least part of a great need in New England industry, particularly on the part of the region's textile manufacturers. Large national companies outside New England, many of which maintain their own laboratories, have been among the leaders in taking advantage of the foundation's specialized facilities. *The research needs of New England's textile and allied manufacturers are so great that they should make the fullest possible use of the Lowell Technological Institute Research Foundation, and it should continue to expand the services and facilities which it offers.*

The New England Industrial Research Foundation was established in

1942, but for a variety of reasons it did not become a going concern. Its basic objective was to further industrial research throughout New England, especially through the study and appraisal of new industrial projects. It was supported by subscriptions and, to some extent, by consulting fees and retainers. Insofar as possible, its small staff sought to supplement the activities of other research organizations rather than compete with them.

The timing of the foundation's organization was unfortunate. The pressure of war soon forced a shift from "emphasis on industrial research to a useful role in assisting the management of New England manufacturers to cope with immediate problems of conversion to wartime operations, development of substitute materials, and so forth." [11] Though it served a useful purpose as a wartime service organization, the foundation had to abandon its fundamental objectives. Inadequate financial support and lack of sufficient interest on the part of the region's manufacturing industries were also factors militating against its success during the war years. Its activities were gradually reduced during 1944 and its residual operations were transferred to the New England Council.

Despite the failure of the New England Industrial Research Foundation, there still seems to be an opportunity for additional nonprofit research foundations in New England, even on a region-wide basis. A launching under more favorable circumstances would greatly increase the probability of success. The present facilities and services of the colleges and universities, which are discussed in a later section, are not yet used to their fullest capacity, and the other research and development facilities in the region can take care of most of the present demand. But as the research consciousness of New England manufacturers grows there will probably be an expanding need for research facilities. Increased use of the foundation device can aid in building a well-rounded research structure in the region.

The greatest problem in increasing the use of nonprofit research institutions, as in any other type of research activity, is to increase the demand for their services. Unless industry is eager to make use of the available services, it is fruitless to provide them. The difference in the response to the New England Industrial Research Foundation and the Lowell Technological Institute Research Foundation, however, suggests that the attitudes of New England management may have changed somewhat during the last 10 or 12 years. A well-conceived organization of this type is much more likely to succeed now than it was a few years ago. The director of one of the nation's largest research foundations, which is located outside the region, has expressed his belief that New England firms have become more progressive in relation to similar firms in other parts of the country than they were in the past. It is of the utmost importance to the region that they maintain this momentum.

11. The New England Industrial Research Foundation, *Report of the Trustees to the Founders,* March 28, 1947.

Commerical Consulting Laboratories

Commericial consulting laboratories are another supplement to the research efforts of individual companies. To some extent their services overlap those of research foundations. They provide specialized knowledge and services which their clients cannot afford themselves or which extend the clients' own facilities. As in other types of research facilities outside a company, a manufacturer can often save money by hiring the services of a consultant instead of carrying out a given research project himself. Even large manufacturing companies which maintain their own laboratories frequently use the special skills and services of consulting firms.

The National Research Council listed 462 independent consulting laboratories in the United States for the year 1950. Forty of them (8.6%) were in New England, all but one in the states of Massachusetts and Connecticut. In terms of professional personnel, however, the New England consultants employed 12.7% of the national total. The largest technical consulting firms in New England are Arthur D. Little, Inc., of Cambridge, Massachusetts, and the Esselen Research Division of the United States Testing Company, Inc., of Boston. Moreover, more than a fifth of the 311 industrial research laboratories in New England listed by the National Research Council for that year also provided consulting services to other manufacturers.

It is evident that New England industry is well provided for in the number and variety of consulting laboratories available within the region. How effectively are New England manufacturers using these facilities?

Like all other problems of appraisal in this field, this is difficult to determine with exactness. The New England business of members of the Association of Consulting Chemists and Chemical Engineers[12] is a somewhat smaller proportion of their total business than one would expect on the basis of the region's relative importance in total manufacturing activity. It is possible but hardly likely that the other, usually smaller, consultant firms that are not members of the association serve New England industry intensively enough to correct the imbalance. *We can advance the tentative conclusion, therefore, that New England manufacturers as a whole might profitably give more serious thought to supplementing their present research activities by greater use of experienced technical consulting firms.*

This conclusion is bolstered by the opinions of New England manufacturers themselves. A study conducted by two students at the School of Industrial Management of the Massachusetts Institute of Technology[13] inquired about the use that 118 responding manufacturers in the region made of con-

---

12. Reported in Staff Memorandum No. 4.
13. Oscar W. Kaalstad and Robert F. King, "Industrial Consulting Services and Their Relationship to Industry in New England" (unpublished paper), May 1952.

sultants and their opinions about that use. A few highlights from the study are summarized in Table 15–5. About three-fourths of the respondents had made occasional use of consultants during the preceding five years. The other fourth was about evenly divided between companies which had used consultants frequently and companies which had not used them at all. There were rather small differences in use of consultants as reported by manufacturers who rated their own research activities as "adequate" and those who rated them as "inadequate." The companies with inadequate facilities who used consultants at all did so somewhat more frequently, but almost as large a proportion of them never used consultants.

Table 15–5. The Use of Outside Consultants by 118 New England Manufacturers, 1952

| | OPINIONS OF COMPANIES ABOUT THEIR OWN RESEARCH ACTIVITIES | |
	ADEQUATE	INADEQUATE
Number of companies	73	45
Per cent of total	62%	38%
Use of consultants in last five years:		
Frequent	8	17
Occasional	77	72
Never	15	11
TOTAL	100	100
Expected future use of consultants:		
Frequent	13	28
Occasional	57	51
If necessary	11	—
None	19	21
TOTAL	100	100

Source: Kaalstad and King, *op. cit.*

It is highly significant that almost two-fifths of the companies reporting assessed their own research activities as inadequate, particularly since most of them were fairly large concerns. Eighty-three per cent had 200 or more employees, and 57% had more than 500 employees. This recognition of present inadequacy by such a large proportion of companies is encouraging. Recognition of a shortcoming is the first step in its correction. While the study did not inquire into the future research plans of the participating companies, it would seem likely that many of them were planning to expand their own research efforts.

There are still too many New England companies with inadequate research facilities of their own that have no intention of seeking outside assistance. In each category of respondents, the proportion that expected to make frequent use of consultants was larger than the proportion that reported frequent use of consultants in the past. But there were also larger proportions that had no future plans to use consultants. While a commercial consultant may or may not provide the best approach to any given technical problem, depending on circumstances, consultants can aid in the solution of a wide variety of problems if they are selected with specific reference to the needs of a company. Some companies which do not plan to use consultants in the future base their position on previous unsatisfactory experiences with particular consultants. Regardless of the merits of their attitudes toward the past relationships, the sweeping generalizations implicit in this stand seem unjustified. *Used wisely, consulting laboratories have much to offer most companies, whether or not they have their own research and development programs.*

University and College Laboratories

Educational institutions are of importance to the technical progress of industry for three principal reasons: (1) they train technical men for employment by industry; (2) they conduct basic research and advance fundamental knowledge; and (3) they provide formal or informal technical assistance to industry. New England is fortunate in having at least 46 colleges and universities that furnish technical training and operate research laboratories, including some of the leading institutions in the country.

According to a study conducted by the United States Bureau of Labor Statistics in 1948 among about 41,000 American scientists,[14] New England institutions were outstanding in training these scientists. Almost 14% of their Ph.D. degrees and 12.5% of their bachelor's degrees were awarded in the region. In terms of the 6.3% of the nation's population that resides in New England, these are impressive proportions. While both northern and southern New England exceeded any other group of states in the proportion of bachelor's degrees granted in terms of population, almost all the New England doctorates in science were awarded by institutions in Massachusetts, Rhode Island, and Connecticut.

A geographical distribution of the 41,000 scientists in 1948 was somewhat different, however, from that of the educational institutions they attended. Only 8.1% of them were employed in New England. Although the New England ratio of scientists employed to population exceeded the national average, it was in turn exceeded by those of the Middle Atlantic region and other individual states. Even southern New England did not maintain the leading position it held in the education of these scientists. Moreover, the proportion of scientists resident in New England was more heavily concentrated in educational institutions than was true of the nation as a whole, and the region's proportion in industry was smaller (see Table 15-6). In view of the intensive industrialization of New England, the number of scientists employed by industry in the region seems low.

New England's industrialization and its extensive technical education facilities largely explain the region's good representation in scientific professions. The excellent scientific staffing of its educational institutions is

14. *Op. cit.*

further attested by their large representation in the membership of the National Academy of Sciences. The Academy, which serves as scientific adviser to the government, had 435 members in 1948.[15] Ninety-two of them (20%) were located in New England, 86 at colleges and universities in the region. Only 15% of the American-born members were born in New England. While 28% of the nationwide membership was affiliated with government, industrial, or nonprofit laboratories, the comparable figure for New England was less than 7%.

Table 15-6. *Scientists Employed in the United States and New England, by Type of Employer, 1948*

	UNITED STATES	NEW ENGLAND	NORTHERN NEW ENGLAND	SOUTHERN NEW ENGLAND
Number of scientists employed	41,430	3,366	409	2,957
Scientists employed per 100,000 in labor force	70	87	58	93
Per cent employed by				
Education	37.4	44.2	63.6	41.5
Government	13.5	4.6	5.1	4.5
Education and government	2.4	2.9	7.1	2.3
Industry	27.1	23.4	7.8	25.6
Foundation	2.2	1.1	2.0	0.9
Independent consultant	1.4	1.6	1.2	1.7
Education and independent consultant	6.8	10.5	7.1	11.0
Other	9.2	11.7	6.1	12.5
TOTAL	100.0	100.0	100.0	100.0

Source: U.S. Bureau of Labor Statistics, *Employment, Education, and Earnings of American Men of Science,* Bulletin No. 1027, Washington, D.C., 1951

We have already noted the net regional outflow of technical graduates of New England educational institutions for the years 1948–50. It appears that this movement has persisted over a considerable period, and the additional evidence further strengthens the conclusion that New England industry is making relatively less use of the trained technical men educated in the region than industry in the rest of the country.

Estimates of research expenditures prior to World War II indicate that universities and endowed research institutions spent about 70% of their research budgets on "basic" research. The comparable proportions of the research budgets for industry and government were estimated at 5% and 15%, respectively. While the percentages have undoubtedly changed since 1940, the relative positions have probably remained about the same. *The universities are the principal source of fundamental scientific advances, and it is to them that industry and government must look for most of the new scientific knowledge needed for technological advancement.*

By 1952 the Federal Government had assumed the major financial burden for "basic" research, but actual conduct of the research rested mainly with

15. Fred E. Wright, *National Academy of Sciences: Distribution and Ages of Membership,* Proceedings of the National Academy of Sciences, Vol. 35, No. 3, March 1949.

private institutions. It was estimated that expenditures for technical research by American educational institutions totaled approximately $380,000,000. The largest portion of that sum, roughly $340,000,000, came from the Federal Government, largely in the form of contracts for specific research projects. The balance was provided by state governments, industry, endowed foundations, and other sources. While most of the federally sponsored research is directed primarily toward national defense and public health, much of it also has important civilian implications.

Separate data are not available for the total research expenditures of New England educational institutions, but it is well known that the Massachusetts Institute of Technology and Harvard University rank among the national leaders. The Federal Government has used their facilities extensively, as well as those of other New England colleges and universities, in its research and development programs. The principal federal agencies which place research and development contracts with educational institutions or make research grants to them are the Army, Navy, Air Force, Atomic Energy Commission, National Advisory Committee for Aeronautics, and Public Health Service. In combination they account for the bulk of all such federal contracts and grants. In the fiscal year 1950, New England institutions held 29% of the value of research and development contracts placed with educational institutions by the military forces. Regional institutions held 21% of the contracts from the National Advisory Committee for Aeronautics, 14% from the Public Health Service, and 10% from the Atomic Energy Commission. In addition, substantial contracts were held from many other government departments and agencies. While precise figures are not available for New England, it seems clear that in 1950 the region's colleges and universities held well over 10% of the national total of government research contracts. There is no reason to believe that the proportion has declined since then.

The defense-related research activities of New England educational institutions have also been studied by the Engineering College Research Council, as part of its examination of the research potential of American colleges and universities.[16] Its concern was with manpower rather than with dollar expenditures. In both the United States as a whole and New England, about half the senior scientific and engineering faculty is actively engaged in research. The council summary shows less difference between the region and the nation in the university manpower devoted to research than might be anticipated on the basis of government contracts held. The region's activity compares favorably with that of the nation, however, and there was apparently a small underreporting for New England which might have depressed the regional percentages slightly (see Table 15–7). As would be expected, Massachusetts and Connecticut institutions are the leaders among the New England states, but Rhode Island and Maine also show up well in the proportion of total scientific and engineering faculty actively engaged in research.

16. *University Research Potential*, Cambridge, Mass., June 1951.

Even though only a small proportion of university research is financed by contracts or grants from industrial concerns, industry can benefit from maintaining close relationship with educational institutions. The scientific findings of university research workers are normally published and made generally available, unless they are covered by security restrictions. In addition, contacts with the technical staffs of nearby institutions can provide manufacturers with an important supplement to their own technical activities.

Table 15–7. University Research Personnel in Science and Engineering,
United States and New England, 1951
(number of persons)

	NEW ENGLAND	UNITED STATES	NEW ENGLAND AS PER CENT OF U.S.
Faculty members and full-time research personnel of equivalent rank	2,212	24,881	8.89
Qualified to participate in research projects	1,841	21,037	8.75
Active, full-time or part-time, in research	1,160	12,866	9.02
Equivalent in full-time research workers	595	6,745	8.82
Equivalent in full-time defense research	309	3,291	9.40
Full-time or part-time instructors, graduate students, and assistants active in research	2,365	24,786	9.54
Equivalent in full-time research by junior staff	1,199	12,143	9.87

Source: Engineering College Research Council, *University Research Potential*

Many colleges and universities, in New England as well as elsewhere, provide research and consulting services directly to industrial concerns and government organizations. Twenty-nine of the nation's 282 colleges and universities that offered consulting services in 1950 were located in New England. In most of them the activity is not highly organized and the amount of such work is small. A few carry on more extensive activities of this sort. Each of the six state universities in New England operates an engineering experiment station which accepts projects from industry. In addition, the University of Connecticut operates a Research Foundation, Norwich University operates the Vermont Bureau of Industrial Research, and the University of Maine and the Massachusetts Institute of Technology maintain divisions of industrial cooperation. We have already mentioned the Lowell Technological Institute Research Foundation, which operates under a separate board of directors.

The M.I.T. Division of Industrial Cooperation is by far the largest of these undertakings. Most of its work, in dollar terms, is for the Federal Government, although it does have a number of contracts with industrial concerns. Only a few of its smaller projects are for New England manufacturers. One reason for the small use made of M.I.T.'s facilities by New England concerns is their failure to recognize the importance to them of basic research and their great concern about production improvements and machine design, which pay off more quickly.

The Vermont Bureau of Industrial Research was originally established in 1939 as a research division of Norwich University. It was reorganized in 1947 and shifted its emphasis to engineering and management consulting services. It serves Vermont manufacturers usually on a no-charge basis except to cover direct expenses, and is financed by an annual appropriation from the State of Vermont. For the most part it concentrates on short-term projects. It served about 200 Vermont manufacturers from 1947 to 1951, and is now well established as a manufacturing aid in the state. The wood products industries, which are a major part of the state's industrial activity, are the most frequent users of the bureau's services.

The Department of Industrial Cooperation was established at the University of Maine in 1945. It accepts research projects and a variety of smaller assignments, on a fee basis, from manufacturers both in and outside Maine. The volume of its activities has increased steadily, and Maine manufacturers are gradually becoming aware of its services. Nevertheless, out-of-state manufacturers have generally used its facilities more than in-state companies.

The engineering experiment stations of the state universities typically provide engineering and research facilities to local manufacturers and to their state governments. They do not always limit their services, however, to clients within the state. The University of New Hampshire Engineering Experiment Station is one of the most active in New England. It has five full-time engineers who are members of the university faculty, plus a dozen part-time workers, and it has access to the services of other members of the university staff. The New Hampshire station is especially concerned with assisting small concerns, which it does by visiting the companies as well as by accepting projects from them.

The Vermont, Maine, and New Hampshire institutions just described are all of considerable importance to manufacturers in the three northern states. Their potential importance is even greater. There are few technical consultants in these states and not many industrial research laboratories. *The organized university facilities should serve as strategic centers of technical knowledge in the northern New England states to a much greater extent than they do now. Their activities should be expanded and encouraged. It would also appear worthwhile for each of the other major colleges in Maine, New Hampshire, and Vermont to step up its facilities and services for industrial engineering and research assistance in its area, probably with the assistance of the state governments.*

While the need for such services may not be as large in the metropolitan centers of southern New England because of the greater availability of alternative sources of assistance, in many parts of Massachusetts, Rhode Island, and Connecticut of the educational institutions could render important local services by increased efforts along these lines. For example, the Engineering

Research Institute of the University of Massachusetts is in a position to serve many small manufacturing concerns in its area. Its program has not been promoted because of staff and financial problems. All income of the university reverts to the general fund of the state government, according to present law, which makes it difficult to develop the activity. A simple change in statute and greater recognition of the importance of such an institute could enhance the local significance of this service.

Government Laboratories

More than half the nation's total expenditures for research and development comes from the Federal Government. As large contractors of research projects to educational institutions and industrial laboratories, government agencies rely heavily on private research facilities. They operate extensive laboratories of their own, however, that do an important part of their work. State and municipal governments also support some research laboratories. All these government laboratories together employed about 25,000 professional scientists and engineers in 1950; most of them worked for the Federal Government.

The proportion of research work done in their own laboratories varies from agency to agency within the Federal Government. The Department of Defense, which accounted for about half of total direct governmental expenditures for research and development in fiscal 1952, carries on about one-fourth of the work in its own facilities and contracts out for the rest. The Atomic Energy Commission, which expends another 35% of the federal total for this purpose, also relies heavily on educational institutions and other nongovernmental laboratories. Some other agencies, such as the Bureau of Mines and the National Bureau of Standards, do a much larger proportion of their own work.

Despite the Federal Government's extensive use of New England's educational research facilities, it has located relatively few of its own laboratories in the region. Of the 60 laboratories and field stations operated directly by the Department of Agriculture, National Bureau of Standards, and Bureau of Mines, which employed more than 3,000 professional workers and 4,500 supporting personnel in 1950, not one was situated in New England. There are a few New England laboratories operated by the other nondefense agencies. None of the Atomic Energy Commission installations is in the region, though some New England educational institutions cooperate in the operation of the Brookhaven laboratory on Long Island. The Fish and Wildlife Service does some technical research in the region, but there are not many other federal laboratories.

The situation has not been much different for the Department of Defense. The Air Force has operated some electronic research facilities at Cambridge and Bedford, Massachusetts, and the Quartermaster Corps has maintained a

Climatic Research Laboratory in Lawrence. The Watertown Arsenal and other manufacturing or operating branches of the armed services also conduct some research and development activities within the region. A new and expanded Quartermaster Laboratory expected to employ 1,500 or more persons is being built at Natick, Massachusetts, to supersede the Lawrence installation. Bedford is to be the site of an enlarged Air Force Electronics Research Laboratory which is expected to employ approximately 3,500.

Even with the addition of these new facilities, New England's representation among the government's research laboratories will remain relatively low. Where a location in New England has the characteristics desired for any future government laboratory to as great or a greater extent than alternative locations, the region's development agencies should actively encourage the selection of a New England site.

Summary of New England Research Facilities

This discussion of the major categories of research and development activity in New England indicates that there has been some unevenness in the region's participation in the various types of effort. Its leadership has been greatest in the work done by educational institutions. Its participation has been rather low in the categories of trade association and industry supported research, nonprofit research foundations and institutes, and government laboratories. New England's industrial laboratories are greater in number but fewer in professional personnel than its proportions of the nation's manufacturing establishments and their employees. Its commercial consulting laboratories present the reverse situation.

On balance, New England seems as active in its total technical effort as the nation as a whole, allowing for the region's relatively greater industrialization and educational development. Though there have been fluctuations in the ratio from year to year New England's proportion of United States patents granted to American citizens in the past 20 years has not increased. (See Chart 15–1.) The average for the period has been fairly consistent with the region's proportion of industrial activity. The patent record is only a rough measure of activity, since it gives the same weight to trivial inventions as to major ones; but the trend over time is of greater significance.

Despite the excellence of certain phases of New England's industrial research effort, however, the region's manufacturers do not yet seem to be taking full advantage of the available research facilities outside their own companies, and they are still far short of the full potentialities of their own development. In an area such as New England, where the manufacturing base is the ability of producers to convert largely imported materials into finished products for sale on a national market, technological leadership is a necessity for the maintenance of competitive position. The inherent cost disadvantages in New England which put a premium on production efficiency put even more on product leadership. New England manufacturers as a group can and should do even better in these respects than they have done so far.

Realization of the importance of research and development work is a prerequisite to expanded industrial research effort. This realization has been growing steadily in New England, especially since World War II, but it has also been growing in the rest of the country. Competition is keen. The recent acceleration in product improvement has tended to reduce the relative

CHART 15–1

New England's Proportion of United States Patents Issued,* 1930–50

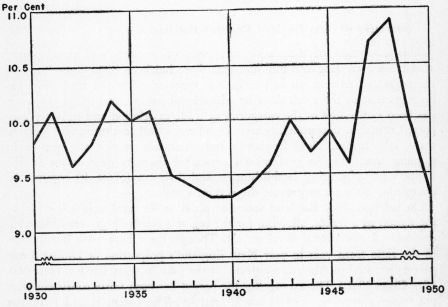

* Patents issued to citizens of the United States.
Source: U.S. Patent Office

importance of cutting costs and to increase the relative importance of developing new sources of revenue. In this situation both short-run and long-run research programs have an important place.

There have been many efforts in New England to stimulate research consciousness during recent years. As the leading region-wide business and development organization, the New England Council has sponsored an annual "research tour" with visits to leading manufacturing concerns in the region. The Boston Chamber of Commerce, Associated Industries of Massachusetts, and New England Council have jointly brought together manufacturers and others for "Research Day" and "New Products Day" exhibits and exchanges of information. The engineering experiment stations and other branches of educational institutions concerned with industrial technology have also helped increase the appreciation of research and development by manufacturers. Other manufacturers' associations, development organizations, and additional groups have similarly aided to a greater or lesser extent. *All these efforts to develop the "idea" of research and to encourage more industrial research in the region should be continued and expanded. In addition, the effort should gradually provide more specific direction to manufacturers in determining the proper focus and objectives for their own research activities.*

PROMISING FIELDS OF RESEARCH FOR NEW ENGLAND

While the need for sustained and expanded technical effort in New England is apparent, it is also plain that the effort must be soundly conceived and directed toward opportunities that offer most to the region. The structure and trends of present industry, the pattern of natural resources, the status and trends of technical knowledge in various fields, and other factors all condition the directions in which future technical effort by New England industry should point. Nevertheless, there are opportunities in a great many fields, and the major limiting factor on New England's success in industrial research is the imagination and initiative of its manufacturers and other business units.

The industrial opportunities for New England have been examined systematically by Arthur D. Little, Inc., in an effort to determine which industries offer the greatest growth possibilities.[17] The summary of the Little report states:

> An appraisal of New England's industrial opportunities inevitably comes back to the proposition that it is primarily men and only secondarily material resources which determine the economic level of a community. New England has the human resources required for the task; it can get access to many of the material factors. The method best calculated to harness material and human resources for the development of New England is systematic application of technical and economic research.

Though vast natural resources are not necessary for economic growth in New England, the region can benefit from improved use of the resources which it has. Research directed toward utilizing these resources has great potential importance.

The forest-based industries provide approximately a tenth of all manu-

17. *A Survey of Industrial Opportunities in New England,* report to the Federal Reserve Bank of Boston (August 1952), p. 30.

facturing employment in New England. Improvements in forest yields and in the use of timber, including logging and manufacturing residues, are of special importance. There is a special need for more technical research on the control and prevention of insect pests and tree diseases, as well as on the economic utilization of low-grade trees and other "waste products." [18]

There is also opportunity for better utilization of the resources of the ocean fisheries. The research needs are many, ranging from increased knowledge of marine biology to improved methods of catching fish and harvesting shellfish and to better ways of preparing and processing fishery products.[19]

Other major natural resources of New England are its soils and climate and mineral resources. Agricultural research is well developed, operating largely through the state experiment stations and private farm groups.[20] In view of the region's limited agricultural land and rising population, there will be a continued need for improvements in seed, breeding of animals, growing and raising methods, and harvesting. While New England's mineral resources are small, the existence of low-grade deposits of manganese, anthracitic coal, mica, and other minerals makes improvements in extraction, separation, and use of these materials of some importance.[21]

As an area with no commercial deposits of mineral fuels, New England is particularly concerned about improvements in the extraction, transportation, and utilization of coal and petroleum in order to lower the region's fuel bill. There are opportunities for research on such divergent but related topics as pipeline transportation of powdered coal, and fuel handling, preparation, and combustion. Advances in any of these fields can benefit New England appreciably, because of the higher than average costs of fuel in the region.

More than three-fourths of the electric power generated in New England is produced by fuel-burning steam plants. That proportion will probably grow, no matter how fully the rivers are developed for hydroelectric power generation. The high fuel costs are the principal factor in the region's higher than average power costs. The increasing trend toward steam generation intensifies the need for research in fuels. It also gives special regional significance to the experiments in power generation with nuclear fuels, as a substitute for combustion fuels. *New England's major electric utilities and principal power users should take an active part in the research and development leading to atomic power, as one electric system in the region is now doing. Industrial firms should study uses of the by-products of nuclear fission.*

Since various parts of New England meet the criteria for location of an early experimental plant for power generation from nuclear fuels, the entire region should strongly urge the location of such a plant in the six-state area. The high level of power costs at present, the existence of a large and growing

18. See our report, "The Forests of New England" (No. 1).
19. See our report, "The Fisheries of New England" (No. 2).
20. Agricultural research is discussed in our report on "Agriculture in New England" (No. 3).
21. New England's mineral resources are discussed in our report, "Minerals and New England" (No. 4).

power market, the availability of adequate water for cooling, and the wealth of technical and scientific manpower and supporting facilities available make the region ideally suited for such an installation. The effect on power rates would probably not be immediate, but New England could get a thorough basic education in the field, as well as make an important contribution to the nation. Moreover, the location of the first or one of the first such plants in New England would stimulate the growth of a whole series of related activities, such as the use of by-products from nuclear fission, and would provide an important psychological impetus to the entire region.[22]

In the manufacturing field as a whole, the opportunities for research are virtually limitless. While large-scale basic research is historically associated more closely with the chemical and electrical-equipment industries than with most other industries, the recent trend has been toward expanded research activities in almost all industries.

The development of new processes, new products, and new materials can help to check the declining industries, as well as help the new industries to grow. There are still great research opportunities in the textile fields, for example, as well as in electrical apparatus. Those opportunities lay dormant, for the most part, until they were picked up by the chemical manufacturers. Textile technology is now in a ferment, and it should be advanced strenuously by New England firms to strengthen their own positions. Saving thousands of jobs that might otherwise be lost is as important to the region as securing an equal number of new jobs. *Research and development offer perhaps the best hope of permanently saving many textile jobs that are now threatened by competitive disadvantages.*

The Little report[23] appraised the growth prospects in most New England industries and found that a large proportion of the industrial opportunities depend heavily on the technological leadership and ingenuity of the manufacturers. The report noted that "the best opportunities are likely to be found in products which satisfy one or more of the following requirements: (1) need for skilled labor; (2) high value added; (3) a unique product or specialty good; (4) need for management ingenuity and patience; (5) small bulk, high value; (6) a material base in the region, in Eastern Canada, or overseas; (7) orientation to a local market; (8) origin in technical research." [24]

The specific possible opportunities listed in the Little report that depend to a greater or lesser degree on research and development cover a broad range. While we cannot list or discuss them all, we can mention a few to illustrate the general nature of the possibilities. The utilization and further development of new techniques of metalworking and new technical uses

22. See our report "Water, Fuel, and Energy in New England" (No. 5) for a discussion of the power situation in the region.

23. *Op. cit.*

24. *Ibid.*, pp. 8–9.

provide opportunities for expansion in the fabrication of aluminum and other light metals in New England. The metal titanium offers especially attractive possibilities.

New types of power tools have been successfully developed in New England, and further opportunities exist. Machinery manufacturers can work out new types of equipment, ranging from machinery for the production of miniature electronic components and for specialized medical equipment to improved electronic computing machines and other office equipment. Photo-typesetting, improved engraving and printing processes provide opportunities in the printing field.

Electronics is a major new field, and New England has already secured an important place in it through its technical leadership. Further progress is possible in such areas as miniature components, printed circuits, semiconductors, electronic instruments, and automation of manufacturing processes. Glass fiber products, pharmaceutical, and specialty chemicals of other types also offer further possibilities. High-grade specialty papers already constitute a large portion of the output of the New England paper industry, but there are other opportunities in such diverse items as paper printing plates, laminated building paper, and food wrappers. Pulp molding is another expanding field.

Other areas for progress through the development, improvement, or use of new materials and processes include unplasterized polyvinyl chloride, reinforced plastics, and many other new plastic materials, new methods of molding plastics, improvements in rubber, the development of various types of new building materials, and many more.

Each industry has its own unique technical opportunities. It is up to the manufacturers to seize them. To the extent that they do—and are successful in their efforts—they will benefit themselves, their workers, and New England as a whole.

TRANSLATING RESEARCH FINDINGS INTO SALES AND JOBS

Even after a research and development program has produced new technical knowledge which leads to a new product, a manufacturer still faces a major task in adapting it to the market, and producing and selling the product. There are important investment, manufacturing, financial, and marketing problems to be resolved for even the most promising development. While it is not possible to present a detailed discussion of these problems in this report, their importance requires a brief consideration of some aspects of the topic.

Large established concerns are generally well equipped to handle the diverse tasks involved in introducing a research-based new product. They usually have new-product departments or other specialized personnel who are experienced in this type of work. Their varied product lines tend to make them familiar with both the opportunities for new products and the attendant risks. Where the new product is closely related to the old, past marketing research and established market contacts make it fairly easy to conduct market appraisals. Manufacturing and cost experience is useful in planning new production processes, capital investment, and pricing. Established financial connections make it relatively easy to finance new investment and meet working capital requirements. Established customer relationships and reputation ease the selling job.

There are pitfalls in introducing new products, even for large companies, however, if the product is quite different from the previous product line. A company must take special care not to allow its thinking about existing products to straitjacket its approach to new and different products, especially in relation to market appraisals and distribution methods. Entirely new and different types of selling may be necessary. There is need for an imaginative approach to each new product which draws on past experience but is not limited by it.

The launching of a new product is much more difficult for a small or new firm. It has little or no experience and reputation to rely on. Its management is usually young and untested and often not well equipped to manage the diversity of problems encountered during the first few difficult years. Financing often constitutes a major obstacle. In addition to all the problems faced by a small or new concern making a standard product,[25] the market, design, production methods, costs, and selling methods all have to be determined from a standing start.

Under these circumstances, the appraisal of the market for a new product in terms of probable production costs takes on great significance even after the technical merit of the product has been proved beyond question. Market surveys must be thorough and realistic, since they provide a principal basis for investment and production decisions.[26] They are also of major importance in determining the availability of financial support from outside the company.

The initial financing of most new or small companies that have developed new products is usually within the capacity of the principals and their relatives or friends. The difficult capital problems usually arise a little later when it is necessary for the business to grow if it is to succeed. By that time technical, cost, and marketing problems must be fairly well worked out if outside capital is to be attracted.

Many small companies with new products rely on retained earnings and new noninstitutional investment to finance their expansion. Changed patterns of saving and investment during recent years and growing capital requirements have made these traditional financing methods less certain. To fill at

25. See "New England's Industrial Management" (No. 14).
26. See Cyril C. Hermann, "Ideas for New Business Firms" and "Market Studies for New Business," *Monthly Review*, Federal Reserve Bank of Boston, June and July 1953.

least part of the need a new type of financial institution has developed, the equity-capital investment company.[27] The American Research and Development Company of Boston was the first such organization formed to invest exclusively in research-based enterprises. It provides both capital funds and management assistance to the concerns in which it invests. Careful screening standards and the restriction to research-based enterprises have limited investments from the company's organization in 1946 to only 27 of the 2,200 applications received by the end of 1952. Even after intensive advance examination and support by American Research and Development, one of the companies has failed and several are still in the struggling stage. The company reports that its investments have been limited more by the shortage of attractive opportunities than by insufficient investment funds. Another such New England investment organization, New Enterprises, Inc., has had a somewhat similar experience.

Despite the limited investments to date by institutional investors in research-based enterprises, this device appears to be an important method of expediting the growth and success of such companies. The number of equity institutions for technically based companies may well increase, and their investments will almost certainly continue to expand. Other institutional investors, such as life insurance companies, might do well to consider expanding their investment operations to this specialized field.

This report has been concerned primarily with research and development activities by manufacturing concerns and other organizations, but there are also many new products that arise out of the work of a private individual. While organized research and development have taken over most of the field in the last 50 years, private inventors still hold a significant place in the flow of new-product ideas. Since most of them are not in a position to manufacture the products themselves, they are often anxious to place their patented developments with established companies on a royalty basis. Existing manufacturers can sometimes supplement their own development activities with new products brought in from outside.

A new type of organization has recently come into existence to aid in finding "a suitable market for an acceptable invention through research, market study, cost comparison and design counsel." [28] The New Products Research Corporation of Boston, organized in 1945, was one of the leaders in this type of organization. Such companies screen thousands of inventions, reject most of them, and try to find markets for those they accept. While most patents are issued for inventions of little commercial value, the small proportion that do succeed can mean added sales and employment. An operation such as this screening can be of assistance to New England, as well as to other parts of the country, in channeling new-product ideas to the region's manufacturers.

27. For a broader discussion of the capital problems of small business, see "The Financial Resources of New England and Their Use" (No. 11).

28. "Bridging the Dreams-and-Dollars Gap," *New England News Letter,* New England Council (Boston, July 1952), p. 9.

CONCLUSIONS

In general, New England is active in technical research and development. The scientific leadership of its colleges and universities is particularly outstanding. The region is also well equipped with commercial consulting laboratories, though it contains relatively few endowed research foundations or government laboratories. The industrial research laboratories maintained by private companies compare favorably with those in the rest of the country in some respects and less favorably in others.

Since technology has increasing importance for American industry, and since New England depends so much on manufacturing for its support, while suffering from certain inherent cost disadvantages because of its geographical location, it is important that manufacturers in the region take maximum advantage of technological opportunities to maintain or improve their competitive positions. Such opportunities exist in most industries, but too few manufacturers have as yet taken advantage of them. The research and development activities of many New England industries are still inadequate, despite numerous outstanding examples by individual companies. Too few manufacturers are aware that a sound research program is often a company's best investment, through the assistance it gives in individualizing and improving products, developing new products, and reducing cost.

Manufacturers should take greater advantage than they do now of the opportunities for research outside their own companies, as well as increase their own research and development efforts. There are various ways in which outside facilities can supplement company laboratories. None is yet used sufficiently in New England.

These are some specific suggestions for improving industrial research efforts:

1. Trade association laboratories and industry-supported research can provide broad benefits to an industry, often more cheaply than action by an individual firm. New England industries might well provide mutual support in this way for fundamental research that would benefit all members.

2. New England manufacturers should make greater use of the Lowell Technological Institute Research Foundation and other specialized nonprofit research foundations and institutes in and outside the region. New England should follow the trend in other parts of the country toward the greater development and use of research laboratories that are oriented to serving the region.

3. Commercial consulting laboratories are not yet employed as extensively and efficiently as they should be in New England, especially by the smaller companies that do not have adequate technical facilities of their own.

4. Manufacturers in the region make too little use of college and university technical facilities, especially those established expressly to provide services

to private businesses and governments, such as divisions of industrial cooperation, engineering experiment stations, and research bureaus. The need for such services is particularly great in the northern states, though it exists also in at least parts of southern New England.

5. The regional and state business and developmental organizations which have sought to increase the research consciousness of manufacturers in the region should maintain and intensify their efforts.

6. New England manufacturers should participate more actively in the research and development programs of the Federal Government, both to acquire new knowledge applicable to their civilian business and to contribute to the national security.

7. New England manufacturers should make greater use than they now do of the technically trained graduates of colleges and universities in the region, who are an important domestic resource.

SELECTED REFERENCES

1. Bush, Vannevar, *Science—The Endless Frontier,* Report to the President by the Director of the Office of Scientific Research and Development, Washington, 1945.
2. Engineering College Research Council, *University Research Potential,* Cambridge, Mass., June 1951.
3. Little, Arthur D., Inc., *A Survey of Industrial Opportunities in New England* (report to the Federal Reserve Bank of Boston), August 1952.
4. National Research Council, *Industrial Research Laboratories of the United States,* 9th ed., compiled by Myron J. Rand, Washington, 1950.
5. ——— *Research and Development Personnel in Industrial Laboratories, 1950,* Report to the National Scientific Register, Scientific Manpower Series, No. 1, Washington, 1951.
6. National Science Foundation, *Annual Reports, 1950–51* and *1951–52,* Washington.
7. U.S. Bureau of Labor Statistics, *Employment, Education, and Earnings of American Men of Science,* Bulletin No. 1027, Washington, 1951.
8. U.S. Bureau of Labor Statistics and the Research and Development Board, U.S. Department of Defense, *Industrial Research and Development: A Preliminary Report,* Washington, January 1953.
9. Gustav E. Larson, *Trade Association Industrial Research,* U.S. Department of Commerce, Industrial Series, No. 77, Washington, 1948.

16

New England's Financial Relations with the Federal Government

*Drafted by Edward K. Smith under the
direction of George H. Ellis*

INTRODUCTION

Since the great depression of the 1930's New Englanders have paid increasing attention to the taxing and spending operations of the Federal Government. They have come to realize that the fiscal activities of the Federal Government not only may redistribute incomes but also strengthen or weaken a region's ability to raise its own income. New England's great dependence on other areas of the country for most of its foodstuffs, raw materials, and markets makes it especially sensitive to both the direct and indirect impact of federal fiscal operations. Increasing awareness of that sensitivity results in more interest in New England's financial relations with the Federal Government.

The combined effects of two world wars and the depression of the thirties shifted the major economic impact of government fiscal activities from state and local governments to the Federal Government. Taxing, borrowing, and spending all advanced much more rapidly at the federal level. Local taxes alone exceeded federal taxes in most every year until 1938. Even up to 1942 combined state and local taxes exceeded total federal taxes. Since 1942, however, the picture has greatly changed and federal taxation now far outweighs state and local taxation.

Practically the same changes occurred in government debt. For a time following the first World War, federal debt exceeded that of the states and localities combined, but during most of the interwar period it was less than the state and local total. By the end of World War II the federal debt clearly dominated. It became about nine and one-half times as large as the total debt of state and local governments combined.

Increased borrowing and taxation have made possible an enormous increase in federal spending. During the 1946–50 postwar years federal expenditures averaged $42.8 billion annually, and during the Korean War they increased to even higher levels. In the prewar years 1935–40 the comparable average was $7.9 billion annually. Clearly the Federal Government is the biggest single spending unit in the economy today, and the effects of its financial operations are inevitably widespread.

The current high level of federal expenditures is not so much a result of present-day philosophy as of the kind of expenditures which have to be made. War outlays, defense and defense-related expenditures must, by their very nature, be large. These outlays have immediate and impressive effects on the economy. For instance, about half the increase in value of our national output since the Korean War started (June 1950) has been accounted for by direct federal defense spending. In the year 1951 the entire rise in federal budget expenditures over 1950 was the result of the increase in defense outlays.

The pre-World War II level of expenditures was related to the "ordinary" business of government and to the newer programs related to the depression. Even though the major portions of federal outlays at present are the results of defense activities, it is well to remember that the absolute level of expenditures for nondefense activities, such as social security, has also increased greatly, although the proportion of expenditures in these categories has fallen. Government financial activities attract special attention because of the power of government to direct collections and make expenditures primarily according to social rather than economic considerations. It is important that the economic impact of federal programs be carefully evaluated.

The revolutionary change in the relative importance of federal expenditures has helped both to solve and to create problems within the American economy. The effects of federal taxing and spending, while felt in some degree by every economic unit within the economy, have been uneven and unpredictable. Accident rather than design has been responsible for much of this. The purpose of this report is to evaluate the major effects of federal financial activities on the New England economy and to see what changes in federal fiscal policies would aid New England's economic development.

TREASURY AND PRIVATE COMMERCIAL AND FINANCIAL INTERREGIONAL FLOWS OF FUNDS

Federal Government transactions set up huge two-way flows of funds which span the nation and have varying effects from region to region.[1] If the Federal Government spends more than it receives in a given Federal Reserve district, it must transfer funds from those districts where it has an excess of receipts over expenditures. Gains in funds on treasury account affect the credit superstructure of a district in much the same way as the importation or production of an equivalent amount of gold. The funds may be used to expand credit or reduce commercial bank borrowing at the Reserve Bank. In the long run, additions to funds stimulate economic development and lead to increased trading with other areas.

"An excess of federal receipts over expenditures and net treasury transfers of funds out of a district have the opposite effect. A loss in funds may lead to increased borrowing by member banks at the Reserve Bank, or to the

1. For additional information on this subject see the selected references listed at the end of this report.

sale of investments, or the reduction of commercial loans. When an individual or corporation pays federal taxes, commercial bank deposits are reduced and the Treasurer's account at the Reserve Bank is increased by the same amount. The member bank's reserve account is decreased in the process. If the government elects to transfer the funds elsewhere and not return them to the district in the form of expenditures and thus restore the reserve funds which had been withdrawn when the taxes were paid, the banking system must make adjustments to compensate for the loss. The net loss of funds on treasury account may be offset, however, by gains in payments on private account arising from transactions in goods or services which will enable the district to maintain a *status quo*." [2]

Some Federal Reserve districts are predominantly industrial while others are mainly agricultural. The different economic structures of the twelve districts cause regional trade and a net movement of funds from one district to another. The movements may be largely seasonal or they may represent longer term adjustments in the regional balance of payments. Shifts in agricultural prices and production in relation to industrial production can cause a net movement of funds from one district to another as do the different seasonal changes in production and the relatively greater seasonal swings in agricultural marketings. The districts which contain money markets with security exchanges and investment banking houses at times attract large amounts of short-term balances and at other times lose them. For instance, bankers' balances (funds due to domestic banks on demand) on the books of the New York City banks have comprised as much as 24% of the total deposits at times. Business funds are raised and accumulated in the financial centers and later transferred in substantial amounts to production areas. Also, at some periods credit expansion supporting economic expansion has proceeded more rapidly in some areas than in others, and the expanding areas presumably tend to lose funds. Some districts are net savings (capital export) areas and others are net investment (capital import) areas. And as World War II and the period of the 1930's has shown dramatically, the government spends its funds in a far different geographical pattern from that by which it raises them through taxes or borrowing.

A precise determination of the components of the interdistrict movement of funds is hampered by the inability to separate trade payments from capital payments. Nor can trade payments be divided into commercial, agricultural, or industrial transactions. It is possible, however, to determine the movements of gold and currency, Treasury transactions, and total commercial and financial payments on private account. Details of the movements of funds on these accounts are shown in Table 16–1 for the years 1934–53.

During the 16 years 1934–49 New England experienced an inflow of funds through private commercial and financial transactions and an outflow of

2. Federal Reserve Bank of Boston, "Federal Receipts and Expenditures in New England—Their Growth and Significance," *Monthly Review* (August 1950), p. 2.

funds through Treasury transactions.[3] In general, the area experienced a net gain except in the recession years 1937 and 1949. Federal Reserve districts in the South, West, and Far West had an opposite movement of funds—a loss of private commercial and financial clearings and a gain from Treasury transactions and a net loss except in 1937 and 1949.

Table 16–1. Gains (+) and Losses (−) of Funds through Treasury and
Private Transactions, First Federal Reserve District, 1934–53
(millions of dollars)

YEAR	TREASURY TRANSACTIONS	PRIVATE COMMERCIAL AND FINANCIAL TRANSACTIONS*	TOTAL GAIN OR LOSS OF FUNDS†
1934	−101.2	+216.9	+115.7
1935	−26.0	+173.3	+147.3
1936	−110.0	+164.4	+54.4
1937	−214.0	+163.9	−50.1
1938	−8.0	+158.1	+150.1
1939	−70.0	+266.2	+196.2
1940	−158.3	+358.7	+200.4
1941	−372.2	+440.9	+68.7
1942	−971.0	+1,247.7	+276.7
1943	−2,116.5	+2,206.6	+90.1
1944	−1,613.9	+1,872.9	+259.0
1945	−1,970.2	+2,166.2	+198.0
1946	−1,181.7	+1,200.3	+18.6
1947	−796.3	+893.8	+97.5
1948	−750.0	+759.2	+9.2
1949	−218.7	+45.6	−173.1
1950	+62.3	−38.2	+24.1
1951	+316.5	−281.5	+80.0
1952	+252.1	−193.0	+59.1
1953	+227.3	−207.7	+19.6

* Including the movement of Federal Reserve notes.
† Excluding inter-Reserve Bank transactions on open market and foreign account.
Source: Federal Reserve Bank of Boston

With the coming of World War II the movement of funds among regions increased and changed. The main factors in the change were the development of defense industry, with consequent restriction of peacetime activities and the large growth in government receipts and expenditures. Some areas experienced greatly increased economic activity through the development of defense industry while in others, such as New England, the expansion of production was relatively less. Funds were raised in the financial centers and spent in the important war production areas. Interior banks also drew upon their accounts in money centers to finance the credit needs of defense industries and to buy government securities. In most districts gains or losses from private commercial and financial activities and from transactions on Treas-

3. This was also true of the period 1919–34. See Beckhart, B. H., *The New York Money Market* (Columbia University Press, 1932), Vol. 2, chap. 17.

ury account were greatly increased, and the net movement of funds between districts was larger. New England continued to gain more from private commercial and financial clearings than was lost on Treasury transactions, but the gains were not as great relatively as those experienced by some other districts. In general, the districts which gained on government transactions had the largest net gains.

Usually the districts which lost through Treasury transactions gained through private clearings and conversely. This relation was in part causal. The financial centers supported Treasury financing, and Treasury expenditures transferred the funds to defense production areas. As the war contractors met their obligations with funds received from the Treasury, the funds were dispersed through private clearings. Profits and unused balances were returned to the financial centers, causing an inflow of financial funds through private channels. The districts which gained from Treasury transactions, i.e. those districts where the Treasury spent more than it received, were those in which war production was important. In some of these areas only small amounts of funds available for investment were invested directly in government securities and most were sent to financial centers to be held or invested.

The New York district has consistently proved to be an exception to these generalizations. During the period 1934–40 the region sustained a net loss of funds from private clearings and Treasury transfers combined. Sometimes the loss arose from private clearings and sometimes from Treasury transfers. During the war years the net loss continued and the losses on Treasury transfers were particularly large. The New York market participated heavily in war financing; receipts were greater than expenditures and transfers were made elsewhere. The movement of bankers' balances also affected New York's position. In 1941 and the war years, as excess reserves of the interior banks declined and as these institutions found employment for their funds in loans to war industries and in purchase of United States securities, they drew down their balances in New York.

New York also lost funds on business transactions during most war years, as Allied governments which had funds in New York transferred them to interior sections for payments for war goods. Our own defense program also caused a shift. This came about not only because corporations used their idle balances on the books of New York banks to increase inventories and expand plant elsewhere but also because of the withdrawal of the proceeds of loans obtained from New York City banks. Throughout the postwar period New York has shown a varying position, losing sometimes from private clearings and sometimes from Treasury transactions.

In the case of New York, it is particularly important that the net domestic movement of funds be considered in connection with foreign gold imports and exports, as gold movements at times have determined net loss or gain of reserves to the district. The large commercial banks in New York City are intermediaries between various parts of the United States and all sections of the United States and abroad.

In the postwar years 1946–50 New England continued to lose funds as a result of Treasury transactions and to gain in private commercial and financial clearings. The net gains, however, were smaller than during the war. A net loss was shown in the recession year 1949. The change in the postwar period reflected the postwar adjustments of the economic relations of the different regions, i.e. the shift of resources from defense to private use, and suggests that the war period brought about a distinct change in New England's economic relations with other areas.

With the outbreak of war in Korea in June 1950 and the accompanying expansion of the defense program, the New England area for the first time experienced a small inflow of funds on Treasury transactions and showed a loss on private commercial and financial clearings. On balance there was a net gain, but it was lower than previous gains. In part the inflow of funds from Treasury transactions represented larger expenditures within the district for purchases of goods and services, but it also represented substantially larger transactions on debt redemption. Insurance companies and other institutional lenders redeemed government securities and used the proceeds to make investments in industry and to acquire residential mortgages. The introduction of the wire transfer of longer term government securities in 1948 tended to reduce the amounts of securities held in custody accounts in New York City. Interest payments and redemptions tended to increase at other reserve banks. Gains on Treasury account continued to be shown through 1953.

In the future, several important factors will influence the movement of funds. The movement of Treasury funds, now such an important factor in interdistrict settlements, will taper off as the defense program levels off or is reduced. A large part of these funds has been obtained by expansion of the public debt, as has been indicated. When the expansion of the public debt slows down or stops, the outflow of funds through Treasury action from the financial centers will at least diminish. As defense financing is replaced by financing with private debt, the funds will probably still be raised in the money markets. At the present time, funds are tending to flow to the important peacetime rather than to defense production centers except insofar as the war and defense-related activities have caused changes in the basic economic relationships of the areas involved. Although New England's relative position in the economic structure of the nation has been lessened in importance as a result of war and its aftermath, the area will probably continue to experience small net gains in payments resulting from transactions with other areas because the nation continues to demand its products. Further loss of competitive position, however, seems likely to bring about an actual net loss of funds. Federal expenditures will continue to be an important part of total expenditures in the economy and will bear importantly on any region's balance of payments. They may prove to be of special interest to New England.

New England has been and still is a high-income region, but more rapid growth of income elsewhere in the nation is indicative of the growing competition and changing trade relationships which New England faces. Alterations in government money flows have much to do with the whole set of conditions which determine whether or not a region can maintain a favorable balance of payments with other regions. This is not to say that government transfers *determine* whether a given region can pay for what it purchases outside, though this becomes more of a possibility as government spending takes a larger and larger share of the national product. However, the influence of federal taxing and spending is great enough today to alter the economic relationships between regions. Government transactions may speed up or retard the changes in regional growth, production, population shifts, and disposable income, which are always taking place in a dynamic economy. This is especially true when the government's actions are the result of a war economy where the type and tempo of economic adjustment may be radically altered from that of peacetime.

FEDERAL ACTIONS AND NEW ENGLAND'S FUTURE

New England is, for the United States, an old region. Age has brought its problems, paramount among them the economic problems of changing productive and competitive relationships. But age also brings its graces. Social maturity is one of them. In exercise of that maturity New England has not gone out of its way to seek federal aid, nor has it in the past followed narrow sectionalism with respect to federal spending in other regions. At present New England must be aware of the real danger that in attempting to solve economic problems she will demand actions which are not in the national interest. Solutions to New England's economic problems may be advanced for political motives, for motives of personal gain, or for narrow interests rather than for the wider interests which must be considered in any measures involving the federal taxing and spending power.

Regional needs must always be placed below, not above, national needs. New England, the South, the West, in fact, every region must recognize that its prosperity is dependent on prosperity in other areas. Each region can legitimately ask from the Federal Government only that which will help the nation. In turn, each region can legitimately expect that the national interest in each federal program will be measured in terms of its total effect on both the newer and older regions. Obviously, it is a problem in economic welfare whether advantages to one area overbalance disadvantages to another. It is equally obvious that the problem must be approached from the viewpoint of the national interest. Narrow sectionalism will not supply the answer.

We must consider also that a region is not an homogeneous economic unit in every sense. For example, New England woolen and worsted manufacturers have much more in common with the national woolen industry than they do with other New England industries. Thus Federal Government action which might benefit one section of the region's population or businesses might harm another section's interest. We must think then in terms of the dominant interests in New England when we advocate changes in federal-New England relationships, always keeping in mind the overriding national interest insofar as we are able to perceive it.

Federal Spending

It is evident that the major part of the federal budget is devoted to purposes which concern *national* rather than *regional* interests. Defense spending is allocated 59% of the fiscal 1954 budget, with funds for international security and foreign relations adding another 10%. The funds which go directly to states or individuals or which are expended by the Federal Government specifically for some given area (e.g. a harbor improvement or flood control) account for a small portion of the budget. Of the programs whose spending is directed toward specific groups, those for veterans and agriculture are the largest. The percentages of the budget devoted to these objectives are not expected to alter greatly over the next few years. *It is evident, then, that the relatively inelastic federal budget is not easily amenable to any changes that can directly benefit any one area.* What of the federal spending which is directed to given areas or individuals?

Federal Aid. The research staff has made some comparisons of federal aids to states and individuals and has computed some indexes of economic ability in order to measure the impact of the various programs by states.[4] Indexes of federal aid were calculated for the 48 states for the years 1941 and 1949. These indexes measure the total financial aid received by state and local units and by individuals in the states from the Federal Government. Average per capita aid grew from $24.73 in 1941 to $36.44 in 1949, but its increase was less than the increases in both wholesale and consumers' prices over the period.

One of the purposes of federal aid, ostensibly, is the equalization of certain public services, and one would suppose that states with low economic ability would typically receive high federal aid relative to the United States average.

4. For a description of the indexes and methods of computation, see our Staff Memorandum No. 8, *Interstate Comparisons of State and Local Tax Burdens and Federal Aid, 1941 and 1949,* August 1952.

To test this hypothesis indexes of state economic ability as measured by per capita income, output, and retail sales were calculated for each of the 48 states for 1941 and 1949. Charts 16–1 and 16–2 show the relationship between federal aid and economic ability for the various states. The charts indicate clearly that there is little general correlation between economic ability and federal aid.

Even the part of federal aid paid to the states does not often depend on formulae which consider economic ability. For the most part, the grants to states are determined on the basis of population, on the basis of fixed payments, on the basis of a matching of funds, or by a combination of these methods. Only a very few aid programs consider the ability of the state to support the service. And most of them require the matching of funds, even if the apportionment of total funds depends in part on some ability measure such as per capita income or "financial need." *On the whole, the easiest way for a state to get more money from the Federal Government is for the state to spend more of its own money.*

The largest part of federal aid payments is still in the form of payments to individuals, though the monies paid directly to state and local governments have been rising rapidly in recent years. For the period 1934–51 about $16 billion were paid to state and local governments, while over $42 billion were paid to individuals. During the period 1946–51, however, the $10 billion paid to governments approached the $14 billion disbursed to individuals. Table 16–2 presents the totals for these and other periods, as well as the principal types of payments to each group.

By far the largest payments to state and local governments have been for old-age assistance and for roads and highways. That was true for both the years before 1946 and for the postwar period. Other welfare type programs, such as aid to dependent children, absorbed most of the other federal grants to states and local governments.

During the depression and early war years, WPA and the other major federal relief expenditures accounted for a very large portion of total payments to individuals, but since World War II veterans' benefits have replaced relief programs as the largest single item. Veterans' benefits and agricultural adjustment payments have absorbed almost 95% of the disbursements to individuals since the end of World War II. The greater part of the funds expended under the programs have been for World War II veterans under the terms of the Servicemen's Readjustment Act of 1944 and the Vocational Rehabilitation Act of 1943. They covered the cost of subsistence, tuition, supplies and equipment for courses in training, payments of readjustment unemployment and self-employment allowances, and vocational rehabilitation for disabled veterans. The importance of New England educational institutions to this flow of funds is evident.

Over the 18-year period, the Veterans' Administration and the Department of Agriculture were the largest disbursers of grants and aid. Next in

CHART 16–1

Relation between Federal Aid and Economic Ability, All States, 1941
(United States average = 100)

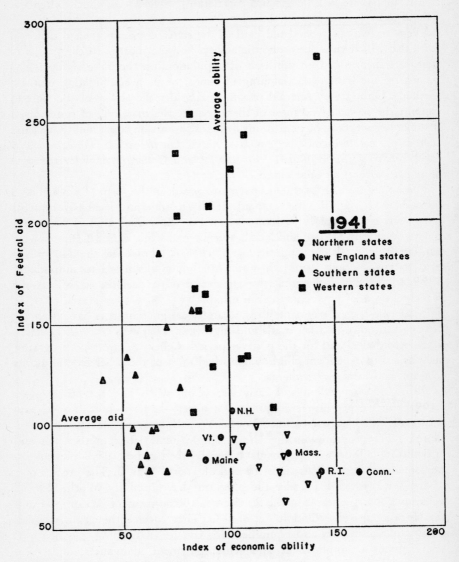

CHART 16-2

Relation between Federal Aid and Economic Ability, All States, 1949
(United States average = 100)

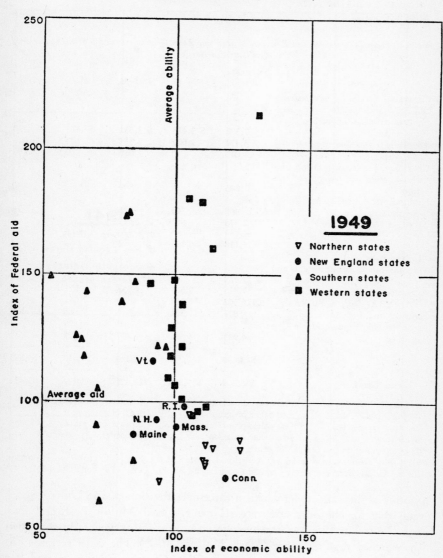

Source: Ibid.

order were the Federal Security Agency, the Federal Works Agency, and the Works Projects Administration. In the two largest items of expenditure and several others, the funds spent were disbursed largely without regard to the economic ability of the states, and economic ability was only one determinant for all the rest.

While for the 48 states as a whole there is little or no correlation between

Table 16–2. *Federal Grants and Aid Payments to State and Local Governments and Individuals, 1934–51 (millions of dollars)*

PROGRAM	TOTAL 1934–51	1934–45	1946–51	1941	1949
To STATE AND LOCAL GOVERNMENTS					
Old-age assistance (including payments to states under Social Security Act)	$ 7,308	$ 3,418	$ 3,891	$ 415	$ 718
Roads and highways (all programs)	3,472	1,607	1,865	174	416
Aid to dependent children	1,010	0	1,010	0	189
Unemployment compensation and Employment Service Administration	885	76	809	k	140
National school milk and lunch program	468	43	425	0	74
All other	2,975[a]	963[b]	2,012[c]	75[d]	320[e]
	$16,118	$6,106	$10,012	$ 664	$1,857
To INDIVIDUALS					
Veterans' readjustment benefits and vocational rehabilitation	11,759	0	11,759	0	3,297
Agricultural adjustment program	7,416	5,564	1,852	721	202
WPA, FERA, CCC, and CWA	16,362	16,362	0	1,541	0
National guard	871	331	541	66	115
Farm Security Administration	758	758	0	58	0
All other	4,923[f]	4,686[g]	237[h]	425[i]	22[j]
TOTAL	$42,090	$27,702	$14,389	$2,812	$3,637
GRAND TOTAL	$58,209	$33,808	$24,401	$3,476	$5,494

Note: Details may not add to totals because of rounding.
  [a] 73 other programs.   [e] 40 other programs.   [i] 9 other programs.
  [b] 38 other programs.   [f] 37 other programs.   [j] 6 other programs.
  [c] 55 other programs.   [g] 26 other programs.   [k] not separately reported.
  [d] 17 other programs.   [h] 24 other programs.
Source: *Federal Grants-in-Aid to States*, Additional Report of the Joint Committee on Reduction of Nonessential Federal Expenditures, 82d Congress, 2d Session, Senate Document No. 101, 1952

economic ability and federal aid, a three-part division of the United States reveals that for the northern states (New England, Middle East, and East North Central sections) above-average economic ability generally coincided with below-average aid. (See Charts 16–1 and 16–2.) The other sections did not show such a consistent pattern. The West Central, Northwest, and Far West showed a peculiar benefit-ability relationship. For both 1941 and 1949 the aid in these states tended to be above average, whether or not economic ability was high or low. For the southern group of states (Southeast and

Southwest) the relationship was haphazard. While all of the southern states were below average in economic ability during both periods, some received above-average aid and some below-average.

In each period only one northern state received above-average aid. None of the western group received below-average aid in 1941, and only three of the 16 received below-average aid in 1949, even though 12 were above average in economic ability. In 1941 most of the highest per capita aid payments were made to the western states. By 1949 the dispersion among all the states was reduced somewhat, and a few southern states entered the high-payments group. The western states moved toward the average, even though they were for the most part still well above average in their aid receipts. By 1949, 13 of the 16 southern states were in the above-average aid group. The northern states, however, showed no change in pattern.

A summary of this interesting pattern is given in Table 16–3. Especially noticeable is the increase in economic ability in the western states without much decrease in aid. For the northern states there was a slight relative change downward in ability but no relative change in aid. Fifteen of the 16 northern states still received below-average aid.

Are there reasons for the great differences in the aid indexes? Any index of this type is a mixture of many elements, and it is necessary to examine those which may push the index up or down. As an aid to evaluation and interpretation of the data, we have taken five states with high aid indexes in 1949 and five with low aid indexes in the same year and have computed the per capita amounts received for eight specific aid programs. Seven of these eight programs account for the greater part of the monies received in all states under federal aid. A large difference from one state to another in per capita aid under any one of them could produce a significant difference between the total aid indexes of the two states.

Differences in the amounts granted under certain of the programs are large. For example, the agricultural states receive large per capita payments under the various farm programs. One of these items, the agricultural adjustment program, accounted for more than $7 billion of the slightly over $11 billion which the Department of Agriculture disbursed in aid during 1934–51. Payments under the program in Wyoming were $6.21 per capita. In New Jersey they were 13 cents. The *difference* between Wyoming and New Jersey in this payment alone was greater than the per capita *total* of five other important aids in New Jersey. The same situation obtains even between two agricultural states, for Virginia received only 99 cents per capita in fiscal 1949 under this program.

Veterans' rehabilitation and the old-age assistance programs showed like dissimilarities in payments. Old-age assistance programs vary greatly from state to state, and the benefits paid are a matter of state decision. The more a state is willing to spend, the more it will receive (up to a limit) from the Federal Government.

Highway aid is another example of interstate disparity which is dependent upon the willingness of a state to spend its own money. Grants are based on a formula which depends upon the miles of various kinds of highways in the state, with the state matching federal funds up to the allocated amount. Though the state need not claim all the money available during a given year, the more it spends the more it usually receives in federal funds. Thus Nevada obtained $27.42 per capita in aid under Public Roads Administration highway grants during 1949 as compared to New York's $1.10. Nevada's per capita highway grants alone approximated *all* of New York's federal grants per person during this particular year.

Table 16–3. Federal Aid Received in States and Economic Ability, by Number of States, 1941 and 1949

AREA	FEDERAL AID		ECONOMIC ABILITY	
	ABOVE AVERAGE	BELOW AVERAGE	ABOVE AVERAGE	BELOW AVERAGE
		1941		
Western	16	0	6	10
Southern	7	9	0	16
Northern	1	15	14	2
		1949		
Western	13	3	12	4
Southern	13	3	0	16
Northern	1	15	12	4

Source: Staff Memorandum No. 8

These examples have been given as an aid in explaining the dispersion in the federal aid indexes. Table 16–4 presents the detailed figures for these ten states. One of the difficulties which such comparisons point up is the inadequacy of per capita measures, but the disparities in aid are not any less real because of this.

Differences in aid, fair or unfair as they may seem, are not easily amenable to change. The basic orientation of federal aid programs seems to be toward *benefits,* without the compensating qualification of need for the benefits. So long as aids are for the most part conditioned upon lump sum payments, population, population ratios, matching of state funds, state laws and the like, the difference in per capita payments will be perpetuated.

Such a system tends toward rigidity. To be flexible, changing needs and changing abilities would have to be considered. To obtain flexibility, however, administrative discretion would have to be increased, and the Congress has always been hesitant to loosen its control of expenditures in this way.

Other Federal Spending. Some types of federal spending are in part controllable and amenable to action on the regional or local level. The greatest part of public spending is not, except insofar as sectional interests are able to promote special projects or developments, or are able to attract to a given location some federal installation. Otherwise, the government buys its materials where it can obtain them most inexpensively and locates

Table 16–4. Per Capita Federal Aid Payments for Major Programs, 10 Selected States, 1949

PROGRAM	FIVE HIGH-AID STATES					FIVE LOW-AID STATES				
	COLORADO	GEORGIA	LOUISIANA	NEVADA	WYOMING	CONNECTICUT	MARYLAND	NEW JERSEY	NEW YORK	VIRGINIA
Agricultural adjustment program	$ 4.24	$ 1.80	$ 3.71	$ 0.81	$ 6.21	$ 0.18	$ 0.44	$ 0.13	$ 0.32	$ 0.99
National school milk and lunch program	0.44	0.91	0.84	0.32	0.57	0.30	0.34	0.27	0.28	0.56
Payments from receipts under Mineral Leasing Act	0.97	—	*	0.05	12.28	—	—	—	—	—
Veterans' readjustment benefits and vocational rehabilitation										
Old-age assistance	32.10	24.01	29.46	12.37	18.04	17.35	14.31	15.15	19.36	14.68
Aid to dependent children	12.40	4.85	14.09	5.14	5.03	2.43	1.36	1.48	2.51	0.98
Aid to the blind	1.69	1.01	2.78	—	0.71	0.59	1.07	0.44	1.33	0.66
Unemployment Compensation and Employment Service Administration	0.83	0.60	0.70	2.90	1.36	1.20	1.06	1.20	1.26	0.48
Public Roads Administration highways	7.69	3.03	1.81	27.42	19.07	1.59	1.70	2.26	1.10	1.44
All other	5.20	6.83	9.81	15.99	14.35	1.91	4.70	2.49	1.54	2.36
TOTAL	$65.56	$43.04	$63.20	$65.00	$77.62	$25.55	$24.98	$23.42	$27.70	$22.15

* Less than one cent.

Source: Federal Grants-in-Aid to States

its facilities where they can be most efficiently used. This is not always so, because intentions are not always fulfilled, but we are not of the opinion that inefficiency predominates. Indeed, much inefficiency is avoided by not yielding to the many pleas for sectional favors.

During and since World War II the greatest part of federal spending has been for the purchase of goods and services rather than transfers or grants. Thus, if the region wishes to derive more income from the Federal Government, its primary step must be to sell more goods and services to the Federal Government. The major problems which arise are easily discernible. They revolve around our competitive abilities, our resources, and our products. Do we manufacture what the government needs? Can we meet competition? Here we are faced with the same problems as exist in the private sphere of the economy. But there are added difficulties.

Many government purchases are made in industries in which New England is not well represented, for example the airframe and motor industries. The airframe industry has shifted westward since 1940, and suppliers in the region have been put at a greater disadvantage. But as aircraft become more complicated and use more and more electronic equipment, New England may gain. The region does not have much of the kind of heavy machinery and equipment manufacturing which the government demands for defense purposes, however. It must depend on selling its lighter, more highly specialized durable goods, or nondurables. In the latter, however, the region faces more competition. The textile and shoe industries are highly competitive as compared to the aircraft industry. Furthermore, the region does not have the type of natural resources to be exploited by the government. Less rather than more federal spending might help instead of hinder New England because much of the war-created industry, growing more rapidly outside New England, remains to be peacetime competitors, often with better buildings and equipment which have been obtained at less than original costs. In peacetime there is less opportunity for such devices as accelerated depreciation which tend to place New England at a disadvantage.[5]

War and defense spending speed up the differential rates of growth between New England and the newer regions. A reduction of such spending would be to the former's advantage even though it might get a smaller *proportion* of the remaining government business. Its tax liabilities would fall in even greater proportion, and the long-run benefits would be larger. Within the foreseeable future major reductions in defense spending do not appear likely. Thus, if New England is to maintain its position, it must obtain a greater share of defense spending. That is a task for its more efficient and enterprising businessmen.

Aside from war or defense spending and the purchases by the Federal Government in more normal periods, there remains another major category

5. See our report No. 11, "New England's Financial Resources and Their Use," pp. 431–433.

of federal expenditures to be discussed. These expenditures have to do with specific federal programs such as farm price supports, river developments, development of underdeveloped areas, and the like. Some of these programs have had a direct adverse effect on New England's competitive position.

Federal farm programs have had three general objectives which varied in emphasis in changing conditions. During periods requiring abundant food supplies, such as those during and after World War II, the major objective was to stimulate farm production. During the great depression the major objective was to raise farm incomes rather than farm production. A third objective has been to reduce the instability of farm income. New England's direct gains from the federal farm support program have been relatively slight, because agriculture plays such a small role in the region and also because New England agricultural products have not been those receiving the greatest attention in support programs.

Undoubtedly the federal farm programs have operated to support farmers' incomes and thereby expand part of the market for New England's manufactured products. In general, however, New England's markets are primarily in the industrial Northeast rather than in the dominantly farm states. On the other hand, the federal farm programs have raised the cost of foodstuffs the region consumes and raised the cost of raw materials used by New England manufacturers. Furthermore, some of the federal farm programs have altered marketing or commercial relationships to the region's disadvantage. The guaranteed price aspects of the wool program had the effect of lowering requirements of financial responsibility for wool brokers to engage in the trade and encouraged the establishment of wool brokers in competition with established New England firms. The potato price support program had the effect of supporting the expansion of potato production outside New England and divorcing New England potato producers from their normal marketing channels. On balance, the region's competitive position seems to have been adversely affected by the federal farm programs.

Federal river basin and other development programs in the South and West build markets for those New England manufactured products which are required to industrialize the underdeveloped areas. Those programs contribute indirectly over the years by building consumer markets for both New England products and the products of New England's industrial customers. Evidently the growth of New England customers in the South and West has been very limited, however. The research staff studies of rail shipments in 1949 indicate that approximately 80% of all New England rail shipments go to the eight states in the Middle Atlantic and Great Lakes regions. Only two per cent of the region's rail shipments go to the southeastern states, and less than 10% ever crosses the Mississippi.[6] It is

6. See our Staff Memorandum No. 1, *Origins and Destinations of New England's Rail Traffic, 1949*, March 1952.

apparent that the federal development programs also contribute to the growth of New England competitors and stimulate further movement of the nation's markets away from New England. In the long run the very success of the federal development programs tends to weaken the competitive positions of the areas which were called upon to support those programs.

The Committee does not wish to leave the impression that it is against all federal programs. What it does object to is programs which are narrow in their benefits, supporting particular groups. The wool and silver interests are examples of small groups whose support is unwarranted. Support for education, on the other hand, is the kind of support from which all groups in the economy can benefit. A reduction of the federal budget in those sectors where the benefits are narrow in favor of improvements in those sectors where the benefits are widely dispersed and multiplied will increase and support the general welfare.

New England's "Share." It is often said that New England is not "receiving its share of federal expenditures." This report has attempted to throw some light on the meaning of that phrase. It is a nebulous concept at best and threatens to become a fiscal cliché. If New England is to receive a greater share of federal purchases, its businesses will have to compete for that share by making the products the government needs. In many fields New England businesses are doing just that. If the New England state and local governments want a greater share of grants-in-aid, they can, within limits, obtain a larger share by spending more of their own funds, as we have explained. New England can also obtain a greater share of federal funds if certain federal programs, which at present benefit other regions, are reduced or eliminated. The best example here would be the price support programs for agriculture. The region can do little more than this without falling into the error of thinking of itself without regard to the national good and asking special favors. If, however, Federal Government actions continue to favor special interests which are in a minority in New England but powerful elsewhere, then it will be more difficult for the people of New England to continue to be unselfish.*

* *Dissenting Opinion by Committee member.* There is little evidence that other regions avoid seeking federal aid which might not be in the national interest. There is evidence that individuals, businesses, and areas of other regions do benefit, often at New England's expense, from the impact of federal taxing and spending policies of recent years.

If we accept the finding that other sections of the country are better equipped to exploit the advantages of heavy industry and their tie-ins with the extractive industries, if we acknowledge the greater proportion of aid going to sections which are primarily agricultural, if we recognize the combined effect of government water power and regional developments such as TVA, which are sometimes coupled with tax exemptions by local governments to set up low-cost competition for New England—if we accept all of the foregoing, should not this region seek out other types of federal spending, assistance, or tax advantage to improve its relative position?

New England businessmen, state and local governments, and educational and research institutions as well as other organizations should seek out and participate in those federal programs which would bring New England more into balance with other regions in terms of federal spending. Urban redevelopment, better schools, improved highways and hospitals can all be obtained by more participation in federal programs.

The Federal Government should feel some responsibility for a decrease in one region's income and employment resulting from some federal action designed to increase the income and employment of other regions. The welfare effects of the TVA, for instance, should not be measured simply by the increases in income and employment which that project has brought to the Tennessee Valley area and elsewhere. From these benefits should be subtracted the costs to older areas in employment and income occasioned by the transfer of businesses out of the older regions as a result of federal actions. Some attempt should be made to assess these costs and to help in the rehabilitation of those who are left behind. The government should also assist unemployed workers who wish to move to areas of growing employment.[7]

Federal Taxation

New England's aggregate tax payments have been discussed. In this section a brief review of certain effects of federal taxation is made with a view toward suggesting improvements in the federal tax structure which may benefit an older economic area in transition.

In its report on the financial resources of New England the Committee has made some suggestions regarding alteration of depreciation allowances, "double taxation" of dividends, carry-over of losses, taxation of capital gains, and rates of taxation on smaller businesses.[8] Other operations of the Federal Government which affect the financial structure of the region are also discussed in that report. On the whole, New England has made less use of these programs than other areas, and many federal lending programs were and are more helpful to other regions.

The federal tax structure has often been criticized for being too heavy a burden on the economy. However heavy the burden may be, it is obvious that in spite of the taxes, national income is very high. Part of present prosperity undoubtedly rests on the artificial base of past deficits and the present unbalanced budget. We have pointed out the difficulties in reducing taxation under our present obligations. Reduction of expenditures should come first, but an increase in debt often appears to be the easier path. As a region, New England tends to hold more debt obligations per capita than many other areas. Thus inflation, by reducing the real value of these obligations, is especially harmful to the region. New England frugality does

---

Still observing and advancing the national interests, New England's congressional delegation should marshal its support for federal programs which will be of particular importance to the region. Federal action in building up port facilities, eliminating rail rate discriminations favoring other regions, developing atomic power in New England, stimulating trade with the Maritime Provinces, supporting the region's research facilities, and establishing historical shrines for the nation's vacationers to visit in New England are all examples of projects worthy of both regional and national support.—Harold D. Hodgkinson.

7. See our report No. 8, "Employment Fluctuations in New England," pp. 323–326.
8. *Ibid.*

not pay under some circumstances, and this is one. If the people of New England inveigh against federal debt creation during prosperous times, they will be doing themselves as well as the nation a service.

On the other hand, prosperity in New England depends on prosperity in the nation. If it is necessary to have unbalanced budgets for a period in order to preserve a high level of employment, the region should favor such a course. In times of full employment, however, fiscal prudence demands balanced budgets or budget surpluses. Federal taxation may then have to be higher rather than lower. In actual practice, deliberate political action to achieve substantial budget surpluses during full-employment periods has not been consummated. The goals of full employment and high income are still desirable, however, and the people of New England should continue to support soundly conceived countercyclical fiscal policies.

Within this context much can be done to improve federal taxation. Many tax loopholes, which allow certain business operations to discriminate against older areas, should be closed. Principal among these is the exemption of state and local bonds from federal taxation, which makes possible municipal construction of tax-free plants for business firms which may be leased at lower costs than plants financed in an orthodox manner. The "certificate of necessity" type of concession is another artificial inducement conducive to migration. Many firms took advantage of such certificates even though expansion would have taken place without them, but many others saw in this kind of an operation opportunity to build a plant for defense purposes which soon could be used for the firm's usual production. Such switching about of productive facilities is seldom made within a small area. The new plants are usually built in less developed areas, and the older, more highly developed area is left after a time with an outmoded plant and a pool of unemployed. Furthermore, the larger companies are in a much better position to take advantage of these arrangements than the small and new firms. In its urgency to build production facilities after Korea, the Federal Government may have been overly liberal in the granting of these certificates. Should the occasion for such an experiment again arise, the New England representatives in Congress should seek methods to prevent abuses of such arrangements rather than protest the results afterward.

The corporate tax laws also discriminate in favor of firms which are permitted depletion allowances. Thus, the extractive industries, such as the oil industries, benefit, and the burden of taxation falls more heavily on other firms. Regions with few mineral resources such as New England cannot claim large depletion allowances in calculating corporate tax liabilities and therefore tend to pay larger corporate taxes in relation to income than areas with extensive extractive industries such as the Southwest.

Federal-State-Local Taxation. Should the Federal Government tax more and increase its aid to state and local governments, or should it yield up some of its sources of revenue to the state governments, decrease the aid programs, and let the states carry out expanded programs? It can be argued that the Federal Government should increase taxes and return the revenues to the states for state use. This argument envisages a federal tax system which is more progressive than state tax systems and bears equally upon equals throughout the nation. Many students of taxation and tax adminstrators have advanced this as one possible solution to the inequities which exist under the present diversity of tax systems. On the other hand, there is a group which wholeheartedly advocates the opposite. They feel that the level of federal taxation is already too great, and envisage a tax system which is much less federal and much more state and local.

A program which is advanced and vigorously advocated in some quarters today is to release from federal taxation some of those sources of revenue which the state governments could use. In turn the state governments would carry out alone those programs which the Federal Government now administers in conjunction with state and local governments. The feeling seems to be that giving up programs on the federal level and returning them to the states will lower the federal budget, reduce administrative costs, and remove the Federal Government from some areas of public assistance, public works, and other public projects which it is believed are better administered on the state level. It has been found, however, that many of the federal programs now in existence are necessary and useful and were inaugurated because state and local governments did not have such programs and seemed to be making no efforts to place them in operation. Many of these programs were started during the depression years and by the late 1930's they had attained a stature and acceptance throughout the nation which ensured their continuance. Would the people give up these programs if the Federal Government did leave these areas for state and for local administration? This is a question which seems not to have been answered by many proponents of the plan for removing these areas of taxation from federal hands. If, however, the intention of the state government is to continue to carry out the programs as they are now established (or to improve upon them), it is not likely that the total cost of these programs would diminish to any appreciable extent. Some cost reductions might take place. Given the variability in resources and personnel, certainly in some states the quality of the programs would deteriorate.

Many government programs were established to help those areas which are unable to carry out the kinds of welfare, school, and other activities which it was felt every area should have. Of course, these programs have not worked out in such a manner as to equalize services among different communities and areas, for they were based mainly on a system of matching grants, as we have shown. It is not possible to conceive of a program which would accomplish this without considering much more directly the needs of different areas. With few exceptions, individual needs are only one of the determinants considered under the present system.

In the absence of federal fund-matching programs, states desiring to maintain their level of services would have to increase their total taxes if they benefited from previous distributions at the expense of other states. It seems hardly likely that much of a decrease in costs can be made through administrative reorganization when the greatest part of the total costs is nonadministrative. Under state sponsorship alone, it is quite obvious that in many states the level of services would be allowed to deteriorate and that the tax differential between the New England states (especially Massachusetts, Connecticut, and Rhode Island) and the southern states would only widen. In this case even louder voices would be raised about tax differentials.

If federal programs are eliminated because they are not useful the action is surely sound. But if the proponents of reduced federal spending are seeking only to lower taxes regardless of the benefits of the programs now in existence, then it is hardly arguable that the changes are meritorious. If the argument that tax differentials among the states are a cause of business relocation is at all valid, then it would follow that to shift the present programs from federal to state level would probably serve only to widen the differentials, and cause further movement of business from "high tax" to "low tax" areas.[9] Indeed, if this were the case, the solution would be to shift taxes from the state to the federal level, to increase federal taxation, and to decrease state and local taxes.

There are no universally valid criteria to determine whether or not federal taxing and spending should increase or decrease in relation to state and local fiscal actions. Whichever way the trend develops, the decision should be made on the basis of an evaluation of the usefulness of each project under consideration and the relative attractiveness of the most likely alternatives. Decisions to expand or contract the federal sphere of action should be carefully weighed in terms of their impacts on all areas of the nation.

FEDERAL RECEIPTS AND EXPENDITURES IN NEW ENGLAND

Much time and effort have been expended on the analysis of federal money transactions among the various states and regions. Usually the more important grants-in-aid and direct expenditures of the Federal Government have been studied, often in isolation from the government receipts derived from the areas under study. The analysis which follows attempts to consider all the major categories of expenditure made by the Federal Government in New England and to relate them to all the major categories of receipts by the Federal Government in the region. It is a continuation of

9. The differences would in part be compensated by the deductibility provisions in the federal tax law.

a similar study first made by the Federal Reserve Bank of Boston.[10] That study compared the three years 1929, 1940, and 1948. Our analysis includes the years 1950–52. Table 16–5 contains this information for the years 1940, 1948, and 1950–52.

Sources of Federal Revenue in New England

Tax receipts are the major source of federal revenue in New England as elsewhere. Personal income taxes account for over half of the tax receipts. In 1929 income taxes provided only about 41% of total tax receipts. Since that time total taxes have increased enormously, and the addition of payroll taxes to the list has made the more than 50% collected via personal income taxation more important than the percentage figure alone would imply. Corporate income taxes have increased in absolute terms but have decreased in relative importance since the twenties. Estate and gift taxes, customs duties, and miscellaneous taxes have likewise decreased in relative importance.

The Federal Government has a variety of other revenue sources, among the largest of which are postal revenues and unemployment trust fund deposits and veterans' insurance premiums. Only the major sources are shown in Table 16–5. Numerous minor sources are not important in this analysis.

The increasing scope of government programs is evidenced by the items given in Section B. Before the thirties Federal Deposit Insurance Corporation assessments and the like were unknown. Price support programs were absent. Since the war years, items bringing revenue to the Treasury such as veterans' premiums and surplus property sales have increased greatly. The latter, however, were insignificant by 1950.

Together these two classifications accounted for practically all the revenue flows into the Treasury account at the Federal Reserve Bank of Boston from the New England area. The exceptions are the net inflows from borrowing during the war years and Treasury transfers from other districts during the years 1950–52. (See Receipts F.)

During the period 1941–46 federal borrowing accounted for over half of total federal revenues. During this period commercial banks and the Federal Reserve banks supplied about $86 billion and nonbank investors about $128 billion of funds for federal use in financing the war. New England banks and private and institutional investors in furnishing part of this immense total of funds brought about a flow of funds which accounted for a large part of the Treasury outflow from the region during the war years. The payment of funds by the private sector to the Treasury account in the region was increased accordingly during that period. During the years

10. See "Federal Receipts and Expenditures in New England," *op. cit.*

1948–52 net debt repayment was the cause of large inflows to the region. They were especially heavy during 1951 and 1952.

It should be noted that Treasury transfers appeared as an inflow for the first time in 1950. Previously the flow was outward to other districts. (See Payments G.) Any decrease in the Treasury general account indicates that

Table 16–5. Receipts and Expenditures of the Federal Government in New England for the Calendar Years 1940, 1948, 1950, 1951, 1952
(millions of dollars)

FEDERAL CASH PAYMENTS IN NEW ENGLAND, BY MAJOR TRANSACTIONS

	1940	1948	1950	1951	1952
A. Direct Cash Payments for Goods and Services					
1. Payments to individuals for services					
a. Military	$ 28.0	$ 167.7	$ 187.5	$ 304.3	$ 367.9
b. Civilian wages and salaries (incl. P.O.)	123.1	273.1	297.7	387.5	450.8
c. Grants-in-aid for performance of special services	19.8	43.3	56.3	53.6	52.8
TOTAL A-1	$170.9	$ 484.1	$ 541.5	$ 745.4	$ 871.5
2. Payments to business					
Public works	$ 37.1	$ 106.0	$ 88.0	$ 250.0	$ 289.0
Other goods and services:					
a. Defense	118.0	200.8	381.5	870.0	1,210.8
b. Civilian	41.0	150.0	93.8	255.0	280.0
TOTAL A-2	$196.1	$ 456.8	$ 563.3	$1,375.0	$1,779.8
B. Transfer Payments to Individuals					
1. Social insurance and public assistance					
a. Federal employees retirement benefits	$ 6.4	$ 17.1	$ 21.5	$ 22.6	$ 25.6
b. Old age and disability benefit payments	3.7	58.5	96.9	182.8	208.7
c. Unemployment insurance benefit payments	51.4	90.0	137.2	89.3	100.8
d. Railroad retirement benefit payments	5.6	10.4	13.1	13.9	18.5
e. Grants-in-aid for public assistance	23.3	47.1	62.0	63.6	64.5
2. a. Readjustment benefits, pensions, and other payments to veterans	29.8	258.4	191.9	204.9	183.2
b. Veterans' NSLI dividend	—	—	217.0	34.0	19.6
c. USGLI and NSLI benefit payments	3.0	28.0	34.1	33.3	33.7
TOTAL B	$123.2	$ 509.5	$ 773.7	$ 644.4	$ 654.6
C. Interest Payments (Cash) to Individuals, Business, etc.	$ 58.6	$ 247.3	$ 210.5	$ 247.3	$ 239.3
D. Work Relief Programs CCC, WPA, NRA	102.6	—	—	—	—
E. Public Debt: net cash repayment	—	23.0	342.9	632.4	461.0
F. Loans, Investments, Subsidies, and other Transfers to Business and Agriculture					
1. Farmers					
a. CCC loans to agriculture	$ —	$ —	$ —	$ 2.5	$ 24.8
b. Price support, *net* (potatoes)	—	40.0	35.6	—	—
c. Other direct subsidies to farmers	6.7	4.8	5.6	4.0	3.7
2. Business					
a. Subsidy arising from postal deficit	2.2	19.8	39.6	30.0	50.0
b. Reimbursement of FRB Boston for fiscal agency and other expenses	—	1.0	0.9	1.0	1.1
TOTAL F	$ 8.9	$ 65.6	$ 81.7	$ 37.5	$ 79.6
G. Total Expenditures Accounted for, A-F	$660.3	$1,785.3	$2,513.6	$3,682.0	$4,085.8
H. Treasury General Account FRB Boston					
1. Increase in Treasury general account during the year	$ —	$ 19.0	$ 8.3	$ —	$ 40.2
2. Net Treasury transfers to other districts	170.0	760.0	—	—	—
TOTAL H	$170.0	$ 779.0	$ 8.3	$ —	$ 40.2
I. Total Expenditures Accounted for and Transfers to Other Districts (G and H)	$830.3	$2,564.3	$2,521.9	$3,682.0	$4,126.0
J. Federal Funds Spent in First District but Unaccounted For	$ 39.8	$ 56.8	$ 65.6	$ 180.6	$ 201.1
TOTAL PAYMENTS	$870.1	$2,621.1	$2,587.5	$3,862.6	$4,327.1

Table 16-5 (continued). Receipts and Expenditures of the Federal Government in New England
for the Calendar Years 1940, 1948, 1950, 1951, 1952
(millions of dollars)

FEDERAL CASH RECEIPTS IN NEW ENGLAND BY MAJOR SOURCE

	1940	1948	1950	1951	1952
A. Tax Receipts					
1. Individual income taxes	$104.9	$1,315.9	$1,328.3	$1,756.7	$2,052.6
2. Corporation income taxes	103.3	635.0	504.9	840.3	1,154.7
3. Payroll taxes	65.4	153.6	148.0	195.1	228.0
4. Miscellaneous taxes	111.2	310.2	299.2	328.3	341.1
5. Customs duties	68.4	62.8	87.0	97.7	89.7
TOTAL A	$453.2	$2,477.5	$2,367.4	$3,218.1	$3,866.1
B. Other Receipts					
1. Gross postal revenues (excl. postal M.O. and savings)	$ 54.0	$ 90.0	$ 118.9	$ 127.5	$ 138.8
2. Deposits by states in unemployment insurance trust funds	78.4	68.5	108.6	148.4	180.0
3. Assessments on deposits by FDIC	2.8	5.5	5.9	2.9	3.2
4. Assessments on deposits of insurance Federal Savings and Loan Associations by FS and LIC	0.3	0.5	0.4	0.4	0.5
5. Veterans' life insurance premiums	3.5	20.6	38.1	34.6	*
6. Sale of surplus property	—	2.3	—	—	
7. CCC sales of wool and sugar under price support program (net)	—	38.0	21.1	—	—
8. Interest paid to Federal Government on Federal Reserve note issue	—	11.1	13.2	17.5	20.4
TOTAL B	$139.0	$ 236.5	$ 306.2	$ 331.3	$ 342.9
C. Total A and B	$592.2	$2,714.0	$2,673.6	$3,549.4	$4,209.0
D. Public Debt: Net Cash Borrowing	$ 86.8	—	—	—	—
E. Transactions in Treasury Currency (U.S. notes, silver certificates, gold certificates, and coin) Net sales by Treasury to FRB Boston	$119.4	$ 10.1	$ 2.0	$ 16.7	$ 12.1
F. Treasury General Account FRB Boston					
Decrease in Treasury general account during year	$ 71.7	$ —	$ —	$ 74.4	$ —
Net Treasury transfers from other districts	—	—	62.3	361.5	252.1
TOTAL A, B, D, E, F	$870.1	$2,724.1	$2,737.9	$4,002.0	$4,473.2
G. Tax Refunds (—)	—	103.0	150.4	139.4	145.9
TOTAL RECEIPTS	$870.1	$2,621.1	$2,587.5	$3,862.6	$4,327.1

* The transfer to Philadelphia of the administrative section which receives New England veterans' life insurance premiums removes this item for 1952 from consideration as a receipt by the Treasury Account at Boston.

the Treasury has spent more than it has received within the district or has transferred some monies out of the district. Thus the decrease is carried as an inflow on one side of the balance sheet to be offset by expenditures within the district or transfers out of the district carried on the other side of the balance sheet. Items which have decreased the Treasury general account are carried under Cash Payments. Increases in the account balance are carried under Item G.

Federal Spending in New England

In 1950 the Federal Government spent about $2.6 billion in New England. Exclusive of debt repayments of $342,000,000, federal spending was slightly more than $2.2 billion. In the nation, the Federal Government had a cash outgo of around $41.9 billion during the calendar year. New England thus accounted for a little over 6 per cent of federal expenditures in that year.

This percentage was a fraction below that of the year 1940 but 1.45% above the 1948 figure. The Korean outbreak during the third quarter of 1950 rapidly pushed government expenditures upward, especially during the fourth quarter of the year. Though the major impact of these expenditures was to be felt in the private sector of the economy later in 1951 and 1952, the beginnings of government spending are evidenced in New England's improved position in government payments for goods and services. Our estimates for 1950 indicate New England businesses sold some $381,000,000 in defense or defense-connected goods and services to federal agencies, as contrasted to an estimated $200,000,000 for 1948. For the nation as a whole, spending on military services advanced from an annual rate of $11.9 billion in the first half of the year to $15.4 billion in the second half.[11]

By 1951 federal expenditures in the region advanced to $3.8 billion and further advanced to about $4.4 billion in 1952. Debt repayment accounted for $632,000,000 in 1951 and $461,000,000 in 1952. Exclusive of debt repayment, federal spending in New England was 5.5% in 1951 and 5.3% in 1952 of the total federal cash outlays in those years. Defense expenditures rose as the impact of the defense programs made itself felt. We estimate that payments to business during 1951 accounted for $1,375,000,000 and in 1952 rose to $1,779,800,000, including public works spending of $250,000,000 and $289,000,000 respectively. Defense spending in the region rose over $300,000,000 in each of the years since 1950.

Federal payments to New England individuals for their services have increased steadily since 1940. Between 1940 and 1948 they increased by 280% and then expanded another 180% in the subsequent four years. The largest increases were recorded in military payments which showed a tenfold increase between 1940 and 1952. During the years shown, federal income payments to individuals in New England held quite steadily at a level of about 20% of all federal cash payments in the region.

During 1950 transfer payments increased in all categories. For the first time a special National Service Life Insurance dividend was paid. New Englanders benefited by $217,000,000 in payments for this one item. Total payments to veterans (or their families) amounted to $443,000,000 in 1950, an amount which was $156,000,000 greater than in 1948. Old-age and disability insurance benefits were increased over the period 1950–52 due both to changes in the benefits obtainable and to the greater number of recipients. As the proportion of aged persons grows, old-age and disability insurance payments will inevitably swell, both in the region and in the nation, even without any change in present laws. However, in 1951 and 1952 total transfer payments were lower than in 1950, the largest difference being in veterans' payments. While New England has over the years received larger transfer payments, it should be noted that a relatively smaller

11. *Economic Report of the President,* January 1951, App. Table C–7.

proportion of total income payments accrues to the region from federal payments of this type than to other regions.

Another very large item which enters into the money flows through the Treasury general account is the borrowings and repayments of federal debt. During 1950–52 this item was unusually large. Our estimates of net cash repayments of debt are $342,900,000 in 1950, $632,000,000 in 1951, and $461,000,000 in 1952. Such large sums more than offset the outflows due to nontax receipts of the Federal Government for those years. During 1948 the net cash repayment of public debt occasioned an inflow of only $23,000,000. Thus it appears that New England's traditional outflow of funds on government account was reversed in 1950, 1951, and 1952 with a good deal of help by way of debt repayment. The reversal of the outflow has continued but cannot be explained, as it has been in some quarters, simply by pointing to increased federal expenditures on grants-in-aid and the like. The explanation must run much more in terms of veterans' expenditures, debt repayment, and increased sales by business. To the business payments we might also add the part of the benefit derived from the postal deficit and a large part of the interest payments on government debt.

Grants-in-aid, while large in themselves, did not add appreciably to the inflow as compared to 1948. All grants-in-aid and public works combined increased about $193,000,000 over the 1948 total by 1952, a small increase compared to those which took place in other categories. The subject of grants-in-aid has been taken up in greater detail in previous sections of this report. Interest payments declined in 1950, rose to the 1948 level in 1951, and fell again in 1952. Price supports and other payments to farmers continued to decline from 1948 levels. The major portion of farm subsidies accruing to New England was due to the potato support program. New England had the largest share of the potato support money of the eastern regions because it was far more economical for the Commodity Credit Corporation to make bulk purchases in Maine. It would be much more to the point to say that Aroostook County, Maine, rather than New England was involved in this particular transaction. The revision of the potato support program has, of course, drastically altered this particular money flow.

The Net Flow

We have described in the previous two sections the major items of receipts and expenditures of the Federal Government in New England. In part two of this report the net flows on Treasury account were discussed. Their relation to New England's balance of payments position was investigated so far as the data available permitted. The change from Treasury drains to Treasury inflows in 1950 and subsequent years is not as encouraging as might be first assumed. Those elements which are nonrecurring have already been described, e.g. the National Service Life Insurance dividend and the large inflow due to debt redemption. The increase in debt redemption may produce favorable effects in the private sector of the New England economy in that New Englanders and New England institutions may find more profitable outlets than government bonds for their funds. The attractions of New England educational institutions to veterans may be evidenced in increased payments to veterans for educational expenses in the area, but the number of veterans eligible for benefits now is much less than in the period immediately after World War II. In addition, however, one other very important element must be considered.

New England's federal tax payments as reported by the Federal Government do not take into consideration those taxes which have been shifted to the region or those which have been shifted out of it. If more taxes are shifted into the region than are shifted outward, then the real net inflow is reduced or net outflows are raised by whatever difference exists. Truly accurate computation of the shifts which do take place is not possible. Some usable estimates which have been made give an indication of the effects, however. On balance it appears that more taxes are shifted to the region than the region's individuals and businesses are able to shift outside. For example, taxes on automobiles and tobacco products are reported as being paid in the states where these items are produced, but it is obvious that the consumers of these products pay most of the taxes. Several careful studies of tax shifting have shown that higher income regions pay more in taxes than the reported tax collections indicate. Estimates have been made which indicate that New England paid out $216,700,000 more in taxes during 1948 than was reported, for example.[12] Every method so far devised has shown New England pays out more than the reported collections. The net flows must be adjusted accordingly. When such adjustments are made, the net Treasury inflows which have occurred during the three years 1950–52 would most likely be offset by the increase in taxes via higher commodity prices on private account. In this sense the positive inflow of funds on Treasury account during 1950–51 only helped to prevent greater losses than would have existed otherwise.

CONCLUSIONS

New England's financial relations with the Federal Government are determined very largely by the nature of the region's economy in relation to other areas of the United States. Higher-than-average incomes, large financial resources, and an advanced industrial structure have all combined to make New England a region with high economic ability to pay Federal Government taxes and invest in government bonds. On the other hand, most federal expenditures outside the field of direct defense spending have been

12. "Federal Receipts and Expenditures in New England," *op. cit.*

disbursed through programs designed to aid individuals and government units, and they have been spent according to formulae based on population, matching of state funds, state laws, and the like. The New England states have tended to receive below-average federal aid payments, partly because New England has not participated as actively in some federal programs as other regions and partly because payments to New England individuals and governments affected by the applicable programs averaged less than in other states.

In the years prior to 1950, New England's private trade and investment relationships with other areas of the United States normally resulted in a net inflow of funds. That inflow generally was adequate to offset a net outflow of funds resulting from direct Treasury transactions in the region and still leave a balance to provide for some needed growth of monetary reserves in New England. Undoubtedly the advancement of industrial growth in other areas as the result of federal programs stimulated sales of New England business in those rapidly growing areas. At the same time, however, industrial growth in other areas was strengthening the competition facing New England manufacturers and changing New England's relative position in the national economy.

After World War II, New England's changed position in the United States economy was reflected in a decreasing net inflow of funds through private commercial and financial transactions. In 1950 and subsequent years the region lost funds as the net result of private transactions. Also in 1950, for the first time in the 35-year period covered by the records, New England gained funds through Treasury transactions. Those gains continued in subsequent years. Unfortunately, however, our analysis indicates that New England's gains through Treasury transactions have not been primarily caused by a general change in New England's participation in federal programs. The change has been largely due to items such as debt repayment by the Treasury and payments to New England manufacturers of defense materials. These cannot normally be considered as permanent sources of net inflow of funds.

Treasury transactions in New England both affect and are affected by private commercial and financial transactions in the region. It is impossible to predict the net effect on the flow of funds through New England's private transactions that will result when Treasury defense expenditures are reduced. Nevertheless, experience since World War II indicates that it may no longer be possible for the region's economy to earn sufficient funds on private account to offset the region's losses according to the historical pattern of Treasury transactions reflecting Federal Government programs.

This situation forces a reconsideration of New England's attitude toward federal programs. New Englanders cannot, in good conscience, adopt a uniform attitude that all federal programs are either good or bad for the region. From the region's point of view, federal programs may be considered in three general categories. In the first category are those programs which are narrow in their benefits, supporting particular groups such as the wool or silver interests. They set up an unwarranted drain on public funds and may rightfully be opposed by regions such as New England which must contribute to their support.

In a separate category are those programs primarily designed to raise the level of living throughout the country. Better education, improved hospitals, fewer slums, and more adequate roads, for example, are all objectives that New England is seeking along with other areas of the nation. National progress in attainment of these goals will surely be greater if the more advanced regions continue their support of such federal programs. These programs do not by themselves directly affect New England's competitive position in the national economy.

New Englanders may logically hold a different viewpoint toward a third category of federal programs which includes river basin developments, farm support programs, and river and harbor improvement expenditures. Unquestionably, New England shares somewhat in the expanded markets attributable to some of those programs. Furthermore, New England's industrial customers in the Middle Atlantic and Great Lakes states buy more in New England because their own markets are expanded. It is also true, however, that these programs raise the cost of the materials and foodstuffs that New England consumes. Also, New England's marketing arrangements are sometimes disrupted and the market moved farther away from the region. In addition, support is given to New England's competitors in the newly developing areas. In effect, the initial stimulus to New England's markets appears to be gradually replaced by a worsening in the region's competitive position in relation to the areas being supported.

New England's prosperity and growth are dependent upon prosperous growth in the national economy. Historically, New England has placed national interests above, not below, regional interests. We must continue to do so. But national and regional interests coincide in the requirement that federal programs be assessed both in terms of gains for growing areas and burdens on older economic areas.

In seeking solutions to regional problems, New England must not resort to recrimination, irresponsible exploitation of federal programs or special pleading for preferred treatment. We may rightfully expect, however, that our own efforts to preserve and strengthen the regional economy will not be undermined by federal programs which concentrate adjustment burdens in older economic regions.

SELECTED REFERENCES

1. Beckhart, B. H., *The New York Money Market,* Vol. 2, Columbia University Press, 1932.

2. Beckhart, B. H., Schairer, Julia E., and Sharpe, Gail E., *Is New York Losing Its Relative Position in the Banking Structure of the Country?* Chase National Bank Department of Financial and Economic Research, 1942. (Mimeographed.)

3. Brown, W. A., *The New York Money Market,* Vol. 4, Columbia University Press, 1932.

4. Buchanan, J. B., "Federal Grants and Resource Allocation," *Journal of Political Economy,* June 1952.

5. —— "A Reply," *Journal of Political Economy,* December 1952.

6. Daane, J. D., *The Fifth Federal Reserve District; A Study in Regional Economics,* Graduate School of Public Administration, Harvard University, October 1948.

7. Federal Reserve Bank of New York, *Annual Report,* 1927, 1934.

8. Federal Reserve Bank of Boston, "New England Gold Reserves and Interdistrict Payments," *Monthly Review,* October 1951.

9. —— "Federal Receipts and Expenditures in New England," *Monthly Review,* August 1950.

10. Hartland, P. C., "Balance of Interregional Payments in New England" (unpublished doctoral dissertation), Harvard University, 1946.

11. Harris, S. E., *The Economics of New England,* Harvard University Press, 1952, chaps. 8–11.

12. Maxwell, James, *Federal Grants and the Business Cycle,* National Bureau of Economic Research, 1952.

13. Scott, A. D., "A Note on Grants in Federal Countries," *Journal of Political Economy,* November 1950.

14. Somers, H. M., "Government Expenditures and Economic Welfare," *Revue de science et de législation financières,* Vol. 43, 1951.

15. Terrill, R. P., "The Interregional Balance of Payments of Southern California, 1920–1934," thesis submitted to Stanford University, Palo Alto, 1941.

16. U.S. Council of Economic Advisors, Committee on the New England Economy, *The New England Economy,* a report to the President, July 1951.

17

State and Local Taxation and Expenditures
in New England

Drafted by Edward K. Smith under the direction
of Arthur A. Bright, Jr., and George H. Ellis

INTRODUCTION

The greatly enlarged role the Federal Government has been playing in the country's economic development has often tended to conceal the importance of state and local government units in economic developments in their jurisdictions. In their taxing, borrowing, and spending decisions, state and local governments determine the varying climates for industrial growth in different sectors of the nation.

The greater than average age of New England's governmental units provides special problems. It also provides the special challenge that this region should demonstrate a maturity in governmental actions which will set standards of leadership for the nation.

This report examines the position of state and local government units in relation to their problems and in relation to achievements in other states. Lack of information made it impossible to provide comparisons with all other states in every instance. For most comparisons, ten states are presented for comparison with New England states. Those ten were chosen because each has characteristics in common with one or more of the New England states. They are, in a sense, "competitive" states.

SOURCES OF TAX REVENUES

There are three major sources of revenue for state and local governments: taxes, borrowing, and aid from other governmental units. On the state level, taxes account for around 75% of revenues. The comparable percentage on the local level is less, but the variations among states are large because of the differences in aid paid to local units. Borrowing, federal aid and miscellaneous fees, licenses, assessments, etc., account for the remainder of state revenues. Tabular summaries of the tax structures of the New England states are given in Appendix 1 of this report. The tables refer only to state taxes. If local taxation were included, property taxes would easily take first rank as a source of revenue. They account for nearly 90% of local taxation in the United States. In the New England states, total local taxes have usually equaled or exceeded the total of state taxes, but the pattern is shifting toward greater state revenues. A full discussion of local property taxation is to be found elsewhere in this report.

The majority of the important state taxes are in use by every New England state, but the exceptions are important. Massachusetts, New Hampshire, and Vermont have no general sales taxes. Personal income is not taxed in Connecticut, Maine or Rhode Island, and only that part of income arising from intangibles is taxed in New Hampshire. Corporate income is not taxed in either Maine or New Hampshire.

The states commonly depend on three or four taxes to raise 50% or more of their tax revenues. For example, during 1951 Massachusetts raised 55.7% of its taxes from levies on income, both personal and corporate, while New Hampshire obtained exactly the same proportion from taxes on gasoline, motor vehicles, and tobacco. Nine separate taxes raise 90% or more of all tax revenues in each of the New England states. This is in distinct contrast to the Federal Government's dependence on income and local governments' dependence on property as the major tax base.

Revenues from payroll taxes are a prominent source of state revenues. In 1951 payroll taxation varied from 9.3% of *all* taxes in Vermont to 34.0% in Rhode Island. These differences are due not only to the differences in rates but also to the varying industrial structures of the states. In Vermont, Connecticut, and Maine unemployment compensation taxes have become a decreasing proportion of total tax collections since 1945, though Connecticut's proportion began to rise in 1950. Massachusetts and New Hampshire have had an increasing proportion of their collections come from this source. Rhode Island has had a decrease from its 1945 proportion, even though in the last three years there has been a rise. The absolute amounts of the collections have varied widely. Appendix Table 3 summarizes this information for selected years and selected states.

The place of all the major types of taxes in state tax structures of selected states may be seen in Table 17–1. Classifications of taxes in this table are according to census definitions. Thus, "sales and gross receipts" includes general sales and gross receipts, admission, alcoholic beverage, insurance premium, motor vehicle, fuels, tobacco, and other taxes. The taxes listed account for 95 to 99% of all taxes collected in the individual states.

In combination, the New England states reveal a pattern of taxation which bears more heavily on personal and corporate income and less on general sales than in most states. New England's avoidance of general sales and gross receipts taxes is very evident, but the selective sales and gross receipts taxes, such as those on alcoholic beverages, cigarettes, and gasoline, nonetheless form an important part of the tax systems of all the states.

Property taxation has been left almost entirely to local governments as the states have turned more and more toward taxation of income and sales. The decreasing emphasis on property taxation by state governments has undoubtedly improved the equity of state taxation a great deal.

Table 17–1. State Tax Collections, by States, for New England and Selected States, 1939 and 1950

1939
(Percentages of total taxes)

STATE	PERSONAL INCOME TAX	CORPORATION INCOME TAX	SALES AND GROSS RECEIPTS	PROPERTY TAXES	LICENSE AND PRIVILEGE TAXES	UNEMPLOY- MENT TAXES
United States	4.7	3.3	38.5	8.8	16.6	22.2
New England	3.8	1.7	24.3	16.2	18.4	27.7
Maine	—	—	28.4	22.7	27.7	17.2
New Hampshire	—*	—	28.8	15.0	29.8	19.8
Vermont	4.9	1.4	33.4	9.8	30.7	13.3
Massachusetts	7.1	1.0	21.4	21.6	9.7	29.9
Rhode Island	—	—	19.8	10.7	28.0	35.3
Connecticut	—	5.3	28.1	4.2	25.7	29.4
Selected States						
California	7.0	6.8	44.1	3.8	9.8	25.5
Illinois	—	—	49.4	1.1	19.4	27.8
Michigan	—	—	54.4	10.5	7.2	24.2
New Jersey	—	—	25.7	9.4	20.9	36.7
New York	18.8	6.4	17.3	2.7	17.8	25.1
North Carolina	3.5	8.8	46.1	5.2	21.6	13.5
Ohio	—	—	54.2	4.9	13.3	26.3
Pennsylvania	—	5.0	24.7	18.1	19.6	25.2
South Carolina	3.9	5.2	52.3	6.5	15.9	14.8
Tennessee	2.1	3.7	46.2	6.1	20.8	17.5

1950
(Percentages of total taxes)

STATE	PERSONAL INCOME TAX	CORPORATION INCOME TAX	SALES AND GROSS RECEIPTS	PROPERTY TAXES	LICENSE AND PRIVILEGE TAXES	UNEMPLOY- MENT TAXES
United States	8.1	7.0	52.2	3.5	13.0	11.5
New England	9.0	14.8	43.2	1.5	12.0	15.7
Maine	—	—	51.0	12.8	19.9	13.1
New Hampshire	4.6	—	46.7	4.8	21.4	18.7
Vermont	13.9	5.3	47.1	1.6	21.3	7.2
Massachusetts	15.8	22.3	32.6	†	8.4	17.3
Rhode Island	—	8.9	52.1	—	13.6	22.2
Connecticut	—	10.3	60.3	0.3	12.9	11.2
Selected States						
California	6.5	8.0	56.6	5.2	7.8	13.7
Illinois	—	—	73.6	0.1	11.8	12.8
Michigan	—	—	63.8	5.3	14.0	14.9
New Jersey	—	—	44.4	1.5	26.3	22.8
New York	23.9	16.5	25.9	†	10.7	19.0
North Carolina	10.6	13.0	51.6	2.0	14.0	7.8
Ohio	—	—	68.8	4.0	15.7	10.4
Pennsylvania	—	12.9	45.2	0.3	25.4	11.7
South Carolina	10.6	14.9	55.4	1.4	9.0	7.6
Tennessee	1.9	6.4	65.7	1.0	15.4	7.6

* Shared taxes prior to 1940 were classified as agency receipts by the Census Bureau.
† Less than 1/20 of 1%.
Source: U.S. Bureau of the Census, *Compendium of City and State Government Finances*, 1947 and 1950.

IMPACT OF TAXATION

While the percentage distribution of revenues from the major types of taxes reveals the general structure of tax systems of the states, it tells us relatively little about the actual impact of taxation on the citizenry. The term impact refers to the initial payment of the tax by the person on whom the tax is imposed. The final resting place of the tax is quite another thing. We are not here discussing the shifting of taxation.

Our present concern is to approximate a division of tax collections into three parts: that paid by individuals, that paid by business, and that paid by both. Table 17–2 gives the approximate percentages of total taxes (including

Table 17–2. Percentage of Total State Taxes Paid by Selected Groups, New England States, 1949 and 1950

STATE	INDIVIDUAL		BUSINESS		OTHER TAXES PAID BY BOTH INDIVIDUALS AND BUSINESS	
	1949	1950	1949	1950	1949	1950*
Maine	22%	22%	26%	24%	52%	54%
New Hampshire	36	34	28	29	35	37
Vermont	45	50	33	27	22	23
Massachusetts	40	40	47	47	13	13
Rhode Island	24	23	49	50	27	27
Connecticut	35	37	38	39	27	24

* Maine: over 50% motor fuels, registration, and operation.
  New Hampshire: motor fuels, registration, and operation.
  Vermont: motor fuel and operators.
  Massachusetts: motor fuels, registration, operation, and excise.
  Rhode Island: motor fuels and operators.
  Connecticut: motor fuels, registration, and operation.
Source: Computed by the Committee of New England from *Compendium of City and State Government Finances,* 1949 and 1950

licenses and permits) which are paid by these groups in each of the New England states. The percentages are rough estimates and should not be taken to be exact. Certain assumptions are made in this compilation. Occupation taxes are considered business taxes even though many of them are levied on individuals—these individuals are usually acting in a business capacity. All cigarette and liquor taxes are assumed to be paid by individuals, although they may be levied on the distributor or manufacturer. In Massachusetts unincorporated business income is taxed under the individual income tax. Thus there is opportunity for argument as to the validity of such a compilation.

This breakdown does, however, help to make clearer the general structure of the tax systems within each state. For example, Rhode Island tends to tax business operations more than the other states, while Vermont tends to levy more on individuals. Also, the taxation of corporation income is very high in Massachusetts. This accounts for part of the shift from the category "both" to the business sector. Note that Massachusetts is lowest for the third group. To arrive at a conclusion as to what each group, business or individual, *eventually* pays is impossible. It would require a complete theory of the shifting and incidence of taxation, but no such theory exists. Lacking such theory, no valid dimensions can be given to tax shifts.

It does not appear that the New England state tax systems are aimed at deriving the greater part of revenues from any one group. It is much more likely that the states are far more pragmatic. They get money where and when they can. The higher percentages of the tax burdens on business in Massachusetts and Rhode Island would immediately change direction if unemployment compensation taxes were excluded, for instance. In those states where the class "both" is large in Table 17–2, improved knowledge of the proportion paid by businesses or individuals could easily result in changing the percentage of taxes falling on either of the other groups.

However revealing such classifications may be, they do not show the total money impact of taxation, nor do they reveal the changing yields over a period of time. A brief survey of the absolute yields of state taxation in New England, together with the per capita collections, is given in Table 17–3.

Table 17–3. *Total State Tax Collections and Collections per Capita, United States, New England, and Selected States; Selected Years*

STATE	TOTAL IN THOUSANDS OF DOLLARS				DOLLARS PER CAPITA			
	1940	1947	1949	1950	1940	1947	1949	1950
UNITED STATES	4,156,903	6,745,438	8,348,656	8,939,889	31.92	48.51	57.59	60.52
NEW ENGLAND	299,968	427,972	507,747	544,206	35.55	48.81	55.03	58.12
Maine	24,667	35,274	46,252	47,233	29.16	40.87	51.50	52.25
New Hampshire	15,833	21,797	23,801	24,302	32.31	42.90	45.51	46.47
Vermont	11,632	17,034	20,492	21,912	32.49	48.53	56.45	59.71
Massachusetts	159,958	221,315	268,064	282,977	36.80	49.13	57.79	59.30
Rhode Island	25,638	39,316	47,579	49,207	36.57	53.05	63.86	62.21
Connecticut	62,240	93,236	101,559	118,575	36.70	48.76	51.06	59.11
SELECTED STATES								
California	335,442	699,079	865,475	934,756	49.44	73.81	85.99	89.03
Illinois	266,879	361,329	439,303	435,796	33.82	45.16	52.62	50.52
Michigan	197,037	341,056	456,768	460,962	38.22	58.10	73.48	73.52
New Jersey	143,967	232,326	191,811	191,557	34.87	51.54	40.23	40.01
New York	585,124	818,815	896,549	1,096,549	43.27	59.23	63.00	74.36
North Carolina	87,536	193,770	231,011	230,369	24.91	52.82	60.82	58.41
Ohio	257,043	356,991	398,307	423,425	37.33	47.72	50.79	52.96
Pennsylvania	338,657	379,416	509,018	496,485	34.20	37.19	48.58	47.69
South Carolina	35,223	81,172	100,226	97,292	18.82	42.67	50.57	48.55
Tennessee	51,885	94,440	155,231	162,166	18.05	31.46	48.83	49.64

Source: *Financial Statistics of States in 1940*, Vol. 3: *Statistical Compendium;* Bureau of the Census, *Compendium of City and State Government Finances*, No. 2, 1947, 1949, and 1950

In absolute terms, the variation in yield among the states is large but reduction of these figures to per capita amounts brings them into better focus. The figures emphasize that since 1940 there has been a very large increase in taxation in each state. Although there was a steady increase in taxation during the war, the major increases came after 1945. The yields in the nation more than doubled between 1940 and 1950. The New England states experienced changes very much like those of comparable states. The states which experienced faster rates of growth in income and other elements of economic change also found their tax yields increasing, without finding it necessary to change tax structures significantly to create this change.

The impact of war is clearly revealed by changes in tax revenues. From 1942 to 1950 tax revenues increased 80% on the state level and 73% on the local level. School district revenues increased over 100%. City revenues gained by 59%.

Generally speaking, the increased revenues were derived primarily from the major tax sources within each state. States dependent on income taxation obtained the largest proportionate increases from this source. States whose major source had been sales taxes derived the largest percentage increases from those taxes. Exceptions may be noted. For example, Massachusetts by 1950 obtained 22% of its tax revenue from corporate income taxation; in 1942 it had received 12% from that source. Its yield from corporate taxation increased 209% over the period, its yield from personal income taxation 113%. Vermont, on the other hand, had an increase of 114% in its corporate tax yield, while its personal income taxation produced 269% more than in 1942. In Vermont's case 6.3% of its revenues were from personal income taxation in 1942 and 13.9% came from this source in 1950.

TAXES IN RELATION TO STATE
ECONOMIC CAPACITIES

While it is apparent that the yields of taxes have increased greatly during the past decade, it is also apparent that personal and corporate income, output, sales, population, and other economic elements have advanced too. Where does the taxpayer stand in this scramble of the economic adjustment of government units to changing costs and needs? Several methods may be employed to measure the changing burden of taxation. Two simple aggregative measures often used are collections as a percentage of income payments and per capita collections as a percentage of per capita income payments. Table 17–4 contains this data.

Comparing the years 1940 and 1950, we find that collections fell in relation to income, both for the total and per capita measures. The rise in income over the period was enough to outweigh the rise in taxation—on the state level. During the war the states were precluded from spending all they might have desired. Taxes did not reflect this deferred spending until after the war. The increases in taxation which have taken place since the end of the war are reflected in the *rising* proportions of income taken by state taxation. In spite of the rising proportions, however, none of the states with which we are concerned took more of the citizens' income than was taken before the war. The New England states followed the United States pattern, though the magnitude of change for the states varied. The rise during 1949 can be explained more by falling incomes than by changes in taxation. However revealing these measures of changing taxation and ability to bear this taxation may be, they are not revealing enough—especially for state comparisons.

A more refined measure has been developed which takes account of both state and local taxation. Table 17–5 presents the summarized results of a

Table 17–4. State Taxes as a Percentage of Income Payments, United States, New England, and Selected States, 1940, 1947, 1949, and 1950

STATE	STATE TAXES AS A PERCENTAGE OF STATE INCOME PAYMENTS				PER CAPITA STATE TAXES AS A PERCENTAGE OF PER CAPITA INCOME			
	1940	1947	1949	1950	1940	1947	1949	1950
UNITED STATES	6.0	3.6	4.3	4.1	5.5	3.7	4.4	4.2
NEW ENGLAND	4.9	3.4	3.8	3.7	4.9	3.4	3.8	3.7
Maine	6.2	3.6	4.5	4.4	5.8	3.6	4.7	4.5
New Hampshire	5.9	3.7	3.9	3.6	5.8	3.5	3.8	3.6
Vermont	6.7	4.2	5.0	4.9	6.2	4.3	5.1	5.0
Massachusetts	5.1	3.4	3.9	3.8	4.8	3.5	4.0	3.7
Rhode Island	5.3	3.6	4.3	4.0	5.1	3.7	4.6	4.0
Connecticut	4.8	2.3	3.2	3.3	4.4	3.0	3.2	3.3
SELECTED STATES								
California	6.6	4.4	5.2	5.0	6.2	4.7	5.4	5.1
Illinois	5.0	2.7	3.1	2.8	4.6	2.8	3.2	2.9
Michigan	6.5	4.0	5.1	4.5	5.9	4.1	5.1	4.6
New Jersey	5.0	3.5	2.7	2.5	4.3	3.3	2.6	2.4
New York	5.2	3.3	3.4	3.9	5.0	3.4	3.6	4.0
North Carolina	8.0	6.0	6.9	5.9	7.9	6.1	7.1	6.1
Ohio	6.2	3.3	3.5	3.4	5.9	3.7	3.6	3.3
Pennsylvania	5.8	2.8	3.6	3.1	5.5	2.7	3.5	3.1
South Carolina	7.1	5.4	6.3	5.5	6.5	5.5	6.4	5.8
Tennessee	6.1	3.4	5.5	5.1	5.7	3.6	5.6	5.1

Source: Compiled from Table 17–3 and Bureau of the Census, Survey of Current Business, "State Income Payments," August 1953

special study by the Committee to find how and in what direction the tax burden has changed, and how these changes compare to those of other states which compete with, or have many elements in common with, one or more of the New England states.[1]

The first two columns of Table 17–5 contain index numbers designed to represent each state's economic ability to pay taxes. The index is an aggregate measure which takes into account income, production, and sales in each state in relation to the national average set at 100. The index reveals that in 1949 the three northern states in New England were slightly below the national average in economic ability to pay taxes.

1. A full discussion of the economic ability indexes, their preparation, use, and sources of data is given in the Staff Memorandum No. 8, Interstate Comparisons of State and Local Tax Burdens and Federal Aid, 1941 and 1949.

The remaining columns in Table 17–5 relate the level of taxation in each state to its economic ability. Tax indexes were computed by relating per capita tax collection in each state to the national average. Indexes of tax burdens were then computed by dividing the tax index by the index of economic ability to pay taxes. These indexes make it possible to compare the burden of taxation, state by state, in a general but meaningful way. The indexes for the combined burden of state and local taxes are presented in Chart 17–1 to illustrate the changes between 1941 and 1949.

Table 17–5. State and Local Tax Burdens, New England and Selected States, 1941 and 1949
(indexes: United States average = 100)

STATE	ECONOMIC ABILITY		STATE TAX BURDEN*		LOCAL TAX BURDEN*		STATE AND LOCAL TAX BURDEN*	
	1941	1949	1941	1949	1941	1949	1941	1949
NEW ENGLAND								
Maine	89	86	105	103	103	103	104	103
New Hampshire	101	94	94	83	145	113	119	97
Vermont	96	92	123	108	147	122	135	115
Massachusetts	129	102	85	97	116	136	100	115
Rhode Island	143	103	82	101	85	94	84	98
Connecticut	161	120	77	78	89	93	83	85
SELECTED STATES								
California	121	112	125	131	98	128	112	129
Illinois	127	125	83	69	99	113	91	90
Michigan	123	125	102	100	79	82	91	91
New Jersey	137	117	83	58	127	123	105	89
New York	126	112	105	103	159	142	131	122
North Carolina	62	71	133	141	69	56	101	101
Ohio	125	111	97	79	66	76	82	76
Pennsylvania	114	106	94	78	90	75	92	76
South Carolina	56	65	119	129	70	46	95	90
Tennessee	58	80	100	104	93	72	97	89

* Indexes of tax collections divided by indexes of economic ability.
Source: Staff Memorandum No. 8

Several important facts stand out. In terms of burden Maine, Massachusetts, and Vermont are above average. Massachusetts and Rhode Island had the largest relative increases in burden of any of the states in the group studied. Maine and Vermont have had falling burdens in relation to the United States average, while New Hampshire's relative burden fell sufficiently to put that state below average. Vermont had a sharp decline but not enough to bring its relative burden down to the average. Connecticut's increase in relative burden was small, and that state was third lowest of the 16 states studied in 1949.

Among the non-New England states shown, only California, New York, and North Carolina had indexes greater than average in 1949, and North Carolina's index was only 1% higher than the average. Ohio and Pennsylvania had the lowest total state and local tax burdens of the 16 states.

There were many reasons for these changes, but a study of Table 17–5 helps to show the role played by state taxes on the one hand and local taxes on the other. For example, the burden of local taxation in Massachusetts in relation to the United States average increased greatly over the years 1941–49, while the state tax burden in New Jersey decreased sharply during the same period. The patterns varied considerably from state to state, though the indexes of both state tax burden and local tax burden moved in the same direction in ten of the 16 states.

CHART 17–1

Total State and Local Tax Burdens, New England and Competing States, 1941 and 1949

(Indexes: United States average = 100)

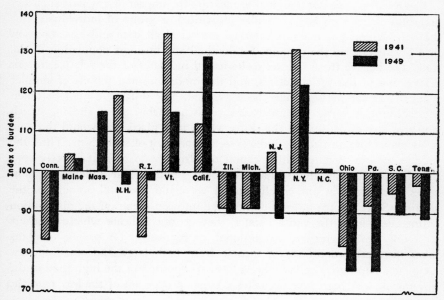

Source: Ibid.

The interregional patterns revealed by this analysis are both interesting and significant. A point of major interest is that the southern and south-western states usually have state tax burdens above the average, while their local tax burdens are usually below average. The northern states, on the other hand, often have state tax burdens which are below average and local tax burdens which are above average. The central and western states show a mixture of both cases. The southern and northwestern states all show a drop in the relative level of taxation and therefore in the total relative tax burden when local taxes are added to state taxes.

In New England the addition of local taxes raises the total state and local tax index, with the exceptions of Maine in both 1941 and 1949 and Rhode Island in 1949. If we were to consider state taxes only, then the New England states would have lower relative burdens than many of the southern states, and even lower indexes of state tax collections in some instances. But local taxes in the South are so low relative to the United States average, while local taxes in the North are usually so much higher, that the final result is sharply lower indexes of total state and local taxation in the South relative to the United States as a whole. Despite the lower southern indexes of total tax collections, however, the *burdens* of those taxes are not always low. Some southern states have lower than average burdens while others have above average burdens. The final result depends on both the tax level and the economic ability of the state.

These indexes *are not* designed to measure the impact of any particular tax or group of taxes on any particular individual or group of individuals. But they *are* designed to measure the total impact of all state and local taxation in a given state on the combined individual and business population of the state. We believe these indexes to be useful measures of the relative impact of taxation in the various states, and the more common pitfalls of simpler types of tax comparisons have been avoided. Tax shifting cannot be taken into account, however, inasmuch as there is no theory of tax shifting which can give any dimension to the shifts which take place, nor would the data be available for constructing indexes to take account of such shifts. Thus, the indexes assume that the shifts cancel out from state to state. We believe, therefore, that only slight changes would result in the indexes of most states, and hence in our conclusions, if we could take full account of the shifting. Since the tax indexes do not take into consideration the distribution of income within the various states, they do not indicate whether the tax structures are progressive, proportional, or regressive. (A proportional tax takes identical proportions of income from both large and small income recipients. A progressive tax takes a larger proportion of the high than of the low incomes. A regressive tax takes a larger proportion of the low than the high incomes.)

The indexes do point up some of the major problems of New England's tax structure in spite of these technical difficulties. They demonstrate the falseness of claims that New England as a region has a "high tax burden." Parts of New England may have a high burden, but the tax situation is far less bleak than many critics would paint it. New England is not homogeneous with respect to taxation.

REVENUES FROM FEDERAL AID

An increasingly important part of state and local revenues is being derived from federal grants. A full discussion of federal aid to states appears in our report on "New England's Financial Relations with the Federal Government." In this section we are only concerned with federal grants to states for state purposes and for distribution to local units. Direct aid to local governments is a much smaller part of the aid program.

During 1951 the states received about $2.4 billion under various federal programs. The New England states received $168,418,000 from federal sources, or 6.7% of the United States total. In 1950 New England obtained 5.8% of the total. In that year federal aid made up 16.5% of total state revenues for the United States as a whole and for the New England states. Vermont derived a greater proportion of its revenues from federal aid than any other New England state, while Connecticut obtained the least. The data for New England and ten selected states are given in Table 17–6.

Table 17–6. Federal Aid per Capita and as a Per Cent of Total Revenues, New England and Ten Selected States, 1950

STATE	PER CAPITA	PER CENT OF TOTAL REVENUES
NEW ENGLAND	$12.76*	16.5%*
Maine	15.04	19.0
New Hampshire	12.33	16.6
Vermont	16.41	20.0
Massachusetts	12.55	16.5
Rhode Island	10.72	14.1
Connecticut	9.49	12.7
SELECTED STATES		
California	17.05	14.8
Illinois	10.85	17.0
Michigan	12.08	12.4
West Virginia	6.69	13.1
New York	8.62	10.0
North Carolina	10.56	14.5
Ohio	10.04	14.7
Pennsylvania	9.08	14.1
South Carolina	12.47	19.3
Tennessee	14.35	21.1

* Mean.
Source: Bureau of the Census, Compendium of City and State Government Finances, 1950

Variation among the states in the proportion of total revenues attributable to federal aid is another indication of differing state revenue structures. Per capita amounts vary greatly, but low per capita aid is not always associated with a low proportion of aid to total revenues. For example, South Carolina's $12.47 per capita accounts for 19.3% of revenues, while Massachusetts' $12.55 per capita accounts for only 16.6% of total revenues. Even though some states receive more aid per person, they do not necessarily depend on this aid in their budgets to the same extent as other states.

It appears that the more industrialized states tend to derive a smaller proportion of their revenues from the Federal Government than the less industrialized states. In addition, those states which have smaller budgets tend to have higher percentages attributable to federal aid because they spend more of their internally raised funds on programs for which federal aid may be sought. The higher income states which have large budgets not only spend on federally aided projects but also provide their citizens with many other services which either are not rendered or are less adequately rendered in the lower income states. Some low income states spend disproportionate sums on such programs as old-age assistance, for example, and their aid receipts reflect these large sums in the revenue totals. *The New England states have, on the whole, been singularly free of those influences which make for obtaining funds "cheaply" and which usually result in distorting the fiscal picture within the state.*

DEBT

Borrowing by government takes place essentially for the same reasons as business borrowing. Either the unit cannot meet its current obligations, or it desires to invest in some capital improvement such as roads or schools, for which money cannot be obtained during the given period. Government units usually experience much less difficulty than private units in obtaining borrowed funds, and the rates of interest paid are invariably lower than rates paid by nongovernment borrowers.

State and local governments are in essentially the same position as individuals and business units in their debt relations. They frequently have to borrow, and their borrowed funds have to come from financial institutions and individuals. Unlike some federal borrowing, state and local borrowing does not create money. The main differences between business and government borrowing are: (1) the greater resources behind government; and (2) the exemption from federal taxation of the interest received on obligations of state and local governments.

A brief review of the recent debt trends in New England and the United States provides a valuable link in the study of taxing and spending. During the war, material and other restrictions prevented state and local governments from spending on needed capital projects. Substantial surpluses were built up because of rising tax yields in conjunction with low expenditures. The release of much of these funds after the war's end was inevitable under the pressures developed by the needs for new roads, schools, and the like. The rising costs of construction in the postwar economy quickly reduced the real value of state surpluses. Resort to borrowing came much earlier than many states anticipated. A further complicating factor intruded when many states reduced taxation, thinking their surpluses sufficient for their needs. Political pressures for veterans' bonuses and some other noncapital uses of funds soon forced the states into heavier debt positions.

Most of the New England states followed the course outlined above. The exception in New England is Maine, which has had sizable retirements of old debts in every postwar year, but at the same time has had a net increase in outstanding debt since the war because of toll road bond issues. Vermont, too, has retired debt in five of the years since 1945, but new issues in two years more than offset the debt retired. Table 17–7 shows the amount of new

Table 17–7. State Debt, New England and United States, 1942–51
(thousands of dollars)

STATE	NET NEW BORROWING BY STATES						
	1945	1946	1947	1948	1949	1950	1951
ALL STATES	−209,622	−154,529	589,474	635,807	457,714	1,164,131	937,675
NEW ENGLAND	−18,233	7,039	114,804	58,412	29,217	94,996	148,684
Maine	−2,001	−2,582	−1,509	−2,231	−1,902	−1,824	−1,659
New Hampshire	−1,726	−1,893	−1,133	3,976	4,332	3,570	2,971
Vermont	−977	−692	−1,118	1,326	−670	4,071	−647
Massachusetts	−9,680	13,881	93,786	1,341	28,100	4,100	77,171
Rhode Island	−2,266	−910	19,430	−570	−420	9,100	571
Connecticut	−1,573	−765	5,348	54,570	−223	75,979	70,277

Note: Negative figures indicate net debt redemption

STATE	DEBT OUTSTANDING, ALL FORMS, END OF YEAR		
	1942	1945	1951
NEW ENGLAND			
Maine	26,485	19,178	28,437*
New Hampshire	19,042	14,443	25,443
Vermont	6,650	3,374	5,664
Massachusetts	111,375	70,288	319,565
Rhode Island	29,333	25,327	54,284
Connecticut	30,213	23,600	228,786
TOTAL	233,098	156,210	662,179

* Census reclassification of debt increased Maine's figure by $21,000,000 in 1951 by including bonds for toll road facilities, heretofore excluded as an independent state agency.
Source: Bureau of the Census, *Revised Summary of State and Local Government Finances in 1942* and *Compendium of City and State Government Finances*, 1945–51

borrowings (debt issued minus debt retired, both long- and short-term) since 1945 for the six New England states.[2] The table clearly reveals that two states have undertaken by far the greatest proportion of new borrowing in postwar years. The proportions of all state debt outstanding in New England accounted for by Massachusetts and Connecticut rose from 60% to 82% of the total between 1945 and 1951.

In most respects, the New England states differ little from selected comparable states. All of them have spent borrowed money on roads, schools, and increased state aid. Indeed, of the 16 states included in this study, seven of them more than doubled their debt since 1942. Two of these were New England states, Connecticut and Massachusetts. Vermont was the only state with a decrease in debt from the 1942 level. Massachusetts, Connecticut, and Rhode Island issued veterans' bonuses after the war which added signifi-

2. The table reflects the census definitions and classification of debt and may disagree with other published reports. For example, our figures show a $4,100,000 increase in Massachusetts debt in 1950, while the Massachusetts Special Commission on Taxation reported a $6,500,000 increase in "net direct debt."

cantly to their total debt, but expenditures for highways, educational facilities, and nonhighway transport account for a very large proportion of the new debt issues.

Local debt remains the largest segment of government debt within the state-local structure. State debt, however, has been increasing at a greater rate than local debt, and the rate of increase in federal debt has been very much larger than either of the former. Communities which have pressing needs for new schools, roads, and water and sewage systems have no choice except to borrow funds for these projects, and growing communities all over the United States have been faced with similar problems. The faster growing cities of the Southwest have had large increases in debt within the past few years to cover such capital outlays. New England's cities, already having developed public facilities, have not had to make such large outlays. On the other hand, increases in the tax base in the faster growing areas make carrying of the debt easier than would first appear from examining the gross debt figures alone. Few large cities have low debt loads, though many smaller cities have larger per capita debt loads than the largest cities. The range of per capita gross debt of cities of all size classes is large and so also is the range within New England cities. Massachusetts and Rhode Island cities tend to have larger per capita debt outstanding than cities of like size in other states. Exceptions may be found, of course, but it is evident that some cities are in difficult positions, either because of population pressures or slow rates of economic growth.

In the case of faster growing communities, the problem does not appear intractable. With proper management and sensible amortization, the cities should be able to handle their present expenditures, even though increases in taxes will have to result. Many New England communities have found, and will continue to find themselves in the difficult position of having to rebuild antiquated public facilities without increases in assessment bases to make the task easier. These cities become problem areas from the fiscal point of view. Confronted with the necessity of increasing current outlays, because of rising costs and demand for better services, they are also faced with the problem of replacing schools and other structures which are outmoded—and in some cases not yet fully paid for because of unrealistic amortization. Thus debt may be piled upon debt, tax rates raised, new building discouraged, and old buildings not improved.

Cities which are integral parts of metropolitan areas find also that space and cost problems force industries and individuals out of their jurisdictions. The movement out of the city into suburban areas only magnifies this situation and creates a further multiplication of the problems confronting these units. Creation of new agencies, such as district commissions, helps to solve the fiscal problems of larger units but does not remove the underlying causes and is not applicable to a wide enough range of problems to constitute a good long-run solution. Resort to deficit financing is often but a temporary expedient. Older areas such as New England are faced with difficult tasks if they wish to alleviate the fiscal burdens of their cities.

STATE AND LOCAL EXPENDITURES IN NEW ENGLAND

State expenditures in New England have expanded more slowly than the national average in the years since 1939. By 1951 total New England expenditures had increased by 195% to reach $961,000,000. The increase was 217% for all states. Expenditure increases were rapid after the war, inflation taking its share in governmental operation as elsewhere in the economy. Operation expenditures for highways, health, hospitals, public welfare, schools, and so forth increased greatly in most states, but in many cases capital outlay increased even more rapidly. The construction of roads, schools, and other projects, deferred because of the war, was largely responsible for the different rates of change. In addition, population growth and the changing demands of the population led to many new capital expenditures.

Distribution of Expenditures

The distribution of total expenditures among general operation, capital outlay, and other expenditures varies considerably from state to state. As a rule, the New England states devote 40% to 50% of their total budgets to operation outlays. Variations in capital outlays are large. During 1950, for example, both Connecticut and New Hampshire allocated over 20% of their expenditures to capital outlays, while Massachusetts spent less than 10% of its expenditures for such purposes. Massachusetts, however, devotes between 30% and 40% of its expenditures to state aid, more than any other New England state. This reduces the percentage which the state may devote to its operation expenditures. In 1950 it spent a greater percentage on state aid than on operation expenditure. New Hampshire devotes the lowest percentage of its expenditures to state aid of any New England state. In 1950 its 5.1% was the lowest in the nation. For all states the average 1950 percentage was 30.4.

The non-New England states also showed large variations in expenditure patterns. General operation expenditures tended to take a smaller share than in the New England states. Aid paid to other governments varied from New York's 41.7% to North Carolina's 11.7% in 1950.

Table 17–8 gives the percentage distribution for these three types of expenditures for four years. The differences over the years reflect changes in the functions as well as amounts spent by state governments for various government services. Some states took over functions which local governments had performed, while others changed the shares allocated to different levels of government. To understand why each shift took place would require detailed analysis of all of the programs under each general division. The broad outlines of the changes can be stated, however.

The changes in patterns of expenditures were more significant in New England than changes in the general pattern for all states between 1939 and

Table 17–8. *Distribution of State Expenditures by Three Selected Major Categories, New England and Selected States, 1939, 1947, 1949, and 1950*

	GENERAL OPERATION				CAPITAL OUTLAY				AID TO OTHER GOVERNMENTS			
STATE	1939	1947	1949	1950	1939	1947	1949	1950	1939	1947	1949	1950
ALL STATES	37.9	40.7	42.2	41.4	15.9	11.6	15.5	16.0	26.8	32.0	30.1	30.4
NEW ENGLAND	n.a.	54.6	46.0	42.1	n.a.	6.9	12.0	13.4	n.a.	22.6	27.0	28.2
Maine	48.2	62.4	58.0	57.8	17.2	10.9	16.6	16.3	18.9	8.3	11.5	12.6
New Hampshire	61.4	62.7	57.4	56.0	16.5	13.5	19.0	22.3	5.5	5.9	8.6	5.2
Vermont	53.15	56.9	54.8	57.9	19.7	11.5	17.9	14.6	14.8	15.8	16.5	18.8
Massachusetts	39.1	51.9	34.6	30.3	3.4	4.2	7.3	9.4	33.6	33.8	41.7	41.4
Rhode Island	40.1	60.2	52.5	47.6	7.6	3.4	8.7	11.6	17.6	9.4	19.1	18.6
Connecticut	45.9	53.5	57.2	56.5	22.5	12.0	17.9	20.2	8.9	9.0	13.8	12.9
SELECTED STATES												
California	33.3	26.4	35.3	36.3	9.7	12.0	14.6	15.0	34.8	41.9	38.3	36.3
Illinois	31.7	52.8	53.0	47.1	12.5	11.0	12.3	13.5	29.1	21.0	20.3	22.5
Michigan	45.1	44.1	33.6	36.1	11.3	10.5	12.2	10.1	24.7	34.5	36.8	38.3
New Jersey	32.1	25.2	31.4	33.0	11.6	9.3	19.4	18.2	20.5	29.9	24.1	25.3
New York	24.3	24.5	36.7	25.4	8.6	8.9	7.8	11.7	41.9	42.8	37.1	41.7
North Carolina	27.4	55.9	55.7	46.8	23.3	20.7	21.5	30.5	31.7	9.0	10.3	11.7
Ohio	33.6	35.3	53.1	36.0	8.3	6.2	8.7	14.9	35.8	43.8	29.7	38.9
Pennsylvania	56.2	49.9	46.7	57.4	18.7	10.4	21.7	18.6	6.3	21.6	19.1	14.8
South Carolina	36.3	36.4	37.0	37.4	24.9	14.6	20.3	18.2	25.9	33.4	29.1	31.1
Tennessee	35.9	35.8	31.4	37.2	16.3	18.8	24.8	21.9	26.9	23.8	31.5	29.8

Note: n.a. means figures are not available.
Source: Bureau of the Census, *Compendium of City and State Government Finances*

1950. General operation expenditures *decreased* in relative importance in the New England states but *increased* in the nation. In relative terms, the New England states moved nearer the national pattern in capital outlays for schools, highways, and hospitals and in aid to other governments.

State Expenditures: Per Capita

Table 17–9 rounds out the picture of state expenditures by showing the amounts per capita which were spent during selected years. New England's per capita total expenditure has kept quite close to the 48-state average. The difference between New England and the United States in 1950 was very small, and the differences among the New England states were not large. New Hampshire, Rhode Island, and Vermont were nearly equal. Maine was the lowest and Massachusetts the highest of the six states. The picture varies from year to year, however, often depending on presence of a large capital outlay and, in the postwar period, on bonuses for veterans.

In the non-New England states the variation among states is large. The

Table 17–9. Per Capita State Government Expenditures, Selected States (in dollars)

STATE	TOTAL EXPENDITURES*				GENERAL OPERATION				CAPITAL OUTLAY				AID TO OTHER GOVERNMENTS			
	1939	1947	1949	1950	1939	1947	1949	1950	1939	1947	1949	1950	1939	1947	1949	1950
UNITED STATES	36.83	56.65	81.28	87.48	13.96	23.85	34.30	36.21	5.88	6.82	12.60	14.01	9.85	18.75	24.45	27.16
NEW ENGLAND	38.63	73.38	73.71	87.76	16.79	40.06	33.94	36.94	4.15	5.07	8.88	11.72	n.a.	16.35	20.06	24.71
Maine	39.81	64.16	79.29	82.32	19.17	40.02	45.97	47.56	6.84	7.00	13.16	13.44	7.52	5.35	9.09	10.36
New Hampshire	39.47	63.54	84.35	85.58	24.25	39.82	48.45	47.93	6.51	8.56	16.01	19.12	2.18	3.78	7.24	4.44
Vermont	40.49	63.68	88.33	85.93	21.52	36.22	48.40	49.75	7.97	7.29	15.80	12.59	6.02	10.09	14.62	16.20
Massachusetts	37.35	77.92	69.53	90.69	14.58	40.46	24.03	27.47	1.28	3.27	5.10	8.53	12.56	26.31	28.96	37.52
Rhode Island	36.34	79.48	77.32	85.95	14.58	47.87	40.60	40.88	2.77	2.69	6.71	10.01	6.41	7.46	14.81	16.02
Connecticut	41.55	64.62	76.72	84.88	19.08	34.57	43.88	47.94	9.33	7.73	13.75	17.11	3.71	5.81	10.60	10.96
SELECTED STATES																
California	56.71	73.03	116.25	130.26	18.87	19.26	41.03	47.34	5.53	8.80	16.93	19.59	19.75	30.57	44.51	47.34
Illinois	34.38	49.96	81.63	70.62	10.90	26.37	43.24	33.28	4.31	5.48	10.07	9.51	10.00	10.50	16.59	15.91
Michigan	42.77	82.34	102.55	104.62	19.28	36.32	34.46	37.74	4.84	8.64	12.54	10.52	10.55	28.46	37.74	40.06
New Jersey	34.62	58.85	53.93	54.48	11.12	14.81	16.93	17.97	4.01	5.46	10.44	9.92	7.10	17.62	13.02	13.78
New York	40.75	65.62	87.29	93.26	9.89	16.05	32.07	23.67	3.52	5.86	6.85	10.94	17.07	28.09	32.38	38.85
North Carolina	28.15	53.26	70.90	86.57	7.71	29.75	39.50	40.49	6.57	11.03	15.28	26.41	8.92	4.78	7.29	10.09
Ohio	37.70	49.77	92.27	74.02	12.67	17.57	49.03	26.62	3.13	3.08	8.02	11.02	13.51	21.81	27.40	28.77
Pennsylvania	44.54	48.15	64.90	92.44	25.03	24.01	30.30	53.06	8.32	5.03	14.08	17.23	2.80	10.39	12.43	13.68
South Carolina	26.85	55.92	73.88	75.25	9.74	20.36	27.36	28.12	6.68	8.18	14.96	13.73	6.95	18.64	21.53	23.43
Tennessee	22.69	41.21	70.27	72.51	8.14	14.75	22.04	26.96	3.71	7.75	17.43	15.88	6.11	9.81	22.14	21.62

* Defined as expenditures for highways, health, hospital, public welfare, schools, public safety, natural resources, etc.

Note: n.a. means figures are not available.

Source: Bureau of the Census, Financial Statistics of States, Vol. 3, and Compendium of City and State Government Finances, Current Population Estimates, Series p-25

large northern and central states tend to spend above average and the southern states below average amounts for all expenditures combined.

The differences among states in tax yields are reflected in the expenditures made by the states. The use of deficit financing complicates the picture, but it remains fundamentally true that one does not get something for nothing. If some states *tax less* than others, those same states *spend less* than others and inevitably state services are thereby reduced. Differences in efficiency of expenditure cannot be expected to make up for the large differences in dollar amounts spent.

Differences in the proportions of total expenditures allocated to general operation, capital outlay, and aid to other governments are reflected in the per capita amounts for each of these classes. For example, in 1950 Massachusetts was the lowest of the New England states in per capita expenditures for operation, while in per capita expenditures for state aid it was the highest. Again, variations in operation expenditures tended to be less than variations in capital expenditures. Differences in expenditure for aid to other governments were pronounced. Fluctuations in state aid were less than those in capital outlays over the years. Most states experienced steady and large increases in per capita outlays for capital purposes over the period 1939–50. The variability after the war increased, but the differences among the New England states did not change significantly except for Massachusetts and Rhode Island.

Local Expenditures

Comparison of local expenditures among cities and towns is extremely difficult because there are overlapping jurisdictions and intergovernmental transfers of funds which are not reflected in the published figures. However, it is clear that local governments spend the greatest part of their revenues on schools and police and fire protection. For the 474 largest cities in the United States 43.4% of operation expenditures and a large part of capital expenditures in 1950 were devoted to those three purposes. Welfare expenditures accounted for another 13%. Sanitation and highway expenditures were next in magnitude. The differences among cities of populations less than one million were not as pronounced as the largest cities. Police and fire protection costs in small towns are a much smaller percentage of expenditures than in the cities, but school expenditures remain high.

There are some important exceptions to the basic rule that where taxes are low the services rendered by government are usually less. For instance, the surburban communities of large cities tend to have an excellent level of police and fire protection and usually have the best school systems. The high level of property values, low levels of exempt property, low delinquencies, and more careful administration of funds, together with dependence upon the adjoining city for many services, e.g. hospitals, combine to put the suburb in a favorable fiscal position such that taxes may be quite low though the essential services are well maintained. Communities in this kind of favorable position are the exception and not the rule.

The presence of industrial properties has sometimes caused a loss in the residential property base and a consequent reduction in the ability to finance education and other services rendered by the community. On the other hand, for some communities the existence of some large industrial plants has been a virtual guarantee of adequate revenue and thus of expenditure.

Local expenditure patterns have undergone changes in recent years in states where state aid has come to play a more important role in local finances. Schools, for instance, have received greater support, as have welfare services. Accompanying this change has been a decreasing emphasis upon property taxation as a revenue source. In the absence of state aid (and federal aid channeled through the states to local units) property taxes would have risen much more than they actually did. *In New England, state aid could be improved in every state, and in New Hampshire the need for state aid to communities is a pressing problem.*

Expenditures of local governments are generally much lower in the southern states, usually reflecting a lower level of services. Nevertheless, the *effort* put forth by these communities is often large in relation to their income. As local governments spend the largest part of their money receipts for schools, protection, and welfare purposes, large differences in tax receipts among local units inevitably reflect differences in the level of services rendered under each of those categories. Furthermore, as property taxes are the mainstay of local revenue systems, these taxes will vary directly with the level of those major services and the proportion of the cost of these services borne by state and federal governments. Because of the increasing needs for schools, some states have passed enabling legislation which has allowed local governments to raise needed revenue by nonproperty taxation in order to keep property taxes down and still keep up the level of educational services. In Maine the state legislature has authorized the sale of bonds by a School Building Authority to build schools for towns and to collect principle and interest, plus administrative costs from the towns under a rented-lease arrangement.

Though welfare costs are today less burdensome than they were during the depression years, they still are one of the most important items of local expenditure. Those states which have assumed more of the welfare burdens have correspondingly lessened the local pressures in this field. Federal aid has also helped to reduce the burden. For *county* governments, public welfare payments are the largest part of expenditures. For towns, cities, and other units they are a lesser proportion.

City government finances of the largest cities often dominate the fiscal picture in a state. Indeed, the major cities of a region are all too often taken as an example of the entire fiscal system of a state. Nothing could be more incorrect, for the large cities are not typical.

The "sore spot" of cities in New England is Boston. In 1950 its total expenditures per capita were the highest in the nation. So were its taxes. Its property taxes, per capita, were the highest in the nation even though its state aid was very high. Boston's expenditure per capita for police exceeded that of any city in the nation over 25,000 population. Its fire expenditures were only exceeded by three other cities—and none of the cities of over 1,000,000 population spent as much per capita on fire and police protection.

Other Massachusetts cities, such as Cambridge, Somerville, Springfield, Worcester, Quincy, Everett, and Gloucester were also high tax, high expenditure cities when compared to their counterparts in other states, yet these cities received more aid from other governments than most cities of their size. Only certain cities in New York, New Jersey, and Michigan tended to have equally large expenditures. Connecticut and Rhode Island cities tended to have higher revenues and expenditures than their counterparts elsewhere. Cities in the three northern New England states did not display these tendencies.

It is a fair conclusion to say that many Massachusetts cities have higher expenditures and taxes than seems necessary in view of their size and the quality of their services. Admittedly, any conclusion on quality of service is subjective to a great degree, but we believe our conclusion fair. Comparative studies on the level, quality, and costs of services rendered by governments should be undertaken. It would be valuable to know why large differences in costs exist.

STATE AND LOCAL TAXATION

Business Taxation and Location

In this section we are concerned with the major taxes paid by business firms in the New England states; more specifically, with comparative tax burdens and the influence of taxation in location decisions, because the establishment of business firms is most important to the future of employment and income in the New England states. The taxes discussed, it may be noted, are not necessarily *borne* by business, as they may be shifted in whole or in part to other firms or individuals both within and outside the political unit involved. The possibility of shifting certain taxes will be mentioned where it seems appropriate. The assumption is that the business units actually bear the money burden of the taxes assessed against them.

Taxation and Location

Do state and local taxes play a dominant role in the location decisions of most business firms? Our conclusion is that they do not. That they are a factor in many location decisions is not questioned. That they are the de-determining factor is a proposition we reject.

Too often a change in taxation, i.e. a decrease in taxation, has been assumed to be a cure-all for whatever economic ills face a community. No doubt certain tax changes can help in many situations. We suggest in the following sections certain changes which we believe will help the New England community. But we do not offer them as new wonder drugs. Where problems arise *because* of taxation, changes in taxation can help. But if the problems are of other origins, revision may be of little assistance.

Several studies have indicated the minor importance taxes have in location decisions.[3] Of prior importance are such factors as nearness to markets, proximity to raw materials, labor supply, available plant space, transportation, labor cost, community attitude and others. Does this mean taxes play no role in location? No, for sometimes taxation may be that marginal element which tips the scales in favor of a certain location.

In practically all industries taxes are a small percentage of costs. If federal taxation is omitted, state and local taxes become a very small part of costs. If all other costs are equal between two locations, taxes can be the element which influences location within a given area. Seldom, however, are "all other costs equal," and it is rarely possible that absolute differences in tax costs can overcome those differences in other costs which are a larger *proportion* of total costs. *Small differences in those costs which are a large proportion of total costs are the important determinants in industrial location, both within and among regions.*

If, however, combinations of cost elements can be minimized in many locations, and these minima are not significantly different, variation in state and local tax costs will make for differences in total costs. Thus, whatever may be the real or imagined effects of tax differentials on plant location, certainly differences in taxes will affect the net returns of firms. Furthermore, plant locations are not always selected on the basis of factual analysis of alternative costs at all possible sites. In many instances potential sites are ruled out of consideration without full analysis because a business executive has strong prejudices against a state or community. *The reputation of being a "high tax state" can be a serious location disadvantage.* Once such a reputation is established, business executives tend to concentrate their attention on other areas in seeking plant locations.

3. Maryland State Planning Commission, *Location Factors in Establishing New Manufacturing Firms in Maryland,* Baltimore, 1951; University of Michigan, Survey Research Center, *Industrial Mobility in Michigan,* Ann Arbor, 1950; U.S. Department of Commerce, *Basic Industrial Location Factors,* Industrial Series No. 74, Washington, 1947.

The question arises: how great are the variations in state and local taxes among and within states? Many attempts to answer this question have failed because of incomplete analysis. There is, however, sufficient evidence available to give some answers. A study of the tax bill of a selected corporation in six southeastern states showed that

> the range of variation in corporation tax loads as between localities in the same state is, on the whole, considerably wider than the range of variation in the average load of corporate taxation as between entire states. As a consequence of the broad variability of local taxes, no matter where a corporation is situated, it is usually possible to pick out individual cities in neighboring states in which the corporation's tax bill would be lower. This generalization holds even when the corporation is located in the state having the lowest average tax burden for concerns of its particular class, unless, of course, the corporation happens to be located in a city with a property tax rate considerably below the state median.[4]

It was also found that the tax advantages of a particular location for a particular corporation changed with changes in three factors, which were: "(1) the character and relative proportions of the corporation's various balance sheet items, (2) the rate of return which the corporation earns on its capital investment and (3) the character and rates of Federal taxation." [5]

One of the more interesting findings of this study was that no one of the six states possessed a tax advantage in every situation. Advantages tended to shift with the changes in (2) and (3) above. A major reason for the shifts in tax advantage was the differing emphasis on property or income as the basis of taxation. Property tax variation is in itself very great because of the many differences in assessment practices both within and among states. Cyclical variation in income, of course, can often change the relative standing of a state depending on what year is chosen for the comparison. It was also found that the interstate variations in state and local taxes were in all cases greater when federal taxes were not included. This reflects the situation which exists when, for example, federal excess profits taxation would wipe out part of the gains of state and local tax savings. It also indicates that higher state and local tax bills are shifted in part toward the Federal Government, and that higher federal income and excess profit taxation reduces the range of variation between states and localities.

Unfortunately, no New England states appeared in Heer's analysis, but inasmuch as each of the New England states has all or some of the same kind of taxes as the southern states involved, the same conclusions as to the causes of variation hold.

4. Heer, Clarence, *Tax Bill of a Selected Manufacturing Corporation in Six Southeastern States,* North Carolina State Planning Board, Raleigh, 1945.
5. *Ibid.*

A similar study which does contain analysis of New England locations was undertaken by Joe S. Floyd.[6] Floyd measured the differences in tax costs for given firms in alternative locations. Ninety-six locations in 19 states were selected for certain hosiery and furniture firms, and four states were chosen for cigarette manufacturing firms. Computations were made for industrial cities within each state with the highest, lowest, and median adjusted property rates, and in some cases for areas adjacent to industrial cities. Floyd's conclusions bear out those of Heer.

It was found that "industrial tax loads at specified locations in specified states vary with the type of industry, with the ratio of earnings to net worth, with changes in the amount and composition of assets and liabilities, with the type of locations compared, and with other factors."[7] Wide ranges in tax bills were found both within and among states for state and local taxes, and when federal taxes were included the magnitude of the differentials was reduced. Few states were found where "taxes were uniformly high or low for all types of corporations and for both urban or rural sites."[8] *Because of the variables which can affect the final tax load, Floyd concludes that what can be a low tax area for one concern may be a high tax area for some other firm, and that a low tax bill may vaporize if the structure of the firm's balance sheet or earnings changes significantly. For these reasons and because other costs may be affected adversely when a firm engages in tax-oriented location, such location tends to be uneconomic.* Where large differences in taxation exist, however, these differences should somehow be reduced, if possible. We shall return to this point shortly.

Interestingly enough, in Floyd's study the tax bills for a seamless hosiery mill in both Massachusetts and Connecticut (median tax city locations) were lower than in North Carolina, yet North Carolina had the highest value added in this industry of the 19 states used in the comparison. Both 1946 and 1947 property tax rates left Massachusetts and Connecticut in the same relative position, eighth and ninth lowest, respectively. All other taxes were computed using 1947 rates.

Massachusetts and Connecticut also had lower tax bills for the median rural sites than most southern states. Because of the high value and low weight of hosiery, transport costs are negligible and for this and other reasons firms in this industry may locate in many different tax jurisdictions. Why, then, would not Massachusetts have a much higher proportion of this industry if low taxes draw firms to an area? The fact is that the high tax area has a greater concentration of the industry than the low tax areas, and the explanation for their location presumably lies in factors other than taxation.

6. Floyd, Joe S., *Effects of Taxation on Industrial Location,* Chapel Hill, University of North Carolina Press, 1952.

7. National Tax Association, *Journal and Proceedings of National Tax Association,* Sacramento, Calif., 1951.

8. *Ibid.*

Many studies of comparative tax burdens have included one or more of the New England states, or specific cities in New England. Despite the variation in methods used and the time at which these studies have been made, Massachusetts, Connecticut, and Rhode Island tend to be high, but not necessarily the highest, tax areas. In all of them, however, there was significant variation among industries. Most of these studies are not definitive. One of the best is that of the Massachusetts Special Commission on Taxation.

The Massachusetts study compared 20 manufacturing corporations in seven alternative locations to their respective Massachusetts locations. In general, it was found that Massachusetts taxes were higher than in most of the cities compared. Table 17–10 summarizes the tax payments made (in index form) for the year 1950. The sample corporations would have paid lower taxes in Buffalo and Philadelphia (with one exception); higher taxes in Charlotte, North Carolina, except in five cases; while in South Bend, Indiana, Lansing, Michigan, and New Haven, Connecticut, taxes varied above and below the Massachusetts levels. Both Lansing and New Haven had median burdens very near that of Massachusetts. Paterson, New Jersey, had the lowest median burden, but in this city and four others, Charlotte, South Bend, Lansing, and New Haven, where taxes on corporate tangible personal property are levied, the results could have changed significantly if alternative valuations were made.

On the state level alone, Massachusetts taxes on manufacturing corporations were higher than in the other states, but local property taxes in the other states tended to reduce the differential, except in the case of Philadelphia.

The limitations to this study deserve mention. The locations of the Massachusetts corporations were in cities and towns throughout the state, while only one location was assumed for each of the other states. North Carolina was the only southern state considered. Variations in local property taxes and assessments *within* those states would without doubt be large, and this would mean the range of the indexes would increase. Personal property valuation increases the likelihood of further variation, as does the assumption of assessment at book value. In addition, Massachusetts' dependence on income taxation would tend to put it at a disadvantage during periods of high economic activity compared to states such as New Jersey with their dependence on property taxation.

Finally, the exclusion of unemployment compensation taxes, one of the most important taxes employers pay, reduces the tax bills of many manufacturing corporations significantly, and for states such as Massachusetts, Rhode Island, and New York where merit rating is not now in effect, tax burdens in most cases would increase relative to burdens in other states. There are other limitations, some of which might be overcome. Thus, even one of the very best studies cannot give conclusive evidence from which

Table 17-10. Comparison of Estimated Taxes Payable by 20 Participating Corporations in Eight States in 1950
(exclusive of Unemployment Compensation Taxes; index: Mass. = 100)

CORPORATION	MASSACHUSETTS	PHILADELPHIA, PA.	SOUTH BEND, IND.	BUFFALO, N.Y.	CHARLOTTE, N.C.	NEW HAVEN, CONN.	PATERSON, N.J.	LANSING, MICH.
A	100	72	71	82	111	114	59	73
B	100	70	127	87	173	162	81	154
C	100	80	62	85	88	90	68	83
D	100	94	—	88	131	99	85	118
E	100	61	152	34	134	131	—	32
F	100	65	—	—	95	63	35	—
G	100	65	266	40	150	121	—	23
H	100	83	118	—	102	—	88	117
I	100	82	80	93	114	95	50	91
J	100	55	—	60	110	104	59	132
K	100	86	—	77	128	124	93	130
L	100	67	59	71	99	71	52	75
M	100	79	—	71	125	155	99	151
N	100	95	252	41	179	170	193	292
O	100	60	61	68	82	67	49	82
P	100	121	259	79	169	284	226	295
Q	100	39	54	60	51	80	48	97
R	100	69	67	76	112	83	65	85
S	100	76	61	66	103	94	114	98
T	100	71*	132	68	132	117	—	—
MEDIAN INDEXES								
Median	—	71.5	80	71	113	104	68	97.5
High	—	121	266	93	179	284	226	295
Low	—	39	54	34	51	63	35	23

* Information on value of buildings indefinite, some not included.

Source: Commonwealth of Massachusetts, Report of the Special Commission on Taxation, Pt. 4, "The Comparative Impact of Corporate Taxes in Massachusetts."

final conclusions may be drawn. *But this study, more than any other, supports the contention of many groups that corporate taxation in Massachusetts is higher than in most other competitive states and that, while consideration of local and other taxes may, to some extent, ameliorate this condition, taxation of corporations in Massachusetts remains high.*[9]

The Massachusetts study did not reveal the nature of the business of the corporations used in the comparisons. It is apparent that different types of businesses are affected differently by tax laws even aside from the problems of shifting and incidence. Of particular importance to New England are the textile industries. The Kendall Company and Barnes Textile Associates have both made tax comparisons for mills in various locations. The Kendall Company operates 15 plants in the United States. Five of these are in New England. The *average* Massachusetts plant had income and excise taxes 207% higher than the *average* plant outside the state in 1950. Its unemployment compensation costs were 227% higher but its property taxes were only 1.87% higher.[10]

The Kendall Company made available to the Committee an analysis which compared actual tax costs in 1950 of all the companies' plants with the probable tax costs if all the outside plants were located in Massachusetts. Payroll and income and franchise taxes would have risen 71% and 82% respectively, property taxes would have risen only 2%, and miscellaneous taxes would have decreased to zero. The net cost of total state and local tax increases would have been $348,471 or 54% higher than the actual 1950 tax bills of all the plants. Though the Kendall Company studies did not include federal taxes, and though the computations might change if actual rather than assumed property assessment ratios had been used and if apportionment factors for income and franchise taxes were known exactly, it is evident that a significant rise in taxes for this company would occur if all its plants were moved to Massachusetts.

The Barnes Textile Associates have made comparative cost computations for textile mills. One comparison for a representative Massachusetts and southern mill producing combed broadcloth showed a tax cost of .36 cents per yard in Massachusetts and .25 cents in the South. Though this was an excess of 44% over southern tax costs, it accounted for only 4.6% of the excess of all costs in Massachusetts over the southern location. The major part of the cost disadvantage was due to other factors, labor costs being dominant.[11] Differences in tax costs per yard of other fabrics varied from .03 to .47 cents per yard, while differences in total costs varied from .94 to 21.42 cents, depending on the fabric being produced. The greatest

9. Massachusetts corporate income *tax rates* are higher than any state in the nation, except Oregon.

10. The figures given were published in a series of three articles by Henry P. Kendall in the *Boston Herald*, March 18–20, 1951.

11. Staff Memorandum No. 10, *The Textile Industries of New England*, August 1952.

percentage differences in total costs were in cotton goods, and in all cases the largest part of these differences was due to labor costs.

Tax costs as a per cent of total costs per yard were very small in both Massachusetts and the South, though they were a larger per cent of costs in Massachusetts. They were in every case the smallest component of total cost.[12] Large variations in tax costs between these alternative locations would have only a small effect on total costs. Though much is unknown about the effects of taxes on locations and development, there is sufficient knowledge available to question many of the loose statements made on this subject. Certainly it is true that taxes do affect the actions of firms. To what extent they do so depends very much on the type of tax, the market for the firm's product, the composition of the balance sheet, the concern's knowledge of other costs, and a host of other factors.

Tax Competition among the States

Whether the results of tax comparisons are favorable or unfavorable to the New England states, it will be a very great error to engage in tax competition with other states. Tax concessions on the tax and expenditure patterns of state and local governments may only result in placing burdens on those least able to pay, or in lowering the standard of public services to a level incompatible with the welfare of the people. If tax competition breaks out into open war, the very few states which are sufficiently alike to compete actively with one another will soon recognize that a system of mutual dependence exists and that competition under the circumstances can only lead in the direction of fiscal suicide.

It is one thing to improve the fairness and reduce the distortions of a tax system in order to encourage business development. It is quite another thing to exaggerate the salubrious effects of little or no business taxation so that the fiscal system is distorted in other directions; the consequences are far more grave. This is not to say that the tax systems of the state should not be improved. Too often, however, improvement is conceived of in terms of lower taxes or taxes on somebody else. Tax improvement should not be so narrowly conceived, and tax competition resulting from such a conception inevitably results in increasing inequity.

NONBUSINESS TAXATION

Tax improvement exclusively concerned with the business sector neglects those taxes having their impact on individuals. The particular taxes paid by individuals have been enumerated in the first section of this report. In this section, we are concerned with the general effects of taxation upon the in-

12. *Ibid.*

dividual. Individuals, like businesses, often complain of the burden of taxation and attribute many undesirable effects to it.

Increased sales and property taxes have accounted for much of the increase in the nonfederal taxes since the war, and state income taxes have also generally increased. In addition, the need for revenues by local governments has led to many forms of nuisance taxes. It must be remembered that this is in addition to increases in federal taxes which have taken place. Any desire to help the business community by shifting tax burdens to individuals must consider the effects such shifts may have. This is a problem of equity, and many complaints of the business community concern not the level of taxes but the distribution of the burden. There is little doubt that the number of complaints about taxation emanating from the business community would be drastically reduced if businesses paid few or no taxes—yet the total taxation in the community could remain the same. Thus, the level of taxation is perhaps less important to those contending groups than the problem of who is to pay the taxes. Reducing the total money burden is one thing; changing its distribution is another. Both these alternatives must be considered in tax planning.

The general level of taxation is important because high levels of taxation invariably cause difficult revenue-raising problems as state and local governments seek new tax sources or further exploit old sources. Inasmuch as the best revenue sources are monopolized by the Federal Government, other units are left to rely upon those taxes which are often the least acceptable from the point of view of equity and yield. As revenue demands increase, recourse is made to less acceptable taxes, and many economic distortions result. This is especially true at the local level of government where much weight is given to property taxation. To distribute the added burdens "fairly" is an ever-present problem. As a general rule, it is best to distribute burdens in such a way as to minimize the distortions resulting from taxation. Some states have a bias in the direction of taxing business, while others favor taxing individuals. Although the dividing line between these two groups is sometimes nebulous, the effects on the tax structure are evident.

Every proposed change in taxation should be reviewed by the authorities to determine what effects these changes will have on the structure of the tax system and on the various groups within the economy. While much has been said in recent years about the effects of taxes on business, much less has been said about the increasing taxation of individually owned properties and the inequities of local property taxes, income taxes, sales taxes, and so forth, which have their impact on individuals. The business community has a much better organized system of watching and evaluating tax changes than does the unorganized and amorphous mass of ordinary taxpayers. Certainly any equitable tax system should consider all groups, and legislatures should not be pressured into poor public policy by those who are most vocal.

LOCAL TAXATION

While state tax systems often contain a great variety of taxes, local tax systems are invariably dependent on one or two major taxes. Property taxes, both real and personal, dominate the picture.

Since colonial times, New England communities have depended on property taxation. The early property taxes, given the kind of economic system then existing, were essentially taxes based upon ability to pay, property then being a quite accurate indicator of income and wealth. Today, however, general property taxation is far removed from that early position. Not only has the structure of the economy undergone revolutionary changes, but the whole meaning and intent of property taxation have altered radically. The system of property taxation has developed over the years into a hodgepodge affair which violates many standards of good tax practice. Generations of citizens have created committees and commissions to study such tax problems. Practically every one of their reports has pointed out the inequities of property taxation, the capricious and unsystematic way in which it works, and a host of related problems. Practically every study has recommended that further study, usually of an "exhaustive" variety, be undertaken. Practically every one has been ignored.

Few changes have been made, especially in New England, to improve local property taxation, primarily because the majority of citizens have not pressed for reform at the local level. Unfortunately, the property tax system must be *improved* rather than eliminated, for no other tax is available to furnish adequate revenues to the cities and towns. It is unwelcome but necessary.

The major problem of the property tax system lies in its administration. A well-administered property tax would remove many of the existing inequities and help to prevent new ones from arising. The major difficulty to be faced is that of assessment. Improper assessment causes inequities among taxpayers not only within a government unit but also in different government units. The government units themselves may be treated inequitably when state aid is measured wholly or in part by the assessment base.

Illustrative of the variations in assessment practices is a 1948 study by the Illinois Department of Revenue.[13] In the city of Chicago, for example, modern stores or offices, vacant lots, factories and warehouses and hotels had median assessments of not less than 55% of market value. Old style residences, cottages and bungalows, private garages, and smaller modern

13. Illinois Department of Revenue, *Illinois Property Tax Statistics, 1948,* Table 11, 1951.

residences had median assessments of not over 33%. In every case variations in assessment ratios within each class of property were large. There were assessments ranging from less than 5% of market value to 120% or more of market value. The dispersions noted were not exceptional. Outside of Cook County the differences in assessment ratios narrowed, but they were still large.

The Illinois experience is not unusual; similar conditions exist everywhere. Some states have made definite corrective attempts, Illinois among them. While every one of the New England states has at some time or other recognized the problem of assessments in one or more reports, no machinery has been set up in any one of the states which would assure more uniform and equitable assessments.[14] Very little control is exercised over local officials by state authorities. Massachusetts does not even have a guide published for the use of assessors to help them arrive at proper assessments. Maine does have such a guide and holds schools for assessors. Every one of the New England states could benefit from training assessors in their duties. In addition, benefits could probably be derived from more centralization of assessors. *Creation of state boards to review assessments, to set up standards of valuation, and to train assessors is a logical first step. In addition to the usual staff of specialized assessors, the boards should have their own research specialists to review and assist towns in fiscal planning.*

Some towns have undertaken complete reassessments, usually with the help of an outside organization. Periodic reassessment could be encouraged by state grants to local units to cover all or part of the costs. It should be realized that reassessment means little if it is not repeated at definite and short intervals. Of course, better qualified and better paid local assessors would reduce the need for complete reassessments by outside organizations. *Well-considered expenditure to establish proper assessments will normally pay for itself by raising tax yields—and at the same time increase the fairness of the property tax.*

One definite shortcoming of property taxation in New England is the continued use of personal property (both tangible and intangible) in the tax base. The inclusion of such property multiplies the assessor's difficulties and greatly increases the inequity of local taxation. The variability with which the tax is applied makes it an unfair nuisance. Valuation and reporting problems become insurmountable and evasion spreads as popular resentment against the tax mounts. As a result, many local governments make only gestures in the direction of enforcement, except for business property. Differences in enforcement among communities only help to cause additional bitterness as the inequities increase. Evidently, the best

---

14. Such steps as have been taken in New England to rectify this situation have been more in the nature of piecemeal attempts at a solution, e.g. a 1950 Massachusetts act "authorizes" cities and towns to engage expert appraisers to revalue real estate.

possible move with regard to this tax is to eliminate it or considerably restrict its application.

Another major problem of property taxation relates to exemption provisions of the various states. In every state religious, charitable, educational, and other similar institutions enjoy substantial tax exemptions. Veterans and other special groups also enjoy partial tax exemption. These exemptions have been growing rapidly and the equity of them ought to be questioned seriously. In certain communities institutional exemptions remove a good deal of valuable land from the tax base with no compensation to the communities for services rendered. In some cases, one community is forced to support an institution used by many communities. Within a community a tax exemption may force contribution by one part of the community to support another part. No matter how laudable the purposes of the exempt institution, the forced contribution may come from those least able to afford it. Communities should consider some system to permit payments in lieu of taxes. The degree of public subsidization of the tax-exempt institutions should be a matter of public record.

Nonproperty Taxation

Nonproperty taxation, though a minor portion of local revenues, is becoming increasingly important. Such taxation usually takes the form of local sales or income levies, though a multitude of other taxes are used, for example, on hotel rooms, cigarettes, liquor, admissions, and gaming devices. More and more communities are turning to these nonproperty taxes as costs mount and revenue needs expand. Many of these taxes become earmarked for special purposes, such as schools. Their administration is sometimes costly but not unworkable. Fortunately New England communities are remarkably free of these taxes.

More effective administration of real property taxation would no doubt reduce the need for such taxes. The distortions introduced by them are too often overlooked, and their vulnerability to cyclical and other changes is seldom considered. Those cities which levy income taxes may find their revenues seriously depleted if strikes occur in the major industries in the area or if plants are closed because of conditions in the industries involved. Falling prices and sales would reduce sales tax receipts far faster than municipal expenditures could be reduced. *Inasmuch as many of the financial difficulties of local units can be avoided by reasonably stable revenue yields, taxes which defeat this purpose should be avoided. A distinct contribution to stability may be made by local governments if they do not cut essential expenditures in depressed times and if they do not increase the less essential services in prosperous periods.* But if the tax systems of local governments become cyclically sensitive, this aim will be impossible to attain without deficit financing.

On the whole, New England local governments have avoided piling new taxes atop those already in existence. This means, of course, continued reliance on property taxation. For some units, especially metropolitan centers, continuing increases in property taxation have been the cause of much dissatisfaction. Relief for these units may force some sort of sales or income taxation into being unless a better system of state taxation and redistribution of revenues is devised. Cities such as Boston, faced with difficult financial problems, strive to keep their tax bases from withering away, but may find that recourse to other tax bases is inevitable. However, multiplication of taxes to allow many or most local units to increase the number of taxes which they levy is poor public policy.

SOME SPECIFIC PROBLEMS OF TAXATION IN THE SIX NEW ENGLAND STATES

Each of the New England states has a tax system which is a result of both its economic and political development. Many of the conditions which gave birth to particular laws or practices in these tax systems no longer exist, so there is in each state a body of outmoded doctrine side by side with the more recent tax law. On the whole, the tax systems of the states in the region do not differ greatly in the *types* of taxes imposed, but they do differ, as was shown earlier, in the degree to which specific taxes are used and in the method of their application. The outmoded provisions of tax law and the use of certain types of taxes bring into being problems which should be corrected if the states are to enjoy healthier fiscal systems.

Connecticut

Connecticut is a rich and prosperous state, and it has an efficiently administered tax department. Connecticut's favorable income picture does not relieve the state of all fiscal problems, but of all the New England states it is probably in the best financial condition. While its long-range fiscal planning has been inadequate, in this respect it does not differ from most states.

The 1948 Report of the Connecticut State Tax Survey Committee suggested minor improvements in the sales tax and recommended against the imposition of a personal income tax. A minority report of that committee took issue with those conclusions because the Connecticut tax system is regressive. The imposition of a progressive income tax could do much to lessen this regressivity, but the peculiar position of Connecticut with respect to New York has to be considered. An important part of the state is tied more closely to New York than to New England, and thus Connecticut is a good tax refuge for New Yorkers. Peculiar pressures thus exist to preserve the present system.

Local property taxation in the state presents all of the difficulties which general property taxation forces on taxpayer and tax administrator alike. Avoidance of personal property taxation is easy, and the four-mills state tax on intangible personal property only increases the incentive for avoidance. Repeal of those sections of the property tax law dealing with personal property and intangibles is in order. In addition, more direct state control over assessing officers would lessen present inequities.

One of the recommendations of the Connecticut Tax Survey was to decrease the difference in impact of the corporation income tax between incorporated and unincorporated businesses. The higher taxation of incorporated business, under current conditions, is due to the alternative measures employed as the tax base. Rather than become involved in various alternative measures of the base, it would be better to insist on a *net income* base for all businesses, incorporated or not, and irrespective of type. Integration of this kind of income tax with a personal income tax would be a further step toward a more efficient and equitable system, though on the state level such integration may be impracticable. Income from unincorporated businesses could be taxed under a personal income tax.

Fortunately Connecticut had accumulated surpluses to meet the deficits of recent years. As in many other states, these wartime accumulations have all but disappeared. It is unfortunate that deficits are appearing at a time when income and employment in Connecticut are so favorable. To make up these deficits, proposals have been advanced for a gross receipts tax as an alternative to raising the retail sales tax. Such a tax would be a variant of an income tax, in essence. While the tax would be "passed on" to the consumer, wholly or in part, it would not be deductible by the consumer in paying his federal income taxes, because this kind of tax is seldom separately stated. The producers, or others, would obtain this benefit. It would be more equitable and efficient if Connecticut chose to tax the income of individuals directly.

Maine

Maine's recently enacted 2% sales tax in its first year yielded $12,500,000 in revenues. Dependence on gasoline and motor vehicle taxes remains as a governing factor in the Maine tax system, however. The recommendation of the Maine Tax Revision Committee (1950) that the sales tax might be used in conjunction with a personal income tax to obtain greater equity was not accepted. The state's tax system remains regressive. The recommendation that the state property tax be revised by exempting all intangibles and household personal property was not adopted.

As with most states, Maine's property taxation could stand many administrative improvements. Clear recognition of the problems associated with the administration of the Maine property tax is evidenced in the report, and the tax administrators have done much toward improving the situation. Assessors' guides are available and meetings to improve assessment practices have been held under the direction of the state tax assessor. Much more could be done if the state could provide more effective direction of local assessors and if assessment districts were set up along the lines suggested by the tax committee's report. Valuation inequities could be considerably reduced. Another problem which demands attention is the reported practice of allowing exemptions or preferential treatment of industrial property. Local authorities are engaging in these practices without the legal authority to do so. Tax competition between local governments can threaten the stability of local tax systems.

The tax revision committee was also impressed with the necessity of reorganizing the tax office and recommended establishing a special committee of tax experts to study the tax system. A better alternative would be to establish a research section in the tax office for continuous study of the state's tax problems. In any case, more funds should be allocated to the tax bureau if it is to carry out effectively all of the tasks assigned to it.

Rhode Island

Rhode Island's fiscal difficulties rival those of Massachusetts. The differences are mainly of magnitude rather than kind. Consumer taxes play a large part in the tax structure of this state and state taxes have been taking an increasing share of per capita income, while the share taken by local taxes has been diminishing. The local tax and expenditure system is essentially like that of most states, and the tax problems confronting local government units are not unlike those of other industrial states.

Rhode Island has no personal income taxation, relying on its various sales taxes to produce up to 50% of its tax revenues. Thus general sales, gasoline, alcoholic beverage, cigarette, and betting taxes occupy important places. Corporation and other business taxes have produced roughly 30% of state taxes since 1935.[15] But payroll taxes dominate Rhode Island's tax picture and, if added, would raise the percentage figure given above to a much higher level, as we have shown in the first section of this report. The very large proportion of covered employment existing in the state and the high tax rate have combined to produce this result. The state has had great difficulty in preserving its unemployment compensation reserves, which were very sharply reduced by the recession of 1949. As in Massachusetts, difficulties with this tax have been a great irritant to business firms. Dissatisfaction with the handling of the system in Rhode Island has been the cause of rancor leading to much of the over-all condemnation of the

15. See the various comparisons in the Rhode Island Development Council's publication on taxation in the state, *The Tax Structure of Rhode Island,* Rhode Island Development Council, Research Division, 1952 (mimeographed).

state's tax structure. Satisfactory solutions here are not easily found. The reports of the Rhode Island Development Council are understandably silent on this aspect of the state's tax structure.

Local property tax revenues in the state have not risen as rapidly as state tax revenues. State aid has been mainly responsible for keeping property levies from rising rapidly. Because Rhode Island is highly urbanized, and because it is such a small state, dominated by the city of Providence, state-local relations could be worked out in such a way as to reduce expenditures significantly. That this has not been done is due in the main to inadequate planning. The state aid program has developed in a haphazard fashion. Many functions performed by the state could be done at the local level in so small a state as Rhode Island. On the other hand, a transfer of some local functions to the state would no doubt save much money. Some changes in the political structure might be necessary to increase the efficiency of the governments involved. The geographical unity of Rhode Island is conducive to close cooperation between state and local units, but even on so simple a matter as state audit of local government accounts this cooperation is lacking.

While increasing state aid in Rhode Island has prevented serious fiscal difficulties for the cities and towns, there is little reason to believe the finances of local units can withstand the pressures of a recession or depression. Dependence on the shared revenues from alcoholic beverages and pari-mutuel taxes, especially the latter, should be avoided. The system of allocating grants should be simplified and as a condition for grants local units should be required to submit to audits and to standardize their accounts and reports. At the present time it is almost impossible to make comparisons among Rhode Island units because of the absence of reports and the use of dissimilar accounting systems.[16]

In addition to improving state-local relationships, there is room for major improvement in the state tax office. Most tax research of value has been done by other than state agencies, yet the state legislature is most in need of the knowledge which continuous surveillance brings. Effective tax administration requires a knowledge of the workings of the tax system and the effects of taxation upon business and individuals in the community. Rhode Island could well utilize such studies.

New Hampshire

State taxation in New Hampshire is relatively unimportant compared to local taxation. The major state taxes are gasoline, motor vehicle, and tobacco levies. Local property taxes consistently exceed the total state taxes by a wide margin. New Hampshire is akin to New Jersey and some of the less

16. Rhode Island Public Expenditure Council, *Local Finances in Rhode Island,* Providence, 1944.

populous western states in its property tax emphasis, ranking around fifth among all states in emphasis on local tax collections. Thus, local governments raise and spend most of the money, while state aid to local government is the lowest of any state in the nation. The major state taxes are earmarked for special purposes, which introduces further elements of rigidity into the expenditure system. The state revenue base is narrow and unstable.

The New Hampshire Interim Committee on Over-all Taxation recommended in 1949 that a gross income tax or a combination sales and net income tax be enacted. The constitutionality of the gross income tax with variable rates is doubtful, but a flat rate income tax is legally possible. So far these taxes have not been passed. While the very large size of the New Hampshire legislature will make it difficult to attain agreement on any comprehensive tax reform, the successive neglect of tax reports and their recommendations means that the tax system becomes outmoded in relation to present-day tax and fiscal policies. The very little help given to local communities by the state places a heavy burden on local communities for schools and other vital functions. The inequities of property taxation are only increased when more revenues are raised through the use of such taxation. The state tax authorities have expended a good deal of effort in attempting to change some of the more inequitable features of the state tax laws, such as the "stock-in-trade" tax and some good work has been done in the field of assessments of real property, but the tax commission lacked the needed public support. Education for a better tax system is one of the state's most pressing needs.

There are many encouraging signs that New Hampshire will improve its system. Its citizens are careful spenders, and projects beyond the state's fiscal resources are unlikely to be undertaken. The state has an excellent forestry taxation program. The state tax office is competently staffed but could use additional help, especially that of qualified assessors. The tax commissioners are interested and active in attempting to improve the system. The provincial outlook of the influential groups in the towns has so far frustrated any far-reaching changes. There is no tax crisis in the state at the moment, but any fairly severe recession would place burdens on the cities and towns which would be difficult to overcome under the present system. It would be wise to make changes now in order to meet the future better.

Vermont

The 1952 report of Vermont's tax commission closed with a discussion of a problem unusual for investigatory bodies of that type.[17] The problem was the commission's inability to estimate the state surplus for fiscal 1952.

17. State of Vermont, *Report of Commission to Study the Question of Taxation*, Montpelier, 1952.

The problem was soon solved. The nearly $5,000,000 surplus was the highest in the state's history. The commission was quick to point out that the combination of circumstances which led to this blissful state was not to be taken as normal.

Vermonters have always been careful of their freedom, and this includes freedom from taxation. Yet in relation to income Vermont's taxation is higher than the United States average. Its per capita expenditures for general operation are above the New England average. Its state aid expenditures are low, however. Vermont has had an accumulated, unappropriated surplus in its general fund since before the war. The surplus fell rapidly after the war but has, since 1951, reached a peak. This situation is not altogether the result of what many would assume to be the foresight of wise fiscal policy. It is due more to passing tax laws which brought in more than had been estimated, and therefore is in part the result of poor estimating methods. The introduction of withholding provisions in the income tax law in 1951 added approximately $400,000 and the additional surtaxes on personal and corporate incomes yielded $1,300,000. A "windfall" of $1,200,000 resulted from stepped-up collections of income taxes. The increased yield resulting from the use of withholding is an excellent example of the efficacy of this device.

Property tax assessment in Vermont was demonstrated to be as badly handled as it is in most other states. The tax commission's report indicated how assessments vary, but the recommendations to improve the system did not go far enough. It is insufficient to ask that local assessors *request* assistance. The commission took a forward step in recommending elimination of taxation on personal property not used for business purposes.

As for new taxes, it was felt that a general sales tax should be levied if additional revenues were necessary. The regressive features of the tax would be mitigated by the progressive features of state and federal income taxation, the commission felt, and it also found appealing the idea that vacationers would be paying the tax.

The report called for the creation of a Fiscal Planning Commission and for additional funds for research to be undertaken by the commission on taxes. It stressed the need for research more strongly than do most tax reports. The increasing emphasis on research, in evaluating fiscal operations, can do much to help the smaller states such as Vermont which have suffered for years from a paucity of information. The expenditure of funds in this direction could provide continuous dividends over the years.

Massachusetts

Though every New England state is confronted with tax and revenue problems, Massachusetts has had more attention directed toward its tax system than any other New England state. Much can be done in Massachusetts to improve tax and expenditure policy on both the state and local level. Reduction in state spending will go a long way toward alleviating the need for more tax sources, while improvements in the existing structure will reduce the inequities now present. Some taxes will have to be changed; others ought to be eliminated. Tax improvements might encourage industrial expansion and investment or improve the psychological climate which is evidently a deterring influence to industrial development in Massachusetts.

Although we cannot describe them here in detail, many opportunities exist for reducing expenditures. The reports of the Massachusetts Special Commission on the Structure of the State Government contain literally hundreds of suggestions for improving state services while decreasing the costs of those services. It has been estimated that increasing the efficiency of the tax department can bring additional tax yields of from $10,000,000 to $20,000,000. If the efficiency of the department can be raised as much as some critics believe to be possible, then the rates on some taxes can be reduced and the less workable and most onerous ones can be eliminated entirely.

Reduction in the rates of certain Massachusetts taxes is necessary to bring them into line with other states. In some cases, changes in the law are needed to improve equity. An excellent and thorough analysis of the tax structure of the state has been made by the Massachusetts Special Commission on Taxation. The commission advised in 1951 that the Commonwealth "refrain from further increases in taxes upon manufacturing corporations." [18]

The commission also advised that the corporate excess measure be repealed and an alternative minimum tax of $2.50 per $1,000 on corporate net assets be imposed. The corporate excess measure is now in addition to net income measure. The new provision would eliminate this and also the present alternative minimum tax of 1/20 of 1% of capital stock value. Thus, the present complicated corporation excise tax would be simplified and employ one of two measures: (1) 6% of net income or (2) $2.50 per $1,000 of net assets (used within the Commonwealth), whichever is greater. The new tax would be a far better levy than the present total net excise which reached a level of 10.7% of income allocable to Massachusetts for all foreign and domestic corporations in 1950. No other state has effective rates of this height. In addition, the present system of basic and surtax rates is confusing and unnecessary.

The differential treatment of business corporations resulting from the exemption of the machinery of manufacturing corporations from local taxation came about when the "in lieu" tax included more elements than those necessary to make up for the value of exempt machinery. The tax on

18. *Report of the Massachusetts Special Commission on Taxation*, Pt. 4, "The Comparative Impact of Corporate Taxes in Massachusetts."

Massachusetts tangibles of nonmanufacturing corporations turned out not to be in lieu of but in addition to the other taxes inasmuch as these corporations did not have the opportunity to exempt machinery. The commission suggested that business and manufacturing corporations be put on the same base and that *all* corporations be exempted from local taxation of machinery and inventory. In place of the present local taxation of such personalty, it recommended that the Commonwealth assess a tax of $6 per $1,000 of the value of tangible personal property, including inventories.[19] The virtues of this proposal, which has been temporarily removed from the commission's proposals regarding state-local relationships, are that surtaxes are eliminated; the base would be the same for commercial and manufacturing corporations; the rate would be lower for most corporations in that they are now subject to corporate excess. The pressures of local assessors would be removed because the Commonwealth would assess but local governments would collect the tax. In addition, the outmoded 1936 base for distributing the tax would be removed, and the towns in which the facilities are now located would receive the funds.

The present computation of alternative minimum measures discriminates against corporations using debt rather than equity financing, those with large inventories, and new companies with large capital investments. Tax policies relating to local taxation of personal property are mainly responsible for these differences, according to the commission, and the "basic objection to the tangibles alternative is that the franchise tax is no place to make adjustments to offset tax policies in other areas." [20] Thus, the attempts in the thirties to alleviate the tax burdens of certain stricken industries have resulted today in the complication of the law and in the unfair treatment of certain taxpayers. Adoption of the commission's recommendation for eliminating the corporate excess tax, revising the capital stock measure, and extending the exemption of machinery to business corporations is necessary to achieve a fairer and more workable corporate tax structure. The present one-sided emphasis on taxation of manufacturing corporations should cease.

The *personal income tax* now levied by the Commonwealth is one of the poorest of any state. The tax discriminates unfairly between incomes received as wages and salaries and incomes arising from intangibles, the latter being taxed much more heavily. The rate structure is based on four classes of income, the highest rate being 7.38% (including 1953 surtaxes) on intangibles while the rate on income derived from "professions, employments, trade or business" is only 2.62%. Income from real estate is excluded from taxable business income. The inequities are obvious and are increased by the system of deductions and exemptions.

Some degree of graduation in the effective rate of the tax exists because

19. *Ibid.*, Pt. 5, p. 72.
20. *Ibid.*, Pt. 4.

taxpayers in the higher income groups tend to have more income of the "unearned" variety than taxpayers in the lower income groups, though the burden is relatively greater for those low-income individuals who receive most of their income from investments.

More than half of the tax yield is derived from the unearned income class and under certain conditions this might have an unstabilizing effect on state revenues. The present exemptions are large enough to permit thousands of residents of the Commonwealth to pay little if any tax. Broadening of the base would provide a substantial increase in revenues and allow a decrease (or at least no further increases) in the less equitable taxes.[21]

Several loopholes in the present law ought to be closed. The most important of these is the exclusion of rents from income. Another is the partial exclusion of interest received from mortgages. The present use of the business trust device to avoid income taxation, especially in the real estate field, should be eliminated. There are other improvements which can be made. A reduction in exemptions to a more reasonable level has been mentioned, and the possibility of eliminating the deduction for federal taxes should be considered. Finally, a simplification of the tax form and the use of withholding provisions ought to be considered. The present cumbersome and confusing form undoubtedly results in many mistakes by the taxpayer and increases the difficulty and time spent in auditing the returns. A special commission on taxation has also pointed out the need for integrating the state income tax with that of the federal law. In addition, the distribution of clear and concise administrative regulations and instructions for taxpayer guidance is urgently needed.

While corporate and personal income taxes account for over half the state's tax revenues, gasoline, cigarette, liquor, and motor vehicle registration revenues are important to the Commonwealth. Not much can be said about these taxes except that they should not be raised at every opportunity. When taxes on cigarettes and liquor become high in relation to the rates in neighboring states, evasion increases and enforcement becomes difficult. The costs of preventing evasion—and prevention is absolutely necessary if any semblance of equity is to be preserved—may outweigh the presumed benefits of higher rates. Better enforcement of the cigarette tax might be obtained through the use of tax stamps.

In recent years the requirements for increased revenues have led to the imposition of sales taxes in many states and in some cities and counties. There is increasing pressure for such a tax in Massachusetts.

Consideration of a sales tax for Massachusetts should involve careful weighing of both its faults and merits, and the effect it might have on the existing tax system. Probably its most serious fault is that sales taxation

21. The present surtaxes result from the need to provide monies for the General Fund. Under the system now existing, proceeds from the normal tax are distributed to the cities and towns. Changes in this system will be necessary to accomplish the above objective.

tends to bear relatively heavily on the lower income receivers, a tendency that can be lessened by exempting sales of food and rent. A decided merit is that a sales tax would provide revenues which could be used to facilitate greatly needed changes in present state and local taxes, including a reduction in the rates of corporate taxation and lower real estate taxation at the local level. Another merit is that a sales tax is a method to secure contributions from out-of-state residents who visit Massachusetts. It also provides a substantial source of relatively stable revenue.

A sales tax should not be considered simply as a temporary addition to an already complex tax structure in Massachusetts. In drawing sales tax legislation the experience of many states with sales tax laws should be closely examined so that a well-devised law could resolve as many conflicts of interest as possible.

STATE-LOCAL FISCAL RELATIONS IN MASSACHUSETTS

The present arrangements for state aid to the cities and towns of the Commonwealth are outmoded and in many ways unworkable. The Special Commission on Taxation has put forward proposals to simplify and improve the present system. A complex of some 40 "aids," "grants," "reimbursements," and so on has grown up over the years. The commission did not attempt to unravel "this snarled skein of financial relationships," but rather suggested improvements in those areas where immediate action appeared possible.[22]

The most serious shortcomings in the aid programs arise in the sharing of state-collected income, corporation, meals, and public service corporation taxes. The commission pointed out that the amount, basis, and mechanism of the distribution are faulty. The unpredictability of revenues from the program preclude intelligent planning by city and town officers. The discretion given in the past to the commissioner of corporations and taxation in determining the total amounts to be shared, and the necessity of his making estimates of distributions to be made, are the major elements in this unpredictability. The commissioner's estimates often fall wide of the mark.

The taxes mentioned are disbursed to the cities and towns on the basis of an "equalized" value of assessments for the cities and towns.[23] The discussion of assessing difficulties given earlier in this report should make the reader well aware of the difficulties and inequities inherent in this system of distribution. It should be changed at the first opportunity. Because of this system, some of the cities and towns most in need of aid receive relatively lower distributions than cities and towns least in need of aid.

22. *Report of the Massachusetts Special Commission on Taxation*, Pt. 6, "State-Local Fiscal Relationships," Boston, 1952.

23. "Equalization" does not imply reassessment. The procedure is really only one of adjusting the over-all valuations of the towns for distribution purposes.

While there are certain equalizing tendencies present, they may be due more to chance than to planning.

The earmarking of certain tax revenues for specific purposes is the root cause of these difficulties. Fluctuations in the yield of certain taxes have a profound effect on the distributions to cities and towns. The rigidities which earmarking introduces into tax and expenditure policy outweigh many assumed benefits. Around 66% of tax collections were earmarked during 1950. Much more flexibility in spending can be had if tax collections go into the General Fund and thence to those areas and functions where there is the most need. *The revenues of a particular tax should not determine the funds available for a specific purpose. Need should be the determinant, and this determination should be made by the legislature.* A much more stable distribution can be made and the impact of cyclical changes on city and town finances can be much reduced. And perhaps more important, the legislature can regain control of the public purse.

A far-reaching change of this sort will be objected to by local governments on the grounds that local control will be lost and the cities and towns will be at the mercy of the General Court. But the cities and towns are now at the mercy of fluctuating tax revenues and the rather arbitrary, unpredictable, and confusing distributions under present laws. These are certainly less merciful than the General Court whose members are the elected representatives of residents in the cities and towns. Advocates of home rule have discovered that revenue stability is one of the most essential ingredients of local freedom. More, not less, freedom is the result.

Without going into the details of the proposals advanced by the special commission, it is sufficient to say that the changes in state aid are designed to relieve the local communities of the greater part of the burdens of public assistance and veterans' assistance, and extend both school and highway aid. A "general government" grant is also included. This is a forward step in state-local relationships, for it is given without reservations as to use.

THE BOSTON PROBLEM

The need for improved taxation in the City of Boston has been obvious for some time. Boston's property taxation is probably the highest in the United States. The administration of the tax is possessed of all the faults of property taxation everywhere, in addition to those faults engendered by Boston's political and economic difficulties. While much might be said of the results of poor political control, it must be realized that many of the higher than normal costs result from the physical composition of the city itself. For example, the heavy police costs arise in part from the need for traffic control, and the latter arises from the cowpath arrangement of the city streets. Boston came of age long before the automobile, and it is almost impossible to remedy traffic congestion without very large outlays. Additional taxation to correct this and other municipal difficulties may take the form of a city sales or income tax. Properly drawn, either of these taxes would be a large revenue raiser.

The real solution of Boston's fiscal problems will probably have to be far more imaginatively conceived, however. It may be that creation of a more inclusive metropolitan district or the sharing of certain costs with the surrounding communities is necessary. More state aid is certainly needed and changes in the aid program will have to be undertaken. Revision in the property tax structure should be made in such a way as to encourage new building rather than discourage it as at present. A solution for the transit deficits is badly needed. The savings to Boston and to the cities and towns in the metropolitan district which can be made if the system is put on a paying basis are enormous. Careful research on this particular problem should be undertaken as soon as possible.

It is indisputable that significant reductions in the cost of the city government can be made by elimination of unnecessary positions, more careful audit and control over expenditures, central purchasing, stricter control of competitive bidding, and the like. These problems are not new. That they have not been solved is in great measure due to public apathy on the part of those who might contribute most to effective solutions. The elimination of noneconomic factors operating to hinder effective government is a prerequisite to any solution to Boston's economic problems. And the solution of Boston's problems is imperative for the economic good of the Commonwealth. Indeed, it may be that an economically healthy Boston is the most essential ingredient for the economic development of the Commonwealth.

ADMINISTRATIVE REFORMS

The proposals which have been advanced for Massachusetts cannot be carried into effect without the help of an informed citizenry. The greater part of the information now reaching the people is put forward by partisan groups and much of it is of little real value in reaching intelligent conclusions. The tax department in past years has been of little help in the matter. The Annual Report is anything but annual; the last published report appeared in 1940. There has been a paucity of information relating to local taxation and assessment procedures in an area where much education is needed if the equity of property taxation is to be improved. There has been little effective liaison between local officials and the state tax office. The department could be made far more efficient. Appointments have frequently been made with little regard to qualifications. Within the department, the section chiefs have had little effective control over their orbit of responsibility. There has been small incentive in the department for imaginative administration.

The situation is difficult but not hopeless. Reform of the tax department is essential and much of the detail for that reform has been given by the Special Commission on the Structure of the State Government.[24] The primary aim is to establish lines of organization and control, most notably lacking at the moment. The new organization of three commissioners in place of one is no guarantee of efficiency, however. Authority and prestige must be restored to those who know their duties best. Modern accounting and processing equipment should be installed to eliminate the backlog of work and provide more effective tax control. This is more than a matter of new organization charts. Reform must have the willing and open cooperation of the public and the state employees.

The major task of informing the public, the executive, and the legislature on taxation and spending in the Commonwealth should be performed by a research section specifically established for that purpose. A legislative research department can coordinate the information gathering of the several departments concerned with the economic development of the Commonwealth. Tax and expenditure policies should be considered an integral part of such research and development. Perhaps the most valuable work of such a unit would be to *define the problems* in the tax field, whose nature is unknown under present arrangements. The benefits would be many: the need for many special investigations would be much reduced; information would be currently available for the legislature and the executive; the public would obtain needed information in clear and concise publications designed to acquaint the citizen with tax and spending problems; and the reporting and analysis of tax and revenue data would be brought together in one place for the first time.

SELECTED REFERENCES

1. City of Boston, reports and recommendations of the Finance Commission.
2. Commerce Clearing House, Publisher of detailed information on all aspects of state tax resources. See especially *Tax Systems,* Chicago, for brief summaries of state resources.
3. Commonwealth of Massachusetts, *Report of the Massachusetts Special Commission on Taxation,* Pts. 1–6, Boston, 1951–52.
4. Floyd, Joe S., *Effects of Taxation on Industrial Location,* Chapel Hill, University of North Carolina Press, 1952.
5. Hansen and Perloff, *State and Local Finance in the National Economy,* New York, 1944.

24. Massachusetts Special Commission on the Structure of the State Government, *Tentative Report on Study Unit No. 15, The Department of Corporations and Taxation,* Boston, May 1952.

6. Heer, Clarence, *Tax Bill of a Selected Manufacturing Corporation in Six South-eastern States,* North Carolina State Planning Board, Raleigh, 1945.

7. Martin, James W., and Morrow, Glen D., *Taxation of Manufacturing in the South,* Bureau of Public Administration, University of Alabama, 1948.

8. National Tax Association, *Journal and Proceedings of National Tax Association,* Sacramento, Calif., 1951.

9. National Tax Association Proceedings, *Report of the Model Plan for State and Local Taxation,* Lancaster, Pa., 1933.

10. State of California, *Report of the Senate Interim Committee on State and Local Taxation,* Pt. 3, State and Local Taxes in California, a Comparative Analysis, Sacramento, Calif., 1952.

11. Tax commissions of the six New England states, annual reports.

12. Tax Institute, publisher of much material on problems of state and local taxation or finance, Princeton, New Jersey.

13. U.S. Department of Commerce, Bureau of the Census, *Compendium of City and State Government Finances,* Washington, 1947, 1949, 1950.

14. U.S. Treasury Department, *Federal-State-Local Tax Coordination,* Washington, 1952.

Appendix Table 1. *Major State Taxes, Rates and Basis of Measure, New England States, 1951*

	CONNECTICUT		MAINE		MASSACHUSETTS		NEW HAMPSHIRE		RHODE ISLAND		VERMONT	
	MEASURE	RATE	MEASURE	RATE	MEASURE	RATE	MEASURE	RATE	MEASURE	RATE	MEASURE	RATE
Sales, gross receipts, and use taxes (1)	Gross income from interstate operation of unincorporated businesses Gross receipts of retail sales of tangible personal property Sales price of tangible property used or consumed within state	$1 per $1,000 3% 3%	Tangible personal property sold at retail—storage and use of tangible personal property	2% of sales price	Meals tax when charge is $1 or more	5%	None		Retail sales, tangible personal property, and certain utility services or use of such	1%	None	
Unemployment compensation (2)	Wages paid up to $3,000 during calendar year	0.25% to 2.7% merit rate	Wages paid up to $3,000	0.25% to 2.7% merit rate	Wages paid up to $3,000	2.7%	Wages paid up to $3,000	0.25% to 2.7% merit rate	Wages paid up to $3,000	2.7%	Wages paid up to $3,000	0.25% to 2.7%
Motor vehicle fuels (3)	Gallons sold or used	4¢ per gallon	Gallons sold or used	6¢ per gallon	Gallons sold or used	4.3¢ per gallon	Gallons sold or used	5¢ per gallon 4¢ for aircraft	Gallons sold or used	4¢ per gallon	Gallons sold or used	5¢ per gallon
Motor vehicle fees (4)	Noncommercial Commercial	$7-$11 30¢-50¢ per cut	Private Trucks	$10-$16 15¢ cut	Private Trucks Automobile excise—value of automobile, scaled rate*	$3-$25 $3 per 1,000 lbs. Av. state tax rate	Motor vehicles generally	35¢-60¢ per cut	Passenger vehicles Trucks	$8-$23 $2.50-$147 + $6 per 2,000 lbs. over 48,000 lbs.	Private—depending on age Trucks	$14 or $22 70¢ to $1.05 per cwt.
Personal Income (5)	None		None		Annuity income Employment and business Dividends and interest Gains from sale of intangibles plus surtax	1½% 2½% 6% 6% 23%	Personal income from intangibles only	Av. state prop. rate	None		Personal income Temporary surtax	graduated 1½%–5½% 15%

Appendix Table 1 (continued)

	CONNECTICUT		MAINE		MASSACHUSETTS		NEW HAMPSHIRE		RHODE ISLAND		VERMONT	
	MEASURE	RATE	MEASURE	RATE	MEASURE	RATE	MEASURE	RATE	MEASURE	RATE	MEASURE	RATE
Corporate Income (6)	Income on value of stocks, surplus, etc. Banks and financial corporations	3% on income 1½ mills per $1 on alternative measure 3%	None		Corporations: corporate excess plus net income plus surtax on income and corporate excess Banks: net income —financial institutions —fixed annually savings banks public utilities —net income	$5 per $1,000 5½% 23% max. 8% of net income ⅓ of 1% of "deposits" 4%	None		Business corporations and banks: net income or corporate excess Banks: net income Unincorporated business Retail or manufacturing wholesale	4% (5% for 1951) or 40¢ per $100 of excess 4% $2 per $1,000 $1 per $1,000	Corporate franchise (income) Surtax	4% 15%
Alcoholic beverage sales (7)	Beer Liquor Alcohol Wine Licenses—class of business and location	$1 per bbl. $1 per gal. $1 per gal. 10¢–25¢ per gal. $5–$1,500	Manufacturers' excise: malt wine—raw material Consumer's tax —cost price Licenses	5⅓¢ per gal. 4¢ per gal. or 2¢ per gal. maximum 61% $50 to $3,000	Excise (manufacturers' or sale): malt beverages wines other plus additional excises plus income from certain organizations and associations selling alcoholic beverages Licenses	$2 per bbl. 30¢–40¢ per gal. 60¢–$1.75 per gal. 50¢ per gal. 1½% or 1/20 of 1% of gross receipt $1–$5,000			Excise on local manufacturer: wines distilled liquor beer alcohol Imported, service charge for liquor: wines beer Licenses	20¢–25¢ per gal. 50¢ per gal. $1 per 31 gal. bbl. $1 per gal. $1.50 per gal. 20¢–25¢ gal. $1 per bbl. $10–$3,000	Excises: malt and alcohol Licenses	depending on content 15¢ per gal. to 45¢ per pint $2–$2,000
Cigarette taxes (8)	Quantity held, stored, used	3¢ per 20	Quantity	4¢ per 20	Quantity sold	5¢ per 20	Retail selling price	15%	Quantity sold or held for sale	3¢ per 20	Quantity held for sale	4¢ per 20

* This tax is assessed by the municipalities at the average state tax rate and retained by the municipalities. The tax is described here to illustrate its comparability with those of the other New England states.

Source: Compiled from Commerce Clearing House, *Tax System of the World*, 13th ed., 1952

Appendix Table 2. *Sources of State Tax Revenues, Excluding Unemployment Taxes, 1951*

TAX	PER CENT OF TOTAL YIELD	CUMULATIVE
MAINE		
Gasoline	31.5%	31.5%
Motor vehicle registration	15.9	47.4
General property[1]	14.1	61.5
Cigarette and tobacco[2]	12.2	73.7
Alcoholic beverages	6.1	79.8
Inheritance	3.8	83.6
Railroad companies	3.7	87.3
Telephone and telegraph company	2.4	89.7
All other	10.3	100.0
NEW HAMPSHIRE		
Gasoline	24.3%	24.3%
Motor vehicle registration	19.5	43.8
Tobacco	11.9	55.7
Income from intangibles	11.3	67.0
Horse racing permits, fees and pari-mutuel pools	7.8	74.8
Alcoholic beverage[3]	5.6	80.4
Public utilities	5.6	86.0
Insurance	4.7	90.7
All other	9.3	100.0
VERMONT		
Gasoline	23.1%	23.1%
Motor vehicle registration	18.7	41.8
Personal income	16.1	57.9
Alcoholic beverages	13.1	71.0
Cigarette	8.1	79.1
Corporate income	6.2	85.3
Insurance companies	5.3	90.6
All other	9.4	100.0

TAX	PER CENT OF TOTAL YIELD	CUMULATIVE
MASSACHUSETTS		
Corporate income	33.3%	33.3%
Personal income	22.4	55.7
Gasoline and motor fuel	9.6	65.3
Cigarette	9.1	74.4
Liquor	8.1	82.5
Motor vehicle registration	3.8	86.3
Insurance	3.6	89.9
Inheritance	3.4	93.3
All other	6.7	100.0
RHODE ISLAND		
Sales and use	15.8%	15.8%
Gasoline	15.4	31.2
Corporate income[3]	15.1	46.3
Motor vehicle registration	11.6	57.9
Cigarette	7.7	65.6
Pari-mutuel pools	7.5	73.1
Public utilities	7.0	80.1
Alcoholic beverages	5.9	86.0
Inheritance	4.5	90.5
All other	9.5	100.0
CONNECTICUT		
Sales	28.0%	28.0%
Gasoline and fuel	16.4	44.4
Corporate income	15.1	59.5
Motor vehicle	8.8	68.3
Liquor	7.6	75.9
Cigarette	6.4	82.3
Insurance premiums	5.7	88.0
Succession and transfer	5.1	93.1
Public utilities	3.9	97.0
All other	3.0	100.0

1 State share only.
2 Includes permits and fees. (No report of 1951 sales taxes given.)
3 Includes banks.
Source: Ibid.

Appendix Table 3. Unemployment Compensation Tax Revenues, United States, New England, and Selected States, 1939, 1947, 1949, 1950

STATE	TOTAL (IN THOUSANDS)				AS PERCENTAGE OF TOTAL TAX COLLECTIONS			
	1939	1947	1949	1950	1939	1947	1949	1950
UNITED STATES	801,111	969,227	972,929	1,028,033	22.2	14.4	11.7	11.5
NEW ENGLAND	69,339	83,718	71,633	85,510	27.7	19.6	14.1	15.7
Maine	4,032	6,421	6,406	6,173	17.2	18.2	13.9	13.1
New Hampshire	2,734	3,636	4,010	4,538	19.8	16.7	16.8	18.7
Vermont	1,506	2,141	2,147	1,569	13.3	12.6	10.5	7.2
Massachusetts	37,803	28,084	43,526	49,018	29.9	12.7	16.2	17.3
Rhode Island	7,594	13,892	7,839	10,927	35.3	35.3	16.5	22.2
Connecticut	15,670	29,544	7,705	13,285	29.4	31.7	7.6	11.2
SELECTED STATES								
California	75,351	116,586	113,240	128,456	25.5	16.7	13.1	13.7
Illinois	65,909	43,043	63,045	56,031	27.8	11.9	14.4	12.8
Michigan	36,563	43,626	79,584	68,839	24.2	12.8	17.4	14.9
New Jersey	43,978	78,750	50,505	43,601	36.7	33.9	26.3	22.8
New York	119,215	169,915	150,270	208,227	25.1	20.8	16.8	19.0
North Carolina	10,691	16,674	20,038	17,987	13.5	8.6	8.7	7.8
Ohio	56,889	52,578	37,964	44,029	26.3	14.7	9.5	10.4
Pennsylvania	75,745	73,955	64,312	57,937	25.2	19.5	12.6	11.7
South Carolina	4,438	6,002	7,751	7,377	14.8	7.4	7.7	7.6
Tennessee	8,486	15,506	14,841	12,396	17.5	16.4	9.6	7.6

Source: Bureau of the Census, *Compendium of City and State Government Finances,* 1947, 1949, 1950; and *Financial Statistics of States in 1939,* Washington

18

Business and Economic Information in New England

*Drafted by George H. Ellis on the basis of material
prepared by Arthur A. Bright, Jr.*

INTRODUCTION

A modern industrial society demands an incredible amount of information for its efficient operation. Information is the basis of decisions, and making decisions is the heart of economic activity. As economic, political, social, technological, and other conditions change, there is a persisting need for new facts and more facts. They must not only be discovered but be organized and distributed where they are most needed.

Business units of all kinds seek out the information they need to carry on their day-to-day operations and to make their long-range plans. Much of that information is highly specialized in order to answer questions of particular interest to the individual concern, such as the credit rating of a new customer, the delivered price of a given raw material, or the market potential for a certain product. Over the years, channels of trade information have grown up to help satisfy the various needs. Just as manufacturers have their own particular informational requirements, so have farmers, retailers, labor unions, banks, railroads, utilities, and all the other kinds of economic units. To supplement their specialized trade data, they also draw on the informational resources of federal, state, and local government organizations and of numerous private ones.

All levels of government also require extensive business and economic information in enacting and administering the laws. They satisfy their fact requirements largely through their own efforts. Most government agencies, especially those of the federal and state governments, make both regular statistical compilations and numerous special investigations to obtain the information they need. Much of that information is made available for the use of private business units and others.

Despite the voluminous outpouring of data, or perhaps because of it, the public at large is often not well informed about business and economic conditions and problems. There is too much detailed information for the average person to gather, much less read and understand. For the most part, the public obtains its business and economic information through piecemeal reports in the newspapers and on radio and television. Only those with particular interests go to the trouble of studying the various reports, pamphlets, and books that deal with these subjects, and even they seldom go to the original material.

While members of the public normally do not feel an urgent or immediate need for economic facts unrelated to their own personal businesses or employment, the importance of their having a basic understanding of the economic life of their community, region, and nation is nonetheless great. Their attitudes, their expressions of opinion, and their votes affect economic policy formulation and actions by both business units and governments. *A genuinely well-informed public is an important element in constructive economic action in any area. It is especially important in New England, where the process of economic transition has created a strong need for unified and aggressive policies and action.*

Perhaps even more important than getting more and better economic information is disseminating that which is already available. Even the best information is of no value if it is not used. The task is twofold: there is first the matter of channeling the facts to those who should have them, and second that of obtaining action on the basis of the facts.

A study of the distribution of business and economic information in New England was an important element in the research program of the Committee of New England. The spread of such information is an integral part of the region's economic process. A comprehensive research program on New England must take into account the organizations which carry on informational activities, by summarizing and evaluating their contributions to economic knowledge. There is still too little understanding by business units, government agencies, and the public of many of the major economic problems of the region.

In this report we are primarily concerned with the informational activities of organizations in New England. We consider the range of actions undertaken, the methods used, and the obstacles faced by those organizations. We shall offer some suggestions for increasing the value and effectiveness of their operations. Our attention is centered on the assembly and distribution of existing business and economic information. We have not attempted a comprehensive survey of the region's needs for economic research to create more information. Nor have we evaluated all the existing economic research agencies in terms of the region's needs. In this, as in our other reports, however, we have pointed out opportunities where additional inquiry would seem to be beneficial.

Any discussion of business and economic information must, of necessity, deal also with promotional and developmental efforts. Promotion and development are the ultimate goals of many of the informational agencies in the region. Any organization which conducts the one type of activity is usually concerned with the other, though the relative emphasis varies greatly. Accordingly, the survey upon which much of this report is based undertook to examine and appraise several aspects of the developmental work under way in the region rather than the informational phases alone.

THE EXTENT AND NATURE OF PRESENT INFORMATIONAL AND DEVELOPMENTAL ACTIVITIES

A great many organizations concern themselves with informational, promotional, and developmental efforts within New England. These groups have a strong influence upon the region's industrial growth, both directly and indirectly. The information which they originate or disseminate is also important in molding public opinion on New England's problems and enlisting it for desirable courses of action.

Kinds and Numbers of Organizations

A mere listing of the organizations currently engaged in informational and developmental work in New England would be impressive. It would cover well over a thousand private organizations and many governmental bodies. Most of them are concerned primarily with local problems, but there are scores with statewide or region-wide interests.

The group concerned mainly with individual communities includes at least 350 chambers of commerce and boards of trade, more than 100 taxpayers' associations, almost 200 agricultural associations, 36 industrial foundations, a score of local area developmental associations, and large numbers of trade and industrial organizations, real estate associations, labor organizations, better business bureaus, community development associations, and other groups. The chambers of commerce typically have the broadest interests and are most active, both in the dissemination of business and economic information and in local promotion and economic development. Many of them have auxiliary organizations such as industrial bureaus or industrial foundations to aid in their programs.

The private statewide organizations are fewer but they cover almost as broad a range. Each New England state has a manufacturers' association, a farm bureau federation, a state federation of labor, a CIO council, a commercial bankers' association, a savings bank association, and a hotel association. It may have a taxpayers' federation, a state chamber of commerce, and various other special groups. Some of these are concerned with rather narrow fields of interest and activity, while others, such as the manufacturers' associations, usually take an active interest in most phases of the economic life of their states.

At the regional level there are relatively few private informational and developmental organizations. The New England Council is the largest and most influential. Its interests encompass all economic aspects of New England as a whole as well as its subdivisions. In addition, there are more specialized groups, such as the Smaller Business Association of New England and various regional trade, industrial, and agricultural organizations.

Besides the associations, a large number of private or quasi-private organizations disseminate business and economic information about New England or promote economic development in the area in support of their own businesses or as part of their other operations. Many railroads and utilities are active in this effort, as are other transportation agencies and some of the larger commercial banks and other financial institutions. The Federal Reserve Bank of Boston occupies a strategic position in the dissemination of information. Some colleges and universities are active in the spread of information, especially those with bureaus of business research. Finally, newspapers, radio, television, and magazines have an important role as reporters of news and molders of public opinion.

Government agencies also take an important part not only in spreading business and economic information about New England but also in the economic development of the region. The Federal Government maintains regional offices of its Department of Commerce and Bureau of Labor Statistics which issue quantities of information about this as well as other parts of the nation. Regional offices of the Department of Agriculture, Bureau of Mines, Fish and Wildlife Service, Forest Service, and many others provide specialized information. Their activities are invaluable for local economic development. And it must be remembered that a tremendous amount of business and economic information about New England is compiled and issued by other branches of the Federal Government in Washington.

The principal concern of the state development commissions is usually industrial development, but they are also active in the development of vacation business and natural resources and in distributing a wide range of material about economic activities in their states. Other state agences include the departments of employment security, which are major sources of business statistics, and the state planning boards, which have important developmental functions. In addition, a number of New England cities have municipal developmental or industrial commissions, city planning boards, and other kinds of agencies with developmental and informational functions.

We shall devote most of our attention here to a general summary and appraisal of the activities of all organizations, but in the final section we shall consider in more detail some of those organizations dealing with the broader aspects of New England's economic problems, such as the New England Council and the Federal Reserve Bank of Boston at the regional level and the six state development commissions and state manufacturers' associations at the state level. We shall conclude with a discussion of the region's newspapers and radio stations because of their very important position as information sources for most citizens.

Personnel and Expenditures of Organizations

To learn more about the one thousand or so private organizations and governmental agencies in New England concerned with business and economic information, promotion, and development, the Committee of New England conducted a questionnaire survey among approximately 300 of the key organizations. The mailing list included 122 of the larger chambers of commerce within the region, all six state development commissions, all six state manufacturers' associations, and a sample group drawn from other trade, industrial, promotional, or developmental organizations. The responses received from 83 organizations form a fairly typical pattern, and while not fully representing all such organizations in the region, do provide a general idea of the scope of their activities. Returns from the promotional and developmental organizations were slightly higher than those from the trade and industrial groups. The differences among most of the subclassifications were not large.

Table 18–1. The 1951 Budgets of 64 Informational and Developmental Organizations in New England

| | | DEVELOPMENTAL ORGANIZATIONS | | | | TRADE, INDUS- TRIAL, AND FINANCIAL ORGAN- IZATIONS |
	TOTAL	TOTAL	CHAMBERS OF COMMERCE	STATE DEVEL- OPMENT COMMIS- SIONS	OTHER	
Number of organizations:	64*	47	32	5	10	17
Size of budget		(Per cent of organization in group)				
$0–10,000	33%	38%	50%	—	20%	18%
$10,001–25,000	28	19	22	—	20	53
$25,001–50,000	17	17	12	—	40	18
$50,001–100,000	6	6	6	—	10	6
$100,001–200,000	11	13	9	60	—	6
$200,001–300,000	5	6	0	40	10	0
TOTAL	100%	100%	100%	100%	100%	100%
Approximate median budget	$20,000	$20,000	$10,000	$200,000	$30,000	$20,000

Note: Details may not add to totals because of rounding.
* Nineteen respondents did not state their budget totals.

What have the various organizations to work with? The budgets of those which responded to our inquiry ranged from almost nothing to nearly $300,000 during 1951. A third of the 64 organizations which provided this information had budgets of $10,000 or less. Almost as many more had budgets between $10,000 and $25,000. The total budget of the 64 organizations was approximately $3,000,000, but 60% of that total was accounted for by ten respondents with the largest budgets. Five of these ten were state development commissions. Table 18–1 provides a breakdown of the budgetary groupings by major types of organizations.

On the basis of these findings, we estimate that the budgets of all such organizations in New England totaled more than $10,000,000 during 1951 This [total] excludes federal agencies which operate in the region and all state agencies other than the state industrial commissions.

There was a similar distribution in the size of the various organizations surveyed as measured by the number of employees. Three-quarters of them had fewer than seven employees, while half had fewer than three full-time employees. Only 11 had more than 15 employees, but they accounted for approximately one-half of the 500 or so employees of all the organizations combined. On the assumption that we have covered the largest and most important of these organizations, we estimate that all informational and promotional organizations (including trade associations) in New England employed about 2,500 persons in 1951. Expenditures per employee ranged from less than $2,000 to more than $20,000, but there was a very large concentration between $4,000 and $8,000 among the organizations surveyed. The average for all such groups in New England was probably between $4,000 and $5,000 per full-time worker.

Not all the organizations spend full time on promotional and informational activities. Many of them, including a large number of the promotional agencies, have other functions as well. In the agencies surveyed, the average time spent on promotional and informational activities was approximately 64%, with each organization weighted equally. A weighting by size would produce a somewhat higher figure. We believe that the proportion of time devoted to informational and developmental activities by the other organizations not included in our sample would be slightly lower, but that over-all these groups devote about two-thirds of their efforts to such activities. *Accordingly, it would appear that in New England there were at least 1,600 equivalent full-time employees working on informational and developmental work for the region, for the states, for subareas within states, for local communities, or for special trade or industrial groups, and that they spent close to $7,000,000 in 1951 for those purposes.*

Informational Activities

What kinds of informational functions do these organizations perform in New England? The participants in our survey were asked to indicate which of 12 specified activities they conducted in 1951 and to describe any additional activities. There were six types carried on by 70% or more of the respondents. In order of relative frequency they were:

1. The publication of bulletins or bulletin-type newsletters.
2. The dissemination of information about government controls and regulations.

3. Speeches by staff or officers relating to business or economic matters.
4. Conferences and meetings on economic and business matters sponsored by the organization.
5. Preparing press releases about economic and business matters.
6. Providing statistical and other data services by mail, phone, or personal visit.

While there were some differences in the frequencies of the kinds of activities carried on by the various types of organization, the general pattern was not significantly different for the subgroups. Moreover, the number of such activities which each organization conducted was remarkably consistent from group to group. State development commissions and chambers of commerce were slightly above the average, the other promotional or developmental organizations were about average, and the various trade and industrial organizations were slightly under average in number of activities conducted per organization (see Table 18–2).

The number of functions does not, of course, indicate their relative importance, but the answers to our question "Which three of the activities absorb the largest proportion of the staff's time?" produced a result not much different from the summary of the number of activities themselves. The same ones ranked high, though there was some change in order. Apparently bulletins and bulletin-type newsletters absorbed the largest proportion of time spent on informational matters, with information about government controls and regulations second in importance. Conferences and meetings were third in rank, followed in turn by statistical and other data services and by "other" activities. Even those activities which were mentioned by a smaller proportion of the organizations occurred fairly frequently, and every one of them was mentioned as among the three most important informational activities by a few of the organizations. It is clear that most of the responding organizations take the initiative in disseminating large quantities of information directly to the user through press releases, conferences, publications of their own, and in many other ways. The patterns revealed for our selected sample are probably fairly close approximations for all such organizations in New England.

The principal topics of concern to the 83 organizations in our survey cover an extremely broad range. Taxation, the most frequent, was mentioned by almost half the organizations which answered the question. Information about business conditions was a close second. Concentration on these matters was evident in both the promotional groups and the trade and industrial groups. Mentioned quite frequently were such other topics as business opportunities, government controls and regulations, and legislation. This emphasis shows a particular interest on the part of organizations of all types in interpreting and spreading information about the actions of government which affect business. The other topics specifically mentioned were

Table 18–2. *The Informational Activities of 83 Organizations in New England during 1951*

	TOTAL	DEVELOPMENTAL ORGANIZATIONS				TRADE, INDUSTRIAL, AND FINANCIAL ORGANIZATIONS
		TOTAL	CHAMBERS OF COMMERCE	STATE DEVELOPMENT COMMISSIONS	OTHER	
Number of organizations:	83	56	39	6	11	27
Activities conducted		(Per cent of organizations in group conducting each activity)				
Bulletins or newsletters	81%	75%	77%	67%	73%	93%
Speeches by staff and officers	75	77	69	100	91	70
Information about government controls and regulations	75	77	92	67	27	70
Conferences and meetings sponsored	73	79	82	100	55	63
Press releases	72	80	82	67	82	56
Statistical and other data services	70	77	85	83	45	56
Special pamphlets and reports	65	68	64	100	64	59
Cooperation with schools	64	64	64	50	73	63
Business opportunity information	59	77	79	83	64	22
Radio programs	39	41	41	17	55	33
Regular statistical reports	35	34	36	50	18	37
Publication of magazines	19	20	13	33	36	19
Other	33	32	23	33	64	33
Average number of listed activities per organization	7.6	8.0	8.1	8.5	7.5	6.7

usually subdivisions of one or another of these broad topics or matters which related to the particular interests of the organization's members.

Despite the similarity in the patterns of informational activities and the topics of interest, it would appear that there is relatively little duplication of activities among the various organizations. Those which concern themselves primarily with local matters, of course, have an interest in problems with which no one else is particularly concerned. Even the statewide and regional organizations tend to supplement the activities of others far more than they overlap them. Most of those organizations keep in touch with each other in their day-to-day operations and exchange information. Where joint problems are involved, they tend to work together at both staff and officer levels. Undoubtedly, additional cooperation would be desirable in many instances, particularly in the planning and execution of major informational activities.[1]

As pointed out above, a large proportion of the organizations covered in our survey concerned themselves chiefly with local affairs. We asked for a specific statement on the geographic area to which their informational activities related. Three-quarters of the respondents indicated primary interest in single geographic areas, and they listed local communities, states, and New England as a whole in the relative frequency 4–2–1 respectively. The other 25% of the respondents indicated combinations of areas without specific stress upon one or another. A few organizations also mentioned information about the United States as a whole as part of their interest. The ratio in favor of locally oriented informational groups would probably be considerably increased if we had data for all such organizations in New England.

The organizations in our sample were about evenly divided between those which carried on their informational activities for the benefit of their own members, and those which acted for the benefit of the public. A sizable number mentioned both groups, and a few indicated other specific groups as the intended beneficiaries. The chambers of commerce were more heavily weighted toward serving their own members, while the state development commissions and other promotional or developmental organizations were more strongly oriented toward general public service. The trade and industrial associations leaned toward service to their members, although a considerable number of them indicated concern with public information.

Developmental and Promotional Activities

Many organizations conduct a considerable range of promotional and developmental activities. The ones most frequently mentioned by our re-

1. In 1950 a businessmen's committee drawn from the area of greater Boston examined the objectives and activities of nine major business-civic organizations which were active in promoting the Boston area. After careful study which involved in particular a search for possible duplication in activities, the committee concluded that there was little duplication.

Table 18–3. The Promotional and Developmental Activities of 80 Organizations in New England during 1951

| | TOTAL | DEVELOPMENTAL ORGANIZATIONS | | | | TRADE, INDUSTRIAL, AND FINANCIAL ORGANIZATIONS |
		TOTAL	CHAMBERS OF COMMERCE	STATE DEVELOPMENT COMMISSIONS	OTHER	
Number of organizations:	80*	54	38	6	10	26
Activities conducted			(Per cent of organization in group)			
Legislative action	61%	59%	68%	50%	30%	65%
Working with individual industrial prospects	56	72	68	100	70	23
Civic improvement activities	56	72	79	50	60	23
Promotional or developmental conferences sponsored	51	50	47	67	50	54
Advertising in publications	36	37	24	50	80	35
Promotional publications	34	41	24	83	80	19
Management assistance to firms	30	35	37	33	30	19
Technical assistance to firms	28	33	29	50	40	19
Direct mail advertising	25	31	29	17	50	12
Other	19	17	16	33	10	23
Average number of listed activities per organization	4.0	4.5	4.2	5.3	5.0	2.9

* Three respondents did not answer this question.

spondents were (1) legislative action; (2) industrial development relating to individual industrial prospects; and (3) civic improvement. (See Table 18–3.) These three activities were also the ones most frequently mentioned by the chambers of commerce included in the sample. State development commissions, on the other hand, stressed promotional publications and promotional or developmental conferences more than civic improvement efforts and legislative action. The other promotional or developmental agencies apparently put more stress on advertising and promotional publications than on any of the other activities. In the trade and industrial groups, legislative action again ranked high, and they tended to do much less in other lines.

Regional Economic and Development Organizations

The New England Council is a unique organization for the conduct of informational and development action. Established in 1925, the Council is a region-wide association of manufacturers, bankers, business concerns, agriculturists, and representatives of labor, government, and other groups. It is a private nonprofit agency directed and financed by more than 2,500 members. It has a small staff of trained personnel working for and with special committees chosen from the membership and with technical experts engaged for special projects. The staff conducts research in limited fields important to the region's economic health. It provides coordination through committee work and quarterly meetings of members in efforts to make full use of New England's resources. As an organization, it can help provide united action on all fronts where the area's economic progress may be concerned. It promotes aspects of the New England economy which merit exploration, consideration, and action, and at the same time it pursues programs of development in industry, agriculture, recreation, transportation, and other fields.

The Federal Reserve Bank of Boston occupies a strategic place in the economy of New England through its obligation to serve the region as a whole. Since the first Federal Reserve district includes all of New England except Fairfield County, Connecticut, the bank has become a major source of information about the entire area.

Part of its responsibility is to provide information about business conditions in New England to the Board of Governors of the Federal Reserve System in order to aid the nation's monetary authorities in the formulation of monetary policy. To do this the Boston bank collects and analyzes a complete range of business and economic information about the region and its component units. Most of the research findings are made available to the 300-odd member banks and to the New England public. Through its extensive program of regional research directed by trained economists with the assistance of a full research staff, the Reserve Bank is in a key position to serve as a general information center about the region's economy. Many of its findings are published in its *Monthly Review* which is distributed free to approximately 14,000 organizations and individuals, mostly in New England.

The bank is also the originator of a broad range of banking and department store statistics and other statistical information, most of which is made public. Its research findings are widely disseminated through extensive newspaper coverage and frequent speeches and radio talks by the staff on subjects of importance to the New England economy. The bank serves as a clearinghouse for statistical and economic information of all kinds for the benefit of those who need specific information. It also maintains a continuous inventory of research pertaining to New England and publishes a quarterly report describing it. In these and a variety of other ways, the bank helps create a greater understanding of New England's economic position both within and outside the region, thereby contributing to constructive action to further its development. While the bank's efforts are concentrated on the informational function, there are developmental aspects implicit in much of its work.

THE ADEQUACY OF INFORMATIONAL AND DEVELOPMENTAL ACTIVITIES IN NEW ENGLAND

It is heartening to find that there are so many organizations actively engaged in informational work and developmental activities in New England As a group, they have large sums of money to use in furthering their efforts, and they have sizable staffs. They work continuously for the benefit of their members, their communities, their states, and for the region as a whole. The critical question is how successful are they? Do they provide the information needed to form intelligent conclusions and to encourage constructive business and economic action? Do the developmental and promotional activities produce enough in results to repay the effort?

Appraisal of Own Success by Organizations

We asked the respondents to our survey to evaluate their own success in carrying on their informational and developmental programs. (See Table 18–4.) Naturally, few organizations when asked point-blank will admit that their efforts are not successful, but it seems rather surprising that only one organization, a chamber of commerce, admitted its informational activities were not successful, and only three organizations, also chambers of commerce, admitted that their promotional and developmental work was unsuccessful. There was apparently doubt in the minds of some respondents, however, for three qualified their answers regarding their informational activities, three more said they did not know whether they were successful or not, and six did not answer. In regard to their developmental activities, five organizations qualified their answers and one admitted not knowing whether it was successful or not. Fifteen by not answering the question revealed their indecisiveness about the success of their own programs.

No doubt many of the organizations were overoptimistic about their own success, but it is interesting to note the reasons they advanced for successful operation. Insofar as informational activities are concerned, there appears to be little agreement on the attributes of a successful program. There were 22 different explanations, no one of which was mentioned more than four times, and 23 organizations gave no explanation for their reported success. The responses are not readily classified, but some of the most frequently mentioned explanations were public interest and support, reputation, co-

Table 18–4. Reasons Advanced by Organizations for Claimed Success
of Their Informational and Developmental Activities

	INFORMATIONAL ACTIVITIES	DEVELOPMENTAL ACTIVITIES
	(NUMBER OF ORGANIZATIONS)	
Number who claimed success:	70	59
Reason claimed*		
Support by public, members, or other external element	22	14
Extent or quality of effort	18	17
Character or nature of information	8	7
Adequacy of program	8	1
No answer	23	28
TOTAL	79	67

* Number of reasons cited exceeded number of organizations, since some mentioned more than one.

operation of outsiders, efficiency, hard work and perseverance, current information, experience, and cooperation by members. In general it appears that the most common evidence of success in the minds of the respondents is the awakening of general interest and support from members and the public.

The respondents also indicated what they thought were various drawbacks or obstacles to the success of their informational activities. (See Table 18–5.)

Nine of the respondents did not answer this question, and 21 more said they had no drawbacks. Of the 53 organizations that cited specific problems 46, or 87%, specified inadequate funds and staff. This applied to all types of organizations, regardless of size, and included three of the state development commissions which are among the largest of these organizations in New England. Eagerness to expand budgets and staff is understandable as a corollary of the desire to achieve greater success, but it is questionable whether shortage of funds plays such a dominant role in obstructing informational work. A substantial minority also referred to lack of support for informational activities by the public or by members or lack of recognition of the organization's objectives. Only two respondents expressed the opinion that the press and radio lacked interest in their aims and thereby hampered their informational activities.

The reasons advanced for success in developmental work showed almost the same pattern as those given for informational activities. There was no one reason which stood out although "hard work and efficiency" edged out all other responses. Similarly, in appraising the drawbacks which they faced

Table 18–5. Drawbacks to Success of Informational and Developmental Activities Cited by Organizations

	INFORMATIONAL ACTIVITIES	DEVELOPMENTAL ACTIVITIES
	(NUMBER OF ORGANIZATIONS)	
Number of responses:	74	65
No drawbacks	21	20
Drawbacks	53	45
Drawbacks cited*		
Inadequacy of funds and staff	46	32
Lack of interest or support by the public	11	11
Fundamental economic difficulties of area	—	11
Lack of demand or support for such activities by members	7	8
Lack of authoritative or reliable information	7	7
Lack of recognition of organization's objectives	6	10
Lack of interest by press and radio	2	—
Other	10	6

* Number of drawbacks cited exceeds number of organizations, since most mentioned more than one.

in their developmental activities, the organizations singled out as most important the inadequacy of funds and staff. There was a wider distribution of answers for this group, however, for almost as many mentioned lack of support by their members or by the public, or lack of recognition of the organization's objectives. In addition, 11 organizations acknowledged as a difficulty the fundamental economic problems in their areas. This applied particularly to local organizations. It is interesting to note that only a few organizations felt they were hampered in either their informational or promotional efforts by inadequate data.

APPRAISALS BY INFORMATIONAL AND DEVELOPMENT ORGANIZATION EXECUTIVES

Subjective evaluations cannot be gathered accurately by questionnaires. To secure an appraisal of New England's needs and problems in the field of business and economic information, the Committee of New England interviewed a selected group of informational and development executives who are intimately acquainted with these subjects. The survey was in no way exhaustive, and no claims can be made that it reveals the complete scope of New England opinions on the subject. However, the survey did reveal many interesting aspects of the problems which concern us here.

Public Understanding of Business Activities

New England's leading development executives underscored the need for expanding the public's understanding of business activities. They observed that the average person does not sufficiently understand the mechanics or appreciate the importance of a freely operating industrial system. They feel that a widespread understanding of the role played by industry in our everyday life is necessary to offset, on the one hand, a tendency to overestimate the benefits from "government" and, on the other, the tendency to take "industry" for granted and load it with excessive community burdens. They endorse the growing efforts to bring local industry and community together by such devices as plant visits by student classes or women's clubs. These executives emphasize the importance of industrial leaders participating in community affairs. Telling industry's story is a major responsibility of development executives and an objective to which they uniformly subscribe.

Offsetting Negative Attitudes

There was widespread agreement among the development executives that they are waging a continuous battle against the idea of a "declining economy," a mental attitude held by many persons both within and outside the region. They feel there is a general lack of understanding and a pessimistic outlook not warranted by the facts. National journals periodically publish special reports which habitually emphasize that New England's growth, while commendable, has not matched that of other areas. Such "relative declines" are mourned in crepe-hung phraseology, and the impression is spread that New England is dead or dying.[2] The attitudes generated by such reports are a liability that weighs heavily on informational and development organizations in New England. They must continually counter with statistical arguments which describe the situation more precisely, and emphasize the positive aspects of growth and adaptation.

Improving News Presentation

Bad news needs no press agent. News of mill closings, strikes, management threats, and growing relief rolls generally receives prominent attention in the region's many newspapers. The vitally important record of achievements which are more commonplace has some difficulty in finding its way into the daily news medium. Informational and development executives are very critical of this tendency, which they regard as an inherent bias in news reporting. In counterargument, publishers and editors emphasize that New

2. For an excellent example of this type of reporting, see "The Deflowering of New England," *Forbes, Magazine of Business and Finance,* July 1953.

England business firms exhibit a traditional reluctance to divulge information. They add that information prepared for newspaper publication should be more interestingly written and more objective, to increase its publishability. Elements of truth in both positions should provide a common ground for joint remedial action. *The Committee feels that it is vital to the region's growth and continued prosperity to achieve understanding between the two groups on this important matter.*

Enlisting Community Support

Industrial development is fast becoming a matter requiring objective planning and directed action. In this process the attitudes and cooperation of the community's citizens are growing to be more important. Local initiative is frequently the agent which sparks an effective industrial development effort; community understanding is often a necessary accompaniment. For example, rezoning may be necessary, but very often inhospitable community attitudes prevent it, thereby hampering or stopping needed industrial growth.

Informational and development organizations are playing a key role in guiding the growth of community understanding. In New Hampshire, for example, the development commission has initiated the formation of separate committees in 48 job-center areas. In Connecticut the development commission has sponsored a Connecticut Federation of Planning and Zoning Agencies which helps guide the work of about 1,400 persons serving on local zoning boards in the state. In these and similar instances, state or regional groups provide know-how and inspiration to the self-help efforts of many New England communities.

Limitations of Money and Personnel

The executives of some informational and development organizations in New England contend that their usefulness is severely limited by insufficient budgets. In some states it is claimed that sharp curtailments in legislative appropriations have on occasion necessitated contraction in activities which were bringing into the state taxable wealth that would substantially offset the cost of the curtailed activity. In some private organizations limitations of staff preclude exploration of potentially effective methods of disseminating information or pursuing useful industrial development work.

Where revenue sources have not been reduced, development executives have worked within their budget limitations to direct their efforts into the most effective channels. In Massachusetts and Rhode Island it was found appropriate to reorganize the basic structure of the development commissions. In both states new executives and new policies are at work to revitalize the state's development program. The executives interviewed in all six states felt that public recognition of the value of informational and development activity should lead to financial support in proportion to the needs to be filled.

OPPORTUNITIES FOR IMPROVING BUSINESS AND ECONOMIC INFORMATION IN NEW ENGLAND

We have described the nature and extent of present informational and development activities in New England and summarized the opinions of representative organizations on the success of their own programs. From these descriptions and appraisals, it is evident that there is a wide range of activities being performed by a large number of informational and development agencies having substantial sums to spend for these functions every year. But these appraisals do not support any conviction that the extent of this activity in New England is greater or more effective than similar activities in other sections of the United States. The basis for a comprehensive evaluation is not available, but it is possible to appraise specific actions and present some evidence that the range of effectiveness of the programs described above can be considerably expanded and improved.

In 1951 the Association of State Planning and Development Agencies compiled a summary of the functions of 29 state planning and development agencies, in addition to those of Puerto Rico and British Columbia. The summary listed 13 functions frequently performed, and described the range of activity in each state. For the 29 states, the average number of activities conducted stood at 9.3; the average for the six New England states was 9.0 in 1951. In this admittedly rough measure, Vermont and Rhode Island were close to the average, while Maine and Massachusetts registered scores below the 29-state average. Important structural changes in the organization of the Massachusetts and Rhode Island development commissions since 1951 have undoubtedly altered their positions in this ranking. With these changes it is evident the variety of activities carried on by New England's state development commissions ranks about on a par with the other 29 states. Evaluation of the quality of the commissions' achievements and of the personnel they employ must inevitably be by subjective judgments based on personal opinions.

Regardless of our personal evaluations of the present effectiveness of our informational and development programs, we cannot be complacent as we judge those activities in relation to the goals to be reached. At least one field study of the location decisions of manufacturing enterprises indicated that in 1947–49 a majority of businessmen who established new enterprises were unaware of the facilities available to assist them in the state development commissions.[3] Our interviews with informational and development execu-

3. Federal Reserve Bank of Boston, "Why New Manufacturing Establishments Located in New England," *Monthly Review,* April 1949.

tives showed a widespread feeling that the task before the development agencies remains very large and that their efforts should be sustained and increased. We endorse that attitude.

Needs for Business and Economic Information

Each of the informational and development agencies in New England is normally concerned with satisfying a particular need of its membership or providing a particular kind of service to its public. When viewed in the aggregate, however, these individual lines of action fall into a pattern. These agencies are striving to fill three general informational needs in the field of business and economic information.

(1) *In national affairs* the citizen and his representatives in Washington and the state capitols need to understand the general functioning of our economic system. A working understanding of the monetary system, productive organizations, public taxation and expenditure, international trade, and the major industrial and occupational groups is necessary to the understanding of our economic system.

(2) *In business affairs* a citizen, and especially the citizen-businessman, needs to understand specific economic and business facts and the complex business, financial, and service occupations which make up our economic structure. He also needs an understanding of the most productive business methods to improve his decision-making in business.

(3) *In community affairs* the citizen needs an understanding of specific economic facts about his community and region in order to help carry out improvements. He needs to understand how people in the community make their living, the historical development of community and region, and the opportunities for further development that lie ahead.

These three general informational needs for business and economic information are not mutually exclusive. They furnish a frame of reference in measuring our efforts to provide for the whole range of needs for business and economic information. *By measuring our efforts in fulfilling this description of needs, we should be able to appraise our effectiveness and delineate areas in which improvements are most needed.*

Methods of Improving Business and Economic Information

There was no unanimity among the persons we interviewed as to the best ways of improving business and economic information in New England. There was considerable agreement that certain activities now being performed are wasteful, or at least not as productive as some other lines of action. For example, many questioned the value of newspaper and magazine advertisements featuring the location advantages of specific geographic areas. On the other hand, few were willing to state that this form of information distribution is worthless. It appears that methods of improving business and economic information will be primarily changes in emphasis among the present methods.

Improved Integration of Activities

Some executives of the informational and development groups expressed concern about lack of coordination among the groups. Some felt they were duplicating the efforts of others. Some were unable to perform at their maximum effectiveness because they were not well informed about the work of other groups dealing with the same general problems. In many areas it was felt that there should be better integration of activities. Some over-all guidance through a coordinating agency is desirable and necessary.

The recent action by the six governors in appointing representatives of their state development commissions to a New England Governors' Regional Committee on Industry and Development may be the first step toward solving the problem at the state level. Community development organizations should also be brought into closer association. *Regardless of the sponsoring agency, there appears to be merit in the proposal that informational and development groups coordinate their activities to delineate common grounds of interest, to determine areas of weakness, and to reinforce each other's programs. With joint effort new devices may often be sponsored which increase the effectiveness of the whole.*

Informational and development groups seldom make use of the services provided by the educational institutions which abound in New England. The general and special training of the staffs of these institutions is an asset which they should rely upon heavily. *Increased efforts to sponsor joint programs by university personnel and informational and development agencies would improve the business and economic information available to the New England public. Credit conferences sponsored jointly by extension services, bankers' groups, and farm groups provide an example.*[4] *Similar conferences on business information would appear to be worthwhile.*

Informational and development groups are concerned about the treatment accorded their news releases by the newspapers. This concern might well be translated into action by improving the form of the material submitted for publication and taking more account of what is newsworthy. For their part, news editors can contribute by assuming a more mature attitude toward the information which their public should receive. "Menu hints" and "Help for the Homemaker" are a daily part of the women's page; *educational features about local, state, and regional labor, business, industry, and finance should also be.*

New England organizations interested in improving the flow of informa-

4. See our reports Nos. 11 and 14, "The Financial Resources of New England and Their Use" and "New England's Industrial Management."

tion might sponsor a newspaper column devoted to business information for consumers. A panel of specialists—a real estate dealer, a lawyer, a tax expert, an accountant, and an economist—might answer questions on particular business and consumer problems submitted by readers, the questions and replies constituting a column for the use of local papers. The column might also become the center of other news about local business developments.

Shifts in Emphasis of Methods Employed

Businessmen are prone to say that the best salesman is a convinced customer. Executives of informational and development agencies might take this cue to increase their efforts among their own members and public rather than among persons outside New England. For example, some of the state development commissions have decided that their budgets and energies are more effectively employed when directed primarily to the residents of their own states. In similar fashion, community organizations might consider that an alert, forward-looking community will promote its own future more effectively than a series of advertisements describing the area in a national publication could.

State and regional agencies might use a shift in emphasis that would expand the number of units working on the problems confronting them. *More attention devoted to the organization of local agencies would in the long run improve the business and economic information available.* New Hampshire's establishing 48 separate job centers and committees to study them is an example. When this program is completed the effectiveness of the state agency will be greatly bolstered by the coordination of these committees.

At present informational and development agencies devote most of their efforts to improving adults' economic understanding of their national business and community affairs. By conferences, speeches, and publications they strive to inform their members and the public about the special topics with which they are primarily concerned. General adult education and civic education of young people are considered to be the responsibility of established schools and colleges. In some cases those responsibilities are being assumed by other organizations with outstanding results. The Civic Education Foundation in Cambridge, for example, has been very active in developing programs and materials.

It is increasingly evident that more emphasis should be put on improving education in the secondary schools about business and economics. The great majority of our young people do not attend college. Even if they do, they may not gain an understanding of economic concepts. Better education at secondary-school levels would equip future citizens to act more wisely and effectively in the situations they will meet as adults. Improved methods for teaching business and economics are plentiful, and their use is increasing. Many corporations are now preparing descriptive and analytical materials for secondary-school use about particular segments of our economy. Many communities and states are adopting teacher-education programs in cooperation with the Joint Council on Economic Education. During 1953 three workshops in economic education were held in New England. Representatives of business, industry, finance, and labor, together with educators, met with a selected group of secondary-school teachers for a three-week period of concentrated study of economic problems. The teachers in workshop committees concerned themselves with planning materials and procedures to be used upon their return to the classroom. *Extension of this economic education device by widespread cooperation from informational and development agencies could greatly improve the level of economic understanding of both secondary-school teachers and the students graduating from our schools.*

Sources of Information

The problem of improving the sources of business and economic information is twofold. Not only must the amount and quality of information be improved but knowledge of sources and distribution channels is important to a smooth flow of information. Increased awareness of the usefulness of business and economic information and increased recognition of the way it can be used would be great stimulants to its flow. *Business firms, for example, could greatly expand the amount of information available to their communities and states by preparing descriptions of the operations they perform and making those descriptions readily available to their local school systems and informational and development agencies.* Larger concerns are already doing this. Smaller firms should be encouraged to, perhaps through cooperative arrangements with schools and colleges. *Community research efforts could greatly increase the amount of useful and critical information. Businesses in New England might find it a profitable investment to support research on the problems of their communities.*

Educational institutions, in general, are expanding service to their local communities in the form of night classes, adult education, forum sponsorship, and similar activities. *In the past few years many colleges and universities have added courses on the New England economy. Some have devoted increased attention to the economic problems of their neighboring communities. These lines of action should be expanded.* For their part, communities could profit by more frequent recourse to these available services.

Government agencies have played a dominant role in expanding the flow of economic information. *The United States Department of Commerce publications, particularly the Census of Manufactures, are vitally important basic sources of data. The census should be firmly established on a periodic basis.* Other federal agencies, such as the Bureau of Labor Statistics, provide a valuable flow of data. Continuation of the basic statistical series is imperative if major economic decisions are to be made informatively.

Special study groups established by government request or sponsorship have made valuable contributions to economic understanding during recent years. With the support of the President's Council of Economic Advisors, a committee of economists prepared a preliminary evaluation of the New England economy in 1950. A request to the National Planning Association by the Joint Committee on the Economic Report of the United States Congress was instrumental in initiating the Committee of New England.

Regional organizations have also improved the flow of economic information. In 1951 the Conference of New England Governors appointed a committee which prepared an extensive report on the New England textile industry. The establishment of the New England Governors' Regional Committee on Industry and Development is another move to aid the flow of economic information.

Economic information is the basis for mature economic decisions. Improvement in the supply and flow of economic information is properly considered a prime obligation of community, state, regional, and national organizations, both private and public. Many New England organizations are working actively to increase this flow. Their achievements compare favorably with similar activities elsewhere, but to meet the needs their services must continue steadily to improve and expand.

SELECTED REFERENCES

1. Boston University, Bureau of Business Research, *New England Community Statistical Abstracts,* Boston, 1953.
2. Council of Economic Advisors, Committee on the New England Economy, *The New England Economy,* a report to the President, Washington, 1951.
3. Federal Reserve Bank of Boston, "Why New Manufacturing Establishments Located in New England," *Monthly Review,* April 1949.
4. ——— Quarterly Inventory of Economic Research, 1947 to present.
5. Joint Committee on the Economic Report, *Handbook of Regional Statistics,* 81st Congress, 2d Session, Washington, 1950.
6. New England Council, *Source Book of New England Economic Statistics,* Boston, 1947.
7. New England Governors' Committee, *Report on the New England Textile Industry,* Cambridge, 1952.
8. State Development Commissions. Each state agency normally publishes a valuable descriptive booklet on its own state's characteristics.
9. U.S. Department of Commerce, *Regional Trends in the United States Economy,* Washington, 1951.
10. ——— *Economic Development Atlas,* Washington, 1950.

II

Goals for New England

Drafted by George H. Ellis on the basis
of material in the preceding reports

INTRODUCTION

In the nineteen reports which have preceded this the Committee of New England has presented a comprehensive analysis of the economic state of New England. Wherever possible, the reports have combined intensive investigation of critical topics with a description and review of general economic issues. With the aid of committee and panel members, the research staff has carried out many path-breaking surveys and inquiries. The results of these studies have appeared in technical staff memoranda on 13 separate topics, ranging from a survey of union-management labor contracts in New England to comparisons of state and local tax burdens. (See Appendix 1.) Although the study concentrated on economic issues, it was recognized that economic motivations are not the only reasons for action.

The Committee of New England reports are independent documents. Each one summarizes studies of problems related to a topic of limited scope. Suggested actions to solve particular problems or to develop new potentials are liberally distributed throughout. Those suggestions point the way to New England's economic goals. They are carefully considered and thoughtfully worded to reflect both the research findings and the relevant decisions of the study panels. Most of the reports conclude with a concise summary of their major recommendations. Wherever the brevity and conciseness of the original statements permit they are repeated unchanged in this summary report. In many instances it has been necessary to condense the original statements of goals. If distortion of meaning has resulted, reference to the wording of the individual reports will establish the original intention.

Every reader is expected to exercise independent judgment in appraising our reports. We have not looked through rose-colored glasses nor have we plodded in old ruts of pessimism. We have tried to examine New England with 20–20 economic vision and then to use perspective in formulating some patterns for its future. If we succeed in stimulating additional thought and study, we will have accomplished part of the Committee of New England's primary objective: to provide the basis for a program of constructive action for New England.

THE ECONOMIC STATE OF NEW ENGLAND:
THREE GENERALIZATIONS

A few sentences cannot adequately convey the findings of the entire research project. Some observations, however, have occurred with such frequency in the separate reports that they may be stated as generalizations which apply to the entire economy.

The New England economy is sound. It is neither stronger nor weaker than the national economy. None of our studies revealed any source of strength which would push New England into a dominant position in the national economy. None revealed any fundamental weakness strong enough to pull the whole regional economy down to disaster levels during a period when the national economy continued to flourish. The common ingredient of the two economies is transition—development and change in use of natural and human resources. As demonstrated in the introductory report, New England leads the nation in this historical process of transition, but this leadership does not necessarily indicate weakness. New England's demonstrated ability to maintain high income levels by manufacture of domestic or imported materials has not been seriously challenged in the findings of our investigations. Our studies have shown that some competitive conditions have seriously weakened some industries. They have also shown that other industries and occupations have originated and continue to flourish in the region. On the whole, we conclude that demonstrated strengths offset demonstrated weaknesses. This view is substantiated by the region's continued growth in population and labor force and by a continued rise in individual incomes.

Critical self-appraisal opens the door to the inflow of new ideas which are the seeds of prosperity for the future New England economy. In many of the region's industries the dominant reason for success is the ability to do something better than competitors elsewhere. In other cases, the biggest disadvantage is an outmoded process or product. In both industrial groups, the necessary ingredient for future success is the application of scientific research techniques which will enable New England producers to maintain competitive advantages. New England's economic prosperity is inextricably linked with industry's ability to adopt new techniques and products. *Continual self-appraisal in the light of constantly changing technology is vitally needed to ensure an open-minded search for new ideas and willingness to adopt new procedures.*

Individuals and organizations in New England must assume the initiative and responsibility for action to advance the region's prosperity, because they have the greatest opportunities for effective action. Government action is important in many instances but it alone will not solve New England's major economic problems. In their churches, social groups, labor unions, financial and industrial organizations New Englanders have traditionally demonstrated their ability to organize and cooperate for effective action. Greater cooperation could increase the effectiveness of many of our industries. Increased cooperation among governmental units could advance the conservation of our resources and improve the education of our citizens.

NEW ENGLAND'S FINANCIAL RELATIONS
WITH THE FEDERAL GOVERNMENT

New England individuals, enterprises, and government units have many contacts with the Federal Government. They transmit funds to the Treasury in the process of paying taxes, buying government securities, or occasionally in paying for government services; they receive them in a multitude of forms such as government payments for munitions, social security payments, interest on bonds, and price support payments. Each of these financial transactions influences the flow of funds to or from New England. The structure of the federal taxing and borrowing system has one impact on the region, the pattern of federal expenditures has another. Viewed in summary form, the flow of funds that result from New England's financial relations with the Federal Government throw light on the region's relative position in the national economy.

Higher than average incomes, large financial resources, and an advanced industrial structure have all combined to make New England a region with high economic ability to pay federal taxes and invest in government bonds. On the other hand, most federal expenditures, outside the field of direct defense spending, have been disbursed through programs designed to aid individuals and government units. They have been disbursed according to formulas based on population, matching of state funds, state laws, and the like. The New England states have tended to receive below average federal aid payments, partly because payments to the individuals and governments affected by the applicable programs averaged less than in other states.

Analysis of financial records indicates that until 1950 New England's loss of funds through federal taxing and borrowing methods exceeded its receipt of funds through federal spending and debt repayment programs of all types. The resulting outflow of funds through Treasury transactions was more than offset by gains through the commercial and financial transactions of the region's businessmen. Industrial growth stimulated in other areas by federal programs undoubtedly assisted New England businessmen by enabling them to sell goods to those areas. At the same time, however, competition for New England manufactures was being stimulated in the other areas.

During World War II New England's relative economic position in the national economy apparently changed markedly, and in the immediate postwar years it was apparent that New England's earnings through private transactions were materially reduced. In 1950 and later years the region showed a net loss of funds through private transactions. Experience during these years indicates that it may no longer be possible for New England's economy to earn, through private transactions, funds to offset losses, according to the historical pattern of Treasury transactions reflecting Federal Government programs.

This situation forces a reconsideration of New England's attitude toward federal programs. Those which are narrow in their benefits, such as the wool and silver support programs, set up an unwarranted drain on public funds and may rightfully be opposed by regions like New England which must contribute to their support. On the other hand, actions designed to raise the level of living throughout the country do not in themselves directly affect New England's competitive position in the national economy. National progress in achieving better education, improved hospitals, fewer slums, and more adequate roads will surely be greater if the more advanced regions continue their support. New Englanders may logically hold a different viewpoint toward a third category of federal programs which includes river basin developments, farm support programs and river and harbor improvement expenditures. While New England markets undoubtedly grow as a result of some of those programs, in the long run the initial stimulus to New England's markets appears to be gradually replaced by worsening in the region's competitive position in relation to the areas being supported.

New England's prosperity and growth are dependent upon prosperous growth in the national economy. Historically, New England has placed national interests above regional interests. It must continue to do so. But national and regional interests coincide in the requirement that federal programs be assessed in terms both of benefit for growing areas and of burden on older economic areas.

In seeking solutions to regional problems New England must not resort to recrimination, irresponsible exploitation of federal programs, or special pleading for preferred treatment. We may rightfully expect, however, that our own efforts to preserve and strengthen the regional economy will not be undermined by federal programs which concentrate adjustment burdens in older economic regions.

New England's representatives in Washington can serve both the national and regional interests in good conscience by unswerving adherence to the principle that national achievements are the net result of gains weighed against losses in all regions. The obvious impossibility of precise measurement of the human values involved does not invalidate the measurement. It only emphasizes the dangers of failing to make conscious attempts to appraise federal programs in their entirety.

GOALS FOR NEW ENGLAND

New England's economic goals can never be satisfactorily defined or neatly packaged for brief description. They are limited only by our present vision. As our attainments multiply, our vision expands and our goals are further advanced.

Our reports on the economic state of New England have concentrated on analysis of the changing methods by which New Englanders use their resources and skills to obtain a better living in terms of material standards. At the same time, we have carefully considered many of the human values which both affect and are affected by economic changes. With due consideration for human motivations, we have endeavored to place New England's economic goals in a meaningful relationship to past achievements and existing potentials.

Attainment of New England's economic goals is dependent on the effectiveness with which natural and human resources are employed by organizations. These three ingredients of the economic future have provided the structure for analysis of the economic state of New England. The first six reports analyzed the resources of forests, farmlands, fisheries, minerals, water, and vacation business and their contribution to the income of the region. The four subsequent reports dealt with human resources, including an analysis of the skills, education, health, income, and employment of the population.

One of man's greatest talents is his ability to achieve by organized effort a goal which is beyond the power of a single man. New England's organizations, both governmental and private, are of paramount importance in advancing its prosperity. Governmental organizations set up the framework for productive activity. They provide protective services, establish and enforce legal procedures, and operate some of the basic utilities. The region's many business organizations direct extensive production facilities. They organize the productive efforts of the labor force, the flow of materials, and the use of machinery and power in production processes. Educational organizations open our minds, and through research open the doors to further developments. New England has pioneered in the development of some of these forms of organization. It seemed important to assess attainment of economic goals in terms of the strengths and weaknesses of some of these organizations. Accordingly, eight of the research reports examined New England organizations and their activities.

NATURAL RESOURCES

It is frequently stated that New England was not bountifully endowed with the basic mineral ores and fuels so important in our present economy.

An obvious corollary is that it must strive for maximum effectiveness in utilizing the resources it does have. Each of the six reports on natural resources emphasizes separate but related steps to be taken in achieving the goal of maximum effective utilization.

New England manufacturers and traders have long exploited the possibilities of importing raw materials used in manufacturing a product for export or sale in the United States. The textile, leather, and other industries are based on that concept. As the nation turns increasingly to foreign sources of raw materials, New England should make maximum use of its seaboard location and nearness to the industrial markets of the northeastern United States. In particular, it should strive to cooperate in developing the latent resources of the nearby provinces of Canada.

Forests

The forests of New England are one of its richest resources. Yet the present forest-timber yield is less than the region's consumption. Moreover, the yield is only a fraction of what the 31,000,000 acres of commercial timberland in New England could produce. There are many positive actions which should be taken by both large and small woodland owners, as well as by private and public organizations, to increase the productivity of the forests and their contribution to the New England economy.

The region has a special stake in the improvement of forest-management practices by large owners. Only a few large forest owners in New England apply intensive management to their properties. Those who do often find that increased yield and improved certainty of future supply more than compensate for the extra costs. Many more large forest owners could benefit from high-level forest management. Large owners could also gain by more vigorous market development of those New England products made from unused and waste wood. An immediate objective could be the reduction of wastes by the use of better harvesting practices and by utilizing much of the timber now left in the forests. Continued intensive research by both private and public agencies should develop new uses for wood wastes and improve wood-using processes.

Small woodland owners are in need of better information and greater understanding of the need for and opportunities offered by better forest management. The effectiveness of many small woodlots could be increased by pooling arrangements. For example, the small woodland owners might engage a marketing specialist such as the New England Forestry Foundation or Connwood, Inc. They might cooperate by pooling their interests in multiple forest holdings such as Timber Owners of New England, Inc. They might also increase their use of forest-fire insurance.

Government agencies can assist materially in improvement of forestry practices. They may sponsor increased research on the prevention and control of destructive insects and diseases. They may make further improvements where opportunities exist in forest-fire protection by cities and states. We recommend also that the New England states adopt progressive forest taxation laws similar to that of New Hampshire. Surely our elected representatives should be in the forefront of efforts to improve management of New England's most valuable natural resource—its forests.

New England's Fisheries

The major problems of the New England fisheries fall into three catagories: increasing the demand for New England fish products, increasing the supply of fish, and solving intra-industry relations. New England's fishing industries are vitally concerned with enlarging the demand for fish among the large inland population of the country. A small shift of consumer preferences in favor of buying fish could produce a greatly expanded demand. To change buying habits and tastes in the face of large commercial expenditures by competing producers, we have recommended increased emphasis on the promotion of New England fish products by individual firms, trade associations, labor unions, and government groups. We have suggested also continuing analysis and improvement of packaging and merchandising techniques on the part of individual firms and trade associations. Sales will be helped if quality can be kept at a high level, either by educational programs among members of the industry, by self-policing, or through the use of a port-wide or New England-wide seal of quality. Increased industrial research and industry-sponsored research for the study of fish processing and technology should be undertaken.

There is apparently no critical scarcity of any major species of New England fish, but better catches could be made in the future if the industry would adopt various recommended conservation measures. The industry should continue to support the International Commission for the Northwest Atlantic Fisheries and its conservation program. As a parallel activity, research by the Fish and Wildlife Service on fish technology and biology, fish-catching methods, and other basic problems of the industry should be augmented. State and local governments could assist in expanding production by adopting a more liberal policy toward leasing shellfish grounds to private persons for the commercial cultivation of clams and other shellfish.

One bargaining group in Boston's fishing industry has been without a contract for six years. Unless the major disagreements can be resolved and a reasonable contract drawn up, each group may suffer seriously, harming others in the process. We have suggested that the Boston vessel owners and the Atlantic Fishermen's Union should reopen negotiations for a collective bargaining contract. As a corollary, the union should establish a cooperative for buying provisions which the fishermen pay for and consume while fishing.

Agriculture

The New England farmer is favored with markets that pay premium prices for high-quality local products. Production of bulky and perishable products close to markets reduces marketing costs and gives producers a higher proportion of the consumers' food dollar than is true in many regions. But if New England farmers are to continue to meet the keen competition from other areas, a better marketing program must be developed, including better grading, standardization, packaging, improvement in transportation techniques to reduce bruising, and more effective promotion of New England farm products. Continued and more aggressive experimentation and research will be necessary to develop the kind of program that is needed. Most of New England's farm products are consumed within the region, and sustained urban prosperity, therefore, is more important to the well-being of the New England rural economy than the present high level of price supports. Nevertheless, supports at a lower level to act as disaster insurance would be desirable.

If the region's dairymen are to continue supplying all the fluid milk needed by our expanding population, New England's milk production will have to be increased. This can be done by further reducing the seasonality of the milk supply, by increasing milk production per cow, by keeping more cows, by raising more high-quality roughage, or by a combination of all these methods.

Transferring farm ownership so that young farmers may get started is an important problem in New England farming communities. The small proportion of rented farms and the high capital investments necessary for modern farming make it necessary to develop new methods of transferring farms as going concerns from older to younger men. Agricultural credit is generally adequate, although some shift in lending, from short to intermediate terms, would be desirable. Present real estate taxes place a significant differential burden on farms in most New England states, a burden that could be lightened through a more equitable distribution of local taxation. To facilitate farm ownership we have recommended a three-step program whereby a young man may first gain experience, then share responsibility, and finally purchase a farm over a period of years.

Mineral Resources

The manufacturing industries of New England are tremendously dependent on minerals brought in from outside. The dependence is absolute for mineral fuels, iron and steel, and many other important mineral products. In spite of the region's age and our familiarity with its characteristics, it is nevertheless true that it has never been subjected to a complete mineral survey using modern prospecting techniques and equipment. A complete inventory of its mineral resources, made with the latest scientific instruments and techniques and considering the changing importance of less common minerals, should be considered as a form of investment in the future.

The dependable availability of most minerals from sources anywhere is far more important to New England than their discovery or development within the six-state area. Minerals generally have a high value relative to weight and can therefore stand the charges of even long transportation hauls. Transportation charges are significantly high, however, and the region should work for transportation economies and improvement in facilities that will assist in making important minerals economically available.

The increasing extent to which the United States is turning abroad for mineral supplies has improved New England's competitive position because of its seacoast location, although the region has not yet taken full advantage of its changing position. New England should support the minerals development of the entire western hemisphere and the rest of the Atlantic basin. In particular, it should work toward a greater integration of its manufacturing structure with the current development of the mineral resources of eastern Canada. In this context, it is obvious that New England shares the broad national interest in low tariffs and the elimination of import restrictions on minerals.

There are some specific developments in mineral use which provide potentialities for the economic progress of the region. These include expansion of mica, cement, and brick production, and the extraction of sulphur and iron from iron sulphide deposits. The establishment of a speciality steel mill to produce carbon and alloy bars is another very important possibility.

Water, Fuel, and Energy Resources

Plentiful supplies of high-quality water are an important industrial and municipal asset in New England. However, years of abuse have impaired the high natural quality of many streams and rivers, and the coastal sections have been particularly affected. Maine should join with the other five states in the New England Interstate Water Pollution Control Commission to maximize effective use of the region's rivers for recreational, industrial, navigational, and other purposes. The New England states should also work together for further flood protection through further dams and warning systems to reduce the economic and social losses in some of the river valleys.

In the absence of regional sources of coal, gas, or oil, New England has capitalized on its seaboard location and ability to import oil from domestic or foreign fields. In 1947 the fuel oil costs of its manufacturing industries were about 5% below the United States average. In those instances where oil competes effectively with other energy sources in industrial use, the fuel costs of New England manufacturers compare favorably with those of most of their competitors. This favorable position is repeatedly threatened by efforts to restrict by quotas the importation of residual fuel oil. In 1951 New England consumed an estimated 40,000,000 barrels of foreign residual oil. This was about a third of all foreign residual oil imported into the United States that year. It is also much more than the 27,000,000 barrels of foreign residual oil that would be admitted to the whole United States under the restrictions proposed by the Simpson Bill.[1] Such a restriction of imports would force New England to be dependent on domestic producers, and in all probability increase the price to New England users. New England's representatives must remain vigilant in opposing efforts to cut off its imports of foreign supplies of oil.

Although the New England power supply is adequate and dependable, the average rate structure for purchased electric power is higher than in most competing states. Higher than average rates result in a small but sometimes important competitive disadvantage for manufacturers and may represent a slight handicap to industrial growth for the region. High fuel prices are a major factor, but other elements of expense controllable in the region have contributed to the higher rates. During recent years progress in expense reduction has been encouraging, but further improvement is both desirable and possible.

By 1970 there will have to be an approximate doubling of generating capacity to meet New England's power needs. All but a small proportion of the expansion will have to be steam plants. While in absolute terms there is considerable undeveloped hydroelectric power which can be economically developed, it is small in proportion to the total need and can have at most only a minor effect on the region's power supply or rates. Further improvements in the efficiency of steam plant generation in the region offer a much greater opportunity for reducing the New England power-rate differential.

Rapid progress in nuclear power development gives hope that New England can look forward to eliminating eventually that part of its power-cost disadvantage which nature has imposed by not supplying the region with indigenous sources of fuel. New England is well suited to nuclear power development and should participate actively in it, including the possibility of providing the location for the first commercial plant to produce power.

1. H.R. 4294. See hearings before House Ways and Means Committee, April 1953.

Vacation Business Resources

New England's vacation business is of importance not only to the operators of the vacation establishments but also to the entire region. Unfortunately, there is far too little information available about the New England vacationist himself to permit of preparing a detailed prescription for the business. We urge the region's development agencies and vacation trade associations to step up their research into these matters in order to increase the efficiency of their promotional efforts.

On the basis of existing information, a threefold approach appears to offer good prospects for strengthening New England's vacation business. As a first step, increased advertising and promotion seems to be in order; such a program should enlist the cooperation of state and private organizations in the joint vacation promotion of New England as a region. A major feature of the program should be a changed emphasis to coincide more closely with the ranking of attractions expressed by vacationists themselves. Special attention in the promotion program should be given to extending the vacation season.

As a corollary development in the program of promotion, operators should undertake a continuing adaptation of the regional vacation facilities to meet the changing pattern of vacationists' desires and characteristics. The program would include modernization and improvement of many existing establishments.

As a third part of the program, the industry should strive to provide a check list of management problems for prospective entrants in the business. Trade associations, banks, development organizations, and others may help raise the business competence of the new operators and increase their prospects of success. An integral part of this effort might be greater provision of management aids for operators of vacation establishments. This might be in the form of printed pamphlets and manuals, and in the form of counseling service, preferably by the industry itself through its trade associations or by area development groups.

The vacation industry in New England has much to gain through active participation in programs to facilitate travel and to improve the areas vacationists will visit. Better roads leading from the border of New York State to the vacation areas would greatly increase the ease of driving and swell the flow of vacationists. Through-ways to resort areas would especially encourage postseason weekend trips in the fall. The vacation industry needs also to press strenuously for more and better state parks, particularly along the seashore, while combatting the danger of spoiling our parks and highways by advertising and commercial developments.

HUMAN RESOURCES

We are not making the best possible use of our most valuable resource, the people of New England. The number of persons unemployed, the people needing vocational training or rehabilitation, the aged forced into retirement all are among the human problems to which we need to devote more attention. We cannot be content simply with matching our neighbors in the training, education, and employment of our workers. Our lack of some basic natural resources must be made up for in other ways. We have the combination of income and facilities to make possible higher levels of education and work experience.

Education

New England's record of school years completed is good, when one takes into account the older average age of its population and the higher proportion of foreign-born residents. The average New Englander has completed more years of school than the average resident of the United States. But we cannot be content with this achievement. There is still room to improve the minimum educational opportunity for the region's youth. The evidence at hand shows the educational needs to be greatest in rural areas and in certain cities where economic distress has followed industrial unemployment. Undoubtedly, low incomes and economic necessity are the principal causes of inadequate educational expenditures and substandard averages of educational attainment where they exist in various parts of New England. The educational problems of such areas are closely entwined, therefore, with their fundamental economic needs and opportunities. Enhancing the basic economic strength of communities would permit raising their educational standards.

The relatively small enrollment in vocational education classes compared to population and industrial distribution suggests that New England is not providing adequately for training the skilled workers which its industries require. Not only must replacement workers be provided but the attractiveness of New England to prospective employers will also be enhanced if they can count on vocational schools to furnish them with well-trained craftsmen. More extensive vocational education is both a need and an opportunity for New England. The quality at present appears to be above average, but there is some room for improvement as well as for a larger scale of activities. In particular, there seem to be opportunities to develop cooperative vocational education methods whereby industries can directly support school instruction in the skills they intend to employ.

Satisfactory use of the labor force requires minimizing the human wastes of physical disability and handicaps by adequate safety measures and by return to employment of those individuals who have become injured or disabled by illness. The record of the New England vocational rehabilitation agencies is good. It could probably be improved if the states adopted more flexible financing methods. State appropriations for vocational rehabilitation should be determined by local needs rather than by the amount of federal contributions.

Health

The average resident of New England appears to be better provided for in terms of health requirements than the average resident of the United States. Except for diseases of older people, the death rates for selected causes in New England are relatively low, but to maintain this relatively favorable health record a major program to replace outmoded or obsolete hospitals and to provide for growing needs is essential.

There are many opportunities to improve the health status of New Englanders. More residents of each state should have the coverage of health insurance programs. Many business concerns might expand the health services provided to their employees. Better control and prevention of communicable diseases and the diseases of old age could contribute to the prosperity and happiness of the region's people. Continued research by private and public groups and close cooperation among all interested parties will point up the need for action.

Employment Growth

New England must take a hard look at its opportunities for raising its income level. We cannot expect in the future to make large gains in income by shifting workers from farming to manufacturing occupations. The opportunity must lie in increasing the value of output that arises out of the working hour of each laborer. This may be done by shifting workers from one industry to another which has a higher value of output per worker. It may also be done by shifting the product emphasis within an industry, by improving the physical output of workers, by use of new tools and methods, and finally, by changes in the price structure.

New England seeks to employ a growing labor force to provide higher individual incomes for a growing population. We have found that if past development processes continue true to form the higher individual incomes in New England will probably be associated with a slowly increasing proportion of the labor force devoted to service occupations. It is apparent that the proportion of the labor force devoted to manufacturing occupations may contract or not expand further. To a region traditionally dependent upon manufacturing, this conclusion has very serious implications. In recent decades New England's labor force has grown at a rate of about 1%, or 34,700 workers a year. Rapid in-migration might permit faster growth, but in its absence we must expect an expansion in the manufacturing labor force of only about 15,000 workers a year during the next few years. This expectation sets a *minimum* employment goal for New England. We must employ our 1,500,000 manufacturing and construction workers continuously; and we must provide about 15,000 new manufacturing jobs a year.

Employment Stability

Manufacturing, the center of New England's economic activity, has been changing materially in recent decades. Expressed simply, the transition in New England manufacturing may be described as an increase in the relative importance of metalworking and metal-using industries. In general, industries producing durable goods have expanded, while industries producing nondurable goods have contracted their employment. As employment in the manufacture of nondurable goods shrinks in relative importance, the region may become subject to wider cyclical swings in total employment and unemployment. The downturns can hurt more and the upturns can come more suddenly and proceed more rapidly. On the other hand, a contracting nondurable-goods industry feels a depression quickly and recovers slowly. Hence it experiences a great deal of cyclical unemployment, as the history of cotton textiles in New England shows. While the best structure is impossible to determine precisely, *a continuation of the shift to durables in New England seems desirable, but it should be brought about by growth in the durable-goods sector and minimizing of losses in nondurable-goods industries.*

The core of New England's long-term unemployment problem is in the group of cities that have relied excessively on a single industry for their livelihood. We join with others in recommending that communities heavily dependent on any single firm or industry work actively to diversify employment opportunities. In the enthusiasm to encourage growth of durable-goods industries in New England, the contribution which the nondurable-goods industries can make to employment stability should not be forgotten.

In the long run, chronic unemployment in specific communities can be most readily corrected by industrial diversification. We should continue efforts to attract new manufacturing plants, including branch plants, where their establishment can economically be justified; and at the same time encourage industrial growth from within the region by providing an environment which will encourage that growth.

Wages

The ideal wage goal for New England is a higher than average wage level, accompanied by a higher than average rate of output per man hour. We have already indicated that some progress toward this goal may be achieved by upgrading our manufacturing employment.

As a broad generalization, it is true that many of New England's nontextile industries pay somewhat lower wages than the same industries in *other highly industrialized regions*. On the whole, however, New England's industrial wages seem to be fairly close to the national average. There are important variations both within and among regions in the levels of hourly earnings and vacation and holiday payments. Except for textiles, there is no clear-cut interregional difference. There are some locations in New England which pay lower than average wages and others which pay above average. New England is clearly a high-wage area for the textile industries, despite the fact that the earnings for most New England textile workers are lower than those of many workers in other manufacturing industries in the region. Our studies of the nonindustrial categories indicate that New England is a low-wage area for the white-collar occupations.

Any attempt to assess the influence of relatively low wages in many New England industries and occupations upon the future economic growth of the region must proceed on an industry-by-industry basis. For the region as a whole, we conclude that New England should strive to be a region of both high wages and low labor costs, with high labor productivity as the means by which the twin goals can be achieved.

Wage Legislation

We do not subscribe to the notion that the Fair Labor Standards Act should be used to narrow interregional wage differentials. From a practical point of view, we do not think increases of the minimum wage could permanently equalize either labor costs or wage rates among regions. We believe that the act should remain an instrument of protection against subminimum standards and that collective bargaining and the normal competition for workers' services should determine wages above the minimum level.

The Walsh-Healey Act is one of a series of laws designed to protect minimum standards for workers. It should continue to fulfill that purpose rather than be used as a means for furthering interregional competition. We favor upward revision of the industry minima if the old determinations are rendered obsolete by inflation. If the law is to protect the workers on government contracts against substandard wages, the legal minimum should be close to the lower limit of the average rates paid by the vast majority of employers in an industry.

Labor-Management Relations

New Englanders are justly proud of the pioneering efforts of some of the region's outstanding businessmen. We have equal reason to be proud of our unions and union leaders. For the most part, unions in New England are stable, responsible, and democratic. Many union leaders in the region play an important part in civic and community affairs, and they are generally aware of the roles played by unions in our modern, complex society. They see the need for educational programs designed for the rank-and-file members and for the general public as well. They are also concerned with taking action to encourage the development of trained and responsible union leaders.

The proportion of workers who are union members is about the same in New England as in the nation as a whole. Massachusetts and Rhode Island, however, are more heavily unionized than the average state in the nation. It is probable that New England's unions display greater stability and maturity than is true in other regions; the strike record has been a favorable one in recent years, reflecting partly mature labor-management relations and partly the industrial structure of the region.

Some New England firms have pioneered in developing advanced methods of industrial relations. The region needs more such firms in which management goes out of its way to develop effective cooperation with the work force. In many cases, management may not be aware that its relations with labor could stand improvement. We urge New England management to take stock of its present relations with the work force, and we recommend a careful study of the cases reported in the Causes of Industrial Peace series published by the National Planning Association. These may contain clues to the solution of problems faced by other firms. If over-all labor-management relations in New England can be improved, the region's competitive position will be strengthened. Workers and management alike will benefit from lower production costs and increases in productivity.

NEW ENGLAND'S ORGANIZATIONS

Cooperative action through voluntary associations has always been a major asset of the New England economy. The results of past achievements of this sort are visible today in the multitude of banks, manufacturing plants, public utilities, stores, schools, colleges, and state and local government organizations. These are the groups whose vital economic decisions determine New England's economic future. They direct the functioning of most of our productive machinery and enlist the resources of our population.

By virtue of these organizations, New England faces its problems with the advantage of working teams with experience in tackling and solving problems. In addition, it has the flexibility to create new organizations to solve different problems as they arise. In some instances, existing organizations have enough flexibility to undertake the solution of new problems; in other instances, new organizations are essential. Flexibility, however obtained, is an essential element in meeting changing conditions.

Financial Organizations

New England has a large and well-organized financial system with ample resources to meet the needs of business in the region. The size of the resources is due largely to the above average incomes of New Englanders and their higher than average personal savings. Institutional wealth in the region is a major source of financial strength.

The limited available evidence indicates that New England's financial institutions more nearly meet the needs of business firms than those in the country as a whole. Nevertheless, there appear still to be some inadequacies, and the most significant comparison for New England is between its present and its potential position. While short-term credit needs are generally met satisfactorily, there is need for better borrower-lender understanding on a local basis. As a step in meeting this need, it would seem desirable for the various state bankers' associations and clearinghouses in New England to take the initiative in bringing together groups of bankers and small businessmen in "clinics" for mutual education and strengthened relations. It would also appear worth while for the banks to check periodically on their past lending judgment by examining the subsequent experience of those whose loan applications were rejected.

New capital investment in New England must certainly increase if the region is to maintain or expand its competitive strength. Every reasonable incentive—economic, legal, and political—should be given to encourage long-term investment in New England enterprises. It is important to New England that individuals who make investment decisions, both as suppliers and as users of funds, should be well informed and as free as possible from prejudices which stand in the way of their investment in the region.

New England has a vital interest in the continued availability of long-term credit and capital for small business. Several basic changes affecting the money markets during recent years have operated to lessen the availability of funds directly to small business. There is a shift away from direct investment by individuals toward more institutional investment. Higher individual and corporation income taxes have played a critical role in this development. The establishment and growth of small enterprises is an important source of strength to New England, and it must be encouraged.

New Englanders have been leaders in the development of new financial institutions and techniques to meet these capital requirements. The continued growth and contribution of such venture-capital organizations as the American Research and Development Corporation are of critical importance to the region. The long-term and venture capital which local industrial foundations and statewide development corporations can make available, in addition to the sale, lease, and construction of plants, helps to establish new businesses in the region. Leasing arrangements by insurance companies and similar investors can also make important contributions to the long-term capital problem of small businesses.

New England has pioneered in the establishment of statewide private development credit corporations to provide risk capital for small enterprises. If these corporations are well financed they may well make the usual concept of a capital bank unnecessary in New England; however, changes in both the supply of long-term and equity capital and the demand for such funds have been so great that the capital bank idea has much to commend it.

Transportation

New England's freight rates are in a period of transition, resulting from a complete revision of the railroad freight classification and rate structure and important changes in the relationship between ocean and rail rates. The effects of the new system of rail rates upon the future development of the New England economy will depend heavily on the way the system is administered. We believe that in making the adjustment from the old to the new rate system the Interstate Commerce Commission should proceed cautiously. If there are sound reasons for granting exceptions to the new rate structure, they should be granted. The revenue needs of carriers and the competitive position of shippers should not be completely subordinated to a desire to achieve simplicity in the rate system. Differences in transportation conditions, composition of traffic, and the industrial composition of various regions indicate the need for exceptions to a rigid formula for rate determination.

The equalization of all railroad grain rates to all North Atlantic ports should result in a greater flow of export traffic through the ports of New England. Since those responsible for setting ocean freight rates have not recognized the distance factor, it is logical to have equalized export and import rail rates as well. If in the future the Interstate Commerce Commission should insist upon restoring rail rate differentials to ports south of New England because of their favored geographic relationship to inland sources and markets, the system of equalized ocean rates should be discarded. If New England should again be penalized for its greater distance from inland markets, it should be permitted to profit by its closer location to the ports of northern Europe and other parts of the world.

New England's railroads today provide more transportation service to the economy than they did before World War II. There are important instances where railroad management has succeeded in shaking off much of the conservatism which characterized its activities in the past. A large part of the rolling stock has been modernized. Locomotives are largely diesel, passenger cars have been brought up to improved standards of comfort and convenience, and freight cars have been increasingly standardized and designed for greater efficiency. In general, the railroads have demonstrated a determination to keep pace with the rest of the economy. However, some New England roads have lagged behind in improvements, partly because the demand for railroad services has not expanded as rapidly as in other sections of the country. Conditions have encouraged motor transportation to a greater degree than in other areas.

To a large extent, railroad regulation is in the hands of the federal authorities. We recommend that greater cognizance be given at both the federal and state regulatory levels to the strong element of competition existing in the transportation field today. Rail management should be permitted more discretion to adjust rates to changing economic circumstances. Carriers should not be required to provide service for revenue that is less than "out-of-pocket" costs.

Motor carriers move more tonnage than all other forms of transportation in New England. This fact alone shows that New England has a particularly strong stake in building truly modern roads and should promptly become a leader in building roads which will meet the commercial and private transportation needs of the area.

The 400,000 registered motor trucks in the region provide a flexible motor transport facility for both city and intercity shipments. There are several factors, however, which inhibit achievement of maximum efficiency of operation. One of the most important of these is regulation. Congressional action in passing the Motor Carrier Act of 1935 imposed upon the motor-carrier industry a pattern of regulation similar to that imposed on the railroads. The route structure of the industry in 1935 was frozen, and responsibility placed upon the Interstate Commerce Commission to supervise all changes in accordance with changing needs. Results have tended to preserve inefficient carriers as well as the efficient. Aggressive firms with the potential to expand have been limited by their inability to obtain I.C.C. approval for expansion. If government controls permitted more leeway for economic forces, it is likely that New England would have a more efficient motor transport system. Regulation of motor carriers should admit more of the stimulating effects of competition. At the same time there should be greater correlation between states in the planning of highways, of freight and passenger terminals, and in achieving uniformity of safety and tax legislation applying to motor vehicles.

In the pattern of world transport by air, New England is in a highly strategic location. Boston is the natural western terminus of North Atlantic air routes. Without question, Logan Airport is one of New England's greatest transportation assets. To capitalize upon that asset, we should obtain more certification for foreign carriers to stop at Boston. We should also try to improve airport managements' initiative and responsibility by increasing their self-sufficiency. The states should provide encouragement and coordination for communities having or planning municipal airports. Airport operations should be placed on a business basis to the greatest possible extent. This involves granting airport managements a high degree of independence from legislative action.

New England's ports, particularly the Port of Boston, are a challenge to our ability to use the advantages they provide. Recent amendments to the law governing the Port of Boston partially overcome some of the previous shortcoming in port administration. Nevertheless, the Port still is not operated with the latitude normally enjoyed by port managers to act in accordance with commercial needs and circumstances. Managerial discretion is severely hampered by legislative control of finances. Much precedent exists for providing port management authority with discretion in the use of funds.

The highly developed and industrial economy of New England is critically dependent upon the effectiveness of its rail, motor, air, and water transport facilities. We believe that greater free play for management initiative in each of these forms of transportation would result in economies and improvement of service to New England.

State and Local Taxation and Expenditures

New England's state and municipal governments are neither extravagant nor uniquely frugal in their expenditures. In the years since 1939 state expenditures in New England have expanded more slowly than the national average. Per capita total expenditures have kept quite close to the 48-state average. Nevertheless, New Englanders should be vitally concerned with improving their municipal and state tax systems. When considered in relation to economic ability, the state tax burdens in three New England states were higher than the United States average in 1949. In four New England states, the local tax burdens exceeded the all-state average for that year. In combination, the burden of state and local taxes in relation to economic ability exceeded the 48-state average in the three states of Maine, Vermont, and Massachusetts. On the other hand, the combined burden of state and local taxes in Connecticut was some 15% below the national average. These comparisons spotlight the possibilities for improving New England's taxation and spending activities.

Information about tax burdens in relation to economic ability to pay taxes does not tell us how taxes affect the decisions of business enterprises that are seeking a location or striving to expand. The level and equity of tax liabilities at competing sites are the critical elements in appraising the effect of taxes on industry. Well-administered economical government is one prime attraction for industry. Here New England has an opportunity to lead the country in establishing high standards of public administration.

Since colonial times, New England communities have depended heavily on property taxation. Gradually the system has become a hodgepodge which violates many standards of good practice. The major problem of the property tax system lies in its administration. A well-administered property tax would remove many of the existing inequities and help to prevent new ones from arising. The critical difficulty to be faced is assessment. Improper assessment results in inequities not only among taxpayers but also between different government units when state aid is measured by the assessment base.

Although each of the New England states recognizes these problems, no machinery has been set up which will ensure uniform and equitable assessments. Creation of state boards to review assessments, set standards of valuation, and train assessors is a logical first step. In addition to the usual staff of assessors, the boards should have their own research specialists to review and assist towns in fiscal planning. Well-considered expenditures to establish proper assessments will normally pay for themselves by raising tax yields, while at the same time increasing the fairness of the property tax.

Soundly reasoned decisions on plant location emphasize such factors as nearness to markets, proximity to raw materials, labor supply, available plant space, transportation, labor cost, and community attitude. In these decisions, state and local taxes can be a determining element only in the rare instances where all other costs are roughly equal between alternative locations. Unfortunately, however, plant locations are not always selected on the basis of factual analysis of alternative costs at all possible sites. In many instances, potential sites are ruled out of consideration without full analysis because a business executive has strong prejudices against a state or community. The reputation of being a high tax state or community can be a serious location disadvantage. New Englanders must have as a goal the equitable taxation of the business enterprises in their jurisdiction. Our studies tend to confirm earlier findings that the taxation of corporations in Massachusetts is relatively high. We endorse the recommendation of the Massachusetts Special Commission on Taxation that the commonwealth "refrain from further increases in taxes upon manufacturing corporations." We urge the other New England states to weigh carefully the impact of their taxation decisions upon the location and expansion decisions of manufacturers.

Communities throughout the United States have been faced with pressing needs for new schools, roads, water, and sewerage systems. The fast-growing cities of the Southwest have had to resort to large increases in debt within the past few years to cover such capital outlays. New England cities, already possessed of developed public facilities, have not had to make such large outlays. On the other hand, increases in the tax base in the faster growing areas make carrying the debt easier than would appear by examining only the increase in debt. Many New England communities have found and will continue to find themselves in the difficult position of having to rebuild antiquated facilities without increases in assessment bases to make the task easier. These cities became problem areas from the fiscal point of view, and the solutions to the problem do not rest simply in improved taxation systems. These communities must strive to preserve and expand their taxable bases. We urge them to early consideration of their problems and prompt action to facilitate and stimulate the growth of new economic activities.

Information and Education Organizations

Our complex industrial economy consumes great masses of economic data. To be useful this information must be put into the hands of those who are concerned with understanding economic aspects of the national, business, and community activities in which they are engaged. Our survey revealed that in 1951 there were in New England at least 1,600 persons working full-time on informational and development activities at the regional, state, or community level. The budgets for these groups totaled approximately $7,000,000 for those purposes. At the same time, our survey revealed lack of confidence that the programs of these organizations were truly effective.

There appear to be three major avenues of improvement in our informational and development activities. Further integration of the many different activities would be a logical move. The recent action by the six New England governors in establishing a permanent regional committee on industry and development may be a first step toward solving the problem of increasing cooperation at the state level. Community groups could also be brought into closer association. Greater efforts to sponsor joint programs by university personnel and informational and development agencies would improve the business and economic information available to the New England public. News editors and development groups should cooperate to increase newspaper coverage of educational features about local, state, and regional labor, business, industry, and finance.

A shift in emphasis of methods employed by informational and development agencies might result in greater efficiency. More attention devoted to the organization of local agencies would, in the long run, better the quality and use of business and economic information. Extension of economic education in our schools would raise the level of economic understanding both of secondary school teachers and of the students graduating from our schools.

Not only should sources of information be improved but distribution channels should be widened. Business firms could expand the amount of information available to their community by preparing descriptions of the operations they perform, and local research efforts could increase the source of useful and critical information to support development in their communities. Many colleges and universities could help by adding courses on the New England economy and devoting more attention to the economic problems of their neighboring communities.

Information is a basis for reasoned economic decisions. Measured against similar activities elsewhere, the achievements of New England's organizations compare favorably. Measured against the needs, it appears that their services could be steadily improved and expanded.

Technical Research Organizations

New England is active in technical research and development. The region has 11% of the nation's industrial laboratories, 8.6% of the independent consulting laboratories, and distinguished representation in university and college laboratories. Nevertheless, it is not active enough in this field. Technology is increasingly important in American industry, and New England's manufacturers, upon whom so much depends, must take maximum advantage of technological opportunities to maintain and advance their competitive position. The research and development activities of many industries are still inadequate despite the outstanding examples set by some individual companies. There is still too little awareness among a large proportion of the region's manufacturers that a sound research program is often a company's best investment, improving products, developing new products, and reducing costs.

Manufacturers in the region should take greater advantage than they do now of the opportunities for research outside their own companies. For example, trade association laboratories and industry-sponsored research can often bring wide benefits to an industry more cheaply than action by an individual firm. The fisheries, textile, jewelry, and some other industries might well provide mutual support in this way for fundamental research that would benefit all members. Another outside source of research assistance is such organizations as the Lowell Technological Research Foundation. New England should lead in the greater development and use of the research facilities that are oriented to serve the region.

Manufacturers in the northern New England states should make more use of the college and university technical facilities, especially those established expressly to provide services to private businesses and governments. Regional and state business and development organizations might assist by encouraging such use, and urging more employment of the technically trained graduates of colleges and universities in the region.

INDUSTRIAL MANAGEMENT

New England's dependence upon manufacturing for its income underscores the fact that adequate industrial management is of the utmost concern to all whose future is tied up with the economy of the region. We have endeavored to answer two questions: Is management making its maximum contribution to regional employment and income? And is that contribution adequate to bring about the growth and expansion needed to provide jobs at good wages for the region's growing population?

Our investigations involved four separate measurements of New England's industrial management: (1) a profits test; (2) a comparison of management ratings assigned by the American Institute of Management to New England and non-New England firms; (3) a pilot study of the relationships between criteria of good management and profitability in a selected sample of New England firms; (4) analysis of the opinions of consulting engineers about New England management.

By the test of profitability such data as we have been able to obtain indicate that on the average New England's industrial concerns are not earning as much as their principal competitors. In the measurement of New England management against standards of excellence for most industries, the data raised doubt that the average New England managements are equal to those elsewhere. It follows that mangement is not making its maximum contribution to New England's employment and income.

The most hopeful finding of this study is the fact that there is considerable room for improvement in management. If in the face of our industrial history during which so many plants have closed and so many adjustments have been required, it were found to be a fact that New England's industrial management were generally of the highest level and showed little potential for improvement, then New England would indeed have cause to be worried. The existence of a large potential for improvement clearly points the way to the solution of many serious problems and should provide the basis for an optimistic outlook on the future.

New England is an economy in transition. Old economic activities are being supplanted by new. In this process the decisions of manufacturing executives are of paramount importance. They are the most important single group in determining the future of the New England economy. *One of the chief goals for the entire region should be to have businessmen focus their attention on making their own businesses operate better by adapting policies, techniques, and operations to changing conditions and by developing and maintaining forward-looking attitudes. The attitudes of management constitute one of the most important keys to New England's future.*

"Research-mindedness" in the broadest sense on the part of management is vital if New England is to maintain and improve its industrial position. In an appendix to our report on management, we have listed 105 questions to stimulate an intensive, continuous, self-examination of all aspects of New England management. We urge any New England management that is uncertain whether it is doing the best job possible to give itself a thorough objective examination or to have its operation appraised to determine whether it is abreast of its competition.

The actions of management will be bolstered or hindered by those of the people of the area. New Englanders have become so accustomed to successful enterprise that they no longer pay the honor they formerly did to those who achieve industrial success. They do not value their industrial leaders and the contributions which those leaders can make so highly as do people in less industrialized areas who experience directly the improvement in living standards resulting from the establishment of new industry. We urge upon every New Englander the value of the economic vision that will both reveal avenues of industrial advancement and induce widespread support of those who are actively seeking to provide jobs at good wages for the population.

APPENDIX: COMMITTEE OF NEW ENGLAND
TECHNICAL STAFF MEMORANDA

The Committee of New England research staff conducted several investigations that yielded significant amounts of new information. In some instances the statistics were too extensive to be reproduced in the published reports. The following memoranda were prepared by the staff for their own use in drafting the Committee reports. They are not official reports of the Committee of New England. They express only the findings and interpretations of the research staff.

A limited supply of copies is available on request to the Research Department, Federal Reserve Bank of Boston.

		Staff Author
No. 1.	*Origins and Destinations of New England's Rail Traffic, 1949*	Ray S. Kelley, Jr.
No. 2.	*Chronic Unemployment in New England from 1947 to 1951*	William H. Miernyk
No. 3.	*Railroad Transportation Charges to New England and Competing Shippers*	William H. Miernyk
No. 4.	*The Use of Professional Consultants by New England Industry and Consultants' Opinions about New England Management*	Arthur A. Bright, Jr.
No. 5.	*Inter-industry Mobility of Workers and the Transfer of Worker Skills in New England*	William H. Miernyk
No. 6.	*The Financing of Small Business in New England: Opinions of Members of the Smaller Business Association of New England*	Edward K. Smith
No. 7.	*The Financing of Small Business in New England: Findings of the National Association of Manufacturers*	Edward K. Smith
No. 8.	*Interstate Comparisons of State and Local Tax Burdens and Federal Aid, 1941 and 1949*	Edward K. Smith
No. 9.	*Wages and Supplementary Payments in Selected New England Industries*	William H. Miernyk

Members of the Committee of New England and the Research Advisory Committee

ELY, Joseph B. (2, 4)
Ely, Bartlett, Thompson & Brown
Boston, Mass.
ERB, Robert C., Pres. (4)
J. F. McElwain Co.
Nashua, N. H.
ERICKSON, Joseph A., Pres. (1)
Federal Reserve Bank of Boston
Boston, Mass.

FILENE, Lincoln, Chairman (4)
William Filene's Sons Co.
Boston, Mass.
FRENCH, Edward S., Chairman (7)
Boston & Maine Railroad
Boston, Mass.
FULHAM, Thomas A., Treas. (5)
Triton Trawling Co.; Fulham Bros.
Boston, Mass.

GAY, Olin D. (4, 7)
Cavendish, Vt.

HAGEMANN, H. Frederick, Jr., Pres. (6)
Rockland-Atlas National Bank
Boston, Mass.
HARRELL, Joe E., Pres. (2, 6, 7)
New England Tel. & Tel. Co.
Boston, Mass.
HAUCK, Arthur A., Pres. (2, 3, 5)
University of Maine
Orono, Maine
HEARD, Marston, Pres. (1, 6)
Amoskeag National Bank
Manchester, N. H.
HIRST, Edgar C., Pres. (1)
First National Bank
Concord, N. H.
HODGKINSON, Harold D., Gen. Mgr.
William Filene's Sons Co.
Boston, Mass.
HOWE, David W., Publisher (6, 7)
Burlington Free Press
Burlington, Vt.

JONES, Howard Mumford, Pres. (2)
Am. Academy of Arts and Sciences
Boston, Mass.
JORGENSEN, A. N., Pres. (2, 3)
University of Conn.
Storrs, Conn.
JUDD, Stanley G., Commiss. (5)
Vermont Dept. of Agriculture
Montpelier, Vt.

KELLEY, Kenneth J., Sec.-Treas., Legis. Agent
(2, 3)
Mass. Federation of Labor
Boston, Mass.
KILLIAN, J. R., Jr., Pres. (3, 4)
Mass. Institute of Technology
Cambridge, Mass.

McGRATH, Michael F., Treas. (1)
Dudley Leather Co.
Lynn, Mass.
McMAHON, John H., Chairman
Berkshire Fine Spinning Assoc., Inc.
Providence, R. I.

MAXWELL, Arthur F., Pres. (1)
First National Bank of Biddeford
Biddeford, Maine
MAXWELL, Rev. Joseph R. N., S.J., Pres. (3)
Boston College
Chestnut Hill, Mass.
MEREDITH, L. Douglas, Exec. Vice Pres. (1)
National Life Insurance Co.
Montpelier, Vt.
MERRILL, Perry H., (5)
State Forester
Montpelier, Vt.
MIRANDO, Felix, Sec.-Treas.
Imperial Knife Company, Inc.
Providence, R. I.
*MONTAGUE, Wallace, Vice Pres. (3)
Norton Company
Worcester, Mass.
MORENCY, Paul W., (7)
Vice Pres. and Gen. Mgr., WTIC
Hartford, Conn.
MORSE, Richard S., Pres. (4, 5)
National Research Corp.
Cambridge, Mass.
MURPHY, Francis S., Publisher (3)
The Hartford Times
Hartford, Conn.

*NEWHALL, Arthur B., Treas. (1, 4, 6)
Dennison Manufacturing Co.
Framingham, Mass.

O'DONNELL, Walter G. (4, 5, 7)
Westport, Conn.
O'HEARN, John A., Managing Ed. (3)
Lawrence Daily Eagle & Evening Tribune
Lawrence, Mass.
O'KEEFE, Adrian F., Pres. (4)
First National Stores, Inc.
Somerville, Mass.
ORR, Dudley W. (6)
Orr & Reno
Concord, N. H.
OTIS, Edward O., Jr., Partner (4)
Otis Company
Providence, R. I.

PENNYBACKER, Miles, Pres. (3, 4)
Voltarc Tubes, Inc.
Norwalk, Conn.
PETELA, Frank S., Field Rep. (2)
United Steelworkers of America, CIO
New Haven, Conn.
PFEIL, John S., Vice Pres. (4, 5)
Stone & Webster, Inc.
Boston, Mass.
PHILLIPS, Dr. Charles F., Pres. (6)
Bates College
Lewiston, Maine
PUTNAM, Roger L., Pres. (2, 4, 6)
Package Machinery Co.
East Longmeadow, Mass.

RALEIGH, Walter, Exec. Vice Pres. (3)
New England Council
Boston, Mass.
REARDON, Harold F., Reg. Grand Lodge Rep.
(2, 5)
Association of Machinists
Hyde Park, Mass.

REYNOLDS, Quentin, Gen. Mgr. (5)
Eastern States Farmers' Exchange, Inc.
West Springfield, Mass.
RICHDALE, J. C., Asst. to Pres. (2, 4)
Esso Standard Oil Co.
Boston, Mass.
ROURKE, Joseph, Sec.-Treas. (5, 6, 7)
Conn. Federation of Labor, AFL
Bridgeport, Conn.

SACHAR, Abram L., Pres. (2, 3)
Brandeis University
Waltham, Mass.
SCHAUFENBIL, Francis M., Vice Pres. (2, 5)
United Textile Workers of America
Lawrence, Mass.
SCHILLER, Avery R., Pres. and Gen. Mgr. (1, 5)
Public Service Co. of N. H.
Manchester, N. H.
*SIMONDS, Godfrey B. (1)
G. H. Walker & Co.
Providence, R. I.
SLAVIN, The Rev. Robert J., O.P., Pres. (2, 3)
Providence College
Providence, R. I.
SMITH, James Barker, Pres. (6)
Wentworth Hotel, Inc.
Portsmouth, N. H.
SMITH, S. Abbot, Pres. (1, 4, 6)
Thomas Strahan Co.
Chelsea, Mass.
STANTON, Seabury, Pres. and Treas. (2)
Hathaway Manufacturing Co.
New Bedford, Mass.

STEINKRAUS, Herman W., Pres. (3, 4)
Bridgeport Brass Co.
Bridgeport, Conn.
STEVENSON, Earl P., Pres. (4)
Arthur D. Little, Inc.
Cambridge, Mass.

*TONER, James V., Pres.
Boston Edison Co.
Boston, Mass.
TRAVERS, Linus, Exec. Vice Pres.
The Yankee Network, Inc.
Boston, Mass.
TROTT, Raymond H., Pres. (1)
Rhode Island Hospital Trust Co.
Providence, R. I.

WALSH, Martin J., N. E. Director (2)
United Steelworkers
Boston, Mass.
WELCH, G. Harold, Vice Pres. (1)
The New Haven Bank
New Haven, Conn.
WHEELER, Walter H., Jr., Pres. (5)
Pitney-Bowes, Inc.
Stamford, Conn.
WILLIAMS, Roy F., Exec. Vice Pres. (3)
Assoc. Ind. of Mass.
Boston, Mass.
WREN, Paul I., Vice Pres. (5)
Old Colony Trust Co.
Boston, Mass.

* Deceased

THE COMMITTEE OF NEW ENGLAND STUDY PANELS

1. Panel on Capital and Credit
2. Panel on Human Resources
3. Panel on Information and Education
4. Panel on Management and Research
5. Panel on Natural Resources
6. Panel on Tax and Fiscal Policies
7. Panel on Transportation

The Research Advisory Committee

Index